# 2nd Workshop on Ancient Language Processing (ALP 2025)

Albuquerque, New Mexico, USA
4 May 2025

ISBN: 979-8-3313-1910-6

**Printed from e-media with permission by:**

Curran Associates, Inc.
57 Morehouse Lane
Red Hook, NY 12571

**Some format issues inherent in the e-media version may also appear in this print version.**



Printed with permission by Curran Associates, Inc. (2026)

For permission requests, please contact the Association for Computational Linguistics at the address below.

Association for Computational Linguistics
209 N. Eighth Street
Stroudsburg, Pennsylvania 18360

Phone: 1-570-476-8006
Fax: 1-570-476-0860

acl@aclweb.org

**Additional copies of this publication are available from:**

Curran Associates, Inc.
57 Morehouse Lane
Red Hook, NY 12571 USA
Phone: 845-758-0400
Fax: 845-758-2633
Email: curran@proceedings.com
Web: www.proceedings.com

NAACL-ALP 2025

# ALP 2025

## Proceedings of the
## Second Workshop on Ancient Language Processing

*associated with*

**The 2025 Annual Conference of the North American Chapter**
**of the Association for Computational Linguistics**
**NAACL 2025**

May 4, 2025

Order copies of this and other ACL proceedings from:

Association for Computational Linguistics (ACL)
317 Sidney Baker St. S
Suite 400- 134
Kerrville, TX 78028
USA
Tel: +1-855-225-1962
acl@aclweb.org

# Preface

The Second International Workshop on Ancient Language Processing (ALP 2025), co-located with the 2025 Annual Conference of the North American Chapter of the Association for Computational Linguistics (NAACL 2025), was held on May 4, 2025, in Albuquerque, New Mexico, USA. This workshop built on the success of its inaugural edition (ALP 2023 at Varna, Bulgaria) and the workshop on Ancient Language Translation (ALT 2023 at Macao, China). ALP 2025 further consolidated the global platform for scholars and practitioners exploring the intersection of natural language processing (NLP) and ancient languages—a domain rich with historical, cultural, and linguistic significance.

Ancient languages, spanning from Sumerian cuneiform (c. 3,400 BCE) to Ancient Greek, Latin, Ancient Chinese and Mayan glyphs, encapsulate humanity's earliest intellectual and cultural achievements. The ALP 2025 workshop sought to advance the application of modern NLP techniques to these languages, addressing challenges such as non-Latin scripts, transliteration variability, fragmented texts, and dialectal diversity. By fostering interdisciplinary collaboration, the workshop aimed to accelerate progress in digitizing and analyzing ancient linguistic resources, thereby unlocking new insights into human history and culture.

ALP 2025 received a diverse array of submissions covering the earliest phases of writing (proto-cuneiform), to the first languages of Mesopotamia (Sumerian and Akkadian), Egypt and Sudan (Egyptian, Demotic, and Meroitic), Anatolia (Hittite), the Mediterranean (Hebrew, Linear B, Ancient Greek, Latin), Iran (Old Persian), India (Sanskrit), East Asia (Classical Chinese, Old Tibetan, Old Japanese), and Mesoamerica (Mayan). Notable themes included: Resource development and Innovations in corpus construction, in Unicode input methods, and linguistically linked data for underrepresented scripts, and the application of Large Language Models (LLMs) in various ancient languages.

The workshop hosted two shared tasks — EvaCun 2025 (cuneiform lemmatization and text restoration using LLMs) and EvaHan 2025 (classical Chinese named entity recognition) — designed to benchmark progress on unique challenges.

The workshop received 43 submissions in total. After rigorous double-blind review, the program committee accepted 33 papers: 10 long papers, 7 short papers, 2 overview papers of shared tasks, and 14 technical reports of shared tasks.

The broad participation in the ALP workshops reflects a rapidly expanding research community, driven by increased digitization of ancient texts and interdisciplinary interest from computational linguists, archaeologists, and philologists. This year's workshop features keynote addressed by Dr. Patrick J. Burns (ISAW, New York University, US), a pioneer in digital philology and developer of the Classical Language Toolkit (CLTK), and Dr. Donald Sturgeon (Durham University, UK), founder of the Classical Chinese Text Project. Their work exemplifies the synergy between traditional scholarship and cutting-edge NLP.

We extend our gratitude to the ALP 2025 Program Committee for their thorough reviews, the NAACL 2025 organizers for their invaluable logistical support, and the student committee members and volunteers whose dedication ensured a smooth process. Special thanks to the shared task coordinators of EvaCun 2025 and EvaHan 2025 for designing evaluation tasks that push the boundaries of ancient language processing.

The ALP 2025 workshop provided an opportunity for all participants to engage in dynamic discussions, share novel ideas, and contribute to a future in which ancient languages are not only preserved, but actively integrated into the global landscape of natural language processing and cultural computation.

# Organizing Committee

**Workshop Organizers**

Adam Anderson, UC Berkeley, USA
Shai Gordin, Ariel University, Israel
Bin Li, Nanjing Normal University, China
Yudong Liu, Western Washington University, USA
Marco C. Passarotti, Università Cattolica del Sacro Cuore, Italy
Rachele Sprugnoli, University of Parma, Italy

**Program Committee**

Alaa Mamdouh Akef, Peking University, China
Masayuki Asahara, National Institute for Japanese Language and Linguistics, Japan
Flavio Massimiliano Cecchini, KU Leuven, Belgium
Claudia Corbetta, Università degli Studi di Bergamo, Italy
Angelo Mario Del Grosso, Istituto di Linguistica Computazionale "A. Zampolli", ILC-CNR, Italy
Sanhong Deng, Nanjing University, China
Minxuan Feng, Nanjing Normal University, China
Lihong Liu, Institute of Information on Traditional Chinese Medicine, China
Renfen Hu, Beijing Normal University, China
Heidi Jauhiainen, University of Helsinki, Finland
Kyle P. Johnson, Berlin-Brandenburg Academy of Sciences, Germany
Orly Lewis, Hebrew University of Jerusalem, Israel
Johann-Mattis List, Max Planck Institute for Evolutionary Anthropology, Germany
Chao-Lin Liu, National Chengchi University, Taiwan
Liu Liu, Nanjing Agricultural University, China
Congjun Long, Chinese Academy of Social Sciences, China
Long-long Ma, University of Chinese Academy of Sciences, China
Francesco Mambrini, Università Cattolica del Sacro Cuore, Italy
Martijn Naaijer, University of Copenhagen, Denmark
Stéphane Polis, Université de Liège, Belgium
Luis Sáenz, Leipzig University, Germany
Aleksi Sahala, University of Helsinki, Finland
Si Shen, Nanjing University of Science and Technology, China
Shahar Spencer, Hebrew University of Jerusalem, Israel
Qi Su, Peking University, China
Xuri Tang, Huazhong University of Science and Technology, China
Toon Van Hal, University of Leuven, Belgium
Dongbo Wang, Nanjing Agricultural University, China
Wenhao Ye, Nanjing Agricultural University, China

**Student Committee**

Stav Klein (Ariel University/TAD Center, Tel Aviv University, Israel)
Zhixing Xu (Nanjing Normal University, China)
Bolin Chang (Nanjing Normal University, China)
Xue Zhao (Nanjing Agricultural University, China)
Ruilin Liu (Nanjing Agricultural University, China)
Jing Chen (Hong Kong Poly University, Hong Kong)
Claudia Corbetta (claudia.corbetta@unibg.it, University of Bergamo, Italy)
Danlu Chen (danlu@ucsd.edu, UC San Diego, USA)
Ercong Nie (nie@cis.lmu.de, Ludwig Maximilian University of Munich, Germany)

# Sponsors

**Workshop Sponsor**

GuLian (BeiJing) Digital Media Tech Co., Ltd

**EvaCun Sponsors**

Digital Pasts Lab - headed by Dr. Shai Gordin (Ariel University)
eBL - electronic Babylonian Library headed by Prof. Enrique Jiménez (LMU Munich)
ARCHIBAB - project headed by Prof. Dominique Charpin (Collège de France), with the assistance of Dr. Marine Béranger (FU Berlin)

**EvaHan Sponsors**

Research Center for Language Big Data and Computational Humanities, Nanjing Normal University

# Table of Contents

# Workshop Program

**9:00–9:05** **Opening Remarks**

**9:05–9:35** **Invited Talk (Dr. Patrick J. Burns: The Role of "Small" Models for Ancient NLP in a World of Large Language Models)**

**9:35–10:35** **Oral Reports A (Part 1)**

*Automatic Text Segmentation of Ancient and Historic Hebrew*
Elisha Rosensweig, Benjamin Resnick, Hillel Gershuni, Joshua Guedalia, Nachum Dershowitz and Avi Shmidman

*Integrating Semantic and Statistical Features for Authorial Clustering of Qumran Scrolls*
Yonatan Lourie, Jonathan Ben-Dov and Roded Sharan

*Assignment of account type to proto-cuneiform economic texts with Multi-Class Support Vector Machines*
Piotr Zadworny and Shai Gordin

*Accessible Sanskrit: A Cascading System for Text Analysis and Dictionary Access*
Giacomo De Luca

**10:35–10:55** **Break**

**10:55–11:10** **Oral Reports A (Part 2)**

*A Dataset of Ancient Chinese Math Word Problems and an Application for Research in Historic Mathematics*
Florian Keßler

**11:10–11:45 Poster**

**11:50–13:30 Lunch**

**13:30–14:00 Invited Talk (Dr. Donald Sturgeon: Ancient languages in the age of LLMs: opportunities and challenges)**

**14:00–15:30 EvaHan**

**Opening Remarks and Invited Talk (Prof. Zhiwei Feng)**

*Overview of EvaHan2025: The First International Evaluation on Ancient Chinese Named Entity Recognition*
Bin Li, Bolin Chang, Ruilin Liu, Xue Zhao, Si Shen, Lihong Liu, Yan Zhu, Zhixing Xu, Weiguang QU and Dongbo Wang

*Exploring the Application of 7B LLMs for Named Entity Recognition in Chinese Ancient Texts*
yicheng zhu and han bi

*Construction of NER Model in Ancient Chinese: Solution of EvaHan 2025 Challenge*
Yi Lu and Minyi Lei

*LLM's Weakness in NER Doesn't Stop It from Enhancing a Stronger SLM*
Weilu Xu, Renfei Dang and Shujian Huang

*Named Entity Recognition in Context: Edit_Dunhuang team Technical Report for Evahan2025 NER Competition*
Colin Brisson, Ayoub Kahfy, Marc Bui and Frédéric Constant

*Simple Named Entity Recognition (NER) System with RoBERTa for Ancient Chinese*
Yunmeng Zhang, Meiling Liu, Hanqi Tang, Shige Lu and Lang Xue

*Make Good Use of GujiRoBERTa to Identify Entities in Ancient Chinese*
Lihan Lin, Yiming Wang, Jiachen Li, Huan Ouyang and Si Li

*GRoWE: A GujiRoBERTa-Enhanced Approach to Ancient Chinese NER via Word-Word Relation Classification and Model Ensembling*
tian Xia, yilin wang, xinkai Wang, Qun Zhao and Menghui Yang

*When Less Is More: Logits-Constrained Framework with RoBERTa for Ancient Chinese NER*
Wenjie Hua and Shenghan Xu

*Multi-Strategy Named Entity Recognition System for Ancient Chinese*
Wenxuan Dong and Meiling Liu

*Multi-Domain Ancient Chinese Named Entity Recognition Based on Attention-Enhanced Pre-trained Language Model*
Qi Zhang, Zhiya Duan, Shijie Ma, ShengYu Liu, Zibo Yuan and RuiMin Ma

**15:30–15:50 Break**

**15:50–16:30 EvaCun**

*EvaCun 2025 Shared Task: Lemmatization and Token Prediction in Akkadian and Sumerian using LLMs*
Shai Gordin, Aleksi Sahala, Shahar Spencer and Stav Klein

*Lemmatization of Cuneiform Languages Using the ByT5 Model*
Pengxiu Lu, Yonglong Huang, Jing Xu, Minxuan Feng and Chao Xu

*Finetuning LLMs for EvaCun 2025 token prediction shared task*
Josef Jon and Ondřej Bojar

*Beyond Base Predictors: Using LLMs to Resolve Ambiguities in Akkadian Lemmatization*
Frederick Riemenschneider

*A Low-Shot Prompting Approach to Lemmatization in the EvaCun 2025 Shared Task*
John Sbur, Brandi Wilkins, Elizabeth Paul and Yudong Liu

**16:30–17:45 Oral Reports B**

*From Clay to Code: Transforming Hittite Texts for Machine Learning*
Emma Yavasan and Shai Gordin

*Towards Ancient Meroitic Decipherment: A Computational Approach*
Joshua N. Otten and Antonios Anastasopoulos

*Detecting Honkadori based on Waka Embeddings*
Hayato Ogawa, Kaito Horio and Daisuke Kawahara

*Incorporating Lexicon-Aligned Prompting in Large Language Model for Tangut–Chinese Translation*
Yuxi Zheng and Jingsong Yu

*ParsiPy: NLP Toolkit for Historical Persian Texts in Python*
Farhan Farsi, Parnian Fazel, Sepand Haghighi, Sadra Sabouri, Farzaneh Goshtasb, Nadia Hajipour, Ehsaneddin Asgari and Hossein Sameti

**17:45 Open Discussion and Closing**

# Automatic Text Segmentation of Ancient and Historic Hebrew

**Elisha Rosensweig[1,‡], Benjamin Resnick[1,‡], Hillel Gershuni[1,2,‡], Joshua Guedalia[1,‡], Nachum Dershowitz[3, §], Avi Shmidman[1,2,†]**
[1]DICTA / Jerusalem, Israel [2]Bar Ilan University / Ramat Gan, Israel
[3]Tel Aviv University / Tel Aviv, Israel
[†]avi.shmidman@biu.ac.il
[‡]{benshafat,benjaminmresnick,gershuni,joshuaguedalia}@gmail.com
[§]nachum@tau.ac.il

## Abstract

Ancient texts often lack punctuation marks, making it challenging to determine sentence boundaries and clause boundaries. Texts may contain sequences of hundreds of words without any period or indication of a full stop. Determining such boundaries is a crucial step in various NLP pipelines, especially regarding language models such as BERT that have context window constraints and regarding machine translation models which may become far less accurate when fed too much text at a time. In this paper, we consider several novel approaches to automatic segmentation of unpunctuated ancient texts into grammatically complete or semi-complete units. Our work here focuses on ancient and historical Hebrew and Aramaic texts, but the tools developed can be applied equally to similar languages. We explore several approaches to addressing this task: masked language models (MLM) to predict the next token; few-shot completions via an open-source foundational LLM; and the "Segment-Any-Text" (SaT) tool by Frohmann et al. (Frohmann et al., 2024). These are then compared to instruct-based flows using commercial (closed, managed) LLMs, to be used as a benchmark. To evaluate these approaches, we also introduce a new ground truth (GT) dataset of manually segmented texts. We explore the performance of our different approaches on this dataset. We release both our segmentation tools and the dataset to support further research into computational processing and analysis of ancient texts, which can be found here https://github.com/ERC-Midrash/rabbinic_chunker.

## 1 Introduction

Ancient languages lack many of the classic features that modern languages use to clarify and disambiguate how to read them. These include spaces between words, diacritics, punctuation and more. This makes it challenging to determine sentence and clause boundaries. Determining these boundaries is a crucial step in any attempt to decipher, analyze and process ancient texts. In the past this would be needed simply as a way to enable humans to read these texts, while in the modern era this need has expanded as more and more NLP tools are coming out, some of which require such sentence segmentation as a prerequisite.

The issue of segmenting text into smaller chunks is a well-known challenge, with a wide range of use-cases and applications. Humans are many times the direct beneficiaries of such a segmentation, in the form of subtitles (Alvarez et al., 2017; Ponce et al., 2023), Easy Read text (Calleja et al., 2024), or text summaries created on a per-segment basis (Cho et al., 2022; Aumiller et al., 2021; Hazem et al., 2020). Furthermore, in recent years we see more and more NLP tools that, while powerful, are limited in the size of text they can accept as input. Accordingly, for each of these tools there arises a need to segment a large text into smaller chunks. These include (but are not limited to) BERT models (Gong et al., 2020) and LLM context windows (Shi et al., 2024).

Although segmenting a text does not change the text itself, the segmentation strategy one selects will impact the quality of downstream tasks that take the segmented text as input. Possible negative impacts include: cutting sentences in half; reduced readability (e.g., in the case of subtitles); loss of information and critical context (e.g. in the case of LLM context and translation), etc. For this reason, different domains and segmentation challenges also require different policies. A sentence segmentation tool, such as discussed in Frohmann et al. (2024), will not be sufficient for handling the needs of chunking large texts for feeding BERTs, where punctuation is assumed to be stable but topic consistency and coherence is a concern. Different tools might be needed for the same task but with changes in the source text properties, such as lan-



*Proceedings of the Second Ancient Language Processing Workshop associated with NAACL 2025*, pages 1–11
May 4, 2025. 

guage and genre (Homburg and Chiarcos, 2016; Aumiller et al., 2021; Hazem et al., 2020).

In this paper, we explore several approaches to the segmentation of ancient and historic Hebrew, as a necessary prerequisite for effective training and running of fine-tuned BERT models for punctuation, morphological tagging, syntactic parsing, and more. The segmented chunks are critical both for creating training samples with which to fine-tune BERT models for the aforementioned tasks, and also at inference time, to ensure accurate results from the models.

As such, our goal is to minimize damage at the sentence level while bounding the length of these segments, which we will refer to as "chunks". A chunk can sometimes be composed of several sentences or, conversely, it may be a syntactically independent part of a single sentence. We are not aware of any work done trying to address this specific challenge w.r.t. ancient and historic Hebrew, and thus draw upon related work from other (similar) domains instead.

Another deficiency in this domain is a lack of ground truth (GT) datasets by which to evaluate these approaches. To this end, our work here also provides the first GT dataset of manually segmented texts for ancient and historical Hebrew, as far as we are aware. We explore the performance of our different approaches on this dataset. We release both our segmentation tools and the dataset to support further research into computational processing and analysis of ancient texts.

The structure of this paper is as follows. In Section 2 we discuss related work, followed by Section 3 where we discuss our GT test set and our approach to curating it, and Section 4 that outlines the metrics we used in this paper. With the background out of the way, we progress to Section 5 to review the various segmentation tools we put to use in this paper. Section 6 presents our results, demonstrating the effectiveness of each of the tools we explore here. We conclude with Section 7 where we discuss the takeaways from this work.

## 2 Related Work

Several approaches have been used in the past for sentence-level segmentation. One approach is to segment the text using masked language models (e.g., BERT models) to predict punctuation marks. This has been done in various contexts. The basic idea is to use the punctuation marks as natural locations in which to segment the text. These ideas worked well for segmenting Easy Read texts (Calleja et al., 2024) and subtitle generation (Ponce et al., 2023), yet it is not clear a-priori that they would work well for other use-cases. Specifically, it is unclear how the various BERT models would behave when facing ancient and historic Hebrew. Some Hebrew models, which we tested here, were trained only on more modern texts, while others were trained on texts where the punctuation is inconsistent and unreliable. Thus, the degree to which this approach can be useful is an open question, which we explore here.

Then there are the approaches that use Generative AI, specifically instruct and few-shot flows. In both of these, the flow prompts the GenAI tool to reproduce the original text with added markers that indicate where to segment it. These are state-of-the-art approaches and very commonly used in the literature for many tasks, well beyond segmentation. One challenge which these approaches have had in the past is that, when asked to reproduce the original text, the GenAI tool does not return a perfect reproduction of the text. Instead, it adds, subtracts or rephrases some of the original text. To manage this issue at scale researchers have proposed auxiliary scoring methods that provide an approximate evaluation of the segmentation quality (Calleja et al., 2024). This issue was also experienced by us in this work. We make note of how it impacted the overall viability of such approaches in Section 6.

In addition to all the above, it is important to note that ancient and historic Hebrew do not always conform to current grammar rules and conventions. Specifically, sentences can formally come out to be hundreds of words long, making a perfect segmentation an impossible goal at times. See more on this in Section 3, where we discuss how this impacts the construction of a GT dataset.

Finally, it is worth noting here how our work relates to existing notation works in ancient Hebrew, specifically the ETCBC project (Eep Talstra Centre for Bible and Computer, 2023). The ETCBC project provides linguistically annotated texts of the Hebrew Bible, offering researchers a comprehensive database with morphological, syntactic, and semantic features encoded in a hierarchical text model that facilitates computational analysis of biblical Hebrew texts. Our work here tackles Rabbinic texts which have a different set of challenges than that of the Bible. Whereas the bible is already pre-

versified into relatively short verses, the texts we tackle are much longer, and can reach hundreds of words. We hope that our work here will enable us in the future to use auto-segmented ancient texts and move to the next level of developing features along the same line as done in ETCBC.

## 3 Methodology - Ground Truth Dataset

### 3.1 Approach

The idea of a ground truth for text segmentation is a fuzzy concept, for several major and distinct reasons.

First, there can be a clash between the natural dynamics of the language and our segmentation goals. On the one hand, for segmentation to be useful, each segment must be capped in length. On the other hand, language in general, and ancient languages in particular, do not have a theoretical bound on sentence length. In Rabbinic texts, for example, it is very common to embed lengthy quotes within a sentence, such that any break between what comes before the quote and what comes after is detrimental to the grammatical structure of the sentence. As such, it is not always possible to segment the text in a manner that both meets the hard length constraints required and simultaneously does no "harm" to the sentence. This, in turn, complicates the process of generating a GT.

Second, to add to the previous point, ancient languages often do not abide by a clear set of grammar rules. As such, it is not always clear where the correct place is to segment the texts, even in cases where length constraints are not an issue.

In light of these two challenges, what is needed is a gradient on which to scale the quality of a segmentation technique. Specifically, we define three levels of segmentation markers:

- Break (B) - Positions that are clear segmentation points. These correspond roughly to ends of sentences, marked in modern Hebrew by a period, a question mark or exclamation point.
- Partial (P) - Positions which reflect a natural pause in the sentence or a completion of an idea. These correspond roughly to semi-colons, colons before a list or a lengthy quote, etc.
- Maybe (M) - Positions which should not be used for segmentation in general, but are clearly superior segmentation positions than one word prior or subsequent to them. Many times these can correspond to where a comma would be placed, but not limited to such cases.

For example, taking a statement from the 3nd century Hebrew treatise Mishnah, Tractate Avot, Chapter 1, Unit 2: שמעון הצדיק היה משירי כנסת הגדולה הוא היה אומר על שלשה דברים העולם עומד על התורה ועל העבודה ועל גמילות חסדים ("Simeon the Just was one of the last men of the Great Assembly. He used to say: the world stands upon three things: the Torah, the Temple service, and the practice of acts of piety.")

One (possible, legitimate) segmentation would be as follows:

שמעון הצדיק [M] (Simeon the Just)

היה משירי כנסת הגדולה [B] (was one of the last men of the Great Assembly.)

הוא היה אומר [P] (He used to say:)

על שלשה דברים ם העולם עומד [P] (the world stands upon three things:)

על התורה [M] (the Torah)

ועל העבודה [M] (the Temple service)

ועל גמילות חסדים [B] (and the practice of acts of piety.)

Note, especially, the usage of "M" markups. An ideal text segmentation would not segment the text at these positions, as they break up the sentence and "destroy meaning" in the process. However, it is clearly worse to break up the sentences in a position one word earlier or later. Therefore, we consider a segmentation tool which would segment at these positions as less than ideal, but which is picking up on language semantics and thus better than a random segmentation tool.

### 3.2 Text Selection

For the work we did in this paper, we completed the annotation of 25 texts, each 200–400 words in length. Table 1 presents the breakdown into different periods, as well as some high-level statistics on the number of words and different markers in our dataset. The core dataset consists of over 4000 words of Hebrew/Aramaic sources from the period of the "Geonim", dated 8th-10th century. To this we add an additional 3177 words of "Rishonim" texts from the High Middle Ages, in order to test whether the extent to which our results are valid for later medieval Hebrew texts as well. This dataset was annotated by a single annotater, with ten years of study in a rabbinic seminary and highly skilled in parsing rabbinic texts. While this is a small test-set and with only a single annotator, it is the first of its kind to the best of our knowledge. In the future, we plan on expanding the coverage of the dataset, as well as gathering annotations from additional annotators to allow for evaluation of interannotator agreement. The latest version of the ground truth dataset can be found here `https://github.com/ERC-Midrash/rabbinic_chunker`.

| | Geonim | Rishonim | Total |
|---|---|---|---|
| # Texts | 11 | 14 | 25 |
| # Words | 4088 | 3177 | 7265 |
| #B | 109 | 132 | 241 |
| #P | 198 | 178 | 376 |
| #M | 1086 | 775 | 1861 |

Table 1: Ground Truth Test Set - Breakdown

## 4 Analysis Metrics

### 4.1 Approach

In order to analyze the performance of a given text segmentation tool, when comparing it with a GT segmentation, we would naturally want both high precision and high recall. Segmentation with high precision would imply we segment only where appropriate, and high recall would imply we capture most meaningful segmentation positions. An important thing to note here is that high recall, after a certain stage, provides diminishing returns, since the downstream NLP tasks that the segmentation will support are met once we do not exceed some upper length limit of segment length. Thus, in this paper we focus on precision, constrained by the requirement that the produced chunks that are reasonably sized. In our experience, having run fine-tuned Hebrew BERT models across many ancient Hebrew texts, we have found that input chunks of up to 50 words work far better than longer chunks. After the 50-word point, accuracy starts to drop precipitously. Thus, our goal is an upper bound of $\approx 50$ words per chunk.

When measuring performance, the question arises: which segmentation markings in the GT should we consider for purposes of evaluation? The reasonable options, using the markup scheme described in Section 3.1, are $\{B\}$, $\{B, P\}$, or all three $\{B, P, M\}$. These represent progressively more permissive/flexible segmentation of the same text. Naturally, the performance scores of any tool will be directly impacted by this decision, with precision monotonically growing and recall decreasing as we move from strict to permissive segmentation. We discuss this impact in the analysis section below (Section 6).

### 4.2 Notation

Let $\mathcal{L}$ be the set of all layer combos we are interested in evaluating. As just discussed, $\mathcal{L} = \{B, \{B, P\}, \{B, P, M\}\}$. For any $l \in \mathcal{L}$ we define $Precision_l^\alpha$ to be the precision of segmentation algorithm $\alpha$ over the GT when considering only segmentation markers in $l$. The same goes for $Recall_l^\alpha$.

## 5 Automatic Text Segmentation Tools

Our research explores several distinct approaches to automatic segmentation of unpunctuated (ancient) texts, each leveraging capabilities of different language models and neural architectures. Each of these approaches offers different advantages in terms of accuracy, computational requirements, and generalizability across different types of texts[1]. Our implementation of the tools described here are publicly available in our repo`https://github.com/ERC-Midrash/rabbinic_chunker`.

### 5.1 Few-Shot Learning with DictaLM2.0

The first approach uses DictaLM2.0, an open-source LLM specifically trained on Hebrew texts (Shmidman et al., 2024a). We use the base model, rather than the instruct-tuned model, in order to leverage the full raw strength of the model. Thus, in order to elicit desired output from the model, we implement a few-shot learning protocol (Brown et al., 2020). The model is presented with several examples of input texts and correctly segmented versions of these texts. This is then followed by the target text requiring segmentation, after which the model proceeds with a completion. This method takes advantage of DictaLM2.0's specialized knowledge of Hebrew language patterns, while requiring minimal fine-tuning or additional training.

In this paper we provided the LLM four examples (shots). Each "shot" was comprised of a JSON object with two entries - *"raw"* to reflect

[1] Our approach in this paper was to explore the type of segmentation information already embedded among various existing models. An alternative approach would be to train models from scratch aimed at chunking, which would enable us to take a variety of approaches, e.g., hierarchical chunking. As explained, this is outside the scope of this work.

the input text, and *"chunked"* to reflect the expected segmented text, which was the same text but with double-slash ("//") markings as indication for where we would expect a segmentation point. See Appendix A.1 for the full specification of the shots used.

### 5.2 Next-Token Prediction using Masked Language Models (MLMs)

Our second approach follows a similar structure to other works (e.g., Calleja et al. (2024)), leveraging the masked language modeling (MLM) head of pre-trained BERT models. Given a long text, we use a sliding window fitted to the model context window. Within that window, taking each word in turn, we mask the word, and predict the subsequent token. When delimiter tokens (periods and/or colons, depending on the configuration we test) appear among the top predictions, we mark these positions as potential segment boundaries. Once a delimiter appears in the top K (K = 5, 15 for different runs) options, we select the earliest point to cut and move the window. This continues until the text is fully processed.

In this paper, we use the following BERT models:

- HeBERT (Chriqui and Yahav, 2021) - The first dedicated Hebrew BERT model, trained with a 30K-token vocabulary
- AlephBERT (Seker et al., 2021) - An expanded dedicated Hebrew BERT model, trained with a 52K-token vocabulary, and a much larger corpus.
- DictaBERT (Shmidman et al., 2023) - Currently the highest-performing BERT for modern Hebrew (Shmidman et al., 2024b), trained with a 128K-token vocabulary.
- BEREL (Shmidman et al., 2022) - A BERT model specifically trained for Historic Hebrew/Aramaic texts (128K-token vocabulary)[2].

### 5.3 Segment Any Text (SaT)

Frohmann et al. (2024) trained models with the express goal of providing a "universal approach for robust, efficient and adaptable sentence segmentation", referred to as *SaT*. They specifically aim to improve over the previous tool, *WtP ("Where's the Point")*, which was presented in (Minixhofer et al., 2023). Improvements include handling of short sentences and code-switching, as well as speeding up the model by moving from character-based to token-based processing.

The authors provided a working github project containing their models and code for running their tool (segment-any text, 2025). For our experiments here, we selected their *sat-12l-sm* model, a 12-layer multilingual model which the authors report had the best multilingual performance (96.0 macro-average F1 score, as reported at the time of writing this paper).

### 5.4 Benchmark: Instruction-Based Segmentation using Closed LLMs

All the methods mentioned thus far are open and free for use. Our final approach utilizes state-of-the-art closed-source language models (GPT-4o and Claude Sonnet) in an instruct flow. One of the main challenges in instruct-based flows is Prompt Engineering (PE), which is notoriously brittle (Errica et al., 2024). However, in our case we utilize the likely fact that these models have seen plenty of punctuated texts during training and are familiar with punctuation tasks. Our approach is therefore a 2-step flow: (a) prompt the LLM to punctuate a given unpunctuated text (see Appendix A.2 for prompt details) and then (b) segment the punctuated text at major punctuation marks (periods, colons, semicolons, and question marks).

Using these commercial models is helpful as an evaluation tool. However, we do not investigate these models in depth, for two reasons. First, these require access to paid services, and also lack transparency (e.g., model weights, open to fine-tuning etc.), thus making them less appropriate for broader use in the research community. Second, as we shall discuss in the analysis section, they have properties that make them unstable and less suitable to building reliable segmentation flows.

## 6 Performance Analysis

### 6.1 The Trouble with Generative LLMs

Generative models are known to be difficult to control via prompts when very precise output is required. In the case of segmentation, we find (as others have commented as well) that using gen-

[2]Note that while BEREL might have seen the GT texts in its training data, the texts BEREL was trained on were almost exclusively without punctuation marks. Thus, it will not have had prior hints to the correct segmentation of the GT dataset.

erative models is fraught with instability, as the LLMs at times inject or delete parts of the text they are asked to segment. While these issues can be handled with further work (modified instructions, modified examples in few-shot, guided decoding, and additional techniques), they are for the most part heuristic improvements that cannot be ensured with total certainty. Table 2 lists the number of texts, out of 25, for which the flow did not add or remove any text. All performance analysis in the rest of Section 6 relates only to this subset of texts.

| Genre | Count |
|---|---|
| Total | 25 |
| AlephBERT | 25 |
| heBERT | 25 |
| Dictabert | 25 |
| BEREL | 25 |
| DictaLM2.0 | 17 |
| SaT-12L-sm | 25 |
| gpt4o | 22 |
| claude-sonnet-3.5 v1 (20240620) | 20 |
| claude-sonnet-3.5 v2 (20241022) | 12 |

Table 2: List of segmentation tools and the number of GT texts that they segment correctly, i.e., w/o adding/removing text to the input text. Generative models demonstrate instability in this flow, making them less suitable to be used as part of a streamlined flow.

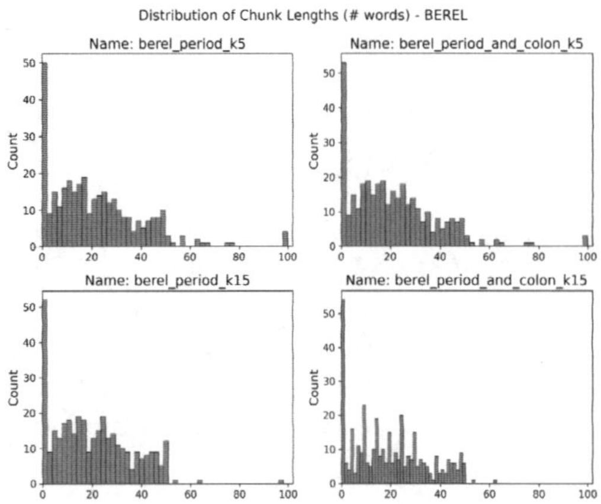


Figure 1

## 6.2 Segmentation Evaluation: Chunk Size

In our problem formulation, we want to have segmentation occur at reasonable places while ensuring that segments are not too long. Let us begin by reviewing the distribution of segment lengths as output by the different tools.

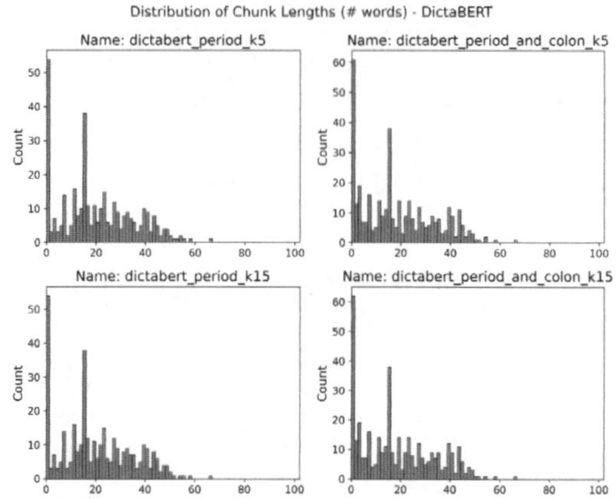


Figure 2

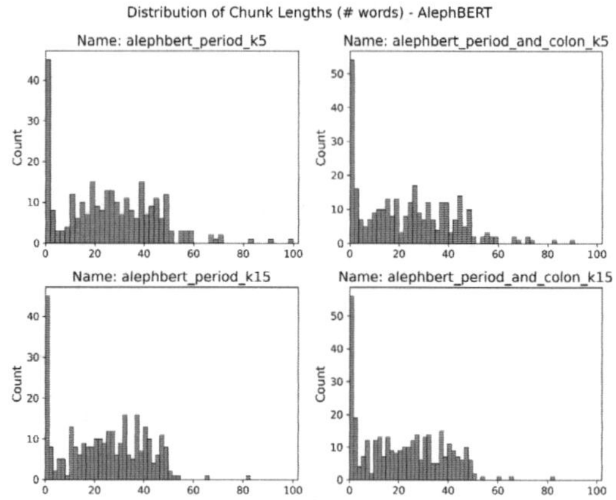


Figure 3

Fig. 1-4 show the performance of BEREL, DictaBERT, AlephBERT and HeBERT respectively, w.r.t. meeting chunk length constraints. In these, we collect all the chunks from across all 25 test samples and plot chunk length histograms. As we can see, all BERT-based models maintain our upper-limit of 50 words, with a small number of outliers. Going deeper in the search for candidate delimiters (K=15) seems to reduce those outliers as well. Note that this is not a straightforward result, as earlier segmentation choices could, at times, cause later segmentation opportunities to be fewer, thus lengthening future chunks.

Finally, we compare this performance to that of the Generative LLMs and SaT (Fig. 6). We can see that they too abide by the limits we were aiming for, though it is clear that the LLMs are concentrating the segment lengths on the shorter side. This might be due to the fact that they start by fully punctuating the text using modern standards, which could result

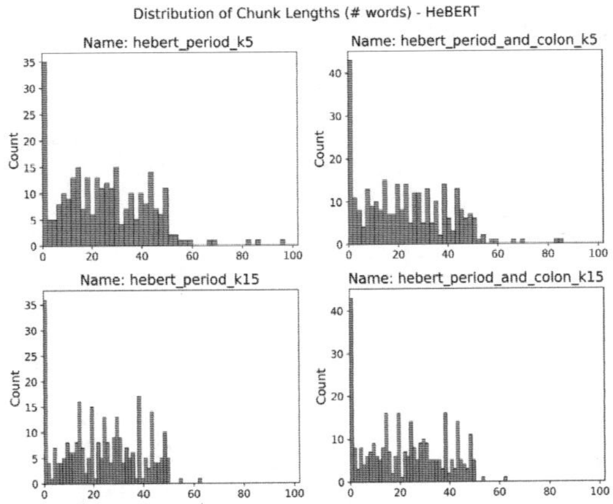


Figure 4

in shorter sentences and therefore shorter chunks.

### 6.3 Segmentation Evaluation: Precision

Satisfied that our segmentation tools are bound by length as required, let us now turn and check how good they are at finding good positions to segment the text. We focus first on the performance regarding Geonic texts of the first millennium and then consider whether to what degree this performance is maintained when the same methods are run slightly later medieval Hebrew texts of the Rishonim period.

Figure 5 shows how precision of segmentation behaves for Geonic texts, as a function of tool and segmentation strictness in GT. Moving from left to right, we see the results for the closed-model LLMs, then the few-shot flow over DictaLM2.0. After that we have *SaT-12L-sm*, and then finally we review our three Hebrew BERT models. For each of the three BERT models we present here, there are four results, corresponding to the four variations of using them: whether we use periods or also colons to predict a segmentation point, and how deep in the options-stack we look in search of these delimiters ($K = 5$ or 15). Figure 7 shows the same plot, but this time for the entire dataset, combining Genoim and Rishonim.

**General Trends.** As expected, as we move from top to bottom and restrict segmentation to more obvious markers, we see a decrease in precision. From a birds-eye view, we can see that most models have similar median performance, and experience the same trends as we move from top to bottom. Specifically, it seems from this that the open models compete well with the closed-model LLMs, at least for the current instruct prompts we used here. Note also that, as mentioned in Section 6.1 and shown in Table 2, the generative models results are not for the full dataset, but rather limited to those where the model did not modify or corrupt the text.

**Best MLM.** The best performance among the MLM solutions was seen with BEREL, the BERT model trained on Historical Hebrew. Especially for the most relaxed mode (BPM) it has near-perfect precision, and outperforms all other solutions. (Note once more that *claude-sonnet-v2*, which also seems to do well for BPM, is scored on only half of the texts, which makes it difficult to draw conclusions from that performance).

**Performance of SaT.** The model provided by Frohmann et al. (2024) seems to do as well and even better than all MLMs, with the exception of BEREL. This holds for all three marker-selection options. As this is a universal model, compared to the other tools which were all trained specifically on some variation of Hebrew language, this is quite impressive and satisfying, considering that the competition has an "unfair advantage".

The above points hold both when limiting our view to the earlier Geonic texts, as well as when expanding our view to include the Rishonim. This is encouraging, as it means our method will serve us well not only for ancient Hebrew, but for broader sections of historic Hebrew as well.

## 7 Conclusion

In conclusion, we have identified a practical and high-performing method of segmenting historic Hebrew texts, using the MLM-based method with the BEREL BERT model for historic Hebrew. We have shown that it far outperforms SaT, and that its performance rivals that of the LLMs, without the instability of the LLMs, and without having to rely on the commercial/closed nature of the big LLMs. Furthermore, we release our code so that this method can be easily run by the NLP community any other Hebrew text, plugging in any desired Hebrew BERT model as desired. Finally, we release the test dataset, the first of its kind, so that future segmentation models developed by the NLP community can be evaluated and compared to the benchmarks that we report here.

## Acknowledgments

This work has been funded by the European Union (ERC, MiDRASH, Project No. 101071829; Principal investigators: Nachum Dershowitz, Tel-Aviv

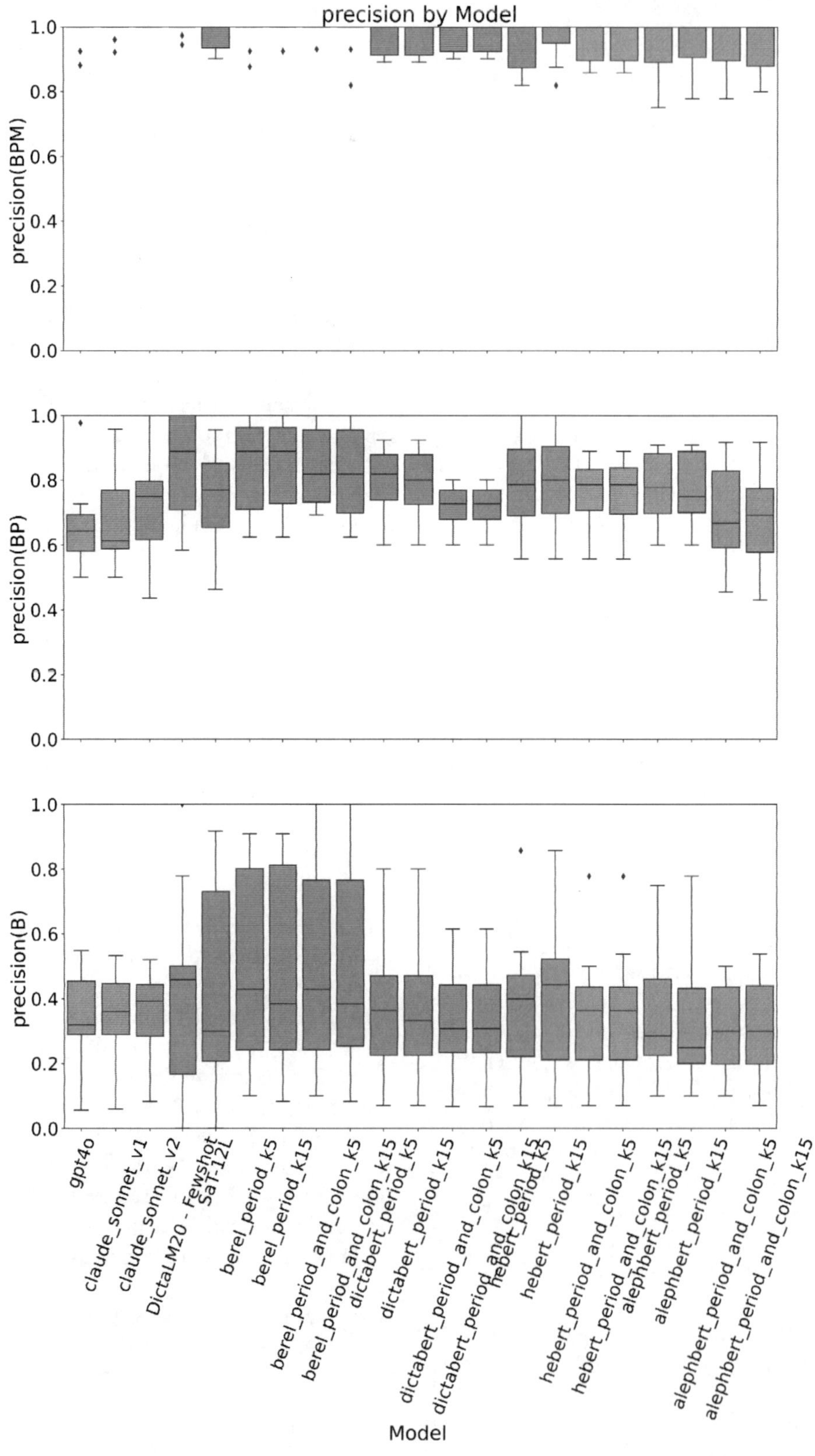


Figure 5: Precision of each method, as dependent on the GT labels we use, for the 8th-10th century Geonic texts. The plots show how precision scores change as we move from more relaxed segmentation demands $l = \{B, P, M\}$ (top), to stricter ones where $l = \{B\}$ (bottom).

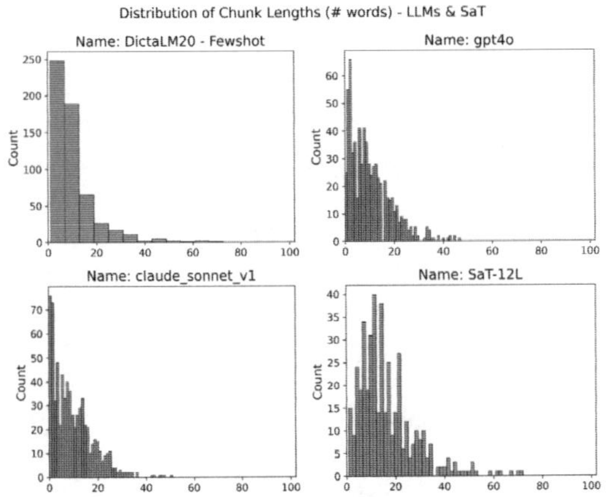


Figure 6

University; Judith Olszowy-Schlanger, EPHE-PSL; Avi Shmidman, Bar-Ilan University, and Daniel Stoekl Ben Ezra, EPHE-PSL), for which we are grateful. Views and opinions expressed are, however, those of the authors only and do not necessarily reflect those of the European Union or the European Research Council Executive Agency. Neither the European Union nor the granting authority can be held responsible for them.

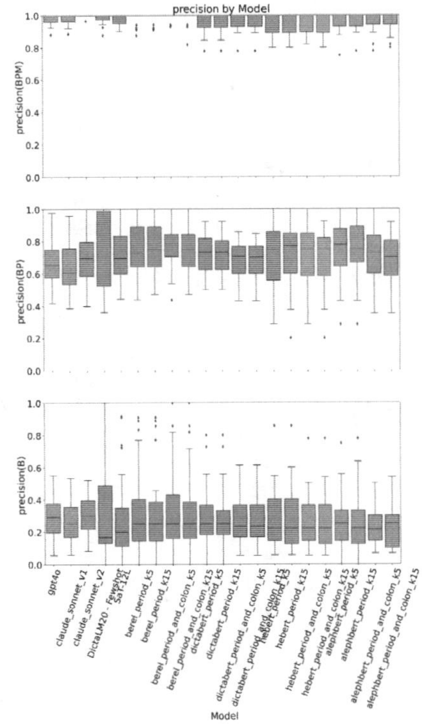


Figure 7: Precision across the combined corpus.

## References

Aitor Alvarez, Carlos-D Martínez-Hinarejos, Haritz Arzelus, Marina Balenciaga, and Arantza del Pozo. 2017. Improving the automatic segmentation of subtitles through conditional random field. *Speech Communication*, 88:83–95.

Dennis Aumiller, Satya Almasian, Sebastian Lackner, and Michael Gertz. 2021. Structural text segmentation of legal documents. In *Proceedings of the Eighteenth International Conference on Artificial Intelligence and Law*, pages 2–11.

Tom B. Brown, Benjamin Mann, Nick Ryder, Melanie Subbiah, Jared Kaplan, Prafulla Dhariwal, Arvind Neelakantan, Pranav Shyam, Girish Sastry, Amanda Askell, Sandhini Agarwal, Ariel Herbert-Voss, Gretchen Krueger, Tom Henighan, Rewon Child, Aditya Ramesh, Daniel M. Ziegler, Jeffrey Wu, Clemens Winter, Christopher Hesse, Mark Chen, Eric Sigler, Mateusz Litwin, Scott Gray, Benjamin Chess, Jack Clark, Christopher Berner, Sam McCandlish, Alec Radford, Ilya Sutskever, and Dario Amodei. 2020. Language models are few-shot learners. *Preprint*, arXiv:2005.14165.

Jesús Calleja, Thierry Etchegoyhen, and David Ponce. 2024. Automating Easy Read Text Segmentation. *Preprint*, arXiv:2406.11464.

Sangwoo Cho, Kaiqiang Song, Xiaoyang Wang, Fei Liu, and Dong Yu. 2022. Toward Unifying Text Segmentation and Long Document Summarization. *Preprint*, arXiv:2210.16422.

Avihay Chriqui and Inbal Yahav. 2021. HeBERT & HebEMO: a Hebrew BERT Model and a Tool for Polarity Analysis and Emotion Recognition. *Preprint*, arXiv:2102.01909.

Eep Talstra Centre for Bible and Computer. 2023. Bhsa: Biblia hebraica stuttgartensia amstelodamensis. `https://github.com/ETCBC/bhsa`. Accessed: 2025-03-18.

Federico Errica, Giuseppe Siracusano, Davide Sanvito, and Roberto Bifulco. 2024. What Did I Do Wrong? Quantifying LLMs' Sensitivity and Consistency to Prompt Engineering. *Preprint*, arXiv:2406.12334.

Markus Frohmann, Igor Sterner, Ivan Vulić, Benjamin Minixhofer, and Markus Schedl. 2024. "Segment Any Text: A Universal Approach for Robust, Efficient and Adaptable Sentence Segmentation". In *Proceedings of the 2024 Conference on Empirical Methods in Natural Language Processing*, pages 11908–11941, Miami, Florida, USA. Association for Computational Linguistics.

Hongyu Gong, Yelong Shen, Dian Yu, Jianshu Chen, and Dong Yu. 2020. Recurrent chunking mechanisms for long-text machine reading comprehension. In *Proceedings of the 58th Annual Meeting of the Association for Computational Linguistics*, pages 6751–6761, Online. Association for Computational Linguistics.

Amir Hazem, Béatrice Daille, Dominique Stutzmann, Christopher Kermorvant, and Louis Chevalier. 2020. Hierarchical text segmentation for medieval manuscripts. In *Proceedings of the 28th International Conference on Computational Linguistics*, pages 6240–6251.

Timo Homburg and Christian Chiarcos. 2016. Akkadian word segmentation. In *Proceedings Tenth International Conference on Language Resource Evaluation.(LREC 2016)*, pages 4067–4074.

Benjamin Minixhofer, Jonas Pfeiffer, and Ivan Vulić. 2023. "Where's the Point? Self-Supervised Multilingual Punctuation-Agnostic Sentence Segmentation". In *Proceedings of the 61st Annual Meeting of the Association for Computational Linguistics (Volume 1: Long Papers)*, pages 7215–7235, Toronto, Canada. Association for Computational Linguistics.

David Ponce, Thierry Etchegoyhen, and Victor Ruiz. 2023. Unsupervised Subtitle Segmentation with Masked Language Models. In *Proceedings of the 61st Annual Meeting of the Association for Computational Linguistics (Volume 2: Short Papers)*, pages 771–781.

segment-any text. 2025. wtpsplit: Toolkit to segment text into sentences or other semantic units in a robust, efficient and adaptable way. `https://github.com/segment-any-text/wtpsplit`. Accessed: 2025-01-22.

Amit Seker, Elron Bandel, Dan Bareket, Idan Brusilovsky, Refael Shaked Greenfeld, and Reut Tsarfaty. 2021. Alephbert:a hebrew large pre-trained language model to start-off your hebrew nlp application with. *Preprint*, arXiv:2104.04052.

Wei Shi, Shuang Li, Kerun Yu, Jinglei Chen, Zujie Liang, Xinhui Wu, Yuxi Qian, Feng Wei, Bo Zheng, Jiaqing Liang, et al. 2024. SEGMENT+: Long Text Processing with Short-Context Language Models. *arXiv preprint arXiv:2410.06519*.

Avi Shmidman, Joshua Guedalia, Shaltiel Shmidman, Cheyn Shmuel Shmidman, Eli Handel, and Moshe Koppel. 2022. Introducing BEREL: BERT Embeddings for Rabbinic-Encoded Language. *Preprint*, arXiv:2208.01875.

Shaltiel Shmidman, Avi Shmidman, Amir DN Cohen, and Moshe Koppel. 2024a. Adapting LLMs to Hebrew: Unveiling DictaLM 2.0 with Enhanced Vocabulary and Instruction Capabilities. *Preprint*, arXiv:2407.07080.

Shaltiel Shmidman, Avi Shmidman, and Moshe Koppel. 2023. Dictabert: A state-of-the-art bert suite for modern hebrew. *Preprint*, arXiv:2308.16687.

Shaltiel Shmidman, Avi Shmidman, Moshe Koppel, and Reut Tsarfaty. 2024b. MRL parsing without tears: The case of Hebrew. In *Findings of the Association for Computational Linguistics ACL 2024*, pages 4537–4550, Bangkok, Thailand and virtual meeting. Association for Computational Linguistics.

# A Appendix: LLM Prompts

In this appendix, we share the prompts used when using Generative AI LLMs for segmentation, to allow full reproducibility.

## A.1 DictaLM2.0 Few-shot prompt

Figure 8 provides the shots we used for the few-shot flow with DictaLM2.0 (Shmidman et al., 2024a). For each shot we provided the raw text (using the *"raw"* key) and the segmented text (using the "chunked" key"). Segmentation points were marked using double-slash ("//"). Few-shot flows work by providing the LLM the shots as context, and then the input text as a new input, and then allowing the LLM to continue by completing the output. LLMs have been found to pick up on patterns in the "shots" and then apply them directly to the new input text.

It is important to note that few-shot flows are very brittle. Specifically, they will react differently even when the order of the shots is changed, or the key names (in our case - "raw" and "chunked") are changed. Thus, for reproducing the results shown in our paper, please make sure to use the exact setup we used, as can be found in our github repo.

## A.2 Closed LLMs Instruct prompt

For the closed LLMs, we used the following prompt template:

"please take the following unpunctuated text, and punctuate it. Punctuation includes periods, commas, question marks, semicolons and colons. Other than punctuating, keep the text exactly as it is. If a word is clipped at the end, like אמ', leave it like that. Return the punctuated text between <punctuation> tags: $text Punctuated text:"

During runtime, the *$text* variable is assigned the value of the inputted text. The *"Punctuated text"* text is the prefix of the reply, which for models such as Claude is a "hint" to nudge the model into following the instructions.

{
"raw":
"הדרך הב' שהמוכר יכול לחזור בלוקח כגון שכיב מרע שמכר נכסיו דלאחר שהבריא אם אותם דמים הם מצויים
בעינה הו"ז יכול לחזור בו ואם לאו אינו יכול לחזור בו כדגר' אבעיא להו ש"מ שמכר כל נכסיו מהו זמנין אר"י אמר
רב אם עמד חוזר וזמנין אר"י א"ר אם עמד אינו חוזר ולא פליגי הא דאיתניהו לזוזי בעיניהו הא דפרעינהו בחובו
והם שני הדרכים שפי' שיכול המוכר לחזור בלוקח,"
"chunked":
"הדרך הב' שהמוכר יכול לחזור בלוקח // כגון שכיב מרע שמכר נכסיו // דלאחר שהבריא אם אותם דמים הם
מצויים בעינה הו"ז יכול לחזור בו // ואם לאו אינו יכול לחזור בו // כדגר' // אבעיא להו ש"מ שמכר כל נכסיו מהו //
זמנין אר"י אמר רב אם עמד חוזר // וזמנין אר"י א"ר אם עמד אינו חוזר // ולא פליגי // הא דאיתניהו לזוזי
בעיניהו // הא דפרעינהו בחובו // והם שני הדרכים שפי' שיכול המוכר לחזור בלוקח"
}

(a) shot #1

{
"raw":
"ודאנא דחמרא דמנחא חירותא בבראזיה אסור למיברזיה לההיא חירותא בשבתא מ"ט דקתני אם היתה נקובה
לא יתן שעוה מפני שהוא ממרח הכי נמי כיון דפתח להאי קירותא לאותביה בגוה קירותא לא אפשר מאי תקנתיה
יטול מגופת חבית ממנה וישתה ממנה כל צרכו אבל כנופה לשעוה מצד זה לצד זה ולדבוקה ולסתמה הוי ליה
ממרח וחייב חטאת וששאלתם,"
"chunked":
"ודאנא // דחמרא דמנחא חירותא בבראזיה אסור למיברזיה לההיא חירותא בשבתא מ"ט // דקתני אם היתה
נקובה לא יתן שעוה מפני שהוא ממרח // הכי נמי כיון דפתח להאי קירותא לאותביה בגוה קירותא לא אפשר //
מאי תקנתיה // יטול מגופת חבית ממנה וישתה ממנה כל צרכו // אבל כנופה לשעוה מצד זה לצד זה ולדבוקה
ולסתמה הוי ליה ממרח וחייב חטאת // וששאלתם"
}

(b) shot #2

{
"raw":
"השביעי מי שקבל לזון את בני אשתו עד זמן ידוע יש עליו לזון אותם כמו שהתנה ואף על פי שגרש את האם יש
עליו לקיים תנאו וכמו כן אם נשאת לאחר והתנה אותו אחר נמי לזון אותם יש על האחר לזון ועל השני לתת דמי
מזו,"
"chunked":
"השביעי // מי שקבל לזון את בני אשתו עד זמן ידוע // יש עליו לזון אותם כמו שהתנה // ואף על פי שגרש את
האם // יש עליו לקיים תנאו // וכמו כן אם נשאת לאחר והתנה אותו אחר נמי לזון אותם // יש על האחר לזון ועל
השני לתת דמי מזונות"//
}

(c) shot #3

{
"raw":
"אמר להם באו וטלו פיתקיכם כל מי שנטל פיתק וכתוב עליו זקן היה אומר לו משה כבר קידשך המקום וכל מי
שהיה נוטל פיתק שלא היה כתוב בתוכו זקן היה משה אומר לו מן השמים הוא מה אני יכול לעשות לך כיוצא בו
אתה אומר ואת פדויי השלשה והשבעים והמאתים,"
"chunked":
"אמר להם באו וטלו פיתקיכם // כל מי שנטל פיתק וכתוב עליו זקן // היה אומר לו משה כבר קידשך המקום // וכל
מי שהיה נוטל פיתק שלא היה כתוב בתוכו זקן // היה משה אומר לו מן השמים הוא מה אני יכול לעשות לך //
כיוצא בו אתה אומר // ואת פדויי השלשה והשבעים והמאתים"
}

(d) shot #4

Figure 8: Shots used in few-shot segmentation flow using DictaLM2.0. Note how we varied the type of input, and specifically ensured that some cases had segmentation points at the end of the text and some not, so as to encourage the model away from simplistic segmentation rules such as "end of line".

# Integrating Semantic and Statistical Features for Authorial Clustering of Qumran Scrolls

**Yonatan Lourie**[1] **Jonathan Ben-Dov**[2] **Roded Sharan**[3]
[1]Department of Statistics and Operations Research, Tel Aviv University
[2]Department of Bible, The Lester and Sally Entin Faculty of Humanities, Tel Aviv University
[3]Blavatnik School of Computer Science and AI, Tel Aviv University

**Abstract**

We present a novel framework for authorial classification and clustering of the Qumran Dead Sea Scrolls (DSS). Our approach combines modern Hebrew BERT embeddings with traditional natural language processing features in a graph neural network (GNN) architecture. Our results outperform baseline methods on both the Dead Sea Scrolls and a validation dataset of the Hebrew Bible. In particular, we leverage our model to provide significant insights into long-standing debates, including the classification of sectarian and non-sectarian texts and the division of the Hodayot collection of hymns.

## 1 Introduction

The discovery of the Dead Sea Scrolls in the mid-20th century represented a turning point in biblical studies and Jewish history, providing a new view into the religious and cultural world of early Judaism and into the theological background of Christianity (VanderKam and Flint, 2005). We discuss the scrolls found in the caves from Qumran, on the shore of the Dead Sea. This is a large collection of approximately 900 scrolls representing a large variety of compositions (i.e. literary entities, books or treatises), each of them featuring its own development history. A large part of the scrolls represents the writings of a community (Collins, 2010) while many other scrolls potentially originate with wider circles of contemporary Judaism. These distinctions, in particular questions of authorship, classification, and origins remain unresolved, fueling scholarly debates for decades. The present study focuses on two such questions.

The first question is the inner division and composition of the collection of Hodayot hymns, particularly the well-preserved copy 1QH[a] from Qumran Cave 1. While earlier research distinguished a class of "Teacher Hymns" from the "Community Hymns" in the rest of the collection (Douglas, 1999), this division is now contested or modified (Newsom, 2021; Johnson, 2022). The second question is the distinction between sectarian and non-sectarian scrolls; While this distinction was once considered consensus (Dimant, 2014), it is now debated (Martínez, 2010).

Compounding these challenges is the fragmentary nature of the scrolls. The title "scrolls" may be misleading, since most of the corpus is preserved in fragments except for a handful of more complete scrolls. Many texts are incomplete, with reconstructed or uncertain words, making traditional manual analysis both laborious and subjective.

Recent advances in Natural Language Processing offer new possibilities for analyzing ancient texts like the DSS. However, applying computational techniques to ancient Hebrew presents unique difficulties. Hebrew is a highly inflected and morphologically rich language with ambiguous word boundaries, inconsistent orthography, and the absence of vowels in many texts. Even modern Hebrew NLP tools face accuracy issues (Tsarfaty et al., 2019). These challenges increase when dealing with ancient forms of the language. This complexity, combined with the fragmentary and noisy nature of the DSS, necessitates robust and innovative computational approaches.

To our knowledge, computational approaches to the DSS are limited. Traditional stylometry methods have been applied, as demonstrated by Starr (Starr, 2019), and classifiers for biblical texts have been explored in the Dicta-Tiberias project[1]. Additionally, Yoffee et al. (Bühler et al., 2024) investigated text partitioning in the Bible, highlighting the potential for structural analysis using computational techniques. Van Hecke's (Van Hecke, 2018) work represents one of the only applications of NLP methods to the DSS, using basic computational linguistics techniques like tri-grams. While

[1]https://tiberias.dicta.org.il/



*Proceedings of the Second Ancient Language Processing Workshop associated with NAACL 2025*, pages 12–21
May 4, 2025. ©2025 Association for Computational Linguistics

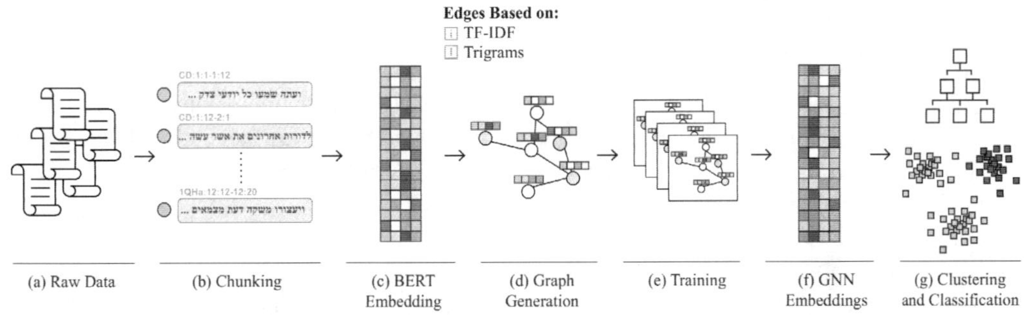


Figure 1: A sketch of the research outline. (**a** and **b**) Data collection and chunking. (**c**) Converting the text to numerical embeddings with BERT semantic model. (**d**) Graph generation based on statistical features. (**e+f**) Graph neural network training and extraction of integrated embeddings. (**g**) Application to clustering and classification questions.

tri-grams can effectively capture local orthographic and morphological patterns (Kulmizev et al., 2017), they are limited in their ability to encode deeper semantic relationships. In our study, we build upon this foundational work by incorporating tf-idf (see definition below) and trigram features, which provide a more nuanced representation of word importance across the corpus. We additionally apply modern semantic embeddings from BEREL (Shmidman et al., 2022), a pre-trained BERT model trained on rabbinic Hebrew literature. This hybrid approach allows us to integrate statistical and semantic features, addressing both the fragmentary nature of the DSS and the inherent challenges of processing ancient Hebrew.

Graph Neural Networks (GNNs) have emerged as powerful tools for representing textual data, particularly for tasks involving relationships between textual entities. Models such as TextGCN (Yao et al., 2018) and BertGCN (Lin et al., 2021) have demonstrated success in text classification by leveraging graph structures, where nodes represent documents or words, and edges capture co-occurrence or semantic relationships. Other works (Yang et al., 2021; Huang et al., 2019), explore alternative GNN architectures, showcasing the versatility of graph-based approaches in text-related tasks.

Unsupervised clustering for text data, particularly ancient and fragmentary texts like our corpus, presents substantial difficulties.

(Kipf and Welling, 2016) have shown good results in unsupervised learning by leveraging graph neural networks to generate latent representations that can be used for clustering. However, their application to textual datasets, particularly ancient and Hebrew corpora, has been limited (some related research exists, such as clustering in the Akkadian language (Stekel et al., 2021)). Our work integrates semantic and statistical features of the DSS within a graph neural network architecture to address the challenges posed by the unique characteristics of this corpus. The resulting embeddings of text chunks are used for clustering and classification of the scrolls, providing significant insights into their structure and content.

## 2 Methods

We developed a novel model for representing the DSS corpus. Below, we describe the data collection and preprocessing, the representation model, hyperparameter tuning and performance evaluation.

### 2.1 Data Collection

We used transcriptions of the DSS based on the data files prepared by Martin Abegg[2]. This data powers popular biblical software like Accordance and DSS Electronic Library. We used the Text-Fabric (Roorda, 2019) package, enabling the extraction of both textual content and morphological features for each word.

The corpus was filtered using several criteria. Paratextual elements such as document name, fragment, column, and line numbers were removed, along with all reconstructed text. Letters marked as probable or possible by the editors were retained, while textual gaps were excluded to prevent their analysis as inherent characteristics of the documents. Additionally, doubt marks, non-Hebrew characters, and redundant spaces were eliminated.

[2]`https://github.com/ETCBC/dss`

We focused exclusively on Hebrew scrolls, excluding Aramaic and Greek. Biblical scrolls were not included in the analysis but rewritten biblical texts like 4Q364 were studied since those texts are comparable to other Qumranic material. Finally, the analysis was restricted to Hebrew scrolls containing a minimum of 300 words.

The texts of each composition were divided into fixed-size chunks; after evaluating various chunk sizes and overlapping ratios (details in Appendix A), a chunk size of 100 words with an overlap of 15 words was chosen. This configuration ensures sufficient representation of smaller scrolls, many of which contain fewer than 500 words, while maintaining granularity for within-scroll analyses. This configuration yielded a dataset with 978 text chunks.

In addition, we curated a set of labels for validation purposes: sectarian / non-sectarian classification and composition name labels, e.g. War Scroll, Instruction, etc (Appendix B).

### 2.2 Document Representation

We represented each text chunk using both *semantic* and *statistical* features. For the semantic component, we rely on two Hebrew BERT-based models: **BEREL**, which is trained on rabbinic texts (closer to DSS Hebrew than modern Hebrew), and **AlephBERT** (Seker et al., 2022), which is more general for Hebrew tasks. Each text chunk is encoded as a 768-dimensional vector by extracting the final hidden representation of the `[CLS]` token from the model's last layer.

For the statistical component, we use *term frequency–inverse document frequency* (tf-idf). Given a term $t$ in a document $d$, tf-idf is defined as:

$$\text{tf-idf}(t, d) = \text{tf}(t, d) \cdot \log\left(\frac{N}{\text{df}(t)}\right),$$

where $\text{tf}(t, d)$ is the frequency of $t$ in $d$, $N$ is the total number of documents, and $\text{df}(t)$ is the number of documents containing $t$. Additionally, we include *tri-grams*: sequences of three consecutive characters, to capture local orthographic and morphological features.

### 2.3 Graph Construction

We use a graph neural network (GNN) framework where adjacency matrices are derived from cosine similarity between text chunk embeddings (*tf-idf* and *trigram*). For each embedding type, we first create a matrix $\mathbf{A}^\star \in \mathbb{R}^{n_{\text{chunk}} \times n_{\text{chunk}}}$ where $\mathbf{A}^\star_{ij} = \text{cosine\_similarity}(\text{chunk}_i, \text{chunk}_j)$ if $\text{cosine\_similarity}(\text{chunk}_i, \text{chunk}_j) > t$, and $\mathbf{A}^\star_{ij} = 0$ otherwise.

Let $\mathbf{D}^\star$ be the degree matrix of $\mathbf{A}^\star$. We then apply symmetric normalization to obtain the matrix $\tilde{\mathbf{A}}^\star \in \mathbb{R}^{n_{\text{chunk}} \times n_{\text{chunk}}}$:

$$\tilde{\mathbf{A}}^\star = (\mathbf{D}^\star)^{-\frac{1}{2}} \mathbf{A}^\star (\mathbf{D}^\star)^{-\frac{1}{2}}.$$

We perform this procedure separately for both embedding types (i.e., *tf-idf* and *trigram*), resulting in $\tilde{\mathbf{A}}^\star_{\text{tfidf}}$ and $\tilde{\mathbf{A}}^\star_{\text{trigram}}$. Next, we combine these normalized matrices via element-wise addition:

$$\mathbf{M}_{ij} = \tilde{\mathbf{A}}^\star_{\text{tfidf},ij} + \tilde{\mathbf{A}}^\star_{\text{trigram},ij}.$$

We then apply a threshold $h$ to $\mathbf{M}$ to form our adjacency matrix $\mathbf{A}$, and normalize it using the same symmetric normalization procedure, yielding our final adjacency matrix $\tilde{\mathbf{A}}$. This adjacency matrix represents edges between text chunks whose combined similarity (over tf-idf and trigram) exceeds the threshold $h$.

### 2.4 Model

For generating refined text embeddings, we use a Graph Auto Encoder model (Kipf and Welling, 2017). Our model uses a two-layer GNN to encode graph structure and node features into a low-dimensional latent space.

The graph is represented by a normalized adjacency matrix $\tilde{\mathbf{A}} \in \mathbb{R}^{N \times N}$. Node features are represented as a matrix $\mathbf{X} \in \mathbb{R}^{N \times D}$, where each node is initialized with a BERT-based embedding vector. The latent space representation is given by $\mathbf{Z} \in \mathbb{R}^{N \times F}$. The GNN layers propagate information through the graph, defined as:

$$\text{GNN}(\mathbf{X}, \mathbf{A}) = \tilde{\mathbf{A}}\text{ReLU}(\tilde{\mathbf{A}}\mathbf{X}\mathbf{W}_0)\mathbf{W}_1, \quad (1)$$

where $\mathbf{W}_0$ and $\mathbf{W}_1$ are trainable weight matrices.

The decoder reconstructs the adjacency matrix $\mathbf{A}$ using the inner product of the latent representations. For a given edge $\mathbf{A}_{ij}$, the decoder predicts the edge probability as:

$$\hat{\mathbf{A}}_{ij} = \sigma(\mathbf{Z}_i \cdot \mathbf{Z}_j^T), \quad (2)$$

where $\sigma(\cdot)$ is the sigmoid function, and $\mathbf{Z}_i$ and $\mathbf{Z}_j$ are the latent representations of nodes $i$ and $j$. The reconstruction loss is computed as:

$$\begin{aligned} \mathcal{L} = -\frac{1}{|\mathcal{E}+|} \sum_{(i,j)\in\mathcal{E}+} \log \hat{\mathbf{A}}ij \\ -\frac{1}{|\mathcal{E}-|} \sum_{(i,j)\in\mathcal{E}-} \log(1 - \hat{\mathbf{A}}ij), \end{aligned} \quad (3)$$

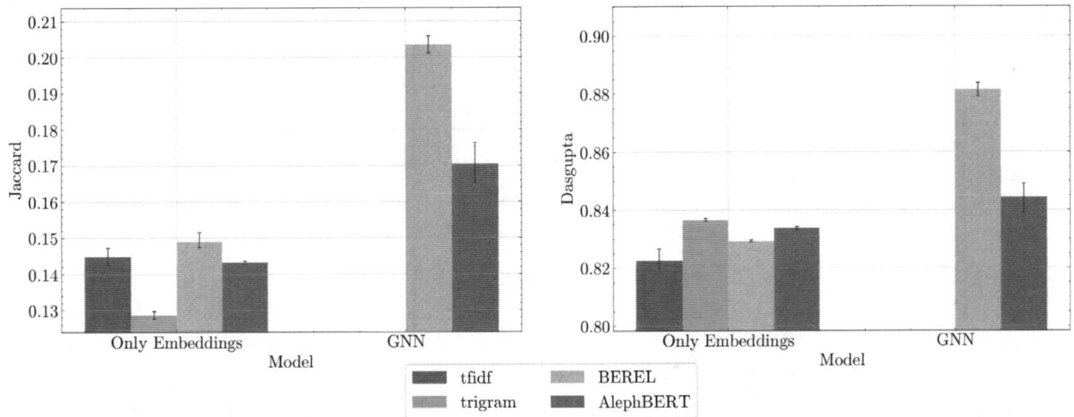


Figure 2: Unsupervised scroll clustering results using different feature extraction methods. Red bars correspond to classical NLP features, blue bars to Hebrew BERT embeddings).

where $\mathcal{E}+$ and $\mathcal{E}-$ are the sets of positive and negative edges, respectively. Negative edges are sampled using negative sampling (Veličković et al., 2018), which is a technique that randomly selects non-existing edges to serve as negative examples in the training. We specifically ensure that the number of negative edges matches the number of positive edges.

During training, we apply a dropout rate of 0.2 along with batch normalization to prevent overfitting.

### 2.5 Clustering and evaluation

We used two clustering algorithms: agglomerative clustering with Ward's linkage (Jr., 1963) for hierarchical clustering, and $k$-means clustering for flat clustering. Both Ward's linkage and $k$-means clustering optimize the same objective: minimizing within-cluster variance, expressed as squared Euclidean distances. The number of clusters is set to the number of compositions in the corpus, reflecting the basic distribution of our dataset.

To assess the clustering performance, we used the Jaccard measure (Rousseeuw, 1987) for external evaluation, where the labels correspond to the **compositions**. We also used the Dasgupta objective (Dasgupta, 2015), which is a custom cost function for evaluating hierarchical clustering models. This method calculates the cost function over a hierarchy of points, given pairwise similarities between those points. In our approach, these similarities are determined by the adjacency of text chunks: for any two consecutive chunks, we assign a similarity score of 1.

### 2.6 Baselines

We compared our method against several baseline embedding models, including character trigrams, tf-idf and BERT. For each baseline, we applied the same clustering procedure as in our proposed method, using $k$-means on the text chunk embeddings, with $k$ set to the number of scrolls or compositions.

### 2.7 Parameter Tuning

To determine the optimal hyper-parameter configuration, we performed a grid search over a range of values for the number of edges (derived from $t$ and $h$), graph construction methods, hidden dimensions, and learning rates. The optimization criterion was based on minimizing the training loss, with early stopping applied when the loss improvement was less than epsilon. For each set of hyper-parameters, we used 10-fold nested cross-validation to evaluate the embedding performance, measured as the average over all folds. The models were trained using the Adam optimizer (Kingma and Ba, 2017) with a weight decay regularization term of 5e-4.

### 2.8 Code and data availability

The code developed for this paper has been made publicly available [3], and the resulting dataset has been uploaded to the Hugging Face Hub [4] to facilitate future research efforts. All of our algorithms were implemented in Python 3.10 and executed on

[3] https://github.com/yonatanlou/QumranNLP

[4] https://huggingface.co/datasets/yonatanlou/QumranDataset

a personal MacBook Pro (M2, 2022, 16 GB RAM, 512 GB SSD).

## 3 Results

We developed a new method that applies a GNN architecture to integrate semantic and linguistic features for clustering of the Qumran Scrolls. First, we identified the optimal parameters by tuning the unsupervised model on the entire Qumran corpus, demonstrating that our algorithm outperforms baseline methods. We then validated the algorithm on the Hebrew Bible dataset, achieving similar performance and confirming its robustness. Finally, we used the trained model to extract improved text embeddings, which were applied to address various well-known research questions. We used the BEREL model which yields the best results across our experiments.

### 3.1 Model evaluation

We evaluated our model based on its performance on the entire Qumran corpus, yielding a GNN with 978 nodes and 9,391 edges. This evaluation explored different initial BERT embeddings and compared them to our baseline methods (see Figure 2). Interestingly, classical methods like tri-grams and tf-idf demonstrated competitive results compared to the BERT embeddings, likely due to the unique characteristics of our corpus. The GNN-based methods in these experiments were based on tf-idf and trigram based similarities, yielding the best overall performance.

### 3.2 Text clustering

The present section will address two research questions about the homogeneity and coherency of the Qumran corpus, both on a large and a smaller scale. It was apparent earlier on that some scrolls reflect the vocabulary, style and theology of a separate community with its ideas and institutions. The core texts of that group were found as well preserved scrolls in Qumran Cave 1 and were published in the 1950s. It was also clear that some compositions did not belong to the Yahad community but were rather a heritage of wider circles. The dividing line between the categories seemed clear at first (Newsom, 1990; Dimant, 2014), but in recent decades it has been debated. Many new fragmentary compositions were found in Cave 4 whose social identity is uncertain, and in addition the definition of a "sect" and the outright connection between it and its literary product was problematized. We therefore venture to test whether these categories could be achieved using advanced clustering techniques. A first research question pertains to the composition and inner-variety of the collection of Hodayot hymns.

**Clustering within the Hodayot.** We examine one of the large scrolls from Cave 1, the Hodayot scroll 1QH$^a$ containing religious hymns on the life of the community. These hymns have parallels in fragmentary copies from Cave 4, but they will not be examined here as the problem is clearest on the largest copy. A prevalent theory distinguished two types of hymns: Teacher Hymns and Community Hymns, as defined in (Douglas, 1999; Johnson, 2022) based on earlier studies. While the hymns are quite similar, experts detected in them different vocabulary and themes. The exact extent of the Teacher Hymns within 1QH$^a$ is debated. Douglas saw them as a block of material concentrated in columns 10-17, and the Community Hymns in columns 2-8, 18-24. Douglas considers Columns 9 and 18-20 as transition material enveloping the Teacher Hymns, that can therefore belong to each of the groups. Other studies saw the Teacher Hymns as a dispersed group through the entire scroll. The existence and extent of Teacher Hymns are examined here. We applied our GNN model to the Hodayot composition. Using these embeddings, we applied hierarchical clustering to perform unsupervised clustering. Our analysis (Figure 3) identified the following clusters:

- Cluster 1 (Purple) and cluster 2 (Red) contain Teacher Hymns from columns 10-16, with two chunks from the enveloping material (columns 18-19).

- Cluster 3 (orange) and cluster 4 (green) contain primarily Community Hymns from columns 1-9, 18-23, with several transitional chunks from column 9 and two hymns from columns 14 and 15. Three chunks from columns 11, 12, 15 stand at the edge of the cluster.

The results overwhelmingly confirm the existence of a distinct category of Teacher Hymns. Moreover, the results confirm that Teacher Hymns are clustered at the center of 1QH$^a$, with only a few outliers. These outliers will be discussed in a dedicated article intended for the Qumran research

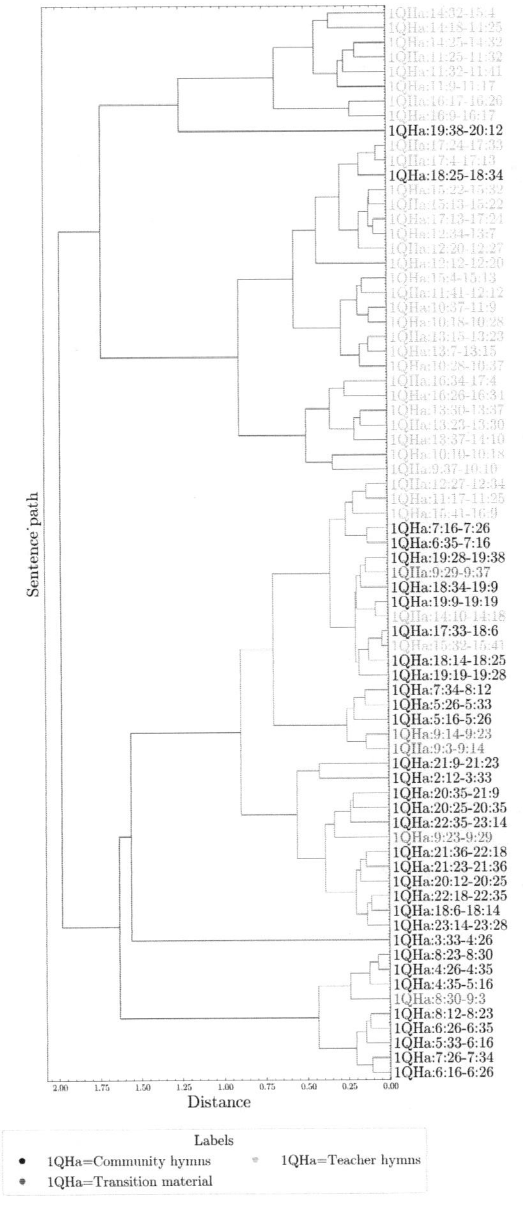


Figure 3: Dendrogram of the Hodayot composition clustering using the best-performing GNN model.

community. Notable is the identity of 3:33–4:26, which received a cluster of its own, as well as the presence of 14:10–18 and 15:32–41 within the cluster of Community Hymns. The blurred identity of the transition passages, as well as some outliers, may be attributed to a unifying "Maskil" redaction (Johnson, 2022).

**Classification of sectarian scrolls.** The clustering of sectarian compositions produced less definitive results although it did point out two main clusters of sectarian compositions. The clustering depends on three categories: 1) core texts of the yahad community based on their vocabulary and content: War Scroll, Community Rule, Rule of the Congregation, Hodayot, CD (Damascus Document), Pesharim and similar documents (Dimant, 2014). 2) texts that do not display sectarian features (such as Apocryphom Jeremiah), 3) Other compositions which, while displaying some similar features, are not fully consistent and their identity remains debated (for example Shir Shabbat - the Songs of the Sabbath Sacrifice). In this section we clustered compositions rather than chunks. To this end, we averaged each composition's chunk embeddings to obtain one vector per composition. Then we performed hierarchical clustering on these composition-level embeddings. The resulting dendrogram is provided in Figure 4. The labeling in this diagram is based on the composition level (e.g., Hodayot), with some labels representing groups of related compositions, such as Pesharim, Rewritten Pentateuch, and Calendrical Texts. The classification as sectarian or non-sectarian is provided in Appendix B. It is important to note that the clustering process was entirely unsupervised and only later compared with predefined labels.

Our expectation was that sectarian and non-sectarian texts would cluster separately. The Calendrical Texts and the Copper Scroll served as test cases, as their distinct linguistic profiles should stand out in an unsupervised clustering scheme. The dendrogram shows two main clusters of sectarian compositions, with text marked in black. Some appear close to texts of uncertain identity, whose sectarian status is now further supported. The yellow cluster includes seven clearly sectarian texts, such as the Pesharim, MMT, the War Scroll, and the Community Rule, making it strongly indicative of sectarian content. The Apocryphal Psalms (11Q11) also appear here, but the composition's small size and the wide dispersion of its embeddings limit the reliability of its clustering, especially after averaging those embeddings. At the edge of the green cluster is CD, a prominent sectarian text. Its proximity to the main sectarian cluster reflects its sectarian character, whereas its literary diversity in terms of genre and content accounts for its location outside the core sectarian cluster.

The gray cluster at the top of the dendrogram contains core sectarian texts such as Hodayot and The Rule of the Blessings, next to the two wisdom texts Instruction and Mysteries. It also includes poetic compositions such as the Collections of Psalms, Barkhi Nafshi, Songs of Maskil, Shir Shabbat, and Daily Prayers, alongside the prayers in Dibre Hameorot. This grouping highlights a set of poetic and prayer texts whose sectarian identity has been debated, now shown to align closely with core sectarian compositions.

The Calendrical Texts and the Copper Scroll cluster separately as expected, forming a distinct group with high distance between other compositions.

Analysis of the embeddings for each composition revealed that the dendrogram representation might be misleading for compositions with high dispersion across text chunks, such as the Apocryphal Psalms, Para Kings, Festival Prayers, and the Book of Tobit. Their average representation in the dendrogram does not fully reflect their true properties. For instance, the entire red cluster consists of such compositions. Upon analyzing these text chunks, we found that most are highly fragmentary, while the Book of Tobit exhibits significant stylistic differences between its text chunks.

The green cluster at the bottom of the dendrogram highlights the model's ability to capture the stylistic characteristics of rewritten Bible texts. This cluster includes the Temple Scroll, Rewritten Pentateuch texts, Dibre Moshe, Books of Tobit, and the Book of Jubilees. This generic grouping overrides the sectarian/non-sectarian division, generally placing the compositions in this cluster in the non-sectarian group and instead aligns them based on genre. While this clustering does not directly address the sectarian question, it demonstrates the model's ability to identify main genres. In summary, the model successfully confirms the grouping of core organizational texts and aligns Dibre Hameorot and Instruction with them. It accurately identifies clear non-sectarian texts such as The Book of Tobit and The Book of Jubilees. These categorizations align with common labels and highlight some unexpected groupings. However, the model does not produce distinct results for the Rewritten Bible and prayer genres, reflecting the complexity of these categories.

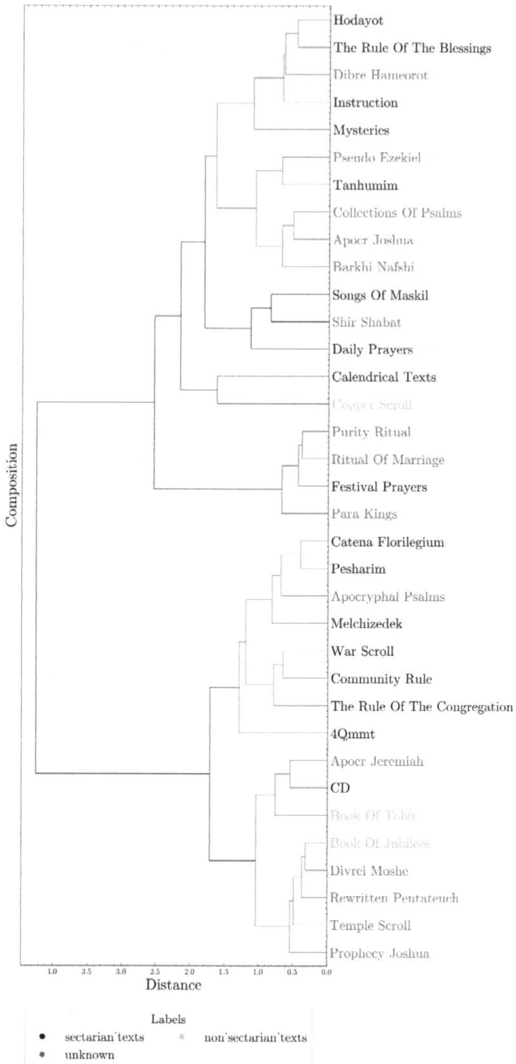


Figure 4: Dendrogram of compositions with sectarian or non sectarian label.

## 4 Conclusions

Our research introduces a novel GNN-based method that effectively integrates semantic and linguistic features for clustering Qumran texts. By training an unsupervised model on the entire corpus, we identified optimal parameters and demonstrated that our approach outperforms baseline methods.

The model's ability to capture complex relationships between text fragments and represent the text with improved embeddings, allowed us to address significant research questions related to authorship and sectarian classification within the DSS corpus. Our clustering results demonstrate that the clustering aligns closely with traditional divisions established in the literature.

While our model provided promising results, some of its aspects could be improved in future work. Sentence-transformer models are particularly effective for processing chunks of text and offer the potential for greater precision. While there is currently no pre-trained Hebrew model available, these models could be fine-tuned on non-debatable text chunks to create a robust embedding space specifically tailored to the DSS corpus.

## 5 Limitations

While our study demonstrates promising results in clustering and classifying the Dead Sea Scrolls, it has several limitations that warrant consideration. Specifically, the fragmentary nature of the DSS corpus poses inherent challenges. The preprocessing steps in this work could be improved, and a comprehensive study dedicated to this topic alone would be beneficial. Moreover, the corpus is continually refined through ongoing manual work, which means that the data used in this study may differ slightly from future versions. The present text of the scrolls is essentially that of the Discoveries in the Judaean Desert (DJD) series, as further refined editions lack a comprehensive electronic repository.

While our clustering results align with traditional scholarly divisions, the evaluation relies on predefined labels that may be subjective. The ground truth for sectarian classification and text authorship is not absolute, thus limiting the objectivity of the performance metrics.

## Acknowledgments

This work was supported by a research grant from the Israel Ministry of Innovation, Science and Technology (grant no. 1001577565).

## References

Axel Bühler, Gideon Yoffe, Nachum Dershowitz, Eli Piasetzky, Israel Finkelstein, Thomas Römer, and Barak Sober. 2024. Exploring the stylistic uniqueness of the priestly source in genesis and exodus through a statistical/computational lens. *Zeitschrift fur die Alttestamentliche Wissenschaft*, 136(2):165–190. Publisher Copyright: © 2024 Walter de Gruyter GmbH. All rights reserved.

John J Collins. 2010. *Beyond the Qumran Community: The Sectarian Movement of the Dead Sea Scrolls*. Wm. B. Eerdmans Publishing.

Sanjoy Dasgupta. 2015. A cost function for similarity-based hierarchical clustering. *Preprint*, arXiv:1510.05043.

Devorah Dimant. 2014. *History, ideology and Bible interpretation in the Dead Sea Scrolls: Collected studies*, volume 90. Mohr Siebeck.

Michael C Douglas. 1999. The teacher hymn hypothesis revisited: New data for an old crux. *Dead Sea Discoveries*, pages 239–266.

Lianzhe Huang, Dehong Ma, Sujian Li, Xiaodong Zhang, and Houfeng Wang. 2019. Text level graph neural network for text classification. In *Proceedings of the 2019 Conference on Empirical Methods in Natural Language Processing and the 9th International Joint Conference on Natural Language Processing (EMNLP-IJCNLP)*, pages 3444–3450, Hong Kong, China. Association for Computational Linguistics.

Michael B Johnson. 2022. Look who's talking: Reconsidering the speaker in the 'teacher hymns'(1qha). In *Emerging Sectarianism in the Dead Sea Scrolls*, pages 313–341. Brill.

Joe H. Ward Jr. 1963. Hierarchical grouping to optimize an objective function. *Journal of the American Statistical Association*, 58(301):236–244.

Diederik P. Kingma and Jimmy Ba. 2017. Adam: A method for stochastic optimization. *Preprint*, arXiv:1412.6980.

Thomas N. Kipf and Max Welling. 2016. Variational graph auto-encoders. *Preprint*, arXiv:1611.07308.

Thomas N. Kipf and Max Welling. 2017. Semi-supervised classification with graph convolutional networks. *Preprint*, arXiv:1609.02907.

Artur Kulmizev, Bo Blankers, Johannes Bjerva, Malvina Nissim, Gertjan van Noord, Barbara Plank, and Martijn Wieling. 2017. The power of character n-grams in native language identification. In *Proceedings of the 12th Workshop on Innovative Use of NLP for Building Educational Applications*, pages 382–389, Copenhagen, Denmark. Association for Computational Linguistics.

Yuxiao Lin, Yuxian Meng, Xiaofei Sun, Qinghong Han, Kun Kuang, Jiwei Li, and Fei Wu. 2021. Bertgcn: Transductive text classification by combining GCN and BERT. *CoRR*, abs/2105.05727.

Florentino García Martínez. 2010. Beyond the sectarian divide: The" voice of the teacher" as an authority-conferring strategy in some qumran texts. In *The Dead Sea Scrolls*, pages 227–244. Brill.

Carol A Newsom. 1990. 'sectually explicit' literature from qumran. *The Hebrew Bible and Its Interpreters*, 1:167–87.

Carol A Newsom. 2021. A farewell to the hodayot of the community. *Dead Sea Discoveries*, 28(1):1–19.

Renyi Qu, Ruixuan Tu, and Forrest Bao. 2024. Is semantic chunking worth the computational cost? *Preprint*, arXiv:2410.13070.

Dirk Roorda. 2019. Text-fabric: handling biblical data with ikea logistics. *HIPHIL Novum Journal for Bible and Digital Resources*, 5(2):126–135.

Peter J. Rousseeuw. 1987. Silhouettes: A graphical aid to the interpretation and validation of cluster analysis. *Journal of Computational and Applied Mathematics*, 20:53–65.

Amit Seker, Elron Bandel, Dan Bareket, Idan Brusilovsky, Refael Greenfeld, and Reut Tsarfaty. 2022. AlephBERT: Language model pre-training and evaluation from sub-word to sentence level. In *Proceedings of the 60th Annual Meeting of the Association for Computational Linguistics (Volume 1: Long Papers)*, pages 46–56, Dublin, Ireland. Association for Computational Linguistics.

Avi Shmidman, Joshua Guedalia, Shaltiel Shmidman, Cheyn Shmuel Shmidman, Eli Handel, and Moshe Koppel. 2022. Introducing berel: Bert embeddings for rabbinic-encoded language. *Preprint*, arXiv:2208.01875.

J. Starr. 2019. Classifying the aramaic texts from qumran: A statistical analysis of linguistic features. *Palestine Exploration Quarterly*, 151(2):160–163.

Moshe Stekel, Amos Azaria, and Shai Gordin. 2021. Word sense induction with attentive context clustering. In *Proceedings of the Workshop on Natural Language Processing for Digital Humanities*, pages 144–151, NIT Silchar, India. NLP Association of India (NLPAI).

Reut Tsarfaty, Shoval Sadde, Stav Klein, and Amit Seker. 2019. What's wrong with Hebrew NLP? and how to make it right. In *Proceedings of the 2019 Conference on Empirical Methods in Natural Language Processing and the 9th International Joint Conference on Natural Language Processing (EMNLP-IJCNLP): System Demonstrations*, pages 259–264, Hong Kong, China. Association for Computational Linguistics.

P. Van Hecke. 2018. Computational stylometric approach to the dead sea scrolls: Towards a new research agenda. *Dead Sea Discoveries*, 25(1):57–82.

James VanderKam and Peter Flint. 2005. *The meaning of the Dead Sea scrolls: their significance for understanding the Bible, Judaism, Jesus, and Christianity*. A&C Black.

Petar Veličković, William Fedus, William L. Hamilton, Pietro Liò, Yoshua Bengio, and R Devon Hjelm. 2018. Deep graph infomax. *Preprint*, arXiv:1809.10341.

Tianchi Yang, Linmei Hu, Chuan Shi, Houye Ji, Xiaoli Li, and Liqiang Nie. 2021. Hgat: Heterogeneous graph attention networks for semi-supervised short text classification. *ACM Trans. Inf. Syst.*, 39(3).

Liang Yao, Chengsheng Mao, and Yuan Luo. 2018. Graph convolutional networks for text classification. *CoRR*, abs/1809.05679.

# A Pre-processing parameter evaluation

## A.1 Chunk Size Evaluation

When dividing the DSS texts into chunks, a critical factor was selecting an appropriate chunk size to balance representation and analytical granularity. Chunk sizes between 25 and 150 words were evaluated, with overlapping ratios of 5%, 10%, and 15%. Smaller chunk sizes increase the granularity of the analysis but risk fragmenting the text excessively, while larger chunk sizes reduce granularity and limit the number of chunks for shorter scrolls. This limitation is particularly problematic for scrolls containing fewer than 500 words, as larger chunks may result in only one or two chunks per scroll, hindering within-scroll clustering. While more advanced chunking techniques exist (Qu et al., 2024), we chose to use a fixed-size chunking method with overlap due to the highly fragmentary and unordered nature of our corpus, which lack the clear structural organization seen in the Bible.

The evaluation showed that chunk sizes of 100 and 150 words yielded the best performance across intrinsic and extrinsic clustering metrics. While 150-word chunks slightly outperformed in some cases, 100-word chunks were ultimately chosen to allow for better representation of shorter scrolls and greater flexibility in downstream tasks. An overlap of 15 words was selected as it provided a good balance between minimizing information loss and computational efficiency.

# B Labeling details

We categorized the compositions into sectarian, non-sectarian, and texts with undetermined identity as follows:

- **Sectarian texts**: Calendrical Texts, Catena and Florilegium, CD, Community Rule, Daily Prayers (4Q503), Festival Prayers (4Q509), Hodayot, Instruction (Musar Lamevin), Melchizedek, Mysteries, Pesharim, Rule of Blessings, Rule of the Congregation, Songs of Maskil, Tanhumim, War Scroll, and 4QMMT.
- **Non-sectarian texts**: Book of Jubilees, Book of Tobit, and Copper Scroll (3Q15).
- **Texts with undetermined identity**: Apocryphal Psalms, Apocryphon Jeremiah, Apocryphon Joshua, Barkhi Nafshi, Collections of Psalms (4Q380-381), Dibre Hameorot,

Dibre Moshe (1Q22), Para Kings (4Q382), Prophecy Joshua, Pseudo-Ezekiel, Rewritten Pentateuch, Ritual of Marriage (4Q512), Shir Olat Hashabbat, Temple Scroll, and Purity Ritual (4Q274).

The full list of labels, including labels for sectarian, composition, and genre, is available online.[5]

[5] https://github.com/yonatanlou/QumranNLP/blob/main/Data/Qumran_labels.csv

# Assignment of account type to proto-cuneiform economic texts with Multi-Class Support Vector Machines

**Piotr Zadworny**
Freie Universität Berlin
p.zadworny@fu-berlin.de

**Shai Gordin**
Ariel University
Dept. of the Land of Israel and Archaeology
shaigo@ariel.ac.il

## Abstract

We investigate the use of machine learning for classifying proto-cuneiform economic texts (3,500-3,000 BCE), leveraging Multi-Class Support Vector Machines (MSVM) to assign text type based on content. Proto-cuneiform presents unique challenges, as it does not encode spoken language, yet is transcribed into linear formats that obscure original structural elements. We address this by reformatting transcriptions, experimenting with different tokenization strategies, and optimizing feature extraction. Our workflow achieves high labeling reliability and enables significant metadata enrichment. In addition to improving digital corpus organization, our approach opens the chance to identify economic institutions in ancient Mesopotamian archives, providing a new tool for Assyriological research.

## 1 Introduction

Proto-cuneiform is a writing system which emerged in southern Mesopotamia at the end of the 4th millennium BCE.[1] It consisted of over 800 signs representing numbers, goods, and administrative procedures, which were impressed on small clay tablets using a reed stylus. The entire corpus consists of almost 7,000 texts, about 5,500 of which are economic accounts, used alongside other tools, such as small clay "tokens", bullae, and cylinder seals, to control the operations of early cities (Fig. 1).

The majority (ca. 80%) of proto-cuneiform artifacts originate from the large Eanna area in the city Uruk (modern-day Warka, Iraq). Excavations at the site since the 1920s by the *Deutsche Orient-Gesselschaft* (DOG), unearthed more than 5,000 texts. The focus of the Eanna excavators was, however, architecture, which determined the choice of a less-than-optimal approach towards other finds (Nissen, 2024).

Figure 1: *MS 4631*. A clay envelope with a seal impression (right) and an array of tokens kept inside it. Artifacts of this kind were the predecessors of writing, and continued to be used by the accountants after writing was invented as well.

Today, our understanding of those accounts' original use context is limited. On the one hand, this is due to the excavation documentation, where information is constrained to a square coordinate in a 20x20 m excavation grid, and occasional comments. On the other hand, it does not help that the tablets were already discarded in antiquity, and used as construction material within Eanna, so their deposition location is not the one in which they were written or stored. As one may expect in such a situation, they are often severely damaged.

Nevertheless, already Englund suggested that the distribution of tablets across the site echoes the original institutions from where they were taken (Englund, 1998). He observed that despite the secondary character of their deposition, accounts documenting the operations of the same sector of the archaic economy tend to be found together. In recent years, scholarly efforts into learning more about this site and the origins of writing, allowed us to gain a better understanding of the archaeological record of Uruk (Nissen, 2024; Naccaro, 2025).

In this article, we offer a machine learning

[1]The debate whether proto-cuneiform is genuine "writing" or just a mnemotechnical tool similar to other used at the time in the Ancient Near East is open. It is rooted in an exclusive definition of writing, which only allows glottographic systems (like later cuneiform), and not semasiographic ones (like proto-cuneiform).



*Proceedings of the Second Ancient Language Processing Workshop associated with NAACL 2025*, pages 22–30
May 4, 2025. 

approach to automatic labeling of those archaic tablets according to the economic sectors they deal with — the account type. Once a trustworthy method of doing this is established, we can measure the accounts' similarity to each other and try to cluster them on that ground to determine local environments — or even offices — they were originally written in. In the future, we may as well try to artificially complete, or at least expand, the damaged artifacts using a model of similar accounts as a template. Those tasks are not innovative on their own — in fact, they are what cuneiform experts traditionally do — however, considering the amount of material to work with, we think that developing an automatic solution is the best approach for measurable results at scale that are also reproducible.

Most importantly, however, automatically generated account labels are an additional metadata point which, together with a method of identifying similar texts in terms of content, allows other researchers to navigate the archaic corpus in a more informed way. As of now, information about account types is dispersed across different publications, which makes exploring the otherwise completely digitized corpus difficult. Account type metadata, either with original citations or an "automated" tag, is available through *4ky* (Zadworny, 2023), an open-source web application.

## 2 Data

To achieve the goal of trustworthy automatic account type classification, we used an existing edition of a comparable (even if much smaller) collection of archaic tablets by Monaco (2007, 2014, 2016) as the main part of the training dataset. Importantly, the texts edited by Monaco come from the antiquities market, and their archaeological origin is unknown. It is accepted as unlikely that they originate from the Eanna area of Uruk (Lecompte, 2023). This set of accounts was extended with some tablets from Uruk and other smaller collections which were discussed by Englund (1998), and few additional texts which we classified ourselves.[2]

The transcriptions of all the accounts used in this study were sourced from the *Cuneiform Digital Library Initiative* (contributors, 2025). The account type tags assigned by the aforementioned authors to the training dataset were extracted and assigned to the transcriptions manually.

Total number of transcriptions used for training was 596. They were divided into seven account types: **animal husbandry**, **cereal**, and **dairy** texts, accounts of **fields**, **fish**, and **humans**, as well as documents concerning **textiles**. Given that some accounts contain a mix of items from multiple economic sectors, we occasionally assigned more than one tag to one text. This influenced the algorithm design, as explained later.

The composition of the training dataset reflects the archaic corpus as a whole. Most of the accounts are **cereal texts** (323 in the training set), followed by **animal husbandry texts** (125). Together, these two types dominate the corpus, making the development of automatic labeling for these accounts particularly useful.

Automatic labeling of **dairy texts** (23), as well as **fish** (22) and **textile accounts** (24) is an interesting task: although they are easily identifiable for human scholars thanks to well-understood semantic sets of signs, they are relatively rare, making training data scarce.

**Field texts** (42) are not as common either, and some of them are entirely mathematical in nature, only identifiable as such if we closely follow the accountant's calculations.

**Human accounts** (58) are challenging for another reason: they usually contain lists of entries understood as individual names and composed of semantically unrelated signs, which may confuse the model. Texts usually assigned to other types, such as grain distributions (a cereal text) or assignments of animal herds (an animal husbandry text) exhibit the same characteristics, adding to the difficulty.

As an additional limitation, we excluded accounts with fewer than 6 signs from the training set, as our experiments showed this led to an improvement of our model's accuracy.

## 3 Method

The main requirements for the model were its trustworthiness and the ability to assign multiple labels to a single text. Additionally, since we intend for scholars to use our tools online, we aimed for a lightweight implementation.

### 3.1 Model architecture

Due to the small and unbalanced training dataset, using a neural network was not the optimal solution. Instead, we decided to use support vector machines (SVMs), which are known to perform better in such

[2]The accounts labeled by us have a "manual" tag in *4ky*.

situations.

To allow for assigning multiple labels to each account, we chose a specific type of SVM: a multi-class support vector machine (Wang and Xue, 2014; Zhang et al., 2021). A standard SVM seeks to optimally divide the dataset into exclusive groups, assigning only one account type per text. In contrast, a multi-class SVM treats each account type as a separate 'true or false' question. This allows one account to appear in the 'true' section of multiple account types, and therefore to have multiple labels assigned to it. This approach also allows the accounts to remain unlabeled when they do not meet the criteria of any of the account types. Together with the ability to assess the certainty of each assignment, this improves the quality of the model.

### 3.2 Approaches to feature extraction

When working with proto-cuneiform accounts, several additional challenges arise that are unique to this writing system. First, the language of those documents is unknown. As the accounts were mainly accounting tools, the writing does not reflect speech. Instead, meaning is encoded through non-linear arrangements of sign sets within *cases*—meaningful subdivisions of the writing surface, similar to text fields in modern forms—making traditional language-oriented methods not applicable.

The second challenge is the non-linearity of the script itself. In Assyriological transcriptions, each proto-cuneiform sign is represented by its *sign name* in Latin script, typically derived from its meaning in later Sumerian cuneiform. The text is also linearized according to the transcriber's intuition, resulting in the loss of information about the original arrangement of the signs (Fig. 2).

As solving the issue of transcriptions' linearity is beyond the scope of this paper, we chose to ignore the arrangements of signs within cases altogether. Instead, we alphabetized the order of the signs within each case to ensure that cases containing the same sets of signs are always represented in the same way.

Aware of those challenges, to feed the account transcriptions into our SVMs, we had to choose a way of tokenizing the texts. To our knowledge, no studies have yet determined the optimal way of doing this in the case of archaic Mesopotamian accounts. Thus, we decided to experiment using a TF-IDF tokenizer[3] with two approaches and compare their accuracy: *case-by-case*, treating the entire group of signs within one case of the document as one unit, and *sign-by-sign*, treating each sign separately.

### 3.3 Adjustments for accuracy

In the course of the study we experimented with other aspects of the dataset as well: we tried to assess the importance of **number signs** and **sign variants**.

The **number signs** were the key that allowed the scholars from the Berlin-based *Archaische Texte aus Uruk* (ATU) project to decipher the archaic accounts in the first place. Through computer-aided statistical analysis, they could show that number signs come in distinct sets depending on what is accounted for, even if some signs are shared across different sets (Green and Nissen, 1987). This observation allowed them to connect the accounts to specific economic sectors, as well as describe sets of semantically similar item signs each sector used.

We were curious if other (non-number) signs alone are enough to make such distinctions. To test this, we prepared for each account an alternative transcription without any numbers, which we then used to train another set of models, and we included the results in the comparison.

Otherwise, when including numbers, we only used the type of the sign, and not its value. For example, the expressions $2N_1$ and $6N_1$ repeat the same sign type — $N_1$ — to express different values, so we treat them both as just $N_1$. Our early tests showed preserving the values decreased the accuracy in the preliminary testing phase. This may have to do with the model giving weight to rare tokens. For instance the rare value $5N_{14}$ may appear unique—and thus significant—to some account types, when in fact this is entirely coincidental, and the sign $N_{14}$ is otherwise common.

The **sign variants** are a palaeographic feature of CDLI transcriptions. They are represented using lowercase letters after the tilde sign (Fig. 2). Although in most cases the variants seem not to indicate semantic differences, there is at least one important example to the contrary: the sign $DUG_a$ usually represents beer, whereas $DUG_b$ and $DUG_c$ stand for dairy fats — each a distinctive entry in different types of accounts. Experiments with excluding them invariably led to dips in model qual-

[3]Part of Scikit-learn *TfidfVectorizer*.

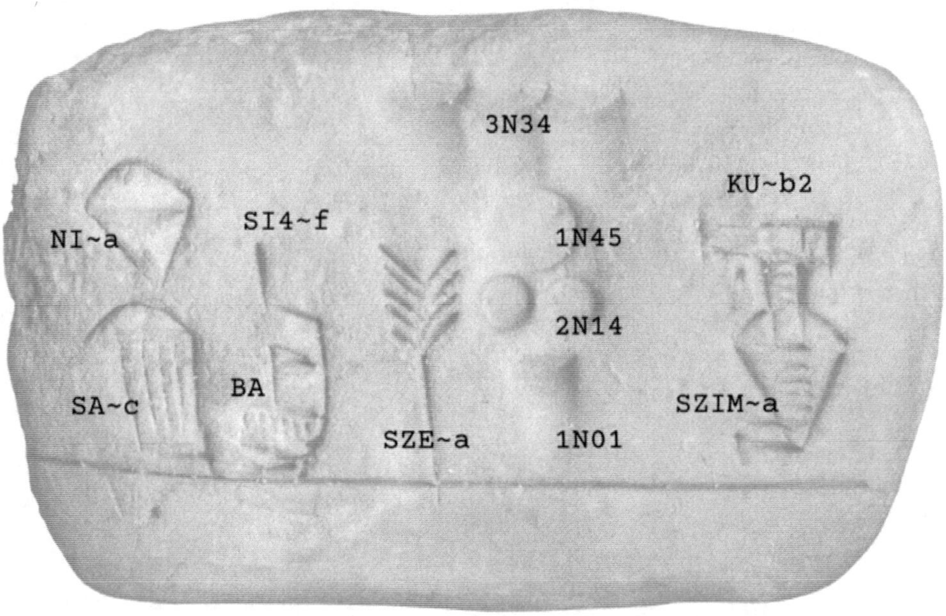


Figure 2: Reverse of *MSVO 3, 64* — metadata section of a cereal account. Here, all signs are inscribed within a single *case*, delineated with a horizontal line.

Transcription in CDLI:
3(N34) 1(N45) 2(N14) 1(N01), SZE∼a KU∼b2 SZIM∼a SI4∼f BA NI∼a SA∼c

ity.

Although it did not make much sense from a methodological point of view to allow the tokenizer to use *n-grams* (sequences of *n*-number of signs), since the signs in the transcriptions were reordered in an arbitrary way, we tested this aspect as well. Surprisingly, allowing for *n*-grams improved the model's accuracy, which made us choose to keep this feature. However, it did not matter whether we set the limit of *n* to 2 or more, so again we opted for the lowest value (2) to reduce its complexity.

### 3.4 Method summary

To summarize, we transformed the original dataset in two ways: through alphabetizing the order of signs within each case, and creating alternative versions of transcriptions without number signs.

Then, we trained four MSVMs to determine which is the most accurate. The variants of tokenization and transcription used were: 1) *line-by-line* with numbers; 2) *line-by-line* without numbers; 3) *sign-by-sign* with numbers; and 4) *sign-by-sign* without numbers.

70% of the dataset was used for training, and 30% for testing the model. The split was random and done once per each model. The models were trained for 10 iterations to see if the outcome changes, and in all cases the results were similar. In the next section, we present the final set of results.

## 4 Results

For convenience, the results of testing the models will be discussed separately for each account type.

### 4.1 Animals

| | with numbers, line by line | | | without numbers, line by line | | | |
|---|---|---|---|---|---|---|---|
| | Precision | Recall | F1-score | Precision | Recall | F1-score | Support |
| no | 0.87 | 1.00 | 0.93 | 0.81 | 1.00 | 0.94 | 148 |
| yes | 1.00 | 0.26 | 0.41 | 1.00 | 0.35 | 0.52 | 31 |
| accuracy | | | 0.87 | | | 0.89 | 179 |
| | with numbers, sign by sign | | | without numbers, sign by sign | | | |
| | Precision | Recall | F1-score | Precision | Recall | F1-score | Support |
| no | 0.93 | 1.00 | 0.96 | 0.93 | 1.00 | 0.96 | 148 |
| yes | 1.00 | 0.61 | 0.76 | 1.00 | 0.61 | 0.76 | 31 |
| accuracy | | | 0.93 | | | 0.93 | 179 |

Table 1: Animal accounts classification

All the values are in the range of 0 to 1, so 0.90 is equal to 90%. The *precision* value shows how many times the model was correct in assigning the label type. So, in the first example, 87% of the negative answers ("the account is not an account of animals") were correct. The *recall* value shows how many matching examples were found—so, together with 87% precision, the 100% value means that although the model assigned the 'not animal' label to too many texts, it caught 100% of the true non-animal texts. The *support* value (last column) is the real number of non-animal and animal accounts in the test set, and it is used as a weight to calculate the *F1 score* — the realistic accuracy measure of the model.

Knowing that, we can see that *line-by-line* tokenization did not work very well in the case of animal accounts: the positive recall scores of 26% (with numbers) and 35% (without numbers) show that the models failed to catch many animal texts in the testing dataset. The performance of the *sign-by-sign* models was slightly better (61% in both). Importantly, neither produced any false positives (the precision score of *yes* is 100%), which is a good sign from the point of view of reliability. Also, it is interesting to see that in this case it did not matter if the numbers were included or not, as the outcome scores were the same.

An additional method of examining the models' performance at this stage is studying **feature importance**. Our models, as they were trained, assigned coefficients (positive and negative) to each token they encountered, to determine how likely each token is to appear in a specific account type. After training, we extracted those coefficients to see what signs or sign combinations models considered as particularly telling for each account type.

In terms of animal accounts, for the *sign-by-sign, with numbers* model, the most positively important tokens were KIŠ (an equid sign), $UD_{5a}$ ("ram"), $U_8$ ("ewe"), and $N_2$ — a numerical sign used to account for dead animals (Englund, 1998).

Among the negatively important tokens we find signs like $N_{19}$ (a quantity sign for emmer, ca. 150 liters), $KISIM_b$ ("sheep's milk butter"), or $SAL.KUR_a$ (metadata sign used for totals of workers). Those findings suggest that the model correctly identifies which signs belong to the semantic set of animal signs, and used them to label the accounts.

## 4.2 Cereals

The performance of the model on cereal accounts was significantly better, and we assume it is due to the dominance of those texts in the training dataset. Here, unlike in the animal texts, *line-by-line* models achieved more success, although they were still worse than those using the *sign-by-sign* approach. With those, we see scores similar to the ones above, with the model with numbers performing slightly better than the one without. Unfortunately, every model produced false positives, with the *sign-by-sign, with numbers* model making the fewest mistakes.

| | with numbers, line by line | | | without numbers, line by line | | | |
|---|---|---|---|---|---|---|---|
| | Precision | Recall | F1-score | Precision | Recall | F1-score | Support |
| no | 0.88 | 0.72 | 0.79 | 0.71 | 0.79 | 0.75 | 78 |
| yes | 0.81 | 0.92 | 0.86 | 0.83 | 0.75 | 0.79 | 101 |
| accuracy | | | 0.83 | | | 0.77 | 179 |
| | with numbers, sign by sign | | | without numbers, sign by sign | | | |
| | Precision | Recall | F1-score | Precision | Recall | F1-score | Support |
| no | 0.89 | 0.97 | 0.93 | 0.81 | 0.92 | 0.86 | 94 |
| yes | 0.98 | 0.91 | 0.94 | 0.93 | 0.83 | 0.88 | 85 |
| accuracy | | | 0.94 | | | 0.91 | 179 |

Table 2: Cereals classification

**Feature importance** analysis shows the significance of number signs in this account type: although the top-scoring signs are $ŠE_a$ ("barley"; also metadata sign for totals of grain) and $DUG_a$ (most often "beer"), among the top ten positively important signs we have $N_{39a}$ (a quantity of ca. 5 liters of barley), $N_{19}$ (ca. 150 liters of emmer), $N_4$ (ca. 25 liters of emmer) or $N_{24}$ (ca. 2.5 liters of barley or malt). Included are also bigrams $N_1$ $ŠE_a$ (ca. 25 liters of barley) and $N_{45}$ $N_4$ (even larger volumes of emmer).

The significance of number signs stands out among the negative features as well: among the top signs are $N_1$ and $N_{34}$ (polyvalent number signs; used in different accounting systems to represent different quantities) as well as $N_{50}$ and $N_{22}$ (used in field measurements).

Overall, this is not surprising, as the accounting systems for cereals were the most varied and contained the most unique numerical signs. Like in the case of animal texts, we see that the model could recognize that and use this feature of proto-cuneiform.

## 4.3 Dairy

The dairy texts are among the most underrepresented in the training set, and this is clearly visible in test scores. In this case, it is difficult to decide which model performed best: the highest score of 22% (*sign-by-sign, without numbers*) is equal to 2 catches, and two other models caught 1 text each. While no model produced false positives, the outcome seems hardly useful. It is also important to

| | with numbers, line by line | | | without numbers, line by line | | | |
|---|---|---|---|---|---|---|---|
| | Precision | Recall | F1-score | Precision | Recall | F1-score | Support |
| no | 0.95 | 1.00 | 0.97 | 0.96 | 1.00 | 0.98 | 170 |
| yes | 0.00 | 0.00 | 0.00 | 1.00 | 0.11 | 0.20 | 9 |
| accuracy | | | 0.96 | | | 0.96 | 179 |
| | with numbers, sign by sign | | | without numbers, sign by sign | | | |
| | Precision | Recall | F1-score | Precision | Recall | F1-score | Support |
| no | 0.96 | 1.00 | 0.98 | 0.96 | 1.00 | 0.98 | 170 |
| yes | 1.00 | 0.11 | 0.20 | 1.00 | 0.22 | 0.36 | 9 |
| accuracy | | | 0.96 | | | 0.96 | 179 |

Table 3: Dairy classification

acknowledge that the very high compound accuracy scores (96%) are inflated by the overwhelming proportion of true negatives, a phenomenon which repeats for other less common account types, and thus *is not* a meaningful measure of success.

Despite that, the **feature importance** analysis shows that the model was still able to learn the signs which are characteristic for dairy accounts. Among positively important signs we have $DUG_c$ ("dairy fat"), $KISIM_a$ (butter from sheep's milk), as well as bigrams $N_1$ $KISIM_a$ ("one vessel of the butter from sheep's milk") or $N_1$ $KU_{3a}$ (a compound number sign representing the quantity of ca. 4 liters of dairy fats).

Interestingly, the negatively important features seem to focus on animal signs, which sometimes do appear in dairy accounts. We find in the report such bigrams as $N_1$ $AB_2$ ("one cow") or AMAR $U_4 \times 1 N_{57}$ ("one-year-old youngling"), which require further study. However, this "prejudice" against animal signs may cause the low score of the model.

### 4.4 Fields

| | with numbers, line by line | | | without numbers, line by line | | | |
|---|---|---|---|---|---|---|---|
| | Precision | Recall | F1-score | Precision | Recall | F1-score | Support |
| no | 0.91 | 1.00 | 0.95 | 0.93 | 1.00 | 0.96 | 163 |
| yes | 0.00 | 0.00 | 0.00 | 1.00 | 0.25 | 0.40 | 16 |
| accuracy | | | 0.91 | | | 0.93 | 169 |
| | with numbers, sign by sign | | | without numbers, sign by sign | | | |
| | Precision | Recall | F1-score | Precision | Recall | F1-score | Support |
| no | 0.95 | 1.00 | 0.98 | 0.93 | 1.00 | 0.96 | 163 |
| yes | 1.00 | 0.50 | 0.67 | 1.00 | 0.25 | 0.40 | 16 |
| accuracy | | | 0.96 | | | 0.93 | 169 |

Table 4: Field texts classification

The outcome here is similar to the one presented in the previous section. Again, we see overall low scores, with the *sign-by-sign, with numbers* model scoring the highest, with 50% of correctly labeled accounts. Again, we have no false positives.

Among the positively **significant features**, we see $GAN_2$ ("field"), as well as several number signs from the appropriate accounting system: $N_{50}$ (an area of ca. 65ha) and $N_{22}$ (ca. 2,16ha), alongside bigrams formed of various combinations of number signs. This reflects the often mathematical character of field texts, many of which are area calculations.

Other than one puzzling bigram, $GAN_2$ $APIN_b$ ("land for ploughing?" or "ploughed field?"), the list of negatively important signs consists of seemingly random entries.

### 4.5 Fish

| | with numbers, line by line | | | without numbers, line by line | | | |
|---|---|---|---|---|---|---|---|
| | Precision | Recall | F1-score | Precision | Recall | F1-score | Support |
| no | 0.97 | 1.00 | 0.98 | 0.97 | 1.00 | 0.99 | 173 |
| yes | 0.00 | 0.00 | 0.00 | 1.00 | 0.17 | 0.29 | 6 |
| accuracy | | | 0.97 | | | 0.97 | 179 |
| | with numbers, sign by sign | | | without numbers, sign by sign | | | |
| | Precision | Recall | F1-score | Precision | Recall | F1-score | Support |
| no | 0.98 | 1.00 | 0.99 | 0.98 | 1.00 | 0.99 | 173 |
| yes | 1.00 | 0.50 | 0.67 | 1.00 | 0.33 | 0.50 | 6 |
| accuracy | | | 0.98 | | | 0.98 | 179 |

Table 5: Fish accounts classification

The fish accounts had the lowest support value out of all the account types, which makes the accuracy scores accidental.

Similarly to other rare account types, we see that the *sign-by-sign, with numbers* model scored the highest, though too by a margin of a single account. The small difference, together with the low support value makes it difficult to judge the quality of the models.

Nonetheless, like in the case of dairy tablets, the model was able to learn some fish-specific signs. Among the positively **important signs** we find entries like SUHUR ("dried fish"), $ZATU759 \times KU_{6a}$ (a container with fish?), or $GA_2 \times KU_{6a}$ ("basket with fish"), all typical for this semantic set.

The list of negatively important features consists mostly of numerals belonging to the cereal system, however, the highest scoring entry is $N_8$ SUHUR: a seemingly valid fish qualification.

### 4.6 Humans

The accounts of humans is an account type where all models failed entirely and did not catch any texts.

Despite this — and in line with what we have seen in the cases of other underrepresented account types — **feature analysis** shows that the model did identify some signs that are indicative of human accounts. We see the bigram $N_1$ $SAL.KUR_a$

| | with numbers, line by line | | | without numbers, line by line | | | |
|---|---|---|---|---|---|---|---|
| | Precision | Recall | F1-score | Precision | Recall | F1-score | Support |
| no | 0.92 | 1.00 | 0.96 | 0.92 | 1.00 | 0.96 | 164 |
| yes | 0.00 | 0.00 | 0.00 | 0.00 | 0.00 | 0.00 | 15 |
| accuracy | | | 0.92 | | | 0.92 | 179 |
| | with numbers, sign by sign | | | without numbers, sign by sign | | | |
| | Precision | Recall | F1-score | Precision | Recall | F1-score | Support |
| no | 0.92 | 1.00 | 0.96 | 0.92 | 1.00 | 0.96 | 164 |
| yes | 0.00 | 0.00 | 0.00 | 0.00 | 0.00 | 0.00 | 15 |
| accuracy | | | 0.92 | | | 0.92 | 179 |

Table 6: Human accounts classification

as well as just SAL.KUR$_a$ (metadata sign for total of male and female workers), accompanied by SAL ("adult female") and N$_1$ AL, a qualification describing groups of laborers.

The list of negatively significant entries is coincidental, though it is interesting to see BA (an administrative qualification) there, as it often features in assignment texts, and is used in personnel lists (Johnson, 2014).

### 4.7 Textiles

| | with numbers, line by line | | | without numbers, line by line | | | |
|---|---|---|---|---|---|---|---|
| | Precision | Recall | F1-score | Precision | Recall | F1-score | Support |
| no | 0.95 | 1.00 | 0.97 | 0.96 | 1.00 | 0.98 | 170 |
| yes | 0.00 | 0.00 | 0.00 | 1.00 | 0.22 | 0.36 | 9 |
| accuracy | | | 0.95 | | | 0.96 | 179 |
| | with numbers, sign by sign | | | without numbers, sign by sign | | | |
| | Precision | Recall | F1-score | Precision | Recall | F1-score | Support |
| no | 0.97 | 1.00 | 0.99 | 0.97 | 1.00 | 0.98 | 170 |
| yes | 1.00 | 0.44 | 0.62 | 1.00 | 0.33 | 0.50 | 9 |
| accuracy | | | 0.97 | | | 0.97 | 179 |

Table 7: Textile accounts classification

The results for textiles, as expected, resemble those for dairy, fish, and human texts. The *sign-by-sign, with numbers* model scored the highest, though with a narrow margin. The models produced no false positives.

In the same manner as above, the model captured the **signs specific** to textiles fairly well: among the positively significant signs we see TUG$_{2a}$ ("garment?"), BARA$_{2a}$ (a type of garment), and SIG$_{2b}$ ("wool?"), as well as combinations of those with number signs.

The negatively important features, again, appear coincidental.

## 5 Corpus-wide experiment and discussion

It seems that the only feasible approach to tokenizing proto-cuneiform is *sign-by-sign, with numbers*, as other approaches consistently scored lower or failed to produce useful results entirely. We see also that the model is conservative, which is good for overall reliability: the precision values for *yes* are almost always 100%, making false positives extremely rare. This meets our basic requirements for experimentally labeling accounts across the entire corpus.

Additionally, feature analysis showed that the model managed to learn semantic sets of signs indicative of all the economic domains, including the underrepresented ones. Despite low scores in the testing phase, we saw this as an optimistic starting point.

To try labeling the entire corpus, we used the *sign-by-sign, with numbers* MSVM to assign labels to the entire corpus of archaic accounts. An advantage of the MSVM architecture is the ability to set a certainty threshold for the model, which allowed us to set the required threshold to a conservative 90%. We also opted to exclude texts containing fewer than 6 signs from labeling entirely, similar to what we did in the training phase. The outcome of this stage of experiment is presented in Table 8.

| | animals | cereals | dairy | fields | fish | humans | textiles |
|---|---|---|---|---|---|---|---|
| training | 125 | 323 | 23 | 42 | 22 | 58 | 24 |
| assigned | 151 | 498 | 68 | 13 | 48 | 31 | 49 |
| increase (%) | +121% | +154% | +296% | +30% | +218% | +53% | +204% |

Table 8: Outcome of applying the model to the entire archaic corpus.

In terms of quantity, the results represent a compound increase of 143% over the training dataset, and together they correspond to 39% of all texts longer than 6 signs (1,454 out of 3,737 texts). It is yet to be determined whether we can decrease the lower limit of account length without sacrificing quality.

Moreover, the results show a large disparity in efficiency: for example, the model found very few new accounts of fields or humans. We can tentatively explain this through the overall scarcity of those texts.

On the other hand, we have large amounts of new dairy, fish, and textile tablets that the model identified, especially interesting due to its low efficiency when dealing with such accounts in the testing phase. To understand the reasons for those disparities, we performed an error analysis of the corpus labels.

### 5.1 Sample error analysis

Analyzing the errors in all automatically labeled tablets was not feasible, so we opted for a sample-based analysis instead.

For each assigned label, we chose 10 random tablets for evaluation and judged the model's work on a three-level scale: *yes* (the assigned label is correct), *unsure* (we were not able to classify the tablet ourselves), and *no* (the tablet was classified incorrectly). The outcome is presented in Table 9.[4]

| | animals | cereals | dairy | fields | fish | humans | textiles |
|---|---|---|---|---|---|---|---|
| yes | 9 | 5 | 10 | 5 | 9 | 6 | 9 |
| unsure | - | 1 | - | 4 | 1 | 4 | 1 |
| no | 1 | 4 | - | 1 | - | - | - |

Table 9: Evaluation of assigned labels.

This demonstrates the merit of the conservative approach. Like in the testing phase, we see only few false positives — which again meets our expectations. Also, they are almost entirely limited to one specific type of texts: cereal accounts.

A closer look at the successfully classified texts shows a distinct limitation of our model. Almost all of the texts the it managed to find were inventories, usually containing few signs other than the semantic sets it learned. The few assignments (accounts of distributions of goods to individuals; see the discussion of human accounts in the Data section) the model caught, tellingly, also contained unusually many signs from those semantic sets.

The model's focus on limited sets of important signs is also what helps us understand its failure when dealing with cereal tablets: this account type is particularly diverse: in addition to inventories, it includes assignments of rations, harvest texts, seed texts, etc., each with new sets of tokens to learn. It is likely that those different subtypes of cereal accounts made them less statistically discernible. Although some degree of diversity exists within other types of texts as well, we think the "confusing" accounts in those cases were not numerous enough to have the same effect.

A reflection of the same issue is illustrated by the misclassified "field" account: the model learned too often that the sign $GAN_2$ is indicative of field texts that it classified an entirely different account, qualified with a known, yet undeciphered administrative term MAŠ $GAN_2$, as a field account too.

## 6 Conclusions

The original goal of this study was to make the exploration of the archaic corpus easier by enriching its metadata and allowing for more detailed statistical studies of the transcriptions. Using the resulting MSVM models trained, we succeeded in more than doubling the number of labeled accounts, although the error analysis suggests that some of the labels assigned (animals, dairy, fish, textiles) are more reliable than others (cereals).

An open question remains: can we label more accounts in a more detailed way? When we refine our typology of tablets and agree on the expected labels for cereal account subtypes, we may have enough data to process those as efficiently as others. The experiment above showed that the model managed well even with little input, as long as it looked at inventories with fixed semantic sets of signs.

The error check hints at the existence of a more fundamental split of account types than according to economic sectors: one according to their administrative use, dividing the texts into assignments and inventories. Assignments, usually consisting of lists of individuals or institutions, are usually more similar to each other across sectors than to inventories of their own sector, leading to the models' trouble with identifying them. In those texts, we can often only understand the account type through studying the sets of numerals used, or through metadata written at the end of the text. A viable method of approaching assignments in an automated way is yet to be discovered.

As described in the introduction, understanding the typology of accounts in greater detail may help us understand their original institutional environments better — in the Eanna district of Uruk, as well as in other sites. The distinction between inventories and assignments is one that we need to further explore, and having recognized it will help us refine our tools and methods, both digital and traditional.

Additionally, we should see expanding the metadata as an important aspect of developing the digital infrastructure. In an effort to make the archaic corpus more accessible, we used the outcomes of this study to develop a tool which allows scholars to find similar tablets based on their content using the *sign-by-sign, with numbers* tokenizer. This similarity measurement tool is one of the features of **4ky** (Zadworny, 2023), and it is freely available for other researchers interested in using or adapting it to their needs.

All datasets, code, and models created during this study are accessible on GitHub.

[4]Detailed scores are available in our GitHub repository.

## Acknowledgments

We wish to thank all the personnel of the *Archaische Texte aus Uruk*, Salvatore Monaco, and CDLI contributors, without whose immense editorial work on the archaic text corpus this paper and future research could not take place.

## References

CDLI contributors. 2025. Cuneiform digital library initiativ home. [Accessed: 29 January 2025].

Robert K. Englund. 1998. *Texts from the Late Uruk Period*, pages 15–233. Universitätsverlag Freiburg Schweiz, Vandenhoek Ruprecht Göttingen.

Margaret Green and Hans J. Nissen. 1987. *Archaische Texte aus Uruk: Zeichenliste der archaischen Texte aus Uruk*. CDL Press.

J. Cale Johnson. 2014. Late uruk bicameral orthographies and their early dynastic rezeptionsgeschichte. *Working Paper No. 2/2014*. (http://dx.doi.org/10.17169/refubium-22792).

Camille Lecompte. 2023. Monaco, salvatore f.: Archaic cuneiform tablets from private collections (review). *Orientalische Literaturzeitung*, 118(3):175–186.

Salvatore F. Monaco. 2007. *The Cornell University Archaic Tablets*. CDL Press.

Salvatore F. Monaco. 2014. *Archaic Bullae and Tablets in the Cornell University Collections*. CDL Press.

Salvatore F. Monaco. 2016. *Archaic Cuneiform Tablets from Private Collections*. CDL Press.

Hugo Naccaro. 2025. La mésopotamie du sud á la transition des ive et iiie millénaires avant notre ère: évolution des cultures proto-urbaines. Dissertation, forthcoming.

Hans J. Nissen. 2024. Uruk and i. *Cuneiform Digital Library Journal*, (1).

Zhe Wang and Xiangyang Xue. 2014. *Multi-Class Support Vector Machine*, page 23–48. Springer International Publishing, Cham.

Piotr Zadworny. 2023. 4ky. [Accessed: 29 January 2025].

Zhiqiang Zhang, Zeqian Xu, Junyan Tan, and Hui Zou. 2021. Multi-class support vector machine based on the minimization of class variance. *Neural Processing Letters*, 53(1):517–533.

# Accessible Sanskrit: A Cascading System for Text Analysis and Dictionary Access

**Giacomo De Luca**
University of Tor Vergata, Via Cracovia 50, 00133 Roma, Italy
University of Tuscia, Via Santa Maria in Gradi 4, 01100 Viterbo, Italy
giacomo.deluca@unitus.it

## Abstract

Sanskrit text processing presents unique computational challenges due to its complex morphology, frequent compound formation, and the phenomenon of Sandhi. While several approaches to Sanskrit word segmentation exist, the field lacks integrated tools that make texts accessible while maintaining high accuracy. We present a hybrid approach combining rule-based and statistical methods that achieves reliable Sanskrit text analysis through a cascade mechanism in which a deterministic matching using inflection tables is used for simple cases and statistical approaches are used for the more complex ones. The goal of the system is to provide automatic text annotation and inflected dictionary search, returning for each word root forms, comprehensive grammatical analysis, inflection tables, and dictionary entries from multiple sources. The system is evaluated on 300 randomly selected compounds from the GRETIL corpus across different length categories and maintains 90% accuracy regardless of compound length, with 91% accuracy on the 40+ characters long compounds. The approach is also tested on the complete text of the Yoga Sūtra, demonstrating 96% accuracy in the practical use case. This approach is implemented both as an open-source Python library and a web application, making Sanskrit text analysis accessible to scholars and interested readers while retaining state of the art accuracy.

## 1 Introduction

Sanskrit, additionally to the difficulties shared with other Morphologically Rich Languages (MRL) (Tsarfaty et al., 2020), presents the unique computationally challenge of Sandhi. Sandhi is defined in (Matthews, 2014) as the written modification and fusion of sounds at or across the boundaries of grammatical units and is used to represent words exactly as they will be pronounced. While the Sandhi application rules are deterministic, the parsing rules are sometimes not (Hellwig and Nehrdich, 2018). The Sandhi phenomenon makes Sanskrit inherently hard to parse for Large Language Models (LLM): the same nominative singular "yogaḥ", may appear as: "yogaś", "yoga", or, as "yogā", when merged with the initial 'a' of the next word. In this last worst case scenario, the word is indistinguishable with the nominative plural, and can only be parsed looking at the context. Without pre-splitting of Sandhi and compounds, the model has to learn multiple representations of the same words in an already scarcely digitalized literature. The ambiguity generated by the multiple parsing solutions of compounds and word blocks agglutinated by Sandhi were known since antiquity: for teaching purpose, alongside the Veda we find the *Padapatha*: a didactic version in which the words are restored to the non morphed grammatical version (Pillai, 1941). If the challenge of parsing created such interpretive complexity that multiple versions of the same poetic text emerged, why was this difficulty deliberately preserved rather than simplified? Before delving in how current computational approaches try to handle this difficulty, it is important to understand the historical reasons for this peculiar phenomenon. Sanskrit, whose name suggests a 'well made' language, is not a naturally arisen language, but a highly refined one which was formalized by the grammarians, starting from Pāṇini's seminal *Aṣṭādhyāyī* (Gillon, 2007) (Cardona, 1988). But what was the ideal leading to keep such a complexity in terms of reading? The reason becomes clear when reading the motivations for the study of language provided by Patañjali the grammarian: "preservation, modification, injunction, brevity and certainty" (Dasgupta, 1991). Those motivations are all related to the preservation of the Vedas and the performance of the sacrifices. From the correct execution of the sacrifice, soteriological immortality was believed to be attainable, as is stated in the



*Proceedings of the Second Ancient Language Processing Workshop associated with NAACL 2025*, pages 31–39
May 4, 2025. 

*Rigveda*(Jamison and Brereton, 2014)[1]. Patañjali presents multiple examples on how just a slight pronunciation error is enough to make the entire sacrifice backfires: the wrong pronunciation of the word "helayaḥ" is imputed as the reason for defeat of the Asuras (Dasgupta, 1991); again the mispelling of the word "Indra—śatru" changes is meaning from 'slayer of Indra' to 'slayed by Indra', resulting in the death of the son of Tvaṣṭṛ. From the correct execution of the sacrifices liberation was expected, and grammar was a mean, if not the primary mean to the right execution. It is easy to see how the performative aspect of language was prioritized over the communicative one. In consequence of this early focus, the language eloquently tells how it should be pronounced, not what words are underneath the pronunciation. To tackle this complexity, multiple approaches to the task of Sanskrit Word Splitting (SWP, splitting Sandhi and compounds) (Hellwig and Nehrdich, 2018) have been proposed, started from the pioneering grammatical based works of Huet (Huet, 2005, 2009). Several approaches to sandhi and compound parsing have been proposed, using both data driven approaches (Nehrdich et al., 2024) and mixed ones (Krishna et al., 2021). This development has not yet translated into improved accessibility to the original texts or the dictionaries. Without previous knowledge, is hard if not outright impossible to search in the dictionaries the words that appears in the texts: most words appear morphed by Sandhi or aggregated in compounds. The Digital Corpus of Sanskrit (Hellwig, 2010–2021) provides access on click to the stemmed and parsed text, with minimal entries derived from the Monier Williams (MW) dictionary (Monier-Williams, 1899). Yet it works just on a manually annotated corpus of texts.

To improve the accessibility of the original texts, we propose an approach to Sanskrit word splitting that retrieves grammatical information and entries from multiple dictionaries. This approach allows for both text annotation and for a dictionary search allowing words to be queried as they appear in text, – inflected, compounded and morphed by Sandhi. This approach has been implemented as an open source Python library which includes a REST API built using Flask and a web application, which is accessible at `https://www.sanskritvoyager.com`. As it can be seen in Figure 1a, the application allows access to the text of the GRETIL[2] library. Words throughout the text become clickable, allowing users to access grammatical analysis and dictionary entries with a single click. Alternatively, text can be provided by the user, either by pasting or typing, receiving the same on demand interactive analysis.

Alternatively, the web application can be used as a more accessible engine to query Sanskrit dictionaries, allowing for inflected form search and multi-dictionary lookup. To check for the capabilities of the current approach to handle complex compounds and Sandhi-blocks, the underlying system has been tested with a random selection of 300 compounds of various length from the GRETIL corpus, and with a practical use case of annotating the entire Yoga Sūtra. The system performed effectively in both tasks, maintaining an accuracy of 92% for all the compounds categories, which increases to an accuracy of the 96% for the Yoga Sūtra task.

## 2 Previous Literature

Sanskrit word processing has seen considerable development over the past few decades, moving from rule-based systems to more data-driven approaches, though it continues to present unique challenges due to the language's complex morphology and phonology. Early approaches often combined Pāṇini's phonetic and morphological rules with lexical resources, using either formal methods or statistical approaches(Huet, 2005) (Huet, 2009). Finite state transducers were employed for automatic segmentation, with the aim of splitting a Sanskrit string into its constituent words (Mittal, 2010). However, a major hurdle is the availability of annotated datasets, which are crucial for training data driven models, particularly when compared to the resources available for other languages. The Digital Corpus of Sanskrit (DCS) has been a significant effort, providing over 650,000 lexically and morphologically tagged sentences. Datasets for word segmentation have also been created, though these often come with their own limitations (Krishnan et al., 2024). The central challenge to Sanskrit computational linguistics remains the handling of sandhi, which obscures word boundaries due to the phonetic merging of words (Krishna et al., 2021). Recent work has explored neural sequence labeling tasks, using recurrent and convolutional neural net-

[1]VIII.48.3: "We have drunk the soma; we have become immortal; we have gone to the light; we have found the gods"

[2]https://gretil.sub.uni-goettingen.de/gretil.html

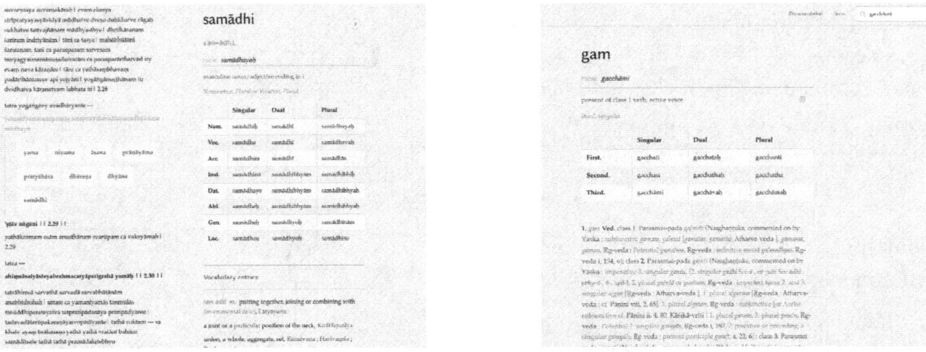


(a) Enhanced text reader with parsing capability

(b) Dictionary interface for inflected forms

Figure 1: Web interface of the Sanskrit analysis system. (a) shows the dictionary lookup for inflected forms, and (b) displays the Yoga Sūtra text from GRETIL with commentary and on-demand word parsing.

works, and seq2seq models for word segmentation (Aralikatte et al., 2018). A graph based framework has been developed for structured prediction tasks including word segmentation and morphological parsing (Krishna et al., 2021). The goal of current computational approaches is developing an unified models capable of handling multiple tasks such as word segmentation, lemmatization and morphological tagging jointly. The approach proposed in (Nehrdich et al., 2024) promise to be handle all those tasks at once, and is the most significant breakthrough in Sanskrit computational linguistic in the recent years. In (Nehrdich et al., 2024) a Byt5 model (Xue et al., 2022) was trained to handle many downstream Sanskrit analysis tasks maintaining state of the art performance.

## 3 Methodology

Our methodology takes a fundamentally different approach from existing solutions by recognizing that not all Sanskrit words require complex processing. Instead of applying sophisticated analysis techniques universally, we implement a cascading system that starts with simple, deterministic methods and progressively moves to more complex approaches only when necessary. The foundation of this approach lies in the observation that many Sanskrit words can be analyzed through straightforward methods with complete certainty. For instance, regular inflected forms like "eṣyāmi" can be directly mapped to their root form through inflection tables, – in this case identifying it as the third person future of the verb "i" (to go). Common Sandhi cases follow predictable patterns: "yogaś" can be restored to its base form "yogaḥ" through simple substitution rules. Additionally, frequently used inflected forms such as "yogena" (the instrumental case of "yoga") often appear in dictionaries as standalone entries, allowing direct lookup without complex analysis. Our system implements this insight through a three tiered processing pipeline, which is shown in the flowchart at Figure 2. The first tier employs computationally inexpensive methods: dictionary lookup and basic substitution rules. This provides deterministic results for a significant portion of Sanskrit vocabulary. When these methods fail to produce a result, the system employs a statistical approach. The quality of this result is evaluated through a scoring system. If the confidence score falls below a predetermined threshold, the system tries again with a quasi brute force compound splitter that tries all possible combination using. The system then retains the highest scoring result from the second or third approach. Finally, for each recovered entry, the system retrieves grammatical information and entries from multiple Sanskrit dictionaries.

### 3.1 Preprocessing

The transliteration scheme of the input is automatically detected using an adaptation of Indic Transliteration Detect [3], and transliterated to IAST through the Indic Transliteration package. The system also supports special character handling for advanced search capabilities. Wildcard searches can be performed inserting underscore ('_') characters, which act as single character wildcards within words. When a word ends with an asterisk ('*'), the system switches to exact dictionary matching mode. If the input is a single word with no diacrit-

[3]https://github.com/indic-transliteration/detect.py/blob/master/detect.py

ics there is first an attempt to match it directly in the UTF-8 decomposed list of words, and it returns all the entries for the possible words with diacritics. This allows for searches without diacritics. For example the term "śiva" can be matched writing "śiva", "siva" and "shiva".

### 3.2 Matching using inflection tables and dictionaries

The rule-based approach draws from the inflected form lookup of the University of Koeln [4]. Through this approach are built inflection tables for the non-indeclinable entries of the Monnier Williams dictionaries. The inflection tables are stored in a SQLite database. Associate to the inflection tables are the grammatical informations relative to the type of the word. The code has been rewritten from php to python, using SQLalchemy as ORM. As was done in (Nehrdich et al., 2024), the tables have been converted from SLP1 to IAST for readability, as it causes minimal storage increase. A multi index increased drastically the speed of the lookup, and future version may benefit from the hash indexes offered by PostgreSQL. The original approach suffers from overgeneration in case of particles (such as "ca") and curious lack of common words such as "vṛtti". To handle those case a post processing cleanup was added.

To match words, the system first tries to match them using the inflection table. Words with uncommon prefixes were a common cause of failure, since they are outside the dictionary. To handle those case, the system looks in a list of prefixes, if the words has one of them it tries again while removing the prefix. If the word initials and endings are inside a list of common sandhi rules, it tries to replace them and to match using again the inflection table. When all of the previous fails, it tries to check if the word is directly inside the hashed list of words of all dictionaries. If a word was matched during any of those steps, the entry (or entries) are retrieved and the function ends. In case the function failed, it means that there are probably multiple words inside and is sent to the multi word processing.

### 3.3 Dictionaries

For the word entries, the digitalized Sanskrit dictionaries from the university of Cologne were employed (Cologne University, 2024). To provide a

[4]https://github.com/sanskrit-lexicon/csl-inflect

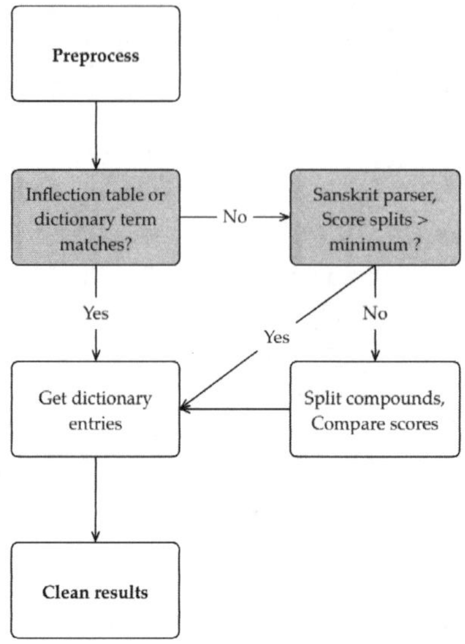


Figure 2: Flowchart of the cascading system, simple words are directly matched using inflection tables, more complex cases are handled with the parser first, then the compound splitter in case the score if too low.

clean interface, dictionaries were manually selected to provide non redundant quality output. The *Concise Pali Dictionary*[5] was later added as well since many terms employed by Vasubandhu could be found there and not in the Sanskrit dictionaries. In table 1 there is the list of the dictionaries and the number of unique entries in each dictionary. The total number of unique words contained in the database is 246,955. Since the system is for web reading and not for print, the majority of the abbreviations (both references and in text) were removed to increase clarity. To increase usability, in the online interface all the Sanskrit words in the entries were made clickable, returning the clicked entry. This way, if "rājapuruṣa" is searched, it returns the entries for the word, but also the split version "rāja—pūruṣa". Selecting one of the splits, the sub-entry is opened. The dictionary lookup accepts a list of dictionary abbreviation as argument, and tries to return the entries from the dictionaries. If the entry is not present in the selected dictionaries, it tries to look in the hashed dictionary with entries and dictionaries that have it, and returns it.

[5]https://buddhistuniversity.net/content/reference/concise-pali-dictionary

| Dictionary Name | Number of Entries |
|---|---|
| Monier-Williams | 194,068 |
| Grassmann | 11,108 |
| Apte Practical | 31,703 |
| Buddhist Hybrid | 17,777 |
| Concise Pali | 23,849 |
| Cappeller | 38,484 |
| MacDonnell | 20,100 |
| Total Unique Words | 246,955 |

Table 1: Number of unique entry in each dictionary, and total of unique words

### 3.4 Sandhi Splitting

For Sandhi and compound splitting the Python library Sanskrit_parser is used as base [6]. The library places every possible split in a graph and attempts to find the most probable split. As stated in the documentation, the first result provided is often not accurate, but the correct one is usually to be found in the first ten splits.

The incorrect splits showed patterns that were incredibly easy to spot: multiple dual letter fragments such as "to" and "ta", non grammatical entries, incorrect sandhi usage. Any application intended for general public use and also for a non professional audience should be providing a single split for a sentence. Recovering the right split amid possible ones may be easy for someone that knows the language, but risks alienating further other kind of interested users.

To select the best split among the offered one, a simple scoring system was made that evaluates the splits on three dimensions: length, morphology and sandhi. The length score tries to predict the number of split, and rewards a number of splits close to the expected. Less splits to the expectation are preferred to more, since errors are usually words being broken up into multiple places. The morphology score punishes multiple very short words that are not in the list of the indeclinable or of the word suffixes (like "tva"). The sandhi score monitors that the sandhi rules were correctly applied. The split with the best score is then selected. If the split is under the confidence threshold, the word is sent to the last cascading fallback. It is to note that every compound with no presence of Sandhi returns none at this stage and is processed by the compound splitter.

[6]https://github.com/kmadathil/sanskrit_parser

| Type | Total | Errors | Err% | Acc% |
|---|---|---|---|---|
| V.Long | 654 | 58 | 8.87 | 91.13 |
| Long | 377 | 22 | 5.84 | 94.16 |
| Medium | 187 | 13 | 6.95 | 93.05 |
| **Total** | 1218 | 93 | 7.63 | 92.37 |
| Y.Sūtra | 665 | 27 | 4.06 | 95.94 |

Table 2: Text Accuracy Analysis. *Total excludes Y.Sūtra

### 3.5 Compound Splitter

The root compound function takes advantage of a characteristic of Sanskrit grammar: in compounds, only the rightmost word is declined. All the words on the left are then in their root form. Assuming it is a pure compound with no Sandhi, it's going to be possible to reach the first word on the left by simply erasing the rightmost letter one by one and trying to match it with the hashed vocabulary with all the dictionary entries. In the ideal pure compound, this returns the leftmost word in O(n) operations, where n is the number of the remainder. Since the rightmost word is inflected, after removing a word on the left, it should be checked if the remainder is in the inflection tables, using replacements in case there is possible sandhi at the endings. Since most compounds contain 2–8 roots, and each root requires O(n) operations to find, with n decreasing at each step, the practical performance remains efficient despite the theoretical $O(n^2)$ worst case.

The complexity of this operation actually increases since pure compounds are rare, and often there is the presence of Sandhi either in the initial position or in the middle. To handle these cases two dictionaries with replacements for the initial and ending position are used. This way if a word if a letter is found that could have been the result of Sandhi, it is tested with all the grammatical possibilities (usually less than two) before getting erased. To handle cases like "kleśakarmavipākāśayair", to avoid it to be split after "kleśaka", which is in the dictionary, when selected suffixes like "ka" are meet, the system tries to split again ignoring the suffix, and measures (in terms of length of words) the quality of the results and pick the best one.

### 3.6 The problem with current Sanskrit Benchmarks

To test the accuracy of the computational approaches to Sanskrit, the Sandhikosh benchmark has been proposed (Bhardwaj et al., 2018) (Aralikatte et al., 2018) , which includes 13,930 annotated sentence splits. The sentence are split only for

Sandhi and not for compounds, which remains agglutinated together. Since this system splits sandhi and compounds in the same pass, the benchmark is not usable to test the proposed approach. It should also be mentioned that the corpus used is extremely unbalanced in favor of Brahmanical text compared to Buddhist ones, drawing extensively from the online corpus of the University of Hyderabad [7]. A more interesting corpus is the Sighum one, presented in (Krishna et al., 2017). The corpus has been used as a benchmark in the inspiring (Nehrdich et al., 2024). The Sighum corpus, similarly from the Hackaton [8], is derived from the Digital Corpus of Sanskrit (Hellwig, 2010–2021). Those corpus provide the roots for all the sandhi and compound split words in the sentence, similarly to the approach proposed there.There is however a important methodological difference which should be considered. This difference can be explained with the parsing of the block "dagdhabījakalpān" which appears in the Yoga Sūtra Bhasya. In the proposed system the block is split in "dagdha", "bīja" and "kalpa". The word "dagdha" is indicated as coming from dah in the provided vocabulary entries (from Apte Practical Sanskrit-English:"dagdha Past passive participle. [dah-kta] 1 Burnt, consumed by fire"). In the DCS the word is directly described as the "PPP" of "dah". While both approaches are grammatically equivalent, the approach used here provides a more specific dictionary entry, with the possibility of accessing the primitive "dah" with an additional click. The DCS approach returns instead directly the primitive without an additional action. Since the current system is built with the explicit goal of vocabulary entry retrieval in mind, rather than stemming, for the current goal is preferable to keep it as it is. For the same reasons common compounds which are present in the dictionaries, such as "rājayoga" are not split. "Rājayoga" and other similarly common compounds have specific dictionary entries, and the entry offers also the detailed parsing "rāja—yoga". The two split parts can be accessed with a simple click on the online interface. This methodological difference makes it so that simply using the smaller corpus derived by the DCS would result in countless errors, derived by the different format of the output. In a benchmark of tens of thousands of sentences it would be impossible to parse manually all those errors. For those reasons is impossible to test the current approach on any benchmark directly derived from the DCS. It also highlight the problem with every current benchmark testing in Sanskrit: each system employs his own convention. A good benchmark should be able to return positive for both "dah" or "dagdha". Since no similar benchmark currently exist, we manually test the system on a random selection of the Gretil corpus and on a practical use case on the Yoga Sūtra text.

### 3.7 Testing

Owing to the problems with the current Sanskrit benchmarks highlighted in the last paragraph, an alternative testing approach was used. Since all the simple words are deterministically parsed, what needed to be tested is the capability of the fallback systems to handle complex compounds and the applicability on the automatic annotation of a real text. All the text of the Gretil corpus was extracted and split in four lists of words in the following categories: medium 10–20, long 20–40, very long 40+. To avoid English words mixed in, only words with diacritics were kept. From each of the four lists 100 random samples were taken. The testing was made to check if the system is resilient enough to handle tasks that cannot be handled by the deterministic matching. The system was applied to each one of those compounds, and manually reviewed. For the practical use case the system was tested on the Yoga Sūtra in the transcription by Philip Maas accessible through Gretil [9]. Both tests can be replicated with the testing module inside the python library.

Undecidable words such as "ālasya" are returned with both possible parsings: the uninflected "ālasya" and the genitive of "āla". Since the only way to decide between the two is looking at the context, both words are returned, and is not counted as an error as long as the correct parsing is there. Even in presence of those cases, the system tends to not overgenerate. Figure 3 present the parsing results from a complex text block from the Yoga Sūtra: some of the words are presented with two possible parsing, such as "ālasya" and "āla" for the "ālasya" in the text. Every non perfect parsing is counted as an error. Errors are counted on a root by root basis: if a compound has 10 roots and only one is incorrect, a single error out of then is counted.

[7]https://sanskrit.uohyd.ac.in/Corpus/

[8]https://sanskritpanini.github.io/

[9]https://gretil.sub.uni-goettingen.de/gretil/1_sanskr/6_sastra/3_phil/yoga/patyogbu.htm

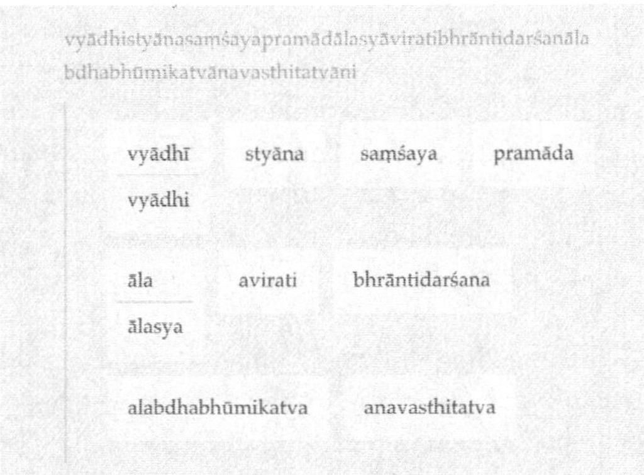


Figure 3: Parsing of one of the Yoga Sūtra verses with multiple possible roots.

In Table 2 are presented the result of the testing, maintaining 90%+ accuracy for all categories. The most surprising result is the high accuracy rate with long compounds considering that the longest one was 283 character long. The practical example of the Yoga Sūtra shows that the accuracy increases with a normal text in which the inflection tables can be used to automatically parse single words such as "atha", "ca" or "iti" or the multiple variations of "yoga".

### 3.8 Error discussion

The majority of the errors come from words which are outside the dictionaries or the inflection tables, and are then unrecognized. The Monnier-Williams dictionary is from 1899 and, while being an incredible work, is oddly missing some reasonably common compounds like "dvandva" (which is instead present in the Macdonnel dictionary). In particular, about 20% of the overall errors come from abstract words produced with the suffix *tva*, which are sometimes recorded (such as "śūnyatva", from "śūnya", emptiness, which is even recorded as the even rarer "sarvaśūnyatva"), but more often than not outside the dictionary entries. The system at the moment returns the root word, the suffix "tva" and the inflected ending as another word, which is clearly not optimal. Since the inflection tables are based entirely on the Monnier Williams entries, all the inflected forms of words outside the Monnier Williams that are not listed as entries may provoke errors. The shape of those errors is typically the word being rightfully recognized plus the inflectional suffix being marked as another word. Less common but still present are the cases in which the word root is morphed. In that case the word is split in small morphemes. Less common verbal forms, like causatives, are often not listed in the inflection tables; the inflection tables are also missing many irregular forms. A possible solution would be to use LLMs to generate the missing inflection tables, and to also use LLMs to search inside the Monnier Williams and other Dictionaries for mentions of irregular forms, and to apply them to the tables.

The sandhi splitter is, even with the scoring, the weakest part of the pipeline. Further versions of this approach could try replacing it entirely with the model developed in (Nehrdich et al., 2024) to increase the accuracy. The other alternative avenue explored was fine-tuning using a Llora (Hu et al., 2021) a middle sized LLM. Since the errors produced by the system are easily identifiable, it is possible to use the output of this system to train a transformer that replaces it. This replacement should be assessed with respect to the increased computational cost and the scalability of the online application. In the best case scenario the current approach resolves annotation with just a few SQL queries. There is no reason to replace the inflection table lookup, as it is deterministically correct and computationally inexpensive.

## 4 Limitations

The cascading system is highly modular; consequently, most limitations stem from the current implementation rather than from the architecture itself.

The system relies heavily on dictionary entries, with the majority derived from the Monier-Williams dictionary (1899), as illustrated in Table 1. While the Monier-Williams dictionary provides a comprehensive foundation, it exhibits notable deficiencies regarding abstract words formed with the "-tva" suffix and numerous compounds of moderate frequency. Although these dictionary limitations are partially mitigated through the integration of multiple dictionaries, the inflection tables are currently constructed solely from the Monier-Williams dictionary. Furthermore, certain common terms, such as "vṛtti" (vortex, mental fluctuation), appear in the dictionary but are notable absent from the inflection tables. The next version of the implementation should take care in reconstructing the inflection table using the correct list of all words as a basis. A possible approach for adding all the irregular forms would be using language models to extract them from dictionaries and grammar books.

Even with the scoring improvements, the Sandhi splitter remains the weakest component in our pipeline. While it works well for most cases, complex Sandhi patterns can still lead to incorrect splits. Future versions can replace this component with neural models such as the one described in (Nehrdich et al., 2024), although this would increase computational costs. The computational increase would still be limited for just the complex cases, since for most words the inflection tables are going to still be enough.

Finally, our approach prioritizes dictionary entry retrieval over stemming, which creates methodological differences when compared to existing benchmarks. This system prioritizes keeping compound and inflected forms intact when the dictionary entry is there: "yogānuśāsanam" (the instruction on yoga) is matched directly with the entry for "yogānuśāsana" that contextualizes the term within Patañjali's framework, rather than being decomposed into the components "yoga" and "anuśāsana". While this is an advantage for a text annotation tool, since the results are more context aware and usually present the split in the dictionary entries, it is a severe limitation when used as a pure stemming tool.

## 5 Conclusions

This work demonstrates that by taking a progressive approach to Sanskrit text processing, starting with simple, deterministic methods and escalating to more complex analysis only when necessary, it is possible to achieve both high accuracy and practical usability. The system's 90%+ accuracy on the long compounds drawn from the GRETIL corpus and 96% accuracy on the Yoga Sūtra validates this approach, showing that it performs reliably across different text types and compound complexities. The system's capability lies in the deterministic lookup for inflected and Sandhi-ed single words, returning entries from multiple dictionaries with accurate grammatical information with minimal computational cost. The approach peculiarity is in keeping compounds and inflected forms which have entries in the dictionaries, returning more contextualised entries than direct stemming. This approach has been implemented as an open source Python library which includes a REST API built using Flask and a web application, which is accessible at `https://www.sanskritvoyager.com`. The system was designed with practical performance considerations in mind. The entire backend requires only 2GB of RAM to operate effectively, making it deployable on modest hardware. Response times vary based on word complexity: simple inflected forms that can be resolved through table lookups are processed in milliseconds, while the most complex compound and Sandhi cases require at most 3 seconds to resolve on a 4GB RAM virtual machine. This performance profile makes the system suitable for both interactive web applications and batch processing of larger texts. The current approach allows dictionary searches for Sandhi-ed inflected and compounded words, without specifying the transliteration scheme and retrieving entries in multiple dictionaries. Future versions may employ a ByT5 based model (Nehrdich et al., 2024) as the last step in the cascading system to handle the most complex cases. The hope of this approach is to open up the treasury of the original Sanskrit literature to any interested reader, regardless of their previous linguistic skills.

## References


Rahul Aralikatte, Neelamadhav Gantayat, Naveen Panwar, Anush Sankaran, and Senthil Mani. 2018. Sanskrit sandhi splitting using seq2 (seq)^ 2. *arXiv preprint arXiv:1801.00428*.

Shubham Bhardwaj, Neelamadhav Gantayat, Nikhil Chaturvedi, Rahul Garg, and Sumeet Agarwal. 2018. SandhiKosh: A benchmark corpus for evaluating Sanskrit sandhi tools. In *Proceedings of the Eleventh International Conference on Language Resources and Evaluation (LREC 2018)*, Miyazaki, Japan. European Language Resources Association (ELRA).

George R Cardona. 1988. *Pāṇini : his work and its traditions*. Motilal Banarsidass, Delhi, India.

Cologne University. 2024. Cologne digital Sanskrit dictionaries. Online resource. Accessed on February 19, 2025.

Surendranath Dasgupta. 1991. *The Mahabhasya of Patanjali (Ahnikas I-IV)*. INDIAN COUNCIL OF PHILOSOPHICAL RESEARCH, New Delhi.

Brendan S Gillon. 2007. Pāṇini's" aṣṭādhyāyī" and linguistic theory. *Journal of Indian philosophy*, 35(5/6):445–468.

Oliver Hellwig. 2010–2021. Dcs - the digital corpus of sanskrit.

Oliver Hellwig and Sebastian Nehrdich. 2018. Sanskrit word segmentation using character-level recurrent and convolutional neural networks. In *Proceedings of the 2018 conference on empirical methods in natural language processing*, pages 2754–2763.

Edward J Hu, Yelong Shen, Phillip Wallis, Zeyuan Allen-Zhu, Yuanzhi Li, Shean Wang, Lu Wang, and Weizhu Chen. 2021. Lora: Low-rank adaptation of large language models. *arXiv preprint arXiv:2106.09685*.

Gérard Huet. 2005. A functional toolkit for morphological and phonological processing, application to a sanskrit tagger. *Journal of Functional Programming*, 15(4):573–614.

Gérard Huet. 2009. Sanskrit segmentation. In *Proceedings of the South Asian Languages Analysis Roundtable XXVIII*, Denton, Ohio.

Stephanie W Jamison and Joel P Brereton. 2014. *The Rigveda: 3-Volume Set*. Oxford University Press.

Amrith Krishna, Bishal Santra, Ashim Gupta, Pavankumar Satuluri, and Pawan Goyal. 2021. A graph-based framework for structured prediction tasks in sanskrit. *Computational Linguistics*, 46(4):785–845.

Amrith Krishna, Pavan Kumar Satuluri, and Pawan Goyal. 2017. A dataset for Sanskrit word segmentation. In *Proceedings of the Joint SIGHUM Workshop on Computational Linguistics for Cultural Heritage, Social Sciences, Humanities and Literature*, pages 105–114, Vancouver, Canada. Association for Computational Linguistics.

Sriram Krishnan, Amba Kulkarni, and Gérard Huet. 2024. Normalized dataset for sanskrit word segmentation and morphological parsing. *Language Resources and Evaluation*, pages 1–52.

P H Matthews. 2014. *The concise oxford dictionary of linguistics*, 3 edition. Oxford Quick Reference. Oxford University Press.

Vipul Mittal. 2010. Automatic sanskrit segmentizer using finite state transducers. In *Proceedings of the ACL 2010 Student Research Workshop*, pages 85–90.

M. Monier-Williams. 1899. *A Sanskrit-English Dictionary: Etymologically and Philologically Arranged with Special Reference to Cognate Indo-European Languages*. The Clarendon Press, Oxford.

Sebastian Nehrdich, Oliver Hellwig, and Kurt Keutzer. 2024. One model is all you need: Byt5-sanskrit, a unified model for sanskrit nlp tasks. *arXiv preprint arXiv:2409.13920*.

PK Narayana Pillai. 1941. The gveda padapāha—a study with special reference to the gveda prātiśākhya. *Bulletin of the Deccan College Research Institute*, 2(3/4):247–257.

Reut Tsarfaty, Dan Bareket, Stav Klein, and Amit Seker. 2020. From SPMRL to NMRL: What did we learn (and unlearn) in a decade of parsing morphologically-rich languages (MRLs)? In *Proceedings of the 58th Annual Meeting of the Association for Computational Linguistics*, pages 7396–7408, Online. Association for Computational Linguistics.

Linting Xue, Aditya Barua, Noah Constant, Rami Al-Rfou, Sharan Narang, Mihir Kale, Adam Roberts, and Colin Raffel. 2022. Byt5: Towards a token-free future with pre-trained byte-to-byte models. *Transactions of the Association for Computational Linguistics*, 10:291–306.

# A Dataset of Ancient Chinese Math Word Problems and an Application for Research in Historic Mathematics

**Florian Kessler**
Friedrich-Alexander-Universität Erlangen-Nürnberg
florian.kessler@fau.de

## Abstract

Solving math word problems, i.e. mathematical problems stated in natural language, has received much attention in the Artificial Intelligence (AI) community over the last years. Unsurprisingly, research has focused on problems stated in contemporary languages. In contrast to this, in this article, we introduce a dataset of math word problems that is extracted from ancient Chinese mathematical texts. The dataset is made available.[1] We report a baseline performance for GPT-4o solving the problems in the dataset using a Program-of-Thought paradigm that translates the mathematical procedures in the original texts into Python code, giving acceptable performance but showing that the model often struggles with understanding the pre-modern language. Finally, we describe how the generated code can be used for research into the history of mathematics, by offering a way to search the texts by abstract operations instead of specific lexemes.

## 1 Introduction

In recent years, using techniques such as Chain-of-Thought (CoT, Wei et al., 2022) or Program-of-Thought (PoT, Chen et al., 2023) prompting, Large-Language-Models (LLMs) have achieved excellent performance in solving mathematical problems formulated in natural language, spiking renewed interest in this area of artificial intelligence. However, while datasets of such math word problems are available in multiple languages, to our knowledge, all of them are contemporary. How do LLMs cope with ancient math problems, which might both involve terms that are unfamiliar to the model, as well as rely on knowledge about a world that differs significantly from what the model is familiar with? In order to answer this question, we will describe in Section 3 the creation of a database of mathematical problems extracted from ancient Chinese texts, using a semi-automatic approach that utilizes the highly structured nature of the textual material. Subsequently, in Section 4 the performance of GPT-4o in solving the problems in the database will be tested, showing that it is able to derive solutions for around two thirds of the problems in the database, but often struggles with unfamiliar expressions in the technical language of pre-modern Chinese mathematics. Figure 1 shows an overview over the setup discussed in this article.

While solving mathematical problems in modern settings with LLMs is useful for real world applications, solving problems in the style of ancient Chinese mathematical texts in itself is presumably of no interest to any user. Also, in the texts considered here, the problems posed are always accompanied by numerical solutions. Hence, being able to automatically compute a solution does not provide the researcher with any new information, aside from being a convenient way of checking for textual errors. However, being able to test the model's understanding of the problems lays the groundwork for confidently applying LLMs for different downstream research tasks. Since historic Chinese mathematics remains an understudied subject, such assistance is especially valuable. In particular, in this article, we suggest a way to use the output of the model for a type of semantic search. All of the state-of-the-art prompting techniques for solving mathematical problems using LLMs cause the model to output intermediate results, either in the form of natural language reasoning steps (Wei et al., 2022), program code (Chen et al., 2023; Gao et al., 2023) or systems of symbolic equations (He-Yueya et al., 2023). In Section 5, we will show how such output, in our case in the form of Python code, that can be aligned to the original algorithms provided in the texts using our prompting technique, can be used by histori-

[1] https://github.com/notiho/ancient-chinese-math-problems.



*Proceedings of the Second Ancient Language Processing Workshop associated with NAACL 2025*, pages 40–51
May 4, 2025. 

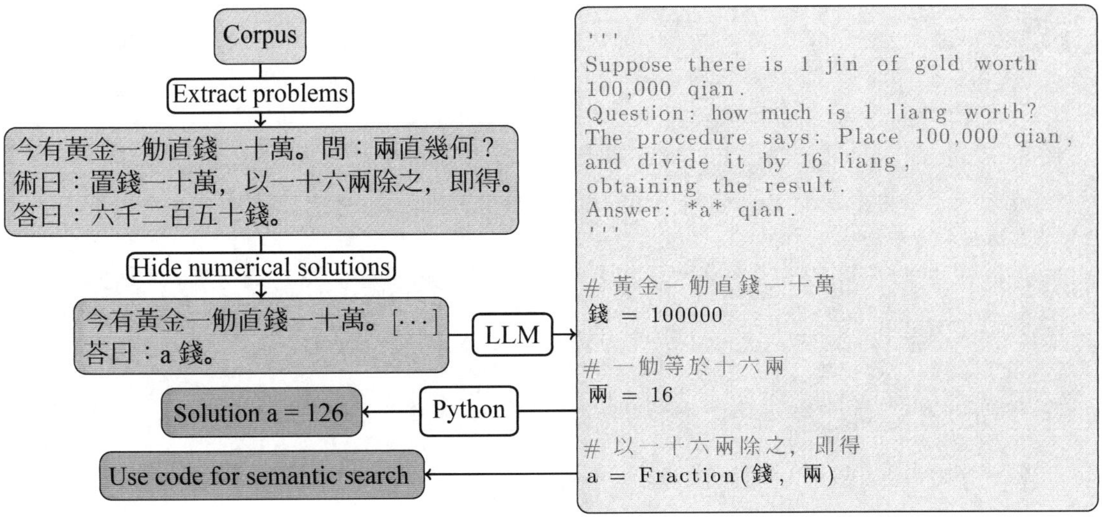


Figure 1: Workflow described in this paper illustrated with problem 18 from chapter 3 of the *Master Sun*

ans of mathematics, by providing a way to search for mathematical contents that abstracts from the language of the texts.

## 2 Related Work

Solving math word problems using artificial intelligence has been an active area of research for a long time, and accordingly, many datasets of problems with different levels of mathematical difficulty and language have been released (see Ahn et al., 2024 for an overview). To our knowledge, none of these contain problems extracted from premodern works.

In solving math word problems with LLMs, program-of-thought (PoT) prompting, that is, having the model emit program code that computes solutions has been one of the most successful paradigms (Chen et al., 2023; Gao et al., 2023). Recent research has shown that for advanced problems, having the model output symbolic equations instead is beneficial (He-Yueya et al., 2023). However, the problems considered here are relatively simple from the point of view of modern mathematics, and can mostly by easily solved using straightforward arithmetic, although the dataset also includes e.g. procedures for square and cube root extractions and solving what is equivalent to a system of linear equations (Martzloff, 2006: 127-41). Furthermore, the potential of transforming ancient Chinese mathematical procedures into imperative languages has long been recognized by the eminent mathematician and historian of mathematics, Wu Wen-Tsun (e.g. Wu Wen-Tsun, 2019: 121).

## 3 Building a Dataset

As the basis of the dataset, a collection commonly known as the *Computational Canon in Ten Books* (*Suanjing shishu* 算經十書) was chosen, containing the most important Chinese mathematical texts up to the Tang dynasty (608-907).[2] Having been compiled from mostly much older sources to serve educational purposes in 656 (Keller and Volkov, 2014: 59-63), among its nine surviving works, there are seven that employ a rigid question-answer-procedure pattern to structure their content that is as typical of ancient Chinese mathematics as it is convenient for automatic extraction. The titles of the seven works as well as dating information are shown in Table 1. In the following, the works will be referred to by the shortened translated titles underlined in the table.

In terms of their structure, these works consist of series of usually thematically grouped triples of questions, numerical answers and procedures ("*shu* 術") to compute the answers (see Table 2 for an example).[3]

[2]In fact, one of the titles included is a later apocryphal text that was not included in the original collection (Wu Wenjun and Shen Kangshen, 2000: 82). However, due to its comparable structure and contents, it was nevertheless included in the dataset.

[3]The strict triplet structure is not entirely followed in one of the works, the *Nine Categories*, where it is common to have several pairs of answers and questions followed by a single procedure that solves them all, and there are a few general procedures that precede a series of triplets, the procedures for which are special cases of the general procedure. In the dataset, these general procedures were not included, unless they were referenced by a stub-procedure specific to

| Title | Date | Chapters | Problems | Punctuated |
|---|---|---|---|---|
| "Computational Procedures of Nine Categories" (*Jiuzhang suanshu* 九章算術) | early 1st century | 9 | 253 | x |
| "Computational Treatise [Beginning with a Problem about a] Sea Island" (*Haidao suanjing* 海島算經) | ca 263 | 1 | 9 | x |
| "Computational Treatise of Five Departments" (*Wucao suanjing* 五曹算經) | after 386 | 5 | 67 | x |
| "Computational Treatise of Master Sun" (*Sunzi suanjing* 孫子算經) | ca 400 | 2 | 61 | x |
| "Computational Treatise of Zhang Qiujian" (*Zhang Qiujian suanjing* 張邱建算經) | ca 450 | 3 | 85 | |
| "Computational Treatise on the Continuation [of Tradition] of Ancient [authors]" (*Jigu suanjing* 緝古算經) | ca 600 | 1 | 20 | x |
| "Computational Treatise of Xiahou Yang" (*Xiahou Yang suanjing* 夏侯陽算經) | 763-779 | 3 | 82 | |

Table 1: Date of compilation, number of chapters (limited to those containing problems), problems in each work and indication whether a punctuated edition was available on Wikisource. Title translations and dating from Keller and Volkov (2014: 62).

As is the case with many modern day math word problem datasets, the problems almost always invoke a real world context in their setting, for example, when asking about the price of purchased goods, although this does not necessarily imply that they were practical in nature (Martzloff, 2006: 54-8).

The procedures that are supplied to compute the solutions can vary in level of detail, but are in general expected to be complete in the sense that following them step by step, one is able to compute the correct answer, although substantial interference might be required in some parts. The procedures often mention the specific numbers used in the problems, and in many cases also contain intermediate numerical results.

In order to build a dataset that is useful for testing automatic solving approaches on these problems, digitized versions were sourced from Wikisource[4] and the Kanseki repository[5] (Wittern, 2016). Since the Wikisource editions have punctuation added to the texts by crowd sourced editors, they were preferred where available.

Since the division of the works into questions, answers, and procedures is expressed in the text using characteristic markers such as "suppose there is" (*jin you* 今有) in the beginning of questions, as well as layout of the text into paragraphs, it is easy to extract triplets in a semi-automated way, taking care of the occasional deviation which is to be expected in natural language documents that have been transmitted over such a long time. Commentaries contained in the texts were removed during the processing.

In total, this process resulted in 577 triplets extracted from the texts. Table 1 shows the number of problems in each work. The table also shows the number of chapters (*juan* 卷), which in mathematical books often correlate with major thematic subdivisions.

In order to use the dataset in an automatic evaluation, the answer strings of each triplet were decomposed into numerical solutions and textual elements, by searching for numerals followed optionally by a unit of measurement (UoM) with a regular expression. This step is necessary because the answers often contain additional verbiage aside from the bare result itself, for which it would be unreasonable to expect the model to correctly predict it. Cases in which a number in the answer does not represent a value to be calculated, but rather helps to structure it textually were manually fixed after-

a problem that is clearly incomplete without the general procedure. For the two general procedures for which such stub-procedures exist (the *Fangcheng* 方程 (equivalent to systems of linear equations) and *Yingbuzu* 盈不足 (double false position) procedures from the *Nine Categories*), the general procedure was appended to the stub-procedure. Furthermore, some of the works feature alternative procedures for solving the same problem. In these cases, only the first procedure given was included in the dataset.

[4] https://zh.wikisource.org/wiki/九章算術, https://zh.wikisource.org/wiki/緝古算經, https://zh.wikisource.org/wiki/海島算經, https://zh.wikisource.org/wiki/孫子算經, https://zh.wikisource.org/wiki/五曹算經 (All accessed 22.12.2024).

[5] https://www.kanripo.org/. The texts used here have numbers KR3f0038 and KR3f0039 in the database.

| | |
|---|---|
| **Question** | 今 有 出 錢 一萬三千五百， 買 竹 二千三百五十 箇 。問 ：箇 幾何 ？<br>now have out *cash* 13 500 , buy bamboo 2350 piece . ask : piece how much ?<br>Suppose one has paid out 13 500 *cash* [unit of currency] and purchased 2350 pieces of bamboo. Question: how much is one piece? |
| **Answer** | 荅 曰 ：一箇 ， 五錢 、四十七分 錢 之 三十五。<br>answer say : 1 piece , 5 *cash* , 47 part *cash* genitive particle 35 .<br>The answer says: 1 piece is 5 *cash* and 35 parts of 47 *cash*. |
| **Converted** | 荅 曰 ：一箇 ， 270/47 錢 。<br>answer say : 1 piece , 270/47 *cash* . |
| **Procedure** | 經 率 術 曰 ：以 所 買 率 為 法 ， 所 出 錢<br>treat ratio procedure say : with relative pronoun buy ratio make divisor , relative pronoun out *cash*<br>數 為 實 ，實 如 法 得 一錢 。<br>number make dividend , dividend match divisor obtain 1 *cash* .<br>The procedure for treating ratios says: take the ratio of what has been bought as divisor, the number of *cash* that has been paid out as dividend, do the division, obtaining one *cash* each time the dividend matches the divisor. |

Table 2: Example of a problem (number 32 from chapter 2 of the *Nine Categories*).

wards, as e.g. in cases where after buying a certain number of goods for an amount of money, the price of *one* item is sought after, and the *one* is repeated in the answer.

In the texts, most answers are in the form of quantities with an UoM attached. Often, a quantity is expressed as a compound of integers or fractions of several UoM at different levels of scale, e.g. "two *chi* [unit of length] and four *cun* [unit of length equivalent to $\frac{1}{10}$ *chi*]" (*er chi si cun* 二尺四寸). When extracting the numerical solutions, such compounds were reduced to a single rational number of the largest UoM, in the example, $2 + \frac{1}{10} \cdot 4 = \frac{12}{5}$ *chi*. The intention of this step is to align the computational steps that need to be taken to compute the result more closely to the procedures that are proscribed in the texts themselves, which in most cases tacitly assume that appropriate conversions are done by the mathematician.[6] The ability of the model to understand and potentially convert pre-modern UoM is still tested, since no conversion of any form is done for the quantities stated in the questions.

In a comparable step, mixed fractions in the answers were reduced to a single improper fraction. In general, fractions which are written in the texts using the notation "$x$ *fen zhi* 分之 $y$", being equivalent to $\frac{y}{x}$ in modern notation, are always considered as a single term in the extracted answers. This runs contrary to the intent of some of the problems, notably 16 problems identified in early parts of the works, which explain basic arithmetic operations on fractions, necessitating an understanding of fractions in the answers as consisting of two numbers to be computed, numerator and denominator.[7] In most other procedures, knowledge of these operations is assumed, so modelling fractions in this way allows us to stay closer to the way procedures are written in most cases.

As opposed to most modern math word problem datasets (Kao et al., 2024), the problems extracted from the ancient Chinese mathematical texts commonly ask for the computation of several unknowns, in one extreme case even 27 (mean 2, sd 2.54). The length of the procedures associated with the problems also varies considerably, ranging (without punctuation) from 8 characters to 681 (mean 55.7, sd 64.1), indicating varying degrees of mathematical complexity of the tasks.

During manual spot-checks, some textual errors in the material were found and corrected. However, it has to be expected that the dataset is not completely free of errors.

## 4 Solving the Problems with a LLM

### 4.1 Experimental setup

In this section, the performance of a state of the art LLM, GPT-4o will be tested in solving the problems in the dataset described in the previous section. The main strategy that will be used for this is PoT (Chen et al., 2023).

[6] It should be noted however that there are some problems the main point of which are unit conversions, which are made significantly easier due to this conversion.

[7] These 16 problems are included in the dataset, but were excluded for the evaluation in Section 4.

Formally, let a problem triplet $(Q_i, A_i, P_i)$ consist of question $Q_i$, answer $A_i$, and procedure $P_i$. Let $\tilde{A}_i$ be the result of decomposing $A_i$ into textual and numerical elements as described in the previous section, containing numerical solutions $a_{i,1}, \ldots, a_{i,k}$. We then test the capability of the model to generate Python code $C$, such that after executing $C$, there are $k$ variables a, b, ... such that a has value $a_{i,1}$, b has value $a_{i,2}$ and so on.

In order to understand the impact of different factors on the performance, various prompts were tested. For the purpose of constructing these prompts in a way that avoids spoiling the result while still giving the necessary structure to give an answer, we define $\hat{A}_i$ as the string that is derived from $\tilde{A}_i$ by substituting the numerical values with letters "a", "b" and so on.

Following the by now well-known few-shot-learning approach (Brown et al., 2020), the model was presented with a series of sample inputs and expected answers. The five problems used as exemplars were chosen in a way that is reasonable for a human researcher, i.e. by pulling respectively the first problems from the first five chapters of the most famous work in the dataset, the *Nine Categories*. For each example $1 \leq j \leq 5$, aside from the solution code $C_j$, an English translation $E_j$ of the problems, including the procedure, was written. One of the exemplars as well as the system prompt $SP$ can be found in Appendix A. For reference, a zero-shot (Kojima et al., 2022) approach was also tested, the prompt for which is also in Appendix A.

Putting the elements together, the full few-shot input for the model when trying to solve problem $(Q_i, A_i, P_i)$ consists of the sequence

$$\begin{aligned} &S(SP), \\ &U(Q_1||P_1||\hat{A}_1), M(E_1||C_1), \\ &\ldots, \\ &U(Q_5||P_5||\hat{A}_5), M(E_5||C_5), \\ &U(Q_i||P_i||\hat{A}_i), \end{aligned} \tag{1}$$

where $||$ denotes concatenation and $S$, $U$ and $M$ system, user and assistant messages respectively.

A solution generated by GPT-4o with this prompt for the problem in Table 2 is shown in Figure 2. The accuracy achieved by GPT-4o using this prompting format is shown in Table 3. The table also shows the accuracy of the zero-shot strategy, as well as several formats that are derived by modifications to (1):

```
'''Suppose there is an expenditure of
13,500 qian to buy 2,350 bamboo pieces.
Question: how much does each piece cost?
The procedure for proportional rates
says: Take the quantity bought as the
divisor , and the amount of money spent
as the dividend. Divide the dividend by
the divisor to obtain the cost per
piece.
Answer: one piece costs *a* qian.'''
# 出錢一萬三千五百 [paid out 13500 cash]
所出錢數 = 13500
# 買竹二千三百五十箇 [bought 2350 pieces
    of bamboo]
所買率 = 2350
# 以所買率為法 [take the ratio of what
    has been bought as divisor]
法 = 所買率
# 所出錢數為實 [the number of cash that
    has been paid out as dividend]
實 = 所出錢數
# 實如法得一錢 [do the division]
a = Fraction(實, 法)
```

Figure 2: Output of the model for problem 32 from chapter 2 of the *Nine Categories*, with English translation in the block comment by the model, and translations of the single-line comments in square brackets added manually afterwards. Empty lines before each single-line comment contained in the original output have been removed for better display.

**Alternative system prompt** For reasons that will be laid out in Section 5, the system prompt used in (1) stresses that the code should stay as close as possible to the structure of the original, and quote appropriate sections from it in comments before each block of code. To test whether this prevents the model from adopting more direct solutions, an alternative system prompt without these restrictions was tried (see Appendix A for the prompt).

**No punctuation** For this configuration, punctuation was removed from all strings in the input. It is important to test the ability of the model to cope with text written without punctuation, as this is the format that the works were transmitted to us, and modern punctuations are not available for all texts. The results for the texts from the dataset without punctuation, for which this was the only configuration tested, are shown in Table 4.

**No translation** In this format, the English translations $E_1, \ldots, E_5$ were removed from the prompt. Doing a complete translation first would be reasonable approach for a human tasked with solving the problems, so we test whether this also helps the model achieve higher accuracy.

| Method | All | | Nine Categories | | Sea Island | | Five Departments | | Master Sun | | Continuation | |
|---|---|---|---|---|---|---|---|---|---|---|---|---|
| | **Mean** | **B-o-5** | **Mean** | **B-o-5** | **Mean** | **B-o-5** | **Mean** | **B-o-5** | **Mean** | **B-o-5** | **Mean** | **B-o-5** |
| Zero-shot | 44.0 | 60.7 | 40.8 | 61.0 | 4.4 | 11.1 | 60.6 | 70.1 | 58.9 | 77.2 | 0.0 | 0.0 |
| Few-shot (default) | 51.1 | 63.0 | 53.0 | 66.1 | 13.3 | 33.3 | 52.5 | 65.7 | 65.6 | 73.7 | 0.0 | 0.0 |
| Few-shot (alternative prompt) | 52.3 | 62.0 | 54.1 | 64.8 | 17.8 | 33.3 | 56.4 | 62.7 | 64.2 | 75.4 | 0.0 | 0.0 |
| No punctuation | 47.8 | 60.7 | 46.6 | 61.0 | 6.7 | 33.3 | 58.2 | 68.7 | 63.9 | 75.4 | 0.0 | 0.0 |
| No translation | 51.1 | 59.4 | 52.6 | 61.0 | 13.3 | 22.2 | 55.2 | 64.2 | 63.5 | 73.7 | 0.0 | 0.0 |
| No procedures | 36.7 | 45.5 | 33.8 | 42.8 | 2.2 | 11.1 | 47.2 | 53.7 | 54.0 | 66.7 | 1.0 | 5.0 |
| Numerical solutions provided | 54.2 | 67.6 | 57.7 | 72.9 | 4.4 | 11.1 | 58.5 | 68.7 | 61.1 | 73.7 | 2.0 | 10.0 |

Table 3: Accuracies of different prompting strategies on the punctuated dataset and by title in percent. Values in the mean columns are averaged over five runs of the model, and in the best-of-5 (B-o-5) columns a problem is counted as solved if it was solved in at least one run.

| All | | Xiahou Yang | | Zhang Qiujian | |
|---|---|---|---|---|---|
| **Mean** | **B-o-5** | **Mean** | **B-o-5** | **Mean** | **B-o-5** |
| 37.4 | 49.7 | 45.6 | 57.3 | 29.4 | 42.4 |

Table 4: Accuracies in percent for the titles in the dataset where no punctuation was available

**No procedures** In order to test whether the information provided in the question alone is sufficient for the model to derive a solution, the procedures $P_1, \ldots, P_5$ and $P_i$ are removed from the prompt. Furthermore, the Python solutions $C_1, \ldots, C_5$ were streamlined to not include steps described in the procedure but unnecessary in Python, and comments that quote the procedures are changed into English comments that explain the reasoning. The system prompt was also changed by removing the instruction to quote the procedure before each block of code. This brings the format much closer to conventional math word problem setups, which usually do not contain procedures for computing results.

**Numerical solutions provided** In this format, the solutions $\hat{A}_1, \ldots, \hat{A}_5$ and $\hat{A}_i$ are modified by adding the values of the unknowns as Arabic numerals, giving the model an opportunity to cheat by knowing the correct solutions.

### 4.2 Discussion

As can be seen in Table 3, the performance in all of the works leaves much room for improvement. Unsurprisingly the setup where the model has access to the solutions it is supposed to compute shows the best accuracy, although even in that scenario, mean accuracy is significantly lower than that reported for the same model on the MATH dataset, 68.5%[8], which was designed to be challenging for expert humans (Hendrycks et al., 2021). While removing procedures outright leads to a large drop in accuracy, telling the model to focus on staying close to the procedure (default prompt) or not (alternative prompt) does not cause a statistically significant difference. Removing punctuation leads to a small but significant drop in mean accuracy. Removing translations did not have a significant effect on mean accuracy.

| **Category** | **Type** | **Count** |
|---|---|---|
| global | misunderstood procedure | 7 |
| | misunderstood procedure (inference required) | 5 |
| | misunderstood question | 4 |
| localized | misunderstood expression | 27 |
| | unit conversion | 17 |
| | code error (fractions) | 16 |
| | math reasoning | 4 |
| | textual error | 3 |
| | code error (variable name) | 2 |
| | code error (syntax) | 1 |
| | result rounded in the text | 1 |

Table 5: Count of errors by type encountered during the evaluation of 50 randomly chosen failed solutions

Looking at the breakdown of the results by title, we can observe considerable differences be-

[8]https://github.com/openai/simple-evals (entry gpt-4o-2024-11-20, accessed 23.01.2025).

tween the accuracy values. In particular, the model was almost unable to solve any problems in the *Sea Island* and the *Continuation*. Inside a single work, the performance can also vary considerably by chapter. For example, the mean accuracy using the default few-shot prompt for the worst performing chapter of the *Nine Categories* is as low as 21%.[9] Since chapters often group thematically related problems, this indicates that the model had more difficulties in solving certain types of problems.[10]

Running a logistic regression shows that both the total textual length of a problem, i.e. the sum of the lengths in characters without punctuation of question, answer, and procedure, and the number of unknowns in it are significant predictors on the model being able to solve it.[11] As a case in point, both of the two works with the worst performances each contain problems or procedures that are much longer than the average of the dataset. The mean number of characters (not counting punctuation) per problem is 164 for the *Sea Island* and 311 for the *Continuation*, but only 106 for the *Zhang Qiujian*, which has the third highest values in this regard. In the *Continuation*, many problems are further complicated by a high number of unknowns to be computed, 6.95 on average per problem, compared to 1.99 for the text with the second highest value. At the same time, it can be considered more advanced in terms of computations involved, as almost all of the problems require the extraction of cubic roots (Lim and Wagner, 2017: 27). Accordingly, in its context as a historic textbook, it was the only one of the works considered here reserved for a program for advanced students (Keller and Volkov, 2014: 61).

In order to gain a deeper understanding of why the model fails to output correct code, a manual error analysis was conducted. 50 problems were randomly sampled from among those where the few-shot prompting strategy failed in all five runs. For each of those, the output for one of these runs was then annotated, by first determining whether the code was in general following the structure of a correct solution and could be fixed by modifying a few localized sections, or whether it was completely unusable, because either the model did not understand the the structure of the procedure provided, or the intent of the question. Table 5 gives an overview of the errors encountered.

In the cases where the code was fixable with localised modifications, the type of error in these locations was further analysed. Of course, there are many possibilities for generating incorrect results. However, a few major categories can be clearly distinguished.[12]

First, there were 27 cases where the model misunderstood an expression in the original text, e.g. translating the expression "*tai ban sheng* 太半升" (two-thirds of a *sheng*) into "half a sheng" in the English translation and "Fraction(1, 2)" in the code section of the output.

Second, there were 17 cases where the model made an error in doing unit conversions, reflecting either a lack of world knowledge or applied mathematical reasoning skill.

Third, there were 19 cases where, judging from the translation and the code it has produced, it intended to do the right thing, but failed to produce working code. 16 of these are related to our choice to force the model to use fractions in computing results, running counter to the semantics of Python defaulting to floating point numbers when doing divisions with "/" or taking square root with "math.sqrt". To our surprise, in two of the examined outputs, the model generated code that was invalid because of wrong variable names, in both cases because it had used the same name with traditional characters in one place in the code, and then with simplified characters in another location. In one case, the syntax of the generated code was incorrect.

Third, there were four cases where the problem seems to have been with the mathematical reasoning of the model. While the procedures supplied with the problems in most cases give a complete solution strategy, they are often not detailed to the level that they could simply be mindlessly followed, and not all mathematics can be left to the

[9]The complete table showing accuracy for each chapter can be found in Appendix B.

[10]As groups of more specifically related problems also tend to cluster inside each chapter, we would have furthermore expected to encounter clusters of easier or more difficult problems when arranging them by their position inside each chapter. However, a runs test only gave a significant result for one single chapter, number 2 in the *Nine Categories*, which is clearly divided into two distinct parts, with the first part containing a family of problems that is much easier than those in the second part.

[11]In the few-shot configuration using best-of-5 for evaluation. $\beta_{text\_len} = -0.0046629$, $SE_{text\_len} = 0.0009004$, $p_{text\_len} < 0.001$, $\beta_{n\_unknown} = -0.3759104$, $SE_{n\_unknown} = 0.0562560$, $p_{n\_unknown} < 0.001$.

[12]Examples of the most commonly encountered categories can be found in Appendix C.

Python interpreter. For example, there was a case where the procedure simply stated to add a "difference", which in the context could refer to two quantities, of which the model chose the wrong one.

Finally, three cases were caused by an error in the original text, and one by the solution provided in the original being rounded, with no indication in the procedure that such a step has to be taken.

## 5 Further Use of the Generated Code

In the previous section, the dataset was used as a benchmark to test a model's ability to output code to calculate correct solutions for the problems. However, as mentioned in Section 1, for the historical problems used here, this may not be the most relevant task. In this section, it will be shown that the code that is generated to compute solutions is interesting in its own right, because it allows us to explore ancient Chinese mathematics from a perspective that was much more difficult to attain before: what were the calculations needed to solve the problems?

Of course, using the digitized full-text editions of the texts, it is trivial to search the procedures for the presence of words that commonly proscribe certain mathematical operations, e.g. "*cheng* 乘" (to multiply). However, this does not necessarily give us a complete picture: On the one hand, there are some polysemous lexemes that can signify different operations, such as "*chu* 除" (to divide, to subtract), or an operation and something entirely else, e.g. "*cong* 從" (length, to accord to, to add). On the other hand, there can be operations that are implicit, and not overtly expressed in the text. For example, as described in Section 3, unit conversions are often left for the practitioner to fill in, and might, due to the system of UoMs used, require non-trivial multiplications or divisions.

By including the instruction for the model to closely follow the structure of the provided procedure, and quote the relevant section of the procedure before each section of code (see Appendix A for the prompt), we ensure that code can be aligned to the original text. While this does of course not ensure a perfect match between the Python implementation and how a practitioner would have done their calculations, the alignment allows a targeted search for the code equivalents of expressions. Furthermore, by restricting ourselves to problems where the Python solution computes the correct answers, without having them spoiled in the prompt, we can be confident that the model understood the problem at least to the level that it could independently solve it.

Among the correct outputs produced by the default few-shot prompt, 76.1% of code blocks divided by empty lines produced by the model were started by a comment that could be matched to a portion of either the question or procedure provided in the prompt. In order to check how reliable this alignment is, a manual analysis of 50 randomly sampled solutions was conducted. In particular, it was examined whether 1) the mathematical operations specified in the text quoted as a comment before each block match the semantics of the code in the block 2) there are calculations specified in the procedure missing from the code 3) there are calculations in the code proscribed neither explicitly nor implicitly (e.g. UoM conversions) in the procedure. Code blocks that contain no calculations but just assign variables were not checked.

In 43 of the 50 cases, no problems were discovered according to the three criteria. In two cases, both from the *Fangcheng* (equivalent to Gaussian elimination) section of the *Nine Categories*, the procedure given contains specific instructions for one paradigmatic problem, which need to be generalized to the problem at hand.[13] Hence, it is impossible to produce code that aligns perfectly to the instructions in the procedure. In two cases, the procedures contained steps needed to deal with fractions, which were rendered unnecessary by using the Fraction class and thus not included in the generated code. In one case each, the comments were translated into English, an algorithm that completely deviated from the procedure was adopted by the model, and one of the code blocks contained code that did not match the quoted section from the procedure.

To demonstrate the potential of this alignment between original text and its translation into code, blocks were searched for multiplication with the operator *, and the accompanying comments were then analysed for the presence of several constructions that commonly denote multiplication. The results, grouped by title, are displayed in Table 6. The table also contains a column for UoM conversions, which are often not explicated in the original text, but for which the model almost always added a separate comment explaining the step. As can

[13]See Footnote 3 above.

| Title | *cheng* 乘 | *n zhi* 之 | *bei* 倍 | *ming* 命 | UoM conversion | other |
|---|---|---|---|---|---|---|
| *Nine Categories* | 141 (56%) | 29 (12%) | 10 (4%) | 0 (0%) | 54 (21%) | 20 (8%) |
| *Five Departments* | 43 (90%) | 0 (0%) | 0 (0%) | 0 (0%) | 4 (8%) | 2 (4%) |
| *Master Sun* | 46 (68%) | 1 (1%) | 4 (6%) | 3 (4%) | 13 (19%) | 5 (7%) |
| *Sea Island* | 5 (62%) | 0 (0%) | 0 (0%) | 0 (0%) | 3 (38%) | 0 (0%) |

Table 6: Constructions in sections of the procedures quoted before code blocks containing multiplications (* in Python). Multiple categories can apply for the same code block.

be seen, "*cheng* 乘" (to multiply), is the most frequently used lexeme to express multiplication. All of the texts also employ other ways for stating this operation. However, the popularity of these differs significantly between the works, with "*n zhi* 之" ("to $n$ it", where $n$ is a natural number) being the most frequent in the earliest text in the dataset, the *Nine Categories*, and seemingly dropping more or less out of fashion in the later texts.

In the current setup, a major drawback is of course that it is limited to those problems that the model has successfully solved. As we have seen, misunderstanding of the text is one of the main reasons for errors in the output, and lexemes that are infrequently used in a certain meaning might be one of the main causes for misunderstandings. For example, "*ming* 命" (to command, to name, to multiply) is used to refer to multiplication in a few procedures in the *Nine Categories* (Chemla and Guo Shuchun, 2004: 963-4), but the model failed to produce correct solutions for these. Hence, at the current stage, the setup is mostly suited to discover larger trends. However, we are confident that with simple means, the accuracy can be further improved. Possible directions for this will be discussed in the next section.

## 6 Conclusions

In this article, we have introduced a dataset of ancient Chinese math word problems, and established a baseline performance for an LLM solving the problems using a PoT approach. While the fact that around two thirds of the problems could be solved in this setting shows the general potential of using LLMs for historic mathematics, it of course leaves much room to improvement. By releasing the dataset, we hope to encourage further research in this direction.

In particular, an obvious first step would be to explore recent advancements over the basic PoT prompting used here, by e.g. giving the model feedback on its solution attempts (Zhou et al., 2023). Of course, more sophisticated models which achieve higher scores in modern day math benchmarks could also be tried. However, as our error analysis in Section 4.2 has revealed, the biggest challenge for GPT-4o does not appear to be in mathematical reasoning, but rather in understanding the language of the texts. In this regard, a fruitful approach to explore could be in using retrieval augmented generation, by giving the model explanations of technical terms contained in the problem. Resources that could be used for this purpose include both pre-modern commentaries that accompany several of the texts in the dataset, as well as modern day glossaries compiled by historians.

A limitation that might require more fundamental changes to the setup is the model of computation used. As outlined in Section 3, the choice taken here was motivated by the consideration to have the code output correspond as directly as possible to the procedures provided in the texts. However, using Python with rational numbers represented by the Fraction class is clearly not ideal. First, it does not align perfectly which what is explicit and implicit in the procedures. Second, as we have seen in Section 4.2, GPT-4o sometimes had considerable problems in producing working code under these conditions. Overcoming these could potentially entail designing a simple custom programming language as the target for translations, or at least providing a set of purpose-built library function that match the semantics of certain compound operations in ancient Chinese mathematics, e.g. root extraction or operations with mixed fractions.

As the sketch of future applications in Section 5 demonstrates, doing further research in this direction might prove very fruitful, because it allows us to approach historical mathematics from a new perspective, guided by a large scale analysis of the actual computations performed, without the need for time-consuming human annotation.

## Limitations

The text in the dataset were not systematically checked to ensure that they are free from errors.

Only a single model and a single set of exemplars was tested.

No comparison was made against human performance on the dataset.

## Acknowledgements

I am grateful for the financial support from the Alexander-von-Humboldt foundation, from a grant awarded to Andrea Bréard. I would like to thank Andrea Bréard and three anonymous reviewers for their helpful remarks on the article.

## References

Janice Ahn, Rishu Verma, Renze Lou, Di Liu, Rui Zhang, and Wenpeng Yin. 2024. Large Language Models for Mathematical Reasoning: Progresses and Challenges. *Preprint*, arXiv:2402.00157.

Tom Brown, Benjamin Mann, Nick Ryder, Melanie Subbiah, Jared D. Kaplan, Prafulla Dhariwal, Arvind Neelakantan, Pranav Shyam, Girish Sastry, and Amanda Askell. 2020. Language Models are Few-Shot Learners. *Advances in Neural Information Processing Systems*, 33:1877–1901.

Karine Chemla and Guo Shuchun. 2004. *Les Neuf Chapitres: Le classique mathématique de la Chine ancienne et ses commentaires*. Dunod, Paris.

Wenhu Chen, Xueguang Ma, Xinyi Wang, and William W. Cohen. 2023. Program of Thoughts Prompting: Disentangling Computation from Reasoning for Numerical Reasoning Tasks. *Transactions on Machine Learning Research*.

Luyu Gao, Aman Madaan, Shuyan Zhou, Uri Alon, Pengfei Liu, Yiming Yang, Jamie Callan, and Graham Neubig. 2023. PAL: Program-aided Language Models. In *Proceedings of the 40th International Conference on Machine Learning*, pages 10764–10799. PMLR.

Joy He-Yueya, Gabriel Poesia, Rose E. Wang, and Noah D. Goodman. 2023. Solving Math Word Problems by Combining Language Models With Symbolic Solvers. *Preprint*, arXiv:2304.09102.

Dan Hendrycks, Collin Burns, Saurav Kadavath, Akul Arora, Steven Basart, Eric Tang, Dawn Song, and Jacob Steinhardt. 2021. Measuring Mathematical Problem Solving With the MATH Dataset. *Preprint*, arXiv:2103.03874.

Kuei-Chun Kao, Ruochen Wang, and Cho-Jui Hsieh. 2024. Solving for X and Beyond: Can Large Language Models Solve Complex Math Problems with More-Than-Two Unknowns? *Preprint*, arXiv:2407.05134.

Agathe Keller and Alexei Volkov. 2014. Mathematics Education in Oriental Antiquity and Middle Ages. In Alexander Karp and Gert Schubring, editors, *Handbook on the History of Mathematics Education*, pages 55–83. Springer, New York.

Takeshi Kojima, Shixiang Shane Gu, Machel Reid, Yutaka Matsuo, and Yusuke Iwasawa. 2022. Large Language Models are Zero-Shot Reasoners. *Advances in Neural Information Processing Systems*, 35:22199–22213.

Tina Su-lyn Lim and Donald B. Wagner. 2017. *The Continuation of Ancient Mathematics: Wang Xiaotong's "Jigu Suanjing", Algebra and Geometry in 7th-Century China*. NIAS Press, Copenhagen.

Jean-Claude Martzloff. 2006. *A History of Chinese Mathematics*, 2nd edition. Springer, Berlin.

Jason Wei, Xuezhi Wang, Dale Schuurmans, Maarten Bosma, Fei Xia, Ed Chi, Quoc V. Le, and Denny Zhou. 2022. Chain-of-Thought Prompting Elicits Reasoning in Large Language Models. *Advances in Neural Information Processing Systems*, 35:24824–24837.

Christian Wittern. 2016. Kanseki Repository. *CIEAS Research Report 2015*, Special issue:1–80.

Wu Wen-Tsun. 2019. 吳文俊全集 - 數學史卷 *[The Complete Works of Wu Wen-Tsun - History of Mathematics]*. Kexue chubanshe, Beijing.

Wu Wenjun and Shen Kangshen, editors. 2000. 中國數學史大系第四卷西晉至五代 *[Compendium of the History of Chinese Mathematics Volume 4: From Western Jin to the Five Dynasties]*. Beijing shifan daxue chubanshe, Beijing.

Aojun Zhou, Ke Wang, Zimu Lu, Weikang Shi, Sichun Luo, Zipeng Qin, Shaoqing Lu, Anya Jia, Linqi Song, Mingjie Zhan, and Hongsheng Li. 2023. Solving Challenging Math Word Problems Using GPT-4 Code Interpreter with Code-based Self-Verification. *Preprint*, arXiv:2308.07921.

## A System prompts and exemplar

Default system prompt: "Translate ancient Chinese math problems into Python code, ensuring that each section of code adheres to the structure of the procedure ('術') provided. Put the part of the procedure that corresponds to each block of code as a comment before the block. Ensure that the complete procedure is encoded. Use the class 'Fraction' to represent numbers that might not be integers and use the appropriate units for each calculation. Don't use any other external functions."

Alternative system prompt: "Translate ancient Chinese math problems into Python code. Ensure that the complete procedure is encoded. Use the class 'Fraction' to represent numbers that might not be integers and use the appropriate units for each calculation."

System prompt for scenario without procedures: "Translate ancient Chinese math problems into Python code. Use the class 'Fraction' to represent numbers that might not be integers and use the appropriate units for each calculation. Don't use any other external functions."

Zero-shot system prompt: "Translate ancient Chinese math problems into Python code that computes the values of the unknowns replaced by letters ('a', ...) in the answer ('荅' or '答'). Write the solutions into variables that have exactly the same name as the unknowns. Use the class 'Fraction' to represent numbers that might not be integers and use the appropriate units for each calculation. Don't use any other external functions."

Exemplar for problem 1 from chapter 1 of the *Nine Categories*:

User: "今有田廣十五步，從十六步。問：為田幾何？
方田術曰：廣從步數相乘得積步。以畝法二百四十步除之，即畝數。百畝為一頃。
荅曰：a 畝。"

Assistant:

```
'''
Suppose there is a field with a
    ↪ width of 15 bu and a length
    ↪ of 16 bu.
Question: how large of a field
    ↪ does it make?

The procedure for rectangular
    ↪ fields says: The numbers of
    ↪ bu in width and length are
    ↪ multiplied with each other
    ↪ , obtaining the [number of]
    ↪ accumulated bu.
When dividing it by the mu-
    ↪ divisor, 240, it is the
    ↪ number of mu.
100 mu make 1 qing.

The answer says: *a* mu.
'''

#廣十五步
廣步數 = 15

#從十六步
從步數 = 16

#廣從步數相乘得積步
積步 = 廣步數 * 從步數

#畝法二百四十步
畝法 = 240

#以畝法二百四十步除之，即畝數
畝數 = Fraction(積步, 畝法)

a = 畝數
```

## B Results by chapter

Table 7 shows accuracy separately for each chapter.

## C Examples of errors

Due to space considerations, only examples of the most frequent categories of localized errors are reproduced here. The complete annotated files can be found at https://github.com/notiho/ancient-chinese-math-problems.

**Misunderstood expression** (Problem 17 from chapter 1 of the *Nine Categories*): The relevant fragment in the original text is "又有三人，三分人之一，分六錢三分錢之一，四分錢之三" (Again, there are three and one third of a person, dividing six *cash*, one third *cash* and three fourth *cash*). The model translates this as "Suppose there are three people. Each person is to receive one-third of the total. The total is 6 qian, plus one-third of a qian, plus three-fourths of a qian." and produces the following code:

```
# 三人
人數 = 3
```

Expected:

```
人數 = 3 + Fraction(1, 3)
```

**Unit conversion** (Problem 21 from chapter 3 of the *Master Sun*): LLM output:

```
# Convert sheng to hu (10 sheng =
    ↪ 1 hu)
a = Fraction(總食量升, 10)  #
    ↪ Total food in hu
```

Expected (100 *sheng* = 1 *hu*):

| Title | Chapter | Problems | Zero-shot | | Few-shot | | Few-shot (alt. prompt) | | No punctuation | | No translation | | No procedures | | Numerical solutions provided | |
|---|---|---|---|---|---|---|---|---|---|---|---|---|---|---|---|---|
| *Nine Categories* | 1 | 25 | 56.0 | 72.0 | 83.2 | 92.0 | 88.8 | 92.0 | 74.4 | 84.0 | 92.0 | 92.0 | 49.6 | 56.0 | 94.4 | 96.0 |
| | 2 | 45 | 24.4 | 46.7 | 52.4 | 64.4 | 50.2 | 57.8 | 40.9 | 53.3 | 57.3 | 62.2 | 7.1 | 8.9 | 56.0 | 73.3 |
| | 3 | 19 | 51.6 | 63.2 | 65.3 | 78.9 | 66.3 | 78.9 | 61.1 | 73.7 | 64.2 | 68.4 | 54.7 | 57.9 | 62.1 | 78.9 |
| | 4 | 23 | 49.6 | 65.2 | 59.1 | 69.6 | 62.6 | 82.6 | 54.8 | 73.9 | 52.2 | 73.9 | 53.0 | 56.5 | 68.7 | 91.3 |
| | 5 | 34 | 37.6 | 64.7 | 58.8 | 70.6 | 56.5 | 64.7 | 56.5 | 64.7 | 49.4 | 55.9 | 34.1 | 41.2 | 63.5 | 73.5 |
| | 6 | 28 | 40.7 | 60.7 | 41.4 | 50.0 | 37.9 | 46.4 | 38.6 | 53.6 | 45.7 | 50.0 | 25.7 | 39.3 | 43.6 | 50.0 |
| | 7 | 20 | 26.0 | 45.0 | 21.0 | 35.0 | 23.0 | 35.0 | 11.0 | 30.0 | 16.0 | 30.0 | 52.0 | 60.0 | 23.0 | 50.0 |
| | 8 | 18 | 53.3 | 66.7 | 40.0 | 55.6 | 40.0 | 61.1 | 35.6 | 55.6 | 46.7 | 72.2 | 45.6 | 72.2 | 50.0 | 77.8 |
| | 9 | 24 | 46.7 | 75.0 | 48.3 | 75.0 | 59.2 | 70.8 | 42.5 | 62.5 | 41.7 | 45.8 | 17.5 | 37.5 | 51.7 | 66.7 |
| *Five Departments* | 1 | 19 | 68.4 | 73.7 | 34.7 | 63.2 | 46.3 | 63.2 | 49.5 | 73.7 | 25.3 | 36.8 | 56.8 | 63.2 | 34.7 | 52.6 |
| | 2 | 12 | 68.3 | 75.0 | 63.3 | 66.7 | 66.7 | 66.7 | 65.0 | 66.7 | 81.7 | 91.7 | 51.7 | 58.3 | 65.0 | 66.7 |
| | 3 | 14 | 84.3 | 92.9 | 78.6 | 85.7 | 85.7 | 85.7 | 81.4 | 85.7 | 84.3 | 85.7 | 55.7 | 57.1 | 87.1 | 92.9 |
| | 4 | 12 | 21.7 | 41.7 | 40.0 | 50.0 | 33.3 | 41.7 | 36.7 | 50.0 | 45.0 | 58.3 | 16.7 | 25.0 | 38.3 | 50.0 |
| | 5 | 10 | 50.0 | 60.0 | 52.0 | 60.0 | 50.0 | 50.0 | 60.0 | 60.0 | 52.0 | 60.0 | 48.0 | 60.0 | 80.0 | 90.0 |
| *Master Sun* | 2 | 23 | 47.0 | 78.3 | 60.9 | 73.9 | 57.4 | 73.9 | 54.8 | 73.9 | 56.5 | 73.9 | 45.2 | 56.5 | 53.0 | 69.6 |
| | 3 | 34 | 67.1 | 76.5 | 68.8 | 73.5 | 68.8 | 76.5 | 70.0 | 76.5 | 68.2 | 73.5 | 60.0 | 73.5 | 66.5 | 76.5 |
| *Sea Island* | 1 | 9 | 4.4 | 11.1 | 13.3 | 33.3 | 17.8 | 33.3 | 6.7 | 33.3 | 13.3 | 22.2 | 2.2 | 11.1 | 4.4 | 11.1 |
| *Continuation* | 1 | 20 | 0.0 | 0.0 | 0.0 | 0.0 | 0.0 | 0.0 | 0.0 | 0.0 | 0.0 | 0.0 | 1.0 | 5.0 | 2.0 | 10.0 |

Table 7: Accuracy in percent by chapter

```
a = Fraction(總食量升, 100)
```

**Code error (fractions)** (Problem 8 from chapter 1 of the *Five Departments*): LLM output:

```
# 以四除之
邊長 = 方周 / 4
```

Expected (division produces fractional result):

```
邊長 = Fraction(方周, 4)
```

# Using Cross-Linguistic Data Formats to Enhance the Annotation of Ancient Chinese Documents Written on Bamboo Slips

**Michele Pulini[1,2] and Johann-Mattis List[2,3]**
[1] Department of Asian and North African Studies, Ca' Foscari University, Venice, Italy
[2] Chair for Multilingual Computational Linguistics, University of Passau, Passau, Germany
[3] DLCE, MPI-EVA, Leipzig, Germany

**Abstract**

Ancient Chinese documents written on bamboo slips more than 2000 years ago offer a rich resource for research in linguistics, paleography, and historiography. However, since most documents are only available in the form of scans, additional steps of analysis are needed to turn them into interactive digital editions, amenable both for manual and computational exploration. Here, we present a first attempt to establish a workflow for the annotation of ancient bamboo slips. Based on a recently rediscovered dialogue on warfare, we illustrate how a digital edition amenable for manual and computational exploration can be created by integrating standards originally designed for cross-linguistic data collections.

## 1 Introduction

Most computational approaches on ancient stages of the Chinese language restrict themselves to the classical canon of writings that have been handed down for several thousand years now. These sources are written in a standardized character system called the *regular script* (楷書 *kǎishū*). From the time when it was introduced more than 2000 years ago until now, this system does not seem to have been modified in any significant form. As a result, one often thinks of Chinese writing as a unified endeavor, unlikely to change, and unlikely to have changed radically throughout most of its history. When going back deeper in time, however, this picture changes drastically. Thanks to an increasing amount of documents written on bamboo slips that have been archeologically excavated in recent times, scholars are now learning more and more about the immense degree of variation in writing that was characteristic for China long before the *regular script* became adopted as the standard. In order to understand the history of the Chinese language, it is indispensable to pay attention to its variety in writing reflected in these sources.

Most bamboo manuscripts date back to the period from the mid-late Warring States Period (*Zhànguó* 戰國, late fourth century to early third century BCE) up to the Hàn dynasty (*Hàn cháo* 漢朝, 206 BCE to 220 CE). They represent a true wealth of new data and evidence for linguistics, paleography, philology, and historiography. However, putting this treasure of knowledge to use in research bears two major challenges that have not been sufficiently addressed so far. A first challenge consists in the *analysis* of the characters observed in bamboo slips. While these follow the general building structure of Chinese characters, allowing us to identify phonetic and semantic components that usually also find their counterparts in the *regular script*, ancient writing shows a much greater variation with respect to the combinations that are possible here (see Figure 1 as an example). As a result, it is often impossible to find the modern counterparts – along with their Unicode values – of characters observed on bamboo slips. A second challenge consists in the digital *curation* of modern editions of excavated texts. Given that scholars often lack digital training, the vast majority of editions is restricted to scans accompanied by comments, while a deeper integration of data is lacking.

Taking one particular text – available in two different bamboo manuscript versions – as example, we illustrate how these problems could be addressed in the future. Using basic concepts from corpus linguistics, Natural Language Processing, and computer science, we show how the original documents can be annotated, how individual characters can be analyzed with respect to their composition, and how an entire digital edition can be constructed, providing scholars interested in manual data exploration with interactive access to the original documents, while the data in standardized, machine-readable form to scholars interested in computational analysis.



*Proceedings of the Second Ancient Language Processing Workshop associated with NAACL 2025*, pages 52–58
May 4, 2025. 

| Original |  |  |  |  |  |  |
|---|---|---|---|---|---|---|
| **Kǎishū** | 㸟 | 㤫 | 既 | 氣 | 𩙣 | 𠂔 |
| **Source** | GD **Lǎozǐ* A 35 | BS **Bǔshì jìdǎo* 223 | SB **fán wù liú xíng* B 3 | QH **Yuègōng qí shì* 20 | QH **Nǎi mìng yī* 9 | SB *Cáo Mò zhī zhèn* 46b |

Figure 1: Illustration of variation in bamboo script. The table lists variants of the character *qì* 氣 "breath, energy", as it can be found across manuscripts, along with projected conversions of the character structure to the modern *regular script*.

## 2 Materials

The text we use to illustrate our workflow is called *Cáo Mò zhī zhèn* 曹沫之陳 (*Cáo Mò's Battle Formations*). It is a long-lost Chinese philosophical dialogue on ethics and warfare between Duke Zhuāng of Lǔ (Lǔ Zhuāng Gōng 魯莊公, reign 693–662 BCE) and his general Cáo Mò, which has resurfaced after millennia in the form of two manuscript copies on bamboo. The Shanghai Museum manuscript (henceforth SB) was first published in print in 2004 in the fourth volume of the collection (Mǎ, 2001–2012), while the Anhui University copy (henceforth AD) was first published in print in 2022 in the second volume of the collection, whose publication is still ongoing (Huáng and Xú, 2019–2022). Though coming from illegal excavations, their authenticity has been proven through radiocarbon dating of the bamboo slips, which has confirmed a mid-third century BCE dating for SB and a late fourth century BCE dating for AD. SB counts 65 bamboo slips (45 intact and 20 broken, average length 47.4 cm, average width 0.6 cm). The manuscript contains 1778 characters written in the Chǔ orthography and carries the title of the text on the back of slip no.2. On the other hand, AD counts 46 slips (slips 4 and 5 are entirely missing, average length 48.2 cm, average width 0.6 cm). The manuscript contains a total of 1623 character entries. Unlike SB, AD lacks a clear title indication on its back, but some inscriptions as well as some oblique lines useful for correct ordering of the slips are present on the verso. Both *folia* were originally held together by three binding cords (*biānshéng* 編繩), secured to the bamboo slips through binding notches (*qìkǒu* 契口). The binding cords, however, have been irreparably lost. A solid study on some codicological aspects, such as scribal hands, manuscripts production, and use of punctuation as been recently published by Zheng (2024) to whom we redirect the reader. The high-quality scans of both AD and SB bamboo slips provided in the the second volume of the Anhui University manuscripts collection has served as starting point and preliminary material for the digital edition.

## 3 Methods

Our workflow for the digital annotation, curation, and publication of bamboo script documents consists of four stages. In the first stage, we carry out a detailed *digital annotation* of the original data. In the second stage, we conduct an extensive *analysis* of the texts by analyzing characters, identifying words, and glossing sentences semantically. In the third stage, we model the data according to the formats proposed by the Cross-Linguistic Data Formats initiative (CLDF, https://cldf.clld.org, Forkel et al. 2018). In the fourth stage, finally, we *deploy* the data in the form of an interactive CLLD application (https://pypi.org/project/clld, Forkel 2014).

### 3.1 Digital Annotation

In order to allow for a flexible reuse of the analyzed data, our workflow starts from the digital annotation of the original documents. The core of this annotation consists in marking individual characters with boundary boxes and annotating the boxes in such a way that the characters can be identified at later stages. For this task, we used Recogito (https://recogito.pelagios.org/, Barker et al. 2019), an interactive tool for semantic annotation that greatly facilitates this task. Other tools could have been used for this step as well, but we selected Recogito for its shallow learning curve and its general openness. Once finished, Recogito's boundary boxes can be easily exported to various file formats and accessed from computer programs, allowing us to cut individual characters out of the original scans in order check how much they vary.

### 3.2 Linguistic Analysis

The linguistic analysis consists in two parts that may go hand in hand, namely *character analysis* and *text analysis*. During character analysis, all characters annotated in the previous step of our workflow must be analyzed carefully, identifying their external and internal structure, – where possible – their modern counterparts, as well as establishing their pronunciation through different stages of Chinese (regarding the distinction between external and internal structure, see List et al. 2016, 50). Since the identification of words and the assignment of readings to the characters attested on the bamboo slips constitute a comprehensive philological enterprise open to criticism and debate, each character was first reproduced as faithfully as possible using *ideographic description sequences* (for details, see Kordek 2013, 62) and then – where possible – assigned a counterpart in standard Chinese characters. The assignment of the modern counterparts was grounded in the extant scholarly literature on the *Cáo Mò zhī zhèn* manuscripts. Aside from the original critical editions of 2004 and 2022 (Mǎ, 2001–2012; Huáng and Xú, 2019–2022), the editions by Yú and Zhāng (2019) and Sūn (2023) proved essential. In addition, it turned out that a basic understanding of word families and language-internal cognates in Old Chinese phonology (compare Pulini and List, 2024) can be of great help during the analysis. This two-level analysis of character structures – one stricter and one broader – ensures transparency and prevents the loss of information during the annotation process. In identifying ancient readings for the characters, we followed the tradition of research on Old Chinese phonology in providing Middle Chinese readings (a language variety documented in rhyme books published around the 6th century CE) in the system of Baxter (1992), and Old Chinese reconstructions, following the system proposed by Baxter and Sagart (2014).

During text analysis, both manuscripts are unified to form one coherent text. Given the status of the sources, the preference is here given to the AD version of *Cáo Mò's Battle Formations*, with apparent gaps being filled in from the SB version. The analysis starts from the identification of words (which may consist of two and more characters at times) and phrases. Once identified, these are glossed semantically, using basic techniques for *interlinear morphemic glossing* (Lehmann, 2004). In this stage, we also handle characters that may be missing entirely from both versions. These are not only marked specifically but can also be identified easily, as they have no image data attached to them. At the end, translations for phrases and entire passages in English are suggested.

Both character analysis and text analysis are carried out in tabular form, using common spreadsheet editors. In character analysis, each row in a table corresponds to a character that is itself linked to the original scan via the boundary boxes that were added during digital annotation, with separate information being placed into different columns of the table. In text analysis, the basic unit assigned to each row is the word, consisting of one or more characters. Both tasks require a detailed knowledge of bamboo slips, Chinese paleography, and Old Chinese etymology, and were therefore exclusively carried out by the first author of this study, while the role of the second author consisted in the design of formal tests of annotation consistency. While this means that tests on inter-annotator agreement (McDonald et al., 2019) are lacking, we hope to improve the data in the future through comments by our colleagues.

### 3.3 CLDF Integration

The CLDF specification has been developed for various forms of cross-linguistic data, including wordlists, dictionaries, and feature collections. More recently, CLDF has been extended to integrate corpus data, offering additional functionality to handle interlinear-glossed texts (List et al., 2021). While CLDF has not been specifically designed to handle Chinese text collections, the format offers many advantages about alternative data formats. First, data provided in CLDF can be easily queried computationally, using the dedicated PyCLDF Python package (Forkel et al., 2025), as well as SQLite (https://sqlite.org, see Shcherbakova and List 2023 for an example querying lexical data in CLDF, and Blum et al. 2024 for an example queryin corpus data). Second, data available in CLDF can be easily imported into CLLD applications (https://clld.org, Forkel, 2014), thus offering facilitated ways to deploy data collections to the web where they can be conveniently inspected by interested users (see § 3.4 for details).

With our main data available in tabular form, it is straightforward to convert the data to CLDF,

| Original | | | | | | |
|---|---|---|---|---|---|---|
| **Analysis** | 魯 | ⿰戕口 公 | ⿰爿酉 | 為 | 大 | 鍾 |
| **Character** | 魯 | 莊公 | 將 | 為 | 大 | 鍾 |
| **Pīnyīn** | lǔ | zhuāng gōng | jiāng | wèi | dà | zhōng |
| **Middle Chinese** | luX | tsrjang-kuwng | tsjang | hjwe | dajH | tsyowng |
| **Old Chinese** | r.ŋˤaʔ | tsraŋ-C.qˤoŋ | tsaŋ | ɢʷ(r)aj | lˤat-s | toŋ |
| **Gloss** | Lu.(place.name) | duke.Zhuang.(personal.name) | aspect.marker | do | big | bell |

*Duke Zhuang of Lu was in the process of having a massive bell cast.*

Figure 2: Interlinear-glossing example from the web application of the digital edition.

since the CLDF format specification itself is mostly based on tabular data. In CLDF, our data is modeled as a generic dataset, consisting of a language table (linking only to one language, Old Chinese), an entry table that stores the words in the text, and an example table consisting of the individual phrases in interlinear-glossed form (following the *Leipzig Glossing Rules*, see Comrie et al. 2015), where Middle Chinese and Old Chinese reading are offered as additional glossing layers. An additional table is used to store individual characters linked to their location in the scans of the original two editions. The CLDF conversion was carried out with the help of CLDF-Bench (https://pypi.org/project/cldfbench, Forkel and List 2020, a tool that facilitates the conversion to Cross-Linguistic Data Formats. Additional data handling was conducted with the help of the SinoPy package (https://pypi.org/project/sinopy, List 2019).

### 3.4 Deployment with CLLD

The clld toolkit (Forkel, 2014) is a Python library that facilitates the deployment of data provided in the form of Cross-Linguistic Data Formats by providing researchers with an interactive web framework that can be interactively explored. The clld application that we created on top of the CLDF data provides the digital edition of the *Cáo Mò zhī zhèn* in the form of an integrated web application in which original characters can be explored in a unique way that integrates the graphemic, phonetic, and semantic analysis underlying the edition.

## 4 Examples

With the data assembled both in the form of CLDF and an interactive web application, our digital edition of the *Cáo Mò zhī zhèn* allows for both computational and manual exploration. Since we provide the data in the form of interlinear-glossed text, standard approaches from corpus linguistics can be used to query the data in order to investigate the text. As a first example, Table 1 shows the ten most frequently recurring words in the source. As can be seen, we do not only find grammatical markers in this list, but also words like *yuē* 曰 "say" that point to the fact that the text is written as a dialogue, and *zhàn* 戰 "war", pointing to the major topic of the text. While the source itself is limited, this example shows the potential for extended computational analysis once more annotated texts become available.

| C | G | OCH | OCC |
|---|---|---|---|
| 之 | conjunction | tə | 76 |
| 曰 | say | ɢʷat | 57 |
| 不 | negative adv. | pə | 56 |
| 有 | have | ɢʷəʔ | 52 |
| 以 | preposition | ləʔ | 40 |
| 而 | conjunction | nə | 30 |
| 於 | preposition | ʔˤa | 29 |
| 其 | poss. pron. | gə | 27 |
| 戰 | war | tar-s | 27 |
| 莊公 | duke Zhuang | tsraŋ C.qˤoŋ | 22 |

Table 1: Most frequent words and particles in the *Cáo Mò zhī zhèn*. C refers to the character (in standardized form), G refers to the gloss (abbreviated for reasons of visibility), OCH refers to Old Chinese readings, and OCC provides information on occurrences in the text.

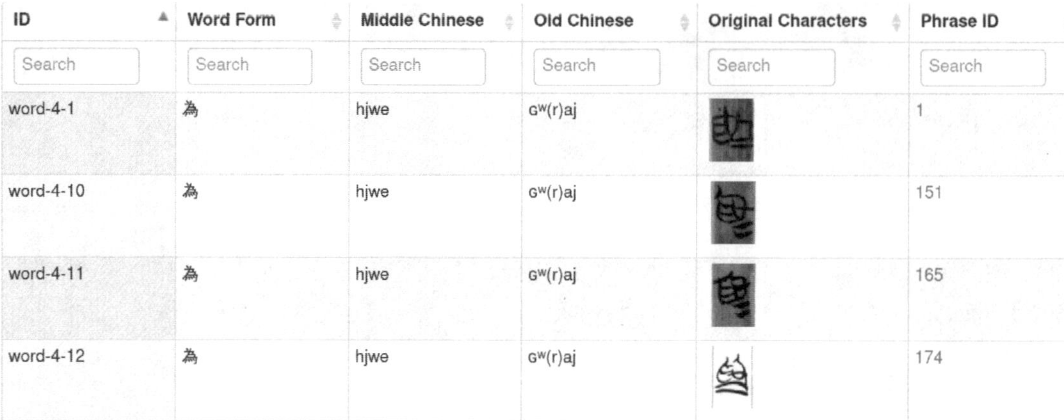

| ID | Word Form | Middle Chinese | Old Chinese | Original Characters | Phrase ID |
|---|---|---|---|---|---|
| Search | Search | Search | Search | Search | Search |
| word-4-1 | 為 | hjwe | Gʷ(r)aj | | 1 |
| word-4-10 | 為 | hjwe | Gʷ(r)aj | | 151 |
| word-4-11 | 為 | hjwe | Gʷ(r)aj | | 165 |
| word-4-12 | 為 | hjwe | Gʷ(r)aj | | 174 |

Figure 3: Comparing individual occurrences of words in the digital edition. The table provides the first 6 out of a total of 16 entries in the digital edition for 為 *wéi* "do, act" MCH *hjwe*, allowing scholars to inspect differences in the writing of the word inside and across editions.

Figure 2 gives a direct example of one interlinear-glossed phrase in the web application, showcasing how the original images are integrated with the two-level analysis of the Chinese characters, the readings in Middle Chinese and Old Chinese, and the semantic glosses. The example also shows how we handle those cases in which the *internal character structure* that we observe in bamboo slips cannot be matched with a counterpart in modern *kǎishū* writing. Since the components of Chinese characters are usually limited and can be easily detected, we use *ideographic description sequences* – a system that allows to systematically analyze characters into their components (Skala, 2015) – to display the way in which the individual components are arranged. Thus, the sequence ⿴戕口, that we identify with the personal name *zhuāng* 莊, refers to a character consisting of *qiāng* 戕 "to kill" with the character radical *kǒu* 口 "mouth" inside.

An additional web view is shown in Figure 3, allowing users to compare individual variants of the same word or character, thus offering direct and convenient ways to assess the variation in writing. In addition, the example not only illustrates how the image annotations are directly integrated with the web application, but also shows how the different backgrounds going back to the original publications of the scans, allow us quickly to see to which of the two sources (AD and SB) the text parts belong, with AD being based on colored images, while SB is given in gray scale.

All in all, we hope that these examples illustrate the advantage of integrated web applications in which data are stored separately, providing access to computers and humans at the same time. Complex web applications often deliberately keep users proficient in computing from accessing the resources with the help of software tools. Resources that focus on providing data exclusively for computational analyses, on the other hand, often underestimate the important role that direct inspection can play in spotting potential errors in annotations.

## 5 Conclusion and Outlook

With this study, we have presented a digital edition of an ancient text on warfare in China that can be accessed both computationally and manually. While computational approaches to bamboo script are still meeting a large number of obstacles, we think that our example application could offer a solution for future studies, by increasing the amount of digitally annotated data that could be used in several kinds of computational studies. Thus, using the annotated images with the associated character structures, one could develop initial models to test the limits of current tools for hand-written text recognition (Kahle et al., 2017). Using tools from corpus linguistics, one could analyze the text in various ways (Hunston, 2022), using it also as the basis for the creation of corpus-based dictionaries (Bowker, 2010). Finally, by providing textual data along with reconstructed pronunciations, such data collections as the one shown here can help to improve and consolidate our knowledge about the ancient pronunciation of Chinese throughout different times and places.

## Supplementary Material

All data and code necessary to replicate the study presented here are freely available for download. The code for the curation of the data is hosted with Codeberg (https://codeberg.org/cldf-datasets/caomozhizhen) and archived with Zenodo (https://doi.org/10.5281/zenodo.15039078, Version 1.0). The application is available online (https://cmzz.digling.org), and the code underlying the application is also hosted with Codeberg (https://codeberg.org/digling/cmzz).

## Acknowledgements

This research was supported by the ERC Consolidator Grant *ProduSemy* (JML, Grant No. 101044282, see https://doi.org/10.3030/101044282). Views and opinions expressed are however those of the authors only and do not necessarily reflect those of the European Union or the European Research Council Executive Agency (nor any other funding agencies involved). Neither the European Union nor the granting authority can be held responsible for them. We thank Robert Forkel for providing important help tips in the preparation of the data in the form of a CLDF package and the deployment of the data as CLLD application.

## Limitations

The workflow we propose is still preliminary. While the extension of *Cáo Mò zhī zhèn* allows for manual transcription and annotation of the data, additional challenges may arise when dealing with longer texts. Moreover, methods for further integrating the critical apparatus into the edition will need to be developed in the future. There are also some concrete points that we hope to improve in the current annotation in the nearer future. Among these are a much more detailed check of glosses and translations, as well as a direct reference to the sources that were employed in the analysis of each individual character and word.

However, the edition we propose serves as a proof of concept and a model for the further development of digital critical editions of early Chinese manuscripts. We thus hope that despite its preliminary status, our work may prove useful for colleagues working on similar research questions and open a broader discussion on the need for consistent annotation and digitalization workflows for data on ancient historical languages.

## References

Elton Barker, Leif Isaksen, Rebecca Kahn, and Rainer Simon Valeria Vitale. 2019. *Recogito [Software Library, Version 3.3]*. Pelagios Network, Vienna.

William H. Baxter. 1992. *A Handbook of Old Chinese Phonology*. Trends in Linguistics: Studies and Monographs. Mouton de Gruyter, Berlin.

William H. Baxter and Laurent Sagart. 2014. *Old Chinese: A New Reconstruction*. Oxford University Press, Oxford.

Frederic Blum, Ludger Paschen, Robert Forkel, Susanne Fuchs, and Frank Seifart. 2024. Consonant lengthening marks the beginning of words across a diverse sample of languages. *Nature Human Behaviour*, 8(11):2127–2138.

Lynne Bowker. 2010. The contribution of corpus linguistics to the development of specialised dictionaries for learners. In Pedro A. Fuertes-Olivera, editor, *Specialised Dictionaries for Learners*, page 155–170. De Gruyter.

Bernard Comrie, Martin Haspelmath, and Balthasar Bickel. 2015. *Leipzig Glossing Rules. Conventions for interlinear morpheme-by-morpheme glosses*. Max Planck Institute for Evolutionary Anthropology, Leizpig.

Robert Forkel. 2014. The Cross-Linguistic Linked Data project. In *Proceedings of the 3rd Workshop on Linked Data in Linguistics: Multilingual Knowledge Resources and Natural Language Processing*, pages 61–66, Reykjavik. ELRA.

Robert Forkel and Johann-Mattis List. 2020. CLDF-Bench. Give your Cross-Linguistic data a lift. In *Proceedings of the Twelfth International Conference on Language Resources and Evaluation*, pages 6997–7004, Luxembourg. European Language Resources Association (ELRA).

Robert Forkel, Johann-Mattis List, Simon J. Greenhill, Christoph Rzymski, Sebastian Bank, Michael Cysouw, Harald Hammarström, Martin Haspelmath, Gereon A. Kaiping, and Russell D. Gray. 2018. Cross-Linguistic Data Formats, advancing data sharing and re-use in comparative linguistics. *Scientific Data*, 5(180205):1–10.

Robert Forkel, Christoph Rzymski, and Sebastian Bank. 2025. *PyCLDF [Software, Version 1.40.4])*. Max Planck Institute for Evolutionary Anthropology, Leipzig.

Susan Hunston. 2022. *Corpora in applied linguistics*, 2 edition. Cambridge University Press, Cambridge.

Dékuān Huáng and Zàiguó Xú, editors. 2019–2022. *Ānhuī Dàxué Cáng Zhànguó Zhújiǎn* 安徽大學藏戰國竹簡. Zhōngxī Shūjú 中西書局, Shanghai. 2 volumes.

Philip Kahle, Sebastian Colutto, Gunter Hackl, and Gunter Muhlberger. 2017. Transkribus – A service platform for transcription, recognition and retrieval of historical documents. In *2017 14th IAPR International Conference on Document Analysis and Recognition (ICDAR)*. IEEE.

Norbert Kordek. 2013. *On Some Quantitative Aspects of the Componential Structure of Chinese Characters*. Wydawnictwo Rys, Poznań.

Christian Lehmann. 2004. Interlinear morphemic glossing. In Geert E. Booij, Christian Lehmann, Joachim Mugdan, and Stavros Skopeteas, editors, *Morphology. An international handbook*, volume 2, pages 1834–1857. De Gruyter, Berlin and New York.

Johann-Mattis List. 2019. *SinoPy: A Python library for quantitative tasks in Chinese historical linguistics [Software Library, Version 0.3.4]*. Max Planck Institute for the Science of Human History, Jena.

Johann-Mattis List, Nathaniel A. Sims, and Robert Forkel. 2021. Towards a sustainable handling of interlinear-glossed text in language documentation. *ACM Transactions on Asian and Low-Resource Language Information Processing*, 20(2):1–15.

Johann-Mattis List, Anselm Terhalle, and Daniel Schulzek. 2016. Traces of embodiment in Chinese character formation. A frame approach to the interaction of writing, speaking, and meaning. In Liane Ströbel, editor, *Sensory-motor concepts. At the crossroad between language & cognition*, pages 45–62. Düsseldorf University Press.

Nora McDonald, Sarita Schoenebeck, and Andrea Forte. 2019. Reliability and inter-rater reliability in qualitative research: Norms and guidelines for cscw and hci practice. *Proceedings of the ACM on Human-Computer Interaction*, 3(CSCW):1−23.

Chéngyuán Mǎ, editor. 2001–2012. *Shànghǎi Bówùguǎn Cáng Zhànguó Chǔ Zhúshū* 上海博物館藏戰國楚竹書. Shànghǎi gǔjí chūbǎnshè 上海古籍出版社, Shanghai. 9 volumes.

Michele Pulini and Johann-Mattis List. 2024. Finding language-internal cognates in Old Chinese. *Bulletin of Chinese Linguistics*, 17(1):53–72.

Olena Shcherbakova and Johann-Mattis List. 2023. Retrieving and analyzing taste colexifications from Lexibank. *Computer-Assisted Language Comparison in Practice*, 6(2):73−86.

Matthew Skala. 2015. A structural query system for Han characters. *International Journal of Asian Language Processing*, 23(2):127–159.

Yǒngbō Sūn. 2023. *Ānhuī Dàxué Cáng Zhànguó Zhújiǎn (Èr) Jí Shì*, volume 38 of *Gǔdiǎn Wénxiàn Yánjiū Jíkān*. Huāmùlán wénhuà shìyè yǒuxiàn gōngsī, New Taibei. 安徽大學藏戰國竹簡（二）集釋.

Shàohóng Yú and Qīngsōng Zhāng, editors. 2019. *Shànghǎi Bówùguǎn Cáng Zhànguó Chǔ Jiǎn Jí Shì* 上海博物館藏戰國楚簡集釋. Social Sciences Academic Press, Beijing. 10 volumes.

Oscar Qiu Jun Zheng. 2024. Scribal hands, errors, and intervention −manuscript production approaches of the cao mie zhi zhen 曹蔑之陣 manuscripts. *Bamboo and Silk*, 7(2):155–201.

# Towards an Integrated Methodology of Dating Biblical Texts: The Case of the Book of Jeremiah

**Martijn Naaijer, Aren Wilson-Wright**
University of Zurich, Switzerland
{martijn.naaijer, aren.wilson-wright}@uzh.ch

**Abstract**

In this paper we describe our research project on dating the language of the Book of Jeremiah using a combination of traditional biblical scholarship and machine learning. Jeremiah is a book with a long history of composing and editing, and the historical background of many of the sections in the book are unclear. Moreover, redaction criticism and historical linguistics are mostly separate fields within the discipline of Biblical Studies. With our approach we want to integrate these areas of research and make new strides in uncovering the compositional history of Book of Jeremiah.

## 1 Introduction

In this paper we present an overview of the research that we will conduct in the following years. The goal of this research is to develop an integrated approach to dating the biblical book of Jeremiah using a combination of traditional biblical scholarship and machine learning.

Dating texts from the Hebrew Bible is a notoriously difficult task. We know that its books are the product of the first millennium BCE, but their exact date within this time span remains debated.

## 2 The book of Jeremiah and its background

At almost 30,000 words, the Book of Jeremiah is the longest book in the Hebrew Bible by word count. It consists of 52 chapters and contains texts from a variety of different genres, the historical background of which is not always clear.

The book itself is set in the turbulent final decades of the 7th century and the first half of the 6th century BCE, during which the kingdom of Judah came under the control of various regional superpowers.

For most of the 7th century BCE Judah was a vassal state of the Neo-Assyrian empire. When the Neo-Assyrian empire began to decline in the latter half of the 7th century, however, Judah enjoyed a brief period of relative independence. Judah's autonomy came to an end in 609 BCE when the Egyptian army under Pharaoh Nekau II killed king Josiah, and brought Judah under Egyptian vassalage. In 605 BCE, control of Judah changed hands, when the Babylonians defeated the Egyptian army at Carchemish. King Jehoiakim stopped paying tribute to king Nebuchadnezzar in 601 BCE, after the Babylonian king suffered heavy losses trying to invade Egypt. Nebuchadnezzar subsequently plundered Jerusalem in 597 BCE, and deported part of the Judean population to Babylon. Zedekiah succeeded Jehoiakim as king, but later revolted against Nebuchadnezzar by withholding tribute and allying himself with Pharaoh Apries sometime in 587 BCE. Nebuchadnezzar then returned and destroyed the city of Jerusalem and its temple in 586 BCE. Another part of the Judean population was deported. The year 586 BCE marks the start of the so-called Babylonian exile, which lasted until 539 BCE, when the Persian king Cyrus conquered Babylon, and allowed the Judean exiles to return home (Crouch, 2021).

The Book of Jeremiah paints a portrait of the prophet with the same name, who receives his prophecies from God. He has a scribe, Baruch the son of Neriah (e.g. Jer. 36:4) who records these prophecies. In the book, we read that the prophet is imprisoned (ch. 37), but is later released (ch. 39)



*Proceedings of the Second Ancient Language Processing Workshop associated with NAACL 2025*, pages 59–64
May 4, 2025. 

and travels to Egypt (ch. 43). Despite this apparent biographical information, it is difficult to say much with certainty about the historical prophet Jeremiah, and to what extent events in the Book of Jeremiah can be related to phases in his life (Leuchter, 2021).

A comparison of the Hebrew version of Jeremiah as preserved in the Masoretic Text (MT) with the later Greek translation, called the Septuagint, reveals several discrepancies between the two text traditions. The Greek text is approximately 8% shorter than its Hebrew counterpart, and locates some passages in a different place in the book.

According to most researchers, the Greek version of Jeremiah reflects an earlier stage in the redaction of the book than MT Jeremiah. An important piece of evidence for this is that the additional material in the MT contains a lot of very specific vocabulary that is absent from the Greek version (Stipp, 2021).

There are strongly varying opinions as to when the book was composed. According to Holladay (1986), the book dates back to the lifetime of the historical prophet ($7^{th}$–$6^{th}$ century BCE) but others date the book later. According to Fischer (2005), for instance, the book was written in the $4^{th}$ century BCE.

## 3 State of the art: Biblical Studies

### 3.1 General

One of the main goals of this research is to combine redaction criticism and historical linguistics. In Biblical Studies, these modes of inquiry are usually kept separate, and their different presuppositions and methods often lead to contradicting results. Here, we introduce both fields briefly.

### 3.2 Linguistics

Even though the Hebrew Bible was written and edited throughout the first millennium BCE, its language, Biblical Hebrew is relatively homogeneous. But it does exhibit some variation. In the literature, the most important explanation for this linguistic variation is diachrony—the change of the language over time. Biblical scholarship distinguishes roughly between Classical (or Early) Biblical Hebrew (CBH or EBH) and Late Biblical Hebrew (LBH).

The CBH corpus consists of the Pentateuch and the Former Prophets[1], and the core LBH corpus contains the books Esther, Daniel, Ezra, Nehemiah and Chronicles. Some scholars also include the book of Qoheleth among the LBH books, but not everyone does so (e.g. Young, 1993, 140–156). Other texts and books are more controversial. For instance, Rendsburg (2012) considers the book of Haggai to be written in LBH, and Paul (2012) observes that there is a concentration of late features in Isaiah 40–66.

The Babylonian Exile (587/6–539 BCE) serves as the dividing line between CBH and LBH with CBH reflecting the written variety of Hebrew used prior to 587/6 BCE and LBH reflecting that used after 539 BCE. LBH differs from CBH in terms of phonology, morphology, syntax, lexicon, and style (Fassberg, 2016, 8). Some of these differences are the result of internal developments within the Hebrew language, while others are the result of language contact between Hebrew and Aramaic, the chancery language of the Persian empire. Fassberg (2016, 11–14) mentions various Aramaic features in LBH. On page 14 he gives some Persian loanwords as well.

Several scholars working on the linguistic dating of Hebrew take it as axiomatic that every text written in CBH must have been written at an early date (e.g. Joosten, 2016, 336). This is a controversial point of view. On the one hand, we know that late texts are late because they deal with late (political) events. However, CBH texts dealing with early events could have been composed at a later date.

Based on the distinction between CBH and LBH, scholars have tried to date biblical texts of unknown date with the help of their language. A prominent scholar who developed a method for linguistic dating is Avi Hurvitz. Hurvitz has published many papers and books on this topic; some of his most important works are Hurvitz (1974) and Hurvitz (2014). According to him a late linguistic feature can be identified on the basis of three criteria. The first is distribution. A late feature should occur predominantly or exclusively in late texts. The second criterion is contrast. A late feature should have a semantic equivalent which occurs in early texts. The third criterion is extra-biblical attestation. A linguistic feature is only a late feature if it is used more broadly than in a single text, because then it could be an idiosyncrasy. If these three conditions are

[1] The Pentateuch or Torah consists of the books Genesis, Exodus, Leviticus, Numbers and Deuteronomy, while the books of Joshua, Judges, Samuel and Kings comprise the Former Prophets.

satisfied, one can say that a feature is late. Finally, for an entire text to be considered late, it must contain an accumulation of late features, because one or two late features could be just a coincidence (e.g. Hurvitz, 2014, 9–10).

In 2014, Aaron Hornkohl published a monograph on the language of the Book of Jeremiah from a linguistic dating perspective. Hornkohl found clear signs of late language in the Book of Jeremiah, but not in such a concentration as in the core LBH books. He describes the language as Jeremiah as a mix of CBH and LBH features that is not found in the early *or* late books (Hornkohl 2014, 59). For some features, Jeremiah uses the early variant, but for others, it uses a mix of early and late language (Hornkohl, 2014, 59–62).

Hornkohl points out that the book of Jeremiah has a complex history of composition and editing (Hornkohl, 2014, 65), and he observes that some parts may contain a higher concentration of late features than others. However, none of these parts have a concentration that is as high as core LBH texts (Hornkohl, 2014, 66).

Various scholars have contested the idea that it is possible to date biblical texts linguistically. Cryer argued that there is not enough linguistic variation in Biblical Hebrew to conclude that the Bible developed over a long period of time. The language is simply too homogeneous (Cryer, 1994).

Another critique from the 90s comes from Philip Davies (1995), who argued that the whole Hebrew Bible was a post exilic composition and that CBH and LBH co-existed in the post-exilic period.

The most comprehensive critique of linguistic dating was given by Young, Rezetko and Ehrensvärd (2 volumes, 2008). In 2 volumes, they discuss the principles and methods of linguistic dating. The authors come to the conclusion that it is not possible to date biblical texts using language alone. They acknowledge that one can distinguish between CBH and LBH, but in their opinion these are two styles that co-existed before and after the exile (Young, Rezetko and Ehrensvärd, 2008, volume 2, chapter 2). In later works they opt for an integrated approach (e.g. Rezetko and Young, 2014).

### 3.3 Redaction criticism

Redaction critical scholarship on Jeremiah owes a lot to the work of Bernhard Duhm (1901) and Sigmund Mowinckel (1914). Duhm distinguished two different categories of prose in the Book of Jeremiah: biographical and nonbiographical. The biographical prose parts appear in chapters 26–45, while the non-biographical parts appear throughout the book. According to Duhm, the non-biographical sections often draw heavily from other biblical texts and were added by later editors (Wilson, 1999, 414).

Mowinckel, by contrast, divided the Book of Jeremiah into three main sources. He assigned the label "A" to the poetic oracles in chapters 1–25, which he saw as the original core of the book. He labelled the biographical sections and the rhetorical prose passage—which he saw as linked with Deuteronomistic literature—"B" and "C" respectively (Wilson, 1999, 414). Mowinckel's work was very influential, and much subsequent work by other researchers was devoted to investigating how C was related to A and to literature outside of the book, especially Deuteronomy. The date of the different sources also became a source of debate.

## 4 State of the art: Large Language Models

### 4.1 LLMs

Recently, Large Langue Models (LLMs), like GPT-4 (OpenAI, 2023) and LLaMA-3 (Llama team, 2024) have set benchmarks in various NLP tasks, including translation, summarization and conversation. Importantly, LLMs do not require hand coded features and thus reduce the risk of replicating traditional biblical scholarship on the segmentation and dating of biblical texts.

These models are able to achieve such a high level of performance by ingesting huge quantities of training data—usually billions or even trillions of words. Biblical Hebrew, however, is a low-resource language comprising approximately 262,934 words. Therefore, it is important to find a solution to the problem of the lack of data.

In recent years, developing LLMs for low-resource languages has become an active field of research. One solution is to reduce the number of parameters in the model. Wdowiak, for example, successfully built a language model for Sicilian using only 266,514 words by reducing BERT's 12-layer architecture to just a single a single layer (Wdowiak 2021). The size of the Sicilian corpus used in this study is similar to that of the Hebrew Bible. Other studies opt for alternative solutions for low-resource languages (e.g. Alam et al., 2024;

Cahyawijaya et al., 2024; Nag et al., 2024 and Nguyen et al., 2023).

Complex models like LLMs are often called black-box models, because it is difficult to get an impression of how they make predictions. For the present project it is important that the models are not only capable of segmenting and classifying strands within the Book of Jeremiah, but also that they do this in an explainable way. The research results should be meaningful from the perspective of linguists. Explainability of LLMs is an emerging and active field of research, and there are various ways in which one can attempt to create transparency (e.g. Sundararajan, 2017. For a survey: Zhao et al., 2023).

### 4.2 Initial experiments

We have done some initial experiments to test whether it is possible to distinguish between different linguistic phases of Biblical Hebrew using Machine Learning.

Wilson-Wright finetuned a RoBERTa Base model with an adapted architecture using the verses of the Hebrew Bible as inputs (Wilson-Wright, "BERiT"). The model features a single attention block with four attention heads, smaller embedding and feedforward dimensions (256 and 1024), a smaller max input length (128), and an aggressive dropout rate (.5) at both the attention and feedforward layers. For further details, see the respective HuggingFace model cards for the architecture, parameters and training data for both BERiT and COHeN. Wilson-Wright then trained a linear classifier on top of the language model using labelled data drawn from CBH and LBH text. (Wilson-Wright, "COHeN"). The classifier also included data from two other hypothetical stages of Biblical Hebrew, Archaic Biblical Hebrew (ABH) and Transitional Biblical Hebrew (TBH). ABH is thought to precede CBH, while TBH represents the transitional phase between CBH and LBH. The classifier model achieved 73.4% accuracy on the validation dataset. The application of an explainability framework in the form of integrated gradients revealed that the classifier had independently learned at least one feature that scholars have argued distinguishes CBH from LBH, namely the occasional spelling of the personal name David as דָוִיד in LBH (vs. דָוִד everywhere else).

Another experiment was done by Naaijer (2020, 149–176). He trained an LSTM-based sequence classifier that distinguishes between CBH and LBH to find out whether the language of the biblical books of Jonah and Ruth shares more characteristics with CBH or LBH. Instead of training the model with the raw Hebrew text, clauses were represented as sequences of parts of speech or phrase functions. Models were trained for narrative and quoted speech. In general, Naaijer found that the language of Jonah and Ruth shares more characteristics with CBH than with LBH. This is an interesting result, but it is somewhat unsatisfying because LSTM models are a black box.

## 5 How to move forward

The main data source for this research is the ETCBC dataset of the Hebrew Bible (e.g. Roorda 2018). The first step will be to figure out how best to train an LLM for Biblical Hebrew using the available data. Questions we will consider include: What is the best architecture, what is the best representation of the Hebrew text (vocalized or unvocalized), and how should the text be tokenized? Also relevant is whether it is possible to use transfer learning by training the model on texts in related languages.

After training a masked language model for Biblical Hebrew, we will finetune the model to be a text classifier with the goal of segmenting and classifying parts of the Book of Jeremiah. Here, it is very important that explainability is one of the key ingredients of the research process.

## 6 Conclusions

There are many interpretations of when and how the Book of Jeremiah was composed and edited. With the newest developments in the field of Natural Language Processing we think it is possible to take groundbreaking new steps in combining redaction criticism and linguistic analysis of the Book of Jeremiah.

## Acknowledgments

We thank the Swiss National Science Foundation for funding this research under grant number 10001381.

## References

Firoj Alam, Shammur Absar Chowdhury, Sabri Boughorbel and Maram Hasanain. 2024. LLMs for Low Resource Languages in Multilingual, Multimodal and Dialectal Settings. In *Proceedings of the 18th Conference of the European Chapter of the Association for Computational Linguistics: Tutorial Abstracts*. 27–33. https://aclanthology.org/2024.eacl-tutorials.5.

Samuel Cahyawijaya, Holy Lovenia and Pascale Fung. 2024. LLMs Are Few-Shot In-Context Low-Resource Language Learners. In *Proceedings of the 2024 Conference of the North American Chapter of the Association for Computational Linguistics: Human Language Technologies (Volume 1: Long Papers)*. 405–433. https://aclanthology.org/2024.naacl-long.24.

Robert Chazan, William W. Hallo, and Lawrence H. Schiffman. 1999. *Ki Baruch Hu, Ancient Near Eastern, Biblical, and Judaic Studies in Honor of Baruch A. Levine*. Eisenbrauns, Winona Lake.

Carly L. Crouch. 2021. The Historical Contexts of the Books of Jeremiah. In Stulman and Silver, 2021, chapter 1.

Frederick H. Cryer. 1994. The Problem of Dating Biblical Hebrew and the Hebrew of Daniel. In Knud Jeppesen, Kirsten Nielsen and Bent Rosendal (eds.). *In the Last Days: On Jewish and Christian Apocalyptic and Its Period.* Aarhus University Press, Aarhus, 185–198.

Philip R. Davies. 1995. *In Search of "Ancient Israel"*, Sheffield Academic, Sheffield, 2nd edition.

Bernhard Duhm. 1901. *Das Buch Jeremia.* Mohr, Tübingen and Leipzig.

Steven E. Fassberg. 2016. What is Late Biblical Hebrew, *Zeitschrift für die Alttestamentliche Wissenschaft*, 128(1). 1–15.

Georg Fischer. 2005. *Jeremia 1-25; Jeremia 26-52.* 2 Volumes. Herders Theologischer Kommentar, Freiburg.

William L. Holladay. 1986. *Jeremiah 1. Commentary on the book of Jeremiah. Chapters 1–25.* Hermeneia, A Critical and Historical Commentary on the Bible, Fortress Press, Philadelphia.

Aaron Hornkohl. 2014. *Ancient Hebrew Periodization and the Language of the Book of Jeremiah, The Case for a Sixth-Century Date of Composition*, Brill, Leiden.

Avi Hurvitz. 1974. The Date of the Prose-Tale of Job Linguistically Reconsidered. *The Harvard Theological Review*, 67(1). 17–34.

Avi Hurvitz. 2014. *A Concise Lexicon of Late Biblical Hebrew, Linguistic Innovations in the Writings of the Second Temple Period.* Brill, Leiden.

Jan Joosten. 2016. Diachronic Linguistics and the Date of the Pentateuch. In Jan C. Gertz, Bernard M. Levinson, Dalit Rom-Shiloni and Konrad Schmid (eds.). *The Formation of the Pentateuch.* Mohr Siebeck, Tübingen.

Llama team. 2024. The Llama 3 Herd of Models. https://ai.meta.com/research/publications/the-llama-3-herd-of-models.

Mark Leuchter. 2021. The Historical Jeremiah. In Stulman and Silver, 2021, chapter 4.

Sigmund Mowinckel. 1914. *Zur Komposition des Buches Jeremia*. Dybwad, Kristiania.

Martijn Naaijer. 2020. *Clause Structure Variation in Biblical Hebrew: A Quantitative Approach.* PhD thesis, Vrije Universiteit Amsterdam. https://research.vu.nl/en/publications/clause-structure-variation-in-biblical-hebrew-a-quantitative-appr.

Arijit Nag, Soumen Chakrabarti, Animesh Mukherjee and Niloy Ganguly. 2024. Efficient Continual Pre-training of LLMs for Low-resource Languages. https://arxiv.org/abs/2412.10244.

Xuan-Phi Nguyen, Sharifah Mahani Aljunied, Shafiq Joty and Lidong Bing. 2023. Democratizing LLMs for Low-Resource Languages by Leveraging their English Dominant Abilities with Linguistically-Diverse Prompts. https://arxiv.org/abs/2306.11372.

OpenAI. 2023. Gpt-4 technical report. https://arxiv.org/abs/2303.08774v6.

Shalom Paul. 2012. Signs of Late Biblical Hebrew in Isaiah 40–66. In Cynthia Miller-Naudé and Ziony Zevit (eds.). *Diachrony in Biblical Hebrew.* Eisenbrauns, Winona Lake.

Gary A. Rendsburg. 2012. Late Biblical Hebrew in the Book of Haggai. In Rebecca Hasselbach and Naama Pat-El (eds.). *Language and Nature. Papers Presented to John Huehnergard on the Occasion of his 60th Birthday.* Studies in Ancient Oriental Civilization. Number 67. The Oriental Institute of the University of Chicago, Chicago.

Robert Rezetko and Ian Young. 2014. Historical Linguistics & Biblical Hebrew, Steps Toward an Integrated Approach. SBL Press, Atlanta.

Dirk Roorda. 2018. Coding the Hebrew Bible. In Research Data Journal for the Humanities and Social Sciences, Volume 3 Issue 1. 27–41. https://doi.org/10.1163/24523666-01000011.

Hermann-Josef Stipp. 2021. Two Ancient Editions of the Book of Jeremiah. In Stulman and Silver, 2021, 93–113.

Mukund Sundararajan, M., Ankur Taly, and Qiqi Yan. 2017. Axiomatic Attribution for Deep Networks. In *Proceedings of the 34th International Conference on Machine Learning.* https://dl.acm.org/doi/10.5555/3305890.3306024.

Louis Stulman and Edward Silver. 2021. *The Oxford Handbook of Jeremiah*, Oxford University Press.

Eryk Wdowiak. 2021. Sicilian Translator: A Recipe for Low-Resource NMT. https://arxiv.org/abs/2110.01938.

Robert R. Wilson. 1999. Poetry and Prose in the Book of Jeremiah. In Chazan, Hallo and Schiffman (1999). 413–428.

Aren M. Wilson-Wright. "BERiT." https://huggingface.co/gngpostalsrvc/BERiT.

Aren M. Wilson-Wright. "COHeN." https://huggingface.co/gngpostalsrvc/COHeN.

Ian Young. 1993. *Diversity in Pre-Exilic Hebrew*. Mohr, Tübingen.

Ian Young., Robert Rezetko and Martin Ehrensvärd. 2008. *Linguistic Dating of Biblical Texts*, 2 Volumes, Equinox Publishing, London.

Haiyan Zhao, Hanjie Chen, Fan Yang, Ninghao Liu, Huiqi Deng, Hengyi Cai, Shuaiqiang Wang, Dawei Yin and Mengnan Du. 2023. Explainability for Large Language Models: A Survey. https://arxiv.org/abs/2309.01029.

# The Development of Hebrew in Antiquity – A Computational Linguistic Study*

**Hallel Baitner**[†], **Dimid Duchovny**[‡]
Tel Aviv University

**Lee-Ad Gottlieb**[§]
Ariel University

**Amir Yorav**[¶]
Afeka College

**Nachum Dershowitz**[‖], **Eshbal Ratzon**[**]
Tel Aviv University

## Abstract

The linguistic nature of Qumran Hebrew (QH) remains a central debate in the study of the Dead Sea Scrolls (DSS). Although some scholars view QH as an artificial imitation of Biblical Hebrew (BH), others argue that it represents a spoken dialect of ancient Judea.

The present study employs computational linguistic techniques, clustering, classification, and machine learning, to analyze the relationship of QH with Biblical and Mishnaic Hebrew. Preliminary findings confirm existing scholarly conclusions regarding the linguistic affinity of certain texts. This demonstrates that our methodology has a fundamental capacity to identify linguistic relationships. They also contribute new leads, on which we are now working to refine and enhance our analytical methods so as to provide founded insights into the historical development of Hebrew and the process of DSS textual composition.

## 1 Introduction

The study of Qumran Hebrew (QH) has long attracted scholars because of its linguistic complexity. Early analyses revealed QH's dual nature: It shares features with Biblical Hebrew (BH), while also displaying unique traits that align with later forms such as Mishnaic Hebrew (MH) and Samaritan Hebrew. This intricate blend has sparked an ongoing debate about QH's origins and its place in the historical development of the Hebrew language. This project aims to leverage computational language tools to deepen our understanding of QH, clarify its relationship to other Hebrew dialects, and refine the relative dating of specific scrolls within the corpus of the Dead Sea Scrolls (DSS).

## 2 The Nature of Qumran Hebrew

Initial scholarly evaluations of QH highlighted both its association with BH and its inclusion of linguistic traits found in later Hebrew forms. Scholars faced the challenge of explaining this duality in a comprehensive way. The predominant view, led by scholars such as Yalon (1967), Kutscher (1974), and Blau (2000), posits that QH represents a literary attempt to replicate BH. They argue that due to the cessation of BH as a living language before the composition of the DSS, this endeavor was only partially successful, allowing contemporary Hebrew features to penetrate. Some of these features are also known from MH. These scholars advocate for focusing on these contemporary linguistic features subtly embedded within QH to reconstruct the historical development of Hebrew during this period.

In contrast, scholars such as Ben-Ḥayyim (1958), Morag (1988), Rendsburg (2015), and notably Qimron (1992, 2018) propose a different model. They argue that QH authentically represents a spoken Hebrew dialect prevalent in ancient Judea. They position QH as a natural continuation of Late Biblical Hebrew (LBH), suggesting these are sequential points along the historical continuum of Hebrew language development. Qimron challenges the notion of shared morphological features between QH and MH, emphasizing their differences and proposing that MH originated from an unidentified Hebrew dialect in the Galilee, rather than from the DSS.

The scholarly debate thus centers on the inter-

*This research was funded in part by the Tel Aviv University Center for AI and Data Science and by the European Union (ERC, MiDRASH, Project No. 101071829). Views and opinions expressed are, however, those of the authors only and do not necessarily reflect those of the European Union or the European Research Council Executive Agency. Neither the European Union nor the granting authority can be held responsible for them.

[†]hallel.baitner@mail.huji.ac.il
[‡]dimidd@gmail.com
[§]leead@ariel.ac.il
[¶]amiryorav@gmail.com
[‖]nachumd@tauex.tau.ac.il
[**]eshbal@gmail.com



*Proceedings of the Second Ancient Language Processing Workshop associated with NAACL 2025*, pages 65–70
May 4, 2025. 

pretation rather than the validity of the evidence. Scholars generally agree on the affinity between QH and LBH, as well as the shared lexical features between QH and MH. This situation underscores the need to expand and deepen comparative analyses of QH against both LBH and MH to provide new evidence regarding the relationships between these dialects. A global quantitative analysis, in addition to qualitative assessments and specific examples, will offer a more comprehensive understanding of these linguistic relationships. Utilizing digital analysis tools promises significant contributions to this discussion. In addition, while the majority of scholarship addresses the language of the scrolls as a whole, only limited research focuses on the distinctive language of specific scrolls, such as Kutcher's work on the Isaiah Scroll and Qimron's on 4QMMT (*Miqsat Ma'ase ha-Torah*). As the composition of the DSS is dated to a period of several centuries, we find this path of research to be promising.

## 3 Computational Linguistics for Hebrew

Before detailing our methodology, it is crucial to review past attempts to use computational linguistic tools for Hebrew text analysis. Early efforts focused on natural language processing (NLP) methods, requiring researchers to create morphological or syntactic descriptions for computers. Later, the field adopted machine-learning techniques, enabling computers to learn data descriptions from large training sets automatically.

Several tools have been adapted for Hebrew tasks, including automated transliteration, root identification, and opinion extraction. Notably, Santacruz (2017) used a bidirectional long-short term memory (LSTM) network to differentiate between Hebrew and Aramaic words. Similar techniques were used by HaCohen-Kerner et al. (2010) to classify Hebrew documents by historical period and ethnic origin, achieving high success rates. Liebeskind and Liebeskind (2020) further refined this approach, using more advanced techniques like recurrent neural networks and convolutional neural networks to differentiate between texts from different centuries. Koppel et al. (2011) and Yoffe et al. (2023) applied NLP methods to computerized source criticism of Biblical texts, focusing on identifying and distinguishing between different source materials within the Bible. Fono et al. (2024) used transformer-based models to reconstruct ancient Hebrew and Aramaic inscriptions, trained on the Hebrew Bible. Additionally, Dicta's Tiberias tool[1] applies modern machine learning to Bible datasets (though not to the DSS), providing stylistic comparisons and classifications based on detailed syntactic and morphological information.

Van Hecke (2018) and Van Hecke and de Joode (2021) explore the use of computational stylometric techniques to analyze BH texts and the DSS, highlighting the methodological challenges and the potential to identify distinct authors and textual variations.

## 4 Approach, Methods and Goals

The linguistic material we have used is based on the linguistic analysis provided by *Accordance*,[2] which includes annotated texts from ancient Hebrew works. We have developed a method to organize the linguistic data from these databases into standardized tables, facilitating computational analysis. Many compositions from the Dead Sea Scrolls have survived only in fragmentary form. We accept the scholarly decisions made in this dataset regarding doubtful letters, but our data is based solely on preserved ink, excluding reconstructions.

Our study involves two distinct types of clustering tasks: general clustering based on overall linguistic features and clustering based on specific morphological criteria. We began with a general clustering analysis of the three corpora based on word frequency. We converted each biblical book, scroll, and mishnaic tractate into a vocabulary vector, a mathematical representation of its lexical profile based on the frequency of word lemmas. To compare the compositions, we sequentially employ the following statistical approaches:

- Raw frequency analysis. Each document of the corpus is represented by a vector: With each word (or more precisely, lemma) of the entire corpus, we associate the same unique coordinate of the document vectors, and so the vector lengths are precisely the number of unique lemmas in the corpus. A document vector $v$ contains in its $i$-th coordinate the number of occurrences in the document of the corresponding lemma.

- TF–IDF (term frequency–inverse document frequency). The raw vector is then normalized

[1] https://tiberias.dicta.org.il

[2] https://www.accordancebible.com

using this method, which reduces the weight of common words while emphasizing unique terms in each book. The TF term for document vector $v$ and coordinate $i$ is $v(i)$ divided by the total number of words in the document (i.e. $\sum_j v(j)$). The IDF term for coordinate $i$ in all document vectors is the logarithm of the percentage of documents containing the corresponding lemma. We normalize the value $v(i)$ to be its TF value, multiplied by the IDF value of coordinate $i$ (i.e. TF∗IDF).

- Cosine similarity. Having computed the representative normalized vector for each document, we can then measure their similarity. For a pair of document vectors $v, w$, their similarity value is given as

$$\frac{\sum_i v(i) * w(i)}{\sqrt{\sum_i v(i)^2} * \sqrt{\sum_i w(i)^2}}$$

For clustering, we use hierarchical clustering with the Ward method, which groups texts based on lexical similarity while minimizing variance within clusters. The results are visualized as dendrograms, where proximity between texts indicates linguistic similarity.

In addition to general clustering, we focus on two specific morphological criteria: (1) the distribution of verb stems (*binyanim*), as previous research has shown shifts in stem usage across different periods of Hebrew (Fassberg, 2001), and (2) verbal valency patterns, which capture variations in the complements verbs can take. To analyze *binyanim*, our algorithm calculates the percentage distribution of each stem relative to the total number of verbs in each text. We then compute the Euclidean distance between these distributions across different texts, identifying those with the smallest inter-distribution distances as the most similar in stem usage. This methodology will be further refined as the research progresses.

To analyze valency, our algorithm systematically processes each verb, inspecting up to four subsequent words to determine whether it is followed by a prepositional particle, an object marker, or a pronominal suffix. Results are stored with detailed morphological attributes, enabling a structured comparison of valency patterns across texts and offering insights into syntactic shifts in Hebrew over time. This method is not yet perfect. In a sample review of the results, compared to a manual examination of the occurrences of the given verb, we observed that some complements were either not covered or incorrectly identified. However, the distribution of the various complements provides a sufficiently accurate representation of their actual occurrence. We will continue working to improve this algorithm.

Beyond clustering, our goal is to train machine learning models on the Hebrew Bible and the Mishnah to identify distinct linguistic features of Classical Biblical Hebrew (CBH), LBH, and MH. Special attention is given to distinguishing literary genres within these corpora to enhance the precision of linguistic classification.

For dialect classification, we aim to leverage recent deep learning models such as ELMo, BERT, XLNet, and RoBERTa, integrating expert knowledge of Hebrew morphology and syntax into statistical learning frameworks. These models, pretrained on large corpora and fine-tuned for specific tasks, will be validated against traditional classification algorithms using metrics such as accuracy, precision, recall, $F_1$-score, and clustering coherence measures like silhouette score and adjusted Rand index. Once the classifier is trained, it will be applied to the DSS to assess linguistic affinity with CBH, LBH, or MH. Special considerations include handling biblical quotations and multiple manuscript versions, ensuring that linguistic features are analyzed independently for each text. To account for textual transmission variations, we will compare rewritten or paraphrased biblical texts separately from non-biblical compositions, assessing linguistic deviations from the original biblical material and applying normalization techniques where necessary.

Since the data on which we relied to build our data set was taken from *Accordance*, it cannot be published without permission. However, the scripts we developed for data extraction will be released at the end of the project, enabling researchers to replicate our experiments

## 5 Preliminary Results

The clustering analysis of three major ancient Jewish textual corpora—the Hebrew Bible, the Mishnah, and the Dead Sea Scrolls—revealed nuanced insights into their linguistic and stylistic structures. The algorithm identified patterns that align with previously observed textual groups, such as the grouping of biblical books (e.g., 1 & 2 Samuel,

1 & 2 Kings, 1 & 2 Chronicles). The Mishnah's tractates generally stood out as a separate cluster. However, in an experiment conducted using the raw frequency model, the tractates *Tamid*, *Middot*, and *Yoma* distinctly differed from the rest of the Mishnah and showed a greater affinity with Qumranic compositions such as the Temple Scroll and Pseudo-Jubilees. This finding aligns well with Mishnah research, which has identified *Tamid*, *Middot*, and *Yoma* as among the earliest tractates (Epstein, 1957).

Additionally, the fragmentary copies of *Miqsat Ma'ase ha-Torah* exhibited, according to the tf–idf model, a closer linguistic proximity to Mishnaic tractates than to any other Qumranic composition (see Figure 1). This finding is consistent with prior research on this text, which has highlighted its distinctive language—deviating from the typical Qumranic linguistic style and resembling Rabbinic Hebrew more closely (Mizrahi, 2020).

Regarding the relationships among Qumranic compositions, further research is required. Preliminary results indicate, on the one hand, a clear affinity between texts such as the *Hodayot* and 4Q511 (The Song of the *Maskil*), as noted in previous studies (Angel, 2012). At the same time, unexpected connections emerged, such as the affinity between the Temple Scroll and a fragment from the Book of Jubilees (4Q219).

Future research should investigate the extent to which content and genre influence the clustering of these texts and strive to develop methodologies that minimize such biases as much as possible.

The analysis of verb stem distribution is still in its early stages. As expected, a close linguistic affinity was observed between related biblical books (e.g., 1 & 2 Samuel). However, other results indicate unexpected connections between compositions whose language appears to be significantly different. These findings require further investigation, and it may be necessary to integrate verb stem distribution data with additional types of linguistic analysis to refine the methods for identifying linguistic affinities between texts.

Valency patterns analysis is also still ongoing. Initial findings indicate distinct patterns in verb complement diversity. Some verbs display clear distributional tendencies, and certain books exhibit marked preferences for specific valency structures. For example, the algorithm successfully identified the various complements of the verb *byn* (*hiphil* stem, "to understand") and correctly detected the tendency of certain biblical books—such as Nehemiah, Daniel, and Chronicles—to use the preposition *b*- as a complement, in contrast to other biblical texts, such as Psalms and Proverbs, which regularly use a pronominal suffix, a direct object, or the preposition *l*-. Future analyses will compare the distribution of valency patterns across different works and corpora, further refining our understanding of verb usage in ancient Hebrew.

Figure 2 presents the normalized distribution of the complements of the verb *byn* in the *hiphil* stem across different books of the Hebrew Bible. The $y$-axis represents the relative distribution of each complement, while the $x$-axis lists the biblical books. The various colors indicate different complements attached to the verb, as shown in the legend.

We have similar graphs for 810 different verbs (where "verb" refers to a specific root in a particular stem), allowing us to quickly map the diversity of valency patterns for each verb.

## 6 Conclusion

This study employs an innovative combination of general clustering, morphological-based clustering, and machine learning techniques to investigate the linguistic landscape of the Dead Sea Scrolls. Our research aims to establish Qumran Hebrew's position within the broader development of ancient Hebrew, while providing new methodologies for the relative dating of scrolls based on linguistic features. By identifying previously unnoticed shared linguistic patterns among dialects and developing a chronological scaling of scrolls from the Hellenistic period to 70 CE, we seek to uncover potential literary connections between scrolls based on linguistic affinity. Our algorithmic approach reveals clusters of texts that share linguistic features with pre- and post-Qumranic corpora, suggesting possible social or chronological commonalities. This methodological framework not only deepens our understanding of Hebrew linguistic development but also contributes significantly to broader discussions on diachronic and dialectal variations in ancient Hebrew.

## References

Joseph L. Angel. 2012. Maskil, community, and religious experience in the *Songs of the Sage* (4Q510–511). *Dead Sea Discoveries*, 19:1–27.

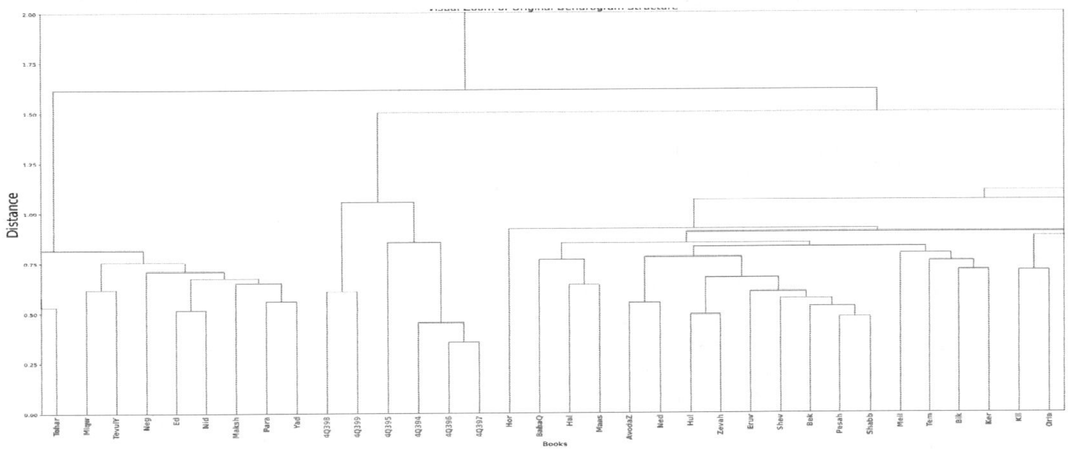


Figure 1: A small section of the dendrogram from the clustering analysis performed using tf–idf, illustrating the affinity between *Miqsat Ma'ase ha-Torah* (4Q394–399, labeled in red) and Mishnah tractates (green). The $x$-axis arranges the different texts; the level of the common ancestor on the $y$-axis indicates the degree of affinity.

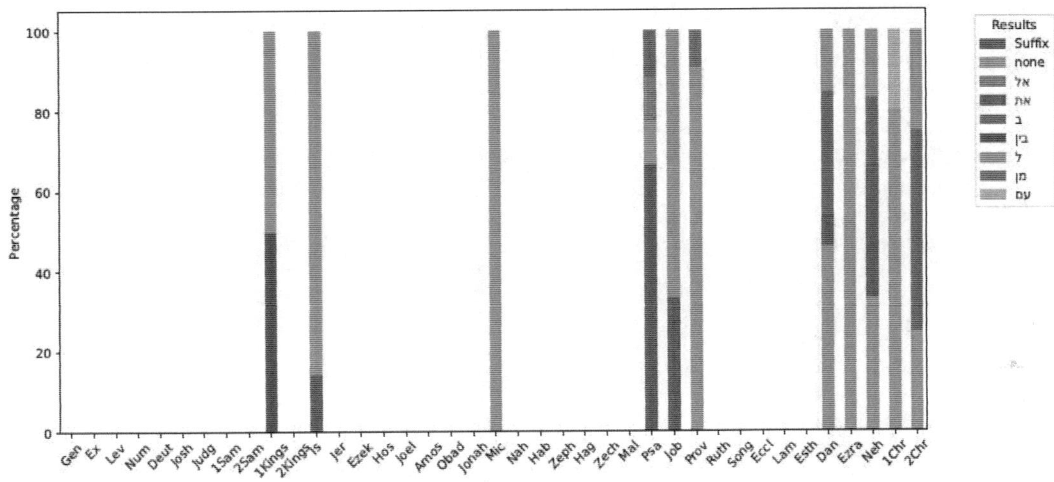


Figure 2: The normalized distribution of the complements of the verb *byn* (in *hiphil*).


Ze'ev Ben-Ḥayyim. 1958. Traditions in the Hebrew language, with special reference to the Dead Sea Scrolls. *Scripta Hierosolymitana*, 5:200–214.

Joshua Blau. 2000. A conservative view of the language of the Dead Sea Scrolls. In J. F. Elwolde and T. Muraoka, editors, *Diggers at the Well: International Symposium on the Hebrew of the Dead Sea Scrolls and Ben Sira*, pages 20–25. Brill, Leiden.

Yaakov N. Epstein. 1957. *Introductions to Tannaitic Literature: Mishnah, Tosefta, and Halakhic Midrashim.* Magnes, Jerusalem. [Hebrew].

Steven E. Fassberg. 2001. The movement from qal to pi"el in Hebrew and the disappearance of the qal internal passive. *Hebrew Studies*, 42:243–255.

Niv Fono, Harel Moshayof, Eldar Karol, Itai Assraf, and Mark Last. 2024. Embible: Reconstruction of ancient Hebrew and Aramaic texts using transformers. In *Findings of the Association for Computational Linguistics: EACL 2024*, pages 846–852, St. Julian's, Malta. Association for Computational Linguistics.

Yaakov HaCohen-Kerner, Hananya Beck, Elchai Yehudai, and Dror Mughaz. 2010. Stylistic feature sets as classifiers of documents according to their historical period and ethnic origin. *Applied Artificial Intelligence*, 24:847–862.

Moshe Koppel, Navot Akiva, Idan Dershowitz, and Nachum Dershowitz. 2011. Unsupervised decomposition of a document into authorial components. In *Proceedings of the 49th Annual Meeting of the Association for Computational Linguistics: Human Language Technologies*, pages 1356–1364, Portland, OR. Association for Computational Linguistics.

Eduard Y. Kutscher. 1974. *The Language and Linguis-*

*tic Background of the Isaiah Scroll (1QIsaa)*. Brill, Leiden.

Chaya Liebeskind and Shmuel Liebeskind. 2020. Deep learning for period classification of historical Hebrew texts. *Journal of Data Mining & Digital Humanities*, 2020:2.

Noam Mizrahi. 2020. The language of 4QMMT. In R. G. Kratz, editor, *Interpreting and Living God's Law at Qumran: Miqsat Ma'aśe Ha-Torah, Some of the Works of the Torah (4QMMT)*, volume 37 of *Sapere*, pages 67–83. Mohr Siebeck, Darmstadt, Germany.

Shlomo Morag. 1988. Qumran Hebrew: Some typological observations. *Vetus Testamentum*, 38:148–164.

Elisha Qimron. 1992. Observations on the history of early Hebrew (1000 B.C.E.–200 C.E.) in the light of the Dead Sea documents. In A. Rappaport and D. Dimant, editors, *The Dead Sea Scrolls: Forty Years of Research*, pages 349–361. Brill, Leiden.

Elisha Qimron. 2018. *A Grammar of the Hebrew of the Dead Sea Scrolls*. Yad Yizhak Ben-Zvi, Jerusalem.

Gary A. Rendsburg. 2015. The nature of Qumran Hebrew as revealed through Pesher Habakkuk. In E. Tigchelaar and P. Van Hecke, editors, *Hebrew of the Late Second Temple Period: Proceedings of a Sixth International Symposium on the Hebrew of the Dead Sea Scrolls and Ben Sira*, pages 132–159. Brill, Leiden.

Noah Santacruz. 2017. PSHAT – part of speech handling for Aramaic in the Talmud. Master's thesis, The Cooper Union for the Advancement of Science and Art, New York, NY.

Pierre Van Hecke. 2018. Computational stylometric approach to the Dead Sea Scrolls: Towards a new research agenda. *Dead Sea Discoveries*, 25:57–82.

Pierre Van Hecke and Johan de Joode. 2021. Promises and challenges in designing stylometric analyses for Classical Hebrew. In S. Fassberg, editor, *Hebrew texts and Language of the Second Temple Period*, pages 349–374. Brill, Leiden.

Hanoch Yalon. 1967. *Studies in the Dead Sea Scrolls: Philological Essays (1949–1952)*. Shrine of the Book/America-Israel Cultural Foundation/Kiryath Sepher, Jerusalem.

Gideon Yoffe, Axel Bühler, Nachum Dershowitz, Thomas Romer, Eli Piasetzky, Israel Finkelstein, and Barak Sober. 2023. A statistical exploration of text partition into constituents: The case of the Priestly source in the books of Genesis and Exodus. In *Findings of the Association for Computational Linguistics: ACL 2023*, pages 1918–1940, Toronto, Canada. Association for Computational Linguistics.

# Evaluating Evaluation Metrics for Ancient Chinese to English Machine Translation

**Eric Bennett**[1,2], **HyoJung Han**[1], **Xinchen Yang**[1], **Andrew Schonebaum**[2], **Marine Carpuat**[1]
[1]Dept. of Computer Science, University of Maryland, College Park
[2]Dept. of East Asian Languages and Cultures, University of Maryland, College Park
ebenne92@umd.edu, hjhan@cs.umd.edu, xcyang@cs.umd.edu,
schone@umd.edu, marine@cs.umd.edu

## Abstract

Evaluation metrics are an important driver of progress in Machine Translation (MT), but they have been primarily validated on high-resource modern languages. In this paper, we conduct an empirical evaluation of metrics commonly used to evaluate MT from Ancient Chinese into English. Using LLMs, we construct a contrastive test set, pairing high-quality MT and purposefully flawed MT of the same Pre-Qin texts. We then evaluate the ability of each metric to discriminate between accurate and flawed translations.

## 1 Introduction

Large Language Models (LLM) make it possible to translate between languages in a zero-shot fashion. This makes it possible for English readers to access previously untranslated texts in ancient languages such as Ancient Chinese (Jin et al., 2023) or Latin (Volk et al., 2024). However, how can we determine how good these translations are? For our language of interest, Ancient Chinese, machine translation (MT) research has relied on standard reference-based metrics to assess translation quality, but these metrics have not been validated specifically for this language.

Ancient Chinese [1] presents a unique challenge in translation to English due to the language's laconic and epigrammatic nature, as well as the relatively limited resources available compared to other languages. There are numerous English translations of the most famous Ancient Chinese texts, including *Tao Te Ching* (Campbell, 2022), *Analects* (Jin et al., 2023), and *Dream of the Red Chamber* (Kong, 2022), but a large majority of texts remain inaccessible to English readers (Fordham, 2021). When translating Ancient Chinese into English, many Chinese characters have multiple meanings depending on their usage in a sentence, requiring disambiguation in the translation process (Zou, 2016). The large amount of idioms and symbolic language also makes translation difficult, along with a lack of sentence boundaries or punctuation, explicit plurals, or conjunctions, making it a uniquely difficult translation problem. (Li et al., 2024). While the advent of LLMs has led to improvements in MT quality for Ancient Chinese to English translation, current models still lag behind human translators. (Jin et al., 2023).

The complexity of translating from Ancient Chinese to English is reflected in the complexity of evaluation. Translations may capture the meaning of a sentence very well, while having very different wording from another valid English translation. This might be problematic when evaluating with metrics such as BLEU (Papineni et al., 2002) and ChrF (Popović, 2015), which measure the word or character $n$-gram overlap between the MT output and a human-written reference translation. Neural metrics based on fine-tuning LLMs (Guerreiro et al., 2024; Rei et al., 2020; Juraska et al., 2023) have been found to correlate better with human ratings of translation quality for modern language pairs evaluated at the Conference on Machine Translation, including English-German and Japanese-Chinese (Freitag et al., 2024), but they have not been evaluated on translation from Ancient Chinese to English.

In this paper, we ask how well existing MT metrics are able to discriminate between 'good' and 'bad' English translations of Ancient Chinese texts. Building on meta-evaluation methods used for modern languages (Karpinska et al., 2022; Edunov et al., 2020), we address this question using a contrastive test set created by prompting an LLM for 'good' and 'bad' translations of the same Chinese inputs. After validating that the 'bad' translations are rated as worse than the 'good' translations by human

[1]The term Ancient Chinese encapsulates thousands of years of linguistic development (Chang et al., 2021). Our experiments use a Pre-Qin dataset from before the establishment of the Qin Dynasty in 221 BCE.



*Proceedings of the Second Ancient Language Processing Workshop associated with NAACL 2025*, pages 71–76

judges, we use this set to evaluate the ability of standard MT evaluation metrics to discriminate between 'good' and 'bad' translations.

## 2 Test Set Construction

### 2.1 Data Collection

The dataset used for this experiment is a collection of texts from the Pre-Qin period (prior to the establishment of the Qin Dynasty in 221 BCE) acquired from Dongbo Wang's team at Nanjing Agricultural University (Li et al., 2024). The format of the Pre-Qin dataset is a collection of Ancient Chinese source texts paired with single human English reference translations.

We cleaned the data for this experiment by removing pairs with the following properties:

1. The source text contains English.
2. The source or target length is greater than one standard deviation from the mean (>61 characters), to simplify human validation.
3. Being a duplicated source text.
4. The text contains portions of the Tao Te Ching, as the high interpretability of the document could interfere with this evaluation.[2]

In total, from the original dataset of 23,686 source-reference pairs 6,794 were deleted in the data cleaning process, resulting in a set of 16,892 source-reference pairs for analysis. The results show insights from both the entire cleaned Pre-Qin dataset, and a 500 entry human validated sample drawn randomly from the Pre-Qin dataset (Table 1).

### 2.2 Synthetic Translations Generation

We used OpenAI's gpt-4o model (Hurst et al., 2024) to generate a 'good' and a 'bad' translation for each of the source texts. We used the following prompts for the 'good' and 'bad' outputs, respectively:

- "Translate the Ancient Chinese text into English. Respond with the translation only."
- "Translate the Ancient Chinese text into English incorrectly, deliberately introducing disambiguation errors, accuracy errors, and tense errors in the text. Respond with the translation only."

The error types listed in the 'bad' translation prompt were chosen based on common errors identified in Chinese to English translations (Freitag et al., 2021), and tense error was drawn from the lack of tense in Ancient Chinese.

[2]Tao Te Ching is one of the most translated texts in the world, with over 2,052 recognized translations in 92 languages. (Tadd, 2022)

Here is a randomly selected example from the evaluation dataset resulting from this process:

**Source:**
鮮卑寇酒泉；種衆日多，緣邊莫不被毒。

**Reference translation:**
*The Xianbi raided Jiuquan. The numbers of their people increased day by day, and there was no region of the border country which did not suffer from them.*

**'Good' translation:**
*The Xianbei raided Jiuquan; their numbers grew daily, and the border regions suffered widespread harm.*

**'Bad' translation:**
*The Xianbei invaded Qiuquan; the people often multiply their seeds, along the edges they refuse to receive poison.*

### 2.3 Human Validation

We asked human judges to validate the LLM-generated translations. A sample of 500 entries was randomly selected from the cleaned dataset, and given to two human evaluators, one being an expert with extensive experience in Classical Chinese to English translation, and one being a native Chinese speaker with an intermediate level of experience with Classical Chinese. 100 entries were randomly selected from the sample as a cross-validation set to ensure coherence between the validators, and each validator was given 200 unique entries to complete the 500 entry sample. The composition of the sample is shown in Table 1.

| | # Entries | # Src Char | # Ref Char | # Ref Words |
|---|---|---|---|---|
| Sample | 500 | 9,641 | 70,902 | 12,916 |
| Pre-Qin | 16,892 | 332,355 | 2,463,235 | 448,386 |

Table 1: Dataset summary

Each validator was given access to the source and reference for an entry, and asked to compare the quality of two unlabelled machine translations A and B by selecting one of 3 options: "A is better than B", "B is better than A", or "too hard to tell". The order in which the 'good' and 'bad' translations were provided was randomly assigned. Annotators did not receive explicit guidelines defining what makes a translation better, and were simply asked to rate based on their own best judgment (Vilar et al., 2007).

The Cohen's Kappa score was 0.78 on the doubly annotated subset, indicating a high strength of agreement. The two validators both chose the 'good' translation as higher quality in 88/100 entries. In entries where both validators decided on one of the translations (neither validator chose the "too hard to tell" option), there was an 88/90 (97.78%) accuracy, and there were no cases where both validators agreed that the 'bad' translation was better. For the compiled validation dataset of 500 entries, when differences between the two evaluators were present, the more expert evaluator response was chosen. Overall, the human validators selected the 'good' translation as higher quality in 471/500 entries (94.2%).

## 3 Metric Selection

When deciding which metrics to test, the first consideration was the metrics used in past papers regarding Ancient Chinese MT. The results of an analysis of 5 recent papers related to Ancient Chinese machine translation is located in Table 2. The "Other" metrics include Ancient Chinese LLM evaluation metrics not related to machine translation in Zhang and Li (2023) as well as LMS (Levenshtein-distance-based Morphological Similarity) and ESS (Embedding Semantic Similarity) for evaluation as proposed in Wang et al. (2023). With this in mind, SacreBLEU (Post, 2018) and ChrF++ were selected for testing.

| Previous Works | BLEU | ChrF++ | Neural | Other |
|---|---|---|---|---|
| Jin et al. (2023) | Multi ref | × | × | ✓ |
| Wang et al. (2023) | Single ref | ✓ | × | × |
| Nehrdich et al. (2023) | Single ref | ✓ | × | × |
| Chang et al. (2021) | Single ref | × | × | × |
| Zhang and Li (2023) | × | × | × | ✓ |

Table 2: Evaluation metrics for Ancient Chinese MT in previous literature.

Furthermore, we decided to test the current state-of-the-art neural metrics for MT evaluation (Freitag et al., 2024) as well, despite them not being trained specifically on Ancient Chinese. From Google, metricx-24-hybrid-xl-v2p6 (Juraska et al., 2024) and metricx-23-xl-v2p0 (Juraska et al., 2023) were chosen. Both metrics are based on the mT5 encoder-decoder language model (Xue et al., 2021). MetricX-23 is finetuned using two stages of training, on direct assessment (DA) followed by MQM training data, as well as synthetic training data. MetricX-24 significantly expands the usage of synthetic data, and mixes DA and MQM data in the second training stage. MetricX-24 Hybrid allows for reference-based or reference-free evaluation in a unified model (in this experiment a reference is given) and had the highest correlation with human evaluation in WMT-24 with the exception of Meta-Metrics-MT (Anugraha et al., 2024).

Two COMET metrics were also chosen for analysis. XCOMET-XL (Guerreiro et al., 2024) is similar to MetricX-24 Hybrid in its ability to evaluate with or without a reference. It is based on the XLM-R XL encoder-decoder model (Conneau et al., 2020), and trained on DA data, followed by MQM data, and finally further high-quality MQM data. It also incorporates error-span detection in the training process, with the error-span detection function of the model sharing a common encoder with the sentence-level score function. COMET-WMT22 (Rei et al., 2022) is based on the XLM-R base model. It is trained primarily on DA data, followed by fine-tuning on z-normalized MQM scores.

For each of the selected metrics, we evaluated the two machine-translated hypotheses for each of the source entries. The provided single human reference translation was used as a single reference.

## 4 Results

To analyze the results of our evaluations using the chosen metrics, a difference score was calculated for each entry by subtracting the metric's score on the 'bad' translation from the score on the 'good' translation. A difference score of >0 represents a 'correct' prediction- that the generated 'good' translation was judged better than the 'bad' translation. A Wilcoxon signed-rank test was also performed for each metric to determine whether the ability of the metric to detect differences in scores is statistically significant. The performance of each metric, both on the entire 16,892 entry Pre-Qin dataset and the 500 entry human-validated sample, is described in Table 3, and Figure 1 compares distributions for each of the metrics in the human validated sample.

One notable performance from the evaluation is the following case, where all four neural metrics performed particularly poorly. The difference score for the evaluation fell within the bottom 10% for each metric, with the 'bad' translation being predicted as being higher quality than the 'good' translation by every metric except for MetricX-24 Hybrid despite the error of the direction 'left' being translated as 'right' in the 'bad' translation:

| metric | Human Validated Sample % predicted correctly | mean | median | stdev | Wilcoxon Test Statistic | P-Value | Pre-Qin Dataset % predicted correctly | mean | median | stdev | Wilcoxon Test Statistic | P-Value |
|---|---|---|---|---|---|---|---|---|---|---|---|---|
| SacreBLEU | 71.600 | 0.027 | 0.011 | **0.064** | 94892 | 9e-28 | 72.241 | 0.029 | 0.012 | **0.066** | 110817290 | **0.0** |
| CHRF++ | 79.200 | 0.062 | 0.053 | 0.082 | 110333 | 1e-49 | 80.440 | 0.064 | 0.054 | 0.084 | 126219585 | **0.0** |
| XCOMET-XL | 88.000 | 0.175 | 0.170 | 0.150 | 119650 | 6e-70 | 88.048 | 0.168 | 0.156 | 0.149 | 136247392 | **0.0** |
| COMET-WMT22 | 93.200 | 0.111 | 0.106 | 0.080 | 122582 | 4e-77 | 93.760 | 0.109 | 0.104 | 0.077 | 140339475 | **0.0** |
| MetricX-24-XL | **95.800** | **0.230** | **0.223** | 0.139 | **124586** | **3e-82** | **95.803** | **0.226** | **0.223** | 0.136 | **141675253** | **0.0** |
| MetricX-23-XL | 94.800 | 0.173 | 0.158 | 0.131 | 123238 | 9e-79 | 93.926 | 0.170 | 0.157 | 0.128 | 140164192 | **0.0** |

Table 3: Difference score metrics on validated sample and Pre-Qin dataset with Wilcoxon Test Statistic. For SacreBLEU and the two MetricX metrics scores were normalized between 0 and 1.

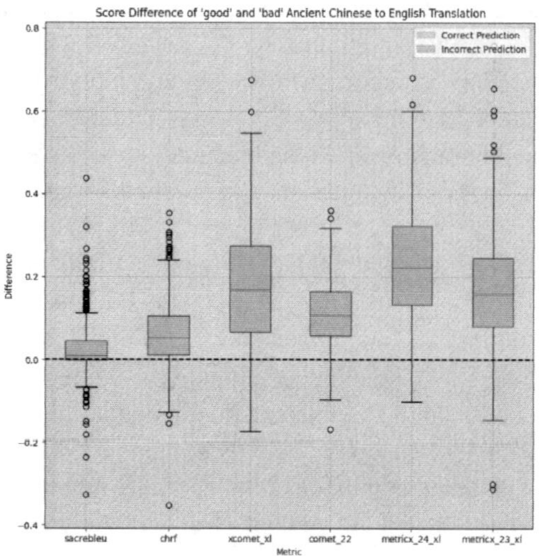


Figure 1: Box plot of difference scores. For SacreBLEU and the two MetricX metrics scores were normalized between 0 and 1.

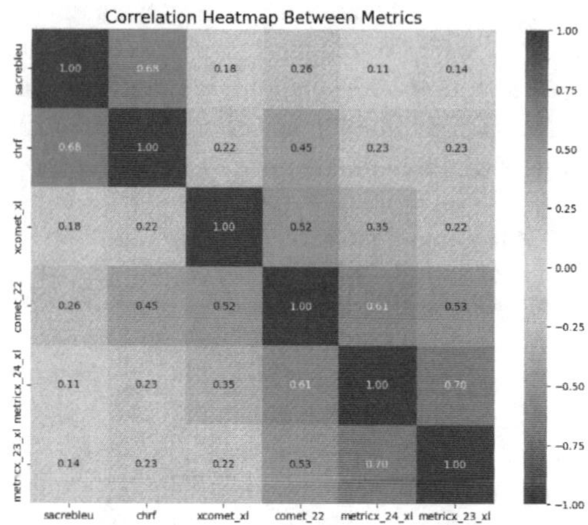


Figure 2: Correlation of difference scores between normalized metrics.

**Source:**
有杕之杜: 有杕之杜、生于道左。
**Reference translation:**
*You Di Zhi Du: There is a solitary russet pear tree,Growing on the left of the way.*
**'Good' translation:**
*A solitary tree in the woods: A solitary tree in the woods, growing by the roadside.*
**'Bad' translation:**
*There is a single pine tree: There is a single pine tree, growing on the right of the road.*

Although all of the metrics were shown to have statistically significant success in the task of determining between the 'good' and 'bad' translations, some metrics performed with greater accuracy or more consistently. Commonly used metrics like BLEU and ChrF++ notably showed a lower standard deviation and therefore more consistency compared to newer metrics, with the exception of COMET-WMT22. While XCOMET-XL has a higher mean than COMET-WMT22, its higher variability results in a worse performance than the older model at predicting the 'good' translation. Furthermore, Figure 2 describes the correlation between metrics, showing that neural metrics tend to agree with each other more than with surface metrics, but still hold disagreements, particularly across families of models.

Overall, these results show that neural metrics are better able to discern 'good' and 'bad' translations than surface metrics, despite not being trained with translation quality ratings of MT from Ancient Chinese to English. Supervision from other MT tasks into English helps identify the problematic outputs in our test set. These results suggest future research on MT from Ancient Chinese would benefit from including neural metrics such as XCOMET-XL or MetricX-24 Hybrid to guide system development. At the same time, it would be useful to design metrics that target error categories known to be problematic for Ancient Chinese MT: the method we used here to generate contrastive synthetic translations could be extended to evaluate each metric's ability to detect specific error categories, and to provide training data for more targeted metrics.

## Acknowledgments

We sincerely thank Professor Dongbo Wang and his team at Nanjing Agricultural University for providing access to the 中古代典籍跨言料 (Chinese Ancient Texts Cross-Language Corpus), which served as the source of Ancient Chinese to English translation data for this paper.

## References

David Anugraha, Garry Kuwanto, Lucky Susanto, Derry Tanti Wijaya, and Genta Winata. 2024. MetaMetrics-MT: Tuning meta-metrics for machine translation via human preference calibration. In *Proceedings of the Ninth Conference on Machine Translation*, pages 459–469, Miami, Florida, USA. Association for Computational Linguistics.

Larry N. Campbell. 2022. *The Parallel Tao Te Ching: A Comparison of English Translations*, volume 1. Aftermath Enterprises LLC, Midland, TX.

Ernie Chang, Yow-Ting Shiue, Hui-Syuan Yeh, and Vera Demberg. 2021. Time-aware Ancient Chinese text translation and inference. In *Proceedings of the 2nd International Workshop on Computational Approaches to Historical Language Change 2021*, pages 1–6, Online. Association for Computational Linguistics.

Alexis Conneau, Kartikay Khandelwal, Naman Goyal, Vishrav Chaudhary, Guillaume Wenzek, Francisco Guzmán, Edouard Grave, Myle Ott, Luke Zettlemoyer, and Veselin Stoyanov. 2020. Unsupervised cross-lingual representation learning at scale. In *Proceedings of the 58th Annual Meeting of the Association for Computational Linguistics*, pages 8440–8451, Online. Association for Computational Linguistics.

Sergey Edunov, Myle Ott, Marc'Aurelio Ranzato, and Michael Auli. 2020. On the evaluation of machine translation systems trained with back-translation. In *Proceedings of the 58th Annual Meeting of the Association for Computational Linguistics*, pages 2836–2846, Online. Association for Computational Linguistics.

Carl Gene Fordham. 2021. English translations of chinese texts from the pre-qin through han period (2010–2020): Publishing trends and quality assurance.

Markus Freitag, George Foster, David Grangier, Viresh Ratnakar, Qijun Tan, and Wolfgang Macherey. 2021. Experts, errors, and context: A large-scale study of human evaluation for machine translation. *Transactions of the Association for Computational Linguistics*, 9:1460–1474.

Markus Freitag, Nitika Mathur, Daniel Deutsch, Chi-Kiu Lo, Eleftherios Avramidis, Ricardo Rei, Brian Thompson, Frederic Blain, Tom Kocmi, Jiayi Wang, David Ifeoluwa Adelani, Marianna Buchicchio, Chrysoula Zerva, and Alon Lavie. 2024. Are LLMs breaking MT metrics? results of the WMT24 metrics shared task. In *Proceedings of the Ninth Conference on Machine Translation*, pages 47–81, Miami, Florida, USA. Association for Computational Linguistics.

Nuno M. Guerreiro, Ricardo Rei, Daan van Stigt, Luisa Coheur, Pierre Colombo, and André F. T. Martins. 2024. xcomet: Transparent machine translation evaluation through fine-grained error detection. *Transactions of the Association for Computational Linguistics*, 12:979–995.

OpenAI: Aaron Hurst, Adam Lerer, Adam P. Goucher, Adam Perelman, Aditya Ramesh, Aidan Clark, AJ Ostrow, Akila Welihinda, Alan Hayes, and et al. 2024. Gpt-4o system card. *arXiv preprint*.

Kai Jin, Dan Zhao, and Wuying Liu. 2023. Morphological and semantic evaluation of Ancient Chinese machine translation. In *Proceedings of the Ancient Language Processing Workshop*, pages 96–102, Varna, Bulgaria. INCOMA Ltd., Shoumen, Bulgaria.

Juraj Juraska, Daniel Deutsch, Mara Finkelstein, and Markus Freitag. 2024. MetricX-24: The Google submission to the WMT 2024 metrics shared task. In *Proceedings of the Ninth Conference on Machine Translation*, pages 492–504, Miami, Florida, USA. Association for Computational Linguistics.

Juraj Juraska, Mara Finkelstein, Daniel Deutsch, Aditya Siddhant, Mehdi Mirzazadeh, and Markus Freitag. 2023. MetricX-23: The Google submission to the WMT 2023 metrics shared task. In *Proceedings of the Eighth Conference on Machine Translation*, pages 756–767, Singapore. Association for Computational Linguistics.

Marzena Karpinska, Nishant Raj, Katherine Thai, Yixiao Song, Ankita Gupta, and Mohit Iyyer. 2022. DEMETR: Diagnosing evaluation metrics for translation. In *Proceedings of the 2022 Conference on Empirical Methods in Natural Language Processing*, pages 9540–9561, Abu Dhabi, United Arab Emirates. Association for Computational Linguistics.

L. Kong. 2022. Bonsall: The first full translation of the dream of the red chamber. *Advances in Literary Study*, 10(3):291–297.

Bin Li, Bolin Chang, Zhixing Xu, Minxuan Feng, Chao Xu, Weiguang Qu, Si Shen, and Dongbo Wang. 2024. Overview of EvaHan2024: The first international evaluation on Ancient Chinese sentence segmentation and punctuation. In *Proceedings of the Third Workshop on Language Technologies for Historical and Ancient Languages (LT4HALA) @ LREC-COLING-2024*, pages 229–236, Torino, Italia. ELRA and ICCL.

Sebastian Nehrdich, Marcus Bingenheimer, Justin Brody, and Kurt Keutzer. 2023. MITRA-zh: An efficient, open machine translation solution for buddhist Chinese. In *Proceedings of the Joint 3rd International Conference on Natural Language Processing for Digital Humanities and 8th International Workshop on Computational Linguistics for Uralic Languages*, pages 266–277, Tokyo, Japan. Association for Computational Linguistics.

Kishore Papineni, Salim Roukos, Todd Ward, and Wei-Jing Zhu. 2002. Bleu: a method for automatic evaluation of machine translation. In *Proceedings of the 40th Annual Meeting of the Association for Computational Linguistics*, pages 311–318, Philadelphia, Pennsylvania, USA. Association for Computational Linguistics.

Maja Popović. 2015. chrF: character n-gram F-score for automatic MT evaluation. In *Proceedings of the Tenth Workshop on Statistical Machine Translation*, pages 392–395, Lisbon, Portugal. Association for Computational Linguistics.

Matt Post. 2018. A call for clarity in reporting BLEU scores. In *Proceedings of the Third Conference on Machine Translation: Research Papers*, pages 186–191, Brussels, Belgium. Association for Computational Linguistics.

Ricardo Rei, José G. C. de Souza, Duarte Alves, Chrysoula Zerva, Ana C Farinha, Taisiya Glushkova, Alon Lavie, Luisa Coheur, and André F. T. Martins. 2022. COMET-22: Unbabel-IST 2022 submission for the metrics shared task. In *Proceedings of the Seventh Conference on Machine Translation (WMT)*, pages 578–585, Abu Dhabi, United Arab Emirates (Hybrid). Association for Computational Linguistics.

Ricardo Rei, Craig Stewart, Ana C Farinha, and Alon Lavie. 2020. COMET: A neural framework for MT evaluation. In *Proceedings of the 2020 Conference on Empirical Methods in Natural Language Processing (EMNLP)*, pages 2685–2702, Online. Association for Computational Linguistics.

Misha Tadd. 2022. *"Laozi" Yi Ben Zong Mu: Quan Qiu Lao Xue Yao Lan = the Complete Bibliography of Laozi Translations: A Global Laozegetics Reference*. Nan kai da xue chu ban she, Tianjin.

David Vilar, Gregor Leusch, Hermann Ney, and Rafael E. Banchs. 2007. Human evaluation of machine translation through binary system comparisons. In *Proceedings of the Second Workshop on Statistical Machine Translation*, pages 96–103, Prague, Czech Republic. Association for Computational Linguistics.

Martin Volk, Dominic Philipp Fischer, Lukas Fischer, Patricia Scheurer, and Phillip Benjamin Ströbel. 2024. LLM-based machine translation and summarization for Latin. In *Proceedings of the Third Workshop on Language Technologies for Historical and Ancient Languages (LT4HALA) @ LREC-COLING-2024*, pages 122–128, Torino, Italia. ELRA and ICCL.

Dongbo Wang, Litao Lin, Zhixiao Zhao, Wenhao Ye, Kai Meng, Wenlong Sun, Lianzhen Zhao, Xue Zhao, Si Shen, Wei Zhang, and Bin Li. 2023. EvaHan2023: Overview of the first international Ancient Chinese translation bakeoff. In *Proceedings of ALT2023: Ancient Language Translation Workshop*, pages 1–14, Macau SAR, China. Asia-Pacific Association for Machine Translation.

Linting Xue, Noah Constant, Adam Roberts, Mihir Kale, Rami Al-Rfou, Aditya Siddhant, Aditya Barua, and Colin Raffel. 2021. mT5: A massively multilingual pre-trained text-to-text transformer. In *Proceedings of the 2021 Conference of the North American Chapter of the Association for Computational Linguistics: Human Language Technologies*, pages 483–498, Online. Association for Computational Linguistics.

Yixuan Zhang and Haonan Li. 2023. Can large language model comprehend Ancient Chinese? a preliminary test on ACLUE. In *Proceedings of the Ancient Language Processing Workshop*, pages 80–87, Varna, Bulgaria. INCOMA Ltd., Shoumen, Bulgaria.

Siyu Zou. 2016. On ancient chinese translation. In *Proceedings of the 2016 6th International Conference on Management, Education, Information and Control (MEICI 2016)*, pages 675–678. Atlantis Press.

# [Neural Models for Lemmatization and POS-Tagging of Earlier and Late Egyptian (Supporting Hieroglyphic Input) and Demotic

**Aleksi Sahala**
University of Helsinki
Helsinki, Finland
aleksi.sahala@helsinki.fi

**Eliese-Sophia Lincke**
Freie Universität Berlin & Berlin-Brandenburg
Academy of Sciences and Humanities
Berlin, Germany
e.lincke@fu-berlin.de

**Abstract**

We present updated models for *BabyLemmatizer* for lemmatizing and POS-tagging Demotic, Late Egyptian and Earlier Egyptian with a support for using hieroglyphs as an input. In this paper, we also use data that has not been cleaned from breakages. We achieve consistent UPOS tagging accuracy of 94% or higher and an XPOS tagging accuracy of 93% and higher for all languages. For lemmatization, which is challenging in all of our test languages due to extensive ambiguity, we demonstrate accuracies from 77% up to 92% depending on the language and the input script.

## 1 Introduction

Since several ancient languages feature complex morphology and a high degree of spelling variation, lemmatization is an essential step for making large text collections of these languages searchable and usable for further computational analysis.

In this paper we present models for lemmatizing and part-of-speech tagging Earlier and Late Egyptian, as well as Demotic, which complements our earlier research on the topic by using larger datasets with *lacunae* (breakages), as well as text represented in Unicode hieroglyphs. Our models are available on https://huggingface.co/asahala.

## 2 Egyptian-Coptic

### 2.1 Diachronic Overview

Egyptian-Coptic was the indigenous language of the lower Nile valley, attested in written form from around 3000 BCE to 1400 CE. It belongs to the Afroasiatic language family and is generally divided into two major phases: Earlier Egyptian, which includes Old and Middle Egyptian, and Later Egyptian, comprising Late Egyptian, Demotic, and Coptic. The transition from Earlier to Later Egyptian is marked by significant linguistic changes in morphology and syntax. While Earlier Egyptian retained a more synthetic structure with root-and-pattern morphology, Later Egyptian initially exhibits increased analytic tendencies, particularly in its verbal system. However, this trend is later followed by a phase of re-synthetization. Another major difference between Earlier and Later Egyptian is the shift from marking main clauses to marking subordinate clauses (Kammerzell, 1998; Winand, 2018). Basic information about the Earlier Egyptian and Demotic language stages has been given elsewhere (Sahala and Lincke, 2024) and will not be repeated here. However, this study also addresses the chronolect Late Egyptian, which was not included in previous work and will briefly be introduced in the following section.

The language phases are represented in distinct corpora and scripts, necessitating different approaches to transcription, lemmatization, and other text processing techniques.

### 2.2 Late Egyptian

The chronolect referred to as 'Late Egyptian' (or French 'Néo-Egyptien') surfaces in the written record in the 14th century BCE although some features can be observed in considerably earlier texts (Kroeber, 1970). Late Egyptian is characterized by an analytical tendency as compared to Earlier Egyptian (fusional) and the later Demotic and Coptic (agglutinative) language stages (McLaughlin, 2022; Stauder, 2020), e.g. by employing periphrastic verb phrases. The word order pattern (AUX-)S-V-O becomes more prominent although it is only fully fledged in Coptic. With respect to the attested sentence types it can be stated that sentences with an adjectival predicate are receding and are being replaced by alternative constructions following the adverbial pattern (Winand, 2018).

As with pre-Demotic Egyptian in general, Late Egyptian texts are recorded in two native Egyptian scripts: monumental hieroglyphs, which were used for inscriptions on stone and, in cursive form,



*Proceedings of the Second Ancient Language Processing Workshop associated with NAACL 2025*, pages 77–82
May 4, 2025. 

for certain texts on papyrus (e.g., the Book of the Dead) or wood; and hieratic, a cursive script written mostly on papyrus and ostraca (pottery and limestone sherds).

## 3 Datasets

The datasets for all language stages discussed here were exported and made available to us by Daniel A. Werning from the database that feeds the Thesaurus Linguae Aegyptiae (TLA), corpus v18 (Richter et al., 2023).[1] The export format is JSONL with each sentence (as defined by the TLA's data model and editors) stored as a separate JSON object and the tokens separated by blanks (Fig. 1). Each sentence is represented both in Unicode hieroglyphs (without quadrat placement) and in Egyptological transcription (i.e., Leiden Unified Transliteration), provided that hieroglyphs have been encoded for the respective text. It is annotated with TLA lemma IDs and POS-tagged using the UPOS tag set[2] and a simplified version of the project-specific subclass tag set of the TLA as the XPOS tag set (Werning, 2024). This XPOS tag set is fine-grained with respect to proper nouns, using different tags for divine names, royal names, personal names, animal personal names, names of institutions, names of artifacts, and place names. It also distinguishes epithets and titles from other types of nouns.


```
{"hieroglyphs": "𓋴𓆓𓂋 <g>G175</g> 𓄂𓄹 𓂝𓂋𓏤 𓌃𓂋𓏭𓀁",
"transliteration": "sḏr r-ḥꜣ.t mdwi̯",
"lemmatization": "150740|sḏr 500053|r-ḥꜣ.t/2 78140|mdwi̯",
"UPOS": "VERB ADP VERB",
"XPOS": "verb preposition verb"}
```


Figure 1: JSON object from the Late Egyptian dataset, *The Teaching of Amenemope* 5,13, pBM EA 10474, TLA ID: IBUBd2RAxJagbkako4lYd0WxDc8.

The lemmatization of the *Thesaurus Linguae Aegyptiae* is fine-grained and tailored to Egyptologists' needs, allowing them to distinguish and search for the individual meanings and functions of a lemma. Consequently, a single lemma may be divided into multiple sub-lemmata, each assigned its own TLA lemma ID, as illustrated in Table 1 for the preposition *m*, the most frequent word in Egyptian. Another reason why lemma IDs are necessary for Egyptian is the high number of homonyms (or more precisely, homographs) in the Egyptological transcription ("transliteration"), which we have described in more detail in Sahala and Lincke (2024).

| | Lemma ID | Meaning / Function |
|---|---|---|
| 1. | 64360 | [preposition] |
| 2. | 400007 | in; to; on; from (spatial) |
| 3. | 64365 | in; on (temporal) |
| 4. | 64362 | in (condition, state) |
| 5. | 400082 | (consisting) of (partitive) |
| 6. | 64364 | by means of (instrumental) |
| 7. | 400080 | together with (comitative) |
| 8. | 500292 | like; as (predication) |
| 9. | 854625 | [connector of the direct object] |
| 10. | 64369 | [with infinitive] |
| 11. | 64370 | when; if [as conjunction] |

Table 1: Sub-lemmata of the preposition *m* in the *Thesaurus Linguae Aegyptiae* lemma list.

The Earlier Egyptian dataset consists of all sentences that predate the Egyptian New Kingdom (c. 1550–1070 BC). The Demotic dataset comprises the entire Demotic text corpus in the TLA. Defining a Late Egyptian dataset is more challenging, as texts in the TLA are not consistently tagged by language phase. Therefore, our Late Egyptian dataset includes only those texts explicitly labeled as Late Egyptian in the TLA metadata.[3]

Other than the material used in Sahala and Lincke (2024), our datasets are not filtered for "premium" sentences that are "fully intact" and "unambiguously readable" (TLA-Dem 2024, TLA-Egy 2024)[4]. The datasets include damaged text, i.e. broken or destroyed individual hieroglyphs or entire word forms that could not be reconstructed by the editors. The respective sizes of the datasets can be found in Table 2.

| Language stage | Sentences | Tokens |
|---|---|---|
| Earlier Egyptian | 43,447 | ~286,000 |
| Late Egyptian | 9,005 | ~86,100 |
| Demotic | 25,822 | ~292,450 |

Table 2: Sentence and token counts for the Earlier Egyptian, Late Egyptian, and Demotic datasets.

Our aim is to train models that can handle two different types of input: (1) Unicode-encoded hiero-

[1]For detailed information on the datasets, see Section *Sources*.

[2]https://universaldependencies.org/u/pos/

[3]TLA ID: J3SNMB4AF5ERPDGE4VPMBZSYRE, Thot Thesauri & Ontology ID: thot-12.

[4]https://huggingface.co/datasets/thesaurus-linguae-aegyptiae

glyphs (e.g. as the output of a successful future hieroglyphic OCR) and (2) transcription, which remains the default digital representation of Egyptian, since many projects still render hieroglyphs only as images. Depending on the availability in the database, not all sentences of Earlier and Late Egyptian in our datasets contain hieroglyphic spellings, some texts were only encoded by means of transcription. Demotic is represented in transcription only, since there is no encoding for the Demotic script itself.

Challenges lie in the complexity of the input data. Currently, not all hieroglyphs are available in Unicode. In such cases, they are encoded using the alphanumerical system known as *Gardiner numbers* enclosed in the tag <g> (Fig. 1, first line, in purple). We test how well our lemmatizer can predict the lemma string plus a numerical index (Fig. 1, third line, in red) replacing the arbitrary TLA lemma IDs (in blue), instead of simply representing a lemma as a string (see Section 6). Effectively, this means training the lemmatizer to disambiguate homonyms caused by the simplified rendering of Egyptian in transcription and by the subdivision of lemmata.

## 4 Previous Work

In their paper on Neural Machine Translation for Egyptian, using the TLA data dump from 2018, De Cao et al. (2024) incorporated the prediction of lemma IDs (lemmatization) and POS tags into the training of some of their models. Their results look promising but cannot be directly compared to ours, as they use SacreBLEU and RougeL as their evaluation metrics, which cannot be converted into accuracy rates, our primary evaluation metric. Díaz Hernández and Carlo Passarotti (2024) manually annotated a dataset of 14,650 tokens from the Old Egyptian Pyramid Texts for the first Egyptian treebank, including lemmatization and POS-tagging. They trained a UDPipe model and evaluated their results with F1 scores of 89.38 (lemma), 90.30 (UPOS), and 76.01 (XPOS). However, their lemmatization approach was string-based and did not account for homonymy by using lemma IDs, making the task significantly simpler than ours, which requires the disambiguation between homonyms and/or multiple sub-lemmata.

Other than that and apart from our own effort (Sahala and Lincke, 2024), models have been created only to lemmatize and POS-tag Coptic. (Zeldes and Schroeder, 2016, 2015; Smith and Hulden, 2016; Dereza et al., 2024).

## 5 BabyLemmatizer

BabyLemmatizer[5] is a lemmatization and POS-tagging pipeline originally designed for the cuneiform languages of Mesopotamia, but is also capable of handling other transliteration and writing systems (Sahala and Lindén, 2023).

The system is based on the Open Neural Machine Translation Toolkit (Klein et al., 2017) and handles POS-tagging and lemmatization as machine translation tasks by mapping character or symbol sequences to each other. It uses a deep attentional encoder-decoder network with a two-layer BiLSTM encoder that reads the input as a character sequence. The output sequence is produced by a two-layer unidirectional LSTM decoder with input feeding attention. We use the default batch size of 64 and start the learning rate decay halfway through the training process.

The neural lemmatizer is followed by a dictionary-based post-corrector to verify the in-vocabulary lemmatizations for better accuracy. The post-corrector also labels lemmatizations with confidence scores that enable easier location of potentially incorrect lemmata.

## 6 Preprocessing and Training

We converted the datasets from the original JSONL format into CoNLL-U to make it usable by BabyLemmatizer. Our CoNLL-U lacks dependency labels and morphology, and uses a simplified lemma notation by representing the disambiguation identifiers in a shorter form (*r-ḥꜣ.t/2* instead of *500053|r-ḥꜣ.t*, see Fig. 1), since our previous experiments proved that the long identifiers are detrimental for OOV word lemmatization.

We use BabyLemmatizer's alphabetic tokenizer for all our models that splits the input strings into character sequences represented as Unicode hieroglyphs or transcribed Latin characters. The POS-tagger input sequence is encoded as a 5-gram of concatenated word forms. The lemmatizer is run after the POS-tagging, and its input sequences are encoded as concatenations of four strings, where the first one represents the input word form (in transliteration or hieroglyphs) and the three following its

[5]The tool is available at https://github.com/asahala/BabyLemmatizer

predicted XPOS tag, as well as the predicted XPOS tags of the preceding and the following words.

## 7 Evaluation

We generate a 80/10/10 train/dev/test split of our datasets and evaluate our models using 10-fold cross-validation. We estimate the performance of our models by using accuracy as our evaluation metric, since we only predict one lemma for each input word (instead of, for example, the most likely three candidates). Our predicted labels are LEMMA, XPOS and UPOS. Due to high lemmatization ambiguity, we do not predict the lemma alone, but also its index, which separates it from other homonymous lemmata. This makes the task significantly more challenging in comparison to typical lemmatization tasks, where only the dictionary forms are predicted. Our final results are summarized in Table 3 with confidence intervals of the cross-validation shown in parentheses.

Our results for Demotic and transcribed Earlier Egyptian show a moderate improvement in comparison to our previous paper albeit the used data contain breakages; for instance, the lemmatization for Earlier Egyptian in transcription improves by 2.04%.

It seems that the hieroglyphic input produces less accurate results than using the transcription. This is due to the increased vocabulary size, and hence a larger number of OOV-vocabulary words, which result from spelling variation that is normalized in transcription (for an example see Sahala and Lincke, 2024, p. 89, Fig. 1).

### 7.1 Data Augmentation and Model Corrector Experiments

We attempted to improve Egyptian lemmatization results by augmenting Late Egyptian training data with Earlier Egyptian data and vice versa, but this did not yield consistently better results for transcription or hieroglyphs.

In addition, we experimented with training a secondary model for post-correcting the lemma identifiers. This process involved first predicting the POS tags and simplified lemmata without identifiers, which can be predicted with an accuracy of ca. 94% for transcribed Earlier Egyptian. The post-corrector attempted to map varying length sequences of simplified lemmata and their POS-tags to the lemmata with identifiers, but we were unable to improve the results.

### 7.2 Error Analysis

In the test set for Earlier Egyptian, 2,960 tokens were erroneously lemmatized from the hieroglyphic input. Of these, 323 (10.91%) correspond to tokens with the hieroglyphic form 𓅓 (*m*), and 313 of these 323 specifically are instances of the preposition *m* 'in', which is divided into multiple sub-lemmata in our corpus (see Table 1). If all these sub-lemmata were assigned to a single lemma—e.g. the hypernym for the preposition *m* (TLA lemma ID 64360, see no. 1 in Table 1)—the total error count could be reduced by 313 (10.57%) solely by addressing this one hieroglyphic input form. The same is true for other frequently used prepositions, such as 𓈖 (*n*) 'for, to' and 𓂋 (*r*) 'to, at'.

In an additional 192 errors (7.14%) in Earlier Egyptian lemmatization with hieroglyphic input, the tokens contain hieroglyphic characters not represented as Unicode points, but rather using the <g> tag and Gardiner numbers (see Fig. 1). This indicates that BabyLemmatizer struggles to effectively learn these non-Unicode representations from the given input data.

With an effective token count of 13.8k in the test set (out of a total size of 28.6k), the 505 instances of two mentioned error types alone account for 3.66%. This means that the accuracy—specifically for lemmatization based on hieroglyphic input—could be significantly improved by simplifying the data, e.g. by avoiding lemmatization at the sub-lemma level and by filtering out tokens with non-Unicode-compliant hieroglyphs.

## 8 Conclusions and Future Work

We presented lemmatization and POS-tagging models for Earlier Egyptian, Late Egyptian, and Demotic with varying results. Whereas the accuracy for Demotic is fairly good (tagger 97%, lemmatizer 92%), the Earlier and Late Egyptian yielded adequate results only for POS tagging (93-96%).

Disambiguating the highly ambiguous Egyptian lemmata is beyond the capabilities of BabyLemmatizer's current model architecture. Therefore, we plan to tackle this issue in the future using more context-aware approaches, including transformers and LLMs, which could perhaps be fine-tuned for disambiguation tasks. Moreover, additional annotation layers, such as dependency parsing, could possibly improve the quality of the lemmatization, as syntactic and morphological labels have previously been used successfully in lemma disambiguation

Whole dataset

| | Demotic | EarlierE T | EarlierE H | LateE T | LateE H |
|---|---|---|---|---|---|
| **XPOS** | 97.13 (±0.09) | 96.20 (±0.08) | 92.97 (±0.16) | 93.98 (±0.08) | 93.13 (±0.26) |
| **UPOS** | 97.45 (±0.09) | 96.62 (±0.15) | 93.64 (±0.04) | 94.48 (±0.16) | 93.52 (±0.23) |
| **LEMMA** | 92.15 (±0.18) | 87.56 (±0.19) | 80.15 (±0.20) | 79.98 (±0.26) | 76.59 (±0.48) |
| **OOV-rate** | 2.51 | 2.62 | 13.54 | 5.54 | 16.75 |

OOV word forms only

| | Demotic | EarlierE T | EarlierE H | LateE T | LateE H |
|---|---|---|---|---|---|
| **XPOS** | 82.12 (±1.45) | 78.00 (±1.04) | 81.39 (±0.69) | 76.09 (±2.02) | 82.19 (±1.67) |
| **UPOS** | 85.70 (±1.94) | 82.45 (±1.28) | 83.89 (±0.48) | 78.28 (±1.20) | 83.35 (±1.43) |
| **LEMMA** | 50.96 (±1.25) | 53.85 (±1.18) | 51.16 (±0.91) | 43.63 (±1.80) | 50.87 (±1.92) |

Table 3: Evaluation results. OOV-rate shows the average percentage of OOV word forms in the test set with respect to training corpus. H = hieroglyphic input and T = transcription.

(Kanerva et al., 2021). We also plan to organize a shared task for Egyptian lemmatization, since the issues are rather unique and are likely to be more easily solved with input from a larger NLP community.

## Acknowledgments

We sincerely thank Daniel A. Werning (Berlin-Brandenburg Academy of Sciences and Humanities) for creating tailor-made exports for all language stages from the TLA, for engaging in discussions on the lemma lists, data model and annotations, and for providing valuable feedback on our work. We also thank the Academy of Finland for funding the project Origins of Emesal (PI Krister Lindén) and the Centre of Excellence in Ancient Near Eastern Empires (PI Saana Svärd).

## Sources

All datasets are taken from **Thesaurus Linguae Aegyptiae, corpus v18, 2023**, ed. by Tonio Sebastian Richter & Daniel A. Werning on behalf of the Berlin-Brandenburgische Akademie der Wissenschaften and Hans-Werner Fischer-Elfert & Peter Dils on behalf of the Sächsische Akademie der Wissenschaften zu Leipzig:

- **TLA-Dem 2025**: Thesaurus Linguae Aegyptiae, Demotic sentences, corpus v18, with destroyed tokens, v1.0, 1/28/2025. Rights reserved.
- **TLA-Egy-L 2025**: Thesaurus Linguae Aegyptiae, Late Egyptian sentences, corpus v18, with destroyed tokens, v1.0, 1/28/2025. Rights reserved.
- **TLA-Egy-E 2025**: Thesaurus Linguae Aegyptiae, Earlier Egyptian sentences, corpus v18, with destroyed tokens, v1.0, 1/28/2025. Rights reserved.

Please refer to the *TLA authors* website for a detailed account of annotators per text/corpus (Werning, 2025).

## References

Mattia De Cao, Nicola De Cao, Angelo Colonna, and Alessandro Lenci. 2024. Deep learning meets egyptology: a hieroglyphic transformer for translating Ancient Egyptian. In *Proceedings of the 1st Workshop on Machine Learning for Ancient Languages (ML4AL 2024)*, pages 71–86, Bangkok, Thailand. Association for Computational Linguistics.

Oksana Dereza, Adrian Doyle, Priya Rani, Atul Kr. Ojha, Pádraic Moran, and John McCrae. 2024. Findings of the SIGTYP 2024 shared task on word embedding evaluation for ancient and historical languages. In *Proceedings of the 6th Workshop on Research in Computational Linguistic Typology and Multilingual NLP*, pages 160–172, St. Julian's, Malta. Association for Computational Linguistics.

Roberto Antonio Díaz Hernández and Marco Carlo Passarotti. 2024. Developing the Egyptian-UJaen treebank. In *Proceedings of the 22nd Workshop on Treebanks and Linguistic Theories (TLT 2024)*, pages 1–10, Hamburg, Germany. Association for Computational Linguistics.

Frank Kammerzell. 1998. *Sprachkontakte und Sprachwandel im Alten Ägypten.* Habilitation thesis, University of Göttingen, Göttingen.

Jenna Kanerva, Filip Ginter, and Tapio Salakoski. 2021. Universal lemmatizer: A sequence-to-sequence model for lemmatizing universal dependencies treebanks. *Natural Language Engineering*, 27(5):545–574.

Guillaume Klein, Yoon Kim, Yuntian Deng, Jean Senellart, and Alexander M. Rush. 2017. OpenNMT: Open-source toolkit for neural machine translation. In *Proceedings of ACL 2017, System Demonstrations*, pages 67–72, Vancouver, Canada. Association for Computational Linguistics.

Burkhart Kroeber. 1970. *Die Neuägyptizismen vor der Amarnazeit. Studien zur Entwicklung der ägyptischen Sprache vom Mittleren zum Neuen Reich.* Dissertation, Universität Tübingen, aku Fotodruck, Bamberg.

Rachael Hannah McLaughlin. 2022. *The Linguistic Cycle in Ancient Egyptian Verbal Constructions.* Phd thesis, University of Liverpool.

Tonio Sebastian Richter, Daniel A. Werning, Hans-Werner Fischer-Elfert, and Peter Dils, editors. 2023. *Thesaurus Linguae Aegyptiae, Corpus issue 18.* Berlin-Brandenburgische Akademie der Wissenschaften and Sächsische Akademie der Wissenschaften zu Leipzig. Web-App-Version 2.1.3, Accessed: 5/16/2024.

A. J. Aleksi Sahala and Krister Lindén. 2023. A neural pipeline for lemmatizing and POS-tagging cuneiform languages. In *Proceedings of the Ancient Language Processing Workshop at the 14th International Conference on Recent Advances in Natural Language Processing RANLP 2023*, pages 203–212.

Aleksi Sahala and Eliese-Sophia Lincke. 2024. Neural lemmatization and POS-tagging models for Coptic, Demotic and Earlier Egyptian. In *Proceedings of the 1st Workshop on Machine Learning for Ancient Languages (ML4AL 2024)*, pages 87–97, Bangkok, Thailand. Association for Computational Linguistics.

Daniel Smith and Mans Hulden. 2016. Morphological analysis of Sahidic Coptic for automatic glossing. In *Proceedings of the Tenth International Conference on Language Resources and Evaluation (LREC'16)*, pages 2584–2588.

Andréas Stauder. 2020. History of the Egyptian Language. In Ian Shaw and Elizabeth Bloxam, editors, *Oxford Handbook of Egyptology*, pages 930–956. Oxford University Press, Oxford.

Daniel A. Werning. 2024. TLA Parts of Speech. In Tonio Sebastian Richter, Daniel A. Werning, Hans-Werner Fischer-Elfert, and Peter Dils, editors, *Thesaurus Linguae Aegyptiae, Corpus issue 19, Web app version 2.2.0, 11/5/2024.* Berlin-Brandenburgische Akademie der Wissenschaften and Sächsische Akademie der Wissenschaften zu Leipzig. Accessed: 2/8/2025.

Daniel A. Werning. 2025. TLA authors. In Tonio Sebastian Richter, Daniel A. Werning, Hans-Werner Fischer-Elfert, and Peter Dils, editors, *Thesaurus Linguae Aegyptiae, Corpus issue 19, Web app version 2.2.1.1, 3/6/2025.* Berlin-Brandenburgische Akademie der Wissenschaften and Sächsische Akademie der Wissenschaften zu Leipzig. Accessed: 3/16/2025.

Jean Winand. 2018. Late Egyptian. In Julie Stauder-Porchet, Andréas Stauder, and Willeke Wendrich, editors, *UCLA Encyclopedia of Egyptology*. Los Angeles.

Amir Zeldes and Caroline T. Schroeder. 2015. Computational Methods for Coptic: Developing and Using Part-of-Speech Tagging for Digital Scholarship in the Humanities. *Digital Scholarship in the Humanities*, 30(suppl1):i164–i176.

Amir Zeldes and Caroline T. Schroeder. 2016. An NLP pipeline for Coptic. In *Proceedings of the 10th SIGHUM Workshop on Language Technology for Cultural Heritage, Social Sciences, and Humanities*, pages 146–155, Berlin, Germany. Association for Computational Linguistics.

# Bringing Suzhou Numerals into the Digital Age: A Dataset and Recognition Study on Ancient Chinese Trade Records


Ting-Lin Wu[♣] Zih-Ching Chen[♦] Chen-Yuan Chen[♥]
Pi-Jhong Chen[♠] Li-Chiao Wang[†]

[♣]National Yang Ming Chiao Tung University [♦]NVIDIA AI Technology Center [♥]National Chengchi University
[♠]National Central University [†]Academia Sinica

[♣]morris0401.cs11@nycu.edu.tw [♦]virginiac@nvidia.com [♥]111301049@nccu.edu.tw
[♠]peter20511@gmail.com [†]lcwang@gate.sinica.edu.tw



## Abstract

Suzhou numerals, a specialized numerical notation system historically used in Chinese commerce and accounting, played a pivotal role in financial transactions from the Song Dynasty to the early 20th century. Despite their historical significance, they remain largely absent from modern OCR benchmarks, limiting computational access to archival trade documents. This paper presents a curated dataset of 773 expert-annotated Suzhou numeral samples extracted from late Qing-era trade ledgers. We provide a statistical analysis of character distributions, offering insights into their real-world usage in historical bookkeeping. Additionally, we evaluate baseline performance with handwritten text recognition (HTR) model, highlighting the challenges of recognizing low-resource brush-written numerals. By introducing this dataset and initial benchmark results, we aim to facilitate research in historical documentation in ancient Chinese characters, advancing the digitization of early Chinese financial records. The dataset is publicly available at our huggingface hub, and our codebase can be accessed at our github repository.


## 1 Introduction

Suzhou numerals, a traditional numerical notation system originating in ancient China, played a crucial role in trade, accounting, and daily transactions in East Asia (Yang and Zhang, 2019). Characterized by their unique brush-based calligraphic style and distinct structural patterns, Suzhou numerals differ significantly from modern numerical systems. Despite their historical and cultural importance, digitization and computational analysis remain underdeveloped (Liu et al., 2021), posing challenges to both preservation and automatic recognition.

Digital preservation of Suzhou numeral is imperative due to their profound historical and cultural significance, yet their survival is at risk. According to Jchi (2011) these numerals evolved from Song dynasty arithmetic rod methods and were widely disseminated in Ming China and Japan via educational. Li et al. (2022) further reveals that, before Arabic numerals prevailed, Suzhou numerals were integral to commerce and measurement. As Suzhou numerals fade from use—gradually replaced by Arabic digits—their preservation becomes increasingly urgent to prevent cultural loss and retain a unique part of China' s mathematical heritage.

Figure 1: Excerpt from a late Qing-era accounting ledger (dated the 4th year of Emperor Guangxu' s reign), preserved in the Hechang Firm in Nagasaki(長崎和昌號) archives.

In the past decade, HTR has made significant progress through the use of deep neural networks Doermann and Tombre (2014). Unlike traditional HTR systems that employ hand-crafted features, these networks are data-hungry and require significant amounts of training data to learn, generalize, and be deployed in real-world scenarios. Suzhou numerals are rarely discussed in current studies, which focus primarily on standard Chinese characters or modern digits. This paper aims to address the gap by introducing a dataset of Suzhou numerals for HTR research.

We introduce the first dataset of Suzhou numer-




*Proceedings of the Second Ancient Language Processing Workshop associated with NAACL 2025*, pages 83–89
May 4, 2025. ©2025 Association for Computational Linguistics

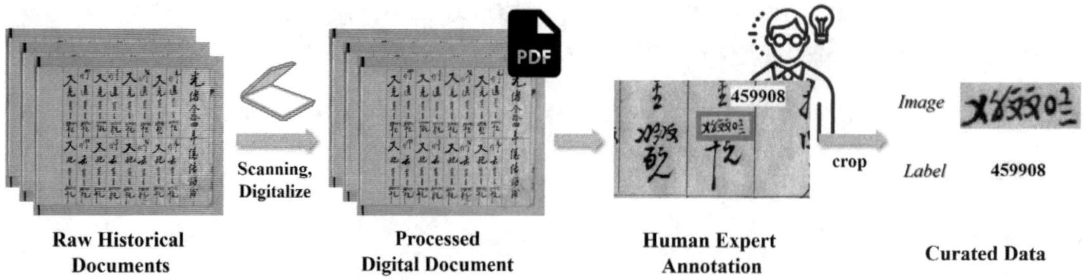


Figure 2: Flow chart of Suzhou Numerals dataset creation

als derived from historical trade records preserved by the Kinmen-based Liang family (1850–1930). These records, originating from the Hechang Firm in Nagasaki, illustrate real-world usage in financial ledgers, contracts, and transactions (Lin, 2020). Fig 1 shows the archievs of Hechang Firm in Nagasaki. Our dataset features:

- High-Quality Suzhou Numeral Samples: 773 manually annotated instances that span various brush styles and levels of degradation.
- Baseline for hand written Suzhou Numeral recognition: CRNN-based baseline model (Shi et al., 2015) for improved recognition of historical scripts .

By bridging cultural heritage preservation and AI-driven OCR, we advance handwritten character recognition for underrepresented scripts, enabling new lines of digital humanities research.

## 2 Related Work

### 2.1 Handwritten Text Recognition

HTR has been extensively studied in computer vision and pattern recognition. With the advent of deep learning, convolutional neural networks (CNN) (LeCun et al., 1998) (Krizhevsky et al., 2012) and recurrent neural networks (RNN) (Graves, 2013) have enabled end-to-end learning for HTR, achieving state-of-the-art results on MNIST (Deng, 2012b) and EMNIST (Cohen et al., 2017). Shi et al. (2015) proposed Convolutional Recurrent Neural Network (CRNN) which integrates CNN-based feature extraction with LSTM-based (Graves and Graves, 2012) sequence modeling, delivering powerful, end-to-end recognition performance for text recognition.

Although these approaches have shown high precision for Latin digits and standard Chinese characters, Suzhou numerals pose unique recognition challenges due to their stroke-based morphology, contextual variations, and historical degradation. Unlike modern printed numerals, their handwritten nature introduces stroke ambiguity, where numerals such as 〢 (2) and 〣 (3) differ by a single stroke, making them susceptible to misclassification. Additionally, numerals appear in both horizontal and vertical layouts, requiring flexible layout analysis for proper segmentation. The multiple variants of Suzhou Numerals, along with its mixed use with Chinese numerals and Manchu numbers, make its recognition extremely challenging (Saarela and Xue, 2023).

### 2.2 Datasets for Handwritten Text Recognition

Large-scale benchmarks have significantly advanced HTR research (Deng, 2012a), yet existing resources primarily target modern digits or standard Chinese text (Cohen et al., 2017; LeCun et al., 1998). Historical East Asian scripts, especially those used in commercial documents, remain notably underrepresented (Zhang et al., 2019). Saeed et al. (2024) introduces the Muharaf dataset which collecting over 1,600 historic handwritten Arabic manuscript images with CRNN-based baseline (Shi et al., 2015). Koch et al. (2023) introduces a tailored end-to-end handwritten text recognition system for Medieval Latin dictionary record cards. Moreover, due to limited archival access and the idiosyncrasies of brush-based writing, most publicly available Chinese OCR corpora do not isolate traditional numeric forms. In response, we introduce a new dataset of 773 annotated Suzhou numerals drawn from late Qing-era trade ledgers. Compared to previous Chinese OCR datasets that focus on general characters, ours specifically highlights the *numeric* brush strokes critical for historical accounting. To our knowledge, this is the first publicly available corpus dedicated solely to Suzhou numerals, providing a foundation for future research in historical OCR and HTR.

Table 1: Suzhou Numerals and Their Unicode Representations

| Arabic | Suzhou numerals | Unicode |
|---|---|---|
| 0 | 〇 | U+3007 |
| 1 | 〡 | U+3021 |
| 2 | 〢 | U+3022 |
| 3 | 〣 | U+3023 |
| 4 | 〤 | U+3024 |
| 5 | 〥 | U+3025 |
| 6 | 〦 | U+3026 |
| 7 | 〧 | U+3027 |
| 8 | 〨 | U+3028 |
| 9 | 〩 | U+3029 |

## 3 Data Collection

### 3.1 Source Material and Archival Records

Our dataset is derived from the **Hechang Firm in Nagasaki** archive (Hec) (Zhu, 2016) (Ichikawa, 1983) (Xu, 1988), which documents trade activities between China, Japan, and Southeast Asia from 1880 to 1930. The collection includes accounting ledgers, trade contracts, and commercial correspondence, where Suzhou numerals appear in transaction records, itemized cost lists, and within handwritten Chinese text (Fig 1). These materials provide a rich historical context, capturing variations in notation style and document formatting over time.

### 3.2 Digitization and Annotation

As illustrated in the flow chart in Figure 2. First, all documents have been scanned and digitized into high-resolution PDF files. Then, the portions containing the Suzhou numerals (0-9) in these documents were manually annotated by human experts. Finally, every portion was individually cropped into an image with an annotated label. Ambiguous cases, particularly those affected by fading or overlapping strokes, were cross-verified by multiple annotators for consistency.

### 3.3 Dataset Statistics

The final dataset comprises **773 annotated instances** of Suzhou numerals. We divide the dataset into training, testing, and evaluation sets with a ratio of 7:1.5:1.5, resulting in 541 samples for training, 116 for testing, and 116 for evaluation. The dataset captures natural variations in stroke thickness, numeral alignment, and stylistic nuances, providing a comprehensive representation of real-world Suzhou numeral usage.

Figure 3 illustrates the frequency distribution of individual digits (0-9) appearing in filename labels, providing insights into numerical biases or inconsistencies within the dataset.

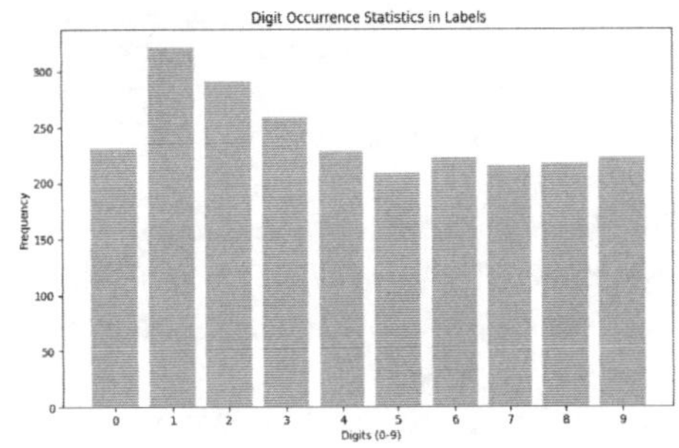


Figure 3: Histogram displaying the frequency of individual digits (0-9) appearing in the filename labels.

## 4 Experiments and Baseline HTR Results

We evaluate our proposed approach using with CRNN (Shi et al., 2015) to recognize brush-based Suzhou numerals. This section details the CRNN pipeline, training procedures, and the effects of rotation, padding, and pretrained checkpoints, for a baseline of our dataset.

**CRNN Pipeline** CRNN architecture introduced by Shi et al. (2015) is adapted as a baseline to address the recognition of handwritten Suzhou numeral sequences. The input to our system is a grayscale image $I \in \mathbb{R}^{H \times W \times 1}$ that contains a series of handwritten Suzhou numerals, where $H = 32$ and $W = 128$.

The brief introduction pipeline is as follows. For more details, please refer to Appendix B. First, the grayscale image is fed into a CNN (LeCun et al., 1998) (Krizhevsky et al., 2012) which extracts high-level feature maps. These feature maps are then reshaped into a sequential feature representation. Subsequently, these features are input to bidirectional LSTM (Graves and Graves, 2012) layers. Finally, the sequence features are fed into MLP and the output sequence is decoded into predicted Arabic digit sequence.

Table 2: Baselines of OCR models on Suzhou Numerals recognition. The table presents results for classic OCR and CRNN-based models under different training configs. The lowest Character Error Rate (CER) is achieved with a pretrained CRNN model incorporating both padding and rotation.

| Model | Pretrained | Padding | Rotation | CER (%) |
|---|---|---|---|---|
| Tesseract | Yes | - | - | 100.00 |
| Tesseract | Yes | No | No | 23.22 |
| CRNN | No | No | No | 5.450 |
| CRNN | No | No | Yes | 5.205 |
| CRNN | No | Yes | Yes | 3.645 |
| CRNN | No | Yes | No | 5.115 |
| CRNN | Yes | No | Yes | 5.150 |
| CRNN | Yes | Yes | Yes | **3.570** |

For the transcription of the sequential output, we adopt the CTC loss (Jaderberg et al., 2014). It proves essential for accommodating irregular spacing and partial strokes.

$$\mathcal{L}_{\text{CTC}} = -\ln p(y \mid \mathrm{x}),$$

which sums over all valid alignments between the input numeral sequence (x) and the ground truth numeral sequence ($y$).

**Training and Data Augmentation** Given the script's variability in stroke density and ink clarity, we apply rotations (up to $\pm 20°$), random scaling (5–15%), and brightness alterations ([0.1, 0.2]). When performing data augmentation, we expand the training data by 3 times (1x original training data and 2x augmented data). We train using Adam (LR=0.0001), a batch size of 4, for 100 epochs. More training details can be found in Appendix C).

**Rotation and Padding Effects** We also investigate how rotation degrees and input padding influence recognition (Table 2). In cases without padding, a moderate rotation (10°) enhances accuracy, but larger angles (20°) start to degrade performance, presumably due to excessive numeral distortion. With padding, the results remain more stable as rotation increases; however, improvements largely plateau beyond 10°. These observations suggest that retaining contextual spacing around numerals helps mitigate augmentation artifacts, especially in heavily degraded scans.

**Baseline Comparisons** We report the baseline of our Suzhou numerals in different models. As shown in Table 2, Tesseract performs poorly

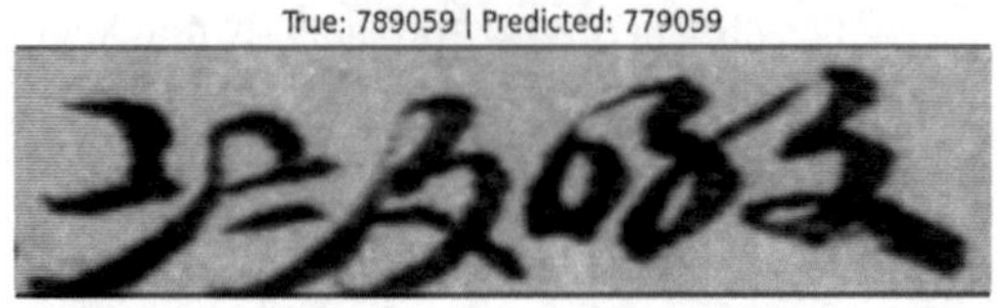


Figure 4: An example of misprediction. The lowest stroke of second character ' 〨' and the top left stroke of the third character ' 〩' is almost connected. Therefore, our model identifies these two strokes as a single stroke, and mistakenly recognized the second character as ' 〧'. See Fig 5 in Appendix for more examples.

(100% CER) on Suzhou numerals, reflecting the script' s brush-based style and close integration with Chinese text. Finetuning CRNN attains significantly lower error rates. Once we incorporate padding and rotations, the CER decreases further to 3.645%.

**Pretrained Checkpoints and Final Results** Leveraging a CRNN checkpoint trained on Synth90k dataset (Jaderberg et al., 2014) yields the best outcome. After fine-tuning on Suzhou numerals, we achieve a CER of 3.57% (Table 2), illustrating that transfer learning is particularly effective in this under-resourced domain. Qualitative inspections reveal that most errors are due to faint strokes, especially confusing 〢 **(2)** with 〣 **(3)** or merging 〤 **(4)** and 〥 **(5)** in severely degraded regions (Figure 4). Despite these issues, the results confirm the viability of specialized neural architectures, even with limited training data, and highlight the importance of careful augmentation strategies when tackling historical scripts.

## 5 Conclusion and Future Work

We introduce the first dataset of Suzhou numerals, providing a critical resource for historical OCR and HTR. Our CRNN baseline, achieving a CER of 3.57%. Future work includes expanding the dataset with additional scribes and degraded samples, integrating attention-based models like Transformers for improved feature extraction, recognizing Suzhou numerals in multilingual documents, and enhancing reproducibility through code and dataset sharing. By bridging cultural preservation with machine learning, this work establishes a foundation for advancing OCR on underrepresented scripts, inviting further research and applications.

## References

《長崎和昌號文書》 (t0856). 中研院臺史所檔案館數位典藏. https://tais.ith.sinica.edu.tw/sinicafrsFront/search/search_detail.jsp?xmlId=0000456122. Accessed: 2025-02-09.

Gregory Cohen, Saeed Afshar, Jonathan Tapson, and Andre Van Schaik. 2017. Emnist: Extending mnist to handwritten letters. *2017 International Joint Conference on Neural Networks (IJCNN)*, pages 2921–2926.

Li Deng. 2012a. The mnist database of handwritten digit images for machine learning research. *IEEE Signal Processing Magazine*, 29(6):141–142.

Li Deng. 2012b. The mnist database of handwritten digit images for machine learning research [best of the web]. *IEEE Signal Processing Magazine*, 29(6):141–142.

David Doermann and Karl Tombre. 2014. *Handbook of Document Image Processing and Recognition*. Springer.

Alex Graves. 2013. Generating sequences with recurrent neural networks. *arXiv preprint arXiv:1308.0850*.

Alex Graves and Alex Graves. 2012. Long short-term memory. *Supervised sequence labelling with recurrent neural networks*, pages 37–45.

Shinai Ichikawa. 1983. 長崎華商「泰益號」🄵🄵文書簡介 昭和 57~ 58 年度科研成果報告の一部. 東南アジア研究年報, (24/25):71–106.

Max Jaderberg, Andrea Vedaldi, and Andrew Zisserman. 2014. Deep features for text spotting. In *European Conference on Computer Vision*.

Shigeru Jchi. 2011. Mathematical books of the song, yuan, and ming dynasties and the "oranda fuch": The japanese transmission of suzhou numerals (studies in the history of mathematics). *RIMS Kkyroku (Proceedings of the Research Institute for Mathematical Sciences)*, 1739:128–137.

Philipp Koch, Gilary Vera Nuñez, Esteban Garces Arias, Christian Heumann, Matthias Schöffel, Alexander Häberlin, and Matthias Assenmacher. 2023. A tailored handwritten-text-recognition system for medieval Latin. In *Proceedings of the Ancient Language Processing Workshop*, pages 103–110, Varna, Bulgaria. INCOMA Ltd., Shoumen, Bulgaria.

Alex Krizhevsky, Ilya Sutskever, and Geoffrey E Hinton. 2012. Imagenet classification with deep convolutional neural networks. *Advances in Neural Information Processing Systems*, 25:1097–1105.

Y. LeCun, L. Bottou, Y. Bengio, and P. Haffner. 1998. Gradient-based learning applied to document recognition. *Proceedings of the IEEE*, 86(11):2278–2324.

Wenhua Li et al. 2022. The application and cultural connotation of suzhou numerals in hainan during the late qing and republican periods. *Library Journal*, 41(12):112.

Man-houng Lin. 2020. Maritime trade networks in east asia: The kinmen merchant archives. *Journal of Chinese Historical Studies*, 30(2):78–96.

Chang Liu, Xu-Yao Zhang, and Qiu-Feng Wang. 2021. A survey of traditional chinese character recognition methods. *Pattern Recognition*, 112:107750.

Mårten Söderblom Saarela and Zhang Xue. 2023. A study on the quantification and reform of chinese characters in a late qing bannerman manuscript. *Bulletin of the Institute of Modern History, Academia Sinica*, (119):1–37.

Mehreen Saeed, Adrian Chan, Anupam Mijar, joseph Moukarzel, Gerges Habchi, Carlos Younes, amin elias, Chau-Wai Wong, and Akram Khater. 2024. Muharaf: Manuscripts of handwritten arabic dataset for cursive text recognition. In *Advances in Neural Information Processing Systems*, volume 37, pages 58525–58538. Curran Associates, Inc.

Baoguang Shi, Xiang Bai, and Cong Yao. 2015. An end-to-end trainable neural network for image-based sequence recognition and its application to scene text recognition. *Preprint*, arXiv:1507.05717.

Zifen Xu. 1988. 🄵支簿記法としての🄵門華僑簿記の事例研究-長崎在留の「泰益号」の簿記(一九〇七-一九三四)-. 🄵🄵史学, 23(3):29–47.

Hongwei Yang and Jianguo Zhang. 2019. Chinese historical numbers: Morphology, evolution and usage. *Journal of Chinese Writing Systems*, 3(1):12–31.

X.Y. Zhang, F. Yin, Y.M. Zhang, C.L. Liu, and Y. Bengio. 2019. A survey of deep learning algorithms for optical character recognition. *IEEE Transactions on Pattern Analysis and Machine Intelligence*.

Delan Zhu. 2016. 公私領域之間 長崎僑領陳世望(1901-1940). 國史館館刊, (50):1–46.

## Appendix

## A Examples of Mispredictions

We list some examples (Figure 5) which our model can't correctly predict the true labels.

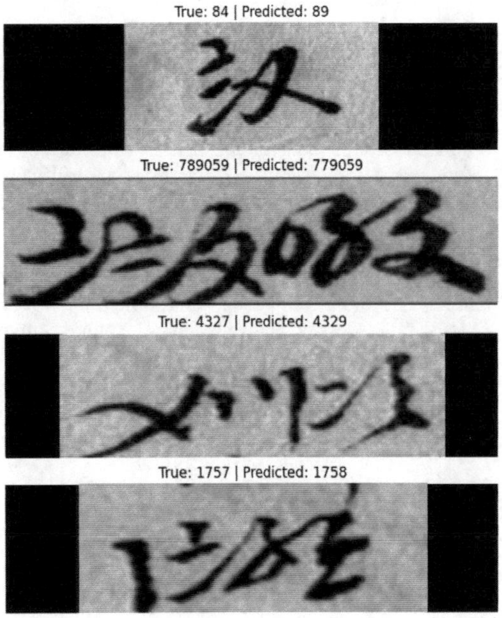


Figure 5: Some examples of mispredictions

## B CRNN Model Pipline

We have the same model architecture as Convolutional Recurrent Neural Network (CRNN) (Shi et al., 2015) because we want to obtain a baseline for our Suzhou Numerals recognition task. The following is the detailed model architecture.

- **Input:** Grayscale image of size $32 \times W$ (Height $\times$ Width), where the height is fixed and $W$ is variable. We set $W = 128$ here.
- **Conv1:**
  - Kernel: $3 \times 3$, Filters: 64, Stride: 1, Padding: 1.
  - Output: $32 \times W \times 64$.
- **Pool1:**
  - Max Pooling: $2 \times 2$ with stride 2.
  - Output: $16 \times \frac{W}{2} \times 64$.
- **Conv2:**
  - Kernel: $3 \times 3$, Filters: 128, Stride: 1, Padding: 1.
  - Output: $16 \times \frac{W}{2} \times 128$.
- **Pool2:**
  - Max Pooling: $2 \times 2$ with stride 2.
  - Output: $8 \times \frac{W}{4} \times 128$.
- **Conv3:**
  - Kernel: $3 \times 3$, Filters: 256, Stride: 1, Padding: 1.
  - Output: $8 \times \frac{W}{4} \times 256$.
- **Conv4:**
  - Kernel: $3 \times 3$, Filters: 256, Stride: 1, Padding: 1.
  - Output: $8 \times \frac{W}{4} \times 256$.
- **Pool3:**
  - Max Pooling with kernel $2 \times 1$ (vertical pooling only).
  - Output: $4 \times \frac{W}{4} \times 256$.
- **Conv5:**
  - Kernel: $3 \times 3$, Filters: 512, Stride: 1, Padding: 1.
  - Output: $4 \times \frac{W}{4} \times 512$.
- **Conv6:**
  - Kernel: $3 \times 3$, Filters: 512, Stride: 1, Padding: 1.
  - Output: $4 \times \frac{W}{4} \times 512$.
- **Pool4:**
  - Max Pooling with kernel $2 \times 1$ (horizontal pooling only).
  - Output: $2 \times \frac{W}{4} \times 512$.
- **Conv7:**
  - Kernel: $2 \times 2$, Filters: 512, Stride: 1, No padding.
  - Output: $1 \times \frac{W}{4} \times 512$.

The final feature map is reshaped into a sequence:

$$\mathrm{x} = \{x_1, x_2, \ldots, x_T\}, \quad T = \frac{W}{4}, \quad x_i \in \mathbb{R}^{512}.$$

**RNN Sequence Modeling**

The sequential features are modeled by two layers of Bidirectional Long Short-Term Memory (BiLSTM):

- **BiLSTM Layer 1:**
  - Hidden Units: 256 in each direction.
  - Output per time step: 512-dimensional feature vector.
- **BiLSTM Layer 2:**
  - Hidden Units: 256 in each direction.
  - Output per time step: 512-dimensional feature vector.

**Transcription Layer and CTC Loss**

A fully connected layer with softmax activation is applied to the output of the final BiLSTM to obtain a probability distribution over the target character set augmented by a blank label for CTC. Formally, for each time step:

$$\text{Output dimension} = |\mathcal{A}| + 1,$$

where $\mathcal{A}$ denotes the set of target characters. In our case, $\mathcal{A}$ means a set of numerals from 0-9.

The network is trained using the Connectionist Temporal Classification (CTC) loss:

$$\mathcal{L}_{\text{CTC}} = -\ln p(y \mid \text{x}),$$

which sums over all valid alignments between the input sequence (x) and the ground truth sequence ($y$).

## C Training Hyperparameters

Table 3: Hyperparameters

| Parameter | Value |
|---|---|
| img_height, img_width | 32, 128 |
| epochs | 100 |
| batch size | 4 |
| learning rate | $1 \times 10^{-4}$ |
| augmentation ratio | 2x |
| rotation degree | 20 |
| brightness | 0.1 |

## D Example of Training and Evaluation loss

Figure 6 shows an basic example of training and evaluation loss graph. Hyperparameters are set same as Appendix C

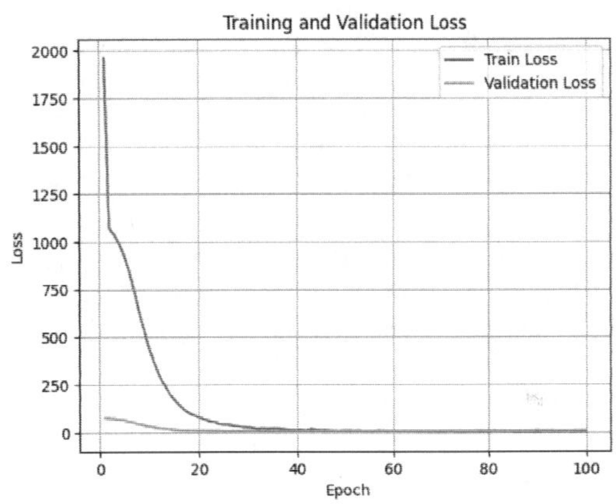


Figure 6: Basic training and evaluation loss graph

# The Historian's Fingerprint

## A Computational Stylometric Study of the Zuo Commentary and Discourses of the States

**Wenjie Hua**
School of Chinese Language and Literature, Wuhan University, China
huawenjie@whu.edu.cn

### Abstract

Previous studies suggest that authorship can be inferred through stylistic features like function word usage and grammatical patterns, yet such analyses remain limited for Old Chinese texts with disputed authorship. Computational methods enable a more nuanced exploration of these texts. This study applies stylometric analysis to examine the authorship controversy between the *Zuo Commentary* and the *Discourses of the States*. Using PoS 4-grams, Kullback-Leibler divergence, and multidimensional scaling (MDS), we systematically compare their stylistic profiles. Results show that the *Zuo Commentary* exhibits high internal consistency, especially in the later eight Dukes chapters, supporting its integration by a single scholarly tradition. In contrast, the *Discourses of the States* displays greater stylistic diversity, aligning with the multiple-source compilation theory. Further analysis reveals partial stylistic similarities among the Lu, Jin, and Chu-related chapters, suggesting shared influences. These findings provide quantitative support for Tong Shuye's arguments and extend statistical validation of Bernhard Karlgren's assertion on the textual unity of the *Zuo Commentary*.

## 1 Background

Stylometry, which also known as authorship identification, is the process of analyzing textual features to determine uncertain authorship (authorship attribution) or verify an author's identity (authorship verification). The fundamental premise of stylometry is that "authors have an unconscious aspect to their style, an aspect which cannot consciously be manipulated but which possesses features that are quantifiable and may be distinctive." This study applies stylometry to old Chinese texts, focusing on two historical works with contentious authorship: *Zuo zhuan* 左傳 (Zuo Commentary) and *Guo yu* 國語 (Discourses of the States).

The *Zuo Commentary* is a chronicle-style historical record documenting events in Central Plains states during the Spring and Autumn period. Regarding its authorship, figures such as Sima Qian 司馬遷 (145-86? BCE), Ban Gu 班固 (32-92 AD), and Du Yu 杜預 (233-285 AD), along with early records from *The Analects*, identify Zuo Qiu Ming 左丘明, the Tai shi 太史 (historian) of the state of Lu 魯, as the author of the work. Relevant sources include:

> The gentleman of Lu (魯君子), Zuo Qiu Ming, compiled the *Zuo Commentary* to the Spring and Autumn Annals. (Sima Qian, *Records of the Grand Historian* - Yearly Chronicle of the Feudal Lords)

However, started in the Tang dynasty (618-907), historians raised doubts about whether Zuo Qiu Ming mentioned in *Records of the Grand Historian* and *The Analects* were the same person. In the late Qing period, New Text scholars argued more broadly that the *Zuo Commentary* was a forgery by Liu Xin 劉歆 (50?-23 BCE). Due to the absence of further archaeological evidence, contemporary views generally accept the reliability of Sima Qian's records.

The *Discourses of the States* is a state-specific historical record. It primarily focuses on events during the Spring and Autumn period, with some content overlapping with the *Zuo Commentary*. The text comprises 21 chapters, each consisting of independent speeches or dialogues.

Concerning its authorship, Sima Qian, followed by Ban Gu, attributed it to the same author as the *Zuo Commentary*:

> Zuo Qiu lost his sight and finished the *Discourses of the States*. (Sima Qian, *Records of the Grand Historian* - Autobiographical Afterword of the Grand Historian)

> Confucius composed the *Spring and Autumn Annals* based on Lu's historical records, and Zuo Qiu Ming organized their accounts as commentary and further compiled divergences into the *Discourses of the States*. (Ban Gu, *Book of Han* - Sima Qian)

Karlgren (1968) conducted the earliest stylometric analysis of the *Zuo Commentary* and the *Discourses of the States*. By manually selecting seven sets of function words from the *Zuo Commentary*, Karlgren compared its linguistic style with *The Analects* and *Mencius*, which represent the linguistic style of the Lu region. He reached two significant conclusions. First, the *Zuo Commentary* is either the work of a single author or represents a specific school, as it exhibits a high degree of internal consistency. However, it does not reflect the style of Lu's "gentlemen of Lu." Second, the grammar of the *Zuo Commentary* is very similar to that of the *Discourses of the States*. Hirase (1998) affirmed Karlgren's judgment and used subsequent research on calendar records to demonstrate a connection between the author of the *Zuo Commentary* and the court of the State of Han 韓.

## 2 Tools and Corpus

Distinguishing from earlier studies reliant on manual annotation and subjective judgment, since the 1980s, the introduction of digital tools and mathematical methods has made stylometry more feasible for processing vast corpora, providing repeatable experimental procedures and objective metrics. Building upon the methodology of Karlgren, who conducted full-text statistics on the *Zuo Commentary* and *Discourses of the States*, we expanded the sample size to uncover linguistic style differences more comprehensively, which aims to conduct a mega-size computational analysis of the *Zuo Commentary* and the *Discourses of the States*, presenting the results visually and intuitively. For word segmentation (WS) and part-of-speech tagging (POS), Jiayan, a professional Python-based NLP tool for old Chinese, Jiayan[1]was utilized for this step. After statistics and calculation processing, we employed visualization tools to output the results.

The version of the *Zuo Commentary* commonly used today originates from the Western Jin dynasty, where Du Yu reorganized the single spread text (單篇別行) by integrating it into the *Chun Qiu* 春秋 (the Spring and Autumn Annals), aligning the commentary years with the corresponding years in the Annals, a process described as "attaching the commentary years to the Annals years" (分經之年与傳之年相附) (Ma, 1992). This version, referred to as *Chun Qiu Zuo zhuan* 春秋左傳 (*Zuo Commentary to the Spring and Autumn Annals*), serves as part of the corpus for our study. In order to facilitate analysis, we divided the *Zuo Commentary* into twelve parts, corresponding to the twelve rulers. Similarly, the *Discourses of the States* was divided into twenty-one parts, based on its chapters.

## 3 Methodology

### 3.1 POS n-grams

POS n-grams, defined as sequences of n consecutive part-of-speech tags, offer significant advantages as higher-order POS features. They capture subtle stylistic differences that can be indicative of authorship. POS n-grams have demonstrated strong performance in previous studies (Martinc et al., 2017; Siagian and Aritsugi, 2019). Similar methods have also been applied to post-Classical Chinese literature. For example, Liu and Xiao (2015)provides valuable insights; however, there are currently no precedents for applying such methods to Old Chinese.

Compared to analyzing individual POS tags or simple POS elements, n-grams demonstrate greater robustness, particularly for short, stylistically diverse texts. This makes them highly suitable for analyzing Old Chinese texts.

After comparing p-values, mean differences, and contrastive analysis for n = 2, 3, and 4, we found that 4-grams offer the best overall performance in terms of statistical significance, contextual coverage, and text differentiation power. Therefore, we computed POS 4-gram statistics for individual chapters and constructed cosine similarity matrices. Retaining only the most frequent n-grams helped reduce noise and sparsity.

If a text exhibited clear clustering patterns among chapters, we computed the group centroid of the $J$ set in the original feature space to represent central stylistic features and identified outlier chapters based on their Euclidean distance to this centroid. Subsequently, we applied multidimensional scaling (MDS) to visualize the distance matrices in low-dimensional space.

[1]https://github.com/jiaeyan/Jiayan

### 3.2 Kullback-Leibler Divergence

Function words reveal writing style (Pennebaker, 2011). Damerau (1975) was the first to propose an authorship identification method based on the frequency of function words. Subsequent studies (Halvani et al., 2020; Zhao and Zobel, 2007) have justified the effectiveness of this approach for alphabetic languages. This stylistic phenomenon is also evident in Old Chinese, where function words are particularly effective in distinguishing writing styles based on authorship, regional characteristics, and temporal context.

Based on previous research, we exhaustively compiled all function words in the two texts and calculated their unary probabilities. Subsequently, we introduced the concept of relative entropy for the same function word across texts and computed its Kullback-Leibler (KL) divergence using the following formula:

$$D(p \parallel q) = \sum_{x} p(x) \log_2 \frac{p(x)}{q(x)} \quad (1)$$

To assess the disparity between two probability distributions, relative entropy is zero when $p = q$ and increases as their difference grows. KL divergence quantifies this disparity by summing the relative differences across elements. To prevent invalid operations (e.g., division by zero), we replaced zero frequencies with a small constant $\epsilon$ for numerical stability.

Using the computed KL divergence as a distance metric, we compiled function word statistics for individual chapters and constructed distance matrices for within-group and between-group comparisons of the *Zuo Commentary* and the *Discourses of the States*. To analyze clustering patterns, we first calculated group centroids in the original feature space and identified outliers via Euclidean distance to these centroids. Then, we used MDS to visualize as well.

## 4 Results

We calculated and visualized POS 4-grams cosine similarity matrices for the chapters of the *Zuo Commentary* and *Discourses of the States*. The *Zuo Commentary* shows high internal similarity, forming distinct clusters (the $J$ set) with minor variations. In contrast, the *Discourses of the States* displays lower internal similarity. MDS provides us a clear view of internal consistency and divergence.

The *Discourses of the States* chapters show wide dispersion in feature patterns, while the *Zuo Commentary* exhibits strong clustering, especially among the last eight dukes recorded in the *Zuo Commentary* — *Dukes Xi, Wen, Xuan, Cheng, Xiang, Zhao, Ding, and Ai* — forming a cohesive group. In contrast, the first four dukes recorded, *Dukes Yin, Huan, Zhuang, and Min*, display more dispersed patterns (see Figure 1). Comparing independent chapters to the *Zuo Commentary*'s group centroid (calculated from its coordinate positions in MDS space) reveals that *Discourse of Lu-1*, *Lu-2*, *Chu-1*, *Jin-4*, and *Jin-8* exhibit similar stylistic proximities, suggesting overlaps with the *Zuo Commentary* (see Figure 2).

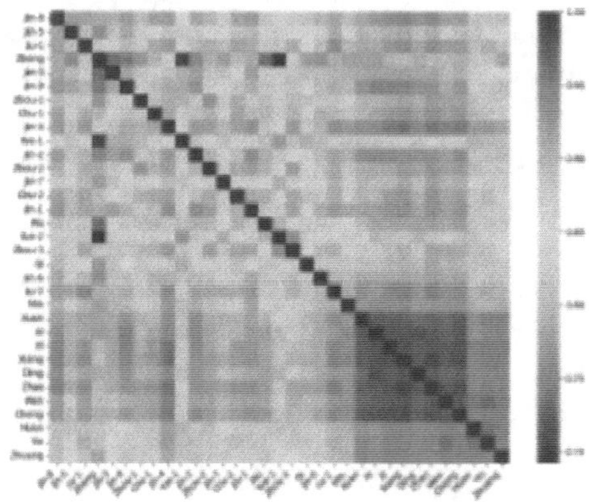

Figure 1: Cosine Similarity of PoS 4-grams in the Zuo Commentary and the Discourses of the States

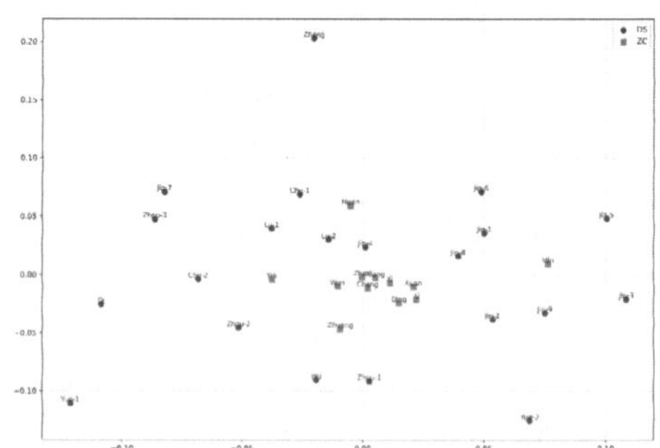

Figure 2: MDS Projection of 4-grams with Chapter Distances

KL divergence values near 0 indicate greater similarity, and its heat-map mirrors the patterns in the prior heat-map (see Figure 3). MDS projection based on KL divergence also aligns with POS 4-grams results, showing clustering for the *Zuo Commentary* and dispersion for the *Discourses of the States*. Notably, the stylistic differences between the first four and last eight dukes are also evident within the *Zuo Commentary*. Furthermore, the *Discourses of the States* chapters with proximity to the *Zuo Commentary*'s centroid align with the previous results (see Figure 4).

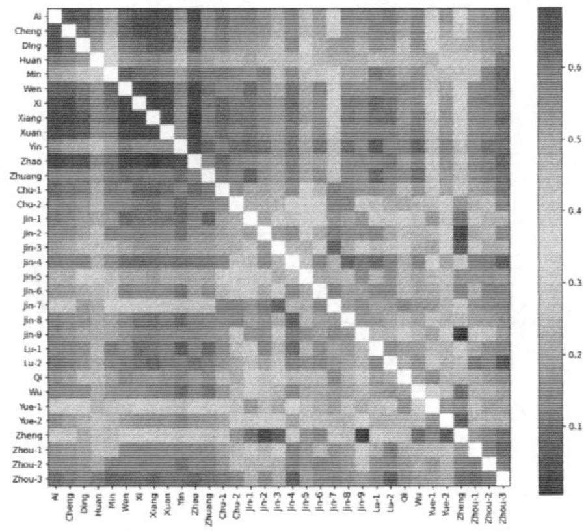


Figure 3: KL Divergence between the Zuo Commentary and the Discourses of the States

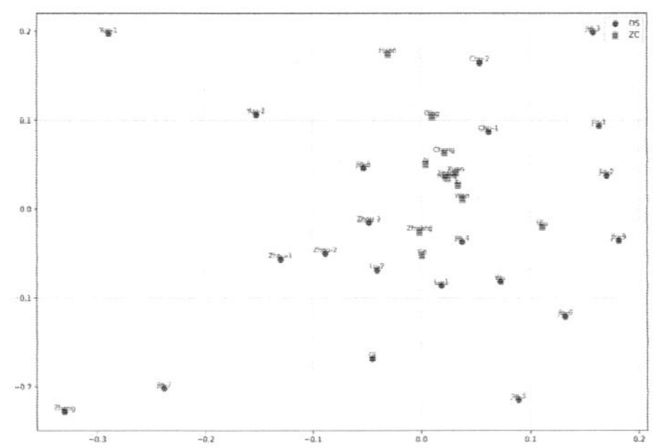

Figure 4: MDS Projection of KL Divergence with Chapter Distances

## 5 Related Work

Revisiting the history of scholarship, Yao Nai was the first to claim that "(Zuo Commentary) has accumulated additional elements, especially influenced by followers of Wu Qi (累有附益, 而由吳起之徒為之者蓋尤多)" Jiao and Shen (2016), but the evidence remains insufficient. Later, Zhang (1982), based on the statement in *Han Feizi* that "Wu Ch'i was a native of Tso-shih in Wei" (吳起, 衛左氏中人也) (Liao, 1959), inferred that Wu Qi was the author of *Zuo Commentary*. Liu (2008) held a similar view. Subsequently, Tong (2006) listed four pieces of evidence from the perspective of national affairs and more clearly delineated the author's affiliation as "persons related to the states of Lu, Jin, and Chu, along with their disciples." Now, we should admit that Tong (2006)'s perspective is well-founded.

## 6 Conclusions

This study provides a new empirical perspective on this academic debate through experiments using part-of-speech 4-grams and KL divergence. First, the significant stylistic differences between the *Zuo Commentary* and the *Discourses of the States* quantitatively refute the most traditional view—that both texts originated from Zuo Qiu Ming. Notably, the internal heterogeneity of the *Discourses of the States* aligns with the "multi-source compilation theory" proposed by Zhang (1939) and Wang (1986), which suggests a layered integration of historical materials from multiple states.

In contrast, while the first four chapters exhibit a relatively scattered stylistic pattern, the latter eight chapters of the *Zuo Commentary*, spanning from *Duke Xi* to *Duke Ai*, demonstrate a high degree of homogeneity. Overall, the *Zuo Commentary* maintains strong internal consistency, lending support to Karlgren (1968)'s conclusion that it was authored by either a single individual or, more precisely, a cohesive scholarly school. Furthermore, combining four scattered chapters, we may hypothesize that the diachronic evolution of authorship followed a convergent trajectory—namely, the emergence of this very school likely occurred after the period of *Duke Xi*. Notably, *Discourse of Lu, Jin,* and *Chu* exhibit high stylistic similarity to the *Zuo Commentary* in both experiments. These localized similarities strongly align with Tong (2006)'s proposition that the text was influenced by scholarly circles associated with the states of Lu, Jin, and Chu.

In conclusion, computational stylometric not only validates the intuition of earlier scholars that the *Zuo Commentary* was not the work of a single author or period, but also reveals, through quantitative evidence, that its textual unity is more likely derived from a school that integrated elements from Lu, Jin, and Chu. This finding echoes the hypotheses of Zhang (1982) and Liu (2008) regarding Wu Qi's involvement in its authorship while also concretizing Tong (2006)'s school-based theory, offering a new approach to the study of classical text formation.

## 7 Limitations

This study demonstrates the potential of stylometric methods in analyzing Old Chinese texts and intuitively presenting abstract linguistic features but acknowledges certain limitations. Our methodology assumes stylistic consistency across an author's works regardless of textual content or temporal variation. This assumption, while foundational to stylometry, remains theoretically contested. An author's style may indeed evolve due to genre adaptation or diachronic linguistic changes. Also, the accuracy of the Jiayan NLP toolkit for old Chinese POS tagging has been challenged by models based on BERT(Devlin et al., 2019) and RoBERTa(Liu et al., 2019) in recent years. We should use newer tools to improve accuracy and avoid passing errors to downstream analysis. We believe that future research should explore additional state-level texts to establish indicators beyond the *Discourses of the States*, thereby determining the regional origin of the *Zuo Commentary*. Furthermore, developing benchmark datasets and establishing standardized evaluation frameworks will advance stylometry as a robust discipline.

## References

Fred J. Damerau. 1975. The use of function word frequencies as indicators of style. *Computers and the Humanities*, 9(6):271–280.

Jacob Devlin, Ming-Wei Chang, Kenton Lee, and Kristina Toutanova. 2019. BERT: Pre-training of deep bidirectional transformers for language understanding.

Oren Halvani, Lukas Graner, and Roey Regev. 2020. Cross-domain authorship verification based on topic agnostic features. In *Conference and Labs of the Evaluation Forum (CLEF)*, Thessaloniki, Greece. European Language Resources Association (ELRA).

Takao Hirase. 1998. *Saden No Shiryō Hihanteki Kenkyū*. Tōkyō Daigaku Tōyō Bunka Kenkyūjo. 101998.

Xun Jiao and Qinhan Shen. 2016. *Supplementary Commentaries on the Zuo Commentary and Additional Annotations to the Zuo Tradition of the Spring and Autumn Annals*. Shanghai Chinese Classics Publishing House, Shanghai.

Bernhard Karlgren. 1968. *On the authenticity and nature of the Tso chuan*. Chengwen Pub. Co., Taipei. Print.

W. K. Liao. 1959. *The Complete Works of Han Fei Tzŭ: A Classic of Chinese Political Science*, volume 2. Arthur Probsthain, 41 Great Russell Street, London, W.C. 1.

Shipei Liu. 2008. *Zuo'an Ji [Collected Works of Liu Shipei]*. China Bookstore.

Ying Liu and Tianjiu Xiao. 2015. Words and n-gram models analysis for "a dream of red mansions". *Data Analysis and Knowledge Discovery*, 31(4):50–57.

Yinhan Liu, Myle Ott, Naman Goyal, Jingfei Du, Mandar Joshi, Danqi Chen, Omer Levy, Mike Lewis, Luke Zettlemoyer, and Veselin Stoyanov. 2019. Roberta: A robustly optimized bert pretraining approach. *arXiv preprint arXiv:1907.11692*.

Su Ma. 1992. *Zuo Zhuan Shi Wei (Chronological Account of the Zuo Commentary)*. Qilu Press, Jinan.

Matej Martinc, Iza Škrjanec, Katja Zupan, and Senja Pollak. 2017. Pan 2017: Author profiling - gender and language variety prediction. In *Conference and Labs of the Evaluation Forum (CLEF)*, Dublin, Ireland. European Language Resources Association (ELRA).

James W. Pennebaker. 2011. The secret life of pronouns. *New Scientist*, 211(2828):42–45.

Al Hafiz Akbar Maulana Siagian and Masayoshi Aritsugi. 2019. DBMS-KU approach for author profiling and deception detection in arabic. In *Working Notes of FIRE 2019 - Forum for Information Retrieval Evaluation*, volume 2517 of *CEUR Workshop Proceedings*, pages 115–121, Kolkata, India. CEUR-WS.org.

Shuye Tong. 2006. *Research on Zuo Zhuan of Spring and Autumn Annals (Revised Edition)*. Zhonghua Book Company.

Shu-Min Wang. 1986. The author and compiler of guo yu. *Studies in Chinese Classics*.

Taiyan Zhang. 1982. Article on "qiuming" in volume one of *Reading of Zuo Zhuan of Spring and Autumn Annals*. In Yihua Jiang, editor, *The Complete Works of Zhang Taiyan (Volume 2)*, pages 58–59. Shanghai People's Publishing House.

Xin-Cheng Zhang. 1939. *General Examination of Forged Books, Vol. 1 (Wei Shu Tong Kao, Vol. 1)*, volume 1 of *Studies in Chinese Forgery*. Commercial Press, Shanghai.

Ying Zhao and Justin Zobel. 2007. Searching with style: Authorship attribution in classic literature. In *Proceedings of the 30th Australasian Conference on Computer Science*, ACSC '07, pages 59–68, Ballarat, Australia. Australian Computer Society.

## A Appendix

### A.1 Corpus Classification

#### The *Zuo Commentary*

Duke Yin 隱, Duke Huan 桓, Duke Zhuang 莊, Duke Min 閔, Duke Xi 僖, Duke Wen 文, Duke Xuan 宣, Duke Cheng 成, Duke Xiang 襄, Duke Zhao 昭, Duke Ding 定, Duke Ai 哀.

#### The *Discourses of the States*

the Discourse of Zhou 1 - 3 周語, the Discourse of Lu 1 and 2 魯語, the Discourse of Qi 齊語, the Discourse of Jin 1 - 9 晉語, the Discourse of Zheng 鄭語, the Discourse of Chu 1 and 2 楚語, the Discourse of Wu 吳語, the Discourse of Yue 1 and 2 越語.

### A.2 Selection of n (Example)

| Text Pair | Statistic | p-value |
|---|---|---|
| Xi & Ai | 1.4920 | 0.1373 |
| Xi & Ding | 7.6496 | 4.77E-12 |
| Xi & Xuan | 7.2402 | 3.02E-11 |
| Xi & Zhuang | 10.0681 | 2.28E-18 |
| Xi & Cheng | 1.4624 | 0.1452 |
| Xi & Wen | 6.7607 | 3.27E-10 |

Table 1: Results of 2-grams on Different Chapters

| Text Pair | Statistic | p-value |
|---|---|---|
| Xi & Ai | 2.7994 | 0.00565 |
| Xi & Ding | 6.2389 | 4.19E-09 |
| Xi & Xuan | 6.4660 | 1.28E-09 |
| Xi & Zhuang | 7.8409 | 3.39E-13 |
| Xi & Cheng | 1.7063 | 0.0896 |
| Xi & Wen | 6.3221 | 2.60E-09 |

Table 2: Results of 3-grams on Different Chaptsers

| Text Pair | Statistic | p-value |
|---|---|---|
| Xi & Ai | 4.3110 | 2.58E-05 |
| Xi & Ding | 7.8073 | 3.69E-13 |
| Xi & Xuan | 8.0324 | 8.73E-14 |
| Xi & Zhuang | 13.6326 | 4.74E-30 |
| Xi & Cheng | 0.2850 | 0.775972457 |
| Xi & Wen | 5.9907 | 1.06E-08 |

Table 3: Results of 4-grams on Different Chapters

### A.3 POS 4-grams Statistics (Example)

| POS 4-grams | Count |
|---|---|
| nt_nt_wp_nh | 8 |
| nt_wp_d_v | 4 |
| wp_d_v_n | 18 |
| d_v_n_wp | 24 |
| v_n_wp_v | 26 |
| n_wp_v_u | 8 |
| wp_v_u_wp | 5 |
| v_u_wp_nt | 5 |
| u_wp_nt_wp | 9 |
| wp_nt_wp_n | 18 |

Table 4: POS 4-grams statistics for Lord Yin

### A.4 Function Words Categories

| Tag | Description | Example |
|---|---|---|
| a | adjective | 幽明 |
| b | other noun - modifier | 男，女 |
| c | conjunction | 與，而 |
| d | adverb | 皆 |
| e | exclamation | 嗚呼 |
| g | morpheme | 甥 |
| h | prefix | 非 |
| i | idiom | 發憤忘食 |
| j | abbreviation | 五帝 |
| k | suffix | 者 |
| m | number | 一，百 |
| n | general noun | 鬼神，山川 |
| nd | direction noun | 東，南 |
| nh | person name | 軒轅 |
| ni | organization name | 遼隊 |
| nl | location noun | 城北 |
| ns | geographical name | 襄平縣 |
| nt | temporal noun | 春，夏 |
| nz | other proper noun | 山海經 |
| o | onomatopoeia | 嗚嗚 |
| p | preposition | 以，為 |
| q | quantity | 年，歲 |
| r | pronoun | 其，斯 |
| u | auxiliary | 之，所 |
| v | verb | 賜 |
| wp | punctuation | ，。！ |
| ws | foreign words | CPU |
| x | non - lexeme | 萄, 翱 |
| z | descriptive words | 默然，區區 |

Table 5: Function Words Categories

### A.5 Function Words Statistics (Example)

| Word | PoS | Count | Unary Probability |
|---|---|---|---|
| 之 | u | 119 | 0.030861 |
| 以 | p | 97 | 0.025156 |
| 不 | d | 94 | 0.024378 |
| 之 | r | 71 | 0.018413 |
| 其 | r | 69 | 0.017894 |
| 而 | c | 66 | 0.017116 |
| 也 | u | 61 | 0.015820 |
| 于 | p | 53 | 0.013745 |

Table 6: Function Words in Chu-1

### A.6 KL Divergence Statistics (Example)

| Comparison | KL Divergence |
|---|---|
| Yin & Ai | 0.4561 |
| Yin & Cheng | 0.4393 |
| Yin & Ding | 0.5129 |
| Yin & Huan | 0.6547 |
| Yin & Min | 1.5357 |
| Yin & Wen | 0.3379 |
| Yin & Xi | 0.2747 |
| Yin & Xiang | 0.2994 |
| Yin & Xuan | 0.2358 |
| Yin & Zhao | 0.3308 |
| Yin & Zhuang | 0.5614 |

Table 7: KL Divergence for Lord Yin

# Overview of EvaHan2025: The First International Evaluation on Ancient Chinese Named Entity Recognition

**Bin Li[1,2✉], Bolin Chang[1,2], Ruilin Liu[3], Xue Zhao[3], Si Shen[4], Lihong Liu[5], Yan Zhu[5], Zhixing Xu[1,2], Weiguang Qu[6,2], Dongbo Wang[3,2]**

[1]School of Chinese Language and Literature, Nanjing Normal University, China,
[2]Center for Language Big Data and Computational Humanities, Nanjing Normal University, China,
[3]College of Information Management, Nanjing Agricultural University, China,
[4]School of Economics and Management, Nanjing University of Science and Technology, China,
[5]Institute of Information on Traditional Chinese Medicine, China Academy of Chinese Medical Science, China,
[6]School of Computer and Electronic Information, Nanjing Normal University, China

**Correspondence:** libin.njnu@gmail.com

## Abstract

Ancient Chinese books have great values in history and cultural studies. Named entities like person, location, time are crucial elements, thus automatic Named Entity Recognition (NER) is considered a basic task in ancient Chinese text processing. This paper introduces EvaHan2025, the first international ancient Chinese Named Entity Recognition bake-off. The evaluation introduces a rigorous benchmark for assessing NER performance across historical and medical texts, covering 12 named entity types. A total of 13 teams participated in the competition, submitting 77 system runs. In the closed modality, where participants were restricted to using only the training data, the highest F1 scores were 85.04% on *TestA* and 90.28% on *TestB*, both derived from historical texts, compared to 84.49% on medical texts (*TestC*). The results indicate that text genre significantly impacts model performance, with historical texts generally yielding higher scores. Additionally, the intrinsic characteristics of named entities also influence recognition performance. It remains challenging to further enhance model recognition performance and to effectively integrate entities from different annotation schemes into a unified system.

## 1 Introduction

The EvaHan series represents an international endeavor focusing on the advancement of information processing for ancient Chinese texts. In 2022, EvaHan was convened in Marseille, France, where it conducted evaluations on word segmentation and part-of-speech tagging in ancient Chinese, contributing to the field' s fundamental tasks (Li et al., 2022). The following year, the series moved to Macao, China, extending its scope to include evaluations on ancient Chinese machine translation, a significant step in computational linguistics for historical languages (Wang et al., 2023). The following year 2024, the series moved to Turin, Italy, extending its scope to include evaluations on ancient Chinese sentence segmentation and punctuation, aiming to address a critical and yet under-explored area in the processing of classical texts (Li et al., 2024). In 2025, EvaHan is set to pioneer a new frontier with its first campaign specifically devoted to the evaluation of ancient Chinese named entity recognition, aiming to enhance the identification and categorization of proper names, places, and temporal expressions in historical and medical texts, thereby fostering deeper insights into ancient Chinese text analysis.

Named Entity Recognition (NER) is a fundamental task in natural language processing that involves identifying and classifying entities (Rau, 1991). NER plays a crucial role in ancient Chinese natural language processing (NLP), facilitating the structuring and analysis of historical texts (Zhang and Yang, 2018; Li Dongmei et al., 2022). Consequently, accurate named entity recognition is essential for various downstream applications, including historical knowledge extraction, document retrieval, and the construction of large-scale historical knowledge graphs (Goyal et al., 2018; Liu Liu and Wang Dongbo, 2018). However, unlike English, ancient Chinese texts lack ex-



*Proceedings of the Second Ancient Language Processing Workshop associated with NAACL 2025*, pages 97–105
May 4, 2025. 

plicit word boundaries. Different from modern Chinese, ancient Chinese texts use traditional characters with a significantly larger set of characters. Additionally, the vocabulary and grammar of ancient Chinese differ from those of modern Chinese, further complicating tasks such as Named Entity Recognition (NER) and making it a particularly challenging endeavor.

The existing studies on ancient Chinese NER face several issues and challenges. First, the ancient Chinese NER mainly focused on historical texts, other types of texts are not well considered. Second, different corpora have different types of named entities. For example, historical texts include persons, locations and temporal expressions, while the medical texts have more entities like illness, cures, and formula. Third, annotation guidelines and tag set are different caused by different system developers. There is not a full named entity hierarchy for ancient Chinese. Each corpus only focus on its own interest. Thus, it is difficult to construct a wide-coverage NER system. Forth, the evaluation of ancient Chinese NER is not well set yet. The basic unit for calculation of Precision and Recall rate to be a character or an entity is still a problem, thus making it hard to compare the performances of different NER systems.

EvaHan2025 is designed as a comprehensive evaluation benchmark to address these issues. The evaluation aims to answer four key questions:

(1) How do different types of ancient Chinese texts influence NER performance?

(2) Is it possible to build an integrated system capable of handling multiple text types and multiple entity categories?

(3) Can large language models effectively generalize across different classical Chinese domains?

(4) How can we ensure a fair and unbiased evaluation, given that many pretraining corpora contain historical texts?

EvaHan2025 collects a dataset of 12 types of named entities from history and medical texts, which is designed to test the NER systems' performance on different genres and entities. And the basic unit for evaluation is the whole named entity, not the character. Considering the fast development of large language models (LLMs) , we encourage the participants to use LLMs as well as traditional models.

| Entity | Meaning | Example | Dataset |
|---|---|---|---|
| NR | Person Name | 蘇秦 | A B |
| NS | Geographical Location | 長平 | A B |
| NB | Book Title | 易 | A |
| NO | Official Title | 中大夫 | A |
| NG | Country Name | 秦 | A |
| T | Time Expression | 三十四年 | A B |
| ZD | Traditional Chinese Medicine Disease | 金疮 | C |
| ZZ | Syndrome | 脾胃虚弱 | C |
| ZF | Chinese Medicinal Formula | 当归散 | C |
| ZP | Decoction Pieces | 当归 | C |
| ZS | Symptom | 烦满 | C |
| ZA | Acupoint | 承扶 | C |

Table 1: 6 Entities involved in the evaluation

EvaHan2025 is proposed as part of the The Second Workshop on Ancient Languages Processing, co-located with The 2025 Annual Conference of the North American Chapter of the Association for Computational Linguistics. The benchmark, scoring methodology, and detailed annotation guidelines are publicly available in our GitHub repository[1], providing an open and transparent evaluation framework for the research community.

## 2 Task

In the EvaHan2025 evaluation task, participants are required to develop systems that automatically identify and label named entities within ancient Chinese texts, transforming raw unstructured text into structured data with entity annotations.

The evaluation focuses on 12 distinct types of named entities, covering key categories relevant to both historical texts and traditional Chinese medicine texts. Table 1 lists 12 entity types, including Person Name (NR), Geographical Location (NS), etc. Systems are assessed based on their ability to accurately detect entity boundaries and correctly classify entity types.

## 3 Dataset

Ancient Chinese texts, covering both historical records and Traditional Chinese Medicine literature. All the data has been annotated and proofread by experts of ancient Chinese language.

### 3.1 Data Source

The EvaHan2025 dataset is designed to evaluate NER performance in ancient Chinese

[1]https://github.com/GoThereGit/EvaHan

| Datasets | Genre | #Char Tokens | #Entity Tokens |
|---|---|---|---|
| A | History | 178167 | 19070 |
| B | History | 115090 | 11931 |
| C | Medicine | 151703 | 11967 |

Table 2: Size of each dataset

texts, covering both historical records and Traditional Chinese Medicine (TCM) literature. The dataset consists of three subsets (A, B, C), each sourced from distinct domains.

DatasetA is made of historical texts extracted from *Shiji*(史記)[2], with 6 types of named entities, developed by Nanjing Normal University.

DatasetB is also historical text extracted from *Twenty-Four Histories*(二十四史)[3], with 3 types of named entities, developed by Nanjing Agriculture University.

DatasetC is extracted from classical Traditional Chinese Medicine (TCM) texts, including TCM ancitent books such as *Liu Juanzi Guiyi Fang* (劉涓子鬼遺方)[4]. It has 6 types of entities, annotated by institute of information on traditional Chinese medicine.

Table 2 presents the size of each dataset, where Dataset A is the largest, while Dataset B is the smallest.

### 3.2 Data Format

All datasets are provided in plain text format, encoded in UTF-8, and include characters, punctuation marks, and a dual-layer entity annotation scheme. This dual-layer annotation structure encodes two crucial types of information: position information to indicate a character' s placement within an entity and entity type to specify its semantic category. To represent position information, the dataset employs the BMES (Beginning, Middle, End, Single) tagging scheme, which is widely used for sequence labeling tasks. In this scheme, the B (Beginning) tag marks the first character of a multi-character entity, the M (Middle) tag is assigned to characters occurring within the entity, the E (End) tag denotes the final character, and the S (Single) tag is used for entities that consist of only a single character.

[2]Also known as *Records of the Grand Historian*, https://en.wikipedia.org/wiki/Shiji

[3]https://en.wikipedia.org/wiki/Twenty-Four_Histories

[4]https://en.wikipedia.org/wiki/Liu_Juanzi_Guiyi_Fang

By utilizing this structured annotation method, the dataset provides a clear and systematic framework for entity recognition, allowing models to effectively learn both entity boundaries and entity types.

### 3.3 Training Data

The training set comprises 80% of the total dataset, ensuring sufficient data for model learning.

### 3.4 Test Data

The test data, comprising 20% of each dataset, serves as a benchmark for evaluating system performance in NER on ancient Chinese texts. Like the training data, the test sets contain annotated entities, but they were not accessible to participants during model training, ensuring an unbiased evaluation.

Given that Datasets A and B belong to the historical text category, they provide a strong basis for assessing system performance on historical texts. In contrast, Dataset C, sourced from Traditional Chinese Medicine texts, allows for a dedicated evaluation of NER models in medical literature, which poses distinct challenges due to its specialized terminology and unique linguistic structures.

Historical texts are commonly used in ancient Chinese NER tasks and constitute a major portion of the pretraining corpora for ancient Chinese large language models. As a result, entity recognition in historical texts is typically less challenging, and models tend to achieve higher accuracy on such data.

To rigorously assess NER capabilities in historical texts, Dataset A and Dataset B are deliberately distinguished despite both belonging to the same genre. Dataset B, sourced from *The Twenty-Four Histories*, includes only three entity types, offering a comparatively simpler entity distribution. In contrast, Dataset A, contains six types of named entities, making it richer and more complex in annotation. This differentiation increases annotation complexity and introduces a higher degree of difficulty in recognizing named entities, thereby enhancing the evaluation depth of the benchmark. This distinction ensures a more precise measurement of model performance and highlights potential areas for improvement in the recognition of historical named entities.

| Limits | Closed Modality | Open Modality |
|---|---|---|
| Machine learning algorithm | No limit | No limit |
| Pretrained model | Only *GujiRoBERTa_jian_fan* | No limit |
| Training data | Only Train | No limit |
| Features used | Only from Train | No limit |
| Manual correction | Not allowed | Not allowed |

Table 3: Limitations on the two modalities

## 4 Evaluation

Initially, each team could only access the training data. Later, the unlabeled test data was released. After the submission, the labels for the test data were also released.

### 4.1 Scoring

The scorer employed for EvaHan is a modified version of the one developed from SIGHAN2008 (Jin and Chen, 2008). The evaluation aligned the system-produced sentences to the gold standard ones. Then, the performance of NER were evaluated by precision, recall and F1 score. In the scoring process, we assess the correctness of entities directly, rather than Chinese characters as done in previous researches. The final ranking was based on F1 score of NER.

### 4.2 Two Modalities

Each participant can submit runs following two modalities. In the closed modality, the resources each team could use are limited. Each team can only use the Training data, and *GujiRoBERTa_jian_fan*[5], a large language model pretrained on a very large corpus of traditional Chinese collection, including *Siku Quanshu* (四庫全書)[6] and *Daizhige* (殆知閣)[7]. Other resources are not allowed in the closed modality.

In the open modality, there is no limit on the resources, data and models. Annotated external data, such as the components or Pinyin of the Chinese characters, word embeddings can be employed, as shown in Table 3. But each team has to state all the resources, data and models they use in each system in the final report.

[5]https://huggingface.co/hsc748NLP/GujiRoBERTa_jian_fan

[6]https://en.wikipedia.org/wiki/Siku_Quanshu

[7]https://github.com/up2hub/daizhige

### 4.3 Procedure

Training data was released for download from January 15, 2025. Test data was released on February 15, 2025, and results were due on 00:00 (UTC) February 21, 2025.

## 5 Participants and Results

### 5.1 Participants

A total of 23 teams registered for the task, and 13 of them submitted 77 running results. Table 4 presents the details of the participating teams. Submissions were primarily concentrated in the closed modality, while there were relatively fewer submissions in the open modality. It is important to mention that lots of submissions were initially presented in incorrect formats. It is caused by the over-generation of large language models. These errors were subsequently rectified automatically to facilitate accurate evaluation.

### 5.2 Results

Tables from 5 and 8 list the performance of the participating teams, arranged in descending order of the F1 scores. The Precision, Recall and F1 score for Named Entity Recognition are abbreviated as P, R and F. We classified the submissions into four categories: *TestA* and *TestB* Closed, *TestA* and *TestB* Open, *TestC* Closed, and *TestC* Open. This distinction was made because *TestA* and *TestB* consist of historical texts, whereas *TestC* is derived from Traditional Chinese Medicine texts, allowing for a comparative evaluation of NER performance across different domains. Most teams participated in the closed tests.

The highest F1 scores on *TestA* and *TestB* are 85.04% and 90.28% in the closed modality. In the open modality, they are 84.11% and 89.64%.

Since *TestA* contains a greater variety of entity categories compared to *TestB*, the performance on *TestA* is generally lower than on *TestB*. For instance, NJU achieved 88.97% and 89.64% in the closed and open modalities, respectively, on *TestB*. However, on *TestA*, NJU' s scores dropped to 83.02% and 84.11% in the closed and open modalities, respectively, reflecting a nearly 5 points decrease compared to *TestB*.

| ID | Name | Affiliation | Close | Open |
|---|---|---|---|---|
| 1 | BUPT | Beijing University of Posts and Telecommunications | 5 | 0 |
| 2 | ECNU | East China Normal University | 0 | 2 |
| 3 | EPHE | École pratique des hautes études | 0 | 1 |
| 4 | HUST | Huazhong University of Science and Technology | 0 | 3 |
| 5 | NFU1 | Northeast Forestry University | 1 | 0 |
| 6 | NFU2 | Northeast Forestry University | 3 | 0 |
| 7 | NJU | Nanjing University | 0 | 0 |
| 8 | RUC | Renmin University of China, Midu Technology Co., Ltd. | 15 | 18 |
| 9 | SXU | Shanxi University | 4 | 0 |
| 10 | TJU | Tongji University | 4 | 0 |
| 11 | UM | University of Macau | 5 | 0 |
| 12 | UT | University of Toronto | 5 | 1 |
| 13 | WHU | Wuhan University | 4 | 0 |

Table 4: Participating teams by modality

| Team | TestA | | | TestB | | |
|---|---|---|---|---|---|---|
| | P | R | F | P | R | F |
| RUC | 88.97 | 81.45 | 85.04 | 90.22 | 90.34 | 90.28 |
| WHU | 87.23 | 80.65 | 83.81 | 89.47 | 89.92 | 89.70 |
| NJU | 86.64 | 79.69 | 83.02 | 88.73 | 89.21 | 88.97 |
| SXU | 86.30 | 78.78 | 82.37 | 87.43 | 90.09 | 88.74 |
| UT | 86.42 | 76.54 | 81.18 | 89.80 | 87.59 | 88.68 |
| NFU1 | 90.77 | 76.75 | 83.17 | 88.42 | 88.75 | 88.59 |
| BUPT | 88.16 | 76.38 | 81.84 | 86.87 | 90.09 | 88.45 |
| NFU2 | 89.13 | 79.32 | 83.94 | 89.34 | 87.30 | 88.31 |
| UM | 84.42 | 73.86 | 78.79 | 86.65 | 85.71 | 86.18 |
| TJU | 65.89 | 70.92 | 68.31 | 70.11 | 71.14 | 70.62 |

Table 5: Results on TestA and TestB in closed modality (%)

| Team | TestA | | | TestB | | |
|---|---|---|---|---|---|---|
| | P | R | F | P | R | F |
| NJU | 88.07 | 80.49 | 84.11 | 90.11 | 89.17 | 89.64 |
| UT | 86.12 | 76.91 | 81.25 | 86.28 | 89.05 | 87.64 |
| ECNU | 83.46 | 75.52 | 79.29 | 89.41 | 85.09 | 87.20 |
| HUST | 83.68 | 73.70 | 78.37 | 88.44 | 84.09 | 86.21 |
| RUC | 73.14 | 84.13 | 78.25 | 82.41 | 82.17 | 82.29 |
| EPHE | 82.16 | 78.51 | 80.30 | 61.29 | 71.80 | 66.13 |

Table 6: Results on TestA and TestB in open modality (%)

| Team | P | R | F |
|---|---|---|---|
| RUC | 81.33 | 87.91 | 84.49 |
| UT | 82.26 | 84.32 | 83.28 |
| NFU2 | 78.37 | 86.32 | 82.15 |
| NJU | 77.63 | 86.14 | 81.66 |
| WHU | 76.52 | 86.82 | 81.35 |
| NFU1 | 75.58 | 87.36 | 81.05 |
| SXU | 75.91 | 86.09 | 80.68 |
| BUPT | 75.57 | 85.50 | 80.23 |
| UM | 70.33 | 83.09 | 76.18 |
| TJU | 44.04 | 56.77 | 49.60 |

Table 7: Results on TestC in closed modality (%)

| Team | P | R | F |
|---|---|---|---|
| NJU | 78.33 | 86.77 | 82.34 |
| RUC | 73.99 | 88.82 | 80.73 |
| UT | 75.35 | 84.05 | 79.46 |
| HUST | 71.32 | 84.32 | 77.28 |
| ECNU | 82.19 | 69.23 | 75.15 |
| EPHE | 46.85 | 59.18 | 52.30 |

Table 8: Results on TestC in open modality (%)

For *TestC*, which derived from the less common domain of Traditional Chinese Medicine texts, the scores were approximately 6 points lower than those on *TestB*. The highest F1 score of *TestC* is 84.49% in the closed modality. In the open modality, it is 82.34%.

### 5.3 Baselines

To provide a basis for comparison, we computed the baseline scores for each of the test sets. The baseline for ancient Chinese

| Test Set | P | R | F |
|---|---|---|---|
| TestA | 85.90 | 77.50 | 81.48 |
| TestB | 87.09 | 87.92 | 87.50 |
| TestC | 71.84 | 72.95 | 72.40 |

Table 9: Baselines (%)

| Test Set | P | R | F |
|---|---|---|---|
| TestA | 88.97(+3.07) | 81.45(+3.96) | 85.04(+3.56) |
| TestB | 90.22(+3.14) | 90.34(+2.42) | 90.28(+2.78) |
| TestC | 81.33(+9.48) | 87.91(+14.95) | 84.49(+12.1) |

Table 10: The improvement of the best system with respect to the baseline (%)

named entity recognition was constructed using SikuRoBERTa-BiLSTM-CRF model, as shown in Table 9.

The scores of most teams exceed the baselines. The best scores from RUC outperform the baselines by around 10 points as shown in Table 10.

## 6 Error Analysis and Discussion

By analyzing the errors in the participating teams' systems, we can further discuss aspects related to the dataset, entity types, and large language models.

### 6.1 Unbalanced training samples

Based on the scores of each team across the three test sets, as shown in Tables 11 to 12, it is evident that most teams performed best on *TestB*, followed by *TestA*, while performance on *TestC* was significantly lower. This trend can be attributed to two key factors.

Firstly, while both *TestA* and *TestB* belong to the historical text category and have similar training set sizes, they differ in entity complexity. *TestB* contains only three entity types: *NR*, *NS*, and *T*, whereas *TestA* includes these three as well as three additional categories: *NO*, *NB*, and *NG*. The inclusion of these extra entity types increases the difficulty of entity recognition.

Secondly, unlike *TestA* and *TestB*, which originate from historical texts, *TestC* is sourced from Traditional Chinese Medicine literature, presenting a distinct linguistic challenge. The GujiRoBERTa model used in this evaluation was pretrained primarily on historical texts, as such texts are more commonly available. In contrast, TCM texts are relatively rare in pretraining corpora, resulting in weaker model performance on entity recognition in TCM texts compared to historical texts. This finding underscores the critical role of pretraining in large language models —a broader and more diverse pretraining corpus can significantly improve model robustness across different text domains in downstream tasks. Expanding the variety of pretraining data could enhance the model' s ability to adapt to diverse text types, leading to more consistent performance across different genres.

### 6.2 Entities of different datasets

Table 11 lists the quantity of annotations and corresponding scores for different entities predicted by the highest-scoring system in close modality submissions by RUC. Table 11 presents the evaluation results obtained by merging *TestA*, *TestB*, and *TestC* into a combined test set, *TestTotal*. In Table 11, *TrainTotal (Total)* means the number of gold entities in train data, *TestTotal (Gold)* means the number of gold entities in *Test Total*. *Machine (Total)* means the total number of entities tagged by the RUC' s system running on Test sets. *Machine (Correct)* means the number of correct entities tagged by RUC' s system. It is evident that *T* exhibits the highest performance, while *NB* less satisfactorily. There are two main issues with the system' s performance in NER.

Firstly, the system's performance in entity recognition is closely correlated with the frequency of entities in the training data. According to Table 11, entities with higher scores, such as *NR* and *ZP*, which achieved 90.67% and 90.24%, respectively, also appear more frequently in the training set, with occurrences of 12,968 and 4,983, respectively. Conversely, entities that are less frequent in the training data tend to have lower recognition accuracy. For example, the *NB* entity appears only 61 times in the training set, making it significantly underrepresented. As a result, the model struggles to effectively learn its patterns, leading to a much lower performance, with a score of only 50%.

Secondly, the system' s entity recognition performance is also influenced by the intrinsic characteristics of the entities themselves,

| Entity | P (%) | R (%) | F (%) | Train (Total) | Test (Gold) | Machine (Correct) | Machine (Total) |
|---|---|---|---|---|---|---|---|
| T | 91.37 | 90.68 | 91.02 | 3,452 | 1,062 | 963 | 1,054 |
| NR | 92.87 | 88.58 | 90.67 | 12,968 | 1,734 | 1,536 | 1,654 |
| ZP | 86.20 | 94.68 | 90.24 | 4,983 | 1,128 | 1,068 | 1,239 |
| ZF | 86.85 | 90.08 | 88.44 | 1,073 | 242 | 218 | 251 |
| ZA | 89.55 | 85.38 | 87.41 | 1,111 | 301 | 257 | 287 |
| NS | 84.49 | 83.36 | 83.92 | 5,550 | 1,124 | 937 | 1,109 |
| NO | 90.14 | 77.11 | 83.12 | 1,318 | 249 | 192 | 213 |
| ZZ | 64.77 | 82.61 | 72.61 | 536 | 69 | 57 | 88 |
| ZD | 63.69 | 79.72 | 70.81 | 640 | 143 | 114 | 179 |
| NG | 74.12 | 64.95 | 69.23 | 3,380 | 97 | 63 | 85 |
| ZS | 65.87 | 69.40 | 67.59 | 1,424 | 317 | 220 | 334 |
| NB | 100.00 | 33.33 | 50.00 | 61 | 6 | 2 | 2 |

Table 11: NER scores by RUC

which can either simplify or complicate the learning process. Even if an entity type is not highly frequent in the training set, its score may still be relatively high if it exhibits consistent and structured patterns. For instance, the *T* entity appears only 3,452 times in the training set but achieves a remarkably high score of 91.02%, the highest among all entity types. This is because *T* entities, unlike other entity categories, typically follow limited and highly regular forms, making them easier for models to learn. Examples include 今 (today), 冬 (winter), and 十年 (a decade).

Additionally, the *ZA* entity, despite being relatively infrequent in the training data, also achieves a high recognition score. This can be attributed to the fact that many instances of *ZA* entities appear in continuous sequences within the training data, and these sequences tend to have fixed-length structures, making them easier for models to identify. For example, in the phrase:

"循 [商阳/ZA][二间/ZA][三间/ZA] 而行，历 [合谷/ZA][阳溪/ZA] 之俞，过 [偏历/ZA][温溜/ZA] 之滨，[下廉/ZA][上廉/ZA]"

the *ZA* entities appear in a structured, repetitive format, allowing the model to recognition them with greater ease, leading to higher accuracy scores.

### 6.3 Character Discrepancies Due to Large Language Models

Large language models, particularly generative models, often alter the original text during prompt engineering, automatically adding, removing, or modifying Chinese characters. This leads to inconsistencies between the generated output and the original text, posing challenges for maintaining textual fidelity.

In EvaHan2024, numerous instances of such discrepancies were observed, where the model, while performing punctuation restoration, simultaneously modified the original sentence, resulting in unintended textual differences (Jin and Chen, 2008). This issue has persisted in the current evaluation, indicating that further attention is required in analyzing model outputs. To ensure that the generated results remain faithful to the original text, post-processing mechanisms should be incorporated into the workflow. Such mechanisms would help correct unintended modifications and restore textual accuracy, ensuring greater consistency between the model's output and the original input.

In this evaluation, most teams encountered issues with character omission and redundancy. The majority of differences of Chinese characters between the submitted results and the test set are around 1% to 2%, with the largest deviation reaching 8%. Although algorithms were employed in this evaluation to rectify the problems of character omission and redundancy in the submissions, teams still struggled to achieve high scores. Hence, to solve the issues of character omission and addition over-generated by large language models, post-processing is needed for the text consistancy. Another way is to constrain the generated characters during model output generation to maintain consistency with the original text.

### 6.4 Teams' Approaches

In this evaluation, several teams adopted unique approaches to address the challenges of ancient Chinese NER, achieving notable improvements. Among them, the RUC team, which achieved the highest performance in this assessment, employed a combination of the GujiRoBERTa pre-trained model and the W2NER word-pair relation prediction framework. By leveraging BiLSTM and convolutional layers for feature extraction, along with five-fold cross-validation and ensemble learning, they significantly enhanced the effectiveness of ancient Chinese NER. Their method demonstrated outstanding results on the EvaHan2025 dataset, as shown in Table 9.

Looking at the overall evaluation results, most teams outperformed the baseline model. A comparative analysis reveals that, in addition to the adoption of innovative algorithms by some teams, the primary factor contributing to the improvement is the superior performance of GujiRoBERTa over SikuRoBERTa, which was used in this evaluation.

Moreover, some teams used prompt engineering techniques of large language models. However, these methods yielded limited improvements in performance and resulted in greater modifications to the original text, making them less effective for this task.

## 7 Conclusions

EvaHan2025 focuses on Named Entity Recognition in Ancient Chinese texts, covering two distinct categories of documents and presenting a significant challenge. Despite the complexity, most participating teams successfully completed the task. In terms of performance across different text types, teams generally performed better on historical texts, while their results on medical texts were comparatively lower, though still surpassing the baseline model.

From a methodological perspective, the majority of teams trained three separate models for each test set, achieving commendable results. However, no team has yet proposed a comprehensive, unified model capable of handling all 12 categories of named entities effectively. Additionally, a comparison of different implementation strategies reveals that prompt engineering based on large language models has shown limited effectiveness, often leading to undesirable modifications to the original text.

In the future, we encourage teams to explore deeper and more innovative approaches. Whether through small, domain-adaptive models or comprehensive frameworks leveraging large language models, we hope to see more efficient and accurate NER solutions for ancient Chinese, ultimately enabling high-performance, integrated recognition of diverse named entities across multiple categories. With the achievements of this shared task, we will move forward to the named entity relation recognition, named entity linking and related tasks in the coming years.

## Acknowledgments

Thank the reviewers for their advices. Thank Yuyun Pan, Mengting Xu and Ye Gao for their data annotation and checking. This research was supported by General Program of the Ministry of Education of China Humanities and Social Sciences Fund (24A10319028), National Social Science Funds of China (21&ZD331) and Beijing Natural Science Foundation (7252253).

## References

Archana Goyal, Vishal Gupta, and Manish Kumar. 2018. Recent named entity recognition and classification techniques: A systematic review. *Computer Science Review*, 29:21–43.

Guangjin Jin and Xiao Chen. 2008. The fourth international Chinese language processing bakeoff: Chinese word segmentation, named entity recognition and Chinese POS tagging. In *Proceedings of the Sixth SIGHAN Workshop on Chinese Language Processing*.

Bin Li, Bolin Chang, Zhixing Xu, Minxuan Feng, Chao Xu, Weiguang Qu, Si Shen, and Dongbo Wang. 2024. Overview of EvaHan2024: The first international evaluation on Ancient Chinese sentence segmentation and punctuation. In *Proceedings of the Third Workshop on Language Technologies for Historical and Ancient Languages (LT4HALA) @ LREC-COLING-2024*, pages 229–236, Torino, Italia. ELRA and ICCL.

Bin Li, Yiguo Yuan, Jingya Lu, Minxuan Feng, Chao Xu, Weiguang Qu, and Dongbo Wang. 2022. The first international Ancient Chinese word segmentation and POS tagging bakeoff: Overview of the EvaHan 2022 evaluation campaign. In *Proceedings of the Second Workshop on Language Technologies for Historical and Ancient Languages*, pages 135–140, Marseille, France. European Language Resources Association.

Li Dongmei, Luo Sisi, Zhang Xiaoping, and Xu Fu. 2022. Review on named entity recognition. *Journal of Frontiers of Computer Science & Technology*, 16(9):1954–1968.

Liu Liu and Wang Dongbo. 2018. A review on named entity recognition. *Journal of the China Society for Scientific and Technical Information*, 37(3):329–340.

L.F. Rau. 1991. Extracting company names from text. In *Proceedings. The Seventh IEEE Conference on Artificial Intelligence Application*, pages 29–32.

Dongbo Wang, Litao Lin, Zhixiao Zhao, Wenhao Ye, Kai Meng, Wenlong Sun, Lianzhen Zhao, Xue Zhao, Si Shen, Wei Zhang, and Bin Li. 2023. EvaHan2023: Overview of the first international Ancient Chinese translation bakeoff. In *Proceedings of ALT2023: Ancient Language Translation Workshop*, pages 1–14, Macau SAR, China. Asia-Pacific Association for Machine Translation.

Yue Zhang and Jie Yang. 2018. Chinese NER using lattice LSTM. In *Proceedings of the 56th Annual Meeting of the Association for Computational Linguistics (Volume 1: Long Papers)*, pages 1554–1564, Melbourne, Australia. Association for Computational Linguistics.

# Exploring the Application of 7B LLMs for Named Entity Recognition in Chinese Ancient Texts

**Chenrui Zheng**[1], **Yicheng Zhu**[1], **Han Bi**[2]
[1]East China Normal University，[2]Shandong Second Medical University
{10194800486,10210110437}@stu.ecnu.edu.cn,
2336007835@qq.com

## Abstract

This paper explores the application of fine-tuning methods based on 7B large language models (LLMs) for named entity recognition (NER) tasks in Chinese ancient texts. Targeting the complex semantics and domain-specific characteristics of ancient texts, particularly in Traditional Chinese Medicine (TCM) texts, we propose a comprehensive fine-tuning and pre-training strategy. By introducing multi-task learning, domain-specific pre-training, and efficient fine-tuning techniques based on LoRA, we achieved significant performance improvements in ancient text NER tasks. Experimental results show that the pre-trained and fine-tuned 7B model achieved an F1 score of 0.93, significantly outperforming general-purpose large language models.

## 1. Introduction

Named Entity Recognition (NER) is a foundational task in natural language processing (NLP) that involves identifying and categorizing entities, such as person names, locations, organizations, and temporal expressions—within unstructured text. Since its inception in the 1990s (Nadeau and Sekine, 2007), NER has evolved significantly, transitioning from rule-based systems to machine learning approaches, and more recently, to deep learning architectures like Bidirectional Long Short-Term Memory networks (Hochreiter and Schmidhuber, 1997) and transformer-based models (Devlin et al., 2019). These advancements have enabled robust performance in modern languages, particularly with the advent of pre-trained language models (e.g., BERT) that capture contextualized representations.

However, applying NER to ancient Chinese texts presents unique challenges. Ancient Chinese, characterized by archaic vocabulary, flexible grammar, and extensive use of homophones, diverges substantially from modern Mandarin. Additionally, historical texts often lack standardized punctuation and contain domain-specific terminology (e.g., official titles in dynastic records or disease names in medical classics), complicating entity boundaries and classification. Furthermore, annotated resources for ancient Chinese are scarce compared to those for contemporary languages, limiting the scalability of data-driven approaches.

## 2. Task Description

In EvaHan2025,[1] our team participates in the open modality track, which allows unrestricted use of external resources, models, and domain-specific knowledge to enhance NER in ancient Chinese texts. The task involves identifying 12 distinct entity categories across three heterogeneous datasets: (1) Shiji（"史记"） (historical records), (2) Twenty-Four Histories ("二十四史"), and (3) Traditional Chinese Medicine Classics ("中医药典籍"). To facilitate our evaluation, we split the dataset into train, development, and test sets using an 8:1:1 ratio. Our objective is to fine-tune the model to achieve the highest possible F1 score, optimizing its performance on the given task.

## 3. Related works

In the domain of NER for ancient Chinese texts, particularly in TCM, the field has witnessed a progression through various methodological approaches. Initially, dictionary-based and rule-based pattern matching methods, such as the maximum matching algorithm (Wang Y et al.,2012), were prevalent. The advent of deep learning ushered in new approaches. For instance, Xie et al.(2022) employed Sikubert and SikuRoBERTa, demonstrating that pre-trained

[1]https://github.com/GoThereGit/EvaHan/tree/main/evahan2025



*Proceedings of the Second Ancient Language Processing Workshop associated with NAACL 2025*, pages 106–111
May 4, 2025. 

models based on ancient texts outperform generic BERT models in these specialized NER tasks.In recent years, Large Language Models (LLMs) have exhibited significant potential in NER tasks. This aligns with contemporary research on LLM applications in NER, such as the work by Raffel et al. (2020), which illustrates that models like GPT and T5, when fine-tuned for NER tasks, can achieve superior performance by leveraging their extensive pre-trained knowledge and contextual understanding.

For NER tasks involving ancient Chinese texts, the flexibility and contextual understanding inherent in LLMs render them especially suitable for addressing the intricacies of these historical documents. He Yuhao's research(2024), for instance, revealed that LLMs outperformed other deep learning models in identifying and extracting entities and relationships from "ZhonghuaYaofang" ( "中华药方"), demonstrating superior performance across precision, recall, and F1-score metrics. This growing body of evidence underscores the rationale behind the present study's objective to further explore and harness the potential of LLMs in processing NER tasks for ancient texts.

## 4. Methods

In our study, we employed a combination of SikuRoBERTa, BiLSTM, and CRF methodologies to establish a robust baseline for our NLP tasks. After conducting 20 epochs, we evaluated our model on a segmented test dataset and obtained the following results in Table 1, which serve as the foundational benchmark for our experimental analysis.

Table 1: Performance Metrics of SikuRoBERTa+BiLSTM+CRF Model on Segmented Test Dataset after 20 Epochs

| Entity Type | Accuracy | Recall | F1 | Num |
|---|---|---|---|---|
| Symptom (ZS) | 54.34% | 66.20% | 59.68% | 142 |
| Traditional Medicine Disease (ZD) | 65.22% | 68.18% | 66.67% | 66 |
| Syndrome (ZZ) | 65.31% | 69.57% | 67.37% | 46 |
| Acupoint (ZA) | 86.36% | 78.08% | 82.01% | 73 |
| Chinese Formula (ZF) | 84.55% | 90.43% | 87.39% | 115 |
| Time Expression (T) | 88.47% | 83.53% | 85.93% | 340 |
| Official Title (NO) | 77.86% | 79.56% | 78.70% | 137 |
| Geographical Location (NS) | 87.97% | 82.01% | 84.88% | 517 |
| Book Title (NB) | 100% | 80% | 88.89% | 5 |
| Decoction Pieces (ZP) | 92.60% | 93.56% | 93.08% | 388 |
| Country Name (NG) | 90.51% | 96.25% | 93.30% | 347 |
| Person Name (NR) | 93.78% | 93.38% | 93.58% | 1194 |
| Overall | 0.878 | 0.8798 | 0.8789 | 3370 |

These metrics, while commendable, revealed a notable shortcoming when applied to Task C (Precision: 82.29%,Recall: 84.37%,F1 Score: 83.33%), which involves the processing of Traditional Chinese Medicine texts. Specifically, the BERT model's accuracy was significantly lower in this context compared to its performance on other tasks. We hypothesize that this discrepancy stems from BERT's limited exposure to and familiarity with the specialized terminology and nuanced semantics inherent in TCM texts.

To address this limitation, we propose the integration of more semantically aware LLMs that are better equipped to comprehend and process the complex linguistic structures found in TCM texts. By leveraging these advanced models, we aim to enhance the accuracy and effectiveness of our NLP applications in the domain of TCM texts, thereby improving the overall performance and reliability of our system in handling specialized medical texts.

※ Prompt1：

你是一名专注于处理中医领域的文献的专家，你的任务是从我提供的中医文献原文中，直接在原文的基础上标注以下实体:<病名>、<证候>、<方剂>、<饮片>、<症状>、<穴位>。

You are an expert specializing in processing literature from the field of Traditional Chinese Medicine. Your task is to annotate the following entities directly on the original text I provide: <Traditional Medicine Disease> , <Syndrome> , <Chinese Formula>, <Decoction Pieces> , <Symptom> , <Acupoint> .

- input:一男子时疫愈后，遍身发作痒，服补中益气汤而愈。
- input: A man who had recovered from an epidemic disease later developed itching all over his body, took Buzhong Yiqi Tang and recovered.

- output:<实体标注结果>一男子<病名>时疫</病名>愈后，遍身发作痒，服<方剂>补中益气汤</方剂>而愈。</实体标注结果>
- output: <Named entity recognition results>A man who had recovered from <Traditional Medicine Disease>epidemic disease</Traditional Medicine Disease>, later developed itching all over his body, took <Chinese Formula>Buzhong Yiqi Tang</Chinese Formula> and recovered.</Named entity recognition results>

※ Prompt2：

你是一名专注于处理中医领域的文献的专家，你的任务是从我提供的中医文献原文中，直接在原文的基础上标注以下实体:{病名}、{证候}、{方剂}、{药材}、{症状}、{穴位}。

You are an expert specializing in processing literature from the field of Traditional Chinese Medicine. Your task is to annotate the following entities directly on the original text I provide: {Traditional Medicine Disease}、{Syndrome}、{Chinese Formula}、{Chinese Formula}、{Symptom}、{Acupoint}.

- input:一男子时疫愈后，遍身发作痒，服补中益气汤而愈。
- input: A man who had recovered from an epidemic disease later developed itching all over his body, took Buzhong Yiqi Tang and recovered.

- output:{实体标注结果}一男子{时疫|病名}愈后，遍身发作痒，服{补中益气汤|方剂}而愈。{实体标注结果}
- output: {Named entity recognition results}A man who had recovered from {epidemic disease|Traditional Medicine Disease}, later developed itching all over his body, took {Buzhong Yiqi Tang|Chinese Formula} and recovered.{Named entity recognition results}

Figure 1 Two distinct prompt formats

### 4.1 Prompt Engineering

To advance our research effectively, the initial step involves the meticulous determination of the prompts to be used with LLMs. This is crucial for structuring both the input and output data in a manner that aligns with our objectives. Drawing upon previous studies, we have meticulously selected two distinct prompt formats that have demonstrated efficacy in similar contexts（Figure 1）.

In our experiments, we utilized the Qwen-Plus[2] model and the Task C test dataset under a 1-shot learning setting to evaluate the performance of the two prompt formats. Our findings revealed that Prompt 2 significantly outperformed Prompt 1 in terms of accuracy（Table 2）. We hypothesize that this is because Prompt 2 provides a more structured and contextually rich input by directly incorporating the original text, which allows the model to better understand the task and generate more accurate outputs. As a result, we decided to adopt Prompt 2 for all subsequent research.

Additionally, we compared the performance of the Qwen-Plus model with the Qwen-7B model. Surprisingly, the Qwen-7B model achieved a higher F1 score than Qwen-Plus on this specific task. We speculate that this may be due to the fact that Qwen-Plus, as a more general-purpose large language model, tends to "overthink" or generalize too much, making it less adaptable to the highly specialized and domain-specific nature of the task at hand. In contrast, the smaller Qwen-7B model, with its more focused architecture, may be better suited for handling the nuances and intricacies of this particular domain. These insights highlight the importance of tailoring both the prompt design and model selection to the specific requirements of

2 https://github.com/QwenLM/Qwen

the task. Moving forward, we will continue to refine our approach by leveraging Prompt Prompt 2 and exploring the potential of smaller, more specialized models like Qwen-7B for domain-specific NLP tasks.

| Prompt | Precision | Recall | F1 Score |
|---|---|---|---|
| Prompt 1 （Qwen-Plus） | 0.7876 | 0.6729 | 0.717 |
| Prompt 2 （Qwen-Plus） | **0.8945** | **0.8398** | **0.8592** |
| Prompt 1 （Qwen-7B） | 0.8015 | 0.7574 | 0.7719 |

Table 2:difference between Prompt 1 and 2

# 5. Experiments

## 5.1 Data Transformation

To prepare the data for our experiments, we performed a series of preprocessing steps on the raw text data provided by Evahan2025. The original data was in TXT format, and our goal was to transform it into a structured format suitable for training and evaluation. The transformation process involved the following steps:

### 5.1.1 Sentence Segmentation:

We first segmented the text into sentence-level units using punctuation marks such as "。", "！", and "？". This step ensured that each sentence was treated as an independent unit for further processing.

### 5.1.2 BEMS to Prompt 2 Conversion:

The original data was annotated using the BEMS (Begin, End, Middle, Single) tagging scheme, which is commonly used for sequence labeling tasks. We converted these annotations into Prompt 2, a more structured and readable format that aligns with our prompt design. For example:

- Original Text: 一男子时疫愈后,遍身发作痒,服补中益气汤而愈。
- BEMS Tags: ['O', 'O', 'O', 'B-ZD', 'I-ZD', 'O', 'O', 'O', 'O', 'O', 'O', 'O', 'O', 'O', 'O', 'B-ZF', 'I-ZF', 'I-ZF', 'I-ZF', 'I-ZF', 'O', 'O', 'O']
- Converted Prompt 2:

{实体标注结果}一男子{时疫|病名}愈后,遍身发作痒,服{补中益气汤|方剂}而愈。{实体标注结果}

This conversion process made the annotations more interpretable and aligned with the input format required by our LLMs.

### 5.1.3 Handling Long Sentences:

After segmentation, we observed that some sentences in the training data were still relatively long. However, given the capability of modern LLMs to handle longer sequences, we decided not to further split these sentences. This approach preserved the contextual integrity of the text while ensuring that the models could still process the data effectively.

By transforming the data into Prompt 2, we created a structured and consistent input format that facilitated better model performance. This preprocessing step was critical for ensuring that the LLMs could accurately interpret and process the specialized terminology and semantic nuances present in the TCM texts.

In the next steps, we will use this transformed dataset to train and evaluate our models, with a focus on improving performance for domain-specific tasks.

## 5.2 Model Training and Results

In this section, we detail the model training process and the results obtained from our experiments. The fine-tuning was primarily conducted using the Unsloth framework[3] from, LLaMA-Factory(Zheng Yaowei,2024) and we explored several approaches to optimize the model's performance on the task of TCM text processing. The results can be seen in Table 3.

### 5.2.1 Pre-Fine-Tuning Baseline

Before fine-tuning, we evaluated the baseline performance of the model on the task. This provided a reference point to measure the impact of our subsequent fine-tuning strategies.

### 5.2.2 Task C Specific Fine-Tuning

We fine-tuned the model using the Task C TCM training data with LoRA (Low-Rank Adaptation). Each training sample included three components: Instructions, Input, and Output, following a SFT(supervised fine-tuning) approach. This method allowed the model to learn task-specific patterns and improve its performance on TCM text processing.

### 5.2.3 Multi-Task Fine-Tuning (Task A, B, C)

To further enhance the model's generalization capabilities, we combined the training data from Task A, Task B, and Task C into a single dataset for multi-task fine-tuning. This approach ex-

[3] https://github.com/unslothai/unsloth

posed the model to a more diverse range of materials, which led to a noticeable improvement in accuracy. The results confirmed that providing the model with more varied and extensive training data significantly enhances its performance. As a result, in all subsequent supervised fine-tuning (SFT) stages, we consistently used the combined dataset from all three tasks (A, B, and C) together. This multi-task approach became our standard practice for fine-tuning, leveraging the synergies between the different tasks to improve overall model performance.

#### 5.2.4 Pre-Training with External Data

To further boost the model's performance, we introduced a pre-training phase before fine-tuning. The pre-training data was sourced from the open-source project "殆知阁", [4]and We selected 12.5MB of unannotated classical Chinese text there, including 1/3 historical texts from the Twenty-Four Histories and 2/3 TCM-related texts.

We conducted training on a single NVIDIA RTX 4090 GPU. The learning rate was set to 5e-05 and the train batch size was 1. We first performed unsupervised pre-training using the unsloth framework on the unlabeled domain-specific text for 3 epochs. This was followed by supervised fine-tuning (SFT) using the same hyperparameters as befores(within a combination of Task A, B, C). After pre-training and fine-tuning, the final loss value decreased to around 0.0005. The loss curves for the SFT stage

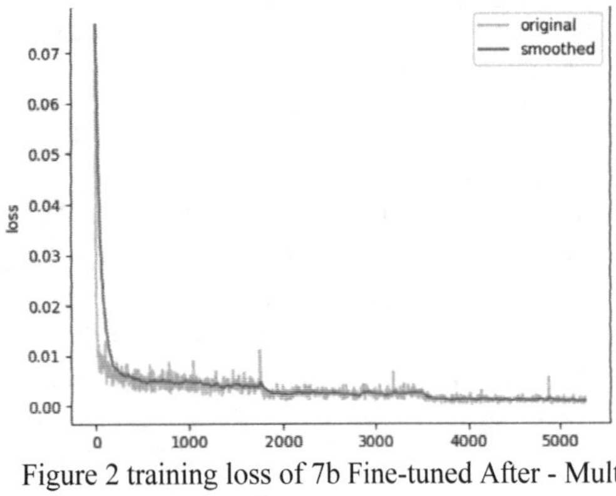


Figure 2 training loss of 7b Fine-tuned After - Multi + Pretrain (Prompt 2)

are shown in Figure 2.

After 3 epochs of pre-training and subsequent fine-tuning, the model **achieved an F1 score of 0.93,** significantly outperforming general-purpose LLMs. This demonstrated the effectiveness of domain-specific pre-training in improving model performance on the target task.

#### 5.2.5 Performance of Smaller Models (3B)

We also experimented with a smaller 3B parameter model using the same training methodology. Surprisingly, this model achieved an F1 score of 0.91, indicating that even smaller models can perform well on specialized tasks when properly trained.

#### 5.2.6 Ensemble Approach with 7B and 3B Models

To further improve accuracy, we implemented an ensemble approach:

- Both the 7B and 3B models generated results independently.
- If their results agreed, the output was considered correct.
- If their results disagreed, we used Qwen-Plus as a teacher model to determine which result was more reliable.

We initially envisioned that both 3B and 7B models could achieve certain accuracy levels. They're like students working on the same NER task - if they give the same answer, there's a higher probability that their results are correct. If they disagree, someone needs to judge who's right and who's wrong. While general large language models might overthink, they could be quite effective at determining which NER result is correct, so we combined these methods together.This ensemble method achieved a final F1 score of 0.9277. We hypothesize that integrating additional reasoning models, such as DeepSeek-R1, could further enhance performance. This represents a promising direction for future innovation.

| **Model** | **Precision** | **Recall** | **F1** |
|---|---|---|---|
| 7b Fine-tuned Before (Prompt 1 ) | 0.8015 | 0.7574 | 0.7719 |
| 7b Fine-tuned (Prompt 1 ) | 0.8199 | 0.7811 | 0.7956 |
| 7b Fine-tuned | 0.8051 | 0.8415 | 0.8142 |
| **7b Fine-tuned - Multi** | 0.8805 | 0.897 | **0.8863** |
| **7b Fine-tuned - Multi + Pretrain** | **0.9297** | **0.9346** | **0.9302** |
| 3b Fine-tuned - Multi + Pretrain | 0.9137 | 0.9173 | 0.9147 |
| 7b+3b+Teacher | 0.9296 | 0.9268 | 0.9277 |

Table 3: Results of the experiments [Prompt 2 used unless otherwise specified]

[4]https://github.com/garychowcmu/daizhige v20

## 6. Conclusion

In this study, we found that domain-specific pre-training and multi-task fine-tuning significantly improved model performance on specialized tasks like TCM text processing. Interestingly, smaller models (e.g., 3B) were able to achieve competitive results when trained with the right methods, showing that model size is not always the limiting factor. Additionally, we found that ensemble methods, combined with teacher models, further enhanced accuracy and reliability. Future work will explore integrating more advanced reasoning models, such as DeepSeek-R1, to push the performance limits of domain-specific NLP tasks. These results highlight the importance of tailored training strategies and the potential of smaller, specialized models to achieve state-of-the-art results in niche domains.

## 7. Limitation

This study has several limitations. **The choice of Qwen-Plus** as the teacher model, while effective, was not extensively compared with alternatives, potentially impacting results. The potential of more advanced inference models remains unexplored. **The quality of data annotations**, crucial in specialized fields like Traditional Chinese Medicine, was not discussed, which could affect result reliability. Additionally, **the evaluation relied primarily on F1 scores**, overlooking other important metrics such as model robustness, inference speed, and performance in resource-constrained environments. These factors collectively suggest areas for future research and improvement in the current approach.

## Reference

Colin Raffel, Noam Shazeer, Adam Roberts, Katherine Lee, Sharan Narang, Michael Matena, Yanqi Zhou, Wei Li, and Peter J. Liu. 2020. Exploring the limits of transfer learning with a unified text-to-text transformer. In *Proceedings of the 37th International Conference on Machine Learning*, pages 4171–4186. https://doi.org/10.48550/arXiv.1910.10683.

David Nadeau, Satoshi Sekine, 2007. A survey of named entity recognition and classification. Lingvisticae Investigationes, 30(1), 3-26. https://doi.org/10.1075/li.30.1.03nad.

He Yuhao, Li Ming, Luo Xiaolan, Liu Lili, Yang Qi, Zhu Bangxian, Lyu Yuhan, 2024. Research on entity and relation extraction from traditional Chinese medicine knowledge graphs based on GPTs. *Shanghai Journal of Traditional Chinese Medicine*, 58(8), 1-6.

Jacob Devlin, Ming-Wei Chang, Kenton Lee, and Kristina Toutanova. 2019. BERT: Pre-training of Deep Bidirectional Transformers for Language Understanding. Computing Research Repository, *Computing Research Repository*,arXiv:1810.04805. V2.https://arxiv.org/abs/1810.04805.

Pan Liu, Yanming Guo, Fenglei Wang, Guohui Li, 2022. Chinese named entity recognition: The state of the art. *Neurocomputing*, 473, 37-53. https://doi.org/10.1016/j.neucom.2021.10.101.

Sepp Hochreiter, Jürgen Schmidhuber. 1997. Long short-term memory. *Neural Computation*, 9(8), 1735-1780.https://doi.org/10.1162/neco.1997.9.8.1735.

Xie Jing, Liu Jiangfeng, Wang Dongbo, 2022. Study on named entity recognition of Traditional Chinese Medicine classics: Taking SikuBERT pre-training model enhanced by the Flat-lattice Transformer for example. *Library Forum*, 42(10), 51-60.

Yaqiang Wang, Zhonghua Yu, Yongguang Jiang, Yongchao Liu, Li Chen, Yiguang Liu, 2012. A framework and its empirical study of automatic diagnosis of Traditional Chinese Medicine utilizing raw free-text clinical records. *Journal of Biomedical Informatics*, 45(2), 210-223.https://doi.org/10.1016/j.jbi.2011.10.003.

Zheng Yaowei, Zhang Richong, Zhang Junhao, Ye Yanhan, Luo Zheyan, 2024. LlamaFactory: Unified Efficient Fine-Tuning of 100+ Language Models. *Proceedings of the 62nd Annual Meeting of the Association for Computational Linguistics,*V3: 400-410.https://doi.org/10.18653/v1/2024.acl-demos.38.

# Construction of NER Model in Ancient Chinese: Solution of EvaHan 2025 Challenge

**Yi Lu**
University of Toronto
tomlu@cs.toronto.edu

**Minyi Lei**
McMaster University
leim13@mcmaster.ca

## Abstract

This paper introduces the system submitted for EvaHan 2025, focusing on the Named Entity Recognition (NER) task for ancient Chinese texts. Our solution is built upon two specified pre-trained BERT models, namely GujiRoBERTa_jian_fan and GujiRoBERTa_fan, and further enhanced by a deep BiLSTM network with a Conditional Random Field (CRF) decoding layer. Extensive experiments on three test dataset splits demonstrate that our system's performance, 84.58% F1 in the closed-modality track and 82.78% F1 in the open-modality track, significantly outperforms the official baseline, achieving notable improvements in F1 score.

## 1 Introduction

Named Entity Recognition (NER) is one of the most fundamental tasks in natural language processing (NLP), playing a crucial role in understanding ancient Chinese corpus. In ancient Chinese texts, identifying entities such as person names, geographical locations, official titles, book names, and time expressions is particularly challenging due to the archaic language, estoteric grammar, ambiguous boundaries, and diverse annotation schemas. In this work, we present a solution that leverages domain-specific pre-trained BERT models combined with a BiLSTM+CRF architecture. Our approach is designed to effectively capture both the semantic representations provided by the pre-trained language models and the sequential dependencies inherent in the text, which are critical for accurate and effective entity boundary detection.

## 2 Related Works

Named Entity Recognition (NER) refers to the task of tagging entities in text with their corresponding type. Early studies in NER mainly relied on using hand-crafted rules (Zhang and Elhadad, 2013) and dictionaries (Pomares-Quimbaya et al., 2016) to capture entity patterns, which obtained satisfiable performance on specific fields, while suffering from suboptimal generality and poor scalability on broader use cases. Statistical machine learning techniques, including Hidden Markov Models (HMM) (Baum and Petrie, 1966) and Conditional Random Fields (CRF) (Lafferty et al., 2001) were widely adopted for NER, incorporating contextual features and further improved the NER systems' performance. Recent advancements, including the application of BiLSTM-CRF (Huang et al., 2015) and pre-trained language models such as BERT (Devlin et al., 2019), GPT (Radford and Narasimhan, 2018), ELMo (Peters et al., 2018) and RoBERTa (Liu et al., 2019).

Specifically, BERT-based models utilize attention mechanisms (Vaswani et al., 2017), which allows models to dynamically focus on relevant parts of the input sequence, thereby mitigating the limitations of fixed-size hidden representations in RNN-based models, achieving human-comparable results on English NER benchmarks.

Prior work in modern Chinese NER, such as (Huang et al., 2015), has demonstrated the benefits of integrating contextualized embeddings with CRF for structured prediction. The CRF layer refines predictions by modeling label dependencies and enforcing valid output sequences, a feature that is particularly beneficial when dealing with the complex annotation schemes often encountered in ancient texts.

Ancient Chinese texts pose additional challenges due to significant linguistic differences from modern Chinese, sparse annotated data, and heterogeneous tag schemes. Some



*Proceedings of the Second Ancient Language Processing Workshop associated with NAACL 2025*, pages 112–116
May 4, 2025. 

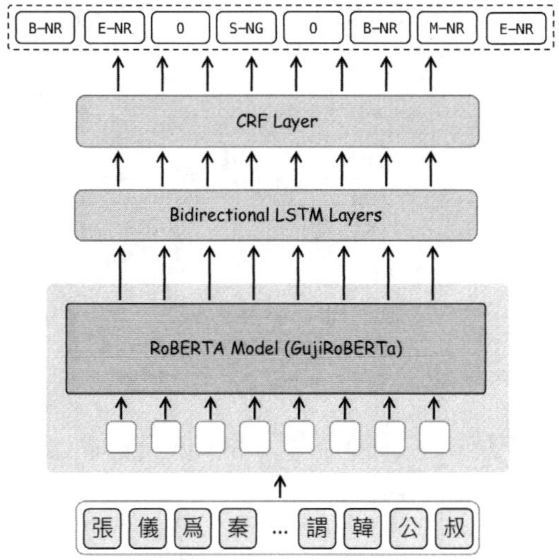


Figure 1: Visualization of our architecture.

works have addressed these issues by building domain-adapted pre-trained models and employing data augmentation or active learning strategies. Our work builds on these advances while specifically tailoring the model and training pipeline for ancient Chinese NER.

## 3 Model Architecture

We strictly follow the competition requirements by only using the provided pre-trained model: "GujiRoBERTa_jian_fan" (Wang et al., 2023) in the closed-modality track. Our solution is based on a two-branch setting:

**Close-Modality**. The pre-trained model: GujiRoBERTa_jian_fan (Wang et al., 2023) is applied as the backbone for extracting information from the corpus. Its output representations are fed into a 4-layer Bidirectional LSTM (BiLSTM) with a hidden dimension of 1024 to capture long-range dependencies. A fully connected layer maps the BiLSTM outputs to the label space, and finally, a CRF layer is employed to model the structural constraints among labels, as shown in Figure 1.

**Open-Modality**. For the open modality track, we adopted the same architecture, and the only difference is the use of the GujiRoBERTa_fan model. Key hyperparameters in our architecture are shown in table Table 1, which is also shared with the close-modality model training.

Specifically, we set the maximum sentence length to 256, as over 98% of sentences fall within this length, according to our analysis of both training and testing datasets. AdamW (Loshchilov and Hutter, 2019) is specifically selected to speed up model training and improve the model's generalization capability. Its base learning rate is set as $2e-5$, along with weight decay being set as 0.01. The gradient clipping is set to 5 to stabilize the model training.

| Parameter | Value |
|---|---|
| Maximum Sentence Length | 256 |
| Model Training Batch Size | 16 |
| BiLSTM's Hidden Dimension | 1024 |
| Number of BiLSTM Layers | 4 |
| Optimizer | AdamW |
| Learning Rate Scheduler | CASwithW |
| Dropout (in BiLSTM layers) | 0.1 |
| Gradient Clipping | 5 |

Table 1: Model and training configuration of our system. "CASwithW" refers to Cosine annealing schedule with warmup.

## 4 Feature Preprocessing

Our preprocessing pipeline involves the following components:

**Sentence Splitting**. During Explorative Data Analysis, we observed that multiple nonstandard Unicode characters are present in the training corpus. Specifically, we observed that quotation marks contain multiple types. To accommodate the dataset, we utilize the Chinese period as the only splitting character. This ensures that the sentences fed to the model are coherent and that over 98% of sentences are within the maximum length.

**Tokenization**. We use the tokenizer provided by GujiRoBERTa, which has been pretrained on an ancient Chinese corpus.

**Label Mapping**. The label vocabulary is constructed based on the training set with splits: A, B, and C. The training set splits are curated from three ancient documents: Shiji, Twenty-Four Histories, and Traditional Chinese Medicine Classics. Each dataset refers to a distinct NER task, whose tags of interest are shown in Table 2.

As the training data from datasets A, B, and C have heterogeneous tag schemes, we ensure that the mapping covers all tags (including prefixes such as B-, M-, E-) for non-"O" tokens. To ensure the existence of "O" label, we specifically set it as the first element in the label-to-id and id-to-label mappings, where it corresponds to the id 0.

| Dataset | Annotation | Meaning |
|---|---|---|
| **Split A** | NR | Person Name |
| | NS | Geographical Location |
| | NB | Book Title |
| | NO | Official Title |
| | NG | Country Name |
| | T | Time Expression |
| **Split B** | NR | Person Name |
| | NS | Geographical Location |
| | T | Time Expression |
| **Split C** | ZD | Disease |
| | ZZ | Syndrome |
| | ZF | Medicinal Formula |
| | ZP | Decoction Pieces |
| | ZS | Symptom |
| | ZA | Acupoint |

Table 2: Combined Tagset for Named Entities in Datasets A, B, and C (without examples).

## 5 Experiments

In this section, we demonstrate the experiment results that we conducted while determining the model's architecture design.

### 5.1 Experimental Setup

We choose overall F1 as the metric for evaluating the model's performance, the metric is compared with the one produced by the baseline model, which is constructed by the committee. The baseline is a simple "SikuRoBERTa-BiLSTM-CRF" model, whose hyperparameters for constructing the BiLSTM and CRF module are not disclosed.

We split the training data with a 90%/10% ratio for the training and validation dataset split. Each model is trained for 40 epochs. During model training, we evaluate the current model at each epoch on the separate test sets of Split A, B, and C. For each split, we evaluate the model's performance on each split using the F1 score metric and update the best F1 that we obtained so far for this dataset split. The best-performed model will be saved and will be used for testing dataset inference after the model training.

The model is trained on a single NVIDIA A6000 40G card. Detailed model training hyperparameter settings are revealed as Table 1.

### 5.2 Model Architecture Ablation

We compared several configurations regarding the model's architecture. Apart from our final design, 'RoBERTa + BiLSTM + CRF' (where, for simplicity, we refer to the "GujiRoBERTa" model used in both close and open modality as "RoBERTa"), we also experimented multiple configurations. Using the same RoBERTa model, we experimented the use of a single CRF layer or SPAN layer. Due to the constraints of time and computational resources, experiments on model architecture are conducted after the submission deadline.

As Table 3 shows, directly applying a CRF layer on top of the RoBERTa output yielded an F1 score of 79.68%, which is slightly lower than the baseline. By replacing the CRF layer with a double-pointer SPAN layer, an F1 score of 80.62% is achieved, which is similar to the baseline. While such simple combinations do not yield substantial improvements, the combination of RoBERTa + BiLSTM + CRF achieved significant improvement, indicating that the incorporation of a deep BiLSTM layer is crucial for capturing sequential context and dependencies.

| Model Arch. | Precision | Recall | F1 Score |
|---|---|---|---|
| Baseline | 81.41% | 79.82% | 80.61% |
| R+C | 78.62% | 80.78% | 79.68% |
| R+S | 84.65% | 76.96% | 80.62% |
| R+B+C | **85.92%** | **83.28%** | **84.58%** |

Table 3: Different model architecture's performance comparison (transposed). The highest metric values in each column are highlighted in bold. Acronyms: "R", "C", "B", "S" refers to RoBERTa Model, CRF, BiLSTM and SPAN, respectively.

### 5.3 Model Hyperparameter Ablation

To determine the optimal model configuration, we performed ablation experiments on two key hyperparameters: "hidden_dim", controlling the hidden dimension size of both the BiLSTM and CRF modules in our system, and "num_layer", setting the depth of the BiLSTM module. Experiment results are summarized in Table 4 and Table 5.

| Hidden Dimension | 512 | 1024 | 1536 |
|---|---|---|---|
| Precision | 80.67% | **85.92%** | 81.87% |
| Recall | 83.71% | 83.28% | **84.45%** |
| F1 Score | 82.16% | **84.58%** | 83.14% |

Table 4: Ablation on Model Width (with 4 BiLSTM layers), highest values are in **bold**.

As the results shown in both Table 4 and Table 5, an appropriate configuration of both the size of hidden dimension and the number of layers is critical for achieving optimal performance. On NER task. In the ablation on model width (with the number of layers fixed at 4), increasing the hidden dimension from 512 to 1024 results in a substantial improvement in the F1 score (from 82.16% to 84.58%). However, further increasing the hidden dimension to 1536 causes a slight drop in performance (83.14%), suggesting that an excessively large hidden dimension may introduce redundancy or overfitting.

| Depth | 4 Layers | 8 Layers | 12 Layers |
|---|---|---|---|
| Precision | **85.92%** | 81.79% | 82.20% |
| Recall | 83.28% | **83.37%** | 81.65% |
| F1 Score | **84.58%** | 82.57% | 81.93% |

Table 5: Ablation on BiLSTM Module's depth, each layer's hidden dimension are fixed as 1024.

Similarly, in the ablation on model depth (hidden dimension fixed at 1024), the best performance is achieved with 4 layers (84.58%). Increasing the number of layers to 8 and 12 leads to a decrease in the F1 score to 82.57% and 81.93%, indicating that although a deeper model might capture more complex patterns, it may also become prone to overfitting or suffer from optimization difficulties.

Overall, these experiments demonstrate that a balanced configuration, a hidden dimension of 1024, and 4 layers provide the most effective trade-off between model capacity and generalization performance.

## 6 Performance of Close and Open Modality Track

Following the finding of the above experiments, we utilized the most optimal model architecture design that we came up with: RoBERTa + BiLSTM + CRF, along with BiLSTM hidden dimension: 1024 and depth set as 4.

For the Closed Modality Track, we utilize "GujiRoBERTa_jian_fan" as requested by the competition, reporting an F1 of 84.58% as our final score in this track.

For the Open Modality Track, we reused the model configuration and hyperparameter settings while utilizing an external RoBERTa model: "GujiRoBERTa_fan", which is being pre-trained on ancient Chinese corpus only. We report the F1 as 82.78% as our final score.

## 7 Future Work

Despite our system's performance on both close and open modality significantly outperforms the baseline: 80.61% F1, there remain avenues for further improvement which were not fully discovered in this work due to time and resource constraints:

**Data Augmentation**. Employing augmentation strategies such as synonym replacement (with domain-specific ancient Chinese synonym dictionaries) or back-translation could increase data diversity and improve the model's tagging accuracy.

**Adversarial Training**. Integrating techniques such as the Fast Gradient Method (FGM) during finetuning BERT models could potentially improve the model's robustness.

**Model Ensembling**. Combining multiple models with diverse architectures (e.g., BERT+Attention+CRF) could further boost performance and improve the F1.

**Open-Modality Exploration**. For the open-modality track, leveraging Large Language Models (LLMs) and prompt-based approaches to transform the NER task into the generative task or utilizing ModernBERT to develop an ancient Chinese-specific BERT could lead to much stronger models that excel in ancient Chinese NER tasks.

Future work could explore these directions to further push the boundaries of ancient Chinese NER, especially under the challenges posed by heterogeneous tag schemes and limited annotated data.

## 8 Summary

To conclude, our system is built on strong foundations provided by domain-specific pretrained models and is enhanced by a BiLSTM+CRF architecture with optimal depth and width. Our solution achieves an F1 score of around 84.6% in the closed-modality track and around 82.8% in the open-modality track, significantly outperforms the baseline of 80.61% F1, and demonstrates our design's effectiveness.

## 9 Limitations

While our system demonstrates strong performance on the EvaHan 2025 NER task, there are several limitations. Firstly, our system is built around the provided pre-trained "GujiRoBERTa" models, which may limit generalization to texts beyond the training domain or unseen linguistic variations in ancient Chinese corpuses. Secondly, due to time and computational resource constraints, we were unable to perform more comprehensive hyperparameter tuning or explore alternative architectures such as Transformer-CRF models in greater depth. Lastly, the diversity in annotation schemes across datasets A, B, and C poses challenges for unified modeling, which were only partially addressed in our current implementation.

## References


Leonard E. Baum and Ted Petrie. 1966. Statistical inference for probabilistic functions of finite state markov chains. *Annals of Mathematical Statistics*, 37:1554–1563.

Jacob Devlin, Ming-Wei Chang, Kenton Lee, and Kristina Toutanova. 2019. BERT: pre-training of deep bidirectional transformers for language understanding. In *Proceedings of the 2019 Conference of the North American Chapter of the Association for Computational Linguistics: Human Language Technologies, NAACL-HLT 2019, Minneapolis, MN, USA, June 2-7, 2019, Volume 1 (Long and Short Papers)*, pages 4171–4186. Association for Computational Linguistics.

Zhiheng Huang, Wei Xu, and Kai Yu. 2015. Bidirectional LSTM-CRF models for sequence tagging. *CoRR*, abs/1508.01991.

John D. Lafferty, Andrew McCallum, and Fernando C. N. Pereira. 2001. Conditional random fields: Probabilistic models for segmenting and labeling sequence data. In *Proceedings of the Eighteenth International Conference on Machine Learning (ICML 2001), Williams College, Williamstown, MA, USA, June 28 - July 1, 2001*, pages 282–289. Morgan Kaufmann.

Yinhan Liu, Myle Ott, Naman Goyal, Jingfei Du, Mandar Joshi, Danqi Chen, Omer Levy, Mike Lewis, Luke Zettlemoyer, and Veselin Stoyanov. 2019. Roberta: A robustly optimized BERT pretraining approach. *CoRR*, abs/1907.11692.

Ilya Loshchilov and Frank Hutter. 2019. Decoupled weight decay regularization. In *7th International Conference on Learning Representations, ICLR 2019, New Orleans, LA, USA, May 6-9, 2019*. OpenReview.net.

Matthew E. Peters, Mark Neumann, Mohit Iyyer, Matt Gardner, Christopher Clark, Kenton Lee, and Luke Zettlemoyer. 2018. Deep contextualized word representations. In *Proceedings of the 2018 Conference of the North American Chapter of the Association for Computational Linguistics: Human Language Technologies, Volume 1 (Long Papers)*, pages 2227–2237, New Orleans, Louisiana. Association for Computational Linguistics.

Alexandra Pomares-Quimbaya, Alejandro Sierra Múnera, Rafael Andrés González Rivera, Julián Camilo Daza Rodríguez, Oscar Mauricio Muñoz Velandia, Angel Alberto Garcia Peña, and Cyril Labbé. 2016. Named entity recognition over electronic health records through a combined dictionary-based approach. In *International Conference on ENTERprise Information Systems/International Conference on Project MANagement/International Conference on Health and Social Care Information Systems and Technologies, CENTERIS/ProjMAN/HCist 2016, Porto, Portugal, October 5-7, 2016*, volume 100 of *Procedia Computer Science*, pages 55–61. Elsevier.

Alec Radford and Karthik Narasimhan. 2018. Improving language understanding by generative pre-training.

Ashish Vaswani, Noam Shazeer, Niki Parmar, Jakob Uszkoreit, Llion Jones, Aidan N. Gomez, Lukasz Kaiser, and Illia Polosukhin. 2017. Attention is all you need. In *Advances in Neural Information Processing Systems 30: Annual Conference on Neural Information Processing Systems 2017, December 4-9, 2017, Long Beach, CA, USA*, pages 5998–6008.

Dongbo Wang, Chang Liu, Zhixiao Zhao, Si Shen, Liu Liu, Bin Li, Haotian Hu, Mengcheng Wu, Litao Lin, Xue Zhao, and Xiyu Wang. 2023. Gujibert and gujigpt: Construction of intelligent information processing foundation language models for ancient texts. *CoRR*, abs/2307.05354.

Shaodian Zhang and Noemie Elhadad. 2013. Unsupervised biomedical named entity recognition: Experiments with clinical and biological texts. *J. Biomed. Informatics*, 46(6):1088–1098.

# LLM's Weakness in NER Doesn't Stop It from Enhancing a Stronger SLM

**Weilu Xu, Renfei Dang, Shujian Huang**
National Key Laboratory for Novel Software Technology, Nanjing University, China
{weiluxu,dangrf}@smail.nju.edu.cn, huangsj@nju.edu.cn

## Abstract

Large Language Models (LLMs) demonstrate strong semantic understanding ability and extensive knowledge, but struggle with Named Entity Recognition (NER) due to hallucination and high training costs. Meanwhile, supervised Small Language Models (SLMs) efficiently provide structured predictions but lack adaptability to unseen entities and complex contexts. In this study, we investigate how a relatively weaker LLM can effectively support a supervised model in NER tasks. We first improve the LLM using LoRA-based fine-tuning and similarity-based prompting, achieving performance comparable to a SLM baseline. To further improve results, we propose a fusion strategy that integrates both models: prioritising SLM's predictions while using LLM guidance in low confidence cases. Our hybrid approach outperforms both baselines on three classic Chinese NER datasets.

## 1 Introduction

Large Language Models (LLMs) (Smith et al., 2022; Du et al., 2022; Rae et al., 2021) have shown remarkable abilities on various NLP applications. LLMs can understand complex semantic information and have extensive knowledge.

However, LLMs often suffer from the hallucination problem, where they confidently classify non-entity words as entities (Wang et al., 2023). In addition, they require significantly higher training costs to achieve performance comparable to supervised Small Language Models (SLMs) (Zhou et al., 2024). In contrast, SLMs can achieve reasonable levels of performance with lower training costs, but struggles with unseen entities and lacks strong semantic understanding in complex contexts.

This raises an important question: Can a relatively weaker LLM in a particular task still provide useful guidance to a smaller but supervised model? If so, integrating LLMs' broad knowledge with SLM's structured learning could boost NER performance while keeping training costs manageable.

In this study, we first trained SLM and LLM baselines with reasonable computational cost. To enhance LLM performance, we applied LoRA-based SFT and retrieved similar examples as prompts for task-specific guidance. These improvements brought LLM closer to the SLM baseline. We then proposed a fusion strategy: SLM's prediction was preferred unless its confidence was low, in which case the LLM output guided the final result. Figure 1 illustrates this process.

Our final hybrid model outperformed both individual baselines, demonstrating that leveraging LLM knowledge can effectively enhance SLM's structured predictions while maintaining efficiency.

## 2 Related Work

### 2.1 Named Entity Recognition

Named Entity Recognition (NER) is a tagging task where each word in a sentence is labeled to indicate whether it is part of a named entity and its corresponding type. A common approach to NER is to model it as a sequence labeling problem, where a multi-layer perceptron with a softmax layer serves as the tag decoder, framing the task as multi-class classification. Additionally, Conditional Random Fields (CRFs) (Liu et al., 2021), which conditionally model dependencies between labels, have been widely used in feature-based supervised learning methods. In addition, deep learning has become a widely used approach for NER, and advances in related upstream and downstream tasks, such as sequence tagging and entity linking, have further improved NER performance.(Roy, 2021)

### 2.2 Collaboration of Large and Small Models

Recent advances in pre-trained large-scale models have enabled training on vast amounts of data, making them adaptable to diverse downstream tasks



*Proceedings of the Second Ancient Language Processing Workshop associated with NAACL 2025*, pages 117–122
May 4, 2025. ©2025 Association for Computational Linguistics

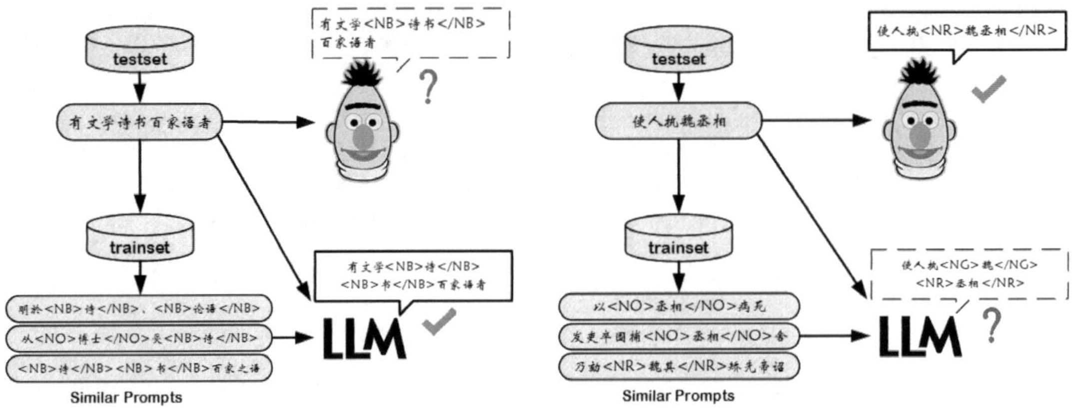


Figure 1: Two cases of the hybrid system. The green tick in the picture represents that the model's annotation for this sentence is confident and correct, while the red question mark represents that its perplexity is high, and it is actually incorrect. Therefore, based on the rules (detailed in Section 4), we select the results with high confidence from both sides. More discussions about these two examples are in Section 5.2.

(Bommasani et al., 2021). However, studies (Ma et al., 2023) suggest that while LLMs excel in extremely low-resource scenarios, they are not always effective for few-shot information extraction. In particular, combining LLMs with SLMs significantly improves performance in difficult cases, demonstrating the potential of hybrid approaches in NER.

## 3 Baseline Approaches for NER

### 3.1 SLM-Based Token Classification

To set a baseline, in the closed modality, we use *GujiRoBERTa_jian_fan*[1], a BERT model pretrained on massive traditional Chinese corpus. For the training data set used to adapt to the downstream NER task, there are three different data sets: Dataset A (from Shiji), Dataset B (from the Twenty-Four Histories), and Dataset C (from Traditional Chinese Medicine Classics).

During data processing, we mainly faced two key issues: sentence segmentation and character tokenization. To better leverage the context information, we use periods, question marks, and exclamation marks instead of a fixed maximum length as the end of a sentence. In terms of tokenization, a character within a single label may be split into multiple tokens, which requires careful processing to keep the boundary information. Details are in table 1.

| Original label (for one char) | Assigned new labels (for multiple tokens) |
|---|---|
| $[B-]$ | $[B-]\ [M-]_{*(i-1)}$ |
| $[M-]$ | $[M-]_{*i}$ |
| $[E-]$ | $[M-]_{*(i-1)}\ [E-]$ |
| $[S-]$ | $[B-]\ [M-]_{*(i-2)}\ [E-]$ |

Table 1: Details of changing labels for multiple-token characters. "B-", "M-", "E-", "S-" are prefixes of labels. *i* is the number of tokens for a single character.

### 3.2 Large Model-Assisted NER

Although LLMs show strong performance in a wide range of tasks, their performance on NER is still significantly below the supervised baselines. To improve the performance of the LLMs in the NER task, we explored two key strategies: LoRA fine-tuning for better model adaptation and similarity-based prompting for more effective few-shot learning. Both methods have a significant impact on performance improvement.

#### 3.2.1 LoRA fine-tuning

Considering the balance between performance and cost, we employed Low-Rank Adaptation (LoRA) (Hu et al., 2022) to fine-tune Qwen2.5-14B-Instruct.

As for the data, we have transformed the token-level training set into a special format that can be understood by LLMs. The specific format is as follows:

<NG>楚</NG>使怒去，归告<NR>怀王</NR>。

[1] https://github.com/hsc748NLP/GujiBERT-and-GujiGPT

In this case, "楚" "怀" "王" are officially annotated as "S-NG" "B-NR" and "E-NR" in the training data set, so we use pairs of "<X></X>" to denote an "X" category.

#### 3.2.2 Similarity-based prompting

Beyond standard fine-tuning, we explored a retrieval-based prompting approach to enhance in-context learning. Specifically, we utilized SIKU-BERT/sikuroberta[2] to generate sentence embeddings and performed similarity matching to retrieve the top 5 most similar sentences from the training set for each test sample. Unlike traditional few-shot prompting, which relies on a fixed set, similarity prompting dynamically selects contextually relevant examples, ensuring better alignment with the input instance. This approach effectively solves the transition labelling problem common to large language models on NER tasks.

## 4 Model Fusion: Combining SLM and LLM Outputs

### 4.1 Method

To leverage the strengths of both SLM-based token classification and LLM-assisted NER, we propose a fusion strategy that integrates their outputs. This method selects the more confident answer when the answers given by the two models are found to be in disagreement.

#### 4.1.1 LLM's Category & Boundary Probabilities

In order to better collaborate with and compare against the small model, we need to define the category probabilities and boundary probabilities for the annotation results of the LLM.

The category probability is defined as the probability obtained after performing softmax normalization on the logits of the positions where the tokens corresponding to that category first appear, while the boundary probability is defined as the average of the probabilities of the first "<" token (denoting the start of an annotation), the first "</" token (denoting the end of one annotation), and the token preceding each of them (denoting whether to start or end an annotation). We will still use the following example:

<NG>楚</NG>使怒去，归告<NR>怀王</NR>。

[2] https://huggingface.co/SIKU-BERT/sikuroberta

In this case, "楚" "怀" "王" are officially annotated as "S-NG" "B-NR" and "E-NR" in the training data set, so we use pairs of "<X></X>" to denote an "X" category. So the category probability for "楚" is $Softmax(Logit(NG))$; and the boundary probability for "怀王" is average of the softmaxed logits of tokens "告" "<" "王" and "</". We do need the token preceding "<", in that the LLM may hesitate whether to start a new entity from token "告" or "怀"; we also need the token preceding "</", in that the LLM may hesitate whether to end this entity in token "怀" or "王".

#### 4.1.2 Hyperparameters and formulas

It was observed that the LLM confidence gap was minimal; therefore, the decision was made to scale it using the exponent of $e$. With regard to the values of the hyperparameters, a search was conducted across the training sets for the optimal results. If $S_S < S_L$, choose the results of SLM; otherwise, let the LLM's results provide guidance. Here is the final formulas.

$$\text{Compare}(S_S, S_L) = S_S < S_L \tag{1}$$

where:

$$S_S = 1 - \text{Entropy}(\text{SLM}) \tag{2}$$

$$S_L = \lambda \cdot e^{P(\text{LLM})} \tag{3}$$

## 5 Experiments

All of our experiments were conducted on at most 4 NVIDIA A6000 GPUs. We train the SLM on training set for 10 epochs, with a batch size of 64 and learning rate of 2e-5. For the SFT of the LLM, we adopted a batch size of 64, learning rate of 2e-5, a LoRA rank of 64 and an alpha of 128. All the evaluation results below are token-level macro scores (on a 10% test set splited from train set).

### 5.1 Results

We conducted ablation experiments for every approach and demonstrated that all approaches were helpful in improving the ability of LLM to perform the NER task on all three test sets.

First, we show that both methods of improving LLM performance are effective. Details are in Table 3.

| Character | Real Label | SLM Output (Entropy) | LLM Output (Category/Boundary Prob.) |
|---|---|---|---|
| 魏 | B-NR | B-NR (0.036) | S-NG (0.7815) |
| 丞 | M-NR | M-NR (0.038) | B-NR (0.9986) |
| 相 | E-NR | E-NR (0.033) | E-NR (-) |
| 诗 | B-NB | B-NB (2.537) | S-NB (0.9062) |
| 书 | E-NB | E-NB (2.425) | S-NB (0.9998) |

Table 2: Cases of SLM guiding LLM and LLM guiding SLM. The one above shows the category probabilities of the LLM, and the one below shows the boundary probabilities of the LLM. Since the LLM only outputs category probabilities for the entire entity once, there is no corresponding category probability for the Chinese character "相" in line 3.

| model | A | B | C |
|---|---|---|---|
| few shot | 0.2626 | 0.4072 | 0.2492 |
| Sim. prompt | 0.4400 | 0.6367 | 0.5182 |
| SFT + few shot | 0.6737 | 0.8329 | 0.5878 |
| SFT + Sim. prompt | **0.8350** | **0.8694** | **0.6381** |

Table 3: Results of two approaches to improve the ability of LLM on NER task. Based on Qwen2.5-14B-Instruct. This 'Sim.' means 'Similarity', and 'SFT' refers to 'Supervised Fine-Tuning'.

Then, despite the close results of SLM and LLM, we merged the two with custom rules and got better results in comparison to both on all three test sets. Details are in Table 4.

| Model | A | B | C |
|---|---|---|---|
| SLM | 0.8305 | 0.8738 | 0.7207 |
| Sim. Prompt | 0.8350 | 0.8694 | 0.6381 |
| Sim. Prompt + SLM | **0.8855** | **0.8824** | **0.7733** |

Table 4: Results from the fusion of the LLM and the SLM model. "Sim. Prompt" refers to a fine-tuned LoRA SFT model with similarity-based prompting.

### 5.2 Case Study

To better demonstrate the effectiveness of our method, we will present two examples below. They are respectively the case where the SLM successfully guides the LLM and the case where LLM successfully guides the SLM. Table 2 presents two typical examples.

**Case 1: SLM guiding LLM.** The phrase "魏丞相" (the Prime Minister of the state of Wei) can be annotated as "Personal Name (NR)" or "Country (NS) + Personal Name (NR)". Although the former is better, it also depends on the annotation style. In this case, due to its professionalism, the SLM grasped the annotation style of the training set more accurately. Therefore, it provided the correct answer with a relatively low entropy (low uncertainty). In contrast, the LLM gave a wrong answer with a relatively low probability (which also reflects its lack of confidence in itself). In such situation, we follow the rules and adopt the result provided by the small-scale model.

**Case 2: LLM guiding SLM.** "诗"(*The Book of Songs*) and "书" (*The Book of History*) are two of the "Six Classics" in ancient China, which is our common cultural knowledge. Since the large-scale model has incorporated a vast amount of knowledge during the pre-training stage, it is highly likely that it has learned this common sense and can accurately annotate the Chinese characters "诗" and "书" as "S-NB" respectively. In contrast, due to the lack of this common sense, the small-scale model tends to mis-annotate things it doesn't recognize with a very high entropy (high uncertainty). According to our rules, this situation can also be successfully corrected.

## 6 Conclusions and Future Work

In this paper, we presents an efficient approach to enhancing LLM performance in NER to match a supervised SLM. Using LoRA fine-tuning and similarity-based prompting, we improved the LLM's entity recognition. We also introduced a fusion strategy that prioritizes SLM's predictions while leveraging LLM guidance when SLM's confidence is low. This hybrid approach consistently outperformed both baselines.

However, our method did not fully utilize the LLM's reasoning and analytical capabilities. In particular, enabling a 14B parameter model with limited domain knowledge of classical Chinese to self-correct remains challenging. Future work may explore ways to enhance LLM's domain adaptation, allowing it to better leverage contextual understanding and reasoning for collaborative NER frameworks.

## References


Rishi Bommasani, Drew A Hudson, Ehsan Adeli, Russ Altman, Simran Arora, Sydney von Arx, Michael S Bernstein, Jeannette Bohg, Antoine Bosselut, and Emma Brunskill. 2021. On the opportunities and risks of foundation models. *arXiv preprint arXiv:2108.07258*.

Nan Du, Yanping Huang, Andrew M Dai, Simon Tong, Dmitry Lepikhin, Yuanzhong Xu, Maxim Krikun, Yanqi Zhou, Adams Wei Yu, and Orhan Firat. 2022. Glam: Efficient scaling of language models with mixture-of-experts. In *International conference on machine learning*, pages 5547–5569. PMLR.

Edward J Hu, Yelong Shen, Phillip Wallis, Zeyuan Allen-Zhu, Yuanzhi Li, Shean Wang, Lu Wang, Weizhu Chen, and 1 others. 2022. Lora: Low-rank adaptation of large language models. *ICLR*, 1(2):3.

Shuai Liu, Tenghui He, and Jianhua Dai. 2021. A survey of crf algorithm based knowledge extraction of elementary mathematics in chinese. *Mobile Networks and Applications*, 26(5):1891–1903.

Yubo Ma, Yixin Cao, YongChing Hong, and Aixin Sun. 2023. Large language model is not a good few-shot information extractor, but a good reranker for hard samples! *arXiv preprint arXiv:2303.08559*.

Jack W Rae, Sebastian Borgeaud, Trevor Cai, Katie Millican, Jordan Hoffmann, Francis Song, John Aslanides, Sarah Henderson, Roman Ring, and Susannah Young. 2021. Scaling language models: Methods, analysis & insights from training gopher. *arXiv preprint arXiv:2112.11446*.

Arya Roy. 2021. Recent trends in named entity recognition (ner). *arXiv preprint arXiv:2101.11420*.

Shaden Smith, Mostofa Patwary, Brandon Norick, Patrick LeGresley, Samyam Rajbhandari, Jared Casper, Zhun Liu, Shrimai Prabhumoye, George Zerveas, and Vijay Korthikanti. 2022. Using deepspeed and megatron to train megatron-turing nlg 530b, a large-scale generative language model. *arXiv preprint arXiv:2201.11990*.

Shuhe Wang, Xiaofei Sun, Xiaoya Li, Rongbin Ouyang, Fei Wu, Tianwei Zhang, Jiwei Li, and Guoyin Wang. 2023. Gpt-ner: Named entity recognition via large language models. *arXiv preprint arXiv:2304.10428*.

Ce Zhou, Qian Li, Chen Li, Jun Yu, Yixin Liu, Guangjing Wang, Kai Zhang, Cheng Ji, Qiben Yan, and Lifang He. 2024. A comprehensive survey on pretrained foundation models: A history from bert to chatgpt. *International Journal of Machine Learning and Cybernetics*. Advance online publication.

## A Detailed Experimental Results

In this section we show detailed experimental results individually. Table 5, table 6 and table 7 are results of LLM Qwen2.5-14B-Instruct on NER tasks **A**, **B** and **C**. Here 'Sim.' means 'Similarity', 'SFT' refers to 'Supervised Fine-Tuning', 'P' refers to 'Precision', 'R' refers to 'Recall', and 'F1' refers to macro F1 scores.

| **Model** | P | R | F1 |
|---|---|---|---|
| few shot | 0.2529 | 0.3167 | 0.2626 |
| Sim. prompt | 0.4369 | 0.4645 | 0.4400 |
| SFT + few shot | 0.6566 | 0.7161 | 0.6737 |
| SFT + Sim. prompt | 0.8143 | 0.8746 | 0.8350 |

Table 5: Results for **A**.

| **Model** | P | R | F1 |
|---|---|---|---|
| few shot | 0.4477 | 0.4087 | 0.4072 |
| Sim. prompt | 0.6528 | 0.6364 | 0.6367 |
| SFT + few shot | 0.8601 | 0.8124 | 0.8329 |
| SFT + Sim. prompt | 0.8823 | 0.8592 | 0.8694 |

Table 6: Results for **B**.

| **Model** | P | R | F1 |
|---|---|---|---|
| few shot | 0.2719 | 0.2642 | 0.2492 |
| Sim. prompt | 0.5280 | 0.5483 | 0.5182 |
| SFT + few shot | 0.6776 | 0.5412 | 0.5878 |
| SFT + Sim. prompt | 0.6874 | 0.6172 | 0.6381 |

Table 7: Results for **C**.

Table 8, table 9 and table 10 are results of the fusion of LLM and SLM model. Here "Sim. Prompt" refers to a fine-tuned LoRA SFT model with similarity-based prompting, 'P' refers to 'Precision', 'R' refers to 'Recall', and 'F1' refers to macro F1 scores.

| **Model** | P | R | F1 |
|---|---|---|---|
| SLM | 0.8223 | 0.8646 | 0.8305 |
| Sim. prompt | 0.8143 | 0.8746 | 0.8350 |
| Sim. prompt +SLM | 0.8841 | 0.8901 | 0.8855 |

Table 8: Results for **A**.

| **Model** | P | R | F1 |
|---|---|---|---|
| SLM | 0.8844 | 0.8648 | 0.8738 |
| Sim. prompt | 0.8823 | 0.8592 | 0.8694 |
| Sim. prompt +SLM | 0.8986 | 0.8685 | 0.8824 |

Table 9: Results for **B**.

| **Model** | P | R | F1 |
|---|---|---|---|
| SLM | 0.6954 | 0.7522 | 0.7207 |
| Sim. prompt | 0.6874 | 0.6172 | 0.6381 |
| Sim. prompt +SLM | 0.7641 | 0.7904 | 0.7733 |

Table 10: Results for **C**.

# Named Entity Recognition in Context: Edit_Dunhuang team Technical Report for EvaHan2025 NER Competition

**Colin Brisson[1, 2], Ayoub Kahfy[2], Marc Bui[1], Frédéric Constant[3],**
[1]EPHE-Université PSL, Paris France, [2]Badiane, Neufchâtel-Hardelot, France,
[3]Université Côte d'Azur, Nice, France
**Correspondence:** colin.brisson@ephe.psl.eu

## Abstract

We present the Named Entity Recognition system developed by the Edit_Dunhuang team for the EvaHan2025 competition. Our approach integrates three core components: (1) `Pindola`, a modern transformer-based bidirectional encoder pretrained on a large corpus of Classical Chinese texts; (2) a retrieval module that fetches relevant external context for each target sequence; and (3) a generative reasoning step that summarizes retrieved context in Classical Chinese for more robust entity disambiguation. Using this approach, we achieve an average F1 score of 85.58, improving upon the competition baseline by nearly 5 points.

## 1 Introduction

The EvaHan2025 competition aimed to evaluate the state-of-the-art in Named Entity Recognition (NER) for Classical Chinese texts. The evaluation was conducted using three distinct datasets, each containing different types of entities. Dataset A comprised texts from the Shiji, the historical records composed by Sima Qian during the late 2nd and early 1st centuries BCE. This dataset included annotations for six entity types: person names, geographical locations, book titles, official titles, country names, and temporal expressions. Dataset B featured more diverse excerpts drawn from the Twenty-Four Histories, the official dynastic histories of China, but contained annotations for only three entity types: person names, geographical locations, and temporal expressions. Dataset C differed significantly from the other datasets, consisting exclusively of medicinal texts annotated for six specialized entities: disease names, syndromes, medicinal formulas, decoction pieces, symptoms and acupuncture points.

Our participation in the competition is part of the Read_Chinese (BnF-Datalab) and Edit_Dunhuang (Biblissima+) projects, which aim to produce digital facsimile of the Chinese documents in the Pelliot collection of the Bibliothèque nationale de France and the Stein collection of the British Library. Both collections consist of documents—primarily manuscripts on paper—discovered in the early 20th century in Dunhuang (Gansu province) in northwest China. These documents provide crucial insights into the history of medieval China as well as the transmission of ideas before the adoption of woodblock printing. As part of these projects, we intend not only to transcribe the text of the manuscripts but also to convert the OCR output into a structured and richly annotated text.

Our strategy was built on three core ideas. First, we developed `Pindola`, a modern transformer-based bidirectional encoder pretrained on a large corpus of Classical Chinese texts. `Pindola` incorporates key enhancements that significantly improve the quality of learned representations. Second, recognizing that target sentences are not isolated fragments but parts of a broader, interconnected context, we enriched our input sequences with external contextual information to support more accurate annotations. Finally, we employed a reasoning generative model to refine and summarize this context, thereby improving the model's capacity for precise entity recognition.

## 2 Related Work

Integrating external context has emerged as a powerful approach to mitigate hallucinations and enhance factual accuracy in generative large language models (LLMs). A prominent example is Retrieval-Augmented Generation (RAG), which supplies models with relevant external context as raw text. RAG has achieved state-of-the-art results on various open-domain question-answering benchmarks, outperforming both standalone gener-



*Proceedings of the Second Ancient Language Processing Workshop associated with NAACL 2025*, pages 123–128
May 4, 2025. 

ative models and specialized retrieval-and-reading pipelines (Lewis et al., 2020). Another promising strategy leverages structured data, notably knowledge graphs. This approach has been effective in improving entity recognition accuracy within traditional Chinese texts (Duan et al., 2025). However, generative LLMs still face significant challenges in Named Entity Recognition (NER), particularly in specialized domains such as historical texts (De Toni et al., 2022), and show a tendency to distort input sequences (Li et al., 2024).

Traditional bidirectional encoder-based NER systems typically analyze sentences independently, often overlooking their broader contextual relationships. Recent studies, however, have demonstrated that integrating relevant external context can substantially improve the performance of these models. For instance, Wang et al. (2021) showed that incorporating context led to an improvement exceeding 2 points over the same model without context on the WNUT-17 dataset (Derczynski et al., 2017), a benchmark designed specifically for recognizing unusual or emerging entities.

Several transformer-based bidirectional encoders have been developed for Classical Chinese, notably the GujiBERT family (Wang et al., 2023), whose use was mandatory in the competition's closed modality and served to establish the competition baseline. However, due to computational constraints, these models were adapted from architectures originally trained for modern Chinese. Consequently, their architectures and performance levels are limited by design decisions made nearly a decade ago. Recent studies indicate that targeted architectural refinements significantly improve learned representations (Warner et al., 2024), especially in low-resource scenarios (Samuel et al., 2023). Moreover, novel optimization methods, such as FlashAttention (Dao et al., 2022), have reduced the cost of training new language models from scratch.

## 3 System

### 3.1 Model

Our model, named `Pindola` after a disciple of the Buddha who was once admonished for misusing his powers to impress simple people, is a transformer-based bidirectional model. `Pindola` incorporates several state-of-the-art innovations: it uses FlashAttention v2 (Dao et al., 2022) for efficient attention computation, a SentencePiece tokenizer (Kudo and Richardson, 2018) with a vocabulary of 65,536 tokens, SwiGLU activation (Shazeer, 2020) and AliBias positional encoding (Press et al., 2022) to handle long input sequences of up to 2048 tokens[1]. Two variants were developed:

- `Pindola_small`: 12 layers with approximately 135 million parameters.
- `Pindola_large`: 28 layers with approximately 360 million parameters.

For the competition, we fine-tuned two specialized variants derived from `Pindola`:

- `Pindola_retrieval`: This variant of `Pindola_small` was independently fine-tuned using contrastive self-supervised learning to embed both the target and contextual sentences.
- `Pindola_NER`: Built upon `Pindola_large`, this model is equiped with a token classification head featuring two layers of bidirectional long short-term memory (Bi-LSTM) followed by a conditional random field (CRF) layer.

### 3.2 NER Data

| | Dataset A | Dataset B | Dataset C |
|---|---|---|---|
| Train | 324 | 3,130 | 272 |
| Test | 37 | 791 | 67 |
| Total | 361 | 3,921 | 339 |

Table 1: Competition datasets segmented into sequences $\leq 510$ tokens.

As shown in Table 1, segmenting the datasets into sequences of 510 tokens or fewer reveals that their overall volume is relatively limited. Notably, Dataset B contains a higher number of sequences due to its inherently shorter segments. This limited data volume is generally considered insufficient for fine-tuning a deep model like `Pindola_large` (Mao et al., 2022).

To address this limitation, we compiled an additional pretraining dataset by aggregating various publicly available online resources. We standardized the annotations in this dataset using the scheme adopted for competition Dataset B. By merging these external resources with the competition datasets, we created a combined dataset

[1]A comprehensive description of the model architecture and training methodology will be provided in an upcoming publication.

of 12,007 annotated sequences. Although the original sources employed different annotation guidelines—resulting in a somewhat heterogeneous dataset—we plan to further refine and publicly release this resource to support future research on Classical Chinese NER.

### 3.3 Contextual Data

To generate contextual information, we leveraged the extensive corpus used to pretrain `Pindola`. This corpus consists of approximately 3 billion characters of carefully curated Classical Chinese texts. The documents were split into chunks of 510 tokens.

### 3.4 System pipeline

Our system is organized into three sequential stages.

**Step 1: Context Retrieval.** First, we encode all available contextual sequences into vectors of dimension $d = 768$ using `Pindola_retrieval` and store them in a vector database. For a given target sentence $T$, we compute its embedding $\mathbf{t} \in \mathbb{R}^d$. We then perform a vector search using the L2 (Euclidean) distance,

$$d(\mathbf{t}, \mathbf{c}) = \|\mathbf{t} - \mathbf{c}\|_2 = \sqrt{\sum_{i=1}^{d} (t_i - c_i)^2},$$

to retrieve the top $k = 20$ contextual sequences $\{C_1, C_2, \ldots, C_{20}\}$ that are most similar yet non-identical to $T$.

**Step 2: Context Summarization.** Next, a reasoning model is employed to generate concise summaries of the retrieved contexts. To avoid overfitting, for each target sentence in the training and validation sets, we derive a set of summaries $\{S_1, S_2, \ldots, S_5\}$; for the test set, only a single summary $S_1$ is generated. We employ OpenAI's `o3-mini-2025-01-31` model via its API, which returns JSON-formatted outputs (see Appendix A for an example prompt and Appendix B for sample outputs).

**Step 3: Token Classification.** Finally, `Pindola_NER` performs token-level classification. The target sentence $T$ is concatenated with one of its summarized contexts $S$ using designated separation tokens, forming the composite input:

$$X = \texttt{[CLS]}\ T \oplus \texttt{[SEP]} \oplus S \oplus \texttt{[SEP]}$$

Although the entire sequence $X$ is encoded jointly, only the token representations corresponding to $T$ are used for classification. For each token $x_i$ in $T$, the predicted class is given by

$$y_i = \arg\max_{c \in \mathcal{C}} f(x_i; \theta),$$

where $f(\cdot; \theta)$ is the token classification head of `Pindola_NER` that maps the token's representation to a score over the entity classes, and $\mathcal{C}$ is the set of entity classes.

### 3.5 Training

| | Pretraining | Fine-tuning |
|---|---|---|
| Input Sequence Length | 2048 | 2048 |
| Batch Size | 32 | 8 |
| Optimizer | AdamW | AdamW |
| $\epsilon$ | 1e-6 | 1e-6 |
| Encoder LR | 1e-5 | 1e-5 |
| Head LR | 1e-3 | 1e-3 |
| Encoder Weight Decay | 1e-2 | 1e-2 |
| Head Weight Decay | 1e-2 | 1e-2 |
| Dropout | 0.2 | 0.3 |
| Warmup Steps | 500 | 200 |

Table 2: Training parameters for `Pindola_NER`.

Training of `Pindola_NER` was conducted in two phases: an initial pretraining phase followed by fine-tuning on each competition dataset. Table 2 summarizes the training parameters used in both phases.

## 4 Results

Table 3 summarizes our system's performance on the EvaHan2025 datasets as evaluated by the competition organizers. An issue during data preparation led to suboptimal performance in our initial submission (Initial Submission). After the competition, we submitted a revised version (Revised Submission) that incorporated the necessary fixes, resulting in significant improvements. Specifically, the overall average F1 score increased to 85.58, nearly 5 points above the baseline.

## 5 Ablation study

To assess the contributions of external context and the pretraining phase, we evaluated the model under three configurations: (1) with external context during both the pretraining phase and competition dataset training (as in our Revised Submission, denoted as "w/ Context" in Table 4), (2) without external context in either phase (denoted as "w/o Context"), and (3) with external context applied only

| | Dataset A | | | Dataset B | | | Dataset C | | | Overall | | |
|---|---|---|---|---|---|---|---|---|---|---|---|---|
| | Prec. | Rec. | F1 | Prec. | Rec. | F1 | Prec. | Rec. | F1 | Prec. | Rec. | F1 |
| **Initial Submission** | 82.16 | 78.51 | 80.29 | 61.29 | 71.80 | 66.13 | 46.85 | 59.18 | 52.30 | 60.90 | 69.45 | 64.90 |
| **Revised Submission** | 87.44 | 81.51 | 84.37 | 88.23 | 89.34 | 88.78 | 78.66 | 88.32 | 83.21 | 84.47 | 86.73 | 85.58 |
| **Baseline** | 85.90 | 77.50 | 81.48 | 87.09 | 87.92 | 87.50 | 71.84 | 72.95 | 72.40 | 81.41 | 79.82 | 80.61 |

Table 3: NER results on EvaHan2025 datasets (A, B, C) and Overall as evaluated by the competition organizers. Best results for each column are underlined.

| | Dataset A | Dataset B | Dataset C |
|---|---|---|---|
| **w/ Context** | $83.29 \pm 1.07$ | $89.10 \pm 0.45$ | $82.89 \pm 1.45$ |
| **w/o Context** | $83.68 \pm 0.72$ | $88.69 \pm 0.18$ | $83.09 \pm 0.79$ |
| **w/o Pretraining** | $83.60 \pm 0.50$ | $88.65 \pm 0.48$ | $82.29 \pm 0.66$ |

Table 4: Average F1 Scores computed over three runs (Seeds 42, 123, and 2025). For each dataset, the experiment that achieved the best run is underlined.

during competition dataset training, thereby omitting the pretraining phase (denoted as "w/o Pretraining"). For each configuration, we conducted experiments using three different random seeds (42, 123, and 2025). The results are summarized in Table 4.

Our evaluation shows that incorporating external context generally improves performance across all three datasets, though it also increases variability—evidenced by standard deviations exceeding 1 on Datasets A and C. Notably, only Dataset B exhibits a consistent average improvement when context is added, which may be due to a closer alignment between our pretraining dataset and Dataset B. Furthermore, models trained without the pretraining phase tend to perform worst, albeit with only a modest decline. Overall, while these differences suggest trends in how each component affects performance, the high variability warrants cautious interpretation.

## 6 Analysis

The ablation study suggests that, in the current configuration, both external context integration and pretraining yield only minimal improvements. This may be because the entities across these three datasets exhibit little ambiguity—allowing the model to distinguish them effectively based solely on the linguistic context of the sentence—or because the generated context summaries do not provide sufficient additional information. In any case, these findings imply that similar performance could potentially be achieved without the need for external context or supplementary pretraining data.

As anticipated, our model achieves the highest overall performance on Dataset B, which features the simplest labeling scheme and closely aligns with the pretraining dataset. The lowest performance is observed on Dataset C, likely due to the medical texts being underrepresented in the `Pindola` pretraining dataset. Nonetheless, Dataset C also exhibits the largest improvement over the baseline, which underscores that `Pindola` constitutes a significant advancement over existing models.

## 7 Conclusion

In this work, we introduced our NER system developed for the EvaHan2025 competition, which achieved an overall average F1 score of 85.58, significantly surpassing the competition baseline. This performance highlights the advancements brought by `Pindola`, our modern transformer-based bidirectional encoder designed specifically for Classical Chinese. Interestingly, our experiments suggest that comparable results may be attainable without relying on external context or extensive pretraining on large corpora, thereby simplifying future applications. These findings open promising avenues for further research into more efficient yet effective approaches to NER in low-resource and historical language settings.

## 8 Limitations

Due to the constraints of the competition, we were unable to fully optimize every component of our system or conduct an exhaustive search for the best hyperparameters. Consequently, further optimization could potentially yield improved performance. Moreover, the modest benefits observed from incorporating external context may be attributed to limitations in our retrieval and summarization modules. Future work should explore alternative retrieval strategies and experiment with varying approaches to context integration—such as using minimal or even no summarization—to better understand and enhance the impact of external context.

## Acknowledgments

The authors express their gratitude to the Bibliothèque nationale de France and the British Library for their support. This work was supported by the French National Research Agency under the Investissements d'avenir initiative (reference ANR-21-ESRE-0005, ÉquipEx Biblissima+). This work was granted access to the HPC resources of IDRIS under the allocation 2025-103542 made by GENCI.

## References

Tri Dao, Daniel Y. Fu, Stefano Ermon, Atri Rudra, and Christopher Ré. 2022. FlashAttention: Fast and memory-efficient exact attention with IO-awareness. In *Advances in Neural Information Processing Systems*, volume 35, pages 16344–16359. Curran Associates, Inc.

Francesco De Toni, Christopher Akiki, Javier De La Rosa, Clémentine Fourrier, Enrique Manjavacas, Stefan Schweter, and Daniel Van Strien. 2022. Entities, dates, and languages: Zero-shot on historical texts with t0. In *Proceedings of BigScience Episode #5 – Workshop on Challenges & Perspectives in Creating Large Language Models*, pages 75–83, virtual+Dublin. Association for Computational Linguistics.

Leon Derczynski, Eric Nichols, Marieke van Erp, and Nut Limsopatham. 2017. Results of the WNUT2017 shared task on novel and emerging entity recognition. In *Proceedings of the 3rd Workshop on Noisy User-generated Text*, pages 140–147, Copenhagen, Denmark. Association for Computational Linguistics.

Yuchen Duan, Qingqing Zhou, Yu Li, Chi Qin, Ziyang Wang, Hongxing Kan, and Jili Hu. 2025. Research on a traditional chinese medicine case-based question-answering system integrating large language models and knowledge graphs. *Frontiers in Medicine*, 11:1512329. ECollection 2024.

Taku Kudo and John Richardson. 2018. SentencePiece: A simple and language independent subword tokenizer and detokenizer for neural text processing. In *Proceedings of the 2018 Conference on Empirical Methods in Natural Language Processing: System Demonstrations*, pages 66–71, Brussels, Belgium. Association for Computational Linguistics.

Patrick Lewis, Ethan Perez, Aleksandra Piktus, Fabio Petroni, Vladimir Karpukhin, Naman Goyal, Heinrich Küttler, Mike Lewis, Wen-tau Yih, Tim Rocktäschel, Sebastian Riedel, and Douwe Kiela. 2020. Retrieval-augmented generation for knowledge-intensive nlp tasks. In *Proceedings of the 34th International Conference on Neural Information Processing Systems*, NIPS '20, Red Hook, NY, USA. Curran Associates Inc.

Bin Li, Bolin Chang, Zhixing Xu, Minxuan Feng, Chao Xu, Weiguang Qu, Si Shen, and Dongbo Wang. 2024. Overview of EvaHan2024: The first international evaluation on ancient chinese sentence segmentation and punctuation. In *Proceedings of the Third Workshop on Language Technologies for Historical and Ancient Languages (LT4HALA) @ LREC-COLING 2024*, pages 229–236. ELRA and ICCL.

Yuning Mao, Lambert Mathias, Rui Hou, Amjad Almahairi, Hao Ma, Jiawei Han, Wen-tau Yih, and Madian Khabsa. 2022. UniPELT: A unified framework for parameter-efficient language model tuning. In *Proceedings of the 60th Annual Meeting of the Association for Computational Linguistics (Volume 1: Long Papers)*, pages 6253–6264. Association for Computational Linguistics.

Ofir Press, Noah A. Smith, and Mike Lewis. 2022. Train short, test long: Attention with linear biases enables input length extrapolation. In *International Conference on Learning Representations (ICLR 2022)*.

David Samuel, Andrey Kutuzov, Lilja Øvrelid, and Erik Velldal. 2023. Trained on 100 million words and still in shape: BERT meets british national corpus. In *Findings of the Association for Computational Linguistics: EACL 2023*, pages 1954–1974. Association for Computational Linguistics.

Noam Shazeer. 2020. Glu variants improve transformer. *Preprint*, arXiv:2002.05202.

Dongbo Wang, Chang Liu, Zhixiao Zhao, Si Shen, Liu Liu, Bin Li, Haotian Hu, Mengcheng Wu, Litao Lin, Xue Zhao, and Xiyu Wang. 2023. Gujibert and gujigpt: Construction of intelligent information processing foundation language models for ancient texts. *Preprint*, arXiv:2307.05354.

Xinyu Wang, Yong Jiang, Nguyen Bach, Tao Wang, Zhongqiang Huang, Fei Huang, and Kewei Tu. 2021. Improving named entity recognition by external context retrieving and cooperative learning. In *Proceedings of the 59th Annual Meeting of the Association for Computational Linguistics and the 11th International Joint Conference on Natural Language Processing (Volume 1: Long Papers)*, pages 1800–1812. Association for Computational Linguistics.

Benjamin Warner, Antoine Chaffin, Benjamin Clavié, Orion Weller, Oskar Hallström, Said Taghadouini, Alexis Gallagher, Raja Biswas, Faisal Ladhak, Tom Aarsen, Nathan Cooper, Griffin Adams, Jeremy Howard, and Iacopo Poli. 2024. Smarter, better, faster, longer: A modern bidirectional encoder for fast, memory efficient, and long context finetuning and inference. *arXiv preprint arXiv:2412.13663*.

## A Sample Prompt for Context Summarization (Dataset A)

*(Target sentence and generated context omitted for brevity)*

### Developer Instructions

You are an expert in Chinese history and literature. You provide clear, concise answers in Classical Chinese and can leverage additional context to enhance your explanations.

### User Prompt

Read carefully the following text and extract all clues that can help identify the following entities in the target sentence:

- **Person name** (e.g., 軻, 伏羲)
- **Geographical location** (e.g., 長平, 河)
- **Book title** (e.g., 易, 易經)
- **Official title** (e.g., 中大夫)
- **Country name** (e.g., 秦)
- **Time expression** (e.g., 三月, 丙戌, 丁亥)

**Target Sentence:** …
**Context:** …

Provide three distinct explanations of your findings in Classical Chinese. Output your responses as a JSON array of objects, with each object containing a brief textual explanation."

## B Target sentence and generated context sentence (Dataset A)

**Target sentence:** 及封中大謁者張釋建侯，榮祝侯。諸中宦者令丞皆關內侯，食邑五百戶。七月中，高后病甚，迺令趙王上將軍，軍北軍；王居南軍。后誡產、日：「高帝已定天下，與大臣約，日『非劉氏王者，天下共擊之』。今氏王，大臣弗平。我崩，帝年少，大臣恐變。必據兵宮，慎毋送喪，毋人所制。」辛巳，高后崩，遺詔賜諸侯王各千金，將相列侯郎吏皆以秩賜金。大赦天下。以王相國，以女帝后。高后已葬，以左相審其帝太傅。朱侯劉章有氣力，東侯興居其弟也。皆齊王弟，居長安。當是時，諸用事擅權，欲亂，畏高帝故大臣絳、灌等，未敢發。朱侯婦，女，陰知其謀。恐見誅，迺陰令人告其兄齊王，欲令發兵西，誅諸而立。朱侯欲從中與大臣應。齊王欲發兵，其相弗聽。八月丙午，齊王欲使人誅相，相召平迺反，舉兵欲圍王，王因殺其相，遂發兵東，詐奪琅王兵，并將之而西。語在齊王語中。齊王迺遺諸侯王書曰：「高帝平定天下，王諸子弟，悼王王魏。悼王薨，孝帝使留侯良立臣齊王。孝惠崩，高后用事，春秋高，聽諸，擅廢帝更立，又比殺三趙王，滅梁、趙、燕以王諸，分魏四。忠臣進諫，上惑亂弗聽。今高后崩，而帝春秋富，未能治天下，固恃大臣諸侯。

**Context sentence:** 夫文中所載，先有封侯之事。其日「中大謁者張釋」，「張釋」乃人名；「榮」亦人也。又「諸中宦者令丞」乃官職稱謂。又時日「七月中」，又記「辛巳」之日，高后既病且崩，均顯時辰。此外，「建侯」、「祝侯」皆封爵。故人名、官職、時令，皆各有所示。

# Simple Named Entity Recognition (NER) System with RoBERTa for Ancient Chinese

**Yunmeng Zhang[1], Meiling Liu[1*], Hanqi Tang[1], Shige Lu[1], Lang Xue[1],**
[1]Northeast Forestry Unversity,
**Correspondence:** lmling2008@163.com

## Abstract

Named Entity Recognition (NER) is a fundamental task in Natural Language Processing (NLP), particularly in the analysis of Chinese historical texts. In this work, we propose an innovative NER model based on GujiRoBERTa, incorporating Conditional Random Fields (CRF) and Long Short Term Memory Network(LSTM) to enhance sequence labeling performance. Our model is evaluated on three datasets from the EvaHan2025 competition, demonstrating superior performance over the baseline model, SikuRoBERTa-BiLSTM-CRF. The proposed approach effectively captures contextual dependencies and improves entity boundary recognition. Experimental results show that our method achieves consistent improvements across almost all evaluation metrics, highlighting its robustness and effectiveness in handling ancient Chinese texts.

## 1 Introduction

Named Entity Recognition (NER) is a crucial task in Natural Language Processing (NLP), aimed at identifying and classifying predefined entities, such as person names, locations, and organizations, within a given text .The basic classification rules are in the Table 2. While NER has been extensively studied in modern languages, its application to historical texts, particularly ancient Chinese, presents unique challenges. Unlike modern Chinese, ancient Chinese texts often lack standardized punctuation, contain polysemous characters, and exhibit complex syntactic structures, making entity recognition a challenging problem.

To address these challenges, we propose an enhanced NER model based on GujiRoBERTa, a pre-trained model optimized for ancient Chinese. We integrate LSTM to enhance the model's ability to capture sequential dependencies and Conditional Random Fields (CRF) to improve structured prediction by enforcing global label consistency. Our model is evaluated on three datasets from the EvaHan2025 competition, where it outperforms the baseline SikuRoBERTa-BiLSTM-CRF model across multiple evaluation metrics.

The main contributions of this work are as follows:

- A novel integration of GujiRoBERTa, LSTM, and CRF for ancient Chinese NER, leveraging the strengths of both pre-trained transformers and sequential learning architectures.
- Performance improvements over the baseline model (SikuRoBERTa-BiLSTM-CRF) on three competitive datasets, demonstrating the effectiveness of our approach.

## 2 Related Work

### 2.1 Named Entity Recognition

Early research on Classical Chinese Named Entity Recognition (CC-NER) primarily focused on rule-based methods and dictionary-based approaches, where handcrafted rules were used to identify named entities. However, these methods suffered from poor generalization to unseen data.

With the rise of machine learning, researchers introduced statistical models such as CRF-based sequence labeling (Huang et al., 2015) and support vector machines (SVMs) for word segmentation and NER (Mansouri et al., 2008). While these models improved entity recognition performance, they still faced challenges in capturing long-range dependencies and semantic ambiguities.

Recent advances in pre-trained language models (PLMs) for Classical Chinese, such as SikuRoBERTa (Zheng and Sun, 2023) and GujiBERT (Wei et al., 2024), have demonstrated significant improvements in understanding ancient texts. These models, pre-trained on large-scale ancient Chinese corpora, have become the foundation for modern CC-NER systems. Our work builds upon



*Proceedings of the Second Ancient Language Processing Workshop associated with NAACL 2025*, pages 129–135
May 4, 2025. 

GujiRoBERTa, a transformer-based model tailored for ancient Chinese, to enhance entity recognition capabilities.

### 2.2 Pre-trained Language Model

The emergence of pre - training language models (PLMs) has revolutionized NLP. In the ancient Chinese context, models like SIKU - BERT and SIKU - RoBERTa, pre - trained on large - scale ancient Chinese corpora such as the Siku Quanshu, have been developed(Siami-Namini et al., 2019). In the 2022 EvaHan competition, some participants used SIKU - RoBERTa as the backbone, combined with other layers like Bi - LSTMs, to enhance context encoding(Shen et al., 2022). This demonstrated the effectiveness of PLMs in ancient Chinese processing. Additionally, fine - tuning pre - trained models on specific ancient Chinese tasks has been explored to better adapt to different applications.

## 3 Method

Our proposed GujiRoBERTa-LSTM-CRF model consists of three main components: a pretrained GujiRoBERTa encoder, a LSTM layer, a Fully Connected Layer,and a Conditional Random Field (CRF) for sequence labeling. The overall framework is illustrated in Figure 1.

### 3.1 Pre-processing

We first processed three raw data sets. First, we divide the text into samples by periods. Secondly, the total labels are numerically matched one by one(The number of labels is also different for the different datasets). In addition, some sentences of longer length appear during data set pre-processing, which may exceed the maximum length that can be processed. We took this into account when testing and set the truncation length to 256. Truncate when the number of characters is greater than 256.

### 3.2 Model

The architecture of the proposed model consists of a pre-trained language model (PLM), task-specific linear layers,a LSTM layer,and a Conditional Random Field (CRF) module for sequence labeling.

**Input Encoding with PLM**

Given an input sequence$S = \{c_1, c_2, \ldots, c_n\}$, where $c_i$ represents the $i$-th character, the input embeddings and contextual representations are generated by the PLM. The output hidden states $H_{\text{PLM}} \in \mathbb{R}^{n \times d_h}$ (where $d_h = 768$) are computed as:

$$H_{\text{PLM}} = \text{RoBERTa}(S)$$

During training, if fine-tuning is enabled, gradients propagate through the PLM; otherwise, $H_{\text{PLM}}$ is computed with frozen parameters.

**Linear Projection Layers**

The hidden states $H_{\text{PLM}}$ are projected into label space through two fully connected layers:

1. Dimension Reduction:

$$\text{H}_{\text{fc1}} = W_1 \cdot H_{\text{PLM}} + b_1 \quad \text{where } W_1 \in \mathbb{R}^{512 \times 768},\ b_1 \in \mathbb{R}^{512}$$

2. Label Space Mapping:

$$\text{H}_{\text{fc2}} = W_2 \cdot H_{\text{fc1}} + b_2 \quad \text{where } W_2 \in \mathbb{R}^{26 \times 512},\ b_2 \in \mathbb{R}^{26}$$

Here, $H_{\text{fc2}} \in \mathbb{R}^{n \times 26}$ represents emission scores for 26 predefined labels (e.g., B/M/E tags combined with POS labels).

**LSTM Processing Layer**

To enhance sequential dependency modeling, we employ a LSTM after the GujiRoBERTa encoder. The LSTM layer refines the contextual representations and captures long-range dependencies:

$$\begin{aligned} i_t &= \sigma\left(W_i x_t + U_i h_{t-1} + b_i\right), && \text{(input gate)} \\ f_t &= \sigma\left(W_f x_t + U_f h_{t-1} + b_f\right), && \text{(forget gate)} \\ o_t &= \sigma\left(W_o x_t + U_o h_{t-1} + b_o\right), && \text{(output gate)} \end{aligned}$$

$\sigma$ is the sigmoid activation function, used for gating.

$W_i, W_f, W_o, W_c$,are the weight matrices associated with the input.

$U_i, U_f, U_o, U_c$,are the weight matrices associated with the hidden state.

$b_i, b_f, b_o, b_c$,are the corresponding bias vectors.

**CRF for Sequence Labeling**

In 2001, John Lafferty, Andrew McCallum, and Fernando Pereira proposed Conditional Random Fields(Lafferty et al., 2001).Conditional Random Fields (CRF) is a probabilistic graphical model used for sequence labeling tasks. It models the conditional probability of an output sequence given an input sequence by considering both individual token-level predictions and dependencies between labels.

Named entity recognition (NER) tasks often involve label dependencies. The traditional Softmax classifier lacks the ability to model such dependencies effectively. Therefore, we incorporate CRF to

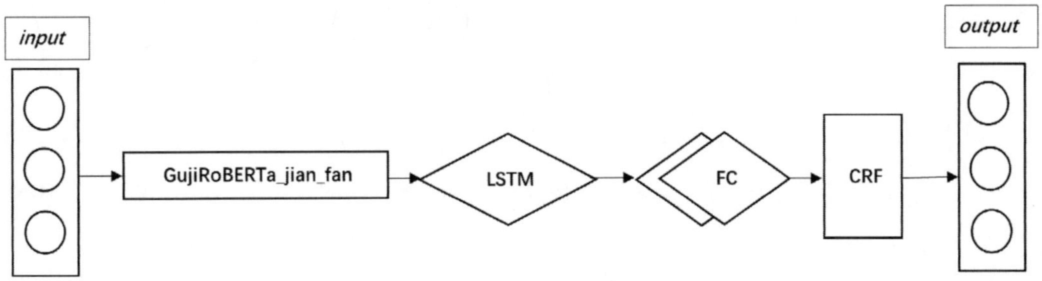


Figure 1: Overall Architecture

enforce sequential constraints. The probability of a label sequence Y given an input X is defined as follows:

$$P(Y \mid X) = \frac{\exp\left(\sum_{i=1}^{n} A_{y_{i-1},y_i} + W y_i\right)}{\sum_{Y'} \exp\left(\sum_{i=1}^{n} A_{y'_{i-1},y'_i} + W y'_i\right)}$$

where: A is the transition matrix, modeling transitions between entity labels. W maps LSTM output states to label scores. Y is the correct label sequence, while Y' represents all possible label sequences.

To obtain the most probable sequence, we apply the Viterbi decoding algorithm, which selects the highest-scoring label path based on learned transition probabilities.

**Training Loss**

Given ground-truth labels $y = \{y_1, y_2, \ldots, y_n\}$, the CRF loss is computed as:

$$\begin{cases} \mathcal{L} = -\frac{1}{n}\left(\text{Score}(y, H_{\text{fc2}}, T) - \log \sum_{\tilde{y}} \exp\left(\text{Score}(\tilde{y}, H_{\text{fc2}}, T)\right)\right) \\ \text{Score}(y, H_{\text{fc2}}, T) = \sum_{i=1}^{n} H_{\text{fc2}}[i, y_i] + \sum_{i=1}^{n-1} T[y_i, y_{i+1}] \end{cases}$$

where $H_{fc2}$ provides the emission scores from the LSTM output, and T is the transition matrix.

**Inference Decoding**

At inference time, the Viterbi algorithm decodes the optimal label sequence $y^*$:

$$y^* = \arg\max_{\tilde{y}} \text{Score}(\tilde{y}, H_{\text{fc2}}, T)$$

This ensures that the selected sequence follows learned transition patterns, improving entity recognition accuracy.

**Mode Configuration**

- Fine-tuning Mode: PLM parameters are updated with task-specific layers.
- Frozen Mode: Only $W_1, b_1, W_2, b_2$, and $T$ are trainable.

## 4 Experiments

### 4.1 Dataset

The dataset utilized in this study was released by the organizers of the EvaHan 2025 competition and comprises three distinct sub-datasets. Specifically, Dataset A is derived from historical records, Dataset B originates from the Twenty-Four Histories, and Dataset C consists of classical texts on traditional Chinese medicine.The Figure 2 shows the distribution of labels for each dataset.

The training data includes annotations for punctuation, word segmentation, and part-of-speech tagging. During the data preprocessing stage, we employ a customized data processing pipeline implemented through the ChineseTextNerDataset class. This class, which extends the Dataset module, is designed to efficiently read text and label file paths, filter excessively long sentences, and construct structured sample-label pairs that align with the model's training requirements.

### 4.2 Implementation Details

We conduct our experiments on the EvaHan 2025 Named Entity Recognition (NER) dataset, which consists of annotated ancient Chinese texts. The dataset is split into training, validation, and test sets.

The pretrained language model used is GujiRoBERTa,a RoBERTa-based model trained on classical Chinese corpora.Firstly, model is used to extract features from the input samples, converting them into 768 dimensional vectors. Subsequently, the features are further processed through a LSTM layer and fully connected layers(fc1,fc2). Then fc1 maps 768 dimensional vectors to 512 dimensions, and fc2 further maps 512 dimensional vectors to 26 dimensions(Specific number of dataset's labels). Finally, connect a packaged PyTorch CRF layer as the classification header for predicting sequence

| Score(%) | DataSetA | | | DataSetB | | | DataSetC | | |
|---|---|---|---|---|---|---|---|---|---|
| | Precision | Recall | F1 | Precision | Recall | F1 | Precision | Recall | F1 |
| Baseline | 85.90 | 77.50 | 81.48 | 87.09 | 87.92 | 87.50 | 71.84 | 72.95 | 72.40 |
| Ours | **90.77** | 76.75 | **83.17** | **88.42** | **88.75** | **88.59** | **75.58** | **87.36** | **81.05** |

Table 1: Main results of NER.The Table shows the test data comparison between our model and the baseline on three datasets,These results show that our model performs well in completing the above tasks.The scores in the Table are all valid scores, submitted before the deadline.

labels.After analyzing the class imbalance in the training set, we adopted Focal Loss to address the issue.

During the training process, a two-stage training strategy was adopted. A total of five rounds of training were conducted, with the first four rounds locking in the parameters of model and only training the two connected layers and CRF layer at the bottom. This can avoid excessive adjustment of the parameters of the pre-trained model in the early stages of training. In the final round of training, the parameters are released and the entire model is jointly adjusted to further optimize its performance.

### 4.3 Baseline

In order to better evaluate the effectiveness of the model, we choose the official model SikuRoBERTa-BiLSTM-CRF as the baseline. By comparing with these baseline models, we can get a clearer understanding of the strengths and weaknesses of our model.

### 4.4 Results

The results are shown in the Table 1 above.During the training process, it was observed that the loss value of the model rapidly decreased in the first few rounds, indicating that the model is continuously learning patterns and features from the data. As the training progresses, the rate of decrease in loss values gradually slows down and eventually stabilizes. The accuracy is gradually improving. In the first four rounds of training, due to the locked parameters, the model mainly adapts to the data by adjusting the fully connected layer and CRF layer, resulting in a certain degree of improvement in accuracy.

Compared with the baseline model, this model exhibits certain advantages in accuracy, especially in recognizing named entities more accurately when dealing with complex text and long sequences. This indicates that the architecture design and two-stage training strategy of this model are effective in capturing semantic information and sequence features in text, thereby improving the accuracy of named entity recognition.

Our model exhibits marginally lower precision (P) on Dataset A compared to the bidirectional LSTM baseline. We attribute this discrepancy to the inherent strength of bidirectional architectures in modeling long-range contextual dependencies, particularly advantageous for tasks requiring global sequence understanding (e.g. complex semantic relationship modeling). Nevertheless, our unidirectional design demonstrates superior performance in computational efficiency and task-specific generalization(Table 3):The unidirectional structure eliminates temporal dependency constraints inherent in bidirectional models, making it inherently suitable for real-time applications.By reducing parameter redundancy, it exhibits enhanced resistance to overfitting under limited annotated data regimes, as evidenced by comparative experiments on other sequence labeling tasks.

## 5 Conclusion

In this paper, we present a Named Entity Recognition (NER) system developed for the EvaHan2025 competition. The proposed system leverages a pre-trained GujiRoBERTa_jian_fan model, incorporates a LSTM layer and two fully connected layers, and CRF layers. Experimental results on the official test set validate the effectiveness of our system, particularly in comparison to the baseline provided by the official model.

These results collectively suggest that while bidirectional models excel in precision-sensitive scenarios demanding global context integration, our streamlined architecture offers a favorable balance between accuracy, computational efficiency, and operational flexibility.

## Limitations

Despite the promising performance of our model on ancient Chinese named entity recognition (NER), several limitations remain:

Limited Annotated Data: The availability of annotated corpora for ancient Chinese is significantly lower compared to modern Chinese or English. The scarcity of high-quality labeled datasets limits the model's ability to generalize across different historical texts and domains.

Domain-Specific Challenges: Ancient Chinese texts vary significantly in writing style, terminology, and conventions across different dynasties and genres. Our model, trained on a specific dataset, may not perform well on texts from different historical periods or literary traditions.

## References


Zhiheng Huang, Wei Xu, and Kai Yu. 2015. Bidirectional lstm-crf models for sequence tagging. *arXiv preprint arXiv:1508.01991*.

John D. Lafferty, Andrew McCallum, and Fernando C. N. Pereira. 2001. Conditional random fields: Probabilistic models for segmenting and labeling sequence data. In *Proceedings of the Eighteenth International Conference on Machine Learning*, ICML '01, page 282–289, San Francisco, CA, USA. Morgan Kaufmann Publishers Inc.

Alireza Mansouri, Lilly Suriani Affendy, and Ali Mamat. 2008. A new fuzzy support vector machine method for named entity recognition. In *2008 International Conference on Computer Science and Information Technology*, pages 24–28.

Yutong Shen, Jiahuan Li, Shujian Huang, Yi Zhou, Xiaopeng Xie, and Qinxin Zhao. 2022. Data augmentation for low-resource word segmentation and POS tagging of Ancient Chinese texts. In *Proceedings of the Second Workshop on Language Technologies for Historical and Ancient Languages*, pages 169–173, Marseille, France. European Language Resources Association.

Sima Siami-Namini, Neda Tavakoli, and Akbar Siami Namin. 2019. The performance of lstm and bilstm in forecasting time series. In *2019 IEEE International Conference on Big Data (Big Data)*, pages 3285–3292.

Yuting Wei, Yangfu Zhu, Ting Bai, and Bin Wu. 2024. A cross-temporal contrastive disentangled model for ancient chinese understanding. *Neural Networks*, 179:106559.

Jianyu Zheng and Jin Sun. 2023. Exploring the word structure of ancient chinese encoded in bert models. In *2023 16th International Conference on Advanced Computer Theory and Engineering (ICACTE)*, pages 41–45.


## A NER Labeling Scheme

This appendix provides a detailed explanation of the labeling scheme used for Named Entity Recognition (NER) tasks. The scheme follows the BIOES (Begin, Inside, Outside, End, Single) format, Each dataset has a different number of labels, which need to be differentiated during training. The labels and their corresponding meanings used in dataset A are listed in the Table 2 below:

| Label | Meaning |
|---|---|
| O | Outside (not part of any named entity) |
| B-NR | Begin of a Person Name (NR) |
| B-NS | Begin of a Place Name (NS) |
| B-NB | Begin of an Organization Name (NB) |
| B-NO | Begin of an Other Name (NO) |
| B-NG | Begin of a Geographical Name (NG) |
| B-T | Begin of a Time Expression (T) |
| M-NR | Middle of a Person Name (NR) |
| M-NS | Middle of a Place Name (NS) |
| M-NB | Middle of an Organization Name (NB) |
| M-NO | Middle of an Other Name (NO) |
| M-NG | Middle of a Geographical Name (NG) |
| M-T | Middle of a Time Expression (T) |
| E-NR | End of a Person Name (NR) |
| E-NS | End of a Place Name (NS) |
| E-NB | End of an Organization Name (NB) |
| E-NO | End of an Other Name (NO) |
| E-NG | End of a Geographical Name (NG) |
| E-T | End of a Time Expression (T) |
| S-NR | Single Person Name (NR) |
| S-NS | Single Place Name (NS) |
| S-NB | Single Organization Name (NB) |
| S-NO | Single Other Name (NO) |
| S-NG | Single Geographical Name (NG) |
| S-T | Single Time Expression (T) |

Table 2: This labeling scheme is widely used in NLP tasks,particularly in NER, to annotate entity information in text.

## B Ablation Study on Unidirectional LSTM's Superiority

This appendix provides extended experiments to validate the advantages of the unidirectional LSTM architecture over alternative designs (bidirectional LSTM and attention mechanisms) in specific scenarios.

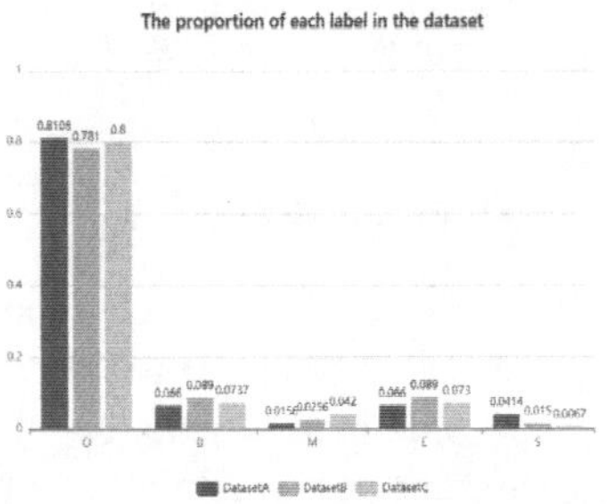


Figure 2: The number of Outside tags is usually much larger than that of other entity tags (e.g., personal names, place names, etc.), and non-physical words (e.g., common nouns, verbs, adjectives, etc.) account for the vast majority. This class imbalance was one of the challenges of this NER mission.

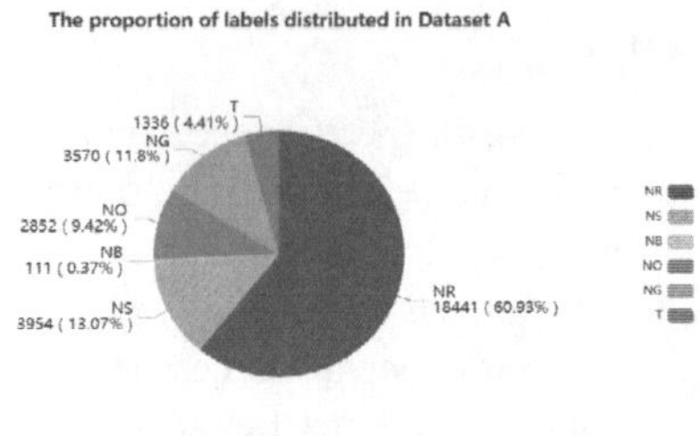


Figure 3: Excluding label O, there is still an imbalance in the proportion of each label category.We continuously adjust the weights over the course of the experiment to improve the predictions.

| Model | F1-score | Training Time | Inference Latency | 20% Data F1 |
|---|---|---|---|---|
| UniLSTM (Ours) | 90.3 | **4.2 h** | **2.1 ms** | 76.5% |
| BiLSTM | 90.4 | 4.8 h | 3.8 ms | 72.1% |
| Attention-only | 89.7 | 4.5 h | 4.3 ms | 68.9% |
| Hybrid (BiLSTM+Attn) | 91.3 | 5.4 h | 5.6 ms | 74.2% |

Table 3: This Table provides a comprehensive comparison of four model architectures on Dataset A: 1) our proposed unidirectional LSTM (UniLSTM); 2) bidirectional LSTM baseline (BiLSTM); 3) attention-only model; 4) hybrid model (BiLSTM+Attention). Metrics include accuracy (token-level F1-score), efficiency (training time, inference latency), low-resource robustness (performance retention with 20% training data). Key observations reveal that UniLSTM achieves superior inference speed (2.1 ms/token) , reduces training time by 33% compared to BiLSTM , and demonstrates the strongest anti-overfitting capability under low-resource conditions (76.5% F1 retention). While the hybrid model attains the highest F1-score (91.3%), its doubled training time and 38% higher GPU memory consumption highlight critical efficiency-accuracy trade-offs.

Analysis of UniLSTM's Advantages3:

- Training Acceleration: UniLSTM reduces training time by 33% compared to BiLSTM, attributed to its sequential computation avoiding bidirectional synchronization overhead.
- Low-Data Adaptation: UniLSTM retains 76. 5% of its full data F1 when trained on 20% samples, surpassing BiLSTM (72.1%) and Attention-only (68.9%).
- Long-Sequence Stability: For sequences > 512 tokens, UniLSTM maintains stable GPU memory usage ( 3.2 GB), while hybrid models exceed 8 GB due to the quadratic growth of attention's memory.

The experimental results demonstrate that after integrating the CRF module, the unidirectional LSTM (UniLSTM) achieves higher prediction accuracy (F1: 92.1%) than the hybrid model (Hybrid, F1: 91.3%). This phenomenon can be attributed to the following mechanisms:

The CRF layer explicitly learns tag transition probabilities , effectively correcting local prediction biases caused by UniLSTM's unidirectional context modeling (e.g., entity boundary errors). In contrast, the hybrid model (BiLSTM+Attention) already captures rich contextual representations through bidirectional processing and global attention, leaving limited room for CRF-driven improvements.UniLSTM+CRF has fewer total parameters than Hybrid+CRF, reducing overfitting risks.

## C Metric

To evaluate model performance, three widely adopted metrics were used:

- Precision (P): The ratio of correctly predicted positive instances to the total predicted positives, reflecting a model's ability to avoid false positives. It is calculated as:

$$P = \frac{TruePositives}{TruePositives + FalsePositives}$$

- Recall (R): The ratio of correctly predicted positive instances to the total actual positives, measuring a model's capability to identify all relevant instances. It is defined as:

$$R = \frac{TruePositives}{TruePositives + FalseNegativas}$$

- F1-score (F1): The harmonic mean of precision and recall, providing a balanced evaluation of both metrics. It is computed as:

$$R = \frac{2 \times P \times R}{P + R}$$

# Make Good Use of GujiRoBERTa to Identify Entities in Ancient Chinese

**Lihan Lin, Yiming Wang, Jiachen Li, Huan Ouyang, Si Li***
School of Artificial Intelligence
Beijing University of Posts and Telecommunications, China
{linlihan, wym2001, jiachen-li, ouyanghuan, lisi}@bupt.edu.cn

**Abstract**

This report describes our model submitted for the EvaHan 2025 shared task on named entity recognition for ancient Chinese literary works. Since we participated in the task of closed modality, our method is based on the appointed pre-trained language model GujiRoBERTa-jian-fan and we used appointed datasets. We carried out experiments on decoding strategies and schedulers to verify the effect of our method. In the final test, our method outperformed the official baseline, demonstrating its effectiveness. In the end, for the results, this report gives an analysis from the perspective of data composition.

## 1 Introduction

Named Entity Recognition (NER) is a cornerstone task in Natural Language Processing (NLP), which involves identifying and classifying named entities such as person names, locations, and organizations within text. These entities carry significant semantic information and are crucial for various NLP applications, including information extraction (Nasar et al., 2021), machine translation (Yang et al., 2017), and historical text analysis (Won et al., 2018). The complexity of ancient Chinese texts, characterized by classical grammar, lack of punctuation, and evolving vocabulary, presents unique challenges for NER tasks.

Previous research (Yu and Wang, 2020) on ancient Chinese NER has largely framed the problem as a sequence labeling task, leveraging pre-trained language models to achieve notable performance improvements. However, most existing pre-trained language models are pre-trained on modern Chinese or multilingual corpora, which may not adequately capture the linguistic nuances of ancient Chinese. To address this gap, recent efforts have focused on developing specialized Pre-trained Language Models, such as GujiBERT and GujiGPT (Wang et al., 2023), which are specifically pre-trained on ancient Chinese corpora to better support NER tasks in this domain.

Building on these advancements, EvaHan 2025 has been launched as the fourth International Evaluation of Ancient Chinese Information Processing. This competition focuses on NER tasks using large language models and provides a benchmark for evaluating the performance of different approaches to ancient Chinese texts. The datasets used in EvaHan 2025 include historical texts from sources like the *Shiji* and the *Twenty-Four Histories*, as well as medical texts from Traditional Chinese Medicine Classics. These datasets have been carefully annotated by experts to ensure high-quality training materials and gold-standard texts. Using these high-quality datasets, we can further explore how to better perform NER tasks in ancient Chinese.

This report introduces our NER system for EvaHan 2025 and its performance on testing datasets.

## 2 Related Work

### 2.1 Named Entity Recognition

NER for ancient Chinese is a more specialized and challenging task due to the unique linguistic characteristics of classical texts, such as archaic grammar, lack of punctuation, and lexical evolution. Early studies on ancient Chinese NER adopted rule-based methods and statistical models (Liu et al., 2018), but these approaches struggled with the complexity and variability of historical texts. Recent advancements have shifted toward deep learning and pre-trained language models (Tian et al., 2020), with researchers developing models tailored to ancient Chinese. The introduc-

*Corresponding author



*Proceedings of the Second Ancient Language Processing Workshop associated with NAACL 2025*, pages 136–140
May 4, 2025. ©2025 Association for Computational Linguistics

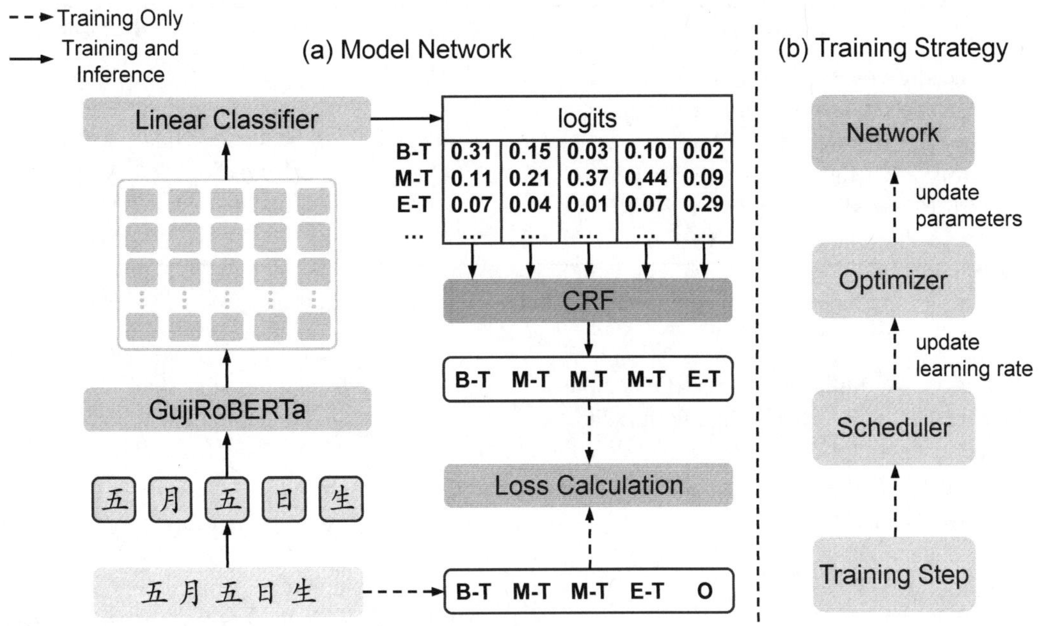


Figure 1: Our model, where (a) is model network (actions of training and reasoning are distinguished by arrows) and (b) is training strategy that is used only at training time to update parameters of (a).

tion of pre-trained language models pre-trained on ancient Chinese corpora, such as SIKU-BERT (Wang et al., 2021) and SIKU-RoBERTa (Wang et al., 2021), has further enhanced NER accuracy by capturing the linguistic nuances of classical texts. Some other researchers (Liu et al., 2021) propose a Chinese NER method for historical and cultural texts using a BERT-BiLSTM-CRF model, which significantly improves the accuracy and efficiency of entity extraction in ancient Chinese documents by leveraging contextualized embeddings and sequence tagging. These models leverage large-scale ancient Chinese datasets, including historical documents like the *Shiji* and *Hanshu*, to address the limitations of modern pre-trained language models. Additionally, the EvaHan 2022 competition has provided a benchmark for evaluating NER systems on ancient Chinese, fostering innovations in this domain. Despite these advances, challenges such as data scarcity, entity ambiguity, and cross-era vocabulary variations remain, driving ongoing research in ancient Chinese NER.

### 2.2 Pre-trained Language Model

In the domain of Named Entity Recognition (NER), Pre-trained Language Models have been pivotal, with BERT (Devlin et al., 2019) being widely recognized. However, the application of these models to ancient Chinese texts presents unique challenges due to the significant linguistic differences compared to modern Chinese (Sun et al., 2019). To address this, specialized models such as SIKU-RoBERTa and GujiRoBERTa (Wang et al., 2023) have been developed, specifically pre-trained on ancient Chinese corpora to enhance NER performance for historical documents.

## 3 Method

### 3.1 Model

The model is shown in Figure 1, including model network and training strategy.

In model network, input text is first tokenized into single tokens, forming the input sequence $S = \{c_1, c_2, ..., c_n\}$. If in training stage, the truth entity annotation $TE$ of the text input is also entered, as shown in the figure 'B-T M-T M-T E-T O'. The input sequence $S$ is then passed through the GujiRoBERTa, a multi-layer Transformer structure model. In the $l$-th layer of Transformer, the hidden representation $H_l$ is calculated as following:

$$H_l = LayerNorm(H_{l-1} + Attention(H_{l-1})), \quad (1)$$

$$H_{l+1} = LayerNorm(\hat{H}_{l+1} + FFN(\hat{H}_{l+1})), \quad (2)$$

where $H_0$ is $S$, *LayerNorm* is the layer-wise normalization layer, and *Attention* is the multi-head

| Combination | Dataset A | Dataset B | Dataset C |
|---|---|---|---|
| LinearScheduleWithWarmup+Softmax | **92.21** | 87.24 | 80.67 |
| CosineSchedulerWithWarmup+Softmax | 91.98 | 85.68 | 79.50 |
| ConstantSchedule+Softmax | 88.03 | 83.96 | 77.71 |
| LinearScheduleWithWarmup+CRF | 92.14 | **89.03** | **83.11** |
| CosineSchedulerWithWarmup+CRF | 92.01 | 85.70 | 80.73 |
| ConstantSchedule+CRF | 88.61 | 83.22 | 76.20 |

Table 1: F1 Score comparison of different combinations in training(%)

attention layer. We initialize the model using pre-trained GujiRoBERTa. After obtaining the encoding representation $H$ from RoBERTa, these embeddings are passed through a linear classification layer to produce logits:

$$R = MLP(H), \tag{3}$$

which represent the raw, unnormalized scores indicating the models confidence for each possible class. Finally, we apply the Conditional Random Field (CRF) to decode the logits into tags:

$$PE = CRF(R). \tag{4}$$

where $PE$ is entity labels predicted by model network, as shown by 'B-T M-T M-T M-T E-T' in Figure 1. During training, $PE$ and $TE$ are used to calculate loss. In inference, $PE$ is the output of the NER task.

In training strategy, we use scheduler, specifically, LinearScheduleWithWarmup, which receives training step and outputs an updates learning rate. The new learning rate is used by optimizer to update parameters of model network.

### 3.2 Decoding Strategy

We employ a Conditional Random Field (CRF) layer as the decoding mechanism. The CRF layer explicitly models sequential dependencies between output tags by incorporating both emission scores (token-level label confidences from the encoder) and transition scores (learnable inter-tag relationships). The CRF layer jointly optimizes these two components to ensure globally coherent predictions. The model computes the most likely tag sequence by maximizing the conditional probability:

$$A = \sum_{i=1}^{T} \psi_{\text{emission}}(x_i, y_i), \tag{5}$$

$$B = \sum_{i=2}^{T} \psi_{\text{transition}}(y_{i-1}, y_i), \tag{6}$$

$$P(y|x) = \frac{1}{Z(x)} \exp(A + B). \tag{7}$$

where $Z(x)$ is the partition function, $T$ is the sequence length, $x_i$ is the hidden state of the $i$-th token, $y_i$ is the tag at position $i$, $\psi_{\text{emission}}$ is the emission score from the encoder, and $\psi_{\text{transition}}$ is the transition score between tags.

### 3.3 Scheduler

As described in 3.1, during training, we employ LinearScheduleWithWarmup as scheduler, updating learning rate based on training step:

$$\text{lr}_{\text{warmup}}(t) = \text{lr}_{\text{base}} \cdot \frac{t}{t_{\text{warmup}}}, \tag{8}$$

$$\text{lr}_{\text{decay}}(t) = \text{lr}_{\text{base}} \cdot \left(1 - \frac{t - t_{\text{warmup}}}{t_{\max} - t_{\text{warmup}}}\right), \tag{9}$$

$$\text{lr}(t) = \begin{cases} \text{lr}_{\text{warmup}}(t), & \text{if } t < t_{\text{warmup}}, \\ \text{lr}_{\text{decay}}(t), & \text{otherwise.} \end{cases} \tag{10}$$

where $\text{lr}_{\text{base}}$ is preset base learning rate, $t_{\text{warmup}}$ is preset warmup timestep, $t$ is training step, and $\text{lr}(t)$ is updated learning rate.

### 3.4 Solution for Long Sentences

The testing datasets contain some long length sentences, which are beyond the maximum length processed by model. Considering this situation, we split these long sentences into some short sub-sentences. We try to keep all sub-sentences semantically complete thus we split the long sentence according to punctuation instead of the maximum length. Then we revert sentences from the output file of system and obtain our final submisson.

| | TestA | | | TestB | | | TestC | | | Test Total | | |
|---|---|---|---|---|---|---|---|---|---|---|---|---|
| | P | R | F | P | R | F | P | R | F | P | R | F |
| Baseline | 85.90 | 77.50 | 81.48 | 87.09 | 87.52 | 87.50 | 71.84 | 72.95 | 72.40 | 81.41 | 79.82 | 80.61 |
| Ours | **88.16** | 76.38 | **81.84** | 86.87 | **90.09** | **88.45** | **75.57** | **85.50** | **80.23** | **82.92** | **84.56** | **83.74** |

Table 2: Baseline and testing results of our model(%)

## 4 Experiments

### 4.1 Dataset

Given the closed modality competition we participated in, our experiments were limited to the datasets provided by EvaHAN 2025, including three different training datasets and their corresponding three test datasets. Dataset A comes from *Shiji*; Dataset B is extracted from *Twenty-Four Histories*; Dataset C consists of texts on Traditional Chinese Medicine Classics.

Models trained on training datasets A, B, and C are then used to test on the corresponding test datasets A, B, and C.

### 4.2 Metric

According to the requirements of EvaHAN 2025, Precision, Recall and F1 Score are selected as metrics, which are simply denoted as P, R and F in tables of this report. The results are presented in percentages (%).

### 4.3 Setting

When training model, we set some hyperparameters. Importantly, we set base learning rate to 5e-5, dropout ratio to 0.1, weight decay to 0.01, and training epoch to 50.

### 4.4 Training

We divided labeled training dataset into training data and validation data in a ratio of 0.95: 0.05. Specifically, in our experiment during training, we used Softmax and CRF for decoding strategies. And we selected LinearScheduleWithWarmUp, CosineScheduleWithWarmup, ConstantSchedule as candidate scheduler respectively. Based on these selected approaches, we obtained six combinations and compared their performance. Each combination was trained on training data A, B, and C and evaluated separately on validation data A, B, and C. In Table 1, we compare the performance of different combinations on the three data sets. For brevity, we only show the F1 Score. Based on the result of comparison, our model finally chosed CRF and LinearScheduleWithWarmup.

### 4.5 Testing

After the test datasets were released, We used trained models to test and got our NER results. After confirming that the number of characters is exactly the same as test datasets and that each line is completely aligned with the test datasets, we submitted our result documents before the deadline. The quantitative results of our model were informed by NER 2025, along with the baseline, which used SikuRoBERTa-BiLSTM-CRF. As shown in Table 2, our approach outperformed the baseline, especially on TestC. In Test Total, compared with baseline, Precision, Recall and F1 Score of our model increased by 1.51%, 4.74% and 3.13% respectively, demonstrating the effectiveness of our model.

However, our method has a slightly lower Recall on TestA and a slightly lower Precision on TestB. To explore the reasons, we carefully examined datasets and found that our model tends to get confused with annotations of certain official positions or time-related terms in TestA and TestB. However, many of the entities in dataset C are medical terms. The individual words that make up these terms appear less frequently in other entities, and the models are less easily confused facing with these terms. In future research, we will try to improve here.

## 5 Conclusion

In this report, we describe our named entity recognition system for EvaHan 2025 task, which proves the rationality of selecting CRF and LinearScheduleWithWarmup through experiments. Additionally, this report proves the effectiveness of the system by comparing to official baseline.

## References

Jacob Devlin, Ming-Wei Chang, Kenton Lee, and Kristina Toutanova. 2019. Bert: Pre-training of deep bidirectional transformers for language understanding. In *Proceedings of the 2019 conference of the North American chapter of the association for computational linguistics: human language technologies, volume 1 (long and short papers)*, pages 4171–4186.

Shuang Liu, Hui Yang, Jiayi Li, and Simon Kolmanič. 2021. Chinese named entity recognition method in history and culture field based on bert. *International Journal of Computational Intelligence Systems*, 14:1–10.

Weiming Liu, Bin Yu, Chen Zhang, Han Wang, and Ke Pan. 2018. Chinese named entity recognition based on rules and conditional random field. In *Proceedings of the 2018 2nd International conference on computer science and artificial intelligence*, pages 268–272.

Zara Nasar, Syed Waqar Jaffry, and Muhammad Kamran Malik. 2021. Named entity recognition and relation extraction: State-of-the-art. *ACM Computing Surveys (CSUR)*, 54(1):1–39.

Yu Sun, Shuohuan Wang, Yukun Li, Shikun Feng, Xuyi Chen, Han Zhang, Xin Tian, Danxiang Zhu, Hao Tian, and Hua Wu. 2019. Ernie: Enhanced representation through knowledge integration. *arXiv preprint arXiv:1904.09223*.

Yuanhe Tian, Yan Song, Xiang Ao, Fei Xia, Xiaojun Quan, Tong Zhang, and Yonggang Wang. 2020. Joint chinese word segmentation and part-of-speech tagging via two-way attentions of auto-analyzed knowledge. In *Proceedings of the 58th annual meeting of the association for computational linguistics*, pages 8286–8296.

Dongbo Wang, Chang Liu, Zhixiao Zhao, Si Shen, Liu Liu, Bin Li, Haotian Hu, Mengcheng Wu, Litao Lin, Xue Zhao, and 1 others. 2023. Gujibert and gujigpt: Construction of intelligent information processing foundation language models for ancient texts. *arXiv preprint arXiv:2307.05354*.

Dongbo Wang, Chang Liu, Zihe Zhu, Jiang, Feng, Haotian Hu, Si Shen, and Bin Li. 2021. Construction and application of pre-training model of siku quanshu oriented to digital humanities.

Miguel Won, Patricia Murrieta-Flores, and Bruno Martins. 2018. ensemble named entity recognition (ner): evaluating ner tools in the identification of place names in historical corpora. *Frontiers in Digital Humanities*, 5:2.

Zhen Yang, Wei Chen, Feng Wang, and Bo Xu. 2017. Improving neural machine translation with conditional sequence generative adversarial nets. *arXiv preprint arXiv:1703.04887*.

Peng Yu and Xin Wang. 2020. Bert-based named entity recognition in chinese twenty-four histories. In *International Conference on Web Information Systems and Applications*, pages 289–301. Springer.

# GRoWE: A GujiRoBERTa-Enhanced Approach to Ancient Chinese NER via Word-Word Relation Classification and Model Ensembling

**Tian Xia, Yilin Wang, Xinkai Wang, Yahe Yang, Qun Zhao, Menghui Yang***

[1]School of Information Resource Management,Renmin University of China, Beijing, China,
[2]Midu Technology Co., Ltd., Shanghai, China

{xiat,wang_yilin}@ruc.edu.cn, xinkaiw18@gmail.com, owyangyahe@126.com,{zhao_qun,yangmenghui}@ruc.edu.cn

## Abstract

Named entity recognition is a fundamental task in ancient Chinese text analysis.Based on the pre-trained language model of ancient Chinese texts, this paper proposes a new named entity recognition method GRoWE. It uses the ancient Chinese texts pre-trained language model GujiRoBERTa as the base model, and the word-word relation prediction model is superposed upon the base model to construct a superposition model. Then ensemble strategies are used to multiple superposition models. On the EvaHan 2025 public test set, the F1 value of the proposed method reaches 86.79%, which is 6.18% higher than that of the mainstream BERT_LSTM_CRF baseline model, indicating that the model architecture and ensemble strategy play an important role in improving the recognition effect of naming entities in ancient Chinese texts.

## 1 Introduction

As an important carrier of Chinese history and culture, ancient Chinese texts preserve thousands of years of civilization and wisdom. It is essential to obtain the information contained in them. Named entity recognition (NER), a crucial natural language processing technique, plays an indispensable role in information extraction from ancient Chinese texts(Long et al., 2016). NER aims to extract entities such as person name, book title, official title and so on, providing a foundation for understanding ancient Chinese texts and constructing ancient Chinese knowledge graphs.

However, NER in ancient Chinese texts faces many challenges. First, Old Chinese (classical Chinese) is highly concise, lacks clear boundary markings between words, and the subject or object is often omitted in sentence structure, which greatly increases the difficulty of identifying named entities. Second, due to historical changes and the diversity of textual contexts, the same word or phrase may refer to completely different entities in different contexts. In addition, in order to promote the task of NER in ancient Chinese texts, the organizers of EvaHan 2025 release a unified dataset and pre-trained pedestal model, hoping to promote the progress of the named entity recognition task through a unified standard.

In this study, we propose a named entity recognition method GRoWE (GujiRoBERTa + Word-Word Relation Prediction + Ensemble) suitable for the characteristics of ancient Chinese texts: based on the pre-trained basic model of ancient Chinese texts GujiRoBERTa, the word-word relation processing of W2NER is reused, and a multi-model ensemble strategy is introduced. On the dataset published in EvaHan 2025, the method achieves significantly better results than the public baseline model.

## 2 Related work

Early NER research primarily relied on rule-based approaches and statistical models; however, the landscape transformed significantly with the advent of deep learning techniques. The BiLSTM-CRF architecture emerged as a pivotal innovation (Huang et al., 2015). This framework established a fundamental paradigm in the NER domain. The application of this method to person name recognition in ancient Chinese literature has shown promising results (Zhang et al., 2021).

In 2018,BERT was proposed(Devlin et al., 2019), characterized by its large-scale unsupervised pretraining and bidirectional Transformer architecture, which delivers robust contextual representations for NER tasks. Extending this technological foundation, the HistoryNER dataset came into being through the implementation of a BERT-BiLSTM-CRF architecture(Liu et al., 2021), specifically engineered for the identification of entity types within historical Chinese texts.

In terms of architectural advancements in NER,



*Proceedings of the Second Ancient Language Processing Workshop associated with NAACL 2025*, pages 141–145
May 4, 2025. 

a unified MRC framework(Li et al., 2022b) materialized, reconceptualizing NER as a machine reading comprehension challenge. This innovative approach extracts entities via natural language queries, harnessing prior knowledge embedded within these queries to enhance the model's comprehension of entity categories. Concurrently, the field benefited from the development of the Global Pointer model(Su et al., 2022), which incorporates relative position encoding and multi-head attention mechanisms, substantially improving the detection of nested and lengthy entities. The evolution of NER methodologies further progressed with the conceptualization of the W2NER framework(Li et al., 2022a), which elegantly models adjacency relationships between entities through word-word relation classification. This novel perspective addresses critical limitations in conventional approaches when handling overlapping and discontinuous entities, contributing significantly to the field with its exceptional capability in processing complex entity structures.

## 3 Method

### 3.1 Model Selection

Mainstream named entity recognition methods use an encoder pre-trained language model to obtain the semantic information of the text, and integrate the features obtained from the encoder into the personalization module for further feature transformation, ultimately outputting probability distribution on different labels. The common personalization modules are as follows: LSTM+CRF combination method, GlobalPointer method which supports multi-head recognition of nested entities, and W2NER method for predicting relations between word pairs. In addition, named entity recognition can be regarded as a reading comprehension task, entities as problems, and text to be labeled as documents, and named entity recognition can be realized by marking the location of the problem in the document.

We cut the training dataset into consistent five-fold divisions, train the four methods mentioned above, and test the model performance. The specific experimental data are shown in Table 1. Based on the model performance, we select the W2NER as the personalized module for the ancient Chinese text named entity recognition task.

### 3.2 Architecture

To better adapt to the characteristics of ancient Chinese texts, we designed the network architecture GRoWE as shown in Figure 1. In order to reflect the characteristics of ancient Chinese texts, the encoder is GujiRoBERTa-jian-fan, a pre-trained model for ancient Chinese texts in the EvaHan2025 part, and the output results of the encoder are further input into the bidirectional LSTM layer, which encodes the features in both directions, and then is sent to the W2NER module, after encoding through Convolution Layer and Co-Predictor Layer, the relation between word pair is classified and the logits are calculated.

In order to explore the potential of model combination, we adopted a multi-model ensemble strategy: the training set was divided into five folds, and the model was trained using the data from four of the folds in turn, resulting in a total of five models. Then, the logits of these five models were directly summed up to form the final ensemble result vector, which was then decoded to obtain the final labeled result.

### 3.3 Main Process

The main process can be formally described as follows:

**Input Representation**: Given an input sentence $X = \{x_1, x_2, \ldots, x_N\}$, the BERT + BiLSTM model generates contextual word embeddings $H = \{h_1, h_2, \ldots, h_N\}$, where $h_i \in \mathbb{R}^{d_h}$ and $d_h$ represents the embedding dimension.

**Word Pair Embedding Computation**: Subsequently, the word-pair embedding $V_{i,j}$ is computed as:

$$V_{i,j} = \gamma_{i,j} \odot \left( \frac{h_j - \mu}{\sigma} \right) + \lambda_{i,j}$$

where:
- $\gamma_{i,j} = W_\alpha h_i + b_\alpha$
- $\lambda_{i,j} = W_\beta h_i + b_\beta$
- $\mu = \frac{1}{d_h} \sum_{k=1}^{d_h} h_{j,k}$
- $\sigma = \sqrt{\frac{1}{d_h} \sum_{k=1}^{d_h} (h_{j,k} - \mu)^2}$
- The symbol $\odot$ denotes element - wise multiplication.

**Multi - Layer Dilated Convolution Application**: Then, multi-layer dilated convolutions (DConv) are applied to $V$:

$$Q^l = \sigma\left(DConv_l(V)\right), \quad l \in \{1, 2, 3\}$$

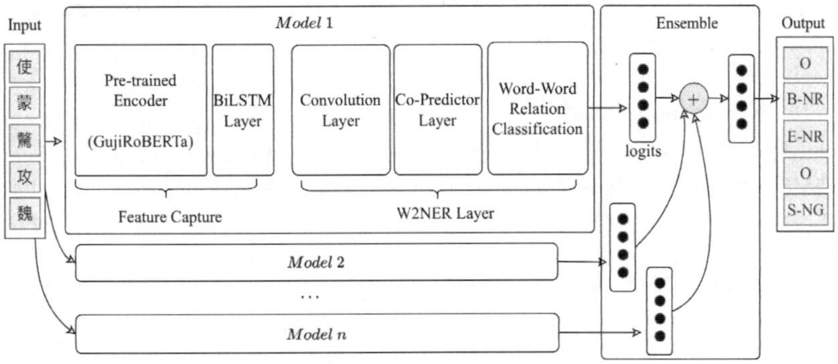


Figure 1: Architecture of GRoWE

The final representation is $Q = [Q^1; Q^2; Q^3] \in \mathbb{R}^{N \times N \times 3d_c}$, where $d_c$ is the hidden dimension of the convolution operation.

**Word-Pair Relation Probability Prediction**: After that, word-pair relation probabilities are predicted by combining Biaffine and MLP:

$$y_{i,j} = Softmax(y'_{i,j} + y''_{i,j})$$

where:

- Biaffine prediction: $y'_{i,j} = s_i^\top U o_j + W[s_i; o_j] + b$

- MLP prediction: $y''_{i,j} = MLP(Q_{i,j})$

- $s_i = MLP_2(h_i)$ and $o_j = MLP_3(h_j)$

**Inference and Aggregation**: During inference, the logits from each model's Co-Predictor Layer are aggregated. For $M$ models, the final logits are the sum of individual model outputs:

$$logits_{final} = \sum_{m=1}^{M} \left( y'^{(m)}_{i,j} + y''^{(m)}_{i,j} \right)$$

The predicted relation is determined by selecting the label with the highest score after applying Softmax:

$$y_{i,j} = Softmax(logits_{final})$$

where $y'^{(m)}_{i,j}$ and $y''^{(m)}_{i,j}$ denote the Biaffine and MLP outputs of the $m$-th model.

**Relation Decoding**: For relation decoding, a directed graph is constructed based on the predicted relations, and entities are extracted via depth-first search.

## 4 Data and experiments

### 4.1 Data preprocessing

The datasets used in this paper are from Shiji (dataset A), Twenty-Four Histories (dataset B), and Traditional Chinese Medicine Classics (dataset C) provided by evahan2025, and are divided into two parts, the training set and the test set. In this study, the preprocessing work is carried out on datasets A, B, and C, and data enhancement process is further carried out on the data in the training set. The preprocessing mainly includes sentence segmentation and de-duplication, while the data enhancement is based on sliding window operations to enrich the training data.

For the data preprocessing, in the initial stage, we cut all the datasets into sentences based on the single character break strategy, using "." , "!" ".", "!", "?" ", "!", "?", ";" as the sentence termination identifiers. For long sentences longer than 120 characters, we implemented a secondary cutting strategy, i.e., we selected the nearest comma or the stop sign to the length of 120 characters as the cutting point to ensure that the cut sentence remained within the appropriate length range. Subsequently, de-duplication is performed on the cut sentences, and the final number of sentences in the training set is obtained as follows: dataset A (8,218 sentences), dataset B (3,507 sentences), and dataset C (6,545 sentences), respectively. After carrying out the same operations, the number of sentences are obtained for the test set: dataset A (994 sentences), dataset B (884 sentences) and dataset C (1,115 sentences).

To enhance the data diversity, we use the sliding window technique to expand the samples in the training set. Specifically, for the preprocessed sentence sequence, $[s_1, s_2, s_3, s_4, \ldots, s_n]$, we implement a sliding window operation with an incremental step of 1 for each sentence $s_i$, generate candidate sets $[s_i, s_i + s_{i+1}, ..., \ldots, s_i + ... + s_n]$, and screen the combined sentences with a length of less than 120 characters as the expanded training samples.Through this processing, the number of training samples in datasets A, B, and C was expanded to 48,797, 14,629, and 65,227, respectively,totaling 128,653 training samples.

For the expanded sample, we implemented stratified sampling according to the sentence entity type, and divided the data into 5 equal parts for cross-validation. It's worth noting that this segmentation strategy can lead to high evaluation metrics due to the potential risk of data breaches. Specifically, when the original sentence that $s_i$ with its derivative samples $s_i + s_{i+1}$. Based on the fact that stratified sampling is randomly assigned to the training and test sets, the models may obtain some information of the test samples from the training data. However, considering that this division only serves the model selection session, and all the comparison models are evaluated under the same dataset and evaluation system, this division is acceptable in the context of this study.

After completing the model selection, we used the sequential cutting method to re-divide the data into five equal parts. In this way, we retrained and reevaluated the optimal models to ensure the reliability and fairness of the final results.

### 4.2 Parameter Settings

When comparing different methods, we use SikuBERT as the base model and the default parameters from each method's public code for training.

For the GRoWE method, the base model is GujiRoBERTa-jian-fan. The training settings are: batch size = 32, learning rate = 5e-6, seed=1234, and 14 epochs in total. We use the model from the last epoch to predict on the test set.

### 4.3 Comparative experiments with mainstream models

In this study, we systematically evaluate the performance of multiple architectures using BERT as encoder in the task of named entity recognizing in ancient Chinese texts, including BERT-BiLSTM-CRF, GlobalPointer, MRC, and W2NER. While keeping the encoder consistent, the experimental results are shown in Table 1, which show that the model based on W2NER architecture performs optimally among all the evaluated scenarios, with F1-score of 88.48%, which is significantly better than other architecture combinations.

Based on this finding, we further use the GRoWE architecture depicted in Figure 1 to train the model and validate it on the public test set.

### 4.4 Comparison of experiments on the Test set

The method of comparison is as follows:

Method1: RoBERTa-BiLSTM-CRF, the official baseline model announced by EvaHan 2025, the pre-trained language model corresponding to the encoder is SikuRoBERTa, and the personalized insertion module is BiLSTM+CRF.

Method2: RoBERTa-W2NER,following the official requirements of EvaHan 2025, the pretrained language model corresponding to the encoder is GujiRoBERTa-jian-fan, and the output of the W2NER Layer is directly used to decode the output for named entity recognition.

Method3: GRoWE,the method proposed in this paper, utilizes five models obtained from five-fold cross-training of the training set, and logits cumulative ensemble is used to obtain the final results.

As shown in Table 2, the combination of the proprietary pre-trained model and W2NER is significantly better than the baseline model, indicating that the W2NER layer embodies a stronger entity recognition ability through convolution and word-word relation prediction processing. GRoWE further adopted the ensemble learning strategy, and the performances were further improved, with the F1-score increasing by 6.18 percentage points compared with the baseline model, and outperforming other methods in all test subsets. It can be seen the word-word relation prediction model can improve the recognition effect of named entities, and the ensemble framework reduces the prediction bias of a single model by integrating the prediction advantages of multiple models.

## 5 Conclusion

This paper proposes a new named entity recognition method GRoWE. It uses the ancient Chinese texts pre-trained language model as the base model, and the W2NER word-word relation prediction model is superposed upon the base model to construct a superposition model. Then ensemble strategies are used to multiple superposition models.The public test set results show that the GRoWE method significantly outperforms the baseline model and improves the overall recognition effect of ancient Chinese texts NER.

## 6 Acknowledgements

This research is supported by the the National Social Science Fund of China (22BTQ068).

| Model Name | Indicator | Fold 1 | Fold 2 | Fold 3 | Fold 4 | Fold 5 | Average |
|---|---|---|---|---|---|---|---|
| BERT-BiLSTM-CRF | Precision | 85.46% | 85.88% | 85.85% | 84.38% | 84.92% | 85.30% |
| | Recall | 86.73% | 87.47% | 88.25% | 87.68% | 87.91% | 87.61% |
| | F1 Score | 86.09% | 86.67% | 86.52% | 86.00% | 86.39% | 86.33% |
| GlobalPointer | Precision | 86.21% | 86.25% | 86.08% | 85.63% | 85.07% | 85.85% |
| | Recall | 89.10% | 89.12% | 88.65% | 88.20% | 89.48% | 88.91% |
| | F1 Score | 87.61% | 87.64% | 87.32% | 86.88% | 87.19% | 87.33% |
| MRC | Precision | 84.58% | 86.39% | 86.29% | 82.84% | 85.03% | 85.03% |
| | Recall | 81.12% | 82.90% | 82.22% | 82.79% | 80.27% | 81.86% |
| | F1 Score | 82.81% | 84.61% | 84.20% | 82.81% | 82.58% | 83.40% |
| W2NER | Precision | 89.60% | 89.88% | 89.32% | 89.05% | 90.19% | 89.61% |
| | Recall | 87.99% | 87.68% | 86.64% | 87.06% | 87.55% | 87.38% |
| | F1 Score | 88.79% | 88.77% | 87.96% | 88.05% | 88.85% | 88.48% |

Table 1: Performance Comparison of Different Models with BERT Encoder across 5-fold Cross-validation

| Model Name | Indicator | Test A | Test B | Test C | Average |
|---|---|---|---|---|---|
| RoBERTa-BiLSTM-CRF (Baseline) | Precision | 85.90% | 87.09% | 71.84% | 81.41% |
| | Recall | 77.50% | 87.92% | 72.95% | 79.82% |
| | F1 Score | 81.48% | 87.50% | 72.40% | 80.61% |
| RoBERTa-W2NER | Precision | 88.17% | 89.55% | 79.53% | 85.47% |
| | Recall | **82.10%** | 89.96% | **88.64%** | **87.24%** |
| | F1 Score | 85.03% | 89.76% | 83.83% | 86.34% |
| GRoWE | Precision | **88.97%** | **90.22%** | **81.33%** | **86.64%** |
| | Recall | 81.45% | **90.34%** | 87.91% | 86.94% |
| | F1 Score | **85.04%** | **90.28%** | **84.49%** | **86.79%** |

Table 2: The Results of the Experiment on the Test set

## References


Jacob Devlin, Ming-Wei Chang, Kenton Lee, and Kristina Toutanova. 2019. BERT: Pre-training of Deep Bidirectional Transformers for Language Understanding. In *Proceedings of the 2019 Conference of the North American Chapter of the Association for Computational Linguistics: Human Language Technologies, Volume 1 (Long and Short Papers)*, pages 4171–4186, Minneapolis, Minnesota. Association for Computational Linguistics.

Zhiheng Huang, Wei Xu, and Kai Yu. 2015. Bidirectional LSTM-CRF Models for Sequence Tagging. *arXiv preprint*. ArXiv:1508.01991 [cs].

Jingye Li, Hao Fei, Jiang Liu, Shengqiong Wu, Meishan Zhang, Chong Teng, Donghong Ji, and Fei Li. 2022a. Unified Named Entity Recognition as Word-Word Relation Classification. *Proceedings of the AAAI Conference on Artificial Intelligence*, 36(10):10965–10973. Number: 10.

Xiaoya Li, Jingrong Feng, Yuxian Meng, Qinghong Han, Fei Wu, and Jiwei Li. 2022b. A Unified MRC Framework for Named Entity Recognition. *arXiv preprint*. ArXiv:1910.11476 [cs].

Shuang Liu, Hui Yang, Jiayi Li, and Simon Kolmanič. 2021. Chinese Named Entity Recognition Method in History and Culture Field Based on BERT. *International Journal of Computational Intelligence Systems*, 14(1):163.

Yunfei Long, Dan Xiong, Qin Lu, Minglei Li, and Chu-Ren Huang. 2016. Named Entity Recognition for Chinese Novels in the Ming-Qing Dynasties. In *Chinese Lexical Semantics*, pages 362–375. Springer, Cham. ISSN: 1611-3349.

Jianlin Su, Ahmed Murtadha, Shengfeng Pan, Jing Hou, Jun Sun, Wanwei Huang, Bo Wen, and Yunfeng Liu. 2022. Global Pointer: Novel Efficient Span-based Approach for Named Entity Recognition. *arXiv preprint*. ArXiv:2208.03054 [cs].

Hailin Zhang, Hai Zhu, Junsong Ruan, and Ruoyao Ding. 2021. People name recognition from ancient Chinese literature using distant supervision and deep learning. In *2021 2nd International Conference on Artificial Intelligence and Information Systems*, ICAIIS 2021, pages 1–6, New York, NY, USA. Association for Computing Machinery.

# When Less Is More
## Logits-Constrained Framework with RoBERTa for Ancient Chinese NER

**Wenjie Hua**
School of Chinese Language and Literature
Wuhan University, China
huawenjie@whu.edu.cn

**Shenghan Xu**
Yuanpei College
Peking University, China
xsh2022@stu.pku.edu.cn

### Abstract

This report presents our team's work on ancient Chinese Named Entity Recognition (NER) for EvaHan 2025[1]. We propose a two-stage framework combining GujiRoBERTa with a Logits-Constrained (LC) mechanism. The first stage generates contextual embeddings using GujiRoBERTa, followed by dynamically masked decoding to enforce valid BMES transitions. Experiments on EvaHan 2025 datasets demonstrate the framework's effectiveness. Key findings include the LC framework's superiority over CRFs in high-label scenarios and the detrimental effect of BiLSTM modules. We also establish empirical model selection guidelines based on label complexity and dataset size.

## 1 Introduction

Named Entity Recognition (NER) is basically a task to identify and classify named entities in texts, such as person name, geographical location, and time expression. It is a crucial research topic in NLP. NER in Ancient Chinese is particularly challenging due to the complex semantic properties of words, which can lead to errors in label sequence predictions. To address this, our model integrates the Logits-Constrained Framework with GujiRoBERTa[2], effectively reducing such errors.

## 2 Related Work

### 2.1 RoBERTa

Large-scale pre-trained language models (PLMs) based on Transformer architectures (Vaswani et al., 2023) have revolutionized sequence labeling tasks. RoBERTa (Liu et al., 2019), an optimized variant of BERT (Devlin et al., 2019), steadily improved Ancient Chinese NER accuracy. GujiRoBERTa, pre-trained on a large corpus of traditional Chinese texts, serves as the backbone model in our EvaHan 2025 close-modality setting and is a fine-tuned version of SikuRoBERTa.

### 2.2 Transition Constraints in Sequence Labeling

Sequence labeling tasks require strict adherence to structural constraints defined by tagging schemes. For instance, under the BMES scheme where valid label sequences must conform to $S_3 = \mathrm{Perm}(\{B, M, E\})$, the transition $(B, M, E)$ is the only valid transition in $S_3$. Traditional approaches employ Conditional Random Fields (CRFs) (Lafferty et al., 2001) with bidirectional LSTMs (BiLSTMs)(Huang et al., 2015) to globally normalize label transition probabilities during inference. However, these methods depend on manually designed transition matrices and often produce illegal paths when decoding under low-resource or label-sparse senarios.

Recent work explores alternative constraint mechanisms. For example, Jiang et al. (2021) proposes a constrained transition framework that dynamically masks invalid transitions during training and inference. Similarly, Wei et al. (2021) develops a masked transition learning approach that implicitly encodes tagging scheme rules through auxiliary language modeling objectives. Our work extends these paradigms by directly incorporating transition constraints into the model's parameterized decision boundary, which eliminates heuristic post-processing while maintaining theoretical guarantees of valid output structures.

## 3 Method

### 3.1 Pre-processing

Punctuation marks provide potential entity boundary information, and preserving and correctly segmenting them can enhance NER performance (Ge, 2022) . Considering the characteristics of punc-

[1] https://github.com/GoThereGit/EvaHan

[2] https://huggingface.co/hsc748NLP/GujiRoBERTa_jian_fan

tuation in the EvaHan 2025 training sets, we adopt different sentence segmentation strategies. Specifically, trainset_c only considers primary sentence-ending punctuation: “。”, “！”, and “？”. In contrast, trainset_a and trainset_b additionally account for “」” and “』”, as well as “”” and “’” as special sentence-final markers.

### 3.2 Framework

Motivated by the Occam's razor principle – that simpler hypotheses consistent with observations are preferable (MacKay, 2003) – we propose a minimally invasive two-stage architecture that maintains model simplicity while enforcing structural constraints. Our design philosophy consciously avoids stacking complex components like CRFs or BiLSTMs, which may introduce interference patterns during learning.Just as illustrated in Figure 1, the framework operates through.

#### 3.2.1 Stage 1: Contextual Encoding with GujiRoBERTa

The pre-trained GujiRoBERTa model generates contextualized embeddings $\mathbf{h}_i \in \mathbb{R}^d$ for each token $x_i$, capturing ancient linguistic patterns through its 12-layer transformer architecture. A linear projection layer then computes initial label logits:

$$\mathbf{l}_i = \mathbf{W}\mathbf{h}_i + \mathbf{b} \tag{1}$$

where $\mathbf{W} \in \mathbb{R}^{k \times d}$ maps to $k$ possible labels. Training uses standard cross-entropy loss without explicit transition modeling.

#### 3.2.2 Stage 2: Logits-Constrained Decoding

We introduce a constraint matrix $\mathbf{M} \in \{0,1\}^{k \times k}$ encoding valid BMES transitions (e.g., B-PER can only transition to M-PER or E-PER). During inference, we modulate the logits sequence $\{\mathbf{l}_1, ..., \mathbf{l}_n\}$ through masked autoregressive refinement:

$$\mathbf{l}'_t = \mathbf{M}[y_{t-1}] \odot \mathbf{l}_t + (1 - \mathbf{M}[y_{t-1}]) \cdot (-\infty) \tag{2}$$

where $y_{t-1}$ denotes the previous token's predicted label. This differentiable masking ensures structurally valid outputs without additional trainable parameters.

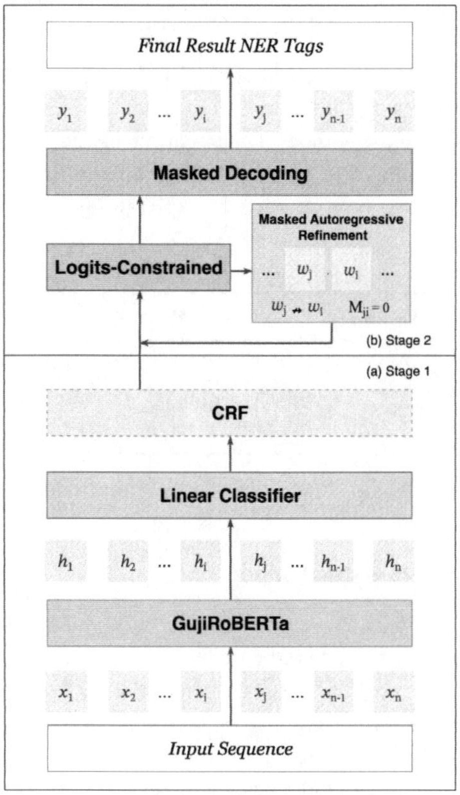


Figure 1: Framework Overview

## 4 Experiments

Following EvaHan 2025 guidelines, we use three training sets—trainset_a, trainset_b, and trainset_c—annotated with 6, 3, and 6 NER categories, respectively, plus a non-NER label “O.” The {B, M, E, S} scheme marks entity positions as Begin, Middle, End, or Single. Since trainset_b's categories are a subset of trainset_a's, the dataset includes 37 classification labels.

### 4.1 Experimental Environment

All experiments were conducted on Google Colab using NVIDIA A100 (40 GB) and T4 GPUs with mixed precision (FP16) training enabled.

### 4.2 Parameter Regulation

The model was trained for 4 epochs with a batch size of 8 for training and 1 for evaluation. The learning rate was set to $2 \times 10^{-5}$ with a warmup ratio of 0.1 and a weight decay of 0.01 to mitigate overfitting. Gradient accumulation was performed over 2 steps, with a linear scheduler adjusting the learning rate progressively.

### 4.3 GujiRoBERTa

We only employed GujiRoBERTa with an additional linear classifier to evaluate the NER tagging results, without incorporating any additional components. Nevertheless, this approach achieved promising performance during training (see Table 1).

| Dataset | P | R | F1 |
|---|---|---|---|
| A | 0.9170 | 0.9190 | 0.9180 |
| B | 0.9251 | 0.9221 | 0.9236 |
| C | 0.7744 | 0.8418 | 0.8067 |

Table 1: Performance of GujiRoBERTa

### 4.4 Cross-Comparison

Therefore, we conducted further cross-comparison experiments, drawing parallels with typical configurations in NER tasks to assess the relative contributions of different model components and potential performance improvements. In the following tables, "+" indicates the inclusion of the corresponding module, while "-" denotes its exclusion.

| BiLSTM | CRF | LC | F1 |
|---|---|---|---|
| - | - | - | 0.9180 |
| + | - | - | 0.9016 |
| - | + | - | 0.9143 |
| - | - | + | 0.9269 |
| + | + | - | 0.8850 |
| - | + | + | 0.9213 |
| + | - | + | 0.8976 |
| + | + | + | 0.8947 |

Table 2: Results of Dataset A

| BiLSTM | CRF | LC | F1 |
|---|---|---|---|
| - | - | - | 0.9236 |
| + | - | - | 0.8617 |
| - | + | - | 0.9278 |
| - | - | + | 0.9218 |
| + | + | - | 0.9100 |
| - | + | + | 0.9308 |
| + | - | + | 0.8594 |
| + | + | + | 0.9012 |

Table 3: Results for Dataset B

| BiLSTM | CRF | LC | F1 |
|---|---|---|---|
| - | - | - | 0.8067 |
| + | - | - | 0.7383 |
| - | + | - | 0.8112 |
| - | - | + | 0.8262 |
| + | + | - | 0.7602 |
| - | + | + | 0.8314 |
| + | - | + | 0.7547 |
| + | + | + | 0.7804 |

Table 4: Results for Dataset C

Through cross-comparison of the results (see Table 2, Table 3, and Table 4), we found that CRF effectively captures sequence patterns in low-dimensional label spaces by leveraging predefined transition constraints. However, as the number of labels increases, the performance of CRF decreases by 1.3% and 0.5% on Datasets A and C, respectively. This is likely because manually designed transition matrices are less capable of covering high-dimensional state spaces.

In contrast, the Logits-Constrained (LC) framework demonstrates greater generalizability. In scenarios with six or more labels ($L \geq 6$) (Datasets A/C), our LC framework exhibits a significant advantage, achieving an average F1 improvement of 1.95%. Notably, on Dataset C, which features a complex entity distribution, the dynamic masking mechanism in LC raises the F1 score from the baseline of 0.8067 to 0.8262 (+2.95%).

Moreover, the introduction of BiLSTM leads to performance degradation across all datasets, with an average $\Delta F_1 = -3.8\%$. We speculate that this is due to the disruption of the inherent attention patterns in the pretrained model caused by the addition of BiLSTM, as well as the increased risk of the bidirectional recurrent structure's parameter updates getting trapped in local optima.

### 4.5 Dataset Expansion

By integrating the annotated data from Dataset A according to the specifications of Dataset B, we expand the sample size of the hybrid Dataset B from 3,434 sentences to 11,307 sentences (+229%), and conduct the same experiments (see Table 5).

| Dataset | Sentences | Label Types |
|---|---|---|
| Dataset B | 3434 | 13 |
| Hybrid | 11307 | 13 |

Table 5: Statistics of Datasets

| BiLSTM | CRF | LC | F1 |
|---|---|---|---|
| - | - | - | 0.9369 |
| + | - | - | 0.8964 |
| - | + | - | 0.9465 |
| - | - | + | 0.9395 |
| + | + | - | 0.8364 |
| - | + | + | 0.9439 |
| + | - | + | 0.8957 |
| + | + | + | 0.9401 |

Table 6: Results for Dataset B (Hybrid)

Table 6 demonstrates a positive correlation between dataset scale and model performance in NER, with the baseline F1 score increasing by 1.33% under consistent model settings. Since the CRF's global normalization enhances long-range dependency modeling and LC's dynamic masking mitigates overfitting in sparse label scenarios, the combined application of the CRF and LC frameworks yields optimal performance, surpassing the performance of individual framework implementations.

### 4.6 Model Selection

As noted earlier, balancing dataset size and label complexity is crucial in sequence labeling tasks. We define the optimal model selection as a function of label cardinality $L$ and sentence count $N$, yielding the following empirically optimized scaling relationship:

$$\Gamma(L,N) = \begin{cases} -\text{ (LC)} & \text{if } L \geq 20 \\ & \quad \wedge N > 0.16L^{2.8} \\ +\text{ (CRF+LC)} & \text{otherwise} \end{cases} \tag{3}$$

Here, the threshold $0.16L^{2.8}$ is derived via parameter tuning across various datasets, and the exponent $2.8$ accurately quantifies the super-linear penalty imposed by increasing label complexity on the required amount of data.

Within this framework, we identify two primary operational regimes. When label complexity is high and data is abundant, the Logits-Constrained (LC) model effectively mitigates the overfitting risk associated with the CRF's transition matrix, leading to significant performance gains. Empirical results show that the LC model explains 82% of the performance variance in this setting. Conversely, for moderate label complexity or limited data, a CRF+LC combination leverages both components: CRF captures tag transitions, while LC acts as a regularizer. The term $L^{2.8}$ quantifies the exponential increase in data required to justify an LC-only approach as label complexity grows.

To refine model selection, we formulate the configuration problem as a constrained optimization:

$$\min_{\alpha,\beta} \sum_{i=1}^{4} \left( F1_{\text{best}}^{(i)} - F1_{\text{pred}}^{(i)} \right)^2 e^{-\alpha \frac{N_i}{L_i^{\beta}}} \tag{4}$$

This is solved via gradient descent, yielding optimal parameters $\alpha = 0.16$ and $\beta = 2.8$.

Ablation studies on BiLSTM integration show consistent performance degradation ($\Delta F1 = -2.4\% \pm 1.1\%$), with the negative impact increasing in high-label, low-data settings:

$$\deg(\text{BiLSTM}) \propto L^{1.7} N^{0.6} \tag{5}$$

This suggests that BiLSTM's detrimental effect is amplified under high label density and limited data.

Based on the above analysis, we provide the following practical guidelines. First, eliminate the BiLSTM module in all configurations. Second, use the CRF+LC model by default when $L \leq 13$ or $N \leq 0.16L^{2.8}$ to fully capture transition dependencies. Third, switch to an LC-only model when $L \geq 20$ and $N > 0.16L^{2.8}$ to avoid overfitting and leverage the benefits of abundant data.

## 5 Conclusion

We propose a Logits-Constrained framework with GujiRoBERTa for ancient Chinese NER. The two-stage pipeline enforces BMES constraints through dynamic logits masking, eliminating invalid transitions while maintaining simplicity. Experiments show that LC outperforms traditional CRF-based methods, improving F1 by up to 2.95% in complex label scenarios. BiLSTM integration degrades performance, while dataset expansion and hybrid CRF+LC improve robustness. A data-driven model selection criterion shows LC alone excels when label count $L \geq 20$ and data size $N > 0.16L^{2.8}$. This work offers a practical, theoretically sound solution for ancient Chinese NER.

## 6 Limitations

Although our framework achieves high accuracy with a compact design, several limitations remain. First, the predefined Logits-Constrained matrix $M$ is based on manual BMES rules, which may not generalize well and is highly sensitive to the accuracy of the initial token. Second, the two-stage pipeline introduces additional inference overhead compared to end-to-end models. Third, performance depends on sentence segmentation quality, making it vulnerable to errors in unpunctuated or irregular historical texts. Future work could explore adaptive constraint learning and unified architectures to address these issues.

## References


Jacob Devlin, Ming-Wei Chang, Kenton Lee, and Kristina Toutanova. 2019. BERT: Pre-training of deep bidirectional transformers for language understanding. In *Proceedings of the 2019 Conference of the North American Chapter of the Association for Computational Linguistics: Human Language Technologies, Volume 1 (Long and Short Papers)*, pages 4171–4186, Minneapolis, Minnesota. Association for Computational Linguistics.

Sijia Ge. 2022. Integration of named entity recognition and sentence segmentation on Ancient Chinese based on siku-BERT. In *Proceedings of the 2nd International Workshop on Natural Language Processing for Digital Humanities*, pages 167–173, Taipei, Taiwan of China. Association for Computational Linguistics.

Zhiheng Huang, Wei Xu, and Kai Yu. 2015. Bidirectional lstm-crf models for sequence tagging. *Preprint*, arXiv:1508.01991.

Haoming Jiang, Danqing Zhang, Tianyu Cao, Bing Yin, and Tuo Zhao. 2021. Named entity recognition with small strongly labeled and large weakly labeled data. *Preprint*, arXiv:2106.08977.

John D. Lafferty, Andrew McCallum, and Fernando C. N. Pereira. 2001. Conditional random fields: Probabilistic models for segmenting and labeling sequence data. In *Proceedings of the Eighteenth International Conference on Machine Learning*, ICML '01, page 282–289, San Francisco, CA, USA. Morgan Kaufmann Publishers Inc.

Yinhan Liu, Myle Ott, Naman Goyal, Jingfei Du, Mandar Joshi, Danqi Chen, Omer Levy, Mike Lewis, Luke Zettlemoyer, and Veselin Stoyanov. 2019. Roberta: A robustly optimized bert pretraining approach. *arXiv preprint arXiv:1907.11692*.

David J. MacKay. 2003. *Information Theory, Inference, and Learning Algorithms*. Cambridge University Press, Cambridge.

Ashish Vaswani, Noam Shazeer, Niki Parmar, Jakob Uszkoreit, Llion Jones, Aidan N. Gomez, Lukasz Kaiser, and Illia Polosukhin. 2023. Attention is all you need. *Preprint*, arXiv:1706.03762.

Tianwen Wei, Jianwei Qi, Shenghuan He, and Songtao Sun. 2021. Masked conditional random fields for sequence labeling. In *Proceedings of the 2021 Conference of the North American Chapter of the Association for Computational Linguistics: Human Language Technologies*, pages 2024–2035, Online. Association for Computational Linguistics.

# Multi-Strategy Named Entity Recognition System for Ancient Chinese

**Wenxuan Dong, Meiling Liu***
Northeast Forestry University, China
{curleydong, lmling2008}@163.com

## Abstract

We present a multi-strategy Named Entity Recognition (NER) system for ancient Chinese texts in EvaHan2025. Addressing dataset heterogeneity, we use a Conditional Random Field (CRF) for Tasks A and C to handle six entity types' complex dependencies, and a lightweight Softmax classifier for Task B's simpler three-entity tagset. Ablation studies on training data confirm CRF's superiority in capturing sequence dependencies and Softmax's computational advantage for simpler tasks. On blind tests, our system achieves F1-scores of 83.94%, 88.31%, and 82.15% for Test A, B, and C—outperforming baselines by 2.46%, 0.81%, and 9.75%. With an overall F1 improvement of 4.30%, it excels across historical and medical domains. This adaptability enhances knowledge extraction from ancient texts, offering a scalable NER framework for low-resource, complex languages.

## 1 Introduction

Named Entity Recognition (NER), a fundamental task in information extraction, identifies key entities such as person names, locations, and organizations within text. It is essential for applications like information retrieval (Fetahu et al., 2021; Wang et al., 2022; Mokhtari et al., 2019). In ancient literature, NER supports the analysis of ancient Chinese texts and the extraction of humanistic knowledge. However, this task faces challenges due to limited public datasets and the unique features of classical texts, including polysemy, continuous structure, and unpunctuated traditional Chinese characters, all of which complicate entity boundary detection.

The EvaHan2025 competition[1] tackles these challenges with a 500,000-character dataset of historical and medical classical texts, expertly curated through automated annotation and manual review. Spanning subsets from *Shiji*, *Twenty-Four Histories*, and *Traditional Chinese Medicine Classics*, it encompasses diverse entity types and linguistic styles. To tackle this complexity, we propose a multi-strategy NER framework for EvaHan2025. Our system integrates a Conditional Random Field (CRF) model to capture intricate sequence dependencies in Tasks A and C, paired with a lightweight Softmax classifier for Task B to optimize efficiency for its simpler tagset. This hybrid approach outperforms official baselines, demonstrating robustness across heterogeneous datasets and advancing NER for ancient Chinese texts.

## 2 Related Work

### 2.1 Named Entity Recognition

Deep learning has shifted NER from rule-based methods to neural networks, which automatically extract features from text, improving efficiency over manual rule design. Huang et al. (Huang et al., 2015) proposed BiLSTM-CRF, combining BiLSTM's long-distance dependency capture with CRF's sequence optimization, excelling on the CoNLL-2003 dataset (Tjong Kim Sang and De Meulder, 2003). (Ma and Hovy, 2016) advanced this with BiLSTM-CNN-CRF, using CNNs for word-level features and CRF for refinement, boosting English NER performance (Wang et al., 2022). Transformer-based models later enhanced results with contextual embeddings (Mokhtari et al., 2019), leading to paradigms like sequence labeling (Lample et al., 2016; Devlin et al., 2019), span-based recognition (Fu et al., 2021), and text generation (Zhang et al., 2022).

While these methods excel in modern languages like English and Chinese (Mokhtari et al., 2019), ancient Chinese NER remains underexplored. The EvaHan2025 competition addresses this by providing an ancient Chinese dataset, advancing domain-specific NER research.

** Corresponding author.
[1] https://github.com/GoThereGit/EvaHan



*Proceedings of the Second Ancient Language Processing Workshop associated with NAACL 2025*, pages 151–158
May 4, 2025. 

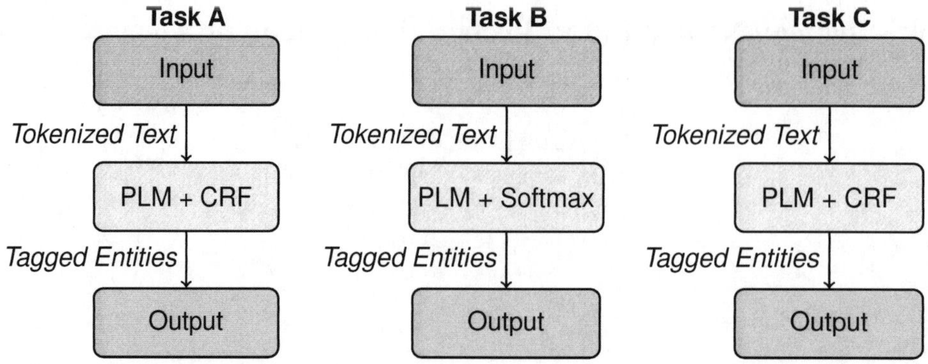


Figure 1: Architecture of the Multi-Strategy NER System. The system employs GujiRoBERTa_jian_fan as the PLM, paired with CRF for Tasks A and C (six entity types) and Softmax for Task B (three entity types).

### 2.2 Pre-trained Language Models

Pre-trained Language Models (PLMs) have revolutionized NLP tasks, including NER, by providing rich contextual representations. BERT (Devlin et al., 2019) pioneered this approach, with variants like RoBERTa (Liu et al., 2019) and ELECTRA (Clark et al., 2020) enhancing efficiency. For ancient Chinese, specialized models like Siku-BERT (Wang et al., 2021) have been developed to address unique linguistic features, significantly improving performance in downstream tasks such as NER.

## 3 Method

### 3.1 Pre-processing

To avoid redundant code, we use the seqeval library for validation—even though it does not support BMES annotations. Thus, we convert BMES prefixes to BIOES during preprocessing, reducing the need for custom evaluation functions. We term this a simplified preprocessing algorithm. Secondly, in the data preprocessing stage, we process it through the custom "NERDataset" class. This class inherits from Dataset, can read text file paths and label file paths, filter out overly long sentences, and form tuples of samples and labels to meet the training requirements of the model. The EvaHan2025 dataset exhibits heterogeneity across Tasks A, B, and C, with varying entity types (six in Tasks A and C vs. three in Task B) and domain styles (*Shiji*, *Twenty-Four Histories*, and *TCM Classics*), necessitating a tailored strategy for each task.

### 3.2 Model

The architecture of our model is shown in Figure 1. To address the heterogeneity of the EvaHan2025 dataset, we propose a multi-strategy NER framework. We adopt GujiRoBERTa_jian_fan[2], a competition-mandated pre-trained model on ancient Chinese texts, to generate contextual representations $\mathbf{H}$ from an input sequence $\mathbf{x} = \{x_1, x_2, \ldots, x_n\}$. The model yields representations $\mathbf{H} = \{\mathbf{h}_1, \mathbf{h}_2, \ldots, \mathbf{h}_n\}$:

$$\mathbf{H} = \text{GujiRoBERTa\_jian\_fan}(\mathbf{x}). \tag{1}$$

For Tasks A and C, which involve six complex entity types (Table 4), we employ a CRF layer to capture intricate label dependencies, computing the optimal sequence:

$$Y = \arg\max_{\mathbf{y}} P(\mathbf{y} \mid \mathbf{H}), \tag{2}$$

where $P(\mathbf{y} \mid \mathbf{H})$ integrates transition and emission scores (Lafferty et al., 2001).

Conversely, for Task B's simpler three-entity tagset (Table 4), we use a Softmax layer to predict tags efficiently:

$$P(y_i = c \mid \mathbf{h}_i) = \frac{\exp((\mathbf{W}\mathbf{h}_i + \mathbf{b})_c)}{\sum_{c'} \exp((\mathbf{W}\mathbf{h}_i + \mathbf{b})_{c'})}, \tag{3}$$

This choice leverages Task B's reduced label transition complexity (three entities vs. six in Tasks A and C), where CRF's sequence modeling is less critical, as validated by ablation studies (Table 3), prioritizing Softmax's computational efficiency without sacrificing accuracy.

This hybrid approach leverages annotated data to bypass boundary ambiguity, with CRF ensuring accuracy for complex tasks and Softmax enhancing efficiency for simpler ones.

[2] https://huggingface.co/hsc748NLP/GujiRoBERTa_jian_fan

| Subset | Task (Domain) | Labeled | Characters | Purpose |
|---|---|---|---|---|
| Training | A, B, C | Yes | 320,000 | Model Training |
| Validation | A, B, C | Yes | 80,000 | Model Selection |
| Blind Test | A, B, C | No | 100,000 | Final Evaluation |

Table 1: Dataset statistics for EvaHan2025. Tasks correspond to domains: A (*Shiji*), B (*Twenty-Four Histories*), C (*Traditional Chinese Medicine Classics*). Total characters: 500,000.

| Method | Test A | | | Test B | | | Test C | | | Overall | | |
|---|---|---|---|---|---|---|---|---|---|---|---|---|
| | P | R | F1 | P | R | F1 | P | R | F1 | P | R | F1 |
| Baseline | 85.90 | 77.50 | 81.48 | 87.09 | 87.92 | 87.50 | 71.84 | 72.95 | 72.40 | 81.41 | 79.82 | 80.61 |
| Ours | **89.13** | **79.32** | **83.94** | **89.34** | 87.30 | **88.31** | **78.37** | **86.32** | **82.15** | **85.16** | **84.66** | **84.91** |

Table 2: Performance Comparison (Precision, Recall, F1, as Percentages) Between Our System and the Baseline Across Test A, B, and C in EvaHan2025 Blind Tests (Close Modality).

# 4 Experiments

## 4.1 Dataset

We used the EvaHan2025 dataset, comprising 500,000 characters across three domains: Task A (*Shiji*), Task B (*Twenty-Four Histories*), and Task C (*Traditional Chinese Medicine Classics*). Statistics are detailed in Table 1, with entity tagsets in Table 4. The labeled data was split into training (80%, 320,000 characters) and validation (20%, 80,000 characters) sets for model training and validation, respectively. The unlabeled blind test set ( 100,000 characters) was used solely for final evaluation by the organizers, with predictions submitted post-training. This separation ensures robust and fair results.

## 4.2 Implementation Details

We built all models atop GujiRoBERTa_jian_fan, a pre-trained model from the Transformers library. For Tasks A and C, we added a CRF task head using the CRF library and applied a layered learning rate strategy. For Task B, we appended a Softmax layer. Models were optimized with AdamW (Loshchilov and Hutter, 2019), and performance was assessed using the seqeval library. Experiments ran on the environment in Table 5, with key hyperparameters listed in Table 10. Full details and code are available on GitHub.[3]

## 4.3 Metrics

In accordance with the conventions of Named Entity Recognition, we use Precision (P), Recall (R), and F1 score (F1) as evaluation metrics across all experiments. All results are reported in percentage form to ensure consistency and facilitate comparison across different models and experimental settings.

## 4.4 Baseline

To better evaluate our model's effectiveness, we use the official SikuRoBERTa-BiLSTM-CRF, trained on the training set without additional resources, as the baseline. Comparing our model with this baseline offers a clearer understanding of its performance and advantages.

## 4.5 Results

Results are presented in Table 2. Our system surpasses the baseline across all metrics for Tasks A, B, and C, achieving average F1 gains of 4.30%. This superiority stems from our multi-strategy approach: CRF effectively captures complex entity dependencies in Tasks A and C, while Softmax enhances efficiency for Task B's simpler tagset, showing strong adaptability to ancient Chinese datasets. Notably, Task C's F1 improves most (9.75%), likely due to CRF leveraging the structured patterns of *TCM Classics*, unlike Task A's diverse *Shiji* or Task B's simpler tagset (Table 4).

## 4.6 Ablation Study

We evaluated our multi-strategy design on EvaHan2025 using GujiRoBERTa_jian_fan as the PLM, reserving 20% of the training data as the validation set for strategy selection. Validation F1 scores are reported in Table 3 as percentages.

[3] https://github.com/wxndong/MSNER4AC

| Configuration | Task A | Task B | Task C | Mean |
|---|---|---|---|---|
| | | *Single-Strategy* | | |
| PLM + CRF (All Tasks) | – | – | – | 85.02 |
| PLM + Softmax (All Tasks) | – | – | – | 84.91 |
| | | *Multi-Strategy* | | |
| PLM + CRF (Per Task) | **91.53** | 86.79 | **80.23** | 86.18 |
| PLM + Softmax (Per Task) | 90.90 | **86.87** | 78.63 | 85.47 |
| Ours (A/C: CRF, B: Softmax) | **91.53** | **86.87** | **80.23** | **86.21** |

Table 3: Validation F1 scores (%). Single-strategy combines all task data; multi-strategy trains per task. '–' indicates unavailable task-specific scores for single-strategy models, as Task B's tagset (NR, NS, T) is a subset of Task A's (Table 4), causing interference that prevents isolated per-task evaluation.

#### 4.6.1 Multi-Strategy vs. Single-Strategy

EvaHan2025 ranks submissions by mean F1 across Tasks A (*Shiji*), B (*Twenty-Four Histories*), and C (*Traditional Chinese Medicine Classics*). Single-strategy models (PLM + CRF and PLM + Softmax), trained on all tasks combined, yield mean F1s of 85.02% and 84.91%. Multi-strategy models (trained per task) reach 86.18% and 85.47%, gaining 1.16–1.27 points. This boost comes from isolating tasks: Task B's tagset (NR, NS, T) is a subset of Task A's (Table 4), causing single-strategy models to overgeneralize. Our approach avoids this interference, improving task-specific performance.

#### 4.6.2 Task-Specific Strategy Selection

Comparing PLM + CRF (Exp. 3) and PLM + Softmax (Exp. 4) (Table 3, Appendix B), CRF excels on Tasks A (91.53% vs. 90.90%, +0.63) and C (80.23% vs. 78.63%, +1.60), handling six-entity dependencies well. Yet, in low-support labels (e.g., NB in Task A, ZZ in Task C), their differences are minor (Appendix B). For Task B, CRF (86.79%) and Softmax (86.87%) perform similarly, but Softmax cuts inference time by 63% (14.28s vs. 38.24s; Appendix 6). Our hybrid design—CRF for A and C, Softmax for B—achieves a mean F1 of 86.21%, balancing accuracy and efficiency.

#### 4.6.3 Lightweight Analysis

For Task B, Softmax's $O(nk)$ decoding complexity (k=3) outperforms CRF's $O(nk^2)$, cutting blind test inference time by 63% (Please refer to Appendix 6) and reducing training/validation time from 202s to 86s, with F1 (86.87 vs. 86.79, +0.08). Here, $n$ is sequence length, and $k$ is label set size. This lightweight efficiency design optimizes efficiency for simpler tagsets without compromising accuracy.

## 5 Conclusion

In this paper, we propose a Multi-Strategy Named Entity Recognition (NER) system tailored for the EvaHan2025 competition. Our system demonstrates superior performance across three distinct datasets by leveraging task-specific strategies, including the use of CRF for complex sequence dependencies in Tasks A and C, and a computationally efficient Softmax classifier in Task B. Our system offers a scalable NER framework for similar low-resource, heterogeneous ancient language datasets, leveraging its multi-strategy adaptability, with potential applications in digital humanities. Future work could explore adaptive hyperparameter tuning and tagset refinement to further enhance generalization.

## Limitations

Our multi-strategy NER system excels in EvaHan2025 but has limitations: inconsistent generalization and challenges with rare entities. Generalization varies across tasks. Task A's F1 drops from 91.53% to 83.94% (-7.59), likely due to overfitting to *Shiji*'s diverse data (Appendix C, Figure 2), while Task C's rises from 80.23% to 82.15% (+1.92), possibly due to a structured medical domain (Figure 3). Task B remains stable (86.87% vs. 88.31%) with a simpler tagset (Table 4). Rare entities (e.g., NB in Task A, ZZ in Task C) with low support (Appendix B) perform inconsistently. Future work could use cross-domain validation to improve generalization and data augmentation to enhance rare entity recognition.

## References

Kevin Clark, Minh-Thang Luong, Quoc V. Le, and Christopher D. Manning. 2020. Electra: Pre-training text encoders as discriminators rather than generators. *arXiv preprint arXiv:2003.10555*.

Jacob Devlin, Ming-Wei Chang, Kenton Lee, and Kristina Toutanova. 2019. Bert: Pre-training of deep bidirectional transformers for language understanding. *arXiv preprint arXiv:1810.04805*.

Besnik Fetahu, Anjie Fang, Oleg Rokhlenko, and Shervin Malmasi. 2021. Gazetteer enhanced named entity recognition for code-mixed web queries. In *Proceedings of the 44th International ACM SIGIR Conference on Research and Development in Information Retrieval*, pages 1677–1681.

Jinlan Fu, Xuanjing Huang, and Pengfei Liu. 2021. SpanNER: Named entity re-/recognition as span prediction. In *Proceedings of the 59th Annual Meeting of the Association for Computational Linguistics and the 11th International Joint Conference on Natural Language Processing (Volume 1: Long Papers)*, pages 7183–7195, Online. Association for Computational Linguistics.

Zhiheng Huang, Wei Xu, and Kai Yu. 2015. Bidirectional LSTM-CRF models for sequence tagging. *arXiv preprint arXiv:1508.01991*.

John Lafferty, Andrew McCallum, and Fernando Pereira. 2001. Conditional random fields: Probabilistic models for segmenting and labeling sequence data. In *Proceedings of the 18th International Conference on Machine Learning*, pages 282–289.

Guillaume Lample, Miguel Ballesteros, Sandeep Subramanian, Kazuya Kawakami, and Chris Dyer. 2016. Neural architectures for named entity recognition. In *Proceedings of the 2016 Conference of the North American Chapter of the Association for Computational Linguistics: Human Language Technologies*, pages 260–270, San Diego, California. Association for Computational Linguistics.

Yinhan Liu, Myle Ott, Naman Goyal, Jingfei Du, Mandar Joshi, Danqi Chen, Omer Levy, Mike Lewis, Luke Zettlemoyer, and Veselin Stoyanov. 2019. Roberta: A robustly optimized BERT pretraining approach. *arXiv preprint arXiv:1907.11692*.

Ilya Loshchilov and Frank Hutter. 2019. Decoupled weight decay regularization. *arXiv preprint arXiv:1711.05101*.

Xuezhe Ma and Eduard Hovy. 2016. End-to-end sequence labeling via bi-directional LSTM-CNNs-CRF. In *Proceedings of the 54th Annual Meeting of the Association for Computational Linguistics (Volume 1: Long Papers)*, pages 1064–1074, Berlin, Germany. Association for Computational Linguistics.

Shekoofeh Mokhtari, Ahmad Mahmoody, Dragomir Yankov, and Ning Xie. 2019. Tagging address queries in maps search. *Proceedings of the AAAI Conference on Artificial Intelligence*, 33(1):9547–9551.

Erik F. Tjong Kim Sang and Fien De Meulder. 2003. Introduction to the CoNLL-2003 shared task: Language-independent named entity recognition. In *Proceedings of the Seventh Conference on Natural Language Learning at HLT-NAACL 2003*, pages 142–147.

Dongbo Wang, Chang Liu, Zihe Zhu, Jiang, Feng, Haotian Hu, Si Shen, and Bin Li. 2021. Construction and application of pre-training model of "siku quanshu" oriented to digital humanities.

Xiao Wang, Shihan Dou, Limao Xiong, Yicheng Zou, Qi Zhang, Tao Gui, Liang Qiao, Zhanzhan Cheng, and Xuanjing Huang. 2022. Miner: Improving out-of-vocabulary named entity recognition from an information theoretic perspective. *arXiv preprint arXiv:2204.04391*.

Xinghua Zhang, Bowen Yu, Yubin Wang, Tingwen Liu, Taoyu Su, and Hongbo Xu. 2022. Exploring modular task decomposition in cross-domain named entity recognition. In *Proceedings of the 45th International ACM SIGIR Conference on Research and Development in Information Retrieval*, pages 301–311.

# A Supporting Tables in References

| Tag | Meaning |
|---|---|
| | *Task A (Shiji)* |
| NR | Person name |
| NS | Geographical location |
| NB | Book title |
| NO | Official title |
| NG | Country name |
| T | Time expression |
| | *Task B (Twenty-Four Histories)* |
| NR | Person name |
| NS | Geographical location |
| T | Time expression |
| | *Task C (TCM Classics)* |
| ZD | TCM disease |
| ZZ | Syndrome |
| ZF | Medicinal formula |
| ZP | Decoction pieces |
| ZS | Symptom |
| ZA | Acupoint |

Table 4: Entity tagsets for EvaHan2025 tasks.

| Environment | Specification |
|---|---|
| CUDA Version | 12.0 |
| GPU | NVIDIA RTX 4090 |
| Memory | 24 GB |

Table 5: Experimental environment.

## B Additional Tables

This appendix provides tables supporting the experiments and ablation studies in Sections 4 and 4.6. Table 6 compares Task B runtime for PLM + Softmax and PLM + CRF, showing Softmax's efficiency (Section 4.6.2). Tables 7–9 detail per-category F1 scores for Tasks A, B, and C on the validation set, complementing Table 3 and guiding our multi-strategy NER design. Due to seqeval, F1 scores are rounded to two decimals and shown as percentages without decimals (e.g., 0.33 to 33%), not affecting comparisons.

| **Model** | **Training + Val. (s)** | **Blind Test (s)** |
|---|---|---|
| PLM + Softmax | 86 | 14.28 |
| PLM + CRF | 202 | 38.24 |

Table 6: Task B runtime comparison (seconds).

| **Category (Support)** | **F1 (CRF)** | **F1 (Softmax)** |
|---|---|---|
| NB (5) | 33.00 | 33.00 |
| NG (731) | 94.00 | 94.00 |
| NO (286) | 77.00 | 74.00 |
| NR (2042) | 95.00 | 95.00 |
| NS (500) | 87.00 | 87.00 |
| T (193) | 79.00 | 77.00 |

Table 7: Task A validation F1 scores (%).

| **Category (Support)** | **F1 (CRF)** | **F1 (Softmax)** |
|---|---|---|
| NR (794) | 91.00 | 89.00 |
| NS (685) | 84.00 | 83.00 |
| T (509) | 85.00 | 89.00 |

Table 8: Task B validation F1 scores (%).

| **Category (Support)** | **F1 (CRF)** | **F1 (Softmax)** |
|---|---|---|
| ZA (294) | 84.00 | 83.00 |
| ZD (166) | 73.00 | 73.00 |
| ZF (197) | 83.00 | 84.00 |
| ZP (1083) | 86.00 | 87.00 |
| ZS (257) | 65.00 | 57.00 |
| ZZ (97) | 47.00 | 33.00 |

Table 9: Task C validation F1 scores (%).

## C Hyperparameters and Transition Matrix

| Hyperparameter | Task A (PLM + CRF) | Task B (PLM + Softmax) | Task C (PLM + CRF) |
|---|---|---|---|
| Batch Size | 32 | 32 | 32 |
| Epochs | 35 | 30 | 35 |
| Learning Rate (PLM) | $5 \times 10^{-5}$ | $5 \times 10^{-5}$ | $5 \times 10^{-5}$ |
| Learning Rate (Head) | $5 \times 10^{-3}$ | $5 \times 10^{-5}$ | $5 \times 10^{-3}$ |
| Warmup Ratio | 0.1 | 0.1 | 0.1 |
| LR Scheduler | Cosine | Linear | Cosine |
| Max Gradient Norm | 1.0 | 1.0 | 1.0 |

Table 10: Key hyperparameter settings.

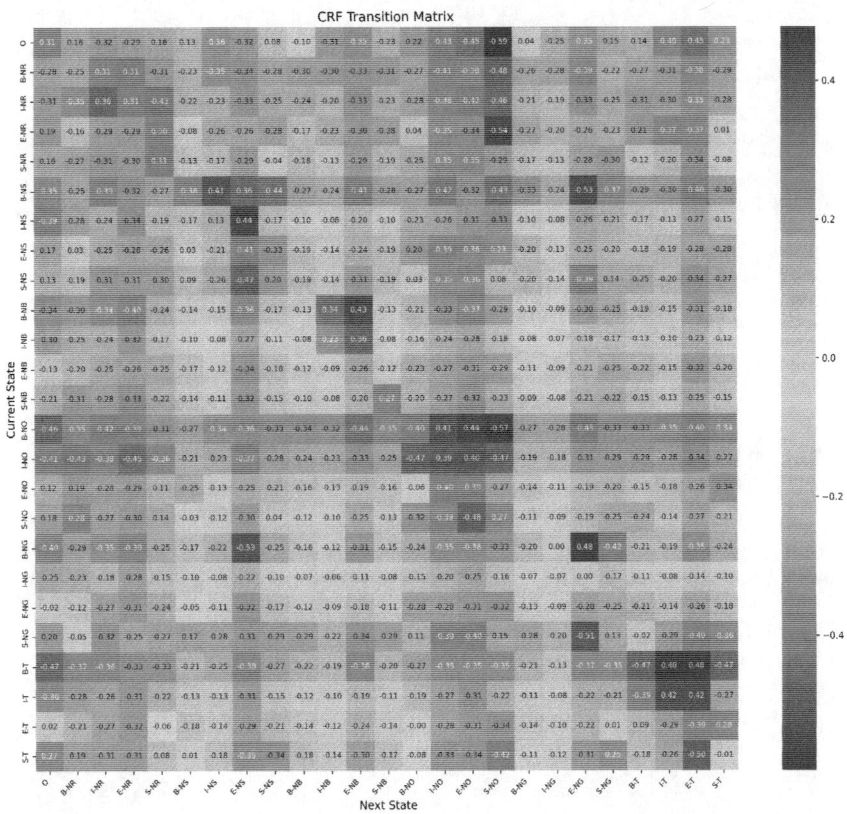


Figure 2: Task A CRF transition matrix (Exp. 3). Rows: current state; columns: next state. Color depth shows transition probability (-0.5 to 0.5).

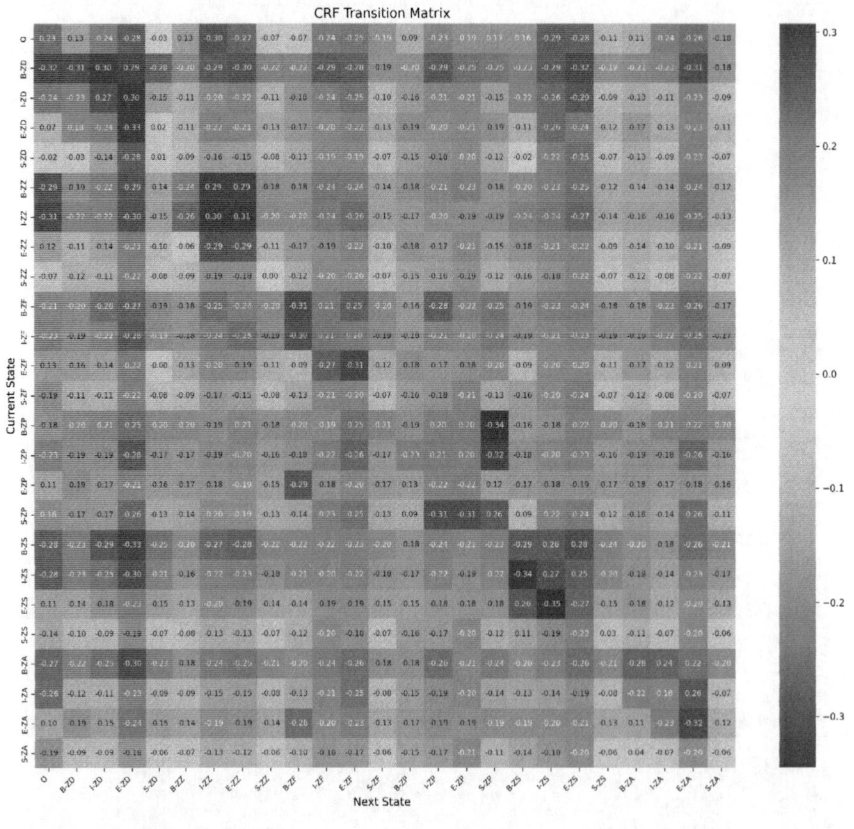


Figure 3: Task C CRF transition matrix (Exp. 3). Rows: current state; columns: next state. Color depth shows transition probability (-0.5 to 0.5).

# Multi-Domain Ancient Chinese Named Entity Recognition Based on Attention-Enhanced Pre-trained Language Model

**Qi Zhang, Zhiya Duan, Shijie Ma, Shengyu Liu, Zibo Yuan, Ruimin Ma**
**School of Economics and Management**
**Shanxi University, China**
***qi.zhang@sxu.edu.cn***

## Abstract

Recent advancements in digital humanities have intensified the demand for intelligent processing of ancient Chinese texts, particularly across specialized domains such as historical records and ancient medical literature. Among related research areas, Named Entity Recognition (NER) plays a crucial role, serving as the foundation for knowledge graph construction and deeper humanities computing studies. In this paper, we introduce a architecture specifically designed for multi-domain ancient Chinese NER tasks based on a pre-trained language model (PLM). Building upon the GujiRoberta backbone, we propose the GujiRoberta-BiLSTM-Attention-CRF model. Experimental results on three distinct domain-specific datasets demonstrate that our approach significantly outperforms the official baselines across all three datasets, highlighting the particular effectiveness of integrating an attention mechanism within our architecture.

**Keywords:** Named Entity Recognition, Ancient Chinese, Multi-Domain GujiRoberta-BiLSTM,-Attention-CRF.

## 1 Introduction

Thousands of years of Chinese civilization have been encapsulated within historical, political, economic, medical and various other types of ancient books. However, due to their vast quantity and significant deterioration over time, these invaluable resources have remained underexplored and underutilized. Recent rapid advancements in frontier technologies, such as big data and artificial intelligence, present unprecedented opportunities for the deep mining and revitalization of ancient texts. In particular, the integration of natural language processing (NLP) and knowledge graph technologies has rejuvenated research into ancient documents. Entities, serving as fundamental knowledge units within ancient texts, play a crucial role in humanities computing studies. Nevertheless, entity recognition from ancient Chinese texts remains significantly challenging, primarily due to the intrinsic complexity of ancient Chinese grammar, archaic vocabulary, semantic obscurity, and the domain-specific nature of texts.

To address these challenges, EVAHAN 2025 proposed a specialized NER task focused on ancient Chinese texts across multiple domains. Based on the PLM called SikuRoBERTa for ancient Chinese provided by EVAHAN 2025, we further propose the incorporation of a BiLSTM-Attention network for enhanced feature extraction, coupled with a CRF layer for decoding to improve the accuracy of entity label classification. Besides, through meticulous hyperparameter tuning, our model better accommodates domain-specific textual characteristics. Extensive experiments conducted on three provided datasets demonstrate the superior performance of our proposed model, significantly surpassing official benchmarks.

## 2 Related Research

Research on named entity recognition (NER) in ancient Chinese has gone through four technical evolution stages: rule-based templates, statistical modeling, neural networks and pre-trained models. Early template and statistical methods were gradually replaced by neural network learning frameworks due to their limited domain transferability (Huang et al., 2002; Li et al., 2023). For instance, Huang et al. (2015) introduced the BiLSTM-CRF model, which captured long-distance syntactic dependencies in ancient texts through bidirectional long short-term memory networks and optimized label sequence prediction through Conditional Random Fields.

The subsequent emergence of pre-trained language models (PLMs) dramatically enhanced the processing efficiency and semantic comprehension capabilities for ancient Chinese



*Proceedings of the Second Ancient Language Processing Workshop associated with NAACL 2025*, pages 159–163
May 4, 2025. 

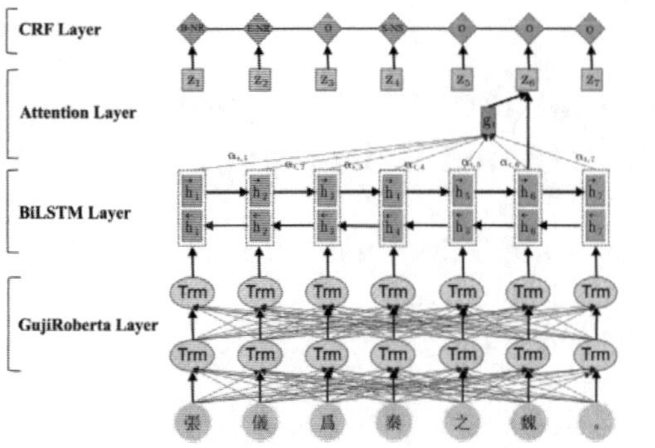


Figure 1: Model Architecture.

texts. The iterations of BERT architecture (Devlin et al., 2019) and the introduction of RoBERTa by (Liu et al., 2019) with dynamic masking mechanisms have redefined the pre-training paradigm. Wang et al.(2022) conducted incremental training using traditional Chinese text from the Complete Library in Four Sections to build SikuBERT and SikuRoBERTa pre-trained models. While generative large language models like GPT demonstrate considerable semantic understanding, they suffer from issues such as entity hallucination and boundary ambiguities, limiting their reliability for precise entity extraction tasks (Zhang et al., 2023) .Recent researches shows BERT-based methods still maintain significant advantages through domain-adaptive fine-tuning in IE tasks (Detroja et al., 2023; Diaz-Garcia and Lopez, 2024; Han et al., 2024).

However, most previous studies on ancient Chinese NER have primarily focused on general entities such as personal names, locations and dates. Recent advancements in digital humanities have broadened the scope, demanding sophisticated processing capabilities for specialized domains such as historical records and ancient medical literature, thus expanding annotation schemas from basic three-element frameworks to more comprehensive multi-element structures, including official titles, pathological terms, and cultural symbols (Zhang et al., 2023). Compared to standard named entity tasks, recognizing specialized domain entities poses greater challenges due to the need for enhanced contextual understanding and domain-specific adaptability.

## 3 Model Construction

### 3.1 Model Introduction

The GujiRoberta-BiLSTM-Attention-CRF model is a deep learning framework designed for the task of ancient text named entity recognition in ancient text. As illustrated in Table1, its process is divided into four stages: Firstly, through the pre-trained model GujiRoberta, context-aware word vectors are generated; Secondly, BiLSTM captures bidirectional long-distance semantic dependencies; Subsequently, the attention mechanism is utilized to enhance key features; Finally, the CRF layer is employed to achieve the global optimal label prediction.

The attention mechanism significantly enhances the model's ability to focus on key information. By introducing attention weights distribution in the output layer of BiLSTM, the importance scores of for each position are calculated through a learnable parameter matrix, and then normalized by softmax to generate a focusing vector. This mechanism can adaptively enhance entity-related features, such as the core verbs in disease descriptions, shile simultaneously suppressing irrelevant noise. It is particularly suitable for processing scattered entity expressions in ancient texts, thereby improving the model's sensitivity to key information.

In the named entity recognition task, CRF, as the decoding layer, solves the label conflict problem of traditional softmax decoding by modeling label transition probabilities. The global score function is constructed by defining emission scores (linear transformation of the BiLSTM-attention output) and transition scores (transition matrix between labels), and the optimal path is solved using the Viterbi algorithm. This design ensures that the output sequence conforms to the ancient text entity annotation specifications (such as the continuity constraint of the BIOES label system), effectively improving the recognition accuracy of entity boundaries.

### 3.2 Experimental Datasets

This competition involves three ancient text named entity recognition datasets: Dataset A is based on "Records of the Grand Historian" and labels personal names (NR), place names (NS), book titles (NB), official titles (NO), dynastic names (NG), and time (T). The complexity of this dataset arises from the evolution of historical naming conventions; Dataset B is selected from "Twenty-Four Histories" and focuses on personal names (NR), place names (NS), and time (T), requiring handling ambiguity issues caused by ancient language abbreviations; Dataset C originates from traditional Chinese medical classics and covers six categories of professional terms: traditional Chinese medicine diseases (ZD), syndromes (ZZ), prescriptions (ZF), medicinal materials (ZP), symptoms (ZS), and acupoints (ZA). It faces the challenge of diverse term expressions.

Data processing adopts a multi-stage optimization strategy: Firstly, perform text data undergoes cleaning and standardization processing, which includes the removal of blank lines and the normalization of characters. Subsequently, dynamic segmentation is executed based on four sets of length thresholds (128/256/400/512) and locate the end symbols, such as periods and quotation marks, etc. through backtracking to ensure semantic integrity. This approach facilitates the model's capability to better learn the correlation information between ancient texts. After randomly shuffling process to eliminate sequence deviations, the dataset should be partitioned into training set and validation set in a 9:1 ratio. Finally, ensure the representativeness of each data subset to meet the multi-dimensional requirements of model training, hyperparameter optimization, and performance evaluation.

### 3.3 Evaluation Metrics

Precision, recall, and F1 score were used as the main metrics to evaluate model performance. Their calculation formulas are as follows:

$$P = \frac{TP}{TP+FP} \times 100\% \quad (1)$$

$$R = \frac{TP}{TP+FN} \times 100\% \quad (2)$$

$$F1 = \frac{2PR}{P+P} \times 100\% \quad (3)$$

Where TP = correctly identified entities, FP = incorrect identifications, and FN = missed entities.

### 3.4 Experimental Environment

The experimental setup utilized a Linux server equipped with an NVIDIA RTX 4090 GPU (24 GB of video memory), facilitating efficient large-scale deep learning model training. A 6-core Xeon Gold 6142 processor provided robust multitasking capabilities, while 64.4 GB of RAM and 420 GB of disk storage were sufficient to meet the computational and data storage requirements.

For the software environment, PyTorch 2.2.2 was chosen, which, although an older version, offered good compatibility and stability. Its dynamic computation graph, user-friendly APIs, and community support made it the preferred choice. Docker containerization technology was utilized to construct a standardized development environment, ensuring research reproducibility and consistency.

### 3.5 Model Training

(1) Loss Function

The objective of model training was to minimize negative log-likelihood loss, measuring prediction error by comparing the predicted label sequences with the true label sequences. The CRF layer calculated probabilities for all possible label sequences, ultimately selecting the most probable sequence as the final prediction.

(2) Optimizer

The AdamW optimizer was used, introducing weight decay to mitigate the risk of overfitting. The learning rate warm-up strategy was implemented to stabilize the initial gradient updates.

(3) Hyperparameter Tuning

This study employs a combined method of grid search and random search to optimize the key hyperparameters of the model. The search space for the learning rate is set from 8e-6 to 4e-5, while the batch size is dynamically adjusted within the range of 8 to 64. The dropout rate is explored within the range of 0 to 0.6, and the input text length is uniformly standardized to the range of 128 to 512 characters. We utilized several pre-trained model architectures, including bert, siku-roberta, GujiRoBERTa_jian_fan, roberta-classical-chinese-large-char, and employed some fine-tuning techniques. Through systematic verification of parameter combinations, the optimal configuration scheme of each model architecture was finally obtained, as shown in Table1.

| Dataset | Dataset_A | Dataset_B | Dataset_C |
|---|---|---|---|
| Pretrained Model | GujiRoBERTa_jian_fan | GujiRoBERTa_jian_fan | GujiRoBERTa_jian_fan |
| Text Length | 128 | 256 | 400 |
| Learning Rate | 0.00005 | 0.00002 | 0.00003 |
| Batch Size | 8 | 8 | 8 |
| Dropout | 0.4 | 0.4 | 0.6 |

Table 1: Hyperparameter Tuning.

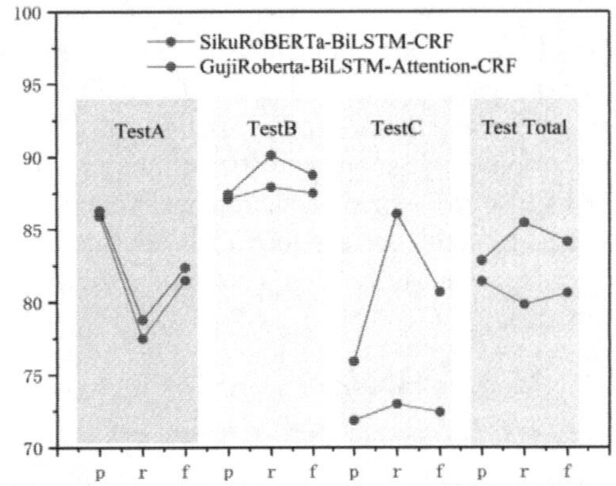


Figure 2: Model Effectiveness Comparison.

## 4 Experimental Results and Analysis

Prior to formal submission, we compared the GujiRoberta-BiLSTM-CRF and GujiRoberta-BiLSTM-Attention-CRF models on the validation set, with individual labels as the smallest unit to calculate P, R and F1-score. Experimental results confirmed that incorporating an attention mechanism consistently improved overall F1-scores. Specifically, under identical parameter configurations, the F1-score increased by over 1% for datasets A and C (the F1-score improved from 0.9103 to 0.9243 for dataset A and from 0.8613 to 0.8765 for dataset C). The attention mechanism significantly boosted global entity recognition by emphasizing critical feature information. Consequently, the GujiRoberta-BiLSTM-Attention-CRF model was selected for the final test

As shown in 错误!未找到引用源。 and Table 2, the test results further validated our model's effectiveness. EVAHAN 2025 adopted the classical SikuRoBERTa-BiLSTM-CRF architecture as its baseline. In the general dataset A, the F1 score of GujiRoberta reached 82.37, reflecting an increase of 0.89. Additionally, there was a significant improvement in the recall rate, which verifies the effectiveness of GujiRoberta's enhanced semantic understanding capabilities and its attention mechanism in capturing key information. In the professional historical dataset B, the F1 score increased to 88.74, representing an enhancement of 1.24, with the recall rate of 90.09. This indicates an advancement in the model's generalization ability concerning ancient terms and abbreviations. Furthermore, in the Chinese medicine classics dataset C, the F1 score improved by 8.28 percentage points to 80.68 compared to the baseline model, demonstrating a comprehensive ability to recognize professional terms. It is noteworthy that the accuracy rate of the three datasets were lower than the recall rates, reflecting that the model still has misidentification phenomena when dealing with complex historical entities, such as names and place names with omitted sentence patterns, as well as the diversity of TCM terms. These insights suggest meaningful directions for future research.

| Dataset | Method | P | R | F |
|---|---|---|---|---|
| A | Ours | 86.3 | 78.78 | **82.37** |
| | Baseline | 85.90 | 77.50 | 81.48 |
| B | Ours | 87.43 | 90.09 | **88.74** |
| | Baseline | 87.09 | 87.92 | 87.50 |
| C | Ours | 75.91 | 86.09 | **80.68** |
| | Baseline | 71.84 | 72.95 | 72.40 |
| Total | Ours | 82.84 | 85.46 | **84.13** |
| | Baseline | 81.41 | 79.82 | 80.61 |

Table 2: Model Effectiveness Comparison.

## 5 Conclusion & Future Directions

The experimental results indicate that the GujiRoberta-BiLSTM-Attention-CRF model proposed in this paper demonstrates a significant improvement over the official baseline on ancient book datasets in different fields such as history and medicine. These findings verify the effectiveness of the attention mechanism and the multi-module integration strategy employed in the model. By enhancing the parsing ability of ancient Chinese complex sentence patterns and long texts, the model significantly improves the entity recall rate, and provides a reliable solution for entity recognition in multi-domain ancient books. However, the accuracy of the model still remains potential for improvement in the face of fine-grained semantic contexts, such as the polysemy of words and variation of professional terms. Future research will focus on optimizing the dynamic attention allocation mechanism, enhancing semantic discrimination ability with domain adaptive pre-training, and further exploring the generalization of multi-domain feature adaptation modules.

## References


Dongbo Wang, Chang Liu, Zihe Zhu, Jiangfeng Liu, Haotian Hu, Si Shen and Bin Li. 2022. *Construction and application of pre-training model of "Siku Quanshu" oriented to digital humanities. Library Tribune*, 42(06):31-43.

Jose A. Diaz-Garcia and Julio Amador Diaz Lopez. 2024. *A survey on cutting-edge relation extraction techniques based on language models. Computing Research Repository*, arXiv: 2411.18157.

Jacob Devlin, Ming-Wei Chang, Kenton Lee and Kristina Toutanova. 2019. *BERT: pre-training of deep bidirectional transformers for language understanding. Proceedings of the 2019 Conference of the North American Chapter of the Association for Computational Linguistics: Human Language Technologies (Volume 1 : Long and Short Papers),* pages 4171-4186, Minneapolis, Minnesota. Association for Computational Linguistics. 10.18653/v1/N19-1423

Jianlong Li, Youren Yu, Xueyang Liu and Siwen Zhu. 2023. *System report for CCL23-Eval task 1;GuNER based on incremental pretraining and adversarial learning. Proceedings of the 22nd Chinese National Conference on Computational Linguistics (Volume 3: Evaluations)*, pages 23-33, Harbin, China.

Kartik Detroja, Ck Bhensdadia and Brijesh S. Bhatt. 2023. *A survey on* relation *extraction. Intell. Syst. Appl.*, 19: 200244.

Liang Huang, Yinan Peng, Huan Wang and Zhenyu Wu. 2002. *PCFG parsing for restricted classical Chinese texts. Series PCFG Parsing for Restricted Classical Chinese Texts. (Volume 18)*, pages 1-6. https://doi.org/10.3115/1118824.1118830.

Ridong Han, Chaohao Yang, Tao Peng, Prayag Tiwari, Xiang Wan, Lu Liu and Benyou Wang. 2024. *An empirical study on information extraction using large language models. Computing Research Repository*, arXiv: 2305.14450.

Xinghua Zhang, Tianjun Liu, Wenyuan Zhang and Tingwen Liu. 2023. *System report for CCL23-Eval task 1: information theory constraint and paragraph based paragraph classical named entity recognition. Proceedings of the 22nd Chinese National Conference on Computational Linguistics (Volume 3: Evaluations)*, pages 1-13, Harbin, China.

Yinhan Liu, Myle Ott, Naman Goyal, Jingfei Du, Mandar Joshi, Danqi Chen, Omer Levy, Mike Lewis, Luke Zettlemoyer and Veselin Stoyanov. 2019. *RoBERTa: a robustly optimized BERT pretraining approach. Computing Research Repository*, arXiv: 1907.11692.

Zhiheng Huang, Wei Xu and Kai Yu. 2015. *Bidirectional LSTM-CRF models for sequence tagging. Computing Research Repository*, arXiv: 1508.01991.

# EvaCun 2025 Shared Task: Lemmatization and Token Prediction in Akkadian and Sumerian using LLMs


**Shai Gordin**
Ariel University
Land of Israel
and Archaeology
shaigo@ariel.ac.il

**Aleksi Sahala**
University of Helsinki
Helsinki, Finland
aleksi.sahala@helsinki.fi

**Shahar Spencer**
The Hebrew University
of Jerusalem
shahar.spencer@mail.huji.ac.il

**Stav Klein**
Ariel University
Land of Israel
and Archaeology
Stav.Klein@msmail.ariel.ac.il



## Abstract

The EvaCun 2025 Shared Task, organized as part of ALP 2025 workshop and co-located with NAACL 2025, explores how Large Language Models (LLMs) and transformer-based models can be used to improve lemmatization and token prediction tasks for low-resource ancient cuneiform texts. This year our datasets focused on the best attested ancient Near Eastern languages written in cuneiform, namely, Akkadian and Sumerian texts. However, we utilized the availability of datasets never before used on scale in NLP tasks, primarily first millennium literature (i.e. "Canonical") provided by the Electronic Babylonian Library (eBL), and Old Babylonian letters and archival texts, provided by Archibab. We aim to encourage the development of new computational methods to better analyze and reconstruct cuneiform inscriptions, pushing NLP forward for ancient and low-resource languages. Three teams competed for the lemmatization subtask and one for the token prediction subtask. Each subtask was evaluated alongside a baseline model, provided by the organizers.


## 1 Introduction

Natural Language Processing for low-resource languages presents unique challenges, especially in an era where bigger models and more data are seen as the key to success. Ancient languages before the spread of the alphabet in the first millennium BCE, were primarily morphosyllabic, written using a combination of logograms (i.e. "word" signs) and syllabic signs (Fedorova; Daniels, 2023). Cuneiform in particular was used to encode more than a dozen languages across Western Asia, from languages of unknown or limited familial origin, like Sumerian or Hurrian, to several Semitic and Indo-European, languages, like Akkadian, Hittite, and Luwian.

Ancient Language Processing deals primarily with solving the challenges of the computational analysis of ancient morphosyllabic scripts, like the pictographic nature of signs, their iconically meaningful and complex visual arrangement, and lexical homonymy to name a few (Gordin, 2014; Gabriel et al., 2021). Some languages, particularly Semitic ones, are even more difficult due to their rich morphology, which leads to complex word forms and intricate grammatical structures (Weninger et al., 2011; Zitouni, 2014). Additionally, ancient languages often suffer from fragmented texts because the sources we rely on—inscriptions, manuscripts, and other historical records—are incomplete due to damage, erosion, and loss over time. These challenges make two key downstream NLP tasks, token prediction (used, for example, in BERT pretraining) and lemmatization, particularly difficult. To address this, we introduce a shared task with two subtasks: lemmatization, which reduces words to their base forms, and token prediction, which predicts the original token replaced with a mask.

The lemmatization and token prediction tasks for EvaCun 2025 focus on Akkadian and Sumerian cuneiform texts. Even though cuneiform was used to write on clay for more than 3,000 years, many cuneiform languages are low-resource languages. Existing corpora of texts consist of a relatively limited amount of data for each historical period of cuneiform, which is moreover divided into different geographical areas, archaeological contexts, and text genres.[1]

Existing language models have relied mostly on the tens of thousands of first millennium BCE Assyrian and Babylonian archival documents and royal inscriptions from the *Open Richly Annotated Cuneiform Corpus* (ORACC) (Gordin et al., 2020; Lazar et al., 2021; Gutherz et al., 2023), as well as the many thousands of sporadic Akkadian and Sumerian sources on the *Cuneiform Digital Library*

[1]For a good textual and linguistic overview of Akkadian and its periodization see (Vita, 2021)



*Proceedings of the Second Ancient Language Processing Workshop associated with NAACL 2025*, pages 164–172
May 4, 2025. 

*Initiative* (CDLI) (Pagé-Perron et al., 2017; Chen et al., 2023). We therefore wanted to introduce new text genres and large scale corpora that have become systematically available over recent decades in the *Electronic Babylonian Library* (eBL) and *Archibab*. For more details on the content and genre of the text in the dataset provided for the shared task see Data section below.

## 2 Previous Research

The origins of Computational Assyriology can be traced back to the 1960s, and since then over 200 relevant papers have been published. Almost all aspects of Assyriological research were experimented with computationally, from artifact reconstruction to transliteration of cuneiform, text annotation, and content analysis. In this section, we briefly summarize past attempts on cuneiform tablet reconstruction and lemmatization of Akkadian. For a more detailed survey on the history of Computational Assyriology see Sahala (2021), on vision related tasks for cuneiform see Bogacz and Mara (2022), and for Assyriological digital resources see Charpin (2014), and the DANES resources on the OpenDANES platform.

### 2.1 Lemmatization

Traditionally Akkadian lemmatizers have been based on dictionary look-ups or morphological analysis. The first[2] published lemmatizer and morphological analyzer of Akkadian was implemented by Kataja and Koskenniemi (1988), but this system was more of a tech-demo to demonstrate, how discontinuative morphology could be implemented as a finite-state grammar (FSG). Further morphology-based models were published for Babylonian by Barthélemy (1998), Macks (2002), Sahala (2014) and Sahala et al. (2020b), and for Old Assyrian by Bamman (2012). To date, the most used lemmatizer for Akkadian, and cuneiform languages in general, is L2 (Tinney, 2019). L2 is a dictionary based lemmatizer, transcriber and POS-tagger that uses bigram look-up for disambiguation. It has been used to annotate ORACC texts, one of the largest open collection of annotated cuneiform texts.

Both, dictionary and morphology based lemmatizers have their shortcomings, which ultimately emerge from the Akkadian spelling variation and discontinuative morphology. Dictionary-based models suffer from spelling-variation and morphology induced out-of-vocabulary words (OOV) that they are unable to lemmatize. Morphology-based models, on the other hand, suffer from the ambiguity and irregularity of the Akkadian writing system, especially concerning the spelling of phoneme quantities. For this reason, morphology-based models rely almost exclusively on phonologically transcribed inputs, which limit their usability, since most unannotated digitized texts exist in transliteration. The only exception to this is Bamman's Old Assyrian morphological analyzer, which uses a brute-force approach to map between transliteration and transcription.

Treatment of discontinuative morphology was a long-standing challenge in Natural Language Processing, since it could not be elegantly expressed with FSGs. Over time, various extensions were introduced to FSGs, such as the compile-replace algorithm, flag diacritics, memory registers and multi-tape automata (Cohen-Sygal and Wintner, 2006), and after the memory requirements allowed it, some implementations relied on linearizing the morphology with procedural pregeneration. Yet, whereas the state-of-the-art analyzers for morphologically concatenative languages had been dominated by FSGs since the 1980s, still in the 2000s, some state-of-the-art computational models of discontinuative morphologies were implemented procedurally, such as Buckwalter (2002) for Arabic.

During the last decade, neural sequence-to-sequence models have opened new avenues for lemmatizing languages (Bergmanis and Goldwater, 2018; Kanerva et al., 2018). These models have introduced promising ways to deal with complex orthographies and morphologies, as well as synchronic and diachronic variation, like those found in Akkadian. Training neural models for lemmatizing Akkadian has been largely possible only due to Oracc's open data policy and the invaluable effort of dozens of Assyriologists, who have contributed their data to Oracc and annotated it semi-automatically using Tinney's L2.

The first neural network based attempt to linguistically annotate Akkadian was Sahala et al. (2020a). This system phonologically transcribed Akkadian using sequence-to-sequence models feeding the output into a finite-state transducer to produce lem-

[2]Giorgio Buccellati built tools for Akkadian already in the 1970s but to our knowledge these have not been published Buccellati (1977); for the goals of his project see the website of Cybernetica Mesopotamica. Tools were also created for the Neo-Assyrian Text Corpus Project by Simo Parpola and Robert M. Whiting. Their dictionary-based lemmatizer, however, remains also unpublished.

mata, POS-tags and morphological labels. This approach suffered from morphological ambiguity and the lemmatization pipeline was later simplified into BabyLemmatizer (Sahala et al., 2022), which predicted the lemmata directly from transliteration without intermediate steps. Another successful Akkadian neural network-based lemmatizer was published by Ong and Gordin (2024), who developed AkkParser, a language model implemented within the spaCy framework, with customized pipeline components for morphological analysis and syntactic dependency parsing specifically adapted to Akkadian cuneiform texts. This model was trained through an iterative bootstrapping methodology on a treebank of Neo-Assyrian letters, with human annotators providing corrections to progressively improve performance across annotation cycles. The only model so far specifically trained to annotate lemmas in Old Babylonian is Smidt et al. (2024), who conducted experiments on Part-of-Speech tagging for Old Babylonian letters using the Flair toolkit, finding that Multilingual BERT Transformer-based embeddings achieved good accuracy, despite working with a limited training corpus.

### 2.2 Token Prediction

Clay tablets, the medium on which the texts of ancient mesopotamia were written, are often found in fragmentery condition, causing a sigificant potential loss of text (Fetaya et al., 2020). Work has been conducted to collate 3D-scanned cuneiform tablet fragments by using join-surface heatmaps (Collins et al., 2014) and script feature analysis (Cammarosano, 2014; Fisseler, 2019). Systems for joining disconnected transliterated fragments have also been implemented (Tyndall, 2012; Simonjetz et al., 2024).

Token prediction differs fundamentally from these reconstruction approaches, as it aims to infer the content of missing text rather than identifying fragment matches in a database. Although relatively underexplored, some studies have employed machine learning models to reconstruct missing sign sequences in cuneiform texts. In Fetaya et al. (2020), RNN models are used to predict missing tokens. Another study, by Lazar et al. (2021), frames the problem using a masked language modeling approach similar to BERT pretraining, leveraging multilingual training with BERT-based models. This task is also popular in works on other ancient languages, see Sommerschield et al. (2023).

## 3 Data

Statistics for the shared task datasets are provided in tables 1, 2 and 3. Our data comes from two primary sources: the Electronic Babylonian Library Dataset (eBL) (Cobanoglu et al., 2024) and Archibab. The eBL data is drawn from transliterated cuneiform tablets via the eBL API provided by Enrique Jiménez on Nov. 2024; an earlier image of the data is also published on Zenodo (Cobanoglu, 2023). The data used is novel for NLP purposes as it focuses on a considerable number of literary texts. Although like ORACC texts it is also dated to the first millennium BCE, the eBL corpus make up very different kinds of literary and scientific genres subsumed here under the term canonical, using the accepted terminology of Hallo (1991). Archibab texts, on the other hand, primarily consist of Old Babylonian archival documents from the early second millennium BCE (2004–1595 BCE), of which a subset mostly made up of letters was provided for the shared task with the kind permission of Dominique Charpin (Collège de France) and Marine Béranger (FU Berlin). Where more metadata was provided in the dataset itself, as in the case of Archibab texts, or available via the eBL API, we included information about genre, find location, and language. To avoid potential bias, we replaced tablet IDs with randomized numbers. Additionally, any words that were entirely missing from the texts were removed.

| Dataset | Split | Fragments | Unique Values |
|---|---|---|---|
| Lemmatization | Total (Train + Test) | 10,214 | 46,966 |
| | Train | 8,171 | 40,640 |
| | Test | 2,043 | 15,539 |
| Token Prediction | Total (Train + Test) | 28,472 | 118,550 |
| | Train | 22,777 | 102,639 |
| | Test | 5,695 | 38,825 |

Table 1: Statistics for Lemmatization and Token Prediction datasets.

| Dataset | Category | Details |
|---|---|---|
| Lemmatization | Akkadian | 377,000 |
| | Sumerian | 51 |
| | Emesal | 2 |
| | test function words | 17,686 / 73,357 samples |
| | test OOV | 7,379 / 73,357 samples |
| Token Prediction | Akkadian | 970,237 |
| | Sumerian | 130,596 |
| | Emesal | 33,237 |
| | test function words | 3,826 / 44,517 samples |
| | test OOV | 4,161 / 44,517 samples |

Table 2: Breakdown for Lemmatization and Token Prediction datasets. Language is reported per word in the dataset as tablets may have words in multiple languages.

| Dataset | Genre | Count |
|---|---|---|
| Lemmatization | Canonical | 4659 |
| | Unclassified | 4217 |
| | Archival | 869 |
| | Administrative letter | 242 |
| | Monumental | 119 |
| | Political letter | 72 |
| | Other | 26 |
| | Private letter | 8 |
| | Diplomatic letter | 2 |
| Token Prediction | Canonical | 11332 |
| | Unclassified | 10994 |
| | Archival | 2940 |
| | Other | 2321 |
| | Monumental | 344 |
| | Administrative letter | 276 |
| | Political letter | 242 |
| | Private letter | 13 |
| | Diplomatic letter | 8 |

Table 3: Lemmatization and Token Prediction Genre Distribution.

Each dataset was split into training and testing sets, with 80 percent of the tablets allocated to the training split, which was provided to participants in the first step. The remaining 20 percent were used for evaluation, and all results are based on this held-out test set. It is worth noting that the two datasets had slight differences in transliteration conventions: this is taken into account during evaluation, as detailed below.

### 3.1 Lemmatization Data

For the lemmatization data, we applied cleaning steps to ensure consistency and usability. If a word in a given context had several possible lemmatic interpretations, we kept only the first lemma from that list. Any words that lacked a corresponding lemma were filtered out, ensuring that all remaining tokens in the dataset had a valid lemmatized form.

### 3.2 Token Prediction Data

For the word completion task, we focused on removing noise and ensuring that only complete, readable words were included. We excluded any words that contained fragmentary markers (such as "...", "[", "]", "x", "X", or "?"), as well as any numbers. Additionally, we cleaned the "value" column by removing non-alphabetical characters like < and #, which are additional editorial marks. We masked 20 percent of the data in each of the splits.

## 4 Shared Task

The task was structured to ensure consistency and transparency in assessing the performance of the lemmatization and token prediction models. Participants submitted both their generated predictions for the test set and technical reports through the SoftConf system. The train datasets provided contained pre-processed cuneiform texts, ensuring all participants worked with the same linguistic resources without modifications. While no strict measures were in place to prevent fine-tuning on the test set, the competition relied on participant integrity to avoid unfair data contamination. The evaluation compared submitted predictions against a held-out test dataset, with participants encouraged to document their methodologies in detail in the technical report, which were reviewed by the organizers. To promote replicability, participants were expected to share their scripts, system source code, and, where possible, trained models on platforms such as GitHub and Hugging Face.

## 5 Evaluation Metrics

We use accuracy as our primary evaluation measure in both, lemmatization and token prediction tasks, that is, the percentage of valid predictions over the whole evaluation category.

We structured our results according to distinct categories to assess performance across different linguistic phenomena:

Function vs. non-function words: Function words (e.g., conjunctions, prepositions) typically have high-frequency, well-attested forms, while non-function words (e.g., nouns, verbs) exhibit more variation and complexity.

In-vocabulary (in-vocab) vs. out-of-vocabulary (OOV) words: In-vocab words appear in the training data, while OOV words do not. OOV performance is particularly important for evaluating a model's generalization ability.

### 5.1 Flexible Matching

We considered predictions valid within the range of certain flexibility to prevent false negatives affecting the lemmatization evaluation results.

Firstly, as the eBL dataset contains Roman numerals indicating homonyms, while the Archibab dataset does not, we removed all numerals from both datasets and from the predictions for both tasks to ensure consistency.

For the evaluation of the lemmatization task, we aimed to allow variations that arise due to differences between the datasets, since dialect or chronolect identification was not part of the task list, and in reality separate models should be trained for different domain s for maximum efficiency. To achieve this, we implemented two steps. First, we wrote a harmonization function that standardizes most lemmatization conventions across datasets. For example, we unified macrons and circumflexes (e.g., *parāsu* vs. *parâsum*; *Anunnakū* vs. *Anunnakû*), made mimation optional (*šarru* vs. *šarrum*) and considered dictionary forms with and without initial waw equivalent (*alādu* vs. *walādu*). Second, we curated a special list of ca. 200 additional lemmatization variants to ensure that reasonable spelling differences did not unfairly impact accuracy. This list handles variation such as *nuhatimmum* vs. *nuhtimmu*. Naturally, all insonsistencies could not be handled, but the implemented rules covered most of the cases where the evaluation could have probably given false negatives. This harmonization was only ran at the evaluation phase when the predictions and the gold standards were matched with each other. Therefore, all models had to deal with the same inconsistencies in the training phase.

For the evaluation of the token prediction task, we focused on exact matches. However, we acknowledge that multiple valid completions can exist. For example, different experts might propose different reconstructions for the same missing segment based on contextual interpretation. Future work should incorporate methods to allow for semantic flexibility in evaluation.

## 6 Baseline Systems

To compare the shared task results with the existing publicly available systems, we used two baselines in lemmatizer evaluation and one baseline for token prediction evaluation

### 6.1 Maximum Likelihood Estimator

Our first baseline lemmatizer is an MLE dictionary look-up that assigns each word form with its most common lemma found in the training data. This simulates the simplest possible lemmatizer for a language and gives an estimate how well the more sophisticated models can handle ambiguity.

### 6.2 BabyLemmatizer 2.2

Our second baseline is BabyLemmatizer 2.2, a hybrid state-of-the-art annotation pipeline that combines the strengths of neural networks and shallow context-aware dictionary look-ups. Previously it has been used for lemmatizing several languages, such as Egyptian, Coptic, Demotic (Sahala and Lincke, 2024), Akkadian, Sumerian, Urartian, Greek and Latin (Sahala and Lindén, 2023). Evaluations have shown an accuracy ranging from 82% to 98% depending on the script and language. In Akkadian lemmatization the reported accuracy is ca. 95% using in-domain training data.

BabyLemmatizer treats lemmatization as a machine translation task. Its neural network architecture comprises a two layer BiLSTM encoder for reading the input sequence, and a unidirectional LSTM decoder with input feeding attention for generating the output. The neural network's output is then validated, corrected and confidence-scored with a heuristic dictionary look-up.

For all BabyLemmatizer models, we split the given training dataset into chunks of ten fragments each, which of we always take the first eight as our training data and the remaining two as development data, yielding 80/20 training/development split.

#### 6.2.1 Lemmatizer Model

Since the dataset used in the shared task does not contain part-of-speech (POS) labels and BabyLemmatizer relies on them for lemma disambiguation, we train two separate models for lemmatization and disambiguation and use them in tandem.

The initial **context-blind model** lemmatizes words without their sentence contexts and estimates their ambiguity using BabyLemmatizer's built-in confidence scoring system. The **disambiguation model** then attempts to correct the low-confidence lemmata by observing their contexts (in transliteration) using a symmetric window of three words. Both models use the default logo-phonemic tokenization that treats logograms and determinatives as indivisible symbols, and syllabograms and phonetic complements as divisible phoneme sequences. This setting collapses homonymous syllabic signs such as **ša** and **ša**$_2$ together but keeps logograms such as **DU** and **DU**$_3$ separate, since their meanings and readings are generally unrelated. The lemmatizer model works only on the word level and does not take the fragment metadata into consideration.

The advantage of the dual-model approach is marginal, providing only ca. 1% increase in lemmatization accuracy in comparison to using either of the sub-models alone.

#### 6.2.2 Token Predictor Model

For the token prediction task we train two models, the basic model and an augmented one. We train BabyLemmatizer similarly to the lemma disambiguation model, but instead of predicting the lemma we predict transliteration for each masked word based on its surrounding context with a symmetric window of three words. We segment the input using BabyLemmatizer's logo-syllabic tokenizer using translitered signs as minimal units, and generate the output sequence similarly. The token prediction model does not take into account the language or genre metadata and relies purely on sign-to-sign relations.

The augmented model is trained in the same manner, but the training data is concatenated with itself for 15 times before the train/dev split. The masked words are then randomized in a way that 15% of the total words are masked. Motivation for this additional model was to provide a more comparable baseline with the team 32's model that used the same augmentation approach.

## 7 Results

Three teams competed for the lemmatization task, and one for the word prediction task. The model numbers refer to submissions in this volume - submission 29 is "Lemmatization of Cuneiform Languages Using the ByT5 Model", submission 33 is "Beyond Base Predictors: Using LLMs to Resolve Ambiguities in Akkadian Lemmatization" and submission 53 is "A Low-Shot Prompting Approach to Lemmatization in the EvaCun 2025 Shared Task". for the token prediction task, submission 32 is "Finetuning LLMs for EvaCun 2025 token prediction shared task".

| Subset | 29 | 33 | 53 | MLE | BL |
|---|---|---|---|---|---|
| all | 0.84 | **0.94** | 0.31 | 0.83 | 0.93 |
| func | **0.98** | **0.98** | 0.83 | **0.98** | **0.98** |
| non func | 0.80 | **0.93** | 0.15 | 0.79 | 0.92 |
| in vocab | 0.89 | **0.97** | 0.34 | 0.92 | 0.96 |
| oov | 0.48 | **0.72** | 0.07 | 0.00 | 0.65 |

Table 4: Accuracy results for lemmatization. Results for teams 29, 33, 53, along with MLE baseline (pick most common lemma for each token), and BabyLemmatizer baseline.

| Subset | 32 | BL | BL+AUG |
|---|---|---|---|
| all | **0.21** | 0.14 | **0.21** |
| func | 0.36 | 0.36 | **0.46** |
| non func | **0.19** | 0.12 | **0.19** |
| in vocab | 0.22 | 0.16 | **0.23** |
| oov | **0.03** | <0.01 | <0.01 |

Table 5: Accuracy results for Token Prediction. Results for Team 32, along with Babylemmatizer baseline, and Babylemmatizer baseline with augmented data.

### 7.1 Lemmatization

The performance of the submitted lemmatization models varied significantly based on the complexity of the word forms and their frequency in the training data. Table 4 presents the overall accuracy results for lemmatization across all systems. One key observation was that function words were significantly easier to lemmatize than non-function words, as seen in the high accuracy scores across all models. This is expected, given their lower morphological variation and higher frequency in the training data. OOV words, by contrast, posed a greater challenge, highlighting the difficulty in handling previously unseen forms. In fact, OOV items represented the only notable bottleneck in lemmatization performance, as in-vocabulary words were almost perfectly lemmatized by BabyLemmatizer and team 33. This suggests that both systems exhibit strong context-awareness, allowing them to accurately determine the relevant lemma based on contextual cues.

### 7.2 Token Prediction

The results in table 5 show that 32 and BL+AUG outperform BL overall (0.21 vs. 0.14), with augmentation significantly improving function-word (0.46) and in-vocabulary (0.23) accuracy. However, OOV handling remains poor across all models, with 32 performing very slightly better (0.03).

## 8 Discussion

The results highlight both progress and remaining challenges in lemmatization and token prediction in ancient Akkadian. For lemmatization, the high accuracy of BabyLemmatizer and team 33's model shows that hybrid models combining neural networks and rule-based approaches are effective for Akkadian's complex morphology. However, the performance gap between in-vocabulary and out-of-vocabulary words suggests that generalizing to unseen forms remains a significant challenge.

Token prediction proved more difficult, reflecting the uncertainty in reconstructing missing text from fragmentary sources. Function words were easier to predict accurately than content in-vocabulary words, which exhibit greater variability. Out-of-vocabulary words were almost impossible to predict.

This shared task reinforces a pattern of successful collaborations between cuneiform specialists and computer scientists, or individuals with expertise in both domains. The complexity of ancient languages like Akkadian and Sumerian, with their rich morphological structures and varied orthographic conventions, demands both computational innovation and philological expertise. The challenges of this field may be noted by the fact that out of sixteen teams that initially expressed interest in the shared task, only four submitted final systems, with three completing the lemmatization task and only one the token prediction task.

The new corpora was made available through the years-long work of cuneiform specialists working on the eBL and Archibab digital projects. Their specialized knowledge ensured high-quality data that enhanced model performance. The original data files were furthermore preprocessed for consistency and machine readability by experts with experience in both computer models and cuneiform texts and their digital representations. Building thus on the works of others, the task force has resulted in robust models for new periods and genres of Akkadian texts that were previously underrepresented in computational studies. These new models enable more comprehensive analyses of Akkadian's diachronic development and genre-specific characteristics, ultimately enriching our understanding of this pivotal language in ancient Near Eastern history.

The task force has demonstrated that the collaboration between domain experts and computational scientists does not need to be direct–their complementary contributions across different stages of the ancient language processing pipeline create an environment conducive to breakthrough results that benefit the entire field. The promising performance on the lemmatization task, particularly by hybrid approaches combining neural networks with rule-based systems, demonstrates that these methodologies can be successfully applied to other under-resourced ancient languages. This could potentially transform our ability to analyze and understand historical texts at scale, opening new avenues for research across multiple disciplines within the humanities.

## Acknowledgments

EvaCun 2025 represents a collaborative scholarly endeavor made possible through the exemplary sponsorship of two foundational digital cuneiform initiatives: the electronic Babylonian Library (eBL), directed by Enrique Jiménez at LMU Munich, and the ARCHIBAB project, led by Dominique Charpin (Collège de France) with substantial contributions from Marine Béranger (FU Berlin). Their provision of extensive textual corpora and competitive financial incentives has fundamentally transformed what would otherwise have remained a theoretical exercise into a vibrant scholarly forum. Their investment in this emerging methodological approach demonstrates remarkable institutional foresight. We would also like to thank Luis Sáenz for creating a comprehensive list of function words for the evaluation splits, the Academy of Finland for funding the Centre of Excellence in Ancient Near Eastern Empires (PI Saana Svärd), and the Origins of Emesal project (PI Krister Lindén).

## References

David Bamman. 2012. *11-712 NLP Lab Report: Akkadian-morph-analyzer*.

François Barthélemy. 1998. A morphological Analyzer for Akkadian Verbal Forms with a Model of Phonetic Transformations. In *Computational Approaches to Semitic Languages*.

Toms Bergmanis and Sharon Goldwater. 2018. Context sensitive neural lemmatization with lematus. In *16th annual conference of the North American chapter of the association for computational linguistics: human language technologies*, pages 1391–1400. Association for Computational Linguistics (ACL).

Bartosz Bogacz and Hubert Mara. 2022. Digital Assyriology—Advances in Visual Cuneiform Analysis. *Journal on Computing and Cultural Heritage*, 15(2):1–22.

Giorgio Buccellati. 1977. The old babylonian linguistic analysis project: goals, procédures and first results. In *Computational and mathematical linguistics: proceedings of the International Conference on Computational Linguistics: vol. I.-(Biblioteca dell'Archivum romanicum; 36)*, pages 385–404. LS Olschki.

Tim Buckwalter. 2002. Buckwalter arabic morphological analyzer version 1.0. *Linguistic Data Consortium, University of Pennsylvania*, pages 86–93.

Michele Cammarosano. 2014. 3d-joins und schriftmetrologie: A quantitative approach to cuneiform palaeography. In *Current Research in Cuneiform Paleography. Proc. of a Workshop held at the 60th Rencontre Assyriologique Internationale. University of Warsaw*.

Dominique Charpin. 2014. Ressources assyriologiques sur internet. *Bibliotheca Orientalis*, 71(3):331–357.

Danlu Chen, Aditi Agarwal, Taylor Berg-Kirkpatrick, and Jacobo Myerston. 2023. CuneiML: A Cuneiform Dataset for Machine Learning. *Journal of Open Humanities Data*, 9(1):30.

Y. Cobanoglu, J. Laasonen, F. Simonjetz, I. Khait, S. Cohen, Z. Földi, A. Hätinen, A. Heinrich, T. Mitto, G. Rozzi, L. Sáenz, and E. Jiménez. 2024. Transliterated cuneiform tablets of the electronic babylonian library platform. *Journal of Open Humanities Data*, 10(1):19.

Yunus Cobanoglu. 2023. Transliterated Fragments of the Electronic Babylonian Literature Project (eBL). *Zenodo*.

Yael Cohen-Sygal and Shuly Wintner. 2006. Finite-state registered automata for non-concatenative morphology. *Computational Linguistics*, 32(1):49–82.

Tim Collins, Sandra I Woolley, Luis Hernandez Munoz, Andrew Lewis, Eugene Ch'ng, and Erlend Gehlken. 2014. Computer-assisted reconstruction of virtual fragmented cuneiform tablets. In *2014 International Conference on Virtual Systems & Multimedia (VSMM)*, pages 70–77. IEEE.

Peter T. Daniels. 2023. "Look with thine ears": Why Writing Is Syllable-based. *WORD*, 69(1):91–116. Publisher: Routledge.

Liudmila L. Fedorova. On the Typology of Writing Systems. In *Grapholinguistics in the 21st Century*, pages 805–824, Online. Fluxus Editions.

Ethan Fetaya, Yonatan Lifshitz, Elad Aaron, and Shai Gordin. 2020. Restoration of fragmentary babylonian texts using recurrent neural networks. *Proceedings of the National Academy of Sciences*, 117(37):22743–22751.

Denis Fisseler. 2019. *Contributions to computer-aided analysis of cuneiform tablet fragments*. Ph.D. thesis, Dissertation, Dortmund, Technische Universität, 2019.

Gösta Gabriel, Karenleigh A. Overmann, and Annick Payne, editors. 2021. *Signs - sounds - semantics: nature and transformation of writing systems in the Ancient Near East*. Number 13 in Wiener offene Orientalistik. Ugarit Verlag, Münster.

Sh. Gordin. 2014. *Visualizing Knowledge and Creating Meaning in Ancient Writing Systems Proceedings of the International Workshop of the Research Group "Notational Iconicity", 24-25 Sep. 2010*. Berliner Beiträge zum Vorderen Orient. PeWe-Verlag, Gladbeck. Type: Edited Book.

Shai Gordin, Gai Gutherz, Ariel Elazary, Avital Romach, Enrique Jiménez, Jonathan Berant, and Yoram Cohen. 2020. Reading Akkadian cuneiform using natural language processing. *PLOS ONE*, 15(10):e0240511.

Gai Gutherz, Shai Gordin, Luis Sáenz, Omer Levy, and Jonathan Berant. 2023. Translating Akkadian to English with neural machine translation. *PNAS Nexus*, 2(5):pgad096.

W. W. Hallo. 1991. The Concept of Canonicity in Cuneiform and Biblical Literature: A Comparative Apprasial. In K. L. Younger, W. W. Hallo, and B. F. Batto, editors, *The Biblical Canon in Comparative Perspective: Scripture in Context IV*, pages 1–19. Edwin Mellen Press, Lewiston. Type: Book Section.

Jenna Kanerva, Filip Ginter, Niko Miekka, Akseli Leino, and Tapio Salakoski. 2018. Turku neural parser pipeline: An end-to-end system for the conll 2018 shared task. In *Proceedings of the CoNLL 2018 Shared Task: Multilingual parsing from raw text to universal dependencies*, pages 133–142.

Laura Kataja and Kimmo Koskenniemi. 1988. Finite-state Description of Semitic Morphology: A Case Study of Ancient Accadian. In *Coling Budapest 1988 Volume 1: International Conference on Computational Linguistics*.

Koren Lazar, Benny Saret, Asaf Yehudai, Wayne Horowitz, Nathan Wasserman, and Gabriel Stanovsky. 2021. Filling the gaps in Ancient Akkadian texts: A masked language modelling approach. In *Proceedings of the 2021 Conference on Empirical Methods in Natural Language Processing*, pages 4682–4691, Online and Punta Cana, Dominican Republic. Association for Computational Linguistics.

Aaron Macks. 2002. Parsing akkadian verbs with prolog. In *Proceedings of the ACL-02 workshop on Computational approaches to semitic languages*.

Matthew Ong and Shai Gordin. 2024. Linguistic annotation of cuneiform texts using treebanks and deep learning. *Digital Scholarship in the Humanities*, 39(1):296–307.

Émilie Pagé-Perron, Maria Sukhareva, Ilya Khait, and Christian Chiarcos. 2017. Machine Translation and Automated Analysis of the Sumerian Language. In *Proceedings of the Joint SIGHUM Workshop on Computational Linguistics for Cultural Heritage, Social Sciences, Humanities and Literature*, pages 10–16, Vancouver, Canada. Association for Computational Linguistics.

Aleksi Sahala. 2014. Babyparser: Muinaisbabylonian morfologian ohjelmallinen jäsentäminen. *Helsinki: University of Helsinki, MA Thesis*.

Aleksi Sahala. 2021. Contributions to computational assyriology. *Helsinki: University of Helsinki*.

Aleksi Sahala, Tero Alstola, Jonathan Valk, and Krister Linden. 2022. Babylemmatizer: A lemmatizer and pos-tagger for akkadian. In *CLARIN Annual Conference*, pages 14–18. CLARIN ERIC.

Aleksi Sahala and Eliese-Sophia Lincke. 2024. Neural lemmatization and pos-tagging models for coptic, demotic and earlier egyptian. In *Proceedings of the 1st Workshop on Machine Learning for Ancient Languages (ML4AL 2024)*, pages 87–97.

Aleksi Sahala and Krister Lindén. 2023. A Neural Pipeline for Lemmatizing and POS-tagging Cuneiform Languages. In *Proceedings of the Ancient Language Processing Workshop at the 14th International Conference on Recent Advances in Natural Language Processing RANLP 2023*, pages 203–212.

Aleksi Sahala, Miikka Silfverberg, Antti Arppe, and Krister Lindén. 2020a. Automated Phonological Transcription of Akkadian Cuneiform Texts. In *Proceedings of the Twelfth Language Resources and Evaluation Conference*, pages 3528–3534.

Aleksi Sahala, Miikka Silfverberg, Antti Arppe, and Krister Lindén. 2020b. BabyFST: Towards a Finite-State Based Computational Model of Ancient Babylonian. In *Proceedings of the Twelfth Language Resources and Evaluation Conference*, pages 3886–3894.

Fabian Simonjetz, Jussi Laasonen, Yunus Cobanoglu, Alexander Fraser, and Enrique Jiménez. 2024. Reconstruction of cuneiform literary texts as text matching. In *Proceedings of the 2024 Joint International Conference on Computational Linguistics, Language Resources and Evaluation (LREC-COLING 2024)*, pages 13712–13721.

Gustav Ryberg Smidt, Katrien De Graef, and Els Lefever. 2024. Keep me PoS-ted: experimenting with Part-of-Speech prediction on Old Babylonian letters. *it - Information Technology*, 65(6):264–274. Publisher: De Gruyter Oldenbourg.

Thea Sommerschield, Yannis Assael, John Pavlopoulos, Vanessa Stefanak, Andrew Senior, Chris Dyer, John Bodel, Jonathan Prag, Ion Androutsopoulos, and Nando De Freitas. 2023. Machine Learning for Ancient Languages: A Survey. *Computational Linguistics*, 49(3):703–747.

Steve Tinney. 2019. *L2: How it Works.*

Stephen Tyndall. 2012. Toward automatically assembling hittite-language cuneiform tablet fragments into larger texts. In *Proceedings of the 50th Annual Meeting of the Association for Computational Linguistics (Volume 2: Short Papers)*, pages 243–247.

Juan-Pablo Vita, editor. 2021. *Vita, J.-P. (Ed.). (2021). History of the Akkadian language. Brill.* Number volume 152/1-2 in Handbook of Oriental studies = Handbuch der Orientalistik : Section one. The Near and Middle East. Brill, Leiden.

Stefan Weninger, Geoffrey Kahn, Michael P. Streck, and Janet C. E. Watson, editors. 2011. *The Semitic Languages: An International Handbook*. Number 36 in Handbooks of Linguistics and Communication Science. De Gruyter, Berlin.

Imed Zitouni, editor. 2014. *Natural language processing of semitic languages.* Theory and applications of natural language processing. Springer, Berlin Heidelberg.

# Lemmatization of Cuneiform Languages Using the ByT5 Model

**Pengxiu Lu[1,2], Yonglong Huang[1,2], Jing Xu[1,2], Minxuan Feng[1,2], Chao Xu[1,2]**
[1]School of Chinese Language and Literature, Nanjing Normal University, China
[2]Center of Language Big Data and Computational Humanities, Nanjing Normal University, China
fomalhaut2001@gmail.com

## Abstract

Lemmatization of cuneiform languages presents a unique challenge due to their complex writing system, which combines syllabic and logographic elements. In this study, we investigate the effectiveness of the ByT5 model in addressing this challenge by developing and evaluating a ByT5-based lemmatization system. Experimental results demonstrate that ByT5 outperforms mT5 in this task, achieving an accuracy of 80.55% on raw lemmas and 82.59% on generalized lemmas, where sense numbers are removed. These findings highlight the potential of ByT5 for lemmatizing cuneiform languages and provide useful insights for future work on ancient text lemmatization.

## 1 Introduction

Cuneiform writing systems, used by ancient Mesopotamian civilizations like the Sumerians and Akkadians, provide valuable insights into early human civilization. However, despite their historical significance, computational methods for processing cuneiform texts remain relatively underdeveloped. One of the key challenges in natural language processing (NLP) for these ancient languages is lemmatization — the task of reducing words to their base or dictionary forms—a process that is particularly complex due to the high degree of inflection, polysemy of signs, and extensive morphological variation characteristic of these languages.

Among the languages written in cuneiform, Akkadian and Sumerian are two of the most extensively documented, yet they pose distinct computational challenges. Akkadian, a Semitic language, exhibits root-based morphology with non-linear inflectional patterns, while Sumerian, a language isolate, follows an agglutinative structure with extensive prefixation and suffixation. Both languages also feature logographic and syllabic writing elements, further complicating automated linguistic analysis.

Among existing approaches, BabyLemmatizer (Sahala and Lindén, 2023) employs a neural encoder-decoder model to perform joint POS tagging and lemmatization, achieving 94–96% accuracy. Similarly, AkkParser (Ong and Gordin, 2024) combines rule-based morphological analysis, dictionary matching, and dependency parsing, providing robust performance on Neo-Assyrian texts. Despite their success, the variability in orthographic forms and the vast morphological richness of cuneiform languages still present challenges.

Recent advancements in transformer-based models, such as T5 (Text-to-Text Transfer Transformer) (Raffel et al., 2020), have significantly improved performance across a wide range of NLP tasks, including sequence-to-sequence applications like translation and lemmatization (Riemenschneider and Krahn, 2024). Building upon this foundation, ByT5 (Xue et al., 2022) was introduced as a variant of T5, designed to process text at the byte level. Unlike traditional token-based models, ByT5 operates directly on raw byte sequences, eliminating the need for predefined vocabularies and tokenization schemes. This token-free approach has proven advantageous in multilingual tasks such as grapheme-to-phoneme conversion (Zhu et al., 2022), where ByT5 has outperformed token-based models. Its architecture has also proven effective in lemmatization tasks—particularly for morphologically rich languages such as Latin (Wróbel and Nowak, 2022)—highlighting ByT5's ability to handle complex morphological variation with minimal preprocessing. Moreover, its strong zero-shot learning capabilities (Stankevičius et al., 2022) enable it to generalize to previously unseen languages, making it especially valuable for under-resourced historical languages such as Akkadian and Sumerian, where annotated corpora remain limited.

The aim of this study is to evaluate the effectiveness of ByT5 in lemmatizing Akkadian and



*Proceedings of the Second Ancient Language Processing Workshop associated with NAACL 2025*, pages 173–181
May 4, 2025. 

Sumerian texts, with a focus on assessing its ability to overcome the challenges posed by the morphological complexity and spelling irregularity of these ancient languages.

## 2 Methodology

### 2.1 Dataset

The original dataset consists of several fields, including: `fragment id`, `fragment line num`, `index in line`, `word language`, `domain`, `place discovery`, `place composition`, `value`, `clean value`, and `lemma`. The primary input to the model during training is the `clean value`, and the target is the `lemma`.

A particular challenge in this task arises from words that have multiple meanings or senses, a phenomenon particularly prominent in cuneiform lexicon. For example, the lemma *abāru* exhibits various senses, each with a specific definition in the *Concise Dictionary of Akkadian* (Black et al., 2000). The different senses of *abāru* are often marked with Roman numerals to denote the specific sense, as outlined below:

1. ***abāru I***: This sense refers to "(the metal) lead." It appears in texts such as A.GAR$_5$ and in 1st millennium royal inscriptions, specifically noted as A.BÁR. In Middle Assyrian, the phrase is also written as *annuku abāru*.

2. ***abāru II***: This sense has two distinct meanings:

    (a) Babylonian literary meaning: "A kind of clamp".

    (b) Standard Babylonian (Jungbabylonisch) transferred meaning: "embrace" or "physical strength", often used in reference to gods or kings.

3. ***abāru III***: This sense refers to "to embrace" in Old and Standard Babylonian. It is often used in magical contexts to mean "embrace intensely" or "bind" (e.g., limbs or persons). In legal contexts, it is used to mean "accuse someone" or "denounce".

Given this ambiguity, two distinct forms of the dataset are created to account for the different levels of semantic granularity.

- **Raw Lemma Dataset** retains sense numbers (e.g., *abāru I*) to capture semantic distinctions, as shown in Table 1.

| Surface Form | Lemma |
|---|---|
| A.BAR$_2$ | *abāru I* |
| a-ba-ri | *abāru II* |
| ub-bir | *abāru III* |

Table 1: Examples from the Raw Lemma Dataset

- **Generalized Lemma Dataset** removes sense numbers for morphological normalization, as shown in Table 2.

| Surface Form | Lemma |
|---|---|
| A.BAR$_2$ | |
| a-ba-ri | *abāru* |
| ub-bir | |

Table 2: Examples from the Generalized Lemma Dataset

### 2.2 Model Architecture

The primary model used for lemmatization of cuneiform languages is the ByT5 model, a variant of the T5 architecture that operates directly on the raw character sequences of texts at the byte level. ByT5 is built on a transformer-based architecture, where input sequences pass through multiple layers of attention mechanisms and feed-forward networks. It employs a standard encoder-decoder framework: the encoder processes the input text, while the decoder generates the corresponding output based on the encoded information.

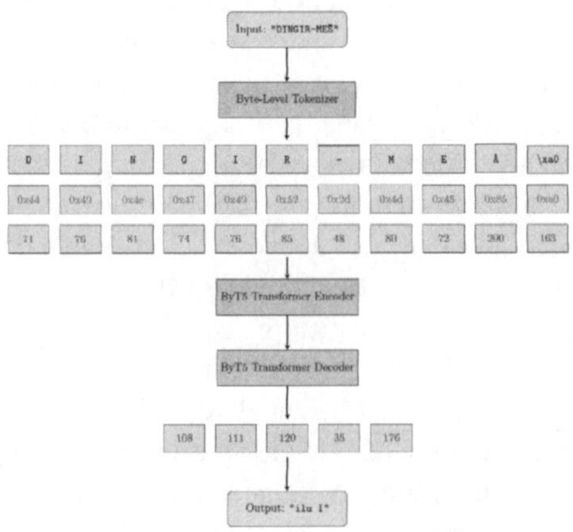


Figure 1: ByT5 Lemmatization Architecture with Byte-Level Tokenization

In this study, ByT5 is trained to map sequences of byte tokens to a sequence of output tokens, where each output token corresponds to the canonical lemma (or generalized lemma) of the input word, as illustrated in Figure 1.

As an additional model for comparison, the mT5 model was also used. mT5 is a multilingual variant of T5, capable of processing text in multiple languages. mT5 also follows a transformer-based architecture, using word-level tokenization and is suited for handling multiple languages with varying scripts. For the purpose of this study, mT5 serves as a baseline model to evaluate how well ByT5 performs relative to a more traditional, multilingual approach.

### 2.3 Training Setup

Both models are trained using a standard sequence-to-sequence learning approach. For ByT5, the input sequence length is limited to 128 tokens, while for mT5, it is restricted to 32 tokens. The input text is prefixed with a task-specific indicator like "Convert:", following the approach inspired by the T5 model. The model's output is the predicted lemma, which can either be a raw lemma with sense numbering (for the Raw Lemma Dataset) or a generalized lemma (for the Generalized Lemma Dataset). Both datasets are split, with 95% used for training and the remaining 5% for validation.

We utilize pre-trained weights from the Hugging Face Transformers library and fine-tune the model on both datasets. The training process uses the Adam optimizer with a learning rate of 2e-5 and a batch size of 16. Models are fine-tuned for 10 epochs or until convergence. Training is conducted on an Apple M3 Pro (18GB) chip, leveraging the MPS backend for accelerated computation.

## 3 Experimental Results

### 3.1 Performance Metrics

To evaluate the effectiveness of the models, we used the following metrics:

**Accuracy (Exact Match):** This metric measures the percentage of instances where the predicted lemma exactly matches the target lemma.

$$Accuracy = \frac{\text{Number of Correct Lemma Predictions}}{\text{Total Number of Words}} \times 100\% \quad (1)$$

Accuracy serves as the primary metric for assessing the accuracy of the lemmatization process.

### 3.2 Results

The following tables present the performance of ByT5-small and mT5-small on the two datasets: one with raw lemmas (where sense numbers are retained) and another with generalized lemmas (where sense numbers are removed).

| Model | Accuracy (%) |
|---|---|
| ByT5-small | 80.55 |
| mT5-small | 77.38 |

Table 3: Performance on Raw Lemmas (Sense Number Retained)

| Model | Accuracy (%) |
|---|---|
| ByT5-small | 82.59 |
| mT5-small | 79.28 |

Table 4: Performance on Generalized Lemmas (Sense Number Removed)

## 4 Error Analysis

### 4.1 Challenges in Lemma Prediction

In this section, we conduct an error analysis based on the predictions made by the ByT5-small model on the raw lemma dataset, which consists of 39,621 unique word forms (transliterations) that have not been normalized and 8,021 unique lemmas, reflecting the diversity and complexity of the cuneiform lexicon. The model was trained on a dataset of 290,294 instances, learning to map surface forms to their corresponding lemmas. To assess its performance, we evaluated it on a validation set of 15,279 instances, where it produced 2,972 erroneous predictions, resulting in an overall accuracy of 80.55%. The detailed statistics of the dataset and its partitions are presented in Table 5 [1].

| Dataset | Instances | Unique Word Forms | Unique Lemmas |
|---|---|---|---|
| Raw Lemma Dataset | 305,573 | 39,621 | 8,021 |
| Training Set (95%) | 290,294 | 38,464 | 7,898 |
| Validation Set (5%) | 15,279 | 5,257 | 2,459 |

Table 5: Detailed Statistics of Raw Lemma Dataset

To better understand the sources of errors, we analyzed the incorrect predictions and categorized

[1] For conciseness, we will refer to the training set as TS and the validation set as VS in following tables.

them into three main groups: (1) surface forms that were most frequently mispredicted, (2) lemmas that were most frequently predicted incorrectly, and (3) erroneous lemma predictions that the model frequently produced. These insights highlight specific challenges in lemma disambiguation and the complex mappings required for accurate lemmatization.

Based on the validation set, the following table summarizes the five most frequently mispredicted surface forms, the five lemmas that were most commonly misclassified, and the five incorrect lemma predictions that the model frequently produced:

| Category | Word/Lemma | Freq |
|---|---|---|
| Most frequently mispredicted surface forms | IGI | 50 |
| | NU | 41 |
| | *ša* | 33 |
| | KI | 32 |
| | BI | 31 |
| Most frequently misclassified lemmas | *amāru I* | 40 |
| | *ul I* | 36 |
| | *ša* | 32 |
| | *ana* | 29 |
| | *šamšu I* | 27 |
| Most frequently produced incorrect lemma predictions | *pānu I* | 77 |
| | *lā I* | 52 |
| | *itti I* | 35 |
| | *ša I* | 33 |
| | *šū I* | 31 |

Table 6: Common Errors in Lemmatization

Building on the analysis above, we can identify three major challenges in the lemmatization process. First, polysemy poses a significant issue: without explicit syntactic or semantic context, the model struggles to accurately disambiguate multiple possible meanings of a given form. Second, inconsistencies in scribal conventions contribute to further complexity, leading to variability in representation. Third, the model exhibits a frequency bias, tending to over-predict high-frequency lemmas even in contexts where they are incorrect. These three challenges will be examined in detail in the following discussion.

#### 4.1.1 Polysemy in Surface Forms

A major source of error in the ByT5-small model's predictions stems from the inherent polysemy in surface forms. Polysemy arises when a single surface form corresponds to multiple meanings or senses, each associated with a distinct lemma. Our analysis identified 2,194 surface forms exhibiting polysemy, accounting for a significant proportion of the dataset.

We observe that many of the most frequently mispredicted surface forms—IGI, NU, KI, BI—are Sumerograms, logographic signs borrowed from Sumerian into Akkadian. Unlike phonetic spellings, Sumerograms encode meaning rather than sound, making them particularly challenging for lemmatization. The interpretation of a single Sumerogram often depends on its contextual usage, as it can correspond to multiple lemmas. For instance, IGI can signify "eye" (*īnu I*) or "to see" (*amāru I*), among other meanings.

The semantic range of the Sumerogram IGI, as documented in the *Concise Dictionary of Akkadian*, along with their frequency distribution in the training dataset, is presented in the table below.

| Sign | Lemma | Meaning | TS Freq |
|---|---|---|---|
| IGI | *pānu I* | face | 772 |
| | *amāru I* | to see | 475 |
| | *mahru II* | front | 270 |
| | *naṭālu I* | to look | 79 |
| | *mahra I* | in front; before; earlier | 51 |
| | *īnu I* | eye | 41 |
| | *mahāru I* | to face; oppose; receive | 10 |
| | *pānātu I* | front | 7 |
| | *lapān I* | in front of | 5 |
| | *mahrum* | / | 4 |
| | *āmeru I* | that sees, reads | 2 |
| | *mehretu I* | opposite side; front | 2 |
| | *panû I* | to face; be ahead | 1 |
| | *nawāru I* | to be(come) bright, shine | 1 |

Table 7: Frequency and Semantic Range of Sumerogram IGI

Similar to IGI, the cuneiform logogram IM can correspond to four distinct lemmas: *ṭuppu I*, *šāru I*, *ṭīdu I*, and *ešēru I*. To illustrate this challenge, Table 8 presents the distribution of IM's lemmas in the training and validation sets and the model's predictions. Despite the diverse occurrences of IM in the dataset, the model consistently predicted *ṭīdu I* across all instances, failing to account for the other possible lemmas.

<table>
<tr><th>Surface Form</th><th>TS Count</th><th colspan="2">TS Lemma Distribution</th></tr>
<tr><td rowspan="4">IM</td><td>226</td><td colspan="2">ṭīdu I (57),<br>ṭuppu I (66),<br>šāru I (102),<br>ešēru I (1)</td></tr>
<tr><td>VS Count</td><td colspan="2">VS Lemma Distribution</td></tr>
<tr><td>16</td><td>ṭīdu I (3),<br>ṭuppu I (9),<br>šāru I (4)</td><td>Prediction:<br>ṭīdu I (16/16)</td></tr>
</table>

Table 8: Distribution of IM's Lemmas in Training and Validation Sets vs. Model Prediction

The majority of most frequently misclassified lemmas and most commonly produced incorrect lemma predictions are closely associated with Sumerograms with multiple semantic variants. As shown in Table 6, *amāru I* and *pānu I* correspond to the Sumerogram IGI, *lā I* corresponds to NU, and *šū I* corresponds to BI. Moreover, these Sumerograms occur with high frequency in the training set, making them some of the most common lexical items (e.g., IGI: 1,720 occurrences; NU: 1,993 occurrences; BI: 1,352 occurrences). This high frequency, combined with their multiple semantic interpretations, constitutes a major source of prediction errors in the model.

Notably, the inclusion of texts from different historical periods and source traditions (as discussed in later sections) may further contribute to inconsistencies in lemmatization, as variations can arise due to differences in transcription conventions for cuneiform signs or historical shifts in the writing system. For example, the original form *ṭup-pi* can be lemmatized as *ṭuppi I*, *ṭuppu I*, or *ṭuppum*, depending on scribal practices. However, the lemma *ṭuppum* appears only twice in the training dataset and is more likely a morphological variant of *ṭuppu I* rather than a distinct lemma.

Overall, these challenges highlight the inherent complexities of cuneiform languages, where a single word form can have multiple interpretations depending on context or transcription conventions. Among all mispredictions, 1,253 errors were attributed to such one-to-many mappings. The model struggles to effectively disambiguate these cases, primarily due to its limited ability to capture the contextual cues that differentiate semantic variants. This issue is fundamentally rooted in the constraints of a simple sequence-to-sequence architecture, in which the model takes a surface form as input and generates a single corresponding lemma as output. Hence, lacking the capacity to incorporate broader contextual information necessary for disambiguation makes the existing model architecture inadequate for handling one-to-many mappings, which eventually leads to frequent misclassifications.

#### 4.1.2 Orthographic Variation in Lemmas

As previously noted, *ṭuppu I* as a lemma may be reconstructed from multiple surface forms, such as *ṭup-pi* or IM, illustrating the intricate mapping between surface forms and lemmas. A single surface form may correspond to multiple lemmas, while a single lemma may also be associated with multiple surface forms (although the latter does not introduce ambiguity in one-to-one lemmatization processes).

Therefore, in addition to polysemy, orthographic variation presents another challenge, wherein a single lemma can be represented by multiple surface forms. Our analysis of the raw lemma dataset revealed that 4,865 lemmas—comprising 60.65% of the total—are associated with multiple surface forms, indicating a significant presence of spelling variants. Noticeably, among the 2,972 lemmas incorrectly predicted by the model (i.e., the lemmas that the model erroneously generated rather than the correct lemmas that were misidentified), 2,788 errors were traced to these orthographic variations. This finding suggests that a substantial proportion of mispredictions can be attributed to the model's inclination to favor frequently occurring variants, likely due to the disproportionate representation of such cases in the training data. A clear example is *pānu I*, which exhibits significant spelling variation and is frequently mispredicted by the model.

Another illustrative case is the lemma *šapârum*, which corresponds to 92 distinct word forms, many of which exhibit considerable morphological complexity and subtle variations (e.g., *ši-ta-ap-pa-ra-am*, *iš-pu-ra-am*, *šu-up-ra-nim*, *áš-tap-ra*, *li-iš-ur-ma*, etc.). While the model successfully predicts the lemma in the majority of cases, it occasionally produces an entirely nonexistent lemma. For instance, for "ša-ap-pa-ra-ak-kum", the model incorrectly generates "*šapparakkum*"—a form unattested in the dataset. This pattern of errors further underscores the model's difficulty in distinguishing between legitimate orthographic variants and erroneous extrapolations, ultimately complicating the lemmatization process.

#### 4.1.3 Frequency Effects in Lemma Prediction

An important consideration in the model's performance is the effect of lemma frequency on prediction accuracy. In the dataset, some lemmas appear far more frequently than others, creating a potential imbalance in the model's learning process. To systematically analyze this, we classified low-frequency lemmas as those appearing at most once (Q1 = 1.0), mid-frequency lemmas as those appearing between Q1 and Q3 (2 to 12 times), and high-frequency lemmas as those appearing 13 times or more (Q3 = 13.0).

Our analysis revealed that 2,349 errors (79.0% of the total errors) were made by the model on high-frequency lemmas, 529 errors (17.8%) on mid-frequency lemmas, and 94 errors (3.2%) on low-frequency lemmas. The relatively high number of errors on high-frequency lemmas suggests that, despite their prominence in the training data, these words still present challenges for the model. This can be attributed to the polysemy and orthographic variation issues discussed above, where the model's familiarity with a lemma's high-frequency forms does not guarantee its ability to handle less common senses or spelling variants. On the other hand, low-frequency lemmas, while less problematic in terms of sheer error counts, may be underrepresented in the training data, leading to occasional mispredictions when these lemmas do appear in the validation set. For instance, in the training corpus (comprising 290,294 instances), there were only nine occurrences of the surface form "*im*", mapping to seven distinct lemmas: *ṣâbum* (2 instances), *ne'rârum* (2 instances), *epêšum* (1 instance), *eqlum* (1 instance), *šapârum* (1 instance), *âlum* (1 instance), and *makârum* (1 instance). Given the extremely limited number of training examples, the model struggled to learn the correct mappings, ultimately producing an erroneous output (e.g., *ṭuppu I*). The lack of sufficient representation of variant forms in the training data makes it even more difficult for the model to generalize accurately.

These findings highlight the impact of data imbalance, where the model's performance is skewed toward frequently occurring lemmas while remaining less reliable on rarer ones.

### 4.2 Comparative Evaluation on Archibab and eBL Corpora

As part of our error analysis, we conducted an additional evaluation by dividing the validation set into two subsets based on their sources: Archibab[2] and the Electronic Babylonian Library (eBL)[3]. This allowed us to assess the model's performance separately on texts from distinct historical periods and linguistic traditions, providing further insights into its strengths and limitations. The division was necessary due to significant differences between these two corpora. Archibab consists of Old Babylonian texts from the early second millennium BCE, primarily legal, administrative, and epistolary documents. These texts adhere to lemmatization conventions shaped by their historical and linguistic context. In contrast, eBL comprises first-millennium BCE literary and scholarly texts, which reflect later linguistic developments and more standardized scribal practices. With approximately 1000 years separating these corpora, their divergent lemmatization practices posed unique challenges for the model.

To conduct this evaluation, we refined the dataset by further splitting the training and validation sets accordingly, after which we obtained the following distribution of instances, as shown in Table 9. Notably, the Archibab dataset does not include sense numbers in its lemmatization annotations, which may influence the ability of certain models to handle this subset effectively.

| Source | Training Set | Validation Set |
|---|---|---|
| eBL | 292,423 | 14,619 |
| Archibab | 13,150 | 660 |

Table 9: Data Distribution across Different Sources

By evaluating performance on each subset independently, we aimed to determine whether the model could generalize across different stages of cuneiform languages or whether it showed biases toward a particular linguistic tradition. Specifically, we evaluated models trained on two different datasets: the *Raw Lemma Dataset* and the *Generalized Lemma Dataset*. The results are summarized in Table 10 and Table 11.

[2]https://www.archibab.fr/home
[3]https://www.ebl.lmu.de

| Model | Dataset | Accuracy (%) |
|---|---|---|
| ByT5 (Raw Lemma) | eBL | 82.39 |
| ByT5 (Raw Lemma) | Archibab | 39.85 |
| mT5 (Raw Lemma) | eBL | 79.30 |
| mT5 (Raw Lemma) | Archibab | 34.85 |

Table 10: Performance of models trained on the Raw Lemma Dataset.

| Model | Dataset | Accuracy (%) |
|---|---|---|
| ByT5 (Generalized Lemma) | eBL | 83.80 |
| ByT5 (Generalized Lemma) | Archibab | 55.76 |
| mT5 (Generalized Lemma) | eBL | 80.60 |
| mT5 (Generalized Lemma) | Archibab | 50.00 |

Table 11: Performance of models trained on the Generalized Lemma Dataset.

Across all models, lemmatization accuracy on the eBL dataset was significantly higher than on the Archibab dataset. This discrepancy can largely be attributed to the imbalance in training data, where eBL data greatly outnumbered Archibab data (292,423 vs. 13,150 instances, a ratio of approximately 22.2:1). This imbalance likely led the model to develop a stronger bias toward the linguistic patterns found in eBL, resulting in higher accuracy for that subset.

Furthermore, models trained on the Raw Lemma Dataset exhibited particularly low performance on Archibab data. This is likely because these models were trained to predict sense numbers, whereas the Archibab dataset lacks sense-number annotations. As a result, the models trained on Raw Lemma data tended to incorrectly assign sense numbers when lemmatizing Archibab instances, leading to a notable decrease in accuracy. In contrast, models trained on the Generalized Lemma Dataset showed higher accuracy on Archibab, as they were explicitly trained to generalize across datasets without relying on sense-number distinctions. This suggests that generalizing lemma annotations can help improve model performance when dealing with corpora that follow different lemmatization conventions.

## 5 Conclusion

The results from our experiments demonstrate that the **ByT5-small** model outperforms **mT5-small** in accuracy across both generalized and raw lemmatization tasks. Results also indicate that predicting raw lemmas (including sense numbers) is more challenging than predicting generalized lemmas, which is reflected in the lower accuracy scores for the raw lemma dataset, suggesting that incorporating sense numbers adds a layer of complexity to the task.

The effectiveness of ByT5's byte-level tokenization is particularly evident in Akkadian and Sumerian lemmatization, as it eliminates the need for complex, language-specific tokenization strategies that traditionally require specialized cuneiform expertise. In previous approaches to processing these ancient languages, pre-tokenization often relied on in-depth linguistic knowledge, such as the logo-syllabic tokenization employed by BabyLemmatizer[4]—a process tailored to the structure of cuneiform writing systems. In contrast, ByT5 leverages a byte-level vocabulary of only 256 basic tokens, enabling it to represent all cuneiform symbols and their transliterations without additional tokenization preprocessing.

This is particularly beneficial for Akkadian and Sumerian transliterations, which often include diacritics (e.g., š, ṭ), subscript numerals (e.g., $_2$ and $_3$, to distinguish between homophones or different readings of the same cuneiform sign), determinatives (e.g., $\{d\}$) and special notations for broken or uncertain readings (e.g., *?*). ByT5's ability to handle these symbols directly allows for a simpler yet effective architecture that achieves competitive performance without relying on intricate domain-specific tokenization rules. This suggests that byte-level models can possibly serve as a more accessible and adaptable approach to lemmatization in low-resource, complex linguistic settings, reducing

[4]`https://github.com/asahala/BabyLemmatizer`

dependence on specialized cuneiform processing techniques.

We acknowledge that a key limitation of our experiment is the lack of contextual integration. Without leveraging broader contextual information, further performance improvements are impossible, particularly in distinguishing sense variations. Future work could explore incorporating sentence- or discourse-level context, as ByT5 with contextual awareness might yield interesting results and further enhance lemmatization accuracy. Additionally, expanding the training data and refining the lemmatization pipeline may further improve performance, particularly for datasets with sparse annotations like Archibab.

## Acknowledgments

This research was supported by the National Language Commission Project of China (YB145-41), the National Social Science Funds of China (21&ZD331, 22&ZD262), and the project *Research on Graded Reading of Children's Chinese Classics*, funded by the Shenzhen IREAD Foundation. We are grateful to the reviewers for comments which helped us to improve the paper.

## References

Jeremy Black, Andrew George, and Nicholas Postgate. 2000. *A Concise Dictionary of Akkadian*, volume 5. Otto Harrassowitz Verlag.

Dominique Charpin. 2014. The assyriologist and the computer. the "archibab" project. *Hebrew Bible and Ancient Israel*, 3(1):137–153.

Evelien de Graaf, Silvia Stopponi, Jasper Bos, Saskia Peels-Matthey, and Malvina Nissim. 2022. Agile: The first lemmatizer for ancient greek inscriptions. In *Proceedings of the 13th Conference on Language Resources and Evaluation (LREC)*, pages 5334–5344. European Language Resources Association (ELRA).

John L. Hayes. 2019. *A Manual of Sumerian Grammar and Texts*, 3rd revised ed. edition. Undena Publications.

Abraham Hendrik Jagersma. 2010. *A Descriptive Grammar of Sumerian*. Ph.d. dissertation, Leiden University.

Tomasz Limisiewicz, Terra Blevins, Hila Gonen, Orevaoghene Ahia, and Luke Zettlemoyer. 2024. Myte: Morphology-driven byte encoding for better and fairer multilingual language modeling. *arXiv preprint*.

Matthew Ong and Shai Gordin. 2024. Linguistic annotation of cuneiform texts using treebanks and deep learning. *Digital Scholarship in the Humanities*, 39(1):296–307.

Colin Raffel, Noam Shazeer, Adam Roberts, Katherine Lee, Sharan Narang, Michael Matena, Yanqi Zhou, Wei Li, and Peter J. Liu. 2020. Exploring the limits of transfer learning with a unified text-to-text transformer. *Journal of Machine Learning Research*, 21(140):1–67.

Frederick Riemenschneider and Kevin Krahn. 2024. Heidelberg-boston @ sigtyp 2024 shared task: Enhancing low-resource language analysis with character-aware hierarchical transformers. In *Proceedings of the 6th Workshop on Research in Computational Linguistic Typology and Multilingual NLP*, pages 131–141. Association for Computational Linguistics.

Aleksi Sahala, Tero Alstola, Jonathan Valk, and Krister Lindén. 2022. Babylemmatizer: A lemmatizer and pos-tagger for akkadian. In *Proceedings of the CLARIN Annual Conference*, pages 14–18. CLARIN ERIC.

Aleksi Sahala and Krister Lindén. 2023. Babylemmatizer 2.0–a neural pipeline for pos-tagging and lemmatizing cuneiform languages. In *Proceedings of the Workshop on Ancient Language Processing*, pages 203–212. INCOMA.

Aleksi Sahala, Miikka Silfverberg, Antti Arppe, and Krister Lindén. 2020. Babyfst: Towards a finite-state based computational model of ancient babylonian. In *Proceedings of the International Conference on Language Resources and Evaluation (LREC)*, pages 3886–3894. European Language Resources Association (ELRA).

Lukas Stankevičius, Mantas Lukoševičius, Jurgita Kapočiūtė-Dzikienė, Monica Briedienė, and Tomas Krilavičius. 2022. Correcting diacritics and typos with a byt5 transformer model. *Applied Sciences*, 12(5):2636.

Chahan Vidal-Gorène and Bastien Kindt. 2020. Lemmatization and pos-tagging process by using joint learning approach: Experimental results on classical armenian, old georgian, and syriac. In *Proceedings of LT4HALA 2020–1st Workshop on Language Technologies for Historical and Ancient Languages*, pages 22–27.

Wolfram von Soden. 1969. *Grundriss der Akkadischen Grammatik*, 3rd ed. edition. Pontificium Institutum Biblicum.

Krzysztof Wróbel and Krzysztof Nowak. 2022. Transformer-based part-of-speech tagging and lemmatization for latin. In *Proceedings of the Second Workshop on Language Technologies for Historical and Ancient Languages*, pages 193–197. European Language Resources Association.

Linting Xue, Aditya Barua, Noah Constant, Rami Al-Rfou, Sharan Narang, Mihir Kale, Adam Roberts, and Colin Raffel. 2022. Byt5: Towards a token-free future with pre-trained byte-to-byte models. *Transactions of the Association for Computational Linguistics*, 10:291–306.

Jian Zhu, Cong Zhang, and David Jurgens. 2022. Byt5 model for massively multilingual grapheme-to-phoneme conversion. *arXiv preprint*.

# Finetuning LLMs for EvaCun 2025 Token Prediction Shared Task

**Josef Jon, Ondřej Bojar**
Charles University, Faculty of Mathematics and Physics
surname@ufal.mff.cuni.cz

## Abstract

In this paper, we present our submission for the token prediction task of EvaCun 2025. Our systems are based on LLMs (Command-R, Mistral, and Aya Expanse) fine-tuned on the task data provided by the organizers. As we only possess a very superficial knowledge of the subject field and the languages of the task, we simply used the training data without any task-specific adjustments, preprocessing, or filtering. We compare 3 different approaches (based on 3 different prompts) of obtaining the predictions, and we evaluate them on a held-out part of the data.

## 1 Introduction

The EvaCun token prediction shared task focuses on missing word restoration in languages originally written in cuneiform – Akkadian and Sumerian. The script is one of the earliest known forms of writing with a history spanning over 3000 years, evolving originally from the proto-cuneiform that was used for accounting and record keeping. One of the most challenging part of interpreting and translating Akkadian and Sumerian text is the polyvalence of cuneiform signs – a single sign can be used as a logogram, i.e. representing a whole word (which is further complicated by the fact that one symbol can represent many different possible words, and that Akkadian texts can contain Sumerian words, even though the languages are not otherwise related), or as a syllable (one sign can represent multiple syllables) or as a determinative that denotes a semantic category of the previous word (diety, person, place, etc.). In the context of the task, our work is greatly simplified by the fact that the task data are already interpreted and transliterated into the Latin alphabet instead of being in the original cuneiform script. As we do not have any knowledge of the languages of the task in our team, we pursued a purely engineering approach of finetuning 3 different LLMs – Aya Expanse 8B (Dang et al., 2024), Command-R v0.1 34B (Cohere4AI team, 2025) and Mistral Small 3 24B (Mistral team, 2025) – on the task data, with 3 slightly different formulations of the problem. We offer our solution as a baseline to be compared with the more informed and task-specific approaches.

## 2 Related work

A more focused effort in NLP for languages written in cuneiform started only recently. A basis for all future work are databases and datasets like the Electronic Text Corpus of Sumerian Literature (Black et al., 2016), Cuneiform Digital Library Initiative, (CDLI contributors, 2025), CuneiML (Chen et al., 2023) and the Open Richly Annotated Cuneiform Corpus (Oracc Team, 2025).

Simmons et al. (2024) created a new corpus based on these previously released datasets that pairs digital Unicode transcription of cuneiform texts with their transliterations as well as a baseline system trained on this dataset to perform this task. Similarly, Gordin et al. (2020) present a method for automatic translation of Akkadian cuneiform. **?** present an MT system for Sumerian with the final goal of an information retrieval pipeline for this language.

## 3 Methods

We fine-tune autoregressive LLMs with 3 different prompts to predict the masked word. A masked language model would be a more natural choice for this task, however causal (autoregressive) language modeling is currently a more popular approach with a larger selection of pretrained models.

### 3.1 Data preprocessing and prompts

The dataset provided by the organizers contains a list of tokens, each token accompanied by its document id, line number in the context of the doc-



*Proceedings of the Second Ancient Language Processing Workshop associated with NAACL 2025*, pages 182–186
May 4, 2025. 

| Method | Prompt |
|---|---|
| All | Fill in the missing {language} words, masked by the [MASK] token. Output "WORDS:" and a comma-separated list of the missing words in original {language}: {masked_document} |
| One by one | Fill in the missing {language} word masked by the [MASK] token: {masked_document_with_unks} |
| Restore | Complete the missing {language} words masked by the [MASK] tokens and print out the restored document: {masked_document} |

Table 1: Prompts for the three token prediction methods we compared.

ument, the word index on that line, language, and extra information, for example, the place where the tablet was found or the type of text. We only make use of the language, word order, and document id, i.e., we do not for example split the inputs into lines or use the additional information. In each document, we mask 15% randomly sampled words with a [MASK] token. For each document, we create at most 15 unique variants with different masks (fewer if the overall possible number of combinations for the given document length is lower). We frame the prediction task in three different ways. The model is shown the masked document in the prompt, and it is asked to:

- Produce a list containing all the original words corresponding to the masked predictions in the correct order (we call this method *All* further in the text).
- All [MASK] tokens except for one are replaced by an [UNK] token, and we ask the model to predict the original word for the single remaining [MASK] token. This is repeated for all [MASK] tokens in the masked document (*One by one*).
- We ask the model to output the full restored text of the masked document. We finetune separate models on each of these prompts (*Restore*).

The specific prompts are shown in Table 1. Our baseline approach, *All*, needs the least effort for data preprocessing and training and inference compute time. However, it could suffer from error propagation due to the autoregressive nature of the inference – the model bases the predictions on previously predicted words as well. *One by one* approach could mitigate this issue, as only one masked word is predicted for each example (others remain masked). *Restore* approach is based on the basic next-word prediction training objective for autoregressive models, but the decoding is complicated by the need for forcing the unmasked parts of the text and keeping the word lengths the same for whole text for both masked and unmasked versions.

## 4 Experiments

We describe the experimental setup, hyperparameters and results in this section.

### 4.1 Data

The full training data from the organizers contains 913252 tokens in 22777 documents. We set aside 1% (227 documents) for the dev set (we filter out single word documents from the dev set). For our evaluation, we used a subset of this dev set containing 135 documents with 1500 different unique masked examples in total.

### 4.2 LLM finetuning

We finetune the pretrained models using QLoRA (Dettmers et al., 2023). We experimented with 3 LLMs: *Command-R V0.1* (4-bit quantized, *CohereForAI/c4ai-command-r-v01-4bit*), *Aya Expanse 8B* and *Mistral Small 3 24B Instruct* (4-bit quantized, *unsloth/Mistral-Small-24B-Instruct-2501-unsloth-bnb-4bit*. We use the `transformers` (Wolf et al., 2020), `peft` and `trl` libraries for the training. We experimented with LoRA rank sizes 8, 16, 32, 64 and 92, $\alpha = r/2$. We finetuned the models by AdamW optimizer, with warmup ratio of 0.03 and learning rate $lr = 2e - 4$. We used batch sizes 40, 36 and 35 for Aya, Command-R and Mistral models, respectively. We trained on a heterogenous cluster on a mix of Nvidia L40, A40 and H100 GPUs. We trained for a maximum of epochs, but the checkpoints we actually used for the prediction were from earlier parts of the training, as we describe in the results section.

### 4.3 Results

We sampled from the models with temperature $t = 0.2$ to obtain the predictions (greedily, without the use of algorithms like beam search) and we measured the accuracy of the predictions on the held-out validation set, i.e the fraction of masked

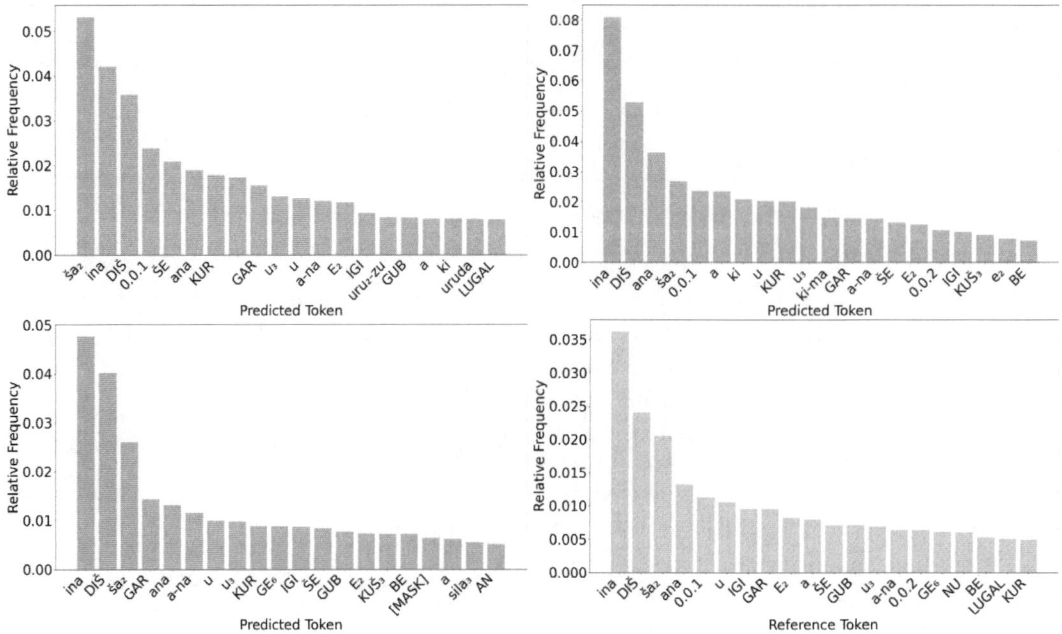


Figure 1: Relative frequencies of the top-20 generated words for masked positions by best checkpoint for each prompt (*All, One by one, Restore* on top left, top right and bottom left, respectively) and of the reference masked words (bottom right).

| | Aya Expanse | Command-R | Mistral |
|---|---|---|---|
| **All** | 0.202 | 0.209 | 0.221 |
| **One by one** | 0.157 | 0.167 | 0.205 |
| **Restore** | 0.136 | 0.139 | 0.137 |
| **Majority voting** | | 0.269 (0.377) | |
| **Most common word** | | 0.04 | |

Table 2: Accuracies of all combinations of models and prompts on held-out part of the task data. We also report top-3 accuracy for the majority voting in the parentheses. The final row shows the accuracy of predicting the most common word for the given language (based on the training data) for each masked position.

| | Aya Expanse | Command-R | Mistral |
|---|---|---|---|
| **All** | 6300 (0.75) | 6300 (0.67) | 5400 (0.55) |
| **One by one** | 8100 (0.15) | 5400 (0.10) | 900 (0.02) |
| **Restore** | 4500 (0.53) | 9000 (0.96) | 2700 (0.27) |

Table 3: Number of updates (and the corresponding fraction of an epoch in parentheses) that the best-performing models were trained for.

positions where the missing word was predicted correctly out of all masked positions. For the *Restore* method, we generate the restored document in parts, by force decoding the known parts and only generating one complete word (possibly consisting of multiple subwords) for each [MASK] token (i.e. after force decoding the unmasked part of the document, we select the most probable subword that starts with a beginning of word symbol and generate next subwords until we reach another beginning of word subword, we discard this last subword and start with force decoding the known continuation again). We ensemble the results by majority voting, pick 60 best-performing checkpoints and select the most common prediction for each position.

We present the results of the 3 methods on the held-out validation set in Table 2. Overall, finetuning the Mistral models resulted in the best accuracies. However, the differences are not large and with a different choice of hyperparameters in the finetuning, we might see different ranking. From the methods point of view, *All* performed the best. Table 3 shows the number of steps and a corresponding fraction of an epoch that the best-scoring checkpoints were trained on. The final line shows the majority baseline – for each language, we only predict the most common word from the training data for all masked positions. For example, in

Akkadian, the most common word is the proposition *ina*, meaning *in, on, onto, at, to, from* and other possible meanings in compound expressions.

We also show the relative frequencies of the top-20 predicted words by each method and of the reference words in Figure 1. We see that while the list of top 10 words is similar to the reference list for all methods, the LLMs overestimate the probability (frequency) of the most popular words. This is a common issue in text-generating models. As a result, probabilities of less common words are underestimated – the methods generated 1567, 1217 and 3164 unique words for *All, One by one* and *Restore* respectively, while the reference contains 2317 unique tokens. We believe that the large number of unique tokens for the *Restore* method is caused by our prediction mechanism that ensures the same word length of both the prediction and the original text but can force the selection of suboptimal predictions as a fallback. Also, note the we did not disallow the generation of [MASK] token in the *Restore* method by mistake. This negatively affects the resulting accuracy of this method.

For the final test set submission, we ran the inference with the best 60 checkpoints on the test dataset and performed the majority voting to obtain top-3 predictions.

## 5 Conclusion

We finetuned various autoregressive LLMs on the token restoration task posed in 3 different ways. We show that the best single model can accurately predict 22.1% of masked tokens on our held-out dev set, while by combining predictions of multiple models by voting, we can reach 26.9% accuracy. However, there might be biases and aspects of the dataset like repetitiveness, which could lead to overestimating the real capabilities of our approach.

In the future, we plan to focus on the much more difficult task of direct translation of cuneiform script into English, either using Unicode transcriptions of the tablets, or a visual LLM to read the tablet photos directly.

## 6 Acknowledgments

This work was supported by Czech Ministry of Education, Youth and Sports (grant MŠMT OP JAK Mezisektorová spolupráce CZ.02.01.01/00/23_020/0008518) and National Recovery Plan funded project MPO 60273/24/21300/21000 CEDMO 2.0 NPO. The computational resources were provided by Ministry of Education, Youth and Sports of the Czech Republic Project Nr. LM2023062 LINDAT/CLARIAH-CZ.

## References

J.A Black, Cunningham, Ebeling, FlückigerHawker, Robson, Taylor, and Zólyomi. 2016. Electronic text corpus of sumerian luterature. `https://etcsl.orinst.ox.ac.uk/`. [Accessed 03-03-2025].

CDLI contributors. 2025. Cdli. https://cdli.mpiwg-berlin.mpg.de/. [Online; accessed 2025-03-03].

Danlu Chen, Aditi Agarwal, Taylor Berg-Kirkpatrick, and Jacobo Myerston. 2023. Cuneiml: A cuneiform dataset for machine learning. *Journal of Open Humanities Data*.

Cohere4AI team. 2025. Command r: Retrieval-augmented generation at production scale. https://cohere.com/blog/command-r. [Online; accessed 2025-03-03].

John Dang, Shivalika Singh, Daniel D'souza, Arash Ahmadian, Alejandro Salamanca, Madeline Smith, Aidan Peppin, Sungjin Hong, Manoj Govindassamy, Terrence Zhao, Sandra Kublik, Meor Amer, Viraat Aryabumi, Jon Ander Campos, Yi-Chern Tan, Tom Kocmi, Florian Strub, Nathan Grinsztajn, Yannis Flet-Berliac, Acyr Locatelli, Hangyu Lin, Dwarak Talupuru, Bharat Venkitesh, David Cairuz, Bowen Yang, Tim Chung, Wei-Yin Ko, Sylvie Shang Shi, Amir Shukayev, Sammie Bae, Aleksandra Piktus, Roman Castagné, Felipe Cruz-Salinas, Eddie Kim, Lucas Crawhall-Stein, Adrien Morisot, Sudip Roy, Phil Blunsom, Ivan Zhang, Aidan Gomez, Nick Frosst, Marzieh Fadaee, Beyza Ermis, Ahmet Üstün, and Sara Hooker. 2024. Aya expanse: Combining research breakthroughs for a new multilingual frontier. *Preprint*, arXiv:2412.04261.

Tim Dettmers, Artidoro Pagnoni, Ari Holtzman, and Luke Zettlemoyer. 2023. Qlora: Efficient finetuning of quantized llms. *Preprint*, arXiv:2305.14314.

Shai Gordin, Gai Gutherz, Ariel Elazary, Avital Romach, Enrique Jiménez, Jonathan Berant, and Yoram Cohen. 2020. Reading akkadian cuneiform using natural language processing. *PLOS ONE*, 15(10):1–16.

Mistral team. 2025. Mistral small 3. https://mistral.ai/news/mistral-small-3. [Online; accessed 2025-03-03].

Oracc Team. 2025. Oracc. `http://oracc.org`. [Accessed 03-03-2025].

Cole Simmons, Richard Diehl Martinez, and Dan Jurafsky. 2024. SumTablets: A transliteration dataset of Sumerian tablets. In *Proceedings of the 1st Workshop on Machine Learning for Ancient Languages (ML4AL 2024)*, pages 192–202, Hybrid in Bangkok,

Thailand and online. Association for Computational Linguistics.

Thomas Wolf, Lysandre Debut, Victor Sanh, Julien Chaumond, Clement Delangue, Anthony Moi, Pierric Cistac, Tim Rault, Rémi Louf, Morgan Funtowicz, Joe Davison, Sam Shleifer, Patrick von Platen, Clara Ma, Yacine Jernite, Julien Plu, Canwen Xu, Teven Le Scao, Sylvain Gugger, Mariama Drame, Quentin Lhoest, and Alexander M. Rush. 2020. Huggingface's transformers: State-of-the-art natural language processing. *Preprint*, arXiv:1910.03771.

# Beyond Base Predictors: Using LLMs to Resolve Ambiguities in Akkadian Lemmatization

**Frederick Riemenschneider**
Dept. of Computational Linguistics
Heidelberg University, Germany
riemenschneider@cl.uni-heidelberg.de

## Abstract

We present a hybrid approach for Akkadian lemmatization in the EvaCun 2025 Shared Task that combines traditional NLP techniques with large language models (LLMs). Our system employs three Base Predictors–a dictionary lookup and two T5 models–to establish initial lemma candidates. For cases where these predictors disagree (18.72% of instances), we implement an LLM Resolution module, enhanced with direct access to the electronic Babylonian Library (eBL) dictionary entries. This module includes a Predictor component that generates initial lemma predictions based on dictionary information, and a Validator component that refines these predictions through contextual reasoning. Error analysis reveals that the system struggles most with small differences (like capitalization) and certain ambiguous logograms (like BI). Our work demonstrates the benefits of combining traditional NLP approaches with the reasoning capabilities of LLMs when provided with appropriate domain knowledge.

## 1 Introduction

Akkadian lemmatization presents significant challenges due to complex morphology, logographic elements, and varying scholarly conventions. Despite significant advances in neural lemmatization approaches (Sahala and Lindén, 2023), ambiguities continue to resist automated resolution. The EvaCun 2025 shared task explores how LLMs can be integrated into lemmatization workflows for Akkadian texts. In this paper, we present our hybrid approach that strategically combines traditional NLP techniques with LLM capabilities. Our system is motivated by the observation that while most Akkadian forms can be reliably lemmatized through conventional methods, a small but significant percentage requires deeper analysis. We leverage this finding by directing our LLM resources specifically toward resolving these difficult cases.

## 2 Related Work

Prior work on Akkadian Lemmatization and neighboring tasks primarily relies on rule-based systems. For instance, Kataja and Koskenniemi (1988) use finite-state transducers to analyze Akkadian morphology, while Macks (2002) employs a Prolog Definite Clause Grammar. Particularly significant in practice is L2 (Tinney, 2019), a dictionary-based tool that has been used to annotate the Open Richly Annotated Cuneiform Corpus (Oracc).[1]

More recently, Sahala et al. (2020) explore finite-state approaches to Ancient Babylonian through their BabyFST model, highlighting the challenges posed by word form ambiguity. The field has since advanced to neural approaches with BabyLemmatizer (Sahala et al., 2022) and its successor BabyLemmatizer 2.0 (Sahala and Lindén, 2023), which represent the current state of the art.

Beyond the Akkadian-focused systems described above, broader lemmatization research in recent shared tasks has established sequence-to-sequence modeling as an effective approach across multiple languages (Wróbel and Nowak, 2022; Yangarber et al., 2023; Riemenschneider and Krahn, 2024). We incorporate this proven methodology while investigating how LLMs can extend and enhance these techniques for Akkadian specifically.

## 3 System Architecture

In this section, we present our lemmatization system architecture, illustrated in Figure 1. Our approach implements a hierarchical approach wherein base predictors handle standard cases, while LLM components address more challenging instances.

### 3.1 Input

The input layer of our lemmatization pipeline accepts two primary data elements: the token of interest to be lemmatized and the full fragment in

[1] https://oracc.museum.upenn.edu/index.html.



*Proceedings of the Second Ancient Language Processing Workshop associated with NAACL 2025*, pages 187–192
May 4, 2025. 

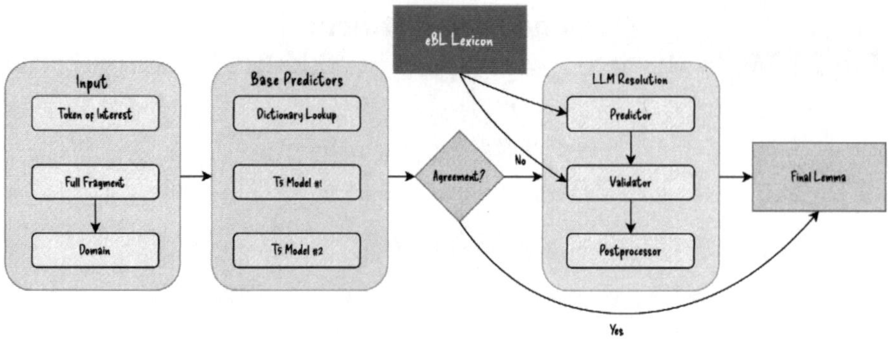


Figure 1: Overview of our system architecture.

which this token appears. In addition to providing contextual information, the full fragment serves an important technical purpose: it enables our system to detect which lemmatization convention should be applied to the output.

**Domain Detection.** An initial analysis of the training data reveals a critical distinction between two different lemmatization conventions that impact how a word should be lemmatized. The dataset contains a mixture of texts following either the Archibab (Charpin, 2014)[2] or the eBL[3] format. For example, "lord" appears as "bêlum" in Archibab (with circumflex accent and mimation) but as "bēlu I" in eBL (with macron, no mimation, and Roman indexing). The transliterated text follows different standards as well: while the data belonging to eBL uses curly brackets for determinatives, Archibab employs parentheses. Moreover, while eBL consistently uses lowerscript indices to distinguish homophones, Archibab uses the acute and grave accents for the indices 2 and 3 (e.g., "u two" is written as "u$_2$" in eBL and as "ú" in Archibab).

To address this challenge, our first processing step determines whether to follow the eBL or Archibab lemmatization format by analyzing the full fragment context. We develop a rule-based domain detection method that determines the target format by analyzing the input format. For example, a transliterated fragment containing parenthesized determinatives and acute accents (e.g., "[...] i-na-an-na ma-ar-ta be-lí-ia (I)-(munus)-ki-ru-ú ša [...]" would be identified as Archibab-style, indicating that "be-lí-ia" should be lemmatized as "bêlum". Conversely, a fragment with subscript numbers and curly braces (e.g., "[...] šu-pi ša$_2$ be-li$_2$-ia lu ṭa-a-bi [...]") would be classified as eBL-style, signaling that "be-li$_2$-ia" should be lemmatized as "bēlu I".

[2] https://www.archibab.fr/home.

[3] https://www.ebl.lmu.de/.

### 3.2 Base Predictors

Our system is built on the observation that lemmatization difficulty varies across tokens, with only a subset requiring complex disambiguation. We therefore leverage a dictionary lookup and T5 models to handle most of the predictions.

**Dictionary Lookup.** When splitting the training data into 95% train and 5% validation data, a simple dictionary lookup already achieves 77.63% accuracy on the validation set. This baseline approach is further improved with a domain-aware dictionary lookup, which reaches 82.63% accuracy. Our domain-aware implementation maintains separate dictionaries for eBL and Archibab; when a token cannot be found in the domain-specific dictionary, the system falls back to a merged dictionary containing entries from both domains.

**T5 Models.** In recent shared tasks, treating lemmatization as a sequence-to-sequence task has proven successful (Wróbel and Nowak, 2022; Yangarber et al., 2023; Riemenschneider and Krahn, 2024). Following this established approach, we pretrain our own Akkadian T5 model on the transliterated texts provided by the task organizers, as additional data was not permitted under the competition rules. Specifically, we train a T5$_{\text{base}}$ model for 100 epochs using nanoT5 (Nawrot, 2023). We fine-tune this pre-trained model twice, each time with a different 5% held-out validation split, continuing until we observe no improvements in lemmatization accuracy for five consecutive evaluation runs.

The input format for both models consists of a domain token followed by a window of three tokens before and after the target, with special tokens delimiting the target: For instance, "[DOMAIN=eBL] BI ip-pal-si-hu ina [special_token_0] MUL.MUL [special_token_1] u {d}30 IGI-šu$_2$-nu-ti-ma" should be lemmatized as "zappu I". Despite this contextualized representation, our two T5 models achieve only 86.96% and 88.25% validation accuracy respectively, barely outperforming the dictionary-based approach and showing limited generalization to unseen forms.

We utilize model disagreement as a signal for identifying challenging lemmatization decisions. When at least two of our three base models produce different predictions for a given token, we invoke a LLM resolution strategy. This targeted approach allows us to process the majority of cases efficiently: 81.28% of the test set was lemmatized using only our base predictors, while the more sophisticated LLM resolution was reserved for the remaining 18.72% of challenging cases.

### 3.3 LLM Resolution

The difficult cases requiring LLM intervention present a dual challenge: on one hand, they require reasoning to determine the correct lemma. On the other hand, we are simultaneously confronted with arbitrary lexicographic conventions that cannot be derived through reasoning alone. For instance, "kasāpu" is a homonym that can mean either "to break (into bits)" or "to make funerary offering", but even after correctly determining the lemma and its meaning, the assignment of Roman indices (I for "break" versus II for "funerary offering") follows arbitrary conventions rather than linguistic principles.

To address this challenge, we prepare the LLM input text with comprehensive contextual information: the full textual fragment, the target token, predictions from all base models, and–importantly–the corresponding dictionary definitions retrieved from the eBL lexicon. Additionally, we augment this information with up to three representative examples from the same textual domain, selected first from exact matches of the target token and then supplemented with similar forms (based on Levenshtein distance) when necessary. We ensure diversity in our examples by including only one example per lemma, thereby presenting three different lemmata to the model. This approach provides information on how lemmatization conventions are structured within the specific domain.

The enriched context supports a two-stage LLM resolution process. First, an LLM Predictor analyzes the available information to generate an initial lemma prediction. Then, a second LLM instance serves as a Validator, reviewing both the original context and the predictor's reasoning to make the final determination. In our implementation, we use Anthropic's `claude-3-7-sonnet-20250219`[4] as both Predictor and Validator.

**LLM Predictor.** The Predictor component leverages the LLM's reasoning abilities while bridging the gap to arbitrary conventions through the selected contextual information. By analyzing the full fragment, the dictionary definitions, and considering domain-specific examples, the Predictor generates both a reasoned explanation and a lemma prediction.

**LLM Validator.** The Validator component receives all the information provided to the Predictor, along with the Predictor's reasoning and lemma choice, as well as the dictionary definition of the Predictor's proposed lemma. This second-stage verification ensures that even when the correct lemma was not present in the base model predictions, it can still be properly evaluated against the eBL lexicon. The Validator considers all available evidence to make the final determination, serving as a safeguard against potential errors in the Predictor's analysis.

**Postprocessing.** The resulting LLM-based prediction system usually follows the domain-specific standards, but exhibits a bias toward eBL conventions due to our reliance on the eBL lexicon. To ensure domain-appropriate outputs, we apply targeted post-processing rules that adapt the lemmata to their domains. For instance, in the Archibab texts, we remove Roman indices and replace macrons with circumflexes (converting ā, ē, ī, ū to â, ê, î, û). Conversely, for eBL texts, we verify the presence of required Roman indices, falling back to the closest base model prediction when necessary. This post-processing ensures that our final lemmata adhere to the expected conventional standards of each domain.

## 4 Error Analysis

**Base Model Performance.** Our system architecture enables a systematic analysis of error patterns at each stage of the prediction pipeline. We begin

[4]`https://www.anthropic.com/news/claude-3-7-sonnet`.

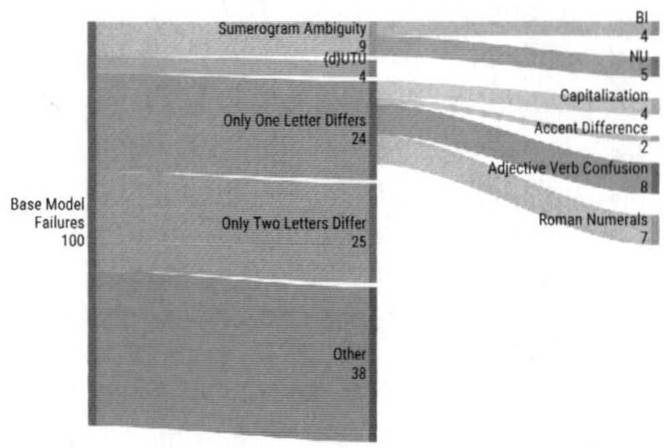


Figure 2: Base Model Failures Despite Agreement (%).

by examining the performance of our base predictors in cases where they unanimously agree, thereby bypassing the need for LLM intervention. Across the two independent train/validation splits, we observe that when both the dictionary lookup and T5 model agree on a lemma prediction, their combined accuracy reaches 97.2% ± 0.04%. This analysis validates our architectural decision to avoid LLM processing when base predictors reach consensus, as the error rate in these cases consistently remains below 3%. Although we cannot directly measure the error rate when all three systems (dictionary and both T5 models) agree due to training data overlap, we can reasonably expect this error to be even lower than the observed 2.8%.

We present an analysis of the 2.8% of cases where base models fail despite agreement in Figure 2. The logogram NU represents the most frequently mispredicted form (5% of all errors), where the system consistently predicts "lā I" instead of the contextually appropriate "lu I" or "ṣalmu II". This pattern reveals a fundamental limitation in the models' ability to disambiguate logogram based on context, highlighting a specific area where targeted improvements could yield significant gains in overall system performance. (ii) Similarly, the logogram BI (3.65% of errors) demonstrates limitations in grammatical reasoning, with the system defaulting to "šū I" instead of contextually appropriate alternatives like "šuāti I" or "šī I".

(iii) The divine name {d}UTU represents the second most frequently mispredicted form (4.2% of errors), where our system consistently predicts "Šamaš I" while the gold standard sometimes requires "šamšu I". This distinction is particularly subtle, as it is often the case that both lemmata are valid, depending on contextual interpretation.

(iv) The largest category of systematically identifiable errors (24.22%) involves cases where predictions differ from gold standards by only a single letter. Within this category, capitalization accounts for 4% of all errors, where the system correctly identifies the lemma but uses incorrect capitalization (e.g., "šarru I" vs. "Šarru I"). Accent differences account for 1.92% of errors. Arguably, lemmata derived from the same root, e.g., "ṣalāmu I" and "ṣalmu I" both being valid lemmata for $GE_6$, also belong in this category as they represent minor variations of the same lexical concept. These "near-miss" errors suggest that a substantial portion of the system's failures involve formatting variations rather than fundamental misunderstandings of the underlying lexical items. Roman index errors represent a more significant issue (7.32% of all errors), where the system identifies the correct lemma but assigns an incorrect index.

**LLM Resolution Performance.** To analyze the performance of our LLM Resolution approach, we examine 500 instances where Base Predictors disagree on the validation data. The overall accuracy on these challenging cases is 77.4%. The LLM Predictor contributes significantly to this performance, correctly resolving 73.6% of cases. The Validator module further improves results by correctly resolving an additional 4% of cases, though it occasionally introduces errors (0.2% of cases). Post-editing rules correct another 1.4% of cases.

Figure 3 presents an error analysis of the remaining cases where our approach fails. The analysis reveals that Roman Indices are particularly well-handled through the LLM's reasoning capabilities, as the model can effectively leverage dictionary entries to reach correct conclusions. Similarly, almost all cases involving the logogram NU are successfully resolved. The logogram BI remains more challenging, with our system failing in 36.37% of all cases involving this logogram.

We hypothesize that these cases are not a limitation of the LLM but rather due to a peculiarity in Akkadian lemmatization, where case and gender variations may require distinct lemma entries (e.g., "šī I" or "šuāti I"). Given that personal pronouns and common logograms like BI appear frequently in the corpus, improving the model's handling of these cases could enhance overall performance. Future improvements could include explicitly instructing the model about the specific lemmatization conventions for these special cases.

Additionally, our analysis reveals several previ-

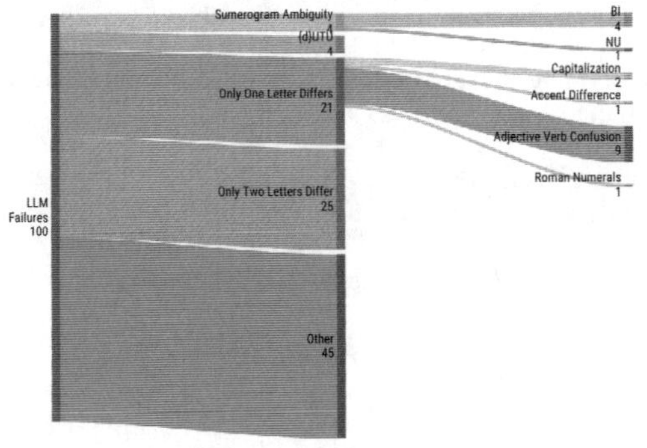


Figure 3: LLM Model Failures (%).

ously unclassified cases of Sumerogram Ambiguity that become apparent as other error types are resolved. These cases are categorized as "Other" in Figure 3 and are beyond the scope of our current qualitative analysis.

## 5 Outlook

Our system was designed specifically for the EvaCun 2025 Shared Task, utilizing only the data provided by the task organizers. In a real-world implementation scenario, several enhancements could substantially improve performance.

A straightforward improvement involves implementing more powerful base predictors. For instance, adapting the BabyLemmatizer or pretraining a more comprehensive T5 model on the full corpus of available digitized Akkadian texts–rather than being limited to the task-provided data–would establish a stronger foundation for the entire system. The BabyLemmatizer has demonstrated accuracy rates of approximately 95% (albeit on different datasets), indicating significant potential improvements for base lemmatizers that could be seamlessly integrated into our architecture.

Another limitation of our current approach stems from working with an LLM with closed weights. As it is not possible to fine-tune Claude, we invested considerable effort in designing prompts that would guide the model to produce appropriately formatted output, creating computational overhead during inference. Parameter-efficient fine-tuning methods such as LoRA (Hu et al., 2022) could potentially streamline this process by teaching the model expected output formats directly. Unfortunately, our initial experiments with Qwen (Yang et al., 2024) and Gemma (Riviere et al., 2024)–models offering accessible weights–yielded suboptimal results, likely due to their limited capabilities with Akkadian language processing.

## 6 Conclusion

We present our system for the EvaCun 2025 Shared Task on lemmatization, which combines traditional NLP approaches with LLM capabilities. Our approach consists of three Base Predictors–a dictionary lookup and two T5 models–augmented with an LLM module that resolves difficult cases, directly accessing the eBL dictionary entries.

In our analysis, we demonstrate that while the Base Predictors achieve already high performance, the LLM Module significantly enhances results by resolving challenging cases. The error analysis reveals that our approach is particularly effective at handling Roman Indices, where the LLM's ability to reason over dictionary entries proves valuable, as it can effectively disambiguate between lemmata by leveraging contextual clues and domain knowledge.

Our work highlights an important methodological consideration in applying AI to specialized linguistic tasks: the trade-off between fine-tuning and prompting approaches. Fine-tuning language models offers the advantage of domain adaptation but risks overfitting to biases present in limited training data. In contrast, prompting LLMs as demonstrated in our approach preserves their general reasoning capabilities but presents challenges in precisely controlling output format and applying domain-specific conventions. While our system successfully augmented the LLM with demonstrations and dictionary entries, future work could benefit from more structured guidance through explicit instructions about lemmatization conventions, particularly for edge cases involving case variations, Sumerian logograms, and personal pronouns.


## Acknowledgements

We thank the anonymous reviewers for their valuable suggestions.


## References


Dominique Charpin. 2014. The Assyriologist and the Computer. The "Archibab" Project. *Hebrew Bible and Ancient Israel*, 3(1):137–153.

Edward J Hu, yelong shen, Phillip Wallis, Zeyuan Allen-Zhu, Yuanzhi Li, Shean Wang, Lu Wang, and Weizhu Chen. 2022. LoRA: Low-rank adaptation of large language models. In *International Conference on Learning Representations*.

Laura Kataja and Kimmo Koskenniemi. 1988. Finite-state description of Semitic morphology: A case study of ancient Accadian. In *Coling Budapest 1988 Volume 1: International Conference on Computational Linguistics*.

Aaron Macks. 2002. Parsing Akkadian verbs with Prolog. In *Proceedings of the ACL-02 Workshop on Computational Approaches to Semitic Languages*, Philadelphia, Pennsylvania, USA. Association for Computational Linguistics.

Piotr Nawrot. 2023. nanoT5: Fast & simple pre-training and fine-tuning of t5 models with limited resources. In *Proceedings of the 3rd Workshop for Natural Language Processing Open Source Software (NLP-OSS 2023)*, pages 95–101, Singapore. Association for Computational Linguistics.

Frederick Riemenschneider and Kevin Krahn. 2024. Heidelberg-boston @ SIGTYP 2024 shared task: Enhancing low-resource language analysis with character-aware hierarchical transformers. In *Proceedings of the 6th Workshop on Research in Computational Linguistic Typology and Multilingual NLP*, pages 131–141, St. Julian's, Malta. Association for Computational Linguistics.

Morgane Riviere, Shreya Pathak, Pier Giuseppe Sessa, Cassidy Hardin, Surya Bhupatiraju, Léonard Hussenot, Thomas Mesnard, Bobak Shahriari, Alexandre Ramé, et al. 2024. Gemma 2: Improving open language models at a practical size. *arXiv preprint arXiv:2408.00118*.

Aleksi Sahala, Tero Alstola, Jonathan Valk, and Krister Linden. 2022. Babylemmatizer: A lemmatizer and pos-tagger for akkadian. In *CLARIN Annual Conference Proceedings, 2022*, CLARIN Annual Conference Proceedings, page 14–18, Netherlands. CLARIN ERIC. CLARIN Annual Conference ; Conference date: 10-10-2022 Through 12-10-2022.

Aleksi Sahala and Krister Lindén. 2023. A neural pipeline for POS-tagging and lemmatizing cuneiform languages. In *Proceedings of the Ancient Language Processing Workshop*, pages 203–212, Varna, Bulgaria. INCOMA Ltd., Shoumen, Bulgaria.

Aleksi Sahala, Miikka Silfverberg, Antti Arppe, and Krister Lindén. 2020. BabyFST - towards a finite-state based computational model of ancient Babylonian. In *Proceedings of the Twelfth Language Resources and Evaluation Conference*, pages 3886–3894, Marseille, France. European Language Resources Association.

Steve Tinney. 2019. L2: How it works. Oracc: The Open Richly Annotated Cuneiform Corpus.

Krzysztof Wróbel and Krzysztof Nowak. 2022. Transformer-based part-of-speech tagging and lemmatization for Latin. In *Proceedings of the Second Workshop on Language Technologies for Historical and Ancient Languages*, pages 193–197, Marseille, France. European Language Resources Association.

An Yang, Baosong Yang, Beichen Zhang, Binyuan Hui, Bo Zheng, Bowen Yu, Chengyuan Li, Dayiheng Liu, Fei Huang, Haoran Wei, et al. 2024. Qwen2.5 technical report. *arXiv preprint arXiv:2412.15115*.

Roman Yangarber, Jakub Piskorski, Anna Dmitrieva, Michał Marcińczuk, Pavel Přibáň, Piotr Rybak, and Josef Steinberger. 2023. Slav-NER: the 4th cross-lingual challenge on recognition, normalization, classification, and linking of named entities across Slavic languages. In *Proceedings of the 9th Workshop on Slavic Natural Language Processing 2023 (SlavicNLP 2023)*, pages 179–189, Dubrovnik, Croatia. Association for Computational Linguistics.

# A Low-Shot Prompting Approach to Lemmatization in the EvaCun 2025 Shared Task

**John Sbur Brandi Wilkins Elizabeth Paul and Yudong Liu**
Computer Science Department
Western Washington University
Bellingham, Washington 98225
{sburj, wilkinb2, paule5, liuy2}@wwu.edu

## Abstract

This study explores the use of low-shot prompting techniques for the lemmatization of ancient cuneiform languages using Large Language Models (LLMs). To structure the input data and systematically design effective prompt templates, we employed a hierarchical clustering approach based on Levenshtein distance The prompt design followed established engineering patterns, incorporating instructional and response-guiding elements to enhance model comprehension. We employed the In-Context Learning (ICL) prompting strategy, selecting example words primarily based on lemma frequency, ensuring a balance between commonly occurring words and rare cases to improve generalization. During testing on the development set, prompts included structured examples and explicit formatting rules, with accuracy assessed by comparing model predictions to ground truth lemmas. The results showed that model performance varied significantly across different configurations, with accuracy reaching approximately 90% in the best case for in-vocabulary words and around 9% in the best case for out-of-vocabulary (OOV) words. Despite resource constraints and the lack of input from a language expert, oour findings suggest that prompt engineering strategies hold promise for improving LLM performance in cuneiform language lemmatization.

## 1 Introduction

In this work, we explore the feasibility of low-shot prompting as a method to leverage the pre-trained knowledge of Large Language Models (LLMs) for cuneiform lemmatization. Low-shot prompting enables the encoding of linguistic patterns and contextual dependencies directly into the model's input format while requiring only a handful of well-chosen examples for adaptation. This is particularly valuable for low-resource languages, such as cuneiform, where large annotated datasets are scarce.

We investigate how carefully designed prompt templates and example selection strategies impact the performance of low-shot lemmatization. Our structured prompts incorporate clear task instructions and illustrative example pairs to guide the model toward accurate lemma predictions. Example selection follows a frequency-driven approach, ensuring a balance between common and rare cases to enhance generalization. Through this experiment, we evaluate a series of configurations in the low-shot prompting framework and assess the effectiveness of this method in handling this specialized task.

In the following sections, we first provide an overview of the low-shot prompting approach. Then, we describe the system architecture and the process of refining it by optimizing configurations on the development set, followed by a report on the corresponding results. Finally, we discuss the limitations of our approach and conclude with insights and directions for future work.

## 2 Low-Shot Prompting with In-Context Learning

The goal of this system is to leverage low-shot prompting through the In-Context Learning (ICL) strategy. As introduced in [1, 2], ICL enables large-scale language models to learn a task by incorporating only a few examples within the prompt, without requiring addtional fine-tuning.

Our proposed approach consists of two key components: (1) designing properly formatted and meaningful prompts and (2) selecting a small but representative set of examples. Together, these are used to enhance an LLM's ability to lemmatize cuneiform languages.

To optimize prompt effectiveness, we adopted the template-based prompt engineering approach described in [3] as a method shown to get better results when interacting with LLMs, especially Ope-



*Proceedings of the Second Ancient Language Processing Workshop associated with NAACL 2025*, pages 193–197
May 4, 2025. 

nAI models [4].

The template pattern guides the model by specifying both the type of information it should expect and the format in which it should interpret and generate responses. We implemented this approach in several prompts, including prompts 3, 4, 10, and 13. Prompt 3 sets up the template and informs the model what kind of information it can expect to receive. This includes a word to identify and relevant background details. Prompt 4 tells it how to respond, which is with a single word representing the lemma of the word. Prompt 10 utilizes the established format by giving the word we need to identify and declaring its correct lemma.

Other template prompts were tasked with providing context alongside prompting or during ICL. For example, Prompt 13 was used to include the provided example sentences before asking for each lemma. We observed that dropping the example sentence led to a decrease in accuracy. In all cases we aimed to form our prompts to be specific and concise so that there was no ambiguity to confuse the model. Appendix A lists the set of prompts that we created for use in this task.

The second part of the prompting low-shot model method is selecting meaningful examples to train the model on. Our implementation focused mainly on the frequency of the lemmas in the process of choosing examples. Selecting a set of frequently occurring lemmas seeks to build context with common lemma recognition. Selecting a set of infrequently occurring lemmas seeks to add diverse examples to the model's context window, with the purpose of better understanding latent grammar rules that make up the outer clusters.

## 3 System Description

The data provided at the beginning of the task was used to create a hashmap of lemmas associated with their clean values. This map of unique lemmas was split into 80-20 partitions. The training set was the larger partition and was used to select examples of lemmas with their clean values to build context while the smaller partition was used to assess the lemmatization accuracy of clean values.

During the ICL process, batches were created by sorting the data by properties such as the total number of occurrences of the lemma. This method of selecting examples on which to build our model's context window allowed us to focus on common words while diversifying our example set so that the model does not become biased. Batch sizes ranged from 4 to 30 lemmas, with batch counts ranging from 2 to 24. Clean values per lemma ranged from 1 to all per lemma. The distribution of lemmas within the batches also varied, including distributions using more infrequently occurring lemmas than frequent ones, where lemmas from specific languages were selected for or ignored, and where sorting by occurrences pertained to the frequency of the clean value rather than the lemma.

During ICL, each clean value in the batch could be sent as a statement and/or question. Statement prompts were sent to the model in the format "[L] is the lemma of [CV]" where a lemma and clean value replaced the [L] and [CV] tokens. Question prompts were in the format "What is the lemma of [CV]?" which would require an answer from the model. We collected data on our ICL accuracy by evaluating the accuracy of the responses given to these question prompts.

This feature was implemented after we noticed a pattern during ICL, in which our accuracy when asking the lemma of each clean value would start low and climb as our model was being trained. It would peak about three-quarters of the way through and then begin to decrease. Thinking that we were likely seeing overfitting, we began to alternate between sending statement prompts and question prompts within the ICL section, a process shown to reduce overfitting. This resulted in improvements in our performance.

## 4 Refining the System Using the Dev Set

To refine the system, we ran our pipeline and performed error analysis on the dev set. The factors we implemented during this stage included variations in prompt wording, alternating between prompts stating rules and prompts asking questions, positive/negative reinforcement, and using mask tokens to note spaces in the example sentences that were missing words.

Positive reinforcement meant sending a prompt indicating that the model's prediction was correct, while negative reinforcement meant sending a prompt indicating that it was incorrect. Tests with positive reinforcement did not result in increased mean accuracy, but implementing negative reinforcement was effective in the general form seen in prompt 14. After some error analysis, we tried to take it a step further by implementing var-

| Batch Properties | | | | | | | Features | | | Reinforcement | | | | Acc. | |
|---|---|---|---|---|---|---|---|---|---|---|---|---|---|---|---|
| Size | Count | | | | Q. | Stmt | Sentence | | Lang. | Neg. | | | Pos. | inv | oov |
| | H. | L. | M. | R. | | | Mask | No M. | | G | S | C | | | |
| 15 | 1 | 2 | | | X | X | | X | | X | | | | 89.82 | 6.26 |
| 30 | 1 | 2 | | | X | X | | X | | X | | | | 90.78 | 8.09 |
| 10 | 3 | 1 | 2 | | X | X | X | | X | X | | | | 84.24 | 6.47 |
| 5 | 7 | 1 | 2 | 2 | X | X | X | | X | X | | | | 83.81 | 6.40 |
| 4 | 8 | 12 | | | X | X | | X | | X | | | | 53.84 | 7.56 |
| 4 | 4 | 6 | | | X | X | | X | | X | | | | 50.46 | 6.57 |
| 4 | 16 | 12 | | | X | X | X | | | X | | | | 63.91 | 9.42 |
| 4 | 16 | 12 | | | X | X | X | | | X | X | X | | 47.12 | 4.01 |
| 4 | 16 | 12 | | | X | X | X | | | X | X | X | X | 43.47 | 1.91 |

Table 1: Accuracy represents mean accuracy from 2 tests per test configuration (except for the highlighted test, which was tested 4 times). "inv" refers to "in vocabulary" and "oov" refers to the accuracy with batches of 30 randomly selected lemmas from the dev set. The highlighted test resulted in the highest scores, and its parameters were used for final testing. High frequency: total appearances > 100; Medium frequency: 50 <= total appearances <= 100; Low frequency: total appearances < 50. Mask refers to mask tokens [MASK] used in place of missing words in example sentences. Abbreviations used: Rand (random lemmas not sorted by frequency), Lang. (language), G (generic negative reinforcement prompts), S (small correction negative reinforcement prompts), C (common mistake negative reinforcement prompts), Q (Question), Stmt (Statement), H. (High), L (Low), M (Medium), and R (Random).

ious degrees of negative reinforcement feedback. This included 'small' corrections, which sent an additional negative response telling the model its answer was close in order to address the common case in which the lemma was mostly accurate but a few letters off (see prompt 15). Commonly mistaken lemmas were addressed by keeping track of how often an incorrect lemma was guessed within each section of clean values within a given lemma and prompting it to avoid making those guesses (see prompt 16). Both of these options seemed promising but ultimately caused worse results, so they were discarded before final testing began.

We used the data from the dev set to test the accuracy of our model post-learning. Batches were created using the dev set. Each clean value associated with a lemma was passed through, with only Prompt 11 alongside background information prompts being used. The responses were collected and evaluated to get our output accuracies.

Table 1 visualizes the various strategies we used to filter and order the data in the batch-formation process ('Batch Properties' section) as well as some features we implemented through prompt engineering ('Features' and 'Reinforcement') and the resulting accuracies we obtained in the tests. Each accuracy is computed by averaging accuracies from two tests (with the exception of the highlighted test). All tests in the table are ran on OpenAI's ChatGPT-4 Mini model.

To create our submission, we ran the pipeline on the test data using the batch parameters that had the best results when testing on the dev set.

## 5 Results

Our results take the form of accuracies representing the portion of words that the model was accurately able to lemmatize. These values are shown in Table 1 as mean accuracies, with each test being run twice. The exception is the highlighted test. It was our highest scoring test, and was tested four times instead to confirm its performance before final testing.

The table displays two mean accuracies: the in-vocab word accuracy (inv) and the dev set accuracy (oov). The proposed lemmas suggested during the ICL process were used to calculate the T accuracy, which represented the percentage of guesses that matched the actual lemma of the clean value the model was to lemmatize. For each lemma in the first four tests seen in the table during training, ICL involved providing both a statement and question prompt of each lemma and its clean value alongside background information; the statements were all provided first followed by questions. For lemmas in the later tests, batches alternated between only questions and only statements. In these tests, batches where questions were used were repeated once with the same question. Repeating questions allowed us to perform negative reinforcement through small mistake and common mistake corrections if needed.

This explains why the inv accuracy varied among tests. The Dev accuracy came from question batches only, which were made of clean values and lemmas from the dev set. Because we partitioned the dataset with no collision of lemmas, this meant that the dev set was entirely composed of out-of-vocabulary terms, which the model had not yet seen. Thus the results we attained in this step are based on proposed lemmas created using the clustering algorithm on clean values whose lemmas have not yet been declared to the model.

The performance of our model varied greatly between tests, which is an indicator that there is more work that can be done here. Despite the low accuracy, our work on this task showed how different data analysis and prompt engineering strategies can improve LLM performance. For example, our tests demonstrated that performance dropped when the example sentences were not included, and increased when telling the model its answers were incorrect or alternating between sending statement and question prompts.

## 6 Resource Limitations

In the process of ICL and performing error analysis, we ran into several limitations. This included time constraints as well as not having access to a language expert to answer language-specific questions. An expert's guidance could lead to the realization of relevant features and context not implemented in our project. The biggest issue we ran into was pricing of various models. Our configurations display results from ChatGPT-4 Mini, but we also ran tests on OpenAI's ChatGPT-4, Anthropic's Claude 3.5 Sonnet, and DeepSeek's DeepSeek Chat. Our best results came from running tests with the Claude 3.5 Sonnet model, but this also ended up being the most expensive option. Since our final testing would need to send a large amount of tokens, Claude required resources beyond those allocated for this task.

## 7 Conclusions and Future Work

Our team began this task with the goal of applying low-shot learning techniques and theories to the lemmatization of cuneiform languages. The success in this project comes from the support of those theories in our results. Positive reinforcement proved ineffective at increasing accuracy while negative reinforcement, relevant context, and a balance of explicit rules and testing the model during ICL was effective at increasing accuracy. The highest accuracy configuration, along with template prompting, demonstrates these findings. Accuracy could increase under the same configuration applied to different AI models such as Claude 3.5 Sonnet or OpenAI's GPT-4 as well as with relevant context provided by a language expert to implement into our prompts and pipeline.

With a better understanding of the lemmatization task and obstacles encountered, we would like to acquire the necessary funding to run more tests using the Claude 3.5 Sonnet model. Additionally, we would like to implement other features that we predict would increase accuracy as well.

Reflection prompts represent a form of chain-of-thought prompting, which would encourage the model to state its 'reasoning' for the response it gave. This would demonstrate its ability to extract lemmatization rules from latent space, hidden features, that are present but cannot be directly observed in the data. With this technique, we could implement another layer of positive and negative reinforcement that addresses chain-of-thought prompting [5]. This would likely allow us to improve accuracy by supporting the formation of outer clusters in the model's hierarchal clustering of cuneiform language grammar rules. The model can then apply these rules to new and untested clean values in order to more accurately determine their lemmas.

Another idea we want to implement is soft prompting where the model is trained on prompts produced by other LLMs based on clean values and other features. This application could lead to better prompts that convey the data to the model without the possibility of human error. Soft prompting has not been tested in this context and could lead to higher accuracy compared to human-produced prompts [6].

## A Appendix

### A.1 Prompts

| Rule | ID | Prompt |
|---|---|---|
| I | 1 | The following is a conversation between two Akkadian language experts. One guesses the lemma of a provided clean value while the other indicates whether they are correct or not. Using your knowledge of linguistic analysis and the information shared in this conversation, you will perform the task of identifying the lemmas of words from Akkadian. |
| I | 2 | A lemma is defined as the root form of a word without conjugation. Also known as one that would be listed in a dictionary entry for the word. |
| I | 3 | You will be given the word which you need to identify. Sometimes you will be given contextual information such as the language the word is found in as well as an example of its use in a sentence. |
| I | 4 | Return a single word without explanation nor formatting when asked for the lemma of a word. |
| RP | 10 | The lemma of [P] is [P]. |
| EP | 11 | What is the lemma of [P]? |
| RP | 12 | This word is found in the language of [P]. |
| RP | 13 | An example sentence using this word is [P]. |
| NC | 14 | Your guess is incorrect. The lemma of [P] is [P]. |
| NC | 15 | The correct lemma is slightly different. |
| NC | 16 | When given words whose lemma is [P], you commonly guess the lemma [P] instead. |
| PC | 17 | Your guess is correct. |

### A.2 Prompt Rules

| Purpose | Symbol | Description |
|---|---|---|
| Param | [P] | Establishes a field that requires input |
| Instruct | I | Gives instructions to the LLM |
| Training | RP | Instills rules to the LLM via ICL |
| PosConf | PC | Sends positive reinforcement |
| NegConf | NC | Sends negative reinforcement |
| Testing | EP | Asks the LLM to perform a task |

## References


[1] Tom Brown, Benjamin Mann, Nick Ryder, Melanie Subbiah, Jared Kaplan, Prafulla Dhariwal, Arvind Neelakantan, Pranav Shyam, Girish Sastry, Amanda Askell, et al. Language models are few-shot learners. *Advances in Neural Information Processing Systems (NeurIPS)*, 33:1877–1901, 2020.

[2] Pengfei Liu, Weizhe Yuan, Jinlan Fu, Zhengbao Jiang, Hiroaki Hayashi, and Graham Neubig. Pre-train prompt predict: A systematic survey of prompting methods in natural language processing. *ACM Computing Surveys*, 55(9):1–35, 2023.

[3] Jules White, Quchen Fu, Sam Hays, Michael Sandborn, Carlos Olea, Henry Gilbert, Ashraf Elnashar, Jesse Spencer-Smith, and Douglas C. Schmidt. A prompt pattern catalog to enhance prompt engineering with chatgpt, 2023.

[4] OpenAI. Gpt-4 technical report. *arXiv preprint arXiv:2303.08774*, 2023. Accessed: March 2025.

[5] Jason Wei, Xuezhi Wang, Dale Schuurmans, Maarten Bosma, Brian Ichter, Fei Xia, Ed Chi, Quoc Le, and Denny Zhou. Chain-of-thought prompting elicits reasoning in large language models, 2023.

[6] Adrian Bulat and Georgios Tzimiropoulos. Language-aware soft prompting: Text-to-text optimization for few-and zero-shot adaptation of v &l models. *International Journal of Computer Vision*, 132(4):1108–1125, 2024.

# From Clay to Code: Transforming Hittite Texts for Machine Learning

**Emma Yavasan** and **Shai Gordin**
Ariel University, Dept. of Land of Israel and Archaeology, Ariel, Israel
emma.yavasan@msmail.ariel.ac.il, shaigo@ariel.ac.il

## Abstract

This paper presents a comprehensive methodology for transforming XML-encoded Hittite cuneiform texts into computationally accessible formats for machine learning applications. Drawing from a corpus of 8,898 texts (558,349 tokens in total) encompassing 145 cataloged genres and compositions, we develop a structured approach to preserve both linguistic and philological annotations while enabling computational analysis. Our methodology addresses key challenges in ancient language processing, including the handling of fragmentary texts, multiple language layers, and complex annotation systems. We demonstrate the application of our corpus through experiments with T5 models, achieving significant improvements in Hittite-to-German translation (ROUGE-1: 0.895) while identifying limitations in morphological glossing tasks. This work establishes a standardized, machine-readable dataset in Hittite cuneiform, which also maintains a balance with philological accuracy and current state-of-the-art.

## 1 Introduction

This paper builds on the advancements in corpus technologies and computational linguistics, contributing to the evolution of corpus linguistics for Hittite studies, making Hittite cuneiform texts accessible for data analysis and machine learning. A corpus-based approach in the area of Ancient Language Processing (ALP) is used to create a dataset of Hittite documents converted primarily into CSV format, with plans to extend to additional formats such as JSON and YAML in future releases.

Hittite is the oldest attested Indo-European language of the Anatolian family written in cuneiform script from the 17$^{th}$ to the 12$^{th}$ centuries BCE. All Hittite documents have been structured according to content and genre in the *Catalogue des textes hittites* (CTH) by Laroche, updated in the digital CTH (see Fig. 1).[1] A more practical way to classify Hittite documents is suggested by van den Hout (2008) who divided the Hittite documents into "prescriptive" (copied over a period of several generations, having a long-term purpose) and "descriptive" (mostly daily economic and administrative texts) categories. This approach, however, is not a formalized one, and there are many exceptions in both groups (van den Hout, 2002; Gordin, 2015).

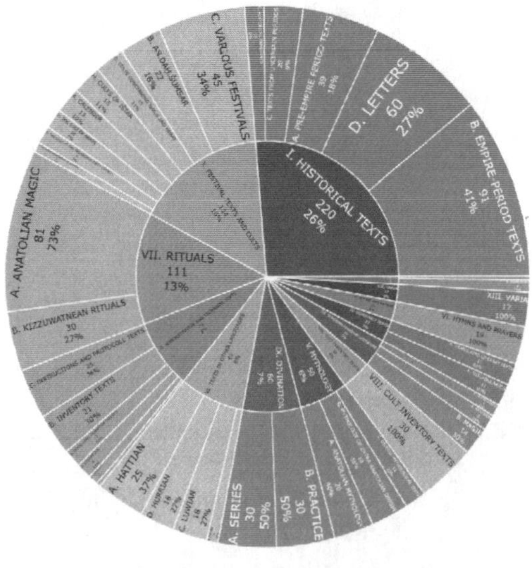


Figure 1: Distribution of texts in CTH

The main digital resource for Hittite is The *Hethitologie Portal Mainz* (HPM), which uses XML mark-up for raw text edition files. By the end of 2024, digital editions of state treaties, laws, myths, prayers, magic rituals and festivals (partly), cult inventories and some administrative texts (mostly inventories) have been published there. Additionally, a searchable annotated ritual and festival corpus of raw transliterations of Hittite documents (**not**

[1] Originally published by Emanuelle Laroche in 1972, this resource has been adopted and updated as part of the CTH online: S. Košak – G.G.W. Müller – S. Görke – Ch.W. Steitler, hethiter.net/: CTH (2025-01-28).



*Proceedings of the Second Ancient Language Processing Workshop associated with NAACL 2025*, pages 198–207
May 4, 2025. 

based on published editions) has been released in 2023 under the *Corpus der Hethitischen Festrituale* (HFR), and in 2024 the *Thesaurus Linguarum Hethaeorum digitalis* (TLH$^{dig}$) was released, which aims to cover eventually the entire known Hittite text corpus. These are the main sources of data for our research (see Acknowledgments).

Corpus linguistics evolved in the early aughts from a narrow methodology primarily concerned with the digitization of printed texts into a cornerstone of linguistic research and applications (Lüdeling and Kytö, 2008). This transformation has been driven by advancements in digital technologies: corpus-derived models use such methods as the fine-tuning of large language models (LLMs) for specific linguistic tasks. This paper aims at creating a dataset for the development of a Hittite corpus, transforming the existing annotated XML data into formats specifically optimized for machine learning applications.

## 2 Background

Research into ancient Near Eastern languages, particularly Hittite, faces unique challenges due to the nature of the source materials. Unlike modern languages, which benefit from vast, well-documented corpora, Hittite studies contend with limited digital resources designed specifically for computational analysis. So far, to our knowledge, two approaches to corpus studies of Hittite have been pursued since 2014: *Goottite* (Digital search of Hittite texts) by D. Frantikova and *Hittitecorpus* (Annotated Corpus of Hittite Clauses) by M. Molina. Both were developed with specific research objectives in mind that differ substantially from our current approach. While these resources allow contextual searches within their text collections, neither was designed to function as a comprehensive, computationally accessible corpus.

The *Hethitologie Portal Mainz* (HPM) represents the most extensive digital resource for Hittite, with richly annotated XML texts primarily optimized for philological accuracy and scholarly reference. However, HPM's complex XML structure, while excellent for digital editions, presents significant challenges for systematic computational processing or machine learning applications. The critical limitation across all these existing resources is that none provides a standardized, machine-readable dataset that researchers can readily extract, manipulate, and process at scale. This represents the fundamental advancement of our approach—transforming philologically rich but computationally challenging materials into structured formats that preserve scholarly annotations while enabling corpus-wide linguistic analysis and computational methods.

Using HPM corpora XML-marked-up material, we are planning to cover a much bigger amount of documents, as well as propose automated parsing and annotation of Hittite texts, taking as a first approach the dataset previously created for fine-tuning a German T5 model for the tasks of glossing and machine translation (Yavasan and Gordin, 2024).

The first problem that emerged in the creation of our Hittite corpus is the convertibility of the annotated data. We worked directly with XML files from TLH$^{dig}$ that incorporate SimTex conventions within their structure[2]. These files are traditionally dense with philological remarks and notations as an addition to grammatical information.

Another significant question is the way to represent all different languages contained in every Hittite document. Traditionally, transliterated texts in Hittite use three types of formatting: italic small caps, italic capital letters, and normal capital letters for Hittite words, Akkadian and Sumerian logograms, accordingly; unfortunately, this textual approach cannot be easily supported in the corpus that makes focus on linguistic analysis rather than on philologically rich digital editions.

There is also the problem of fragmented, often damaged, primary texts (see Fig. 2).

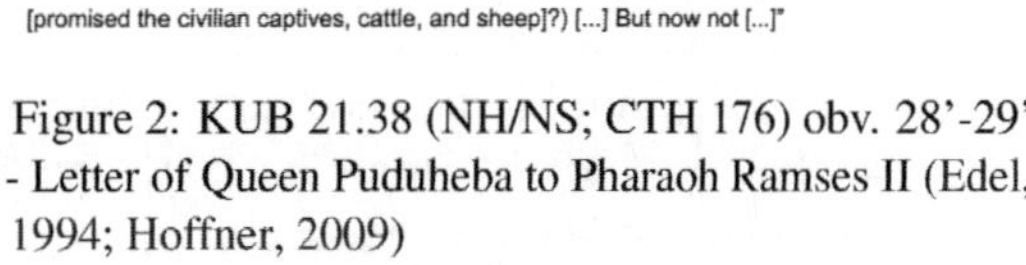

Obv. 28': mān=ta mān DUMU.MUNUS=pat *ŪL* kuwapi peḫḫun mān=ta [...]

Probable reconstruction in the lacuna (Edel 1994; Hoffner 2009: 284):
[NAM.RA.MEŠ GU$_{4}$.ḪI.A UDU.ḪI.A memaḫḫun]

Obv. 29': [.......................................................] **kinun=ma *ŪL*** [...]

"(If I had not at any time (sincerely) given my own daughter to you, would I have you [promised the civilian captives, cattle, and sheep]?) [...] But now not [...]"

Figure 2: KUB 21.38 (NH/NS; CTH 176) obv. 28'-29' - Letter of Queen Puduheba to Pharaoh Ramses II (Edel, 1994; Hoffner, 2009)

Several scholars have proposed solutions for dealing with fragmented texts (Zemánek, 2007; Inglese, 2016; Molina, 2016; Molina and Molin,

[2]For the SimTex format description, see HPM Guide.

2016). In our approach to the Universal Dependencies (UD) treebank, we previously proposed a syntactic annotation method in which every fragmented block is treated as dependent on a verb and marked as FRGM (Yavasan and Molina, 2024). However, this approach introduces ambiguity in the linguistic analysis of Hittite syntax. Therefore, outside the dependency grammar framework, we need to identify an alternative solution that preserves the integrity of the information.

## 3 Methodology & Implementation

### 3.1 Data Sources and XML Encoding

For this research we chose to create a dataset out of a subset available to us from the existing repository of annotated texts, called *Thesaurus Linguarum Hethaeorum digitalis* (TLH$^{dig}$). It is an open-access digital repository that provides structured linguistic and philological annotations in XML format for Hittite cuneiform manuscripts. The data within TLH$^{dig}$ ensures a precise representation of the original inscriptions and at the same time preserves information critical for scholarly research. Note, however, that it does not faithfully represent published text editions.

The dataset chosen for the transformation consists of 8,898 XML files, each corresponding to a unique text ID, and encompasses 145 CTH entries (see Fig. 3). The majority of the texts belong to ritual and festival genres, which are the most represented, accounting for 115 entries (107 entries under festival and cultic texts, 8 entries under rituals). This includes such texts as the Kizzuwatna rituals and seasonal festivals, with other genres significantly less represented. Foreign-language texts in Hattic, Hurrian, Luwian, and Palaic account for 24 entries, while cult inventories, administrative texts, mythology, and divination are represented by 1 entry each. Additionally, miscellaneous texts are categorized under Varia comprising 2 entries. These files serve as the raw material for transformation, requiring extensive processing to extract and structure the information for further linguistic, philological, and computational analysis, including applications in machine learning and deep learning.

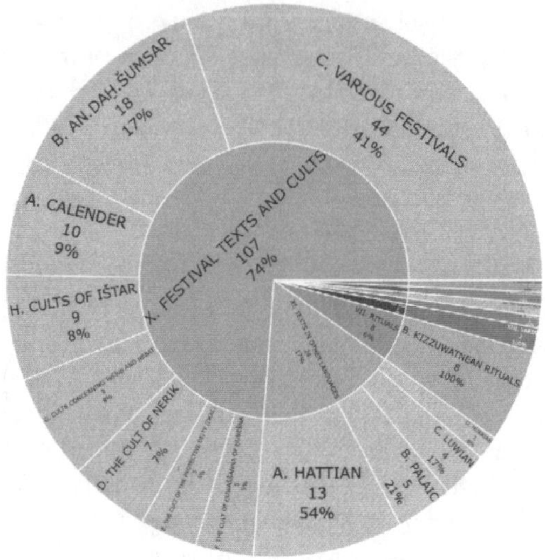


Figure 3: Distribution of texts in the dataset

The XML format captures multiple layers of information essential for Hittitological studies. Both transliteration and transcription (also known as normalization in the literature) are included, allowing for a comprehensive analysis of the texts. About 50% of the texts are glossed, while 16% are completely broken, making glossing impossible. Of the glossed texts, 15% (8% of the total dataset) have been manually validated. Instead, a large number of morphological glossing possibilities has been generated through a rule-based system (Rieken, 2021). These glossing possibilities include multiple grammatical interpretations for individual words, often structured in a format where different cases, numbers, and forms are suggested (see Fig. 4). This variation is a direct consequence of the ambiguities inherent in cuneiform writing, where the same sign can represent multiple sounds or words depending on context (Weeden, 2011). The lack of explicit vowel notation and the polyvalence of signs require multiple possible readings to be considered in the glossing process.

This challenge of multiple possible interpretations and the need for disambiguation is precisely what led us to consider glossing as a task for LLM fine-tuning. Given that traditional rule-based approaches generate numerous possibilities but lack contextual decision-making capabilities, a large language model (LLM) fine-tuned on Hittite data could assist in predicting the most probable gloss based on broader linguistic patterns. By leveraging machine learning, we aim to improve the efficiency of annotation and enhance consistency in glossing, addressing the inherent uncertainties in cuneiform interpretation and at the same time incorporating philological insights.

```
⌜LUGAL⌝-uš {'lg': 'Hit',
'mrp1': 'LUGAL=u-@König@{ a → FNL(u).NOM.SG.C} { b → ACC.PL.C}@28.3.1.1@',
'mrp2': 'LUGAL=ma-@Šarrumma@{ a → DN.STF} { b → DN.HURR.ABS}@36.1.1 += uš@PPRO.3PL.C.ACC@@D',
'mrp3': 'LUGAL=ma-@Šarrumma@{ a → DN.STF} { b → DN.HURR.ABS}@36.1.1 += uš@PPRO.3PL.C.ACC@@D',
'mrp4': 'LUGAL=u-@König@{ a → NOM.SG(UNM)} { b → ACC.SG(UNM)} { c → NOM.PL(UNM)}
{ d → ACC.PL(UNM)} { e → GEN.SG(UNM)} { f → GEN.PL(UNM)} { g → D/L.SG(UNM)}
{ h → D/L.PL(UNM)} { i → ALL(UNM)} { j → ABL(UNM)} { k → INS(UNM)}
{ l → VOC.SG(UNM)} { m → VOC.PL(UNM)}@28.3.1.1 += uš@PPRO.3PL.C.ACC@@'}

da-⌜a-i⌝ {'lg': 'Hit',
'mrp1': 'dā-/d-@nehmen@3SG.PRS@II.2@',
'mrp2': 't=aye/a-@stehlen@2SG.IMP@I.7.5@',
'mrp3': 'dai-/te-/ti(ya)-@setzen@{ a → 3SG.PRS} { b → 2SG.IMP}@II.6.1@',
'mrp4': '@()@@HURR@'}

GA⌝.KIN.AG {'lg': 'Hit',
'mrp1': 'GA.KIN.AG=@Käse@{ a → NOM.SG(UNM)} { b → ACC.SG(UNM)} { c → NOM.PL(UNM)}
{ d → ACC.PL(UNM)} { e → GEN.SG(UNM)} { f → GEN.PL(UNM)} { g → D/L.SG(UNM)}
{ h → D/L.PL(UNM)} { i → ALL(UNM)} { j → ABL(UNM)} { k → INS(UNM)}
{ l → VOC.SG(UNM)} { m → VOC.PL(UNM)}@29.1.1@'}

ḪUR.SAG-n]i {'lg': 'Hur',
'mrp1': '① ḪUR.SAG@Bild eines Berges@FNL(n).D/L.SG@28.14.2@',
'mrp2': '① ḪUR.SAG-n=i-@Berg@{ a → FNL(-i).HURR.ABS.SG} { b → STF}@30.10.4.1@'}

[{LÚ}S]ANGA {'lg': 'Hit',
'mrp1': 'SANGA=@ Priester @ { a → NOM.SG(UNM)} { b → ACC.SG(UNM)} { c → NOM.PL(UNM)}
{ d → ACC.PL(UNM)} { e → GEN.SG(UNM)} { f → GEN.PL(UNM)} { g → D/L.SG(UNM)}
{ h → D/L.PL(UNM)} { i → ALL(UNM)} { j → ABL(UNM)} { k → INS(UNM)} { l → VOC.SG(UNM)}
{ m → VOC.PL(UNM)} @ 28.1.1 @ (LÚ)',
'mrp2': 'SANGA=@ Priester @ { a → NOM.SG(UNM)} { b → ACC.SG(UNM)} { c → NOM.PL(UNM)}
{ d → ACC.PL(UNM)} { e → GEN.SG(UNM)} { f → GEN.PL(UNM)} { g → D/L.SG(UNM)}
{ h → D/L.PL(UNM)} { i → ALL(UNM)} { j → ABL(UNM)} { k → INS(UNM)} { l → VOC.SG(UNM)}
{ m → VOC.PL(UNM)} @ 28.2.1.1 @ (LÚ)',
'mrp3': 'SANGA=@ Priester @ { a → NOM.SG(UNM)} { b → ACC.SG(UNM)} { c → NOM.PL(UNM)}
{ d → ACC.PL(UNM)} { e → GEN.SG(UNM)} { f → GEN.PL(UNM)} { g → D/L.SG(UNM)}
{ h → D/L.PL(UNM)} { i → ALL(UNM)} { j → ABL(UNM)} { k → INS(UNM)}
{ l → VOC.SG(UNM)} { m → VOC.PL(UNM)} @ 28.1.1.1 @ (LÚ)'}
```

Figure 4: A word-by-word annotation of a Hittite text made by a rule-based algorithm

Besides linguistic glossing, the XML data also encodes a range of philological annotations that provide critical context for text interpretation. Elements such as Sumerian and Akkadian logograms are explicitly marked, preserving distinctions between phonetic and logographic writing. Additional annotations track features such as scribal corrections, erasures, and textual additions, including elements that were likely intended by the scribe but are missing, as well as those that appear in the text but may not belong based on scholarly evaluation. These details are crucial for reconstructing the original meaning of the texts, reflecting both the complexities of the writing system and the interpretative challenges faced by modern researchers.

Additionally, the morphological glossing contains references to Hoffner and Melchert (2024), which is the most up-to-date Hittite reference grammar. Annotations often include language identifiers such as Hittite, Hattian, Hurrian, Luwian, and Palaic, along with a set of grammatical possibilities for each term. An additional field is included where one or more glossing options are marked as preferable. In cases where only one option is selected, it is typically human-verified, but for a portion of the material, selections have been made automatically without direct manual confirmation.

XML provides a structured and detailed encoding format, yet, it is not always suitable for computational analysis. Many statistical and corpus-based research methods require a tabular structure, such as CSV, to efficiently process and compare large datasets. Transforming XML into CSV allows for easier searching, filtering, and querying of linguistic features and at the same time makes the data more accessible for machine learning models and text analysis tools. The structured format also facilitates cross-document comparisons, ensuring that the rich philological and linguistic information in TLH$^{dig}$ can be efficiently analyzed and used by other researchers, both in computer and data science, as well as ancient language scholars.

### 3.2 Reframing Text and Annotation

The transformation of XML-encoded Hittite texts required careful consideration of both segmentation practices and annotation preservation. Unlike modern languages, Hittite cuneiform is commonly written on clay tablets[3] and lacks sentence level punctuation, which requires setting up additional algorithms for sentence boundaries mark-up. According to standards in the field, our dataset is primarily segmented at the cuneiform tablet line level, rather than the sentence or clause level. While some genres and text types contain explicit clause divisions (e.g. rituals and festivals), many do not, making line-based segmentation the most consistent and practical approach (Gordin, 2015). Additionally, the fragmentary nature of many sources further complicates sentence segmentation, because missing portions often obscure syntactic structure at the sentence level.

Although the source dataset is organized around line divisions, the transformation process ultimately operates at the word level. We extract and process individual words from the XML structure, so that each token retains its full set of grammatical, lexical, and philological annotations. At the same time, we preserve metadata from the original line structure, including line numbers, obverse and reverse distinctions (Vs./Rs. in the German annotation, or obv./rev. in the English one), and other positional markers, allowing for alignment with the

[3]While clay tablets were the primary medium for Hittite cuneiform writing, several other materials were also used. Of special importance were metal tablets, particularly bronze (exemplified by the unique Bronze Tablet containing the treaty between Tudhaliya IV and Kuruntiya, Bo 86/99), where wedges were incised rather than impressed. Stone was used for monumental inscriptions in Hieroglyphic Luwian, and wooden writing boards played a significant role in Hittite administration, economy, and cult practices, though few examples survive due to their perishable nature (Cammarosano, 2024).

manuscript layout.

The transformation process was designed to maintain a clean primary text representation while storing all linguistic and philological annotations as additional structured fields. Initially, we assumed that achieving both readability and full annotation retention would require compromises. However, as the transformation progressed, it became evident that all linguistic and philological annotations could be preserved as additional fields. This method yields a structured format, in which the core text remains readable, and every nuance documented in the original annotations is retained.

The processed text uses Hittite transcription conventions, including broken marks, determinatives, and other editorial notations for scribal practices, complying with HPM standards. Meanwhile, all philological and linguistic metadata—such as glossing, language identification, restorations, erasures, uncertain readings, *mater lectionis*, and editorial comments—are preserved separately in structured fields. This approach, which is the key methodological insight of this paper, enables researchers to work both with the text without annotations and with its full scholarly annotations, ensuring that no interpretative detail is lost.

### 3.3 Data Processing and Transformation

The transformation of XML-encoded Hittite texts into a structured tabular format follows a multi-step pipeline designed to extract, normalize, and organize linguistic and philological data. This process was implemented using Python, utilizing lxml for XML parsing (Shipman, 2014), pandas for data handling, and regular expressions (re) for text cleaning and refinement.

Each XML file was processed to extract and structure relevant linguistic and philological information. Using lxml's XPath functionality, the script identified line markers to track text segmentation, tokenized words with all their attributes. Additionally, it distinguished between different language layers, identifying content in Hittite, Akkadian, Sumerian, Hurrian, Luwian, Palaic, and Hattic. Once extracted, the data was mapped to a structured format, preparing it for subsequent normalization, parsing, and computational analysis.

As for the annotations directly within the text, they were preserved as independent fields. This step helps maintain that each annotation type was correctly mapped. The structured parsing of linguistic and philological data served as the foundation for normalization.

An essential part of our approach was to expand the annotation structure by introducing additional fields that retained philological and linguistic information separately from the core text. These fields included annotations for subscript markings, *matres lectionis*, numerical markers, sign-based annotations, corrections, erased text, editorial insertions, *rasura* and uncertain *rasura*, missing text markers, editorial comments, and references to other texts or glossaries (see example in Figs. 5 and 6).

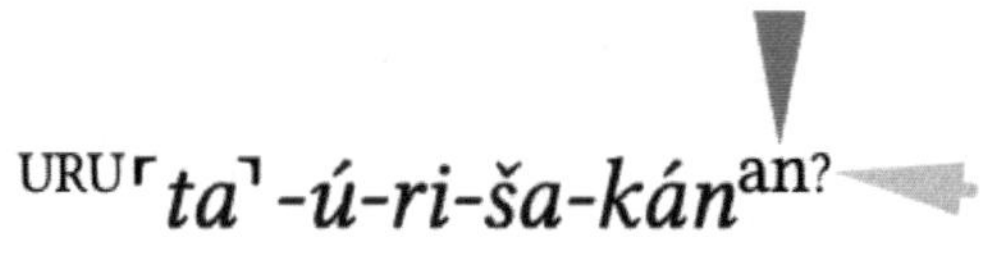


Figure 5: KBo 51.127+ (CTH 615) (Frg. 1+2) Rs.? III 7'/3'

Figure 6: An example of a word's annotation as represented in XML and in CSV.

Since the XML format includes glossing generated by a rule-based algorithm, producing up to 40 possible glossing variations for a single word, parsing requires identifying and extracting these multiple interpretations. In addition to preserving all algorithmically generated glossing possibilities, the parsing process searched for and isolated the human-validated selection whenever available. This step allowed us to distinguish between computationally generated glosses and those verified by scholars.

In cases where no human-validated gloss was available, the dataset retained all generated possibilities without assigning a default selection, which allowed for future verification and computational processing. We preserved these alternative interpretations specifically to support future research efforts, ensuring that subsequent scholars would have access to the complete range of potential readings rather than being limited by our preliminary assessments.

One of the primary challenges in the parsing process was establishing an optimal parsing sequence to prevent data loss or unintended modification. Due to the complexity of the XML structure, executing transformations in an incorrect order risked removing or altering certain elements before they could be fully extracted.

The final stage of data processing involved the integration of Unicode representations to enhance the dataset's interoperability with computational tools and digital cuneiform research frameworks. Transliteration sequences were systematically mapped to their corresponding cuneiform Unicode characters which allows the use of Unicode in further analysis.

### 3.4 Format selection

The selection of an appropriate data format was a crucial consideration in ensuring both computational accessibility and philological integrity. Given the structured nature of the dataset and its diverse applications, three primary formats were evaluated: CSV, JSON, and YAML. Each format presents distinct advantages depending on the intended mode of analysis and data processing requirements.

The dataset was initially released in CSV format, prioritizing simplicity, interoperability, and compatibility with statistical analysis tools, machine learning frameworks, and database management systems. The tabular structure of CSV facilitates efficient numerical and textual data processing, making it well-suited for corpus-based linguistic research. However, CSV lacks the ability to encode hierarchical relationships, requiring additional strategies to represent nested linguistic annotations.

In contrast, JSON and YAML provide hierarchical and flexible data structures, making them more appropriate for storing multi-layered annotations, glossing alternatives, and complex linguistic metadata. JSON, widely used in computational linguistics and NLP applications, supports structured querying and integration with automated processing pipelines, while YAML offers a human-readable alternative for philological research (Wang, 2022).

CSV was selected as the primary output format for the initial dataset release, future expansions will incorporate JSON for structured annotation storage and YAML for enhanced interpretability in philological studies.

## 4 Analysis and Insights

The processed dataset consists of 558,349 tokens, structured with detailed linguistic and philological annotations. The data was analyzed to assess the distribution of glossed words, the extent of human validation, and the proportion of broken or fragmentary text (see Table 1).

| | Glossed | Validated | Broken |
|---|---|---|---|
| True | 297,095 | 47,908 | 87,782 |
| False | 261,159 | 510,346 | 470,472 |

Table 1: Distribution of glossed, validated, and broken tokens.

Of the total tokens, 297,095 (53.2%) were assigned glosses through rule-based annotation. However, only 47,908 glosses (16.1%) of those annotated received human validation, confirming the need for further refinement in automatic glossing methods. Text integrity analysis showed that 87,782 tokens (15.7%) were identified as broken or fragmentary, limiting their potential for linguistic annotation.

These findings highlight both the strengths and limitations of the dataset, particularly regarding the reliance on rule-based glossing and the importance of human validation in refining automatic annotation strategies. We are, however, postponing enhancing glossing accuracy through machine learning to future research, where manually validated glosses would create a probabilistic glossing model.

The additional philological and linguistic annotations are not as widely represented across the dataset, but are still retained due to their significance for the analysis. Various elements of markup, such as subscript markings, determinatives, corrections, and editorial interventions, appear in relatively small proportions, with some features occurring in only a few thousand or even hundred instances. Despite their lower frequency, these annotations provide critical insights into scribal practices, textual transmission, and linguistic variation.

The presence of so many glossing possibilities for a single word highlights the morphological ambiguity inherent in the corpus. This is particularly evident in polysemous words, homographs, and inflected forms, where multiple interpretations arise due to overlapping grammatical or lexical functions. Despite the extensive output of the rule-based glossing system, only 16.1% of glossed words received

| | txtid | inv_nr | cth_number | lnr | word | text_tags | text | subscr | matlect | num | sign | corr | deleted |
|---|---|---|---|---|---|---|---|---|---|---|---|---|---|
| 215 | KBo 58.129b+ | | 636 | Rs. VI 4′ | QA-TAM-MA | <aGr>QA-<ras_in/>TAM</aGr><corr c="!"/><aGr><ras_fin/>-MA</aGr> | --QA-TAM---MA-- | | | | | TAM<corr c="!"/> | |
| 712 | KUB 32.54+ | Bo 10293 | 628 | r. Kol. 7′ | attaniuina | at-ta-ni-wi<subscr c="i"/>-na | at-ta-ni-wi$_i$-na | <subscr c="i"/> | | | | | |
| 739 | FHL 32 | | 668 | 8′ | tianzi | <ras_in/>ti<ras_fin/>-an-zi | ti-an-zi | | | | | | |
| 1609 | KUB 10.100+ | | 627 | Vs. III 6 | tuḫša | túḫ<materlect c="uḫ"/>-ša | túḫ-ša | | túḫ<materlect c="uḫ"/> | | | | |
| 2467 | Bo 3889 | Bo 3889 | 668 | Rs. 7 | šipanti | ši-pa-a<del_fin/>n-<daes_in/>ti<daes_fin/><corr c="(?)"/> | ši-pa-a]n-⸢ti⸣ | | | | | ⸢ti⸣<corr c="(?)"/> | |

| | added | ras | rasx | gap | note | link | gloss_sel | gloss | translation | lg | unicode | combined |
|---|---|---|---|---|---|---|---|---|---|---|---|---|
| 215 | | <ras_in/>TAM<ras_fin/> | | | | | 1 | ADV | ebenso | Hit | [illegible] | {'lg': 'Hit', 'mrp1': 'QĀTAMMA@ebenso@ADV@@'} |
| 712 | | | | | | | 1 | HURR.RLT.SG.GEN.RLT.PL.ABS | Vater | Hur | [illegible] | {'lg': 'Hur', 'mrp1': 'att=ai-@Vater@HURR.RLT.SG.GEN.RLT.PL.ABS@30.10.1.3@', 'mrp2': 'att=a-@Vater@HURR.RLT.SG.GEN.RLT.PL.ABS@30.10.1.2@'} |
| 739 | | <ras_in/>ti<ras_fin/> | | | | | 1 | 3PL.PRS | setzen | Hit | [illegible] | {'lg': 'Hit', 'mrp1': 'dai-/te-/ti(ya)-@setzen@3PL.PRS@II.6.1@', 'mrp2': 'tiye/a-@treten@3PL.PRS@I.7.2@'} |
| 1609 | | | | | | | 1 | 3SG.PRS.MP | abschneiden | Hit | [illegible] | {'lg': 'Hit', 'mrp1': 'tuḫš=@abschneiden@3SG.PRS.MP@III.1.6@'} |
| 2467 | | | | | | | 1a | 3SG.PRS | libieren | Hit | [illegible] | {'lg': 'Hit', 'mrp1': '① šipant= @ libieren @ { a → 3SG.PRS} { b → 2SG.IMP} @ II.1.3 @ '} |

Figure 7: Example of the final dataset

human validation, underscoring the challenges of automated glossing in cuneiform languages.

With 28,656 unique word forms distributed across 558,349 total tokens, the corpus demonstrates a relatively low type-to-token ratio of 0.051 (5.1%), indicating a high degree of lexical repetition, which is an essential characteristic of many Hittite genres, esp. rituals and festivals. These contain formulaic expressions, specialized terminology, and recurring syntactic structures. The prevalence of frequently repeated words suggests a stable core vocabulary, likely influenced by the standardized nature of the texts.

## 5 First Results and Applications

A preliminary version of the dataset was published on Zenodo under the title *Glossed Hittite Texts with German Translation for Machine Learning* (Yavasan and Gordin, 2024). The complete up-to-date version of the dataset accompanying this paper can be found in the following link (for a full list of CTH entries see Appendix). Figure 7 presents an example of the final dataset structure, showcasing the comprehensive annotation fields that preserve both linguistic and philological information from the original XML sources.

In Yavasan and Gordin (2024), the dataset retains only words with human-verified glosses, with a high degree of reliability for machine learning applications. Each text entry includes linguistic glossing, textual alignment, and German translations, structured to facilitate computational analysis (see Fig. 8). By prioritizing verified annotations, this dataset provides a foundation for morphological processing, syntactic parsing, and translation modeling, supporting further research in digital humanities and historical linguistics.

Our initial attempt at fine-tuning focused on the Hittite glossing task, using the dataset published in Yavasan and Gordin (2024). This dataset provided a reliable subset of manually validated annotations, allowing us to assess whether a T5 model could learn the correspondence between Hittite words and their assigned glosses. However, the results were highly unsatisfactory, as the model failed to generate accurate predictions. Our analysis reveals fundamental limitations in the T5 architecture when applied to morphological glossing of Hittite. The model operates primarily at the token level rather than the morpheme level, creating a significant mismatch with the requirements of morphological analysis. Hittite's rich inflectional system—with its numerous cases, verbal endings, and participle formations—encodes multiple grammatical categories within single words, a complexity that T5 struggles to disentangle accurately. Furthermore, the pre-trained T5 model's exposure to primarily non-inflecting languages creates a substantial transfer gap when confronted with Hittite's synthetic morphology. Upon further investigation, we found that T5 struggles with glossing tasks even in English, suggesting that its architecture is not inherently suited for morphological annotation. This led us to conclude that T5 is not an appropriate model for this type of linguistic prediction.

Following this, we redirected our efforts toward fine-tuning the model for Hittite-to-German translation, using a German version of T5[4]. This model contains approximately 247.5 million parameters, all of which were trainable during our fine-tuning process.

For evaluation, we used the ROUGE metric (Lin, 2004), which measures the overlap between the generated text and the reference text. Specifically, ROUGE-1 measures the overlap of unigrams (single words) as defined in Equation 1, while ROUGE-2 extends this concept to measure the overlap of bigrams (word pairs).

[4]GermanT5/german-t5-oscar-ep1-prompted-germanquad

| txtid | lnr | cth_number | word | translit | gloss | trans_de |
|---|---|---|---|---|---|---|
| IBoT 1.30+ | Vs. 1 | 821 | LUGALuš | ⌜LUGAL⌝-uš | FNL(u).NOM.SG.C | König |
| IBoT 1.30+ | Vs. 1 | 821 | kuapi | ku-wa-pí | CNJ | sobald als |
| IBoT 1.30+ | Vs. 1 | 821 | DINGIRaš | DINGIR{MEŠ}-aš | D/L.PL | Gottheit |
| IBoT 1.30+ | Vs. 1 | 821 | aruaizi | a-ru-wa-a-ez-zi | 3SG.PRS | sich verneigen |
| IBoT 1.30+ | Vs. 1 | 821 | $GUDU_{12}$ | {LÚ}$GUDU_{12}$ | NOM.SG(UNM) | Gesalbter |
| IBoT 1.30+ | Vs. 1 | 821 | kišan | kiš-an | DEMadv | in dieser Weise |

Figure 8: First lines of the published dataset

$$\text{ROUGE-1} = \frac{\sum_{unigram \in \text{Reference}} \text{Count}_{\text{match}}(unigram)}{\sum_{unigram \in \text{Reference}} \text{Count}(unigram)} \quad (1)$$

The original pre-trained model showed very poor results, with ROUGE-1 at 0.0255 and ROUGE-2 at 0.02, indicating that it failed to generate meaningful translations. However, after fine-tuning, the instructed model demonstrated a substantial improvement, achieving **ROUGE-1 at 0.895** and **ROUGE-2 at 0.27**, reflecting a significant gain in translation accuracy.

These results suggest that while T5 was ineffective for glossing, it can be successfully fine-tuned for translation tasks in a structured linguistic dataset. This highlights the importance of task selection in NLP applications for low-resource languages. Future work could explore alternative transformer-based architectures specialized for glossing, such as morphology-aware models, or integrate linguistic priors to improve the accuracy of morphological annotation in Hittite and other ancient languages.

```
Input: ekuzi
Expected translation: trinken
Generated translation: (Gefäß)

Input: QA-TAM-MApat
Expected translation: ebenso
Generated translation: ebenso

Input: DINGIRnana
Expected translation: Gottheit
Generated translation: (Priesterin)
```

Figure 9: Examples of translation by instructed model

## 6 Conclusion

This study has outlined the creation and implementation of a computationally annotated corpus of Hittite texts, leveraging XML-encoded linguistic and philological data for structured analysis. The research contributes to the evolving field of Ancient Language Processing (ALP) by providing a standardized and machine-readable dataset, facilitating advanced linguistic inquiries and computational methodologies for Hittite studies.

Through the transformation of XML-based textual data into structured formats such as CSV, this work ensures accessibility for both traditional philological research and modern computational applications. The challenges inherent to Hittite corpus development—such as the complexity of XML annotations, the representation of multiple linguistic layers, and the integration of fragmented texts—demand a methodological approach that preserves philological accuracy. This transformation from XML to more computationally accessible formats represents not just a technical conversion but an essential paradigm shift for ancient language processing, moving from formats optimized for philological documentation toward those that enable computational analysis at scale.

The study also underscores the limitations of current transformer-based language models, such as T5, for morphological glossing in low-resource ancient languages, highlighting the need for hybrid approaches that integrate rule-based linguistic knowledge with probabilistic modeling.

Certain questions that have not been considered in this paper are postponed for future research. These include: refining syntactic annotation through dependency-based models, improving neural network performance for gloss prediction via fine-tuning on enriched datasets, and expanding the corpus to include a broader range of Hittite textual genres. In this way, the current study provides solid foundation for these tasks.

Our data is available as supplementary information to this paper via the following link.

## 7 Acknowledgments

This work would not have been possible without the constant collaboration of Daniel Schwemer and Gerfrid Müller (JMU Würzburg), who provided early access to the XML files, as well as all the contributors to the HPM projects, whose work allowed us to release this new dataset. All data is made available under a CC BY-SA 4.0.

## References

Michele Cammarosano. 2024. Writing on wood in hittite anatolia. In Marilina Betrò, Michael Friedrich, and Cécile Michel, editors, *The Ancient World Revisited: Material Dimensions of Written Artefacts*, volume 37 of *Studies in Manuscript Cultures*, pages 165–205. De Gruyter, Berlin-Boston.

Elmar Edel. 1994. *Die Ägyptische-hethitische Korrespondenz aus Boghazköi*, volume 2. Westdeutscher Verlag, Opladen.

Shai Gordin. 2015. *Hittite Scribal Circles. Scholarly Tradition and Writing Habits*. StBoT 59. Harrassowitz Verlag, Wiesbaden.

Harry Hoffner. 2009. *Letters from the Hittite Kingdom*. Society of Biblical Literature, Atlanta.

Harry Hoffner and H. Craig Melchert. 2024. *A Grammar of Hittite Language. Part 1. Reference Grammar*. Penn State Press.

Guglielmo Inglese. 2016. Annotating the syntax of fragmentary texts: The case of hittite. Presentation at the Workshop "Formal Representation & Digital Humanities: text, language and tools", University of Verona.

Chin-Yew Lin. 2004. Rouge: A package for automatic evaluation of summaries. In *Text Summarization Branches Out*, pages 74–81, Barcelona, Spain. Association for Computational Linguistics.

Anke Lüdeling and Merja Kytö, editors. 2008. *Corpus Linguistics: An International Handbook*. De Gruyter, Berlin-New York.

Maria Molina. 2016. Syntactic annotation of the hittite corpus: Problems and principles. In *Proceedings of the Workshop on Computational Linguistics and Language Science*, CEUR Workshop Proceedings.

Maria Molina and Alexei Molin. 2016. In a lacuna: Building a syntactically annotated corpus for a dead cuneiform language (on the basis of hittite). In *Proceedings of the International Conference "Dialogue-2016"*.

Elisabeth Rieken. 2021. hethiter.net/: Hfr-annotation (2021-12-31). Online resource.

John W. Shipman. 2014. Python xml processing with lxml. Technical report, New Mexico Tech Computer Center.

Theo van den Hout. 2002. Another view of hittite literature. In S. de Martino and F. Pecchioli Daddi, editors, *Anatolia Antica. Studi in Memoria di Fiorella Imparati*, pages 857–878. Florence.

Theo van den Hout. 2008. A classified past: Classification of knowledge in the hittite empire. In R. D. Biggs, J. Myers, and M. T. Roth, editors, *Proceedings of the 51st Rencontre Assyriologique Internationale held at the Oriental Institute of the University of Chicago, July 18-22, 2005*, pages 211–219. Chicago.

Blair Wang. 2022. Programming for qualitative data analysis: Towards a yaml workflow. *ACIS 2022 Proceedings*.

Mark Weeden. 2011. *Hittite Logograms and Hittite Scholarship*. StBoT 54. Harrassowitz Verlag, Wiesbaden.

Emma Yavasan and Shai Gordin. 2024. Glossed hittite texts with german translation for machine learning. Zenodo.

Emma Yavasan and Maria Molina. 2024. Universal dependencies for the queen puduheba. Presentation at Digital Humanities and Social Sciences (DHSS) in Israel, Tel Aviv University.

Petr Zemánek. 2007. A treebank of ugaritic. annotating fragmentary attested languages. In *Proceedings of the Sixth International Workshop on Treebanks and Linguistic Theories*, NEATL, pages 212–218, Bergen.

## Appendix: List of CTH entries in the newly released dataset

See Fig. 10

| topic | category | cth_list | cth_count | txt_count | total_word_count |
|---|---|---|---|---|---|
| II. ADMINISTRATIVE AND TECHNICAL TEXTS | B. INVENTORY TEXTS | CTH 231 Lists of administrators (LÚAGRIG) | 1 | 2 | 188 |
| IX. DIVINATION | B. PRACTICE | CTH 581 Letters about oracles | 1 | 1 | 86 |
| V. MYTHOLOGY | A. ANATOLIAN MYTHOLOGY | CTH 330 Ritual for the Storm-god of Kuliwišna | 1 | 45 | 5781 |
| VII. RITUALS | B. KIZZUWATNEAN RITUALS | CTH 475 Ritual of Palliya, king of Kizzuwatna, CTH 479 Ritual of Kizzuwatna, CTH 480 Ritual of Šamuḫa, CTH 481 Expansion of the cult of the goddess of the night, CTH 482 Reform of the cult of the goddess of the night of Šamuḫa by Muršili II, CTH 488 Ritual referring to Ḫamrišḫara, CTH 494 Ritual of the queen and her sons for the goddess NIN.GAL, CTH 500 Fragments of Kizzuwatnaean festival and magical rituals | 8 | 579 | 39543 |
| VIII. CULT INVENTORY TEXTS | VIII. CULT INVENTORY TEXTS | CTH 523 Provisions (melqētu) for local festivals | 1 | 18 | 1188 |
| X. FESTIVAL TEXTS AND CULTS | A. CALENDER | CTH 591 Festival of the Month, CTH 592 Spring and Herbst festival in Zippalanda, CTH 593 Spring festival on Mt. Tapala, CTH 594 Spring festival at Tippuwa, CTH 595 Spring festival fragments, CTH 596 Autumn festival fragments, CTH 597 Winter festival, CTH 598 Winter festival for the Sun-goddess of Arinna, CTH 599 Journey of the sacred hunting bag in winter, CTH 600 New year's festival | 10 | 181 | 18097 |
| | B. AN.DAḪ.ŠUMSAR | CTH 604 AN.DAḪ.ŠUMSAR, outline tablets, CTH 605 AN.DAḪ.ŠUMSAR, day 1, CTH 606 AN.DAḪ.ŠUMSAR, day 2, CTH 608 AN.DAḪ.ŠUMSAR, days 7–8, CTH 609 AN.DAḪ.ŠUMSAR, day 11, CTH 610 AN.DAḪ.ŠUMSAR, days 12–13: temple of Ziparwa, CTH 611 AN.DAḪ.ŠUMSAR, days 14–15: for the Sun-goddess of the earth, CTH 612 AN.DAḪ.ŠUMSAR, day 16: temple of Zababa, CTH 613 AN.DAḪ.ŠUMSAR, days 18–19: for the Storm-god of lightning, CTH 614 AN.DAḪ.ŠUMSAR, day 21?: for the deity IB/URAŠ, CTH 615 AN.DAḪ.ŠUMSAR, days 22–25: for Ištar of Ḫattarina, CTH 616 AN.DAḪ.ŠUMSAR, day 29: for Ea and his circle, CTH 617 AN.DAḪ.ŠUMSAR, day 32: for the protective deity of Tauriš, CTH 618 AN.DAḪ.ŠUMSAR, day 33–34: on Mt. Puškurunuwa, CTH 619 AN.DAḪ.ŠUMSAR, day 38: rain festival, CTH 620 AN.DAḪ.ŠUMSAR in Ankuwa for the goddess Kataḫḫa, CTH 621 unassigned (formerly "AN.DAḪ.ŠUMSAR, 'first tablet'"; see CTH 608), CTH 625 Fragments of the AN.DAḪ.ŠUMSAR festival | 18 | 346 | 37606 |
| | C. VARIOUS FESTIVALS | CTH 626 Festival of haste (EZEN$_4$ nuntarriyašḫaš), CTH 627 KI.LAM festival, CTH 628 (ḫ)išuwa- festival, CTH 629 Regular festival (EZEN$_4$ SAG.UŠ), CTH 630 Moon and thunder festival, CTH 631 Thunder festival, CTH 632 Festival for the ancestors?, CTH 633 Festival of the investiture of royal successor (EZEN$_4$ ḫaššumaš), CTH 634 Great festival of Arinna, CTH 635 Fragments of the festival of Zippalanda and Mt. Daḫa, CTH 636 Festival of Šarišša, CTH 637 Festival for the God of Ḫiššašḫapa, CTH 638 Festival for Telipinu, CTH 639 Fragments of the festival for Titiwatti, CTH 640 Fragments of festivals for Luwian deities, CTH 641 Cult of Išḫara, CTH 642 Festival fragments referring to the vegetation god Zinkuruwa, CTH 643 Festival fragments referring to the god Ziparwa, CTH 644 Festival or ritual fragments referring to Pirinkir, CTH 645 Fragments of festivals for the netherworld deities, CTH 646 Fragments of festivals celebrated by the queen, CTH 647 Festivals celebrated by the Prince (DUMU.LUGAL... | 44 | 5291 | 284621 |
| | D. THE CULT OF NERIK | CTH 671 Offering and prayer to the Storm-god of Nerik, CTH 672 Monthly festival at Nerik, CTH 674 Fragments of the purulliya- festival of Nerik, CTH 675 Fragments of the festival in the ḫešta- house, CTH 676 Fragments of a purifications ritual in Nerik, CTH 677 Ration lists (tarnatt-), CTH 678 Festival fragments concerning the cult of Nerik | 7 | 135 | 12517 |
| | E. THE CULT OF THE PROTECTIVE DEITY (DKAL) | CTH 681 Festival of Karaḫna, CTH 682 Festival for the protective deities, CTH 683 Renewal of the hunting bag for the protective deities, CTH 684 Festival for the protective deities of the river, CTH 685 Fragments of festivals for the protective deities | 5 | 101 | 9988 |
| | F. THE CULT OF ḪUWAŠŠANNA OF ḪUBEŠNA | CTH 690 List of festivals for Ḫuwaššanna, CTH 691 The witašš(i)aš festival, CTH 692 Fragments of the witašš(i)aš festival, CTH 693 The šaḫḫan festival, CTH 694 Fragments of festivals for Ḫuwaššanna | 5 | 255 | 22050 |
| | G. CULTS CONCERNING Teššup AND ḪEBAT | CTH 698 Cults of Teššup and Ḫebat of Aleppo, CTH 699 Festival for Teššup and Ḫebat of Lawazantiya, CTH 700 Enthronement ritual for Teššup and Ḫebat, CTH 701 Drink offering for the throne of Ḫebat, CTH 702 Ritual after the renewal of a temple of Ḫebat, CTH 703 Rituals of Muwalanni, priest of Kummanni, for Teššup of Manuzziya, CTH 704 Lists of Hurrian Gods in festivals, CTH 705 Lists of Hurrian Gods in festivals, CTH 706 Fragments of festivals for Teššup and Ḫebat | 9 | 492 | 51473 |
| | H. CULTS OF IŠTAR | CTH 711 Autumn festival for Ištar of Šamuḫa, CTH 712 Festival for Ištar of Šamuḫa, CTH 713 Ritual for Ištar of Tamininga, CTH 714 Festival for Ištar of Nineveh, CTH 715 Winter festival for Ištar of Nineveh, CTH 719 Festival for Ištar, Ḫu(r)dumana, Aruna, CTH 720 Fragments of festivals for Ištar, CTH 721 Festival for Ištar of Mt. Amana, CTH 722 Festival for the Great Sea and the tarmana- Sea | 9 | 90 | 10576 |
| XI. TEXTS IN OTHER LANGUAGES | A. HATTIAN | CTH 733 Invocation of Hattian deities: language of gods, language of men, CTH 735 Hattian prayers or incantations, CTH 736 Song of the zintuḫi-women for the Sun-goddess, CTH 737 Festivals of Nerik (with Hattian recitations), CTH 738 Festival for the goddess Tetešḫapi, CTH 739 Festivals of the city of Tuḫumiyara, CTH 740 Hattian litanies, CTH 741 Hattian songs of the women of Tiššaruliya, CTH 742 Hattian songs (SÌR), CTH 743 Hattian antiphonal songs, CTH 744 Festival fragments with Hattian recitations, CTH 745 Hattian fragments, CTH 746 Hattian strophic songs | 13 | 495 | 29617 |
| | B. PALAIC | CTH 750 Festival for Ziparwa, CTH 751 Festival for the Palaic pantheon – bread-, meat- and drink-offerings in Palaic, CTH 752 Festival for the Palaic pantheon – ritual for the disappearing and returning deity, CTH 753 Festival with Palaic recitations, CTH 754 Palaic fragments | 5 | 58 | 4723 |
| | C. LUWIAN | CTH 770 Luwian ritual fragments, CTH 771 Tablet of Lallupiya (with Luwianisms), CTH 772 Festival(ritual)s of Ištanuwa, CTH 773 Songs of Ištanuwa | 4 | 145 | 11669 |
| | D. HURRIAN | CTH 785 Ritual for Mt. Ḫazzi, CTH 786 Hurrian deity lists | 2 | 25 | 3364 |
| XIII. VARIA | XIII. VARIA | CTH 821 Kingship and divine authority, CTH 832 Hittite fragments with diverse content | 2 | 652 | 15167 |

Figure 10: Table of CTH entries

# Towards Ancient Meroitic Decipherment: A Computational Approach

**Joshua Otten, Antonios Anastasopoulos**
Department of Computer Science, George Mason University
{jotten4,antonis}@gmu.edu

## Abstract

The discovery of the Rosetta Stone was one of the keys that helped unlock the secrets of Ancient Egypt and its hieroglyphic language. But what about languages with no such "Rosetta Stone?" Meroitic is an ancient language from what is now present-day Sudan, but even though it is connected to Egyptian in many ways, much of its grammar and vocabulary remains undeciphered. In this work, we introduce the challenge of Meroitic decipherment as a computational task, and present the first Meroitic machine-readable corpus. We then train embeddings and perform intrinsic evaluations, as well as cross-lingual alignment experiments between Meroitic and Late-Egyptian. We conclude by outlining open problems and potential research directions.[1]

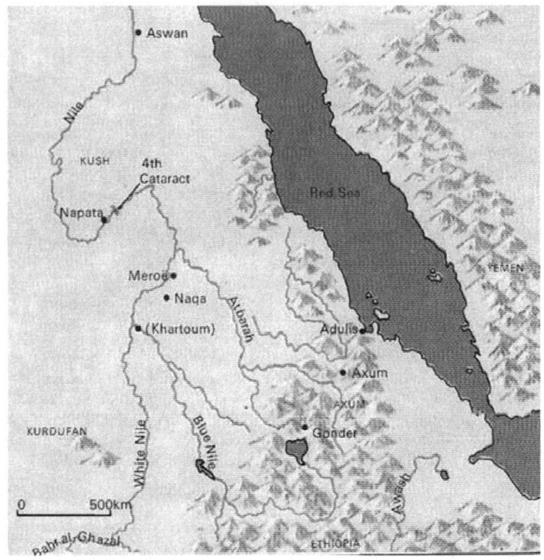


Figure 1: Ancient Meroë (Kush) between approximately 100 BC - 300 AD.

## 1 Introduction

Perhaps one of the most critical elements to deciphering an unknown language is a collection of bilingual texts. From a known language, one can make conclusions about phonetic, morphological, and lexical aspects of the target language, hopefully leading to eventual decipherment. Without such a text, translation of a lost language is practically inconceivable. Only in this day and age, where computer technological applications appear to nearly reach the limits of human imagination, is decipherment with a monolingual corpus potentially feasible, and Meroitic is a great candidate for such work.

Meroitic is the language of the ancient state of Meroë, a Kushite-ethnic group living in approximately 270 BC - 330 AD of what is now present-day Sudan (see Figure 1). Partly due to its geographic location, the Meroë civilization has been studied relatively little, despite its significant presence in the ancient and classical world (Shinnie, 1967; Rilly and de Voogt, 2012). One of the largest obstacles to understanding the Meroitic state, however, is that its language is not well understood, and we currently possess no bilingual texts large enough to illicit an attempt at decipherment. As stated by Shinnie (1967), a British africanist and archaeologist, "... *until this language has been successfully read and the inscriptions translated, much of the story of Meroë will remain unknown.*"

While there have been past attempts to understand the language, few have been made by Computer Scientists. Our hope is that by leveraging machine translation techniques, one could bridge the gap that has hindered progress in this language for decades. In the encouraging words of Griffith: "If new eyes, whether of trained decipherers or of scholars expert in North African philology, will exert themselves upon it, the secrets of Meroitic should soon be yielded up" (Griffith, 1911).

[1]The corpus, along with data and code necessary to replicate our experiments: `https://github.com/Joshua-Otten/Meroitic-Corpus`



*Proceedings of the Second Ancient Language Processing Workshop associated with NAACL 2025*, pages 208–219
May 4, 2025. 

To our knowledge, this is the first work to use modern NLP techniques towards Meroitic decipherment. Our contributions include the following:

- First, we introduce the task of Meroitic decipherment to the NLP community, and provide an overview of the language and its unique challenges.
- Additionally, we present the first machine-readable Meroitic corpus.
- Then, we train embeddings on this and Late-Egyptian data, and provide intrinsic evaluations of each.
- Finally, we perform alignment experiments between the Meroitic and Late-Egyptian embeddings, and lay groundwork for future research in this area.

Meroitic decipherment would allow us to read one of Africa's oldest written languages as well as to better understand the Meroitic civilization and its historical and cultural role across the ancient world.

## 2 The Meroitic Language

A great deal of what we currently know of Meroitic vocabulary and grammar comes from funerary inscriptions, which represent about one third of the available corpus and contain formulas that have been extensively analyzed by Griffith, Hintze, and Rilly (Rilly and de Voogt, 2012). Fortunately, (aside from a few vowel uncertainties) the writing system has already been understood, which allows us to successfully transliterate Meroitic hieroglyphic texts. Scholars have already been able to uncover a number of grammatical elements, allowing them to identify such features as determinants, genitival constructions, and appositions[2] (Rilly and de Voogt, 2012).

The grammar of Meroitic appears to be agglutinative (Rilly and de Voogt, 2012), minimizing the complexity of analyzing roots and grammatical structure. The writing system utilizes an alphasyllabary (Rilly and de Voogt, 2012), which allows for nearly one-to-one phonetic mapping. This removes many of the challenges present in MT for Ancient Egyptian or Cuneiform languages, where signs are neither consistently phonetic or logographic (Sahala and Lindén, 2023). Finally, Meroitic's separator character, ' : ', although not consistently used (Rilly and de Voogt, 2012), greatly improves our ability to identify roots, suffixes, and postpositions.

Scholars have also proposed linguistic affiliations, and we are by now confident that Meroitic is Nilo-Saharan of the Eastern Sudanic group's Northern branch, making it 'North East Sudanic.' The closest language group to Meroitic is Nubian, followed by Nara, whereas Taman and Nyima are separate branches within the same family (Rilly, 2008).

One of the most critical goals for Meroitic decipherment will be expanding our limited vocabulary (Lobban Jr, 1994), the hope being that once we have identified more words, a better understanding of the grammar should be forthcoming. Cognate detection has presented one of the most promising avenues for this, especially with regard to prior scholarly efforts. To this end, we present a cognate investigation by hand for two common Meroitic words in Appendix C. However, since scholars have already been searching the cognate space since the writing system was deciphered by Griffith (Rilly and de Voogt, 2012), we consider it more fruitful to first focus on new computational methods that have never been tried before.

### 2.1 Challenges

**Data Scarcity** Over time, scholars have aggregated approximately 2,200 Meroitic texts. While it is a sizeable amount of material for a lost language, it still would of course be considered a drop in the bucket for standard computational linguistics tasks.

Additionally, collecting data for comparison will become an important task in the future. In particular all close language relatives to Meroitic are also extremely low-resource languages. Although some dictionaries (e.g. Nubian, Old Nubian, Nara) are available, there exist hardly any complete corpora for these relatives in machine readable format. Ideally, analysts would perform experiments on not merely one, but many languages, and use those results cumulatively to better understand Meroitic.

**Orthographic Variation** An additional challenge for those hoping to decipher Meroitic is the orthographic variation across the language. "All researchers since Griffith who have worked on Meroitic have observed and sometimes complained about the great variability of the writing. ... [T]here are frequent examples of different spellings at the same site and from the same era for the more commonly used terms" (Rilly and de Voogt, 2012). It is possible that these may partly con-

[2] Where two adjacent noun phrases refer to the same object; for instance when Meroitic titles precede personal names.

sist of dialectal differences, but the fact that we find examples from the same place and time undermines dialect as a primary suspect. Of course, variations also include scribal mistakes (Rilly and de Voogt, 2012), as well as differences in region and time period (Rilly, 2007). For instance, Osiris and Isis epithets often began with an initial /$q$/ in places near Meroë and the third cataract, whereas they primarily began with /$w$/ around the second cataract; /$qetneyineqeli$/ and /$wetneyineqeli$/ are two valid writings for Isis epithets. Also, the word for "sister" was written /$kdise$/ as well as /$kdite$/.

## 3 Related Work

Schenkel (1972) used computational systems to search Meroitic texts, identifying verbs and common suffixes in three long royal narratives, and comparing them to verbal suffixes in the Barya language. Later, Ouellette and Longpre (1999) used a computer program called "Thoth: Language Cognate Program" to search for cognates in Meroitic, and concluded that "From these word lists it may be possible to continue the work of deciphering the Meroitic writing system until such time as a bilingual text becomes available."

More recently, several works have used machine translation, statistical techniques, and Bayesian probability to decipher foreign scripts (Knight et al., 2006; Snyder et al., 2010; Luo et al., 2019, 2021). These include methods to determine probable phonetic mappings (Knight et al., 2006), morphological segmentation, cognates (Snyder et al., 2010), and language relatedness (Luo et al., 2021).

A foundational experiment deciphered Ugaritic with machine translation techniques.[3] Comparing the "unknown" Ugaritic texts with a closely related language, Hebrew, the computers iteratively theorized alphabetic mappings based on character frequency. They then searched for cognates in the roots and particles using assumptions about morphology, "correctly translat[ing] over 60% of all distinct Ugaritic word-forms with Hebrew cognates and over 71% of the individual morphemes that compose them, outperforming the baseline by significant margins" (Snyder et al., 2010).

Luo et al. (2021) built on this work by generalizing it for other lost languages using a neural approach, which additionally improved the Ugaritic decipherment by 5.5%. This work is particularly relevant since it extracts cognates in undersegmented texts between a known and a lost language, even when the two languages are not particularly related.

Another statistical experiment was performed by Smith (2008), who tested whether Meroitic's word frequency distribution followed Zipf's law, concluding that, like all other human languages, it does indeed adhere to a Zipfian distribution.

## 4 A Machine-Readable Meroitic Corpus

As part of this project, we present the first machine-readable transcribed corpus by manually converting pre-transcribed Meroitic examples into machine-readable format, using examples from three main works: the vocabulary list of Lobban Jr (2021), as well as example phrases from Rilly (2007) and Millet (1968). We have also refitted three lengthy royal narratives from previous word-frequency experiments: Tañyidamani, the Hamadab Stela of Amanirenas and Akinidad (Hofmann, 1998), and the Kalabsha Inscription of Kharamadoye (Hägg, 2000). These data will be made publicly available on Github. Some corpus statistics are listed in Table 1, and examples of this data can be found in Appendix A. Some data instances include proposed translations; however, these translations are often constrained to titularies, toponyms, and anthroponyms (Lobban Jr, 2021), so they offer limited use for full decipherment.

Despite the existence of a Unicode font for Meroitic cursive and hieroglyphs,[4] we opt to use an ASCII-mapping of transcription characters already in use by scholars, both for ease of compatibility (e.g. users might not possess this font) and because our data sources usually provided examples as transcriptions rather than hieroglyphs. The mappings are specified in the corpus, and could certainly be changed to the Unicode if necessary.

In the past, no one transcription standard for Meroitic has been consistently used by scholars. Since we use solely pre-transcribed text, it is important to ensure that differing conventions are not inter-mixed. Thus, we create separate files of Meroitic examples designated by scholar. For a corpus, we combine the data from all files, but first convert to one standard; in this paper, we conform to Millet's paradigm; however, we provide information on our mapping scheme for each file, and characters can easily be replaced by others, so this

[3] Ugaritic had already been deciphered prior to this, but not using computers.

[4] Link to Meroitic font

| Type | Statistics |
|---|---|
| Translated Meroitic words | 193 |
| Meroitic Phrases | 897 |
| Late-Egyptian complete texts | 302 |
| Scanned Nubian pages | 708 |

Table 1: Data-collection statistics; does not include the Meroitic royal narratives.

should not pose an issue for reproducibility.

Additional data for Meroitic may be taken from REM (Le Répertoire d'Épigraphie Méroïtique), a corpus with over 1,000 Meroitic digitized inscriptions[5] (Leclant et al., 2000); however, many of these texts still require transcription[6] (Rilly and de Voogt, 2012) if they are to be analyzed through use of computer technology.[7]

As for data from other relevant languages, we scrape the Ramses Online Corpus of Late-Egyptian texts into JSON files, and use a cleaned version of the corpus for our experiments. Additionally, we are currently in the process of scanning and organizing materials from Old Nubian, Dongolese Nubian, and a few other modern Nubian varieties, in order to broaden the set of possible cognate candidates. We hope to soon develop a large enough sample set to conduct further experiments that may hopefully lead to an increased understanding of the Meroitic language. Note that all these languages are severely under-resourced, and almost all materials come in the form of books that require digitization and/or optical character recognition to be rendered useful. One challenge will be fine-tuning the OCR; for instance, we are currently unaware of any OCR developed for the Nubian or Old Nubian script, and up until now, our OCR attempts have yielded less-than ideal results. Eventually we will need an OCR model for the Meroitic REM texts as well.

## 5 Experiments

In this paper, we use our Meroitic corpus to train word embeddings. We evaluate their quality intrinsically with semantic similarity tests.

Afterwards, we attempt to align them with embeddings from Late-Egyptian. Creating cross-lingual representations is a method for lexicon induction, where embeddings can be aligned on a small dictionary of translation pairs (Mikolov et al., 2013b; Anastasopoulos and Neubig, 2020). We try this here with Meroitic and Egyptian, inducing lexemes of known words for evaluation. Through alignment to Egyptian, we hope to gain an understanding of the meaning (or grammatical function) of unknown words.

### 5.1 Why Egyptian?

Even though Ancient Egyptian is not phylogenetically related to Meroitic,[8] there are good reasons to believe the content of some Egyptian texts may be very relevant, both topically and chronologically, due to geographic and cultural similarities of the neighboring entities.

Napatan texts, Egyptian writings from the Napatan period (circa 800-300 BC), could be especially useful for translating words in the long royal narratives. Unfortunately, the number of long royal narratives and corresponding Napatan texts is not nearly large enough alone for comparison, and even what is available is not in ready machine-readable format. Additionally, unlike many Napatan texts, it is likely that the royal narratives came from oral tradition, since there are no dates, coronations, etc. apparent in the texts; this minimizes our ability to find similarities in format or structure.

Therefore, as a preliminary investigation, we choose to use Late-Egyptian (written between approximately 1550-700 BC (Hoch, 2023)) texts and stories for comparison, as they are openly accessible on the Ramses Online annotated corpus.

### 5.2 Data and Cleanup

For Late-Egyptian data, we scrape 302 texts, ranging from a few sentences to many paragraphs, into JSON format from the Ramses Online Corpus[9] (Polis et al., 27 August 2015).

Note that we use the phonological transcribed version of the Egyptian texts, rather than representations for the specific hieroglyphs used. This is in part because we did not see Gardiner Code representations (alphanumerical codes for individual hieroglyphs) in the Ramses Online texts. Egyptian Hieroglyphic writing makes use of non-phonetic

[5] Many of these can be found at https://ancientworldonline.blogspot.com/2017/11/repertoire-depigraphie-meroitique.html

[6] They include photographs of the physical carvings/documents, along with drawings of scholars' reconstruction of the hieroglyphs, but they have not been converted to an alphanumeric script.

[7] At this point, the texts from REM are image files, and hence not amenable for text-based language technologies.

[8] Egyptian is classified as Afro-Asiatic, Meroitic is a Nilo-Saharan language.

[9] http://ramses.ulg.ac.be/

features, such as determinatives, in order to contribute semantic and sometimes grammatical (eg. plurality) information of words (Allen, 2000). Using only the phonetic representation of texts leaves open the possibility of losing linguistic information, and may even result in ambiguity over certain lexical items. On the other hand, it may make sense to compare the words phonetically, considering that Meroitic hieroglyphs are purely alphasyllabic and do not use determinatives.

We create machine-readable corpora for both Meroitic and Egyptian by eliminating translations, metadata, dashes, colons, etc. and separate each example or text by a new line. Many of the Meroitic words are pre-segmented, so eliminating certain punctuation helps to separate words by morpheme in each language. This Meroitic corpus contains 871 example texts or phrases, and the Egyptian contains 1,729 unique types for 99,338 total tokens.

**Data Augmentation** Additionally, since scholars have been able to detect many words that are anthroponyms (people names), we augment the Meroitic data by swapping out royal names with each other, and then non-royal names with other non-royal names, thereby creating additional synthetic (yet valid) Meroitic examples. The resulting Meroitic corpus contains 1,868 unique word forms from 17,257 sentences or phrases: 782,761 words in all.

**Evaluation Dictionaries** We also compile seven small dictionaries (statistics in Table 2), pairing known Meroitic word forms with Egyptian counterparts that appear in the corpora; these act as our training and evaluation sets. The combined sets include over 90 pairs, with our largest dictionary (of nouns) containing 26. Known orthographic variants are present as distinct entries. Words are grouped by categories, such as part of speech, and these serve as training and test sets. We note that certain Egyptian words can be written with multiple independent morphemes yet have a distinct meaning. For instance, the word for "priest" is written as a genitival construction with two words: $hm\text{-}n\underline{t}r$, literally meaning "servant of god." The dash in transcription is important because it implies the single meaning in the presence of two independent morphemes. Therefore, to account for this kind of issue, we include certain punctuation, such as periods, and we also add dashes back into the Egyptian corpus for specific word pairs, just as they were written in the pre-cleaned version of the corpus.

### 5.3 Methods

We train `Word2Vec` embeddings (Mikolov et al., 2013a) on the Meroitic and Egyptian data. Although we considered using `fastText` which is good for learning subword information (Bojanowski et al., 2017), our cleaning process separated words into their constituent morphemes, so this would not be as helpful here. In order to consider how the small size of the corpora may affect the embedding space, we test with varying word vector dimensions: 20, 50, 100, and 120.

Next, we perform intrinsic evaluation on both embedding spaces (of dimension 100) with respect to semantic similarity, including both nearest-neighbors and word analogy tests. We carefully select known (or hypothesized) words and observe the top 10 most similar lexemes, with the hope that other known words that appear will be semantically related in some way. We also do this for numerals, expecting numerals to align with other numerals. Since most Meroitic words are unknown, our results may not include many known words; in these cases it is difficult to tell how semantically similar the words are. Therefore, we also compare cosine similarity scores to determine how close the words are in the embedding space.

Finally, we attempt embedding space alignment between the Egyptian and Meroitic in three settings: unsupervised, aligning on numbers (mostly shared numerals), and on our dictionary of nouns. We use `VecMap` (Artetxe et al., 2018b,a), since Anastasopoulos and Neubig (2020) found that it can perform better than other methods (`MUSE` (Conneau et al., 2017) and `UMWE` (Chen and Cardie, 2018)) for lexicon induction when the languages or writing-systems are distant.

We then evaluate with a lexicon induction task on each of our dictionaries, using a neighborhood of 10 words (reporting precision@10). Additionally, we perform a similar experiment with French and English Wikipedia-trained embeddings, using a hand-crafted alignment dictionary of 26 pairs, and testing on nearly 5,000 pairs from Anastasopoulos and Neubig (2020). This serves as a skyline to demonstrate the level of accuracy we might expect using higher-quality embeddings but still using a minimal amount of training word pairs. If we receive low accuracy on Meroitic/Egyptian but high

| Type | # entries |
|---|---|
| nouns | 26 |
| names | 18 |
| numbers | 15 |
| verbs | 14 |
| titularies | 9 |
| adj/adv | 6 |
| prepositions | 3 |

Table 2: Alignment dictionaries

accuracy on French/English, this suggests our problem lies in the sparsity/quality of embeddings.

## 6 Results

Overall, our intrinsic evaluation for both Meroitic and Egyptian embeddings shows promise. However, our lexicon induction experiments are found lacking. None of our models could correctly translate terms that had not been seen before, and of the terms that had been seen, only a maximum of 20% were correctly aligned.

### 6.1 Intrinsic Evaluation

We evaluate our embeddings by calculating the cosine similarity between known words.

**Egyptian** Overall, the Egyptian embeddings do very well on our tests considering the limited nature of the dataset. To begin with, lower numerals tend to be paired with low numerals (ex. 1, 5, 3, 6, 8), while high numerals match higher numerals (ex. 1000, 500, 800, 2000).

We find that words associated with kingship or gods often have high cosine similarities and often appear in the top 10 nearest neighbors of each other. For instance, /$nswt$/ ("king"), /$r'$/ ("Ra"), and /$jmn$/ ("Amun") all have over 92% cosine similarities with each other.

In addition, we perform several word analogy tests (similar to the famous "man" is to "woman" as "king" is to "queen" paradigm). Not all these are successful, but we do obtain certain interesting results:

- `nswt`→`wr` as `ms`→`b3k`, meaning "'king' is to 'great' as 'child' is to 'servant,'" which is exactly something we might expect.
- `rmt`→`hm.t` as `nswt`→`mry`, which means "'man' is to 'woman' as 'king' is to 'beloved.'" Ideally, the result would be /$nswy.t$/, meaning 'queen,' but 'beloved' may still contain a relevant connotation; it should also be noted that /$mry$/ was often used in the context of a king's relationship to a god.

We provide cosine similarity scores for some selected Egyptian word comparisons in Table 3, and note that all scores are high.

**Meroitic** The Meroitic embeddings do not perform quite as well on the intrinsic evaluations, but we do find that they capture some semantic information. For instance, the embeddings of the numerals 2, 12, and 6 are all very near to each other, and the gods Isis and Osiris are similar—this in particular is expected since in mythology Isis is the wife of Osiris. Testing with /$qor$/[10] for "ruler" returned /$abrse$/ (a nominal group, meaning "every man" when containing an article: /$abr$-$se$-$l$/), /$qorte$/ (literally "in the king's," probably meaning "palace"), and /$amnp$/ ("the God Amun of Napata"). We also find certain titularies grouped with titularies, for example: /$perite$/ ("local official"), /$ttnylkh$/[11] (some official title), and a word seemingly related to /$pelmo\hat{s}$/[12], which has to do with regional military administration (Millet, 1968).

Additionally, variant word forms appear as nearest neighbors, for example /$mni$/ and /$mnpte$/ for "Amun" and "Amun of Napata," and /$(a)\hat{s}or(i)$/ and /$(a)\hat{s}oreyi$/ (vocative form) for Osiris. This gives hope to future orthographic variation detection efforts. Note that this is despite the fact that we use a method that does *not* take into account character $n$-grams (like `fasttext` would, much more suitable for modeling orthographic variation) and hence this confirms that these are indeed variants of the same word, as opposed to them being two distinct words with very similar forms.

Word analogy results prove difficult to analyze, since it is first more complicated to construct them with our limited vocabulary, and most of the words that are returned are unknown. However, one very good result within the top-10 turns out to be `qor`→`pqr` as `abr`→`yetmdelo`, which means "'ruler' is to 'crown prince' as 'man' is to 'nephew[13].'"

It should also be noted that unlike the Egyptian embeddings (whose nearest neighbors often had cosine similarity scores greater than 95%), many of

[10] written as 'qEr' in our corpus; all $o$'s are written as 'E', since some of Millet's publications transcribed as /$\hat{e}$/. However, it should be noted that $o$ is the standard convention.

[11] written 'ttNlX' in our corpus

[12] written 'pelmES' in our corpus. The actual word returned was /$pelmo\hat{s}lispqebete$./

[13] Note that technically /$yetmde$-$l$-$o$/ is a nominal clause meaning "he is the nephew" or "she is the niece"

| Word 1 | | Word 2 | | Cosine |
|---|---|---|---|---|
| egy | en | egy | en | Similarity |
| $r'$ | Ra | $n\underline{t}r$ | god | **0.96** |
| $r'$ | Ra | $wsr$ | power | 0.93 |
| $r'$ | Ra | $\dot{h}m - n\underline{t}r$ | priest | 0.88 |
| $jmn$ | Amun | $\dot{h}m - n\underline{t}r$ | priest | **0.98** |
| $nswt$ | king | $stp$ | choice/elite | **0.96** |
| $\dot{h}m.t$ | woman | $rm\underline{t}.t$ | woman | 0.95 |
| $\dot{h}m.t$ | woman | $s$ | man | 0.86 |
| $ms$ | child | $s3$ | son | 0.91 |
| $\dot{h}m.t$ | woman | $sn.t$ | sister | **0.98** |
| $'3$ | large | $wr$ | great | 0.93 |

Table 3: Cosine similarity scores between Egyptian words. egy is the Egyptian word; en is its English translation. We choose words that we feel are related, so we get high similarity for the majority of tests. Notice that woman/man is slightly lower than the rest, which may be expected due to the difference in gender.

| Word 1 | | Word 2 | | Cosine |
|---|---|---|---|---|
| xmr | en | xmr | en | Similarity |
| $qor(e)$ | ruler | $qr$ | ruler | **0.91** |
| $qor(e)$ | ruler | $pqr$ | prince | -0.04 |
| $qor(e)$ | ruler | $mlo$ | head | **0.62** |
| $kdi$ | woman | $kdileb$ | women | 0.42 |
| $kdi$ | woman | $sem(l)$ | wife | 0.44 |
| $kdi$ | woman | $abr$ | man | 0.522 |
| $kdi$ | woman | $kdis$ | sister | 0.46 |
| $dd$ | infant/son[14] | $as$ | child | **0.69** |
| $kdis(e)$ | sister | $wi(de)$ | brother | -0.11 |
| $tr$ | big | $lx$ | large/high | **0.73** |

Table 4: Cosine similarity scores between Meroitic words. xmr is the Meroitic word; en is its hypothesized English translation. We choose words that we feel are related, so we would expect similarity to be high. However, while we do get some high scores, results are somewhat inconsistent.

these Meroitic "nearest neighbors" display cosine similarities below 60 or even 50%, indicating that related words are not as near to each other in the embeddings space. We believe this can be attributed to the extremely low training data. Nonetheless, we still present the cosine similarity scores between several known Meroitic words in Table 4. Some pairs have reasonably high scores, but the results are inconsistent.

### 6.2 Alignment Results

Our alignment results (Table 6 in Appendix B) are far from ideal. None of our Meroitic-Egyptian cross-lingual embeddings were able to do lexicon induction for a dictionary they had not seen before. Our best setting appears to be on numerals with 100-dimension vectors; however, even for the training dictionary they were not able to achieve more than 20% accuracy. In contrast, our French-English cross-lingual embeddings performed 70% on the training dictionary, and close to 68% on the test set.

The most obvious explanation for this poor performance is twofold. Firstly, our Meroitic-Egyptian test sets are so small that we cannot expect our models to correctly pair the specific words we have chosen. We should remember that the accuracy on these few words is not an indication of complete failure. However, the fact that we could not achieve better than 20% on the very words we aligned on is an indication that these embeddings are insufficient for proper alignment and lexicon induction. This is likely due to the extreme low-resource nature of the training sets, although it is possible that we may be able to achieve better accuracy when aligning Meroitic to a different language, such as Old Nubian or Coptic, despite the differences in content. One might also try with modern, higher-resourced languages, such as Hebrew or Egyptian Arabic; however, we could hardly expect these to bear any meaningful resemblance to the language in question.

## 7 Discussion and Future Work

Despite the extremely limited nature of our corpora, our embeddings are still able to capture semantic information. This is especially true in our Egyptian embeddings, but Meroitic also shows promise, suggesting that our corpus and embeddings can be useful for future experiments to further understand Meroitic. We believe the Egyptian embeddings were better due to the difference in example length; many Egyptian texts were equivalent to several paragraphs, but most of the Meroitic examples were short sentences or fragments, and heavily augmented using anthroponyms. Regardless, there is still a long way to go before achieving results that may be useful for scholars in any major decipherment effort, which is clear when considering the abysmal performance of our lexicon induction tasks. Future work should attempt the same alignment but with other languages, such as Coptic or Old Nubian. However, we believe the prime reasons for this is simply the lack of quality training data. If more Meroitic examples could be gathered and made machine-readable, then we could expand our corpus and obtain more reasonable results.

Other avenues for future work, now made possible with our new corpus, include cognate detection, orthographic variant recognition, NER tasks, and

POS-tagging. Additionally, Meroitic inscriptions tend to use substantially different vocabulary in different contexts. Thus, performing a study of lexical elements common to various genres would also be useful.

### 7.1 Cognate Detection

One important direction for Meroitic research includes attempting to find cognates in related languages. We hope to first benchmark methods similar to Snyder et al. (2010), Luo et al. (2019), and Luo et al. (2021) (see Section 3). The idea is to search for cognates in related languages by comparing their high-frequency word roots and particles with Meroitic's, based on phonetic values and overall frequency.

We present an initial attempt on cognate detection (by hand, as not all resources are digitized) for two common but unknown words in Appendix C.

### 7.2 Leveraging Related Languages

In contrast to previous machine translation attempts for language decipherment (Snyder et al., 2010), we currently know of no language that serves as a very close relative to Meroitic. However, because we can find similarities between Meroitic and other languages, such as Old Nubian, which shares with it both lexical and grammatical features (van Gerven Oei, 2020), the hope is that we could perform experiments using multiple semi-relatives, perhaps using methods established in Luo et al. (2021) (see Section 3), and combine the data to build a comprehensive understanding of the Meroitic language. At this stage, Old Nubian presents one of the most likely candidates for comparison, although unfortunately its content is primarily Christian-oriented (van Gerven Oei, 2020), contrasting sharply with Meroitic's Kushite Pantheon of gods, and its lexicon is more limited compared to modern Nubian dictionaries[15]. Hopefully there exists enough of a connection to use in computer analyses, but other Nilo-Saharan languages, such as Nara, Tama, and Dinka, may also be useful for comparison. Ideally, analysts would perform experiments on not merely one, but many languages, and use those results cumulatively to better understand Meroitic.

[15]Modern Nubian dictionaries (e.g. Khalil (1996) and Armbruster (1965)) have many more words than the Old Nubian dictionary Browne (1996).

### 7.3 Handling Orthographic Variation

We suspect that orthographic variation may play a significant role in the quality of our embeddings, since each distinct form would erroneously appear to have an entirely new meaning. We plan to attempt the same experiments after modifying the training data to eliminate all known variants, similarly to methods used in Sahala and Lindén (2023). However, it is quite possible that many more variants exist than scholars have previously been able to uncover. One solution would be to compare the words in Meroitic texts of related genres with each other, either considering cosine similarity, or word frequency and phonemes, perhaps taking region and time-period into account as well; in this way we may guess which words are orthographic variants of each other. Seeing how words were written and therefore pronounced by different people might also give insight into Meroitic phonology and where language variations occurred, which would be important not only for knowledge of Meroitic, but for linguistics and history as well. Regardless, this test should improve our ability to read the Meroitic language, as it minimizes the number of terms that are truly unknown, and could lead to higher-quality embeddings.

Our current corpus provides the raw texts as they currently appear, i.e., including all the above-mentioned variations. But we hope to release a "normalized" version in the near future.

## 8 Conclusion

The use of computational methods to decipher Meroitic looks hopeful. Large-scale programs can search for cognates much more effectively than any human, and statistical brute-force comparisons can help to identify word roots and grammatical particles. Meroitic is an ideal language on which to attempt translation, as we already have some knowledge of vocabulary and grammar (albeit limited). The primary challenges will be finding the right language to effectively map word and particle meanings (Lobban Jr, 2003), paired with acquiring enough machine-readable data on both ends.

The corpus, embeddings, and analyses we present here constitute a step in that direction. Despite the disappointing results of our lexical induction tests, our embeddings appear to have the capacity to capture non-trivial semantic information. With additional attempts with other languages, as well as methods to handle orthographic variation, perhaps we may achieve more promising results. Ultimately, decipherment of Meroitic–or any untranslated language–will require computer efficiency and persistence, paired with human ingenuity and intuition.

## Limitations

Creating a machine-readable Meroitic corpus is not a trivial task. Firstly, the language is so obscure that it is difficult to obtain access to Meroitic materials, and putting them into machine-readable format requires extensive care and some expertise. Thus, we had to use some materials that were fairly old and may contain outdated transcriptions and translation hypotheses. However, we believe that even a possibly outdated machine-readable corpus is better than no corpus at all, and given some of our positive results for the intrinsic evaluation, it seems that what we do have is still worthwhile. We hope to eventually curate an up-to-date machine-readable corpus, perhaps based on the recent publication of Hallof (2024). Note, however, that this book is not currently available in any digital format, and our attempts at contacting the author have been unsuccessful. Should we manage to eventually obtain access to this book, it may also lead to substantial improvements in results.

## Acknowledgments

This work was generously supported by the Presidential Scholarship awarded by the George Mason University Graduate Division. It was also partially supported by NEH Award PR-276810-21 and NSF Award IIS-2327143. Computational resources for experiments were provided by the Office of Research Computing at George Mason University (URL: `https://orc.gmu.edu`).

Special thanks to Dr. Richard Lobban Jr., Professor Emeritus at Rhode Island College, for his invaluable mentorship, access to his extensive library, and the sharing of his expertise on Meroë and ancient Nubia; and to Dr. Jeremy Pope from the College of William and Mary, for his guidance and inspiration throughout this project; also to Dr. Claude Rilly, director of research at the CNRS, the Sedeinga Excavations, and professor at École pratique des hautes études in Paris, France, for his thorough review and advice for this paper. Their expertise has proved invaluable for our research thus far.

## References

James P Allen. 2000. *Middle Egyptian: An introduction to the language and culture of hieroglyphs*. Cambridge University Press.

Antonios Anastasopoulos and Graham Neubig. 2020. Should all cross-lingual embeddings speak English? In *Proceedings of the 58th Annual Meeting of the Association for Computational Linguistics*, pages 8658–8679, Online. Association for Computational Linguistics.

Charles Hubert Armbruster. 1965. *Dongolese Nubian: A Lexicon*. Cambridge University Press.

Mikel Artetxe, Gorka Labaka, and Eneko Agirre. 2018a. Generalizing and improving bilingual word embedding mappings with a multi-step framework of linear transformations. In *Proceedings of the Thirty-Second AAAI Conference on Artificial Intelligence*, pages 5012–5019.

Mikel Artetxe, Gorka Labaka, and Eneko Agirre. 2018b. A robust self-learning method for fully unsupervised cross-lingual mappings of word embeddings. In *Proceedings of the 56th Annual Meeting of the Association for Computational Linguistics (Volume 1: Long Papers)*, pages 789–798.

Piotr Bojanowski, Edouard Grave, Armand Joulin, and Tomas Mikolov. 2017. Enriching word vectors with subword information. *Transactions of the Association for Computational Linguistics*, 5:135–146.

Gerald Browne. 1996. *Old Nubian dictionary*. Peeters Publishers.

Xilun Chen and Claire Cardie. 2018. Unsupervised multilingual word embeddings. In *Proceedings of the 2018 Conference on Empirical Methods in Natural Language Processing*, pages 261–270, Brussels, Belgium. Association for Computational Linguistics.

Alexis Conneau, Guillaume Lample, Marc'Aurelio Ranzato, Ludovic Denoyer, and Hervé Jégou. 2017. Word translation without parallel data. arXiv:1710.04087.

Francis LLewellyn Griffith. 1911. *The Meroitic Inscriptions of Shablul and Karanòg*. Pennsylvania University.

Tomas Hägg. 2000. T. eide, t. hägg, rh pierce, l. török (edd.): Fontes historiae nubiorum, vol. iii. textual sources for the history of the middle nile region between the eighth century bc and the sixth century ad: From the first to the sixth century ad. pp. 751–1216. bergen: University of bergen, 1998. paper, nok 220. isbn: 82-91626-07-3. *The Classical Review*, 50(1):1103–1107.

Jochen Hallof. 2024. *Analytic Meroitic Dictionary*. J H Roll Verlag; Bilingual edition.

James Hoch. 2023. Egyptian language.

Inge Hofmann. 1998. Fontes historiae nubiorum: Textual sources for the history of the middle nile region between the eighth century bc and the sixth century ad. vol. ii: From the mid-fifth to the first century bc.

Mokhtar M. Khalil. 1996. *Wörterbuch der nubischen Sprache (Fadidja/MaḥasDialekt): Arbeitfassung/Vorabdruck.*

Kevin Knight, Anish Nair, Nishit Rathod, and Kenji Yamada. 2006. Unsupervised analysis for decipherment problems. In *Proceedings of the COLING/ACL 2006 Main Conference Poster Sessions*, pages 499–506.

Jean Leclant, Claude Rilly, Catherine Berger-El-Naggar, Claude Carrier, and André Heyler. 2000. Répertoire d'épigraphie méroïtique.

Richard Lobban Jr. 1994. Problems and strategies in the decipherment of meroitic. *Northeast African Studies*, 1(2):159–164.

Richard A Lobban Jr. 2003. *Historical dictionary of ancient and medieval Nubia*, volume 10. Scarecrow Press.

Richard A Lobban Jr. 2021. *Historical Dictionary of Ancient Nubia*. Rowman & Littlefield Publishers.

Jiaming Luo, Yuan Cao, and Regina Barzilay. 2019. Neural decipherment via minimum-cost flow: From Ugaritic to Linear B. In *Proceedings of the 57th Annual Meeting of the Association for Computational Linguistics*, pages 3146–3155, Florence, Italy. Association for Computational Linguistics.

Jiaming Luo, Frederik Hartmann, Enrico Santus, Regina Barzilay, and Yuan Cao. 2021. Deciphering undersegmented ancient scripts using phonetic prior. *Transactions of the Association for Computational Linguistics*, 9:69–81.

Tomas Mikolov, Kai Chen, Greg Corrado, and Jeffrey Dean. 2013a. Efficient estimation of word representations in vector space. arXiv:1301.3781.

Tomas Mikolov, Quoc V Le, and Ilya Sutskever. 2013b. Exploiting similarities among languages for machine translation. arXiv:1309.4168.

Nicholas Byram Millet. 1968. *Meroitic Nubia*. Yale University.

Monica Ouellette and Helene Longpre. 1999. *Thoth: Language Cognate Program*. Ph.D. thesis.

Stéphane Polis, Serge Rosmorduc, and Jean Winand. 27 August 2015. Ramses goes online. an annotated corpus of late egyptian texts in interaction with the egyptological community. F.R.S.-FNRS - Fonds de la Recherche Scientifique [BE].

Claude Rilly. 2007. *La langue du royaume de Méroé: un panorama de la plus ancienne culture écrite d'Afrique subsaharienne*. Honoré Champion.

Claude Rilly. 2008. Linguistic position of meroitic. new perspectives for understanding the texts. *The Sudan Archaeological Research Society*.

Claude Rilly and Alex de Voogt. 2012. *The Meroitic language and writing system*. Cambridge University Press.

Aleksi Sahala and Krister Lindén. 2023. A neural pipeline for pos-tagging and lemmatizing cuneiform languages. In *Proceedings of the Ancient Language Processing Workshop*, pages 203–212.

Wolfgang Schenkel. 1972. Meroitisches und baryaverb: Versuch einer bestimmung der tempusbildung des meroitischen. *Meroitic Newsletter*, 11:1–16.

Peter Lewis Shinnie. 1967. *Meroe: A civilization of the Sudan*, volume 55. FA Praeger.

Reginald D Smith. 2008. Investigation of the zipf-plot of the extinct meroitic language. arXiv:0808.2904.

Benjamin Snyder, Regina Barzilay, and Kevin Knight. 2010. A statistical model for lost language decipherment. In *Proceedings of the 48th Annual Meeting of the Association for Computational Linguistics*, pages 1048–1057.

Vincent van Gerven Oei. 2020. Old nubian crash course – day 1.

| Meroitic Corpus Examples |
| :---: |
| plSn aqmks penn 5 ni ye teke lE |
| xbxN wES qer qE sskemxr qE wESi yntke pipl pxilX pli ptrEti pipn pbx wErEteliye krErE |
| t dxe mlEqErebr qEre s l xrws |
| pestE aberEtemte pestE n. yetmde betewi |

Table 5: Example lines from our corpus, where each line is a unique example.

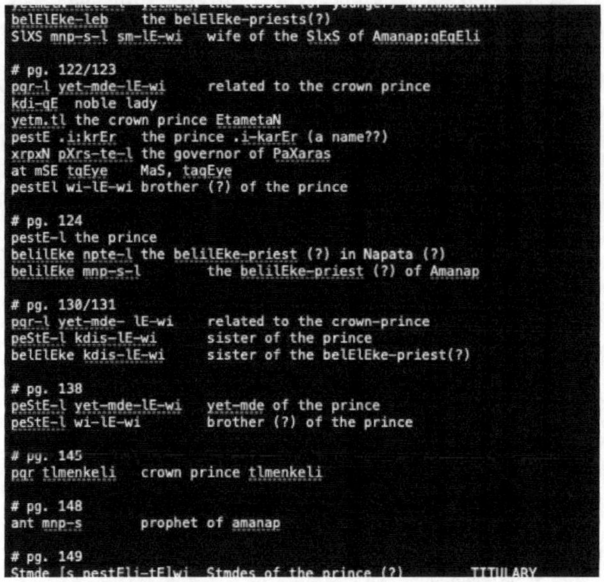

```
belElEke-leb    the belElEke-priests(?)
SlXS mnp-s-l sm-lE-wi   wife of the SlxS of Amanap;qEqEli

# pg. 122/123
pqr-l yet-mde-lE-wi      related to the crown prince
kdi-qE  noble lady
yetm.tl the crown prince EtametaN
pestE .i:krEr   the prince .i-karEr (a name??)
xrpxN pXrs-te-l the governor of PaXaras
at mSE tqEye    MaS, taqEye
pestEl wi-lE-wi brother (?) of the prince

# pg. 124
pestE-l the prince
belilEke npte-l the belilEke-priest (?) in Napata (?)
belilEke mnp-s-l         the belilEke-priest (?) of Amanap

# pg. 130/131
pqr-l yet-mde- lE-wi     related to the crown-prince
peStE-l kdis-lE-wi       sister of the prince
belElEke kdis-lE-wi      sister of the belElEke-priest(?)

# pg. 138
peStE-l yet-mde-lE-wi   yet-mde of the prince
peStE-l wi-lE-wi         brother (?) of the prince

# pg. 145
pqr tlmenkeli   crown prince tlmenkeli

# pg. 148
ant mnp-s       prophet of amanap

# pg. 149
Stmde [s pestEli-tElwi  Stmdes of the prince (?)         TITULARY
```

Figure 2: Screenshot of lines from the Millet examples.

## A Corpus Example

Table 5 displays example lines taken from our Meroitic corpus, and Figure 2 shows a screenshot image of the examples from Millet.

## B Alignment Results

Table 6 shows the results from aligning Meroitic to Egyptian embeddings on numerals and nouns. The columns represent the cross-lingual embeddings, while the rows are the test dictionaries.

| **Dict** | **unsup** | **num-20** | **num-50** | **num-100** | **num-120** | **nn-20** | **nn-50** | **nn-100** | **nn-120** |
|---|---|---|---|---|---|---|---|---|---|
| `numer` | - | 6.67 | 13.33 | **20** | 13.33 | - | - | - | - |
| `nouns` | - | - | - | - | - | 8 | 4 | **16** | 12 |
| `other` | - | - | - | - | - | - | - | - | - |

Table 6: Results from Meroitic-Egyptian cross-lingual embeddings. The `-numbers` are the dimensions of the word vectors. `unsup` stands for an unsupervised model on 100-dimension vectors; `num-` models are aligned on numbers, and `nn-` are aligned on nouns. The results are abysmal, suggesting that we cannot reliably perform lexicon induction between the Meroitic and Late-Egyptian corpora.

## C Preliminary Cognate Study

Once we had compiled the three long royal narratives in machine-readable format, we calculated overall word frequency within the texts. Then, consulting with an expert in Nubian and Meroitic history and languages, we focused on two of the most frequent words, and hand-identified possible cognates from related languages. Tables 7 and 8 show our results for the words /*seb*/ and /*kek*/, respectively. Current theories suggest that /*seb*/ is a noun related to kingship and that /*kek*/ may possibly be a coordinating conjunction (although this is fragile).

| Word | Meaning | Language |
|---|---|---|
| *seb* | unknown | Meroitic |
| *sab* | cat | Nubian Kenzi/Dongolawi |
| *esbyni* | villager | Nubian Kenzi/Dongolawi |
| *sablo* | waterfall | Nubian Kenzi/Dongolawi/Fadija/Mahas |
| *sablo* | obstruction to the flow, irrigation canal | Nubian Kenzi |
| *sablo* | trough (especially for a waterwheel) | Nubian Dongolawi |
| *sib* | to fly | Nubian Kenzi/Dongolawi |
| *sab* | clouds | Nubian Dongolawi/Mahas |
| *sabe* | wall | Nubian Kenzi/Dongolawi |
| *saab* | downstream end | Nubian (17th century) |
| *asab* | sinew/muscle | Nubian |
| *seb* | intelligent | Coptic |
| *sabat* | basket | Old Nubian |

Table 7: Hand-identified possible cognates/borrowings for the Meroitic word /*seb*/.

| Word | Meaning | Language |
|---|---|---|
| *kek* | Unknown | Meroitic |
| *kakke* | small scorpion | Nubian Kenzi |
| *kok* | hammer | Nubian Kenzi/Dongolawi/Fadija/Mahas |
| *kuk* | to hatch | Nubian Kenzi/Dongolawi/Fadija/Mahas |
| *kk* | darkness | Egyptian |
| *ukk* | wean | Nubian Kenzi/Dongolawi/Fadija/Mahas |
| *kkki* | lineage name of island land cultivators | Nubian |
| *kak* | room | Nubian |
| *kikko* | chop | Nubian |
| *Kuk*/*Kek* | God of darkness | Egyptian |
| *Keket* | Goddess of darkness | Egyptian |

Table 8: Hand-identified possible cognates/borrowings for the Meroitic word /*kek*/.

Interestingly, the cognates found for these two words do not appear to directly support the current scholarly theories. Based purely on these results, any hard translation for /*seb*/ or /*kek*/ would be speculative. However, there appears to be somewhat of a theme regarding "earth," "wall," "blockage," "water," or "cataract" relating to the word /*seb*/. Therefore, considering the importance of the Nile in Meroë geography and culture, one possibility is that this Meroitic word means or is related to a cataract. For /*kek*/, many of the Nubian/Egyptian words appear to have a dark or destructive connotation, so one possibility is that /*kek*/ means "to cut" or perhaps "hurt," "hit," or "break." This also makes sense in context of conquest, which is likely a prevailing theme in the royal narratives.

The hope is that once we acquire enough data from languages in addition to Meroitic, we will be able to automate the process of cognate detection. In future work, we also expect to take into account word clusters and *n*-grams.

# Detecting *Honkadori* based on *Waka* Embeddings

**Hayato Ogawa, Kaito Horio, Daisuke Kawahara**
Waseda University
{cookie3120@ruri.,kakakakakakaito@akane.,dkw@}waseda.jp

## Abstract

We develop an embedding model specifically designed for Waka poetry and use it to build a model for detecting *Honkadori*. *Waka* is a traditional form of old Japanese poetry that has been composed since ancient times. *Honkadori* is a sophisticated poetic technique in Japanese classical literature where poets incorporate words or poetic sentiments from old *Waka*s (*Honka*) into their own work. First, we fine-tune a pre-trained language model using contrastive learning to construct a *Waka*-specialized embedding model. Then, using the embedding vectors obtained from this model and features extracted from them, we train a machine learning model to detect the *Honka* (original poem) of *Waka*s that employ the *Honkadori* technique. Using paired data of *Honka* and *Waka*s that are considered to use *Honkadori*, we evaluated the *Honka* detection model and demonstrated that it can detect *Honka* with reasonable accuracy.

Figure 1: Example of *Honkadori*. The upper poem shows the HONKA: "How painful it is, the rain falling at Miwa promontory—at the riverbank of Sano (佐野の渡り), there is not even a house to shelter in." The lower poem shows the HONKADORI: "At dusk, I stopped my horse at the riverbank of Sano (佐野の渡り), brushing off the snow from my sleeves, yet finding no shelter anywhere." The HONKADORI alludes to the phrase "佐野の渡り" (the riverbank of Sano) from the HONKA, sharing the common theme that there is nowhere to hide from the weather.

## 1 Introduction

*Waka* is a traditional form of Japanese poetry based on combinations of 5- and 7-syllable units. First appearing in the *Nara* period (early 8th to late 8th century), *Waka* continued to be composed through the *Edo* period (early 17th to late 19th century). *Waka* can take various forms, such as repetitions of 5-7-5 syllable patterns or a 38-syllable structure (5-7-7-5-7-7), but the most common form is the 31-syllable structure (5-7-5-7-7), known as *Tanka*. Since its inception in the *Nara* period, people have gathered to compose and recite *Waka* on common themes, and it became so deeply rooted in Japanese culture that emperors would sometimes order the compilation of *Waka* collections.

*Honkadori* is a sophisticated poetic technique in Japanese classical literature for composing *Waka*, where poets incorporate words or poetic sentiments from old *Waka*s (*Honka*) into their own work. This technique creates layered meanings while expressing their own poetic voice (Ooka, 2009). In the practice of *Honkadori*, the original *Waka* that serves as the source of borrowed words or expressions is called *Honka*. This technique differs from simple quotation or plagiarism, as it requires deep understanding and creative reinterpretation of classical works. Interestingly, a similar practice exists in modern music, particularly in hip-hop, called sampling. Sampling is a music production technique where parts of existing songs (such as drums,



*Proceedings of the Second Ancient Language Processing Workshop associated with NAACL 2025*, pages 220–227
May 4, 2025. 

bass, melody, or vocals) are extracted and reconstructed within new compositions. For example, Kanye West's "Gold Digger" is known for sampling Ray Charles's "I Got a Woman," adding new interpretations to the original work. Like *Honkadori* in *Waka*, sampling represents a creative technique where modern musicians show respect for classic works while adding their own interpretations. An example of *Honkadori* is shown in Figure 1.

*Honkadori* is said to have been established during the *Heian* period (late 8th to late 12th century). *Teika Fujiwara*, a prominent poet from the *Heian* period, established the following rules for *Honkadori* in his poetic treatise *Eikataigai* (The Editorial Committee of the Great Dictionary of Waka Literature, 2014):

- One should not borrow from *Waka*s of contemporary poets.
- The borrowed phrases from classical *Waka*s should be limited to approximately two phrases.
- The theme must be different from the *Honka*.

We propose a method for automatically detect *Honkadori* in *Waka*. While shared characters between *Waka*s provide important clues for *Honkadori* detection, the second rule from *Eikataigai* often results in relatively short common subsequences between the *Honka* and the *Waka* employing *Honkadori* (hereafter, this is denoted as HONKADORI to distinguish it from the technique itself, and the original *Waka* that serves as the source of this HONKADORI is denoted as HONKA). Therefore, character-based methods alone struggle to automatically distinguish *Honkadori* from other similar *Waka*s. To address this problem, we first develop a *Waka*-specialized embedding model and then create a model that calculates the probability of any given pair of *Waka*s being in a *Honkadori* relationship. Our study is expected to contribute to classical literature studies through the detection of previously undiscovered instances of *Honkadori*.

## 2 Related Work

### 2.1 Character-based Similar *Waka* Detection Methods

Yamazaki et al. (1998) and Takeda et al. (2000) have proposed methods for detecting similar *Waka*s based on character similarity. These methods enable the detection of various types of similar *Waka*s, including *Honkadori*, expressions used in specific poetic situations, variant *Waka*s that developed different expressions through transmission, and *Waka*s that share rhetorical devices such as *makurakotoba* (set epithets in classical Japanese poetry). However, these studies do not focus on the semantic aspects of *Waka*s, making it difficult to detect pairs of similar *Waka*s that do not share significant character similarities.

### 2.2 Allusion Detection Methods Using Embedding Vectors

Kondo (2024) has proposed a method for detecting *Hikiuta* (poetic allusions) using embedding vectors. In their study, they focused on identifying allusions between two significant classical Japanese works that are *The Tale of Genji* and *Kokin Wakashū*. *The Tale of Genji* is a long narrative work, or novel, written by Murasaki Shikibu during the middle Heian period. The *Kokin Wakashū* is a *Waka*'s anthology compiled in the early Heian period under the Imperial command of the Emperor at that time. *The Tale of Genji* contains several passages that use *Hikiuta* based on *Waka* poems included in the *Kokin Wakashū*. *Hikiuta* is a technique similar to *Honkadori*, where a famous *Waka* passage is quoted within prose text or an emotional passage (Nishizawa, 2002).

To detect such *Hikiuta*, Kondo (2024) has proposed a method using embedding vectors. This method first embeds text segments from *The Tale of Genji* and *Kokin Wakashū* into a vector space using OpenAI's text-embedding-ada-002 model (OpenAI, 2022). Then, it calculates cosine similarities between the embedding vector of each *Waka* from *Kokin Wakashū* and the embedding vectors of text segments from *The Tale of Genji* and identifies high-similarity pairs as potential allusions. Furthermore, the study reports that applying N-gram character matching as a filter increases the proportion of verifiable allusions among the candidates in *The Tale of Genji*. This method has also led to the discovery of previously unidentified allusions. However, the study does not evaluate either the accuracy of classical text embeddings of text-embedding-ada-002 or the precision of the allusion detection method itself.

# 3 Construction and Evaluation of *Waka* Embedding Models

We develop *Waka* embedding models. We first construct a training dataset and then use it to fine-tune a pre-trained encoder model with unsupervised SimCSE (Gao et al., 2021). We evaluate the resulting models using pairs of *Waka*s from *Hyakunin Isshu* (en: One Hundred *Waka*s by One Hundred Poets) and their modern Japanese translations.

## 3.1 Construction of Training Datasets

To train *Waka* embedding models, we use literary works from the *Nara* period through the *Edo* period recorded in the Corpus of Historical Japanese (CHJ) (NINJAL, 2024). Additionally, we use *Tanka*s from the Modern *Tanka* Database (Yuna et al., 2022) and literary works in classical Japanese orthography published in the *Aozora Bunko* digital library.

From CHJ, we obtained approximately 100,000 sentences including approximately 17,000 *Waka*s (referred to as the **CHJ dataset**), approximately 140,000 *Waka*s from the Modern *Tanka* Database (referred to as the **Modern *Tanka* dataset**), and approximately 335,000 sentences from *Aozora Bunko* (referred to as the ***Aozora* dataset**).

## 3.2 Construction of *Waka* Embedding Models

In supervised learning for text embedding models, we need annotations indicating which sentences are semantically similar and which are different. However, creating such annotations for large amounts of text is time-consuming and costly. To avoid the annotation cost, we fine-tune a Japanese RoBERTa model (Liu et al., 2019)[1] using unsupervised SimCSE, a contrastive learning approach. Unsupervised SimCSE generates two slightly different embedding vectors by applying dropout twice to the same sentence and treats these as positive examples. This approach allows us to train effective embedding models without the need for manual annotation. When inputting text into this model, we perform word segmentation using the Juman++ morphological analyzer (Tolmachev et al., 2018). We compare the performance of unsupervised SimCSE using individual datasets constructed in Section 3.1 and combined datasets.

[1] https://huggingface.co/nlp-waseda/roberta-base-japanese

### 3.2.1 Models with Individual Datasets

We trained a model for 5 epochs using each of the CHJ dataset, Modern *Tanka* dataset, and *Aozora* dataset individually.

### 3.2.2 Models with Combined Datasets

We trained a model for 5 epochs using a dataset created by merging and shuffling the *Aozora*, Modern *Tanka*, and CHJ datasets. Furthermore, we implemented curriculum learning (Bengio et al., 2009) that gradually adapts the training data to the *Waka* format as follows. In this curriculum learning process, datasets other than the CHJ dataset were used for only 1 epoch of training, followed by 5 epochs of training with the CHJ dataset.

- *Aozora dataset* → CHJ dataset
- Modern *Tanka* dataset → CHJ dataset
- *Aozora* dataset → Modern *Tanka* dataset → CHJ dataset

## 3.3 Evaluation of *Waka* Embedding Models

### 3.3.1 Evaluation Method

To quantitatively evaluate the performance of the trained *Waka* embedding models, we adopt an evaluation method using a parallel corpus of all 100 *Waka*s from *Hyakunin Isshu* and their modern Japanese translations. *Hyakunin Isshu* is an anthology of 100 *Waka*s, with a *Waka* carefully selected to represent each of one hundred distinct poets. The parallel corpus was obtained from the website "History of Hyakunin Isshu"[2 3 4]. The evaluation was conducted according to the following procedure:

1. Convert an original *Waka* into an embedding vector using the target model.
2. Similarly, convert each of the 100 modern translations into an embedding vector using the same model.
3. Calculate cosine similarities between the embedding vectors of the original *Waka* and each of all modern translations.
4. For the original *Waka*, consider the modern translation with the highest similarity as the model's predicted translation.
5. Count a prediction as correct if the predicted translation matches the true translation and evaluate the model using accuracy over all 100 *Waka*s.

[2] https://hyakunin.stardust31.com/gendaiyaku.html
[3] https://hyakunin.stardust31.com/gendaiyaku-itiran.html
[4] https://hyakunin.stardust31.com/yaku.html

| Model | text-embedding-small | text-embedding-large | text-embedding-ada-002 | *Waka* embedding model |
|---|---|---|---|---|
| Accuracy | 0.95 | 0.91 | 0.92 | 0.95 |

Table 1: Accuracy comparison between OpenAI models and *Waka* embedding model.

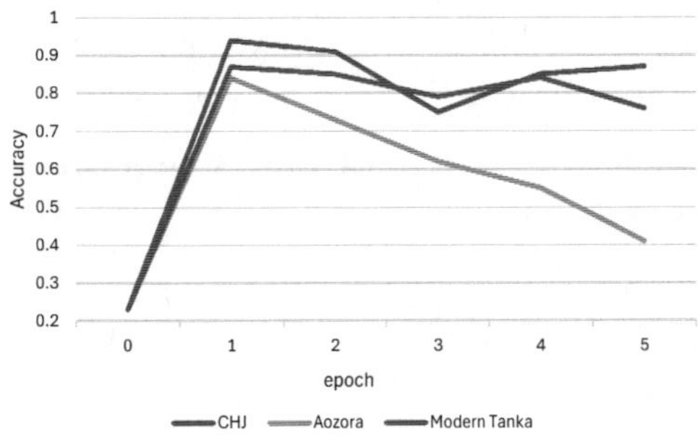


Figure 2: Accuracy transitions by epoch for training with individual datasets.

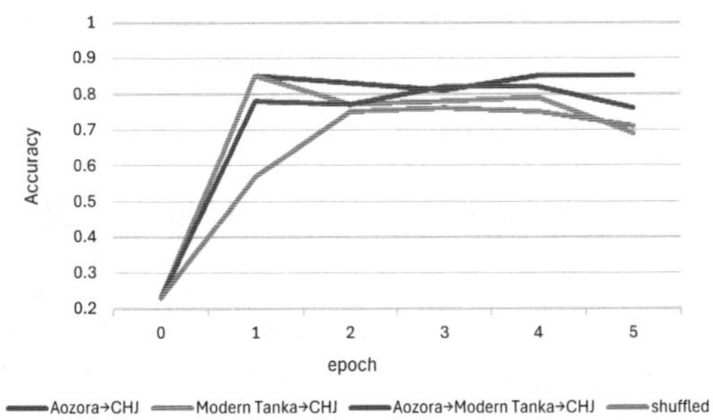


Figure 3: Accuracy transitions by epoch for training with combined datasets.

#### 3.3.2 Evaluation Results

Figure 2 shows the accuracy transitions for each epoch in training with the individual datasets. The best-performing model using a single dataset was the one trained for 1 epoch on the CHJ dataset, achieving an accuracy of 0.95. Figure 3 shows the accuracy transitions for each epoch in training with the combined datasets. Multiple models achieved the highest performance with a combined dataset, with an accuracy of 0.85. Therefore, the model trained for 1 epoch on the CHJ dataset demonstrated the highest performance. Based on these results, we adopted the model trained for 1 epoch on the CHJ dataset as our *Waka* embedding model and used it in the subsequent experiments.

#### 3.3.3 Comparison with OpenAI Models

We compared OpenAI's text embedding models with our *Waka* embedding model using the evaluation method described in Section 3.3.2. The results are shown in Table 1. Among the OpenAI models, text-embedding-3-small achieved the highest performance with an accuracy of 0.95. Our *Waka* embedding model demonstrated performance equivalent to it.

## 4 Construction of HONKA Detection Models

To automatically detect the *Honkadori* technique, we need to consider not only surface similarities between *Waka*s but also their semantic relationships. Therefore, we construct a HONKA detection model that uses machine learning to understand the relationship between HONKA and their HONKADORI by using features obtained from our *Waka* embedding model. The construction of this model involves three steps: first collecting training data of *Honkadori* pairs, then training machine learning models using features extracted from *Waka* pairs, and finally evaluating the model's performance.

### 4.1 Dataset Construction

To construct our training and evaluation datasets for the *Honka* detection model, we collected positive examples and two distinct types of negative examples.

First, as positive examples, we manually collected 300 pairs of HONKA and their corresponding HONKADORI from the Eight Imperial Anthologies[5] as documented in the 日本うたことば表現辞典本歌本節取編 (en: Dictionary of Japanese Poetic Expressions - Compilation of Honka and Honsetsudori). From these collected pairs, we allocated 200 pairs for the training dataset and the remaining 100 pairs for the evaluation dataset.

We created two distinct sets of negative examples. First, we constructed a dataset of 200 randomly combined *Waka* pairs from the Eight Imperial Anthologies. These pairs serve as our first type of negative examples, representing arbitrary combinations of poems without any intentional relationship. For our second set of negative examples, we focused on poems sharing *makurakotoba*, i.e., fixed epithetic expressions that precede and modify

[5]The Eight Imperial Anthologies (*Hachidaishū*) are the most prestigious collections of *Waka*, compiled by imperial order.

specific words through conventional associations. We collected these pairs from the Dictionary of Japanese Poetic Expressions: Makurakotoba Volume 1 and 2 (日本うたことば表現辞典枕詞編(上・下)) (Ooka, 2007). To manage the collection process efficiently, we selected 10 types of *makurakotoba* and collected 6 *Waka*s for each type. We then created all possible unordered pairs from each set of 6 *Waka*s, which resulted in 15 pairs per *makurakotoba* type. This process yielded a total of 150 pairs of *Waka*s that share *makurakotoba* but are not classified as HONKADORI.

In summary, we constructed a dataset with 300 pairs of *Honka* and their corresponding *Honkadori* (200 pairs for training and 100 pairs for evaluation) as positive examples. We also constructed 350 pairs of *Waka*s as negative examples, including 150 pairs that serve as hard negative examples. All negative examples are used only for training purposes.

### 4.2 Machine Learning Model Construction

We constructed the HONKA detection model based on embedding vectors obtained from the *Waka* embedding model. The HONKA detection model calculates the probability that a pair of *Waka* is in a *Honkadori* relationship based on features extracted from the pair. Our *Waka* embeddings (RoBERTa base) are 768-dimensional, meaning that using embedding vectors for both *Waka*s in a pair would result in a $768 \times 2$ dimensional input. Due to the limited amount of training data, we intended to restrict the input dimensionality of the machine learning model. Therefore, instead of using embedding vectors directly, we used the following seven features:

- Cosine similarity between *Waka* pairs
- Top 5 highest cosine similarities from the 25 similarities between corresponding phrases (5-7-5-7-7) of the *Waka* pairs
- Longest common subsequence length between *Waka* pairs

To minimize the impact of orthographic variations, the longest common subsequence length between *Waka* pairs is calculated by obtaining readings using the morphological analyzer MeCab (Kudo et al., 2004). These readings are obtained with the *Waka*-specific morphological dictionary *Waka* UniDic (Ogiso et al., 2012). The readings are then converted to *kana* characters with voiced and semi-voiced sound marks removed. Using these features,

| Method | 1st | 2nd | 3rd | 4th | 5th |
|---|---|---|---|---|---|
| Nearest Neighbor | 8 | 9 | 2 | 0 | 1 |
| Logistic Regression | 8 | 9 | 2 | 0 | 1 |
| SVM | 7 | 0 | 0 | 0 | 1 |
| LightGBM | 1 | 6 | 2 | 1 | 2 |
| MLP | 9 | 11 | 1 | 2 | 0 |
| Meta-model | 10 | 5 | 0 | 0 | 0 |

Table 2: Rank distribution of HONKA detection results of each method.

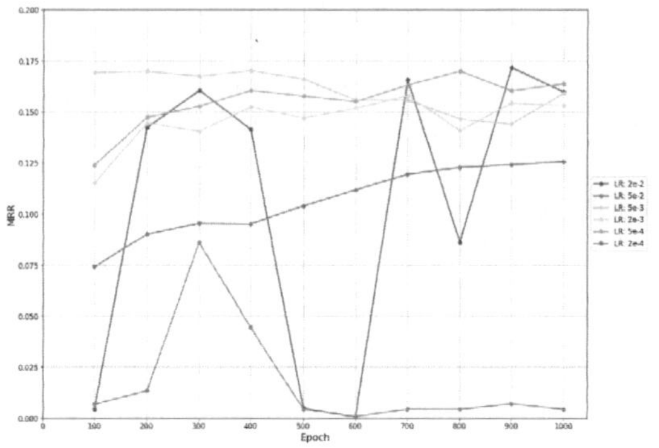


Figure 4: MRR transitions for different learning rates in MLP.

we trained logistic regression, SVM, LightGBM, MLP models, and a meta-model (logistic regression) that blends these models. For MLP, we conducted training with multiple learning rates. The detailed training settings are provided in Table 6.

### 4.3 Experiments

#### 4.3.1 Evaluation Method and Baseline

**Evaluation Method** We evaluated the accuracy of HONKA detection using approximately 9,600 *Waka* from the Eight Imperial Anthologies in the Corpus of Historical Japanese (referred to as the **Eight Imperial Anthologies Dataset**) and the *Honkadori* evaluation dataset (100 pairs). The evaluation was conducted according to the following procedure:

1. Apply the HONKA detection method to each HONKADORI in the evaluation dataset and all *Waka*s in the Eight Imperial Anthologies Dataset.
2. Sort the Eight Imperial Anthologies Dataset based on the probabilities output by the model in descending order of HONKA likelihood.
3. Evaluate using the following two metrics:

| Nearest Neighbor | Logistic Regression | SVM | LightGBM | MLP | Meta-model |
|---|---|---|---|---|---|
| 0.149 | 0.147 | 0.0793 | 0.0650 | 0.172 | 0.137 |

Table 3: MRR for each HONKA detection method.

| HONKADORI | 九重の (imperial court) にほひなりせば (if still as precious) さくらばな (cherry blossoms) **春知りそむる** (just learning spring) かひやあらまし (would have had meaning)<br>(en: If this place was still as precious as it was back then, these cherry blossoms would have held more meaning.) |
|---|---|
| Rank | Predicted HONKA |
| 1 (HONKA) | ことしより (from this year onward) **春しりそむる** (just learning spring) **さくらばな** (cherry blossoms) ちるといふことは (the act of scattering) ならはざらなん (please do not learn)<br>(en: Please don't learn how to scatter, oh cherry blossoms that have just begun to bloom this year as if you've only just discovered spring.) |
| 2 | さくら花 (cherry blossoms) そこなる影ぞ (reflection there) おしまるる (is regrettable) しづめる人の (of the sad people) 春とおもへば (when I think of spring)<br>(en: The cherry blossoms are blooming. When I see their reflection in the pond, it reminds me of those who are unhappy.) |
| 3 | さくら花 (cherry blossoms) 匂ふなごりに (in their lingering fragrance) 大かたの (all of) 春さへ (even spring) おしくおもほゆるかな (feels precious indeed)<br>(en: In the lingering beauty of the cherry blossoms in full bloom, even the entire spring becomes precious, and I cannot help but feel this way.) |

Table 4: Example of correct HONKA prediction ranked first by the model. The bold text represents the shared character sequences between HONKADORI and HONKA.

- Top-5 correct count: The number of times the correct HONKA appeared in the top 5 entries of the sorted Eight Imperial Anthologies Dataset.
- MRR (Mean Reciprocal Rank): The average of the reciprocal of the rank at which the correct HONKA appeared.

**Baseline** As a baseline for comparing our proposed method, we used HONKA detection based on nearest neighbor search. We calculated cosine similarities between the vectors of HONKADORI in the evaluation dataset and each of the *Waka*s in the Eight Imperial Anthologies Dataset. The evaluation was performed by sorting the Eight Imperial Anthologies Dataset in descending order of cosine similarity.

#### 4.3.2 Experimental Results

Table 2 shows the rank distribution of HONKA detection results of each method. Table 3 shows the MRR of each model alongside the baseline MRR. The specifications of each model are shown in Table 6.

While logistic regression and MLP showed relatively good results, SVM and LightGBM performed significantly worse than the baseline. The model with the highest top-5 correct count was MLP (learning rate 2e-2, 700 epochs) with 23 cases. The model with the highest MRR was MLP (learning rate 2e-2, 900 epochs) with 0.172, indicating higher detection accuracy for HONKADORI than the nearest neighbor search. Table 4 shows an example where the model correctly identified the HONKA with the highest probability. Additional examples of *Honkadori* pairs that were included in the top-3 predictions by the model are shown in Table 5. In Table 5, "rank" refers to the position of each HONKA when sorted based on the probability output by the model in descending order of HONKA likelihood. Furthermore, Figure 4 shows the results of comparative experiments with different learning rates for MLP.

## 5 Conclusion

We constructed *Waka*-specialized embedding models and HONKA detection models. Furthermore, by building machine learning models using features extracted from the embedding vectors output by these models, we demonstrated that HONKA detection is possible with reasonable accuracy.

This study has several challenges to address. First, Juman++, which was used for input to the *Waka* embedding model, is a morphological analyzer designed for modern Japanese and is not well-suited for tokenizing old Japanese texts. Next is the amount of training data. While we manually collected 300 pairs of *Waka* with *Honkadori* relationships, higher accuracy could be expected with

| Rank | HONKA | HONKADORI |
|---|---|---|
| 1 | あだなりと (vainly known) 名にこそたてれ (though bearing the name) 桜花 (cherry blossoms) としにまれなる (rarely each year) 人もまちけり (still I wait for someone)<br>(en: Though cherry blossoms are known to scatter so easily, I still wait for those who visit but rarely in a year.) | 嵐吹く (storm-blown) 花の梢は (the tips of blossoms) あだなりと (vainly known) 名にこそたてれ (though bearing the name) 花の白雲 (white clouds of flowers)<br>(en: Though the storm-blown cherry blossoms are known to scatter easily, they still grace the sky like clouds of white flowers.) |
| 2 | けふこずは (if you don't come today) あすは雪とぞ (tomorrow surely snow) 降なましき (will fall like) えずは有とも (even if they remain) 花とみまし (would you see them as flowers?)<br>(en: If you do not come today, these cherry blossoms will scatter and fall like snow. Unlike snow, even if they remained without fading, would they still be seen as flowers?) | さくら色の (cherry-colored) 庭の春風 (spring breeze in the garden) あともなし (no trace remains) 訪はばぞ人の (if someone were to visit) 雪とだにみん (might see them at least as snow)<br>(en: The spring wind that once carried cherry blossom petals through my garden has left no trace behind; if only someone would visit, they might see the scattered petals as fallen snow and find beauty in the scene, but with no visitors, not even footprints remain.) |
| 3 | 山たかみ (high in the mountains) 人もすさめぬ (ignored by people) 桜花 (cherry blossoms) いたくなわびそ (do not grieve so deeply) 我見はやさむ (I shall come to see you)<br>(en: Cherry blossoms on the high mountain, though others pass you by without care, do not grieve so deeply —for I shall admire you and sing your praise.) | 春くれど (though spring has come) 人もすさめぬ (ignored by people) 山桜 (mountain cherry blossoms) 風のたよりに (guided by the wind) 我のみぞとふ (only I come to visit)<br>(en: Though spring has come, no one pays heed to the mountain cherry blossoms—only I, guided by the wind, go to visit them.) |

Table 5: Examples of correctly predicted HONKADORI within Top-3 rankings.

access to more data. Additionally, while the *Waka* embedding model evaluation uses classical texts and their modern Japanese translations, it would be preferable to construct an evaluation dataset composed entirely of classical texts. By addressing these challenges, we can expect further improvements in model accuracy and greater contributions to classical literature research. Moreover, it is expected to have a wide range of applications not only in classical literature research but also in identifying text reuse in modern internet memes, literature, visual works, and other media.

## Acknowledgments

We would like to express our sincere gratitude to Ms. Yuna Murata for providing the Modern Tanka Database for this research. This work was supported by JSPS KAKENHI Grant Numbers JP23K22374 and JP24H00727.

## References

Yoshua Bengio, Jérôme Louradour, Ronan Collobert, and Jason Weston. 2009. Curriculum learning. In *Proceedings of the 26th Annual International Conference on Machine Learning*, ICML '09, page 41–48, New York, NY, USA. Association for Computing Machinery.

Tianyu Gao, Xingcheng Yao, and Danqi Chen. 2021. SimCSE: Simple contrastive learning of sentence embeddings. In *Proceedings of the 2021 Conference on Empirical Methods in Natural Language Processing*, pages 6894–6910, Online and Punta Cana, Dominican Republic. Association for Computational Linguistics.

Yasuhiro Kondo. 2024. Detecting implicitly quoted waka within ' the tale of genji' through vector search. *The 38th Annual Conference of the Japanese Society for Artificial Intelligence*.

Taku Kudo, Kaoru Yamamoto, and Yuji Matsumoto. 2004. Applying conditional random fields to Japanese morphological analysis. In *Proceedings of the 2004 Conference on Empirical Methods in Natural Language Processing*, pages 230–237, Barcelona, Spain. Association for Computational Linguistics.

Yinhan Liu, Myle Ott, Naman Goyal, Jingfei Du, Mandar Joshi, Danqi Chen, Omer Levy, Mike Lewis, Luke Zettlemoyer, and Veselin Stoyanov. 2019. Roberta: A robustly optimized bert pretraining approach. arXiv. Abs/1907.11692.

NINJAL. 2024. The corpus of historical japanese.

Masashi Nishizawa. 2002. *Dictionary of Terms for Reading Japanese Classical Literature*. Tokyodo Shuppan.

Toshinobu Ogiso, Mamoru Komachi, Yasuharu Den, and Yuji Matsumoto. 2012. Unidic for early middle japanese: a dictionary for morphological analysis of classical japanese. In *Proceedings of the 8th International Conference on Language Resources and Evaluation (LREC 2012)*, pages 911–915.

Mkoto Ooka. 2007. 日本うたことば表現辞典枕詞編(上・下)*(en: Dictionary 275 of Japanese Poetic Expressions: Makurakotoba Volume 1 and 2)*. yushikan.

| Model | Parameter | Value |
|---|---|---|
| **MLP** | Input layer | Dimension: 7 |
| | Hidden layer 1 | Fully connected layer (7 $\rightarrow$ 32), Activation function: ReLU, Dropout rate: 0.2 |
| | Hidden layer 2 | Fully connected layer (32 $\rightarrow$ 16), Activation function: ReLU, Dropout rate: 0.2 |
| | Output layer | Fully connected layer (16 $\rightarrow$ 1), Activation function: Sigmoid |
| | Batch size | 8 |
| | Weight decay | $1 \times 10^{-3}$ |
| | Optimizer | Adam |
| | Loss function | Binary Cross Entropy |
| | Input preprocessing | StandardScaler |
| **Logistic Regression** | Maximum iterations | 1000 |
| | Regularization | L2 |
| **SVM** | Kernel function | RBF |
| | Probability estimates | Enabled |
| | Regularization parameter (C) | 1.0 |
| **LightGBM** | Objective function | binary |
| | Evaluation metric | binary error |
| | Number of boosting rounds | 100 |
| **Meta-model** | Input features | First-layer prediction probabilities (Logistic Regression, SVM, LightGBM, MLP) |
| | Data split configuration | 60% of training data used for first-layer learning<br>40% of training data used for meta-model learning |
| | Maximum iterations | 1000 |
| | Regularization | L2 |
| | Tolerance for stopping criteria | $1 \times 10^{-4}$ |

Table 6: Specifications of HONKA detection models.


Mkoto Ooka. 2009. 日本うたことば表現辞典本歌本節取編*(en: Dictionary of Japanese Poetic Expressions - Compilation of Honka and Honsetsudori)*. yushikan.

OpenAI. 2022. New and improved embedding model. Accessed: 2024-10-26.

Masayuki Takeda, Tomoko Fukuda, Ichiro Nanri, Mayumi Yamazaki, and Tamari Koichi. 2000. 和歌データからの類似歌発見(en: Discovery of similar waka from waka datas). 統計数理*(en: Statistical Mathematics)*, 48(2):289–310.

The Editorial Committee of the Great Dictionary of Waka Literature. 2014. 和歌文学大辞典*(en: the Great Dictionary of Waka Literature)*. Tokyodo Shuppan.

Arseny Tolmachev, Daisuke Kawahara, and Sadao Kurohashi. 2018. Juman++: A morphological analysis toolkit for scriptio continua. In *Proceedings of the 2018 Conference on Empirical Methods in Natural Language Processing: System Demonstrations*, pages 54–59, Brussels, Belgium. Association for Computational Linguistics.

Mayumi Yamazaki, Masayuki Takeda, Tomoko Fukuda, and Ichiro Nanri. 1998. 和歌データベースからの類似歌の自動抽出(en: Automatic extraction of similar poems from a waka database). 人文科学とコンピュータ*(en: Humanities and Computing)*, 40(8):40–48.

Murata Yuna, Kiyonori Nagasaki, and Ikki Ohmukai. 2022. 近代短歌全文テキストデータベースの構築(en: Building a comprehensive text database of modern tanka poetry). *Digital Humanities*, 3(1):17–26.

# Incorporating Lexicon-Aligned Prompting in Large Language Model for Tangut–Chinese Translation

**Yuxi Zheng**[1] and **Jingsong Yu**[2]
[1]Department of Chinese Language and Literature, Peking University, China
[2]School of Software and Microelectronics, Peking University, China
zhengyuxi@stu.pku.edu.cn
yjs@ss.pku.edu.cn

## Abstract

This paper proposes a machine translation approach for Tangut–Chinese using a large language model (LLM) enhanced with lexical knowledge. We fine-tune a Qwen-based LLM using Tangut–Chinese parallel corpora and dictionary definitions. Experimental results demonstrate that incorporating single-character dictionary definitions leads to the best BLEU-4 score of 72.33 for literal translation. Additionally, applying a chain-of-thought prompting strategy significantly boosts free translation performance to 64.20. The model also exhibits strong few-shot learning abilities, with performance improving as the training dataset size increases. Our approach effecttively translates both simple and complex Tangut sentences, offering a robust solution for low-resource language translation and contributing to the digital preservation of Tangut texts.

## 1 Introduction

The Tangut script, an intricate logographic writing system developed by the Tangut people in the 11th century, served as the official script of the Western Xia dynasty (1038–1227 CE). As a vital cultural artifact, Tangut texts encompass extensive historical, religious, and sociopolitical insights into this once-flourishing Silk Road civilization (Sun, 2023). Despite its scholarly significance, the decipherment and translation of Tangut texts remain formidable challenges. The script's structural complexity, lack of continuous usage traditions, and scarcity of parallel corpora have hindered efficient scholarly access to these invaluable historical records (Kong, 2018). Traditional translation methodologies, reliant on manual "four-line aligned translation" (comprising original text, phonetic transcription, literal translation, and idiomatic translation), demand specialized expertise and labor-intensive efforts, severely limiting the scalability of Tangut studies.

Recent advances in natural language processing (NLP), particularly the emergence of large language models (LLMs), offer unprecedented opportunities to automate low-resource language translation tasks (Lu, 2025). However, existing research has yet to address Tangut translation systematically. Prior work has focused on dictionary compilation, such as A Concise Tangut-Chinese Dictionary (Li, 2012), and manual text analysis, leaving a critical gap in computational methods tailored for Tangut's unique linguistic characteristics. The absence of machine translation systems for Tangut-Chinese conversion underscores both the urgency and innovation potential of this research.

This paper presents the first systematic study on neural machine translation for Tangut texts, targeting two critical tasks: literal translation (character-to-character alignment) and idiomatic translation (semantic restructuring into fluent Chinese). Below are two example sets. For each set: The first line contains the original Tangut text. The second line provides the Chinese character-by-character translation. The third line offers the English character-by-character translation. We performed word-level alignment for the first three lines. The fourth line presents the idiomatic Chinese translation. The fifth line gives the idiomatic English translation.

(1) Tangut

| | | | | | |
|---|---|---|---|---|---|
| [illegible] | [illegible] | [illegible] | [illegible] | [illegible] | [illegible] |
| 愿 | 永 | 缘 | 同 | 道种 | 为 |
| wish | forever | pratyaya | same | wisdom-seed | BE |

'愿永同缘为道种'
'May we always share the same pratyaya as a seed of the wisdom'

(2) Tangut

| | | | | | | |
|---|---|---|---|---|---|---|
| [illegible] | [illegible] | [illegible] | [illegible] | [illegible] | [illegible] | [illegible] |
| 实 | 正 | 法 | 中 | 入 | 当 | 能 |
| truly | correct | dharma | in | enter | should | be.able |

'当能真正法中入'
'we should be able to enter the truly correct dharma'



*Proceedings of the Second Ancient Language Processing Workshop associated with NAACL 2025*, pages 228–237
May 4, 2025. ©2025 Association for Computational Linguistics

Our work addresses three core challenges: (1) the extreme scarcity of parallel Tangut-Chinese data, (2) the need for precise alignment with authoritative lexicons, and (3) the requirement to adapt Tangut syntax to Classical Chinese expressions. To overcome these barriers, we propose an expert knowledge-enhanced LLM framework that integrates domain-specific dictionaries and chain-of-thought (CoT) prompting strategies. By fine-tuning a pre-trained Classical Chinese LLM (QwenClassical) with carefully curated Tangut datasets, our system achieves robust performance in both translation modes.

Our contributions are threefold:

- **Resource Development**: We compile and release the first publicly available Tangut-Chinese parallel corpus, derived from the *Three Generations Illuminated Collection* and *Avataṃsaka Sūtra*, with 569+525 sentence pairs annotated for literal and idiomatic translation.
- **Methodological Innovation**: We design a hybrid approach combining dictionary-guided character alignment and CoT-based semantic restructuring, enabling accurate translation even with minimal training data.
- **Empirical Validation**: Experiments demonstrate state-of-the-art performance, with BLEU-4 scores of 72.33 (literal) and 64.20 (idiomatic). Ablation studies confirm the effectiveness of domain-adapted LLMs and CoT prompting in low-resource scenarios.

This work not only advances the computational analysis of Tangut texts but also establishes a replicable framework for other under-resourced historical languages. By bridging the gap between ancient script studies and modern NLP, our system empowers historians and linguists to explore Tangut heritage with unprecedented efficiency, fostering new insights into the multicultural dynamics of medieval Eurasia.

The remainder of this paper is organized as follows: Section 2 reviews related work in Tangut linguistics and low-resource machine translation. Section 3 details our methodology, including data preparation and model architecture. Sections 4–5 present experimental results and case analyses, followed by discussions of limitations and future directions.

## 2 Related Work

This section reviews prior research in two key areas relevant to our study: (1) Tangut linguistics and script decipherment, and (2) low-resource machine translation, with a focus on historical and under-resourced languages. By situating our work within these domains, we highlight the unique challenges and opportunities of applying modern NLP techniques to Tangut texts.

### 2.1 Tangut Linguistics and Script Decipherment

The Tangut script, also known as Fanwen or Xixia script, is a logographic system comprising over 6,000 characters, developed under the Western Xia dynasty. Early efforts to decipher Tangut texts began in the 20th century, spearheaded by scholars such as Nikolai Nevsky (1960) and Luo Fuchang, who laid the groundwork for understanding its phonetic and semantic structures.

Recent advances in Tangut linguistics have focused on phonology, grammar, and textual analysis. For instance, studies have elucidated the script's phonetic components and syntactic patterns, enabling more accurate transcriptions and translations. The "four-line aligned translation" method, widely adopted in Tangut studies, exemplifies the meticulous process of converting Tangut texts into modern Chinese. This method involves four steps: (1) presenting the original Tangut text, (2) providing a phonetic transcription, (3) generating a literal translation, and (4) producing an idiomatic translation. While effective, this approach is labor-intensive and heavily reliant on expert knowledge, underscoring the need for computational solutions.

Despite these advancements, the field faces persistent challenges, including the scarcity of parallel corpora, the ambiguity of Tangut characters, and the lack of standardized tools for automated analysis (Liu, 2022). These limitations have hindered the scalability of Tangut research, making it an ideal candidate for NLP-driven innovations.

### 2.2 Low-Resource Machine Translation

Machine translation (MT) for low-resource languages has gained significant attention in recent years, driven by the success of neural models and transfer learning techniques. Early approaches relied on rule-based and statistical methods, which struggled to handle the morphological and syntactic complexities of under-resourced languages. The advent of neural machine translation, particularly sequence-to-sequence models and transformer architectures, has revolutionized the field, enabling more robust and context-aware translations (Zoph, 2016).

For historical and ancient languages, MT systems must address unique challenges, such as incomplete lexicons, fragmented texts, and the absence of native speakers. Recent work has demonstrated the potential of LLMs in this domain (Jiao et al, 2023). For example, BERT-based models have been adapted for Classical Chinese(Yu et al, 2020), while GPT variants have been fine-tuned for ancient Greek (Lu et al, 2025) and Latin (Stüssi et al, 2024) . These models leverage pre-training on large corpora and domain-specific fine-tuning to achieve state-of-the-art performance.

A key innovation in low-resource MT is the use of auxiliary resources, such as dictionaries, parallel texts, and multilingual embeddings (Ammar et al, 2016), to enhance model performance. Techniques like back-translation, data augmentation, and transfer learning (Zoph et al, 2016) have proven effective in scenarios with limited parallel data. Additionally, prompting strategies, including chain-of-thought (CoT) (Wei et al, 2022) and few-shot learning (Wang et al, 2020), have emerged as powerful tools for guiding LLMs in low-resource settings.

Despite these advances, the application of MT to Tangut texts remains unexplored. The script's logographic nature, combined with its historical and cultural specificity, presents unique challenges that require tailored solutions. Our work bridges this gap by integrating domain-specific lexicons and CoT prompting into a fine-tuned LLM framework, enabling accurate and scalable Tangut-Chinese translation.

### 2.3 Bridging the Gap

By synthesizing insights from Tangut linguistics and low-resource MT, our research addresses a critical gap in both fields. We build on the foundational work of Tangut scholars while leveraging cutting-edge NLP techniques to automate and enhance the translation process. This interdisciplinary approach not only advances Tangut studies but also contributes to the broader field of historical language processing, offering a replicable framework for other under-resourced scripts.

In the following sections, we detail our methodology, which combines expert knowledge with neural models to achieve robust and interpretable translations of Tangut texts.

## 3 Methodology

Our methodology addresses the dual challenges of translating Tangut texts into Chinese through two interconnected tasks: literal translation (character-level alignment) and idiomatic translation (semantic restructuring). We propose a hybrid framework that integrates domain-specific lexicons with a fine-tuned large language model (LLM), enhanced by chain-of-thought (CoT) prompting strategies. This section details our data preparation, model architecture, and training protocols.

### 3.1 Data Preparation

#### 3.1.1 Lexical Resources

We utilize the *Concise Tangut-Chinese Dictionary* (Li, 2012), which provides 6,703 Tangut character entries with 8,245 annotated Chinese definitions. Each processed entry includes:

- **Full Definitions** (Dict): Multi-sense explanations with part-of-speech tags (e.g., "1. 種、苗、裔[名詞] 2. 胤 3. 明").
- **Simplified Definitions** (DictSingle): Single-sense keywords derived from Dict (e.g., "种、苗、裔、胤、明").

These definitions serve as lexical anchors for character-level alignment during translation.

#### 3.1.2 Parallel Corpus Construction

We compile a Tangut-Chinese parallel corpus from two primary sources:

- **Three Generations Illuminated Collection**: 569 sentence pairs with four-line aligned translations (original Tangut, phonetic transcription, literal Chinese, idiomatic Chinese), sourced from Sun (2022).
- **Avataṃsaka Sūtra Vol. 77**: 525 sentence pairs, supplemented by ChatGPT-generated literal translations from existing Japanese paraphrases (Arakawa, 2011).

The corpus is split into:

- **Training Set:** 95% of the *Three Generations* data (541 pairs).
- **Test Set:** 5% of the *Three Generations* data (28 pairs).
- **Generalization Test**: the Avataṃsaka Sūtra Vol. 77 data(525 pairs).

### 3.2 Model Architecture

#### 3.2.1 Base LLM: QwenClassical

We employ QwenClassical, a variant of Qwen1.5-14B-Chat (Bai et al., 2023), pre-trained on 36GB of Classical Chinese texts (e.g., Shiji, Zizhi Tongjian) and fine-tuned with 390K task-specific examples (e.g., classical-modern Chinese translation, poetry generation). The specific training process refers to the existing classical Chinese model (Zhang, 2024). This domain adaptation enables robust handling of Tangut-to-Chinese syntactic and semantic divergences.

### 3.2.2 Expert Knowledge Integration

To inject Tangut-specific linguistic knowledge, we change each Tangut character with its Dict or DictSingle definitions during input encoding. For the term '[illegible]', when using DictSingle, its prompt is shown in Table 1.

| Tangut Script | Prompt |
|---|---|
| [illegible] | The candidate words for each Tangut Character are<br>The first character:<br>[罪、过]<br>The second character:<br>[非、否、不]<br>The third character:<br>[皆、咸、俱、普、悉、总、极、周、竟]<br>The fourth character:<br>[不]<br>The fifth character:<br>[做、作、为] |

Table 1: DictSingle Definitions for the Tangut Characters '[illegible]'

This approach grounds the model in authoritative lexical semantics while preserving contextual flexibility. By explicitly associating each Tangut character with its possible meanings, the model can better disambiguate polysemous characters and generate more accurate translations. Additionally, the use of simplified definitions (DictSingle) reduces noise and improves computational efficiency, as the model focuses on the most relevant semantic information.

## 3.3 Training Strategy

### 3.3.1 Literal Translation

We constructed input-output pairs as shown in Table 2 for fine-tuning the model for literal translation.

### 3.3.2 Idiomatic Translation

Idiomatic translation is framed as a two-step CoT task:

1. **Literal Drafting**: Generate a provisional literal translation $L = \{l_1, \dots l_n\}$.
2. **Semantic Refinement**: Restructure $L$ into fluent Classical Chinese $Y = \{y_1, \dots y_n\}$ using in-context examples.

We constructed input-output pairs as shown in Table 3 for fine-tuning the model for Idiomatic translation.

This CoT strategy mimics human translation workflows, reducing semantic drift in low-resource scenarios.

| Input | Output |
|---|---|
| Provide the literal translation of the Tangut script. The candidate words for each Tangut Character are<br>The first character: [...]<br>The second character: [...]<br>The third character: [...]<br>The fourth character: [...]<br>The fifth character: [...] | The literal translation is: ... |

Table 2: Input-Output Pairs for Fine-Tuning the Model for Literal Translation

| Input | Output |
|---|---|
| First, provide the literal translation of the Tangut script, and then give the idiomatic translation based on the literal translation.<br>The candidate words for each Tangut Character are<br>The first character: [...]<br>The second character: [...]<br>The third character: [...]<br>The fourth character: [...]<br>The fifth character: [...] | The literal translation is: ...<br>The idiomatic translation is: ... |

Table 3: Input-Output Pairs for Fine-Tuning the Model for Idiomatic Translation

## 3.4 Implementation Details

- **Hardware**: 2×NVIDIA A800 GPUs (80GB VRAM).
- **Optimization**: AdamW (learning rate 3e−4, cosine decay), mixed-precision (bfloat16).
- **Training**: 5 epochs, batch size 8, gradient accumulation steps 1.
- **Tokenization**: SentencePiece (32K vocabulary) with Tangut Unicode block extensions.
- **Finetuning**: LoRA finetuning with Zero2 technique.

# 4 Experiments

This section evaluates the performance of our Tangut-Chinese machine translation system through quantitative metrics, ablation studies, and qualitative analyses. We assess both literal and idiomatic translation tasks, investigate the impact of training data scale, and validate the model's generalization capability across diverse Tangut texts.

## 4.1 Experimental Setup

### 4.1.1 Datasets

- **Primary Dataset**: 569 sentence pairs from Three Generations Illuminated Collection, split into 541 training and 28 test pairs.
- **Generalization Dataset**: 525 sentence pairs from Avataṃsaka Sūtra Vol. 77, with 200 held-out pairs for cross-domain evaluation.
- **Lexical Resources**: 6,703 Tangut characters annotated with 8,245 Chinese definitions from A Concise Tangut-Chinese Dictionary.

### 4.1.2 Baselines and Variants

We compare two base models:

- **Qwen:** Original Qwen1.5-14B-Chat.
- **QwenClassical:** Our pre-trained Classical Chinese variant.

For each model, we test four configurations:

- **Dict**: Full dictionary definitions.
- **DictSingle**: Simplified single-keyword definitions.
- **Prompt-0-shot**: Direct translation instruction.
- **PromptCoT**: Chain-of-thought prompting.

### 4.1.3 Evaluation Metrics

- **BLEU-4**: Measures n-gram overlap between machine and reference translations (Papineni, 2002).
- **Human Evaluation**: Three Tangut linguistics experts rate translations on a 5-point Likert scale (1: Incoherent, 5: Fluent and Faithful).

## 4.2 Main Results

### 4.2.1 Literal Translation Performance

Table 4 compares BLEU-4 scores across configurations. QwenClassical with DictSingle achieves the highest score (72.33), outperforming the base Qwen model by 2.83 points. Simplified definitions (DictSingle) consistently improve performance over full definitions (Dict), likely due to reduced lexical ambiguity.

| Model | Dict | DictSingle |
|---|---|---|
| Qwen | 69.78 | 71.50 |
| QwenClassical | 70.86 | **72.33** |

Table 4: Performance of Tangut-Chinese Literal Translation on Test Set (BLEU-4)

### 4.2.2 Idiomatic Translation Performance

Table 5 demonstrates the superiority of CoT prompting (PromptCoT) over direct prompting (Prompt-0-shot), with a 12.14 BLEU-4 improvement. QwenClassical+DictSingle+PromptCoT achieves the best performance (64.20), validating the effectiveness of stepwise semantic restructuring.

| Model | Prompt-0-shot | PromptCoT |
|---|---|---|
| QwenClassical+Dict | 51.06 | 62.54 |
| QwenClassical+DictSingle | 52.58 | **64.20** |

Table 5: Performance of Tangut-Chinese Idiomatic Translation on Test Set (BLEU-4)

## 4.3 Impact of Training Data Scale

To assess data efficiency, we vary the training set size from 100 to 500 pairs (Table 6). Both tasks exhibit steady performance growth, with literal translation saturating at ~500 samples (BLEU-4: 73.41). Notably, the model achieves 62.83 BLEU-4 for literal translation with only 100 samples, demonstrating strong few-shot learning capabilities.

| Training Set Size | Literal Translation | Idiomatic Translation |
|---|---|---|
| 100 | 62.83 | 59.53 |
| 200 | 70.06 | 62.34 |
| 300 | 69.57 | 62.73 |
| 400 | 71.31 | 65.94 |
| 500 | **73.41** | **66.05** |

Table 6: BLEU-4 Scores with Varying Training Data Sizes

## 4.4 Cross-Domain Generalization

We evaluate generalization by fine-tuning on incremental subsets of Avataṃsaka Sūtra data (Table 7). With 200 supplementary pairs, the model achieves 30.62 (literal) and 37.00 (idiomatic) BLEU-4 on the out-of-domain test set, confirming its adaptability to new Tangut genres.

| Added Pairs | Literal Translation | Idiomatic Translation |
|---|---|---|
| 40 | 23.88 | 30.92 |
| 80 | 24.58 | 32.62 |
| 120 | 25.45 | 34.76 |
| 160 | 27.28 | 35.49 |
| 200 | **30.62** | **37.00** |

Table 7: Generalization Performance on Avatamsaka Sūtra Dataset (BLEU-4)

### 4.5 Comparison with other high performance models

To clarify the need for fine-tuning, experiments were conducted on ChatGPT-4o, Gemini-2.0-Flash and DeepSeek V3, which currently have excellent comprehensive performance, using a few-shot method. Dictsingle and Dictsingle+PromptCoT is used for the translation. Five samples were randomly selected from the training set as examples and input into the model, and then the BLEU-4 score was calculated on the generated results. The experimental results are summarized in Table 8.

| Model | Machine Literal Translation | Machine Idiomatic Translation |
|---|---|---|
| ChatGPT-4o | 20.13 | 14.96 |
| DeepSeek V3 | 38.85 | 24.33 |
| Gemini-2.0-Flash | 32.07 | 19.68 |
| ours | **72.33** | **64.20** |

Table 8: Comparison with other high-performance models (using few-shot methods) (BLEU-4)

From the experimental results, whether it is automatic literal translation or automatic idiomatic translation, the model proposed in this paper scores significantly higher than ChatGPT-4.0, DeepSeek V3, and Gemini-2.0-Flash under few-shot learning methods. This indicates that general models struggle to meet the demands of literal and free translation tasks for Tangut texts due to a lack of relevant content in their training data aimed at the design tasks of this study. However, through fine-tuning, we have significantly improved the model's adaptability to specific tasks, resulting in a substantial increase in the quality of both automatic literal and idiomatic translations. Based on the above comparative results, we can further validate the effectiveness and necessity of fine-tuning strategies.

### 4.6 Human Evaluation

Three experts rated 50 randomly sampled translations (Table 9). QwenClassical+DictSingle+PromptCoT received the highest fluency (4.12/5) and faithfulness (4.35/5) scores, aligning with automated metrics.

| Model | Fluency | Faithfulness |
|---|---|---|
| Qwen+Dict | 3.45 | 3.78 |
| QwenClassical +DictSingle +PromptCoT | **4.12** | **4.35** |

Table 9: Expert Ratings of Translation Quality (5-point Likert Scale)

### 4.7 Case Study

To visually demonstrate the effects of automatic translation and automatic interpretation, typical examples are selected for analysis separately. The results are shown in Table 10 and Table 11.

| Tangut Script | Reference Literal Translation | Machine Literal Translation |
|---|---|---|
| [illegible] | 香花布列 | 香花排列 |
| [illegible] | 凡君子者，他利故已不忘，不学者无 | 夫子者，他利为己不忘，不学者，则无 |

Table 10: Example of Literal Translation

| Tangut Script | Reference Literal Translation | Reference Idiomatic Translation | Machine Idiomatic Translation |
|---|---|---|---|
| [illegible] | 此复退难自何见 | 此复难退自何见 | 此复遣返难自见 |
| [illegible] | △想△则人悲痛 | 我等每思则悲哭 | 我等每思则悲哭 |

Table 11: Example of Idiomatic Translation

The machine literal translation examples of simple sentences and complex sentences are shown in Table 10. The analysis results show that for the translation of simple sentences, the model can accurately capture the semantic information of the source language and achieve accurate conversion. For the translation of complex sentences, although there are slight differences in local expression between machine translation output and reference translations. Overall, they still maintain a high level of semantic integrity and expression accuracy. This indicates that the model proposed in this study has good robustness in handling translation tasks of different language complexities.

Table 11 presents examples of machine idiomatic translation, where omitted content in the standard translation is represented by the symbol "△". When automatically paraphrased, the model is able to effecttively identify and supplement this implicit information, thus generating a more complete translation.

### 4.8 Error Analysis

Common failure modes include:

1. **Ambiguous Characters**: Misinterpreting Tangut homographs.

2. **Syntactic Divergence**: Over-literal restructuring (e.g., retaining Tangut SOV order in Chinese SVO contexts).

3. **Cultural References**: Missing context-specific terms (e.g., Buddhist technical vocabulary).

## 5 Conclusions

This paper presents the first systematic study on neural machine translation for Tangut texts, addressing the critical challenges of translating a historical logographic script with extremely limited parallel resources. By integrating domain-specific lexicons, chain-of-thought prompting, and a pretrained Classical Chinese LLM, we develop a hybrid framework that achieves robust performance in both literal and idiomatic translation tasks. Our key findings and contributions are summarized as follows:

- Effective Resource Utilization: The integration of expert-curated dictionaries (A Concise Tangut-Chinese Dictionary) with neural models significantly improves translation accuracy, achieving state-of-the-art BLEU-4 scores of 72.33 (literal) and 64.20 (idiomatic). This demonstrates the viability of leveraging domain knowledge to compensate for data scarcity in historical language processing.

- Methodological Innovation: Our two-stage CoT prompting strategy, which decouples literal alignment from semantic restrucktturing, mimics human translation workflows and reduces error propagation. Ablation studies confirm that this approach outperforms direct translation by 12.14 BLEU-4 points in idiomatic tasks.

- Practical Impact: The release of the first publicly available Tangut-Chinese parallel corpus (1,094 sentence pairs) and the trained models provides foundational resources for accelerating Tangut studies. Case analyses show that our system can handle complex syntactic divergences and culturally specific references, such as Buddhist terminology in Avataṃsaka Sūtra.

- Broader Implications: This work establishes a replicable framework for other under-resourced historical languages, demonstrating how LLMs can bridge the gap between computational linguistics and philology. The model's strong few-shot learning capability (62.83 BLEU-4 with 100 samples) highlights the potential for scaling to other extinct or low-resource scripts.

## 6 Limitations and Future Work

While our system marks a significant advance, three limitations warrant further investigation:

- Data Scarcity: Expanding the parallel corpus to include more genres (e.g., legal documents, poetry) and dialects could enhance generalization.

- Context Handling: Current models struggle with long-range dependencies in multi-sentence Tangut texts. Future work should explore document-level translation and multimodal approaches (e.g., integrating textual and glyph features).

- Human-in-the-Loop Optimization: Developing interactive tools for expert validation and error correction would improve practical utility.

By addressing these challenges, we aim to transform Tangut studies from a niche philological endeavor into a data-driven interdisciplinary field. Our work underscores the transformative potential of NLP in preserving linguistic heritage and fostering cross-cultural understanding.

## References


Bojun Sun. 2023. The Current Situation and Future of Literature Research in the Western Xia Regime. *Journal of Southwest Minzu University (Humanities and Social Science)*, 44(1):14-21.

Xianghui Kong. 2018. The Construction and Research of Tangut Corpus from the Perspective of Corpus. *Northwestern Journal of Ethnology*, (4):199-205.

Arakawa Shintaro. 2011. Annotated Translation of the Princeton University Collection of Tangut Huayan Sutra Chapter 77. *Journal of Asian and African Studies*, 81:147-305.

Changqing Liu. 2022. *Digital Research on Tangut Script*. Guangzhou: Sun Yat-sen University Press.

Bojun Sun. 2022. *Compilation and Study of Yuan Dynasty Baiyun Sect Tangut Documents*. Beijing: China Social Sciences Press.

Fanwen Li. 2012. *Concise Tangut-Chinese Dictionary*. Beijing: China Social Sciences Press.

Kishore Papineni, Salim Roukos, Todd Ward, and Weijing Zhu. 2002. Bleu: A Method for Automatic Evaluation of Machine Translation. In *Proceedings of the 40th Annual Meeting of the Association for Computational Linguistics*, pages 311-318.

Wenxiang Jiao, Wenxuan Wang, Jen-tse Huang, Xing Wang, Shuming Shi, and Zhaopeng Tu. 2023. Is ChatGPT A Good Translator? Yes With GPT-4 As The Engine. *arXiv preprint arXiv*:2301.08745v4.

Jinze Bai, Shuai Bai, Yunfei Chu, et al. 2023. Qwen Technical Report. *arXiv preprint arXiv*:2309.16609.

Yuyan Zhang. 2024. *Research and Design of Ancient Chinese Large Language Models*. Master's thesis, Peking University.

Kaiwen Lu, Yating Yang, Fengyi Yang, Rui Dong, Bo Ma, Aihetamujiang Aihemaiti, Abibilla Atawulla, Lei Wang, and Xi Zhou. 2025. Low-Resource Language Expansion and Translation Capacity Enhancement for LLM: A Study on the Uyghur. In *Proceedings of the 31st International Conference on Computational Linguistics*, pages 8360–8373, Abu Dhabi, UAE. Association for Computational Linguistics.

Nevsky Nikolai. 1960. *Tangut Philology: Research and Dictionary*. 2 vols. Moscow: Oriental Literature Publishing House.

Barret Zoph, Deniz Yuret, Jonathan May, and Kevin Knight. 2016. Transfer Learning for Low-Resource Neural Machine Translation. In *Proceedings of the 2016 Conference on Empirical Methods in Natural Language Processing*, pages 1568–1575, Austin, Texas. Association for Computational Linguistics.

Yu Peng and Wang Xin. 2020. BERT-Based Named Entity Recognition in Chinese Twenty-Four Histories. In *Proceedings of the International Conference on Web Information Systems and Applications*. Cham: Springer International Publishing.

Elina Stüssi and Phillip Ströbel. 2024. Part-of-Speech Tagging of 16th-Century Latin with GPT. In *Proceedings of the 8th Joint SIGHUM Workshop on Computational Linguistics for Cultural Heritage, Social Sciences, Humanities and Literature (LaTeCH-CLfL 2024)*, pages 196–206, St. Julians, Malta. Association for Computational Linguistics.

Jason Wei, Xuezhi Wang, Dale Schuurmans, Maarten Bosma, Brian Ichter, Fei Xia, Ed Chi, Quoc Le, and Denny Zhou. 2022. Chain-of-Thought Prompting Elicits Reasoning in Large Language Models. In *Advances in Neural Information Processing Systems*, volume 35, pages 24824–24837.

Yaqing Wang, Quanming Yao, James Kwok, and Lionel M. Ni. 2020. Generalizing From a Few Examples: A Survey on Few-Shot Learning. *ACM Computing Surveys*, 53(3):1–34.

Barret Zoph, Deniz Yuret, Jonathan May, and Kevin Knight. 2016. Transfer Learning for Low-Resource Neural Machine Translation. In *Proceedings of the 2016 Conference on Empirical Methods in Natural Language Processing*, pages 1568–1575, Austin, Texas. Association for Computational Linguistics.

Waleed Ammar, George Mulcaire, Yulia Tsvetkov, Guillaume Lample, Chris Dyer, and Noah A. Smith. 2016. Massively multilingual word embeddings. *arXiv preprint arXiv*:1602.01925.

## A Examples of Translation Results

**Examples of Tangut-to-Chinese Literal Translation (Closed Test)**

Tangut Script:
[illegible]，[illegible]。
Reference Literal Translation:
盛衰孰知何长短，名利实虚不殆谓
Machine Literal Translation:
盛忍谁知何长短，名利实虚不怠谓。

Tangut Script:
[illegible]，[illegible]。
Reference Literal Translation:
菩提道上山关无，般若眼内翳何熏。
Machine Literal Translation:
报日道上山关无，瞿昙眼内翳何熏。

Tangut Script:
[illegible]，[illegible]。
Reference Literal Translation:
家宅宝钱九亲及，禄福于至弃毁者。
Machine Literal Translation:
家宅宝财九亲及，禄福上至弃毁者。

Tangut Script:
[illegible]，[illegible]。
Reference Literal Translation:
性喜早因多乃说，△降皆惧毁。
Machine Literal Translation:
性爱早因多乃说，△雨皆消毁。

Tangut Script:
[illegible]
Reference Literal Translation:
若复实不说，一时名利思。
Machine Literal Translation:
若复实不说，一时名利想。

**Examples of Tangut-to-Chinese Literal Translation (Open Test)**
Tangut Script:
[illegible]
Reference Literal Translation:
凡君子者，他利故已不忘，不学者无
Machine Literal Translation:
夫子者，他利为己不忘，不学者，则无

Tangut Script:
[illegible]
Reference Literal Translation:
己利故他不绝，不教亦无。
Machine Literal Translation:
自利依他不舍，不教亦无。

Tangut Script:
[illegible]
Reference Literal Translation:
金真铃铎云如布
Machine Literal Translation:
金真铃铎云如偈

Tangut Script:
[illegible]
Reference Literal Translation:
宝枝杂布严好为
Machine Literal Translation:
宝支杂行长卷为

Tangut Script:
[illegible]
Reference Literal Translation:
宝王间错严饰为
Machine Literal Translation:
宝王混行金刚为

**Examples of Tangut-to-Chinese Idiomatic Translation (Closed Test)**
Tangut Script:
[illegible]
Reference Idiomatic Translation:
盛衰孰知何短长？名利实虚不懈怠。
Machine Idiomatic Translation:
盛忍孰知何长短？名利实虚不怠谓。

Tangut Script:
[illegible]
Reference Idiomatic Translation:
菩提道上无山险，般若眼内无翳熏。
Machine Idiomatic Translation:
报日道上无关山，瞿昙眼内翳熏何。

Tangut Script:
[illegible]
Reference Idiomatic Translation:
家宅宝财和九亲，上至福禄均毁弃。
Machine Idiomatic Translation:
家宅宝财及九亲，福禄至弃毁家宅。

Tangut Script:
[illegible]
Reference Idiomatic Translation:
因大旱多言性喜，降雨皆惧毁。
Machine Idiomatic Translation:
性爱旱依多乃说，而雨皆毁坏。

Tangut Script:
[illegible]
Reference Idiomatic Translation:
若复不实说，一时名利思。
Machine Idiomatic Translation:
若复不说实，一时名利想。

**Examples of Tangut-to-Chinese Idiomatic Translation (Open Test)**
Tangut Script:
[illegible]
Reference Idiomatic Translation:
凡君子者，利他故不忘己，无不学者；
Machine Idiomatic Translation:
凡君子者，于他利故，己忘不忘，不学者无；

Tangut Script:
[illegible]
Reference Idiomatic Translation:
利己故不绝他，亦无不教。
Machine Idiomatic Translation:
为利自己故不断他，亦不施教。

Tangut Script:
[illegible]
Reference Idiomatic Translation:
真金铃铎如云布
Machine Idiomatic Translation:
真金铃铎如云布

Tangut Script:
[illegible]
Reference Idiomatic Translation:
宝枝杂布为严好

Machine Idiomatic Translation:
宝枝杂布好严密

Tangut Script:
[illegible]
Reference Idiomatic Translation:
宝王间错为严饰
Machine Idiomatic Translation:
宝王间错严饰为

# ParsiPy: NLP Toolkit for Historical Persian Texts in Python

**Farhan Farsi**[1], **Parnian Fazel**[2], **Sepand Haghighi**[3], **Sadra Sabouri**[3,4],
**Farzaneh Goshtasb**[5], **Nadia Hajipour**[5], **Ehsaneddin Asgari**[6], **Hossein Sameti**[7]
[1]Amirkabir University of Technology, [2]University of Tehran, [3]Open Science Laboratory,
[4]University of Southern California, [5]Institute for Humanities and Cultural Studies,
[6]Qatar Computing Research Institute, [7]Sharif University of Technology
farhan1379@aut.ac.ir, parnian.fazel@ut.ac.ir, sepand@openscilab.com, sabourih@usc.edu,
f.goshtasb@ihcs.ac.ir, n.hajipour@ihcs.ac.ir, easgari@hbku.edu.qa, sameti@sharif.edu

**Abstract**

The study of historical languages presents unique challenges due to their complex orthographic systems, fragmentary textual evidence, and the absence of standardized digital representations of text in those languages. Tackling these challenges needs special NLP digital tools to handle phonetic transcriptions and analyze ancient texts. This work introduces ParsiPy[1], an NLP toolkit designed to facilitate the analysis of historical Persian languages by offering modules for tokenization, lemmatization, part-of-speech tagging, phoneme-to-transliteration conversion, and word embedding. We demonstrate the utility of our toolkit through the processing of Parsig (Middle Persian) texts, highlighting its potential for expanding computational methods in the study of historical languages. Through this work, we contribute to computational philology, offering tools that can be adapted for the broader study of ancient texts and their digital preservation.

## 1 Introduction

Ancient languages serve as windows into the past, offering valuable insights into human history and the evolution of communication. The connection between language and culture has long been recognized, with scholars using ancient languages such as Greek (Ostwald, 2009), Italian (Lomas, 2013), and Latin (Farrell, 2001) to uncover the social contexts of historical civilizations. These languages not only preserve cultural heritage but also provide a lens for studying the development of linguistic structures and thought patterns (Kaplan, 2013). Despite significant advancements in Natural Language Processing (NLP), which have transformed the study of modern languages, the application of these technologies to ancient languages remains underexplored (Magueresse et al., 2020). As preliminary attempts, some researchers have tailored NLP tools developed for Pre-modern English (Johnson et al., 2021b) and Sumerian (Guzman-Soto and Liu, 2023), yet many historically significant languages, such as Old Persian and Middle Persian (Pārsīg), still lack sufficient computational resources and tools. Expanding NLP research to include these underserved languages can help bridge critical gaps in historical linguistics while contributing to the preservation of invaluable cultural knowledge.

Pārsīg, represents one such language (Haug, 1870). Despite its historical importance as a bridge between ancient Iranian languages and modern Persian (see Appendix A for more details), Pārsīg has received minimal attention in computational linguistics. Its challenges include a highly limited digital corpus, complex writing system variations, and the absence of standardized computational resources for processing Pārsīg texts in the originally written form.

To address this gap, we introduce ParsiPy, the first NLP toolkit in Python specifically designed for processing Pārsīg. Our framework includes tools for word embeddings, lemmatization, tokenization, and part-of-speech (POS) tagging. Our POS tagging system includes three models—Hidden Markov Model with Viterbi decoding, logistic regression, and random forest.

Pārsīg was written in multiple scripts, but the Book Pahlavi script, widely used in Zoroastrian texts, lacks a Standard Unicode encoding[2]. As a result, most digital resources rely on phonetic transcriptions. To address this, ParsiPy includes a phoneme-to-transliteration module with rule-based and LSTM models. We also provide a tool for converting this transliteration to Book Pahlavi. Future work could develop Unicode support, enabling broader computational applications.

ParsiPy addresses the challenges of processing

[1]https://github.com/openscilab/parsipy

[2]https://www.unicode.org/standard/unsupported.html



*Proceedings of the Second Ancient Language Processing Workshop associated with NAACL 2025*, pages 238–250
May 4, 2025. 

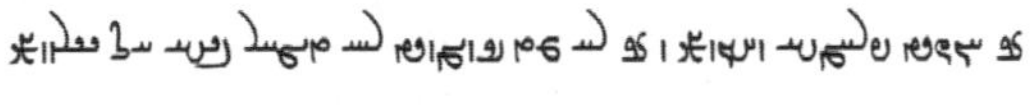

Figure 1: An example of Pārsīg text in original written form from *Andarze Azarabade Mehrsepandan* database. It reads *"ān uzīd frāmōš kun ud ān nē mad ēstēd rāy tēmār bēš ma bar"* and it means *"Forget what is gone and do not worry about what has not yet come."*

Pārsīg texts by using rule-based and statistical methods, which are more effective than large language models for this low-resource language. As a foundational NLP toolkit, ParsiPy enhances computational analysis of Pārsīg, supports digital research, and serves as a model for similar efforts in other ancient languages. The code is available as a Python package on GitHub.

In this paper, we outline the structure of the Pārsīg language in Section 2, followed by related works on NLP toolkits for ancient languages in Section 3. Section 4 details the system design of ParsiPy, while Section 5 describes the dataset used for training and evaluation. We then assess our toolkit in Section 6 and discuss future research directions in Section 7.

## 2 Pārsīg Language Structure

Pārsīg, the language of the Sassanian Empire (224–651 CE), an ancestor of modern Persian (Farsi), has a unique linguistic structure that can be divided by specific features in phonology, morphology, syntax, and orthography. In this section, we go through its specific characteristics.

**Phonology and Orthography** of Pārsīg is similar to that of modern Persian, though there are important historical phonetic differences.

The Pārsīg alphabet consists of only fourteen letters to represent the entire range of sounds, as illustrated in the Appendix. Consequently, several letters possess multiple phonetic values. This variation in phonetic values presents challenges in reading Pārsīg.The difficulty is further compounded by the different shapes the letters can take, depending on their position in the word (MacKenzie, 1971). A significant portion of Pārsīg words is written using Aramaeograms (known as uzwārišn), where words of Aramaic origin are spelled using Pārsīg characters (Farzaneh Goshtasb and Ghayoomi, 2023).

**Morphology** of Pārsīg is primarily inflectional, with both nouns and verbs marked for grammatical roles such as case, tense, and mood. Pārsīg originally had two cases: one reserved for the grammatical subject, and the other for all other syntactic functions (oblique). These cases are commonly referred to as the 'direct' case (used for the subject of the sentence) and the 'oblique' case (used for objects, indirect objects, and other syntactic functions) (Brown, 2005). Verbs are inflected for various grammatical features such as tense, mood, and person (Brunner, 1977). Additionally, Pārsīg verbs often include the use of verbal particles and suffixes to convey different meanings and functions, which can make morphological analysis complex. Another common feature is enclitic pronouns, short pronoun-like elements that attach to words to show possession or objects, which can make segmentation tasks complex.

**Syntax** of Pārsīg follows a Subject-Object-Verb (SOV) word order (Mohammad Dabir Moghaddam, 2014), but this structure is flexible depending on context or emphasis. This variability makes syntactic parsing more challenging. The language also uses prepositions and postpositions, and relative clauses often form with subordinators, requiring tools to detect clause boundaries accurately.

**Semantic and Lexical Features.** The vocabulary of Pārsīg includes many loanwords from Aramaic (Shaked, 2005), which creates challenges for distinguishing between native and borrowed words. Also, due to the script's lack of vowel markings, polysemy (words with multiple meanings) and tomography (identical spellings with different pronunciations) present challenges. These features complicate tasks like word sense disambiguation and machine translation.

Developing NLP tools for Pārsīg requires addressing these unique linguistic features. Techniques such as character-level models for handling logograms, graph-based parsing for non-fixed word order, and morphological analyzers for suffix-rich structures can be particularly effective. This paper uses an excerpt from a Zoroastrian manuscript (Goshtasb and Hajipour, 2022), originally written in P=ars=ig, as an example. Figure 1 shows the original handwritten text. The passage is from *Andarze Azarabade Mehrsepandan*, a collection of life advice, with an English translation: *Forget what is gone and do not worry about what has not yet come.* This example was chosen for its variety of words, characters, and POS tags. The phonetic transcription is as follows:

```
s='ān uzīd frāmōš kun ud ān nē mad ēstēd rāy
      tēmār bēš ma bar'
```

## 3 Related Work

**NLP on Ancient Languages.** Despite the growing interest in computational approaches for ancient languages (Vico and Spanakis, 2023; Long and An, 2023), the Pārsīg language remains entirely unexplored in this domain. Farsi itself is classified as a low-resource language (Shamsfard, 2019), and ancient Farsi, such as Pārsīg, suffers from even greater limitations. To the best of our knowledge, except for (Rahnamoun and Rahnamoun, 2025) who recently presented a set of word embeddings for Pārsīg language, work on this language is scarce. These limitations include the lack of annotated corpora, standardized scripts, and linguistic resources. Existing efforts in the broader area of ancient language processing have focused on better-documented languages. For instance, (Sahala and Lindén, 2023) developed a neural pipeline for POS-tagging and lemmatization of Cuneiform languages, while (Vico and Spanakis, 2023) introduced resources for Etruscan machine translation. Similarly, (Naaijer et al., 2023) proposed a transformer-based parser for Syriac morphology, demonstrating the applicability of modern NLP techniques to ancient scripts.

**Tools for Ancient Languages.** In the broader domain of tool development for ancient languages, (Guzman-Soto and Liu, 2023) introduced an open-source library for Sumerian text analysis, while (Koch et al., 2023) presented a handwritten text recognition system for Medieval Latin manuscripts. Recognizing the unique challenges of ancient languages, researchers like (Johnson et al., 2021a) have developed toolkits to simplify their processing and bridge initial research gaps. These open-source toolkits are especially valuable, streamlining foundational tasks and making further research more accessible. Another prominent example is DadmaTools, a comprehensive open-source NLP toolkit for Modern Farsi that supports tokenization, lemmatization, and part-of-speech tagging (Jafari et al., 2025). However, ancient languages like Pārsīg require additional considerations, such as handling non-standardized scripts, logograms, and transcription-transliteration tasks.

These works highlight the challenges and opportunities in processing ancient languages while emphasizing the importance of creating specialized tools for their unique linguistic and orthographic features. Addressing the lack of research on Middle Persian, ParsiPy is the first computational framework for the language, featuring transcription-transliteration module and morphological analyzers to tackle its challenges.

## 4 System Design

The ParsiPy toolkit is built upon three main components: the embedding module, the NLP task modules, and Parsig character generator. The first component provides a semantical representation for words and sentences while the second one analyzes the input sentence syntactically. Since there is no well-known Unicode representation for the Parsig language we decided to set the input to Parsipy modules as a more well-accepted form of this language which is phonetics representation. However, we present a middle form (transliteration) which can be used to be converted into Parsig characters.

An overview of the ParsiPy structure is presented in Figure 2. The blue dotted parts are current works' contributions. Yellow boxes are embedding modules, purple boxes are NLP modules and green boxes are Parsig character generator modules. Tokenized input can be passed to the embedding module to get embeddings for each token, Lemmatizer, POS Tagger and Transliteration yield lemmization, part-of-speech tagger, and transliteration of each token. Transliterations can be converted to chunks of originally Parsig character set and hence stack together to form sentences in Parsig original form.

### 4.1 Embedding Module

We integrated support for state-of-the-art embedding methods for textual data, including FastText (Bojanowski et al., 2017), GloVe (Pennington et al., 2014), and Word2Vec (Church, 2017), which are well-suited for minimal data sizes, aligning with prior works on low-resource tasks (Nazir et al., 2022; Gaikwad and Haribhakta, 2020; Saadatinia et al., 2025; Fesseha et al., 2021). Parsipy's embedding module enables the transformation of words and sentences into continuous vector spaces. These vector representations capture semantic relationships between words, facilitating downstream tasks such as word similarity (Islam and Inkpen, 2008), sentiment analysis (Medhat et al., 2014), and text classification (Kowsari et al., 2019). They also enable models to identify patterns, improving performance on tasks like document clustering (Shah and Mahajan, 2012), and question answering.

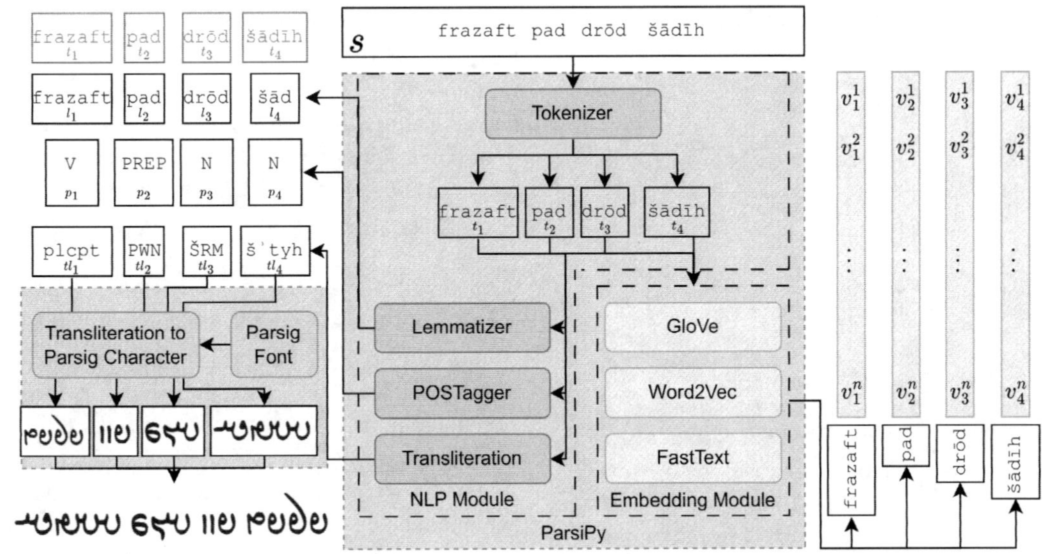


Figure 2: Parsipy Framework Overview. Input string $s$ goes into tokenized into $n$ tokens $(t_1, \cdots, t_n)$ and the embedding module would generate word embeddings for each token $(v_1, \cdots, v_n)$. Lemmatizer extracts the lemma for each token $(l_1, \cdots, l_n)$, POSTagger tags each token with its part-of-speech in the sentence $(p_1, \cdots, p_n)$, and Transliteration module (Phoneme to Transliteration: P2T) generates a middle-form representation of tokens by which they can transform into Parsig in hand-written form. The example sentence is from Corpus Of Pahlavi Texts (Jamaspji Dastur Minochehrji Jamasp Asana) which is gathered and translated by (Goshtasb and Hajipour, 2022). The English translation of it is "It ended with greetings (= happiness)" and it is chosen for the sake of simplicity.

### 4.2 NLP modules

The embedding module focuses on the semantic aspects of language, while other ParsiPy components handle syntactical analysis through tasks like part-of-speech tagging, offering insights into grammatical relationships. We included key NLP tasks—tokenization, lemmatization, and part-of-speech tagging—with easy-to-use APIs for researchers. Additionally, we provide a middle-form transliteration of Parsig, which can be converted into its original character representation.

We developed a pipeline API that covers NLP tasks, including phoneme representation to transliteration, with a usage and output style similar to the Stanza toolkit (Qi et al., 2020).

```
from parsipy import pipeline, Task
result = pipeline(sentence=s,
    tasks=[Task.TOKENIZER, Task.LEMMA,
    Task.POS, Task.P2T])
```

We now explain each part separately showcasing Parsipy's output to give better insights on the matter. The output of the above code fills `result` with a dictionary with a field for each of the provided tasks, i.e., `Task.TOKENIZER` (tokenization), `Task.LEMMA` (lemmatization), `Task.POS` (part-of-speech tagging), and `Task.P2T` (transcription to transliteration).

**Tokenizer.** Tokenization is the process of transforming sentences into smaller units, such as words or sub-words like word pieces and byte pairs (Mielke et al., 2021). Effective tokenization is particularly important for historical and low-resource languages like Parsig, where complex morphology and script variations present unique challenges.

For the tokenization module in ParsiPy, we developed a SentencePiece unigram language model (Kudo, 2018) with a vocabulary size of 40,000 tokens. We chose SentencePiece because it operates directly on raw text without requiring predefined word boundaries, making it particularly suitable for Parsig with inconsistent or non-standardized orthography. Additionally, its subword-based approach helps efficiently handle out-of-vocabulary words and rare morphological variations which ensures better adaptability for low-resource languages with limited digital resources.

The tokenized version of our example sentence is shown below. To enhance identification, we assign a unique token ID to each token, making it easier for traceability during analysis.

```
[
    {'id': 0, 'text': 'ān'},
    {'id': 1, 'text': 'uzīd'},
    {'id': 2, 'text': 'frāmōš'},
    {'id': 3, 'text': 'kun'},
    {'id': 4, 'text': 'ud'},
    {'id': 5, 'text': 'ān'},
    {'id': 6, 'text': 'nē'},
    {'id': 7, 'text': 'mad'},
    {'id': 8, 'text': 'ēstēd'},
    {'id': 9, 'text': 'rāy'},
    {'id': 10, 'text': 'tēmār'},
    {'id': 11, 'text': 'bēš'},
    {'id': 12, 'text': 'ma'},
    {'id': 13, 'text': 'bar'}
]
```

**Lemmatizer.** Lemmatization reduces words to their canonical form, using linguistic rules and context, unlike stemming, which simply removes affixes (Khyani et al., 2021). This is particularly essential for historical languages like Parsig, where inflectional variations and complex morphology require a more nuanced approach to text normalization. In ParsiPy, considering the static nature of the Parsig language and its fixed vocabulary size, we constructed a comprehensive table to store the lemma of each word. Additionally, we formulated linguistic rules to effectively handle specific cases, particularly compound words. This approach facilitated the development of a rule-based lemmatization module that accurately determines the lemma for each word in a text by applying linguistic rules tailored to the Parsig language. Our approach accounts for common morphological transformations. In the following example, the lemma of *ēstēd* is extracted as *ēst*, while other words remain unchanged. For out-of-vocabulary words, the original word itself is returned as the lemma.

```
[
    {'lemma': 'ān', 'text': 'ān'},
    {'lemma': 'uzīd', 'text': 'uzīd'},
    {'lemma': 'frāmōš', 'text': 'frāmōš'},
    {'lemma': 'kun', 'text': 'kun'},
    {'lemma': 'ud', 'text': 'ud'},
    {'lemma': 'ān', 'text': 'ān'},
    {'lemma': 'nē', 'text': 'nē'},
    {'lemma': 'mad', 'text': 'mad'},
    {'lemma': 'ēst', 'text': 'ēstēd'},
    {'lemma': 'rāy', 'text': 'rāy'},
    {'lemma': 'tēmār', 'text': 'tēmār'},
    {'lemma': 'bēš', 'text': 'bēš'},
    {'lemma': 'ma', 'text': 'ma'},
    {'lemma': 'bar', 'text': 'bar'}
]
```

**Part of Speech Tagger.** Part-of-speech (POS) tagging is the task of assigning grammatical roles to words in a sentence. POS tags aid downstream tasks such as syntactic parsing, machine translation, and information retrieval. We have support for three different POS taggers: I) HMM & Viterbi model, II) Logistic Regression model, and III) Random Forest Classifier model. We evaluated them on our dataset and reported the results in Section 6.

Our POS tagger supports a complete tag set for Parsig, covering categories such as nouns (`N`), adjectives (`ADJ`), verbs (`V`), adverbs (`ADV`), pronouns (`PRO`), prepositions (`PREP`), postpositions (`POST`), conjunctions (`CONJ`), determiners (`DET`), numerals (`NUM`), particles (`PART`). Additionally, we incorporated morphological features unique to Parsig, such as automatic recognition of adverbial suffixes (e.g., *īhā*) and verb conjugation patterns. We report the performance of the POS tagger on these different categories in Section 6.

The following example illustrates the output generated by our POS tagging module. For instance, the word *uzīd*, which means *go*, should be tagged as a verb.

```
[
    {'POS': 'DET', 'text': 'ān'},
    {'POS': 'V', 'text': 'uzīd'},
    {'POS': 'N', 'text': 'frāmōš'},
    {'POS': 'V', 'text': 'kun'},
    {'POS': 'CONJ', 'text': 'ud'},
    {'POS': 'DET', 'text': 'ān'},
    {'POS': 'ADV', 'text': 'nē'},
    {'POS': 'V', 'text': 'mad'},
    {'POS': 'V', 'text': 'ēstēd'},
    {'POS': 'POST', 'text': 'rāy'},
    {'POS': 'N', 'text': 'tēmār'},
    {'POS': 'N', 'text': 'bēš'},
    {'POS': 'ADV', 'text': 'ma'},
    {'POS': 'N', 'text': 'bar'}
]
```

**Phoneme to Transliteration (P2T) Module.** Parsig is predominantly represented in a phonemic script in digital resources. Transliteration is a representation in middle form between the phonetic representation and the actual Parsig character set. Therefore, transliterations are crucial components of Parsig linguistic processing since they bridge between these two modalities. A key challenge in this domain is bridging the gap between phonemic representation and standardized transliteration. In our approach, we explored rule-based models, as data scarcity limits the effectiveness of data-driven machine-learning methods. By leveraging linguistic rules specific to Parsig, we developed a robust system that produces high-quality transliteration.

We used character sets from *Huzwārěš*, borrowed from Aramaic (Goshtasb et al., 2021), as initial transliterations, represented in capital letters in ParsiPy's output (e.g., ZK for ān). This exploration refines our model, enhancing accuracy in Parsig text representation.

```
[
    {'translite': 'ZK', 'text': 'ān'},
    {'translite': ''wcyt', 'text': 'uzīd'},
    {'translite': 'pl'mwš', 'text': 'frāmōš'},
    {'translite': 'OBYDWNty', 'text': 'kun'},
    {'translite': 'W', 'text': 'ud'},
    {'translite': 'ZK', 'text': 'ān'},
    {'translite': 'LA', 'text': 'nē'},
    {'translite': 'mt', 'text': 'mad'},
    {'translite': "YKOYMWyt'", 'text': 'ēstēd'},
    {'translite': 'l'd', 'text': 'rāy'},
    {'translite': 'tym'l', 'text': 'tēmār'},
    {'translite': 'byš', 'text': 'bēš'},
    {'translite': 'AL', 'text': 'ma'},
    {'translite': 'YBLWN', 'text': 'bar'}
]
```

### 4.3 Transliteration to Written Form

To encourage the use of the Parsig language in the original form we present an enhanced version of the Parsig font and an executable file for converting translation into a written format of Parsig language texts with the original character set using that font.

**Parsig Font.** We have refined and expanded an existing font set for the Parsig alphabet. This involved adjusting the positioning of letters relative to the baseline to achieve better alignment. The enhanced version of the font set is included in the supplementary materials.

**Transliteration to Parsig Character Module.** Additionally, we introduce an executable tool that converts Parsing sentences from their transliterated form, aligned with ParsiPy's output formats, into their original script using this font set.

## 5 Dataset (Parsig Database)

| Statistic | Value |
|---|---|
| Total Documents | 120 |
| Total Words | 93,518 |
| Unique Tokens | 8,839 |
| Distinct Lemmas | 4,641 |

Table 1: Summary of the Pārsīg Database

We used Pārsīg Database as a comprehensive resource for Pārsīg texts, meticulously curated by domain experts (two authors from this work) with advanced linguistic backgrounds for our training and evaluation. It contains 120 documents with a total of 93,518 words, including 8,839 unique tokens and 4,641 distinct lemmas (Table 1). Each entry is carefully annotated with multiple linguistic layers, such as lemmatization, part-of-speech (POS) tagging, and transliterations. The data set also includes translations in both English and Persian for its usability for researchers studying the evolution of the Psārsīg language and its relationship with modern Persian.

The project was initiated in December 2018 and officially launched in 2020 with an initial corpus of around 40,000 words. Over time, the database has expanded, and it remains an ongoing initiative aimed at further enriching Parsig linguistic resources. The Pārsīg Database adheres to strict annotation standards, including transcriptions, transliteration preserving original spellings, and *Huzvāreš* annotations for ideographic forms. It is accessible for research in Persian language processing[3].

## 6 Evaluation

To ensure the quality of the models used in PasriPy, we evaluated our models using texts from the P = ars = ig database, which includes content from well-known books in that language. Our dataset for evaluation consists of texts from the following books: Jamasp-Asana (1913), Dhabhar (1930), Anklesaria and Modi (1913), and Anklesaria (1935).

**Metrics.** ParsiPy consists of modules for different tasks that require different metrics for evaluation. For the P2T module, due to its resemblance to the P2G (phoneme-to-grapheme) module, we measured performance using Word Error Rate (WER) (Klakow and Peters, 2002) and Character Error Rate (CER) (Morris et al., 2004) which are type of Levenshtein distance (Levenshtein, 1966) in word and character level respectively. Comparing two strings (one predicted and one actual) then projected down to finding the number of substitutions $S$, deletions $D$, and insertions $I$ needed to change one to another and the error rate is calculated as follows, where $N$ is the total number of parts (words or characters) in both two strings.

$$ER = \frac{S + D + I}{N} \quad (1)$$

For the Lemmatizer module, accuracy is used to assess performance, reflecting the proportion of words correctly lemmatized into their base forms out of the total words evaluated.

[3]https://www.Parsigdatabase.com/

For the POS tagger, we used standard accuracy, precision, recall, and F1-score as our evaluation metrics since POS tagging is fundamentally a token classification task. Here, we report the evaluation results of various parts of the ParsiPy framework across different models.

## 6.1 P2T

ParsiPy's rule-based P2T module yielded 29.764% WER and 13.525% CER on the Pārsīg dataset. We also tested other methods for P2T which we report the results in Table 2 (The lower WER and CER, the better it is).

| Model | WER | CER |
|---|---|---|
| Rule-based model | **29.764** | **13.525** |
| LSTM | 31.009 | 22.125 |

Table 2: P2T Models Performance on the Pārsīg Dataset

## 6.2 Lemmatizer

The Lemmatizer module of the ParsiPy toolkit achieved an accuracy of 0.894, indicating that 89.4% of the words were correctly reduced to their base forms during the evaluation.

## 6.3 POS Tagger

Given the limited dataset for POS tagging as a multi-class classification task, we initially hand-crafted linguistic features, a common approach in data-scarce settings (Lee and Lee, 2023; Shumilov et al., 2024). We then experimented with foundational machine learning models such as logistic regression and random forest, following methodologies used by other researchers working with small datasets (Jahara et al., 2020; Ashrafi et al., 2024; Liao and Chin, 2007). We split the dataset into training and test sets, using 10% of the data for testing. We also tried other methods for POS Tagging, which are presented in Table 3. Finally, we compared these models' performance with our heuristic approach, which uses an HMM-based model and a Viterbi decoder for POS tag prediction.

**Features.** As hand-crafted features for the input of the POS tagger, we incorporated the following attributes of each word: the string representation of the word itself, whether it ends with *īhā* (indicating adverb), whether it is the first or last word of the sentence, the string representation of the previous and next words, the first two and last two characters of the word, the first and last character as prefixes and suffixes, the tag of the previous word in the sentence, and the word length.

| Model | Accuracy | F1 | Recall | Precision* |
|---|---|---|---|---|
| Viterbi | 0.98319 | 0.74465 | 0.70933 | 0.89071 |
| Logistic Regression | **0.98984** | 0.8213 | 0.81977 | **0.93396** |
| Random Forest Classifier | 0.98874 | **0.84832** | **0.9268** | 0.9268 |

Table 3: The performance comparison of the different POS tagger models is presented, with all metrics reported as macro averages, except for Precision, which is reported in micro due to the absence of some classes, rendering the macro Precision score unavailable.

**Models.** We implemented three models for the POS tagger classification model. First, we implemented a Hidden Markov Model (Eddy, 1996) with the Viterbi decoding algorithm (Forney, 1973) for sequence labeling. This model relies on emission probabilities (word-to-tag likelihoods) and transition probabilities between adjacent tags. To handle out-of-vocabulary words, we applied Laplace smoothing with a constant of 0.001. For the other two models we fed the feature representations of the sentences into a `DictVectorizer` pipeline (Pedregosa et al., 2011) to obtain vector representations, which were subsequently used to train our baseline POS taggers with two foundational machine learning classifiers: `LogisticRegression` and `RandomForestClassifier`.

To optimize performance, we conducted a grid search over a wide range of hyperparameters, evaluating models using 10-fold cross-validation. The best hyperparameters for the logistic regression model were `penalty='l2'`, `C=1.0`, and `solver='lbfgs'`, while for the random forest model, they were `n_estimators=100`, `criterion='gini'`, `min_samples_split=2`, and `min_samples_leaf=1`. These two models outperformed our baseline hubristic model and the random forest POS tagger yielded a slightly higher f1-score (0.84832). Class-based performance of this classifer has been presented in Table 4.

While some of the categories like Numbers are easy to detect for our model due to their nature, other categories like particles were harder to detect due to the low presentation rate in the training data. For a more detailed analysis of various model evaluations, please refer to Appendix B.

# 7 Discussion

We now outline potential future directions for advancing NLP research in low-resource languages and particularly Pārsīg.

| | ADJ | ADV | CONJ | DET | EZ | N | NUM | PART | POST | PREP | PRON | Unknown | V |
|---|---|---|---|---|---|---|---|---|---|---|---|---|---|
| **ACC** | 0.97273 | 0.98359 | 0.98518 | 0.99325 | 0.99431 | 0.96056 | 0.99735 | 0.99947 | 0.99682 | 0.99457 | 0.98968 | 0.99907 | 0.98703 |
| **AUC** | 0.86275 | 0.91874 | 0.96979 | 0.9433 | 0.98586 | 0.96373 | 0.95177 | 0.9373 | 0.86387 | 0.98768 | 0.89477 | 0.61111 | 0.97294 |
| **F1** | 0.80675 | 0.87321 | 0.95345 | 0.87531 | 0.95459 | 0.93786 | 0.94118 | 0.77778 | 0.78182 | 0.97468 | 0.83884 | 0.36364 | 0.94912 |
| **Precision** | 0.8977 | 0.90466 | 0.95983 | 0.86058 | 0.93388 | 0.90612 | 0.9816 | 0.7 | 0.84314 | 0.97048 | 0.89035 | 1.0 | 0.94421 |
| **Recall** | 0.73254 | 0.84387 | 0.94715 | 0.89055 | 0.97624 | 0.97191 | 0.90395 | 0.875 | 0.72881 | 0.97891 | 0.79297 | 0.22222 | 0.95407 |

Table 4: Performance metrics for different POS classes with Random forest POS Tagger and Random Forest Classifier. Accuracy (ACC) Macro = 0.98984, F1 Macro = 0.84832. The evaluation was conducted using the PyCM library (Haghighi et al., 2018).

**Expandability of ParsiPy.** Due to its modular design, ParsiPy offers a flexible framework that allows researchers to integrate new tasks and train additional models, improving the accuracy of existing functionalities. The exploratory path we followed in developing this library can serve as a foundational scaffolding for other researchers aiming to build an NLP toolkit for low-resource languages. To facilitate this process and ensure easier integration, we will open-source the training code and toolkit package. This approach enables researchers to seamlessly build upon our work, and with transparent ML model transportation frameworks like Pymilo (Rostami et al., 2024), these models can be deployed and served effectively. Community engagement and collaboration will be key to refining and expanding ParsiPy's capabilities.

**Parsig Unicode.** One of the next steps in enhancing resources for the Pārsīg language is establishing a standardized Unicode representation. To our knowledge, previous attempts at Unicode representation have remained incomplete or faced significant challenges, and currently, there is no standard Unicode for this script. A future direction is to develop a Unicode standard for Pārsīg that accounts for both intra-language character similarities and cross-language relations, improving encoding quality and enhancing Pārsīg's accessibility for linguistic research.

Furthermore, the creation of linguistic resources, such as annotated corpora and lexicons, will significantly enhance computational efforts for this historically significant language. By providing structured datasets, we aim to facilitate NLP advancements, ensuring better text processing, character recognition, and model training for Parsig.

## 8 Limitations

Our work has certain limitations. While we concentrated on fundamental NLP tasks to establish a strong foundation for the Parsig language, some tasks, such as Named Entity Recognition (NER), were not included in this phase of development. Expanding support for these tasks remains an important goal for future iterations of our work.

Additionally, the scarcity of high-quality annotated data posed a significant challenge. Due to these limitations, we were unable to fully leverage state-of-the-art transformer-based models, which have demonstrated superior performance over traditional approaches in various NLP applications. Addressing this data gap would allow us to explore more advanced architectures.

Despite these constraints, we are committed to the continued development of ParsiPy. In future work, we plan to expand its capabilities to support a broader range of NLP tasks, incorporate cutting-edge deep learning techniques, and perform a more comprehensive error analysis. By refining our methodologies and leveraging new data sources, we aim to improve the accuracy, robustness, and overall effectiveness of ParsiPy for the research community and practical applications.

## 9 Conclusion

ParsiPy provides a vital NLP toolkit for analyzing Pārsīg texts, addressing challenges like the lack of computational tools. With modules for tokenization, lemmatization, part-of-speech tagging, and phoneme-to-grapheme conversion, it facilitates linguistic analysis and digital preservation. By combining rule-based and statistical methods, ParsiPy proves effective for low-resource languages and serves as a model for similar efforts. Future work could enhance transliteration accuracy, expand deep learning models, and develop Unicode support for Book Pahlavi, further advancing historical linguistics and computational philology.

## References

Jaleh Amouzgar and Ahmad Tafazzoli. 1994. *Pahlavi language, literature and instructions*. Moein, Tehran. In Persian.

B. T. Anklesaria. 1935. Kārnāmag ī ardaxšīr ī pābagān. *Encyclopædia Iranica.*

Ervad Tehmuras Dinshaw Anklesaria and Jinvanji Jamsedji Modi. 1913. *Dānak u Mainyō-ī Khard.* Messrs. T.D. ANKLESARIA & Sons.

Negin Ashrafi, Armin Abdollahi, Jiahong Zhang, and Maryam Pishgar. 2024. Optimizing mortality prediction for icu heart failure patients: Leveraging xgboost and advanced machine learning with the mimic-iii database. *arXiv preprint arXiv:2409.01685*.

Piotr Bojanowski, Edouard Grave, Armand Joulin, and Tomas Mikolov. 2017. Enriching word vectors with subword information. *Transactions of the Association for Computational Linguistics*, 5:135–146.

Keith Brown. 2005. Pahlavi. In *Encyclopedia of Language and Linguistics*, volume 9, page 126. Elsevier Science.

Christopher J. Brunner. 1977. *A Syntax of Western Middle Iranian.* University of Pennsylvania ProQuest Dissertations & Theses.

Kenneth Ward Church. 2017. Word2vec. *Natural Language Engineering*, 23(1):155–162.

Ervad Bamanji Nasarvanji Dhabhar. 1930. *Andarj-i aōshnar-i dānāk.* Trustees of the Parsee Panchayet Funds and Properties.

Desmond Durkin-Meisterernst. 2004. Huzwāreš. *Encyclopædia Iranica*, XII(6):585–588.

Sean R Eddy. 1996. Hidden markov models. *Current opinion in structural biology*, 6(3):361–365.

Joseph Farrell. 2001. *Latin Language and Latin Culture: from ancient to modern times.* Cambridge University Press.

Nadia Hajipour Farzaneh Goshtasb and Masood Ghayoomi. 2023. Statistical analysis of uzwarišn in pahlavi texts. In *5th International Conference of Iranian Languages and Dialects*, pages 285–308. (in Persian).

Awet Fesseha, Shengwu Xiong, Eshete Derb Emiru, Moussa Diallo, and Abdelghani Dahou. 2021. Text classification based on convolutional neural networks and word embedding for low-resource languages: Tigrinya. *Information*, 12(2):52.

G David Forney. 1973. The viterbi algorithm. *Proceedings of the IEEE*, 61(3):268–278.

Vijay Gaikwad and Yashodhara Haribhakta. 2020. Adaptive glove and fasttext model for hindi word embeddings. In *Proceedings of the 7th ACM IKDD CoDS and 25th COMAD*, pages 175–179.

Farzaneh Goshtasb, Masood Ghayoomi, and Nadia Hajipour Artarani. 2021. Corpus-based analysis of middle persian texts based on the pārsīg database. *Language Studies*, 12(1):255–280.

Farzaneh Goshtasb and Nadia Hajipour. 2022. Description and explanation of the nature of justice in khosrow anushirvan's era in persian texts and exploring its historical background in middle persian texts. *Quarterly Journal of Cultural History Studies, Iranian History Association*, 14(53):101–125.

Hansel Guzman-Soto and Yudong Liu. 2023. Introducing an open source library for sumerian text analysis. In *Proceedings of the Ancient Language Processing Workshop*, pages 133–137, Varna, Bulgaria. INCOMA Ltd., Shoumen, Bulgaria.

Sepand Haghighi, Masoomeh Jasemi, Shaahin Hessabi, and Alireza Zolanvari. 2018. Pycm: Multiclass confusion matrix library in python. *Journal of Open Source Software*, 3(25):729.

Martin Haug. 1870. *Essay on the Pahlavi language.* Guttenberg, K. Hofbuchdruckerei.

Aminul Islam and Diana Inkpen. 2008. Semantic text similarity using corpus-based word similarity and string similarity. *ACM Transactions on Knowledge Discovery from Data (TKDD)*, 2(2):1–25.

Sadegh Jafari, Farhan Farsi, Navid Ebrahimi, Mohamad Bagher Sajadi, and Sauleh Eetemadi. 2025. DadmaTools v2: an adapter-based natural language processing toolkit for the Persian language. In *Proceedings of the 1st Workshop on NLP for Languages Using Arabic Script*, pages 37–43, Abu Dhabi, UAE. Association for Computational Linguistics.

Fatima Jahara, Adrita Barua, MD Asif Iqbal, Avishek Das, Omar Sharif, Mohammed Moshiul Hoque, and Iqbal H Sarker. 2020. Towards pos tagging methods for bengali language: a comparative analysis. In *International Conference on Intelligent Computing & Optimization*, pages 1111–1123. Springer.

Dastur Jamaspi Minocheherji Jamasp-Asana. 1913. *The Pahlavi Texts (Contained in the Codex MK copied in 1322 AC by the Scribe Mehr-Âwân Kaî-khûsrû)*, volume II. Fort Printing Press, Bombay.

Kyle P. Johnson, Patrick J. Burns, John Stewart, Todd Cook, Clément Besnier, and William J. B. Mattingly. 2021a. The Classical Language Toolkit: An NLP framework for pre-modern languages. In *Proceedings of the 59th Annual Meeting of the Association for Computational Linguistics and the 11th International Joint Conference on Natural Language Processing: System Demonstrations*, pages 20–29, Online. Association for Computational Linguistics.

Kyle P Johnson, Patrick J Burns, John Stewart, Todd Cook, Clément Besnier, and William JB Mattingly. 2021b. The Classical Language Toolkit: An NLP framework for pre-modern languages. In *Proceedings of the 59th Annual Meeting of the Association for Computational Linguistics and the 11th International Joint Conference on Natural Language Processing: System Demonstrations*, pages 20–29, Online. Association for Computational Linguistics.

Robert B Kaplan. 2013. Cultural thought patterns. *Landmark Essays on ESL Writing: Volume 17*, page 11.

Divya Khyani, BS Siddhartha, NM Niveditha, and BM Divya. 2021. An interpretation of lemmatization and stemming in natural language processing. *Journal of University of Shanghai for Science and Technology*, 22(10):350–357.

Dietrich Klakow and Jochen Peters. 2002. Testing the correlation of word error rate and perplexity. *Speech Communication*, 38(1-2):19–28.

Philipp Koch, Gilary Vera Nuñez, Esteban Garces Arias, Christian Heumann, Matthias Schöffel, Alexander Häberlin, and Matthias Assenmacher. 2023. A tailored handwritten-text-recognition system for medieval Latin. In *Proceedings of the Ancient Language Processing Workshop*, pages 103–110, Varna, Bulgaria. INCOMA Ltd., Shoumen, Bulgaria.

Kamran Kowsari, Kiana Jafari Meimandi, Mojtaba Heidarysafa, Sanjana Mendu, Laura Barnes, and Donald Brown. 2019. Text classification algorithms: A survey. *Information*, 10(4):150.

Taku Kudo. 2018. Subword regularization: Improving neural network translation models with multiple subword candidates. In *Proceedings of the 56th Annual Meeting of the Association for Computational Linguistics (Volume 1: Long Papers)*, pages 66–75, Melbourne, Australia. Association for Computational Linguistics.

Bruce W. Lee and Jason Lee. 2023. LFTK: Handcrafted features in computational linguistics. In *Proceedings of the 18th Workshop on Innovative Use of NLP for Building Educational Applications (BEA 2023)*, pages 1–19, Toronto, Canada. Association for Computational Linguistics.

Vladimir I Levenshtein. 1966. Binary codes capable of correcting deletions, insertions, and reversals. *Soviet Physics Doklady*, 10(8):707–710.

JG Liao and Khew-Voon Chin. 2007. Logistic regression for disease classification using microarray data: model selection in a large p and small n case. *Bioinformatics*, 23(15):1945–1951.

Kathryn F. Lomas. 2013. Language, identity, and culture in ancient italy. *Bulletin of the Institute of Classical Studies. Supplement*, pages 71–92.

Congjun Long and Bo An. 2023. On the development of interlinearized ancient literature of ethnic minorities: A case study of the interlinearization of ancient written tibetan literature. In *Proceedings of the Ancient Language Processing Workshop*, pages 222–231, Varna, Bulgaria. INCOMA Ltd., Shoumen, Bulgaria.

David Neil MacKenzie. 1971. *A Concise Pahlavi Dictionary*, 1st edition edition. Routledge.

Maria Macuch and Ronald E. Emmerick. 2008. Pahlavi literature. In *The Literature of Pre-Islamic Iran*, History of Persian Literature, pages 116–190. Bloomsbury Academic.

Alexandre Magueresse, Vincent Carles, and Evan Heetderks. 2020. Low-resource languages: A review of past work and future challenges. *CoRR*, abs/2006.07264.

Walaa Medhat, Ahmed Hassan, and Hoda Korashy. 2014. Sentiment analysis algorithms and applications: A survey. *Ain Shams engineering journal*, 5(4):1093–1113.

Sabrina J Mielke, Zaid Alyafeai, Elizabeth Salesky, Colin Raffel, Manan Dey, Matthias Gallé, Arun Raja, Chenglei Si, Wilson Y Lee, Benoît Sagot, et al. 2021. Between words and characters: A brief history of open-vocabulary modeling and tokenization in nlp. *arXiv preprint arXiv:2112.10508*.

PhD Mohammad Dabir Moghaddam. 2014. *Typology of Iranian Languages*, volume 1. SAMT. (in Persian).

Andrew Morris, Viktoria Maier, and Phil Green. 2004. From wer and ril to mer and wil: improved evaluation measures for connected speech recognition. In *Interspeech 2004*, pages 2765–2768.

Martijn Naaijer, Constantijn Sikkel, Mathias Coeckelbergs, Jisk Attema, and Willem Th. Van Peursen. 2023. A transformer-based parser for syriac morphology. In *Proceedings of the Ancient Language Processing Workshop*, pages 23–29, Varna, Bulgaria. INCOMA Ltd., Shoumen, Bulgaria.

Shahzad Nazir, Muhammad Asif, Shahbaz Ahmad Sahi, Shahbaz Ahmad, Yazeed Yasin Ghadi, and Muhammad Haris Aziz. 2022. Toward the development of large-scale word embedding for low-resourced language. *IEEE Access*, 10:54091–54097.

Martin Ostwald. 2009. *Language and History in Ancient Greek Culture*. University of Pennsylvania Press.

Fabian Pedregosa, Gaël Varoquaux, Alexandre Gramfort, Vincent Michel, Bertrand Thirion, Olivier Grisel, Mathieu Blondel, Peter Prettenhofer, Ron Weiss, Vincent Dubourg, et al. 2011. Scikit-learn: Machine learning in python. *Journal of Machine Learning Research*, 12(85):2825–2830.

Jeffrey Pennington, Richard Socher, and Christopher Manning. 2014. GloVe: Global vectors for word representation. In *Proceedings of the 2014 Conference on Empirical Methods in Natural Language Processing (EMNLP)*, pages 1532–1543, Doha, Qatar. Association for Computational Linguistics.

Peng Qi, Yuhao Zhang, Yuhui Zhang, Jason Bolton, and Christopher D. Manning. 2020. Stanza: A python natural language processing toolkit for many human languages. In *Proceedings of the 58th Annual Meeting of the Association for Computational Linguistics:*

*System Demonstrations*, pages 101–108, Online. Association for Computational Linguistics.

Rashin Rahnamoun and Ramin Rahnamoun. 2025. Semantic analysis of jurisprudential zoroastrian texts in Pahlavi: A word embedding approach for an extremely under-resourced, extinct language. In *Proceedings of the New Horizons in Computational Linguistics for Religious Texts*, pages 23–41, Abu Dhabi, UAE. Association for Computational Linguistics.

AmirHosein Rostami, Sepand Haghighi, Sadra Sabouri, and Alireza Zolanvari. 2024. Pymilo: A python library for ml i/o. *arXiv preprint arXiv:2501.00528*.

Mehrshad Saadatinia, Minoo Ahmadi, and Armin Abdollahi. 2025. Enhancing multi-modal video sentiment classification through semi-supervised clustering. *arXiv preprint arXiv:2501.06475*.

Aleksi Sahala and Krister Lindén. 2023. A neural pipeline for pos-tagging and lemmatizing cuneiform languages. In *Proceedings of the Ancient Language Processing Workshop*, pages 203–212, Varna, Bulgaria. INCOMA Ltd., Shoumen, Bulgaria.

Neepa Shah and Sunita Mahajan. 2012. Document clustering: A detailed review. *International Journal of Applied Information Systems*, 4:30–38.

Shaul Shaked. 2005. Aramaic loan-words in middle persian. *Bulletin of the Asia Institute*, 19:159–168.

Mehrnoush Shamsfard. 2019. Challenges and opportunities in processing low resource languages: A study on persian. In *International conference language technologies for all (LT4All)*.

Arseniy Shumilov, Yueting Zhu, Negin Ashrafi, Gaojie Lian, Shilong Ren, and Maryam Pishgar. 2024. Data-driven machine learning approaches for predicting in-hospital sepsis mortality. *arXiv preprint arXiv:2408.01612*.

Ahmad Tafazzoli. 1999. *Pre-Islamic Persian Literature*, 3 edition. Sokhan, Tehran. In Persian.

Gianluca Vico and Gerasimos Spanakis. 2023. Larth: Dataset and machine translation for etruscan. In *Proceedings of the Ancient Language Processing Workshop*, pages 39–48, Varna, Bulgaria. INCOMA Ltd., Shoumen, Bulgaria.

# A Parsig Language

## A.1 Overview of Middle Iranian Languages

The Middle Iranian languages span a long period (about 1,200 years) from the fall of the Achaemenid Empire to the 9th century CE. Written documents from this period exist in six languages: Middle Persian (Sasanian Pahlavi or Pārsīg), Parthian Pahlavi, Sogdian, Bactrian, Khotanese, and Khwarezmian. Among these, Pārsīg is particularly significant, as it is the precursor to modern Persian and the only Iranian language with written records from its ancient phase, including Old Persian inscriptions.

Parsig was the language of Zoroastrian Middle Persian texts, Sasanian inscriptions, Manichaean writings, and Christian Middle Persian texts, while each written in different scripts. The majority of surviving Pārsīg texts are religious Zoroastrian writings, composed in the Book Pahlavi script, also known as cursive Pahlavi.

**Zoroastrian Middle Persian Texts.** The surviving Pahlavi texts encompass a wide range of topics, with the largest category being Zand texts—translations and interpretations of the Avesta into Pahlavi—along with works derived from these interpretations, such as *Dēnkard*, *Bundahišn*, *Selections of Zādspram*, *Dādestān ī Dēnīg*, and *Pahlavi Rivayats*.

Beyond these, Pahlavi literature includes various other genres: philosophical-theological works like *Škand Gumānīg Wizār* and *Pas Dānišn-kāmag*; mystical and prophetic texts such as *Ardā Wīrāz-namag* and *Jāmāsp's Prophecies*; ethical and didactic literature including *Yādgar ī Buzurgmihr* and *Dādestān ī Mēnōg ī Xrad*; debates and boastful compositions like *The Assyrian Tree*; historical and geographical accounts such as *Kārnāmag ī Ardaxšīr ī Pāpakān* and *Šahrestān-hā ī Ērān*; epic literature like *Yādgar ī Zarērān*; and legal texts including *Šāyest nē Šāyest* and *Mādayān ī Hazār Dādestān*. Additionally, educational treatises, such as *Xusraw ud Rēdag* and *The Chess and Nard Treatise*, and lexicons like the *Pahlavi Lexicon* further enrich the corpus.

These texts are invaluable for understanding Iran's cultural, religious, and historical heritage, while their linguistic analysis significantly contributes to Persian language studies, historical linguistics, and lexical research (Durkin-Meisterernst, 2004; Macuch and Emmerick, 2008; Tafazzoli, 1999; Amouzgar and Tafazzoli, 1994)

## A.2 The Book Pahlavi Script

All Western Middle Iranian scripts originate from the Aramaic script and were used to write Parthian and Middle Persian (Sasanian Pahlavi) texts. The major script variations include Parthian (Inscriptional Pahlavi), used for Parthian inscriptions and early Sasanian texts; Inscriptional Pahlavi, which appeared in royal and noble inscriptions of the Sasanian period; Book Pahlavi, primarily used for Zoroastrian Middle Persian texts; and Psalter

| Alphabet | Description |
|---|---|
| | A symbol that functions as both '' and 'h' in writing, with pronunciations varying between 'a', 'ā', and 'x', effectively representing four different letters in the system. |
| | This letter is commonly transliterated as 'b' and its phonetic transcription is also 'b'. This letter doesn't connect to the following letter (in writing). |
| | A multi-purpose symbol that can be transliterated as 'y', 'g', 'd', or 'z', with corresponding phonetic values of 'j' (when 'y' appears word-initially), 'g', 'd', 'y', and occasionally 'z'. |
| | A multi-function symbol that's transcribed as 'w' word-initially, but as 'u', 'ū', 'o', or 'ō' elsewhere. It also represents 'r' and 'n'. This letter is non-connecting to the following letter. |
| | A letter consistently represented as 'z' in both transliteration and phonetic transcription. |
| | Transliterated as 'k', pronounced as either 'k' or 'g', and is non-connecting to the following letter. |
| | Transliterated as 'l', with phonetic values of either 'l' or 'r'. |
| | A letter consistently represented as 'm' in both transliteration and phonetic transcription. |
| | Transliterated as 's', with phonetic values of either 's' or 'h'. |
| | Transliterated as 'p', pronounced as either 'p', 'f', or 'b', and is non-connecting to the following letter. |
| | Transliterated as 'c', primarily pronounced as 'č' (ch), occasionally representing 'z' and 'j', and is non-connecting to the following letter. |
| | A letter consistently represented as 'š' (sh) in both transliteration and phonetic transcription. |
| | Transliterated as 't', pronounced as either 't' or 'd', and is non-connecting to the following letter. |
| | A letter used in Huzwāreš words, transliterated as 'E', and is non-connecting to the following letter. |

Figure 3: The 14 letters of the Pārsīg alphabet, used in the Middle Persian language.

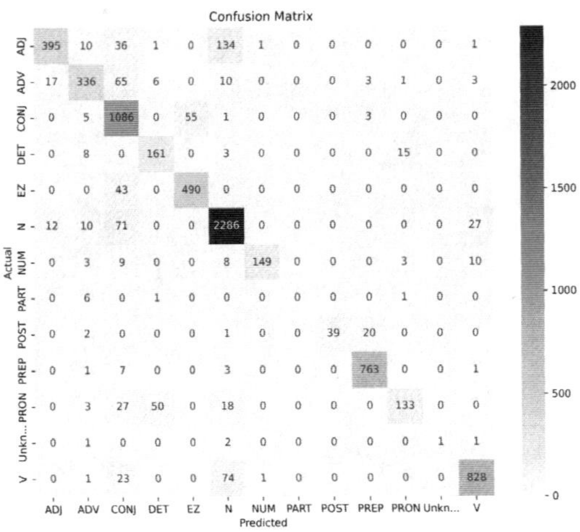


Figure 4: Confusion matrix for HMM & Viterbi

Pahlavi, employed in Middle Persian Christian texts. The script specifically used for Zoroastrian Middle Persian writings is called *Book Pahlavi*, a cursive script referred to by Islamic-era writers as *ram dabīra* or *hām dabīra*, meaning "common script." *Book Pahlavi* consists of 14 letters and is written from right to left (shown in Figure 3).

# B POS Tagger Classification Results

In this part we present class-based metrics confusion matrices for POS tagger classifiers. The evaluation was conducted using the PyCM library (Haghighi et al., 2018).

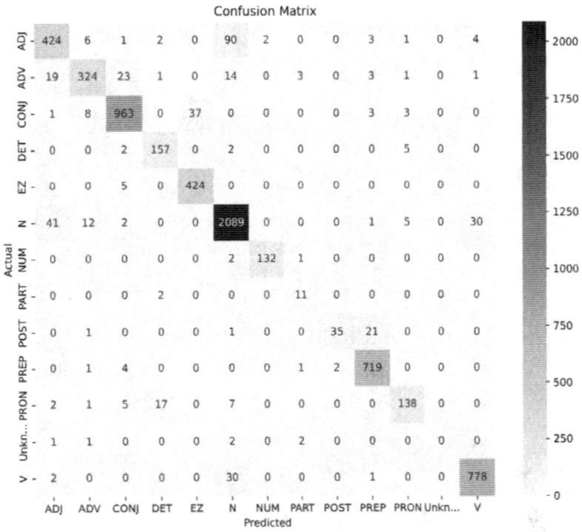


Figure 5: Confusion matrix for Logistic regression

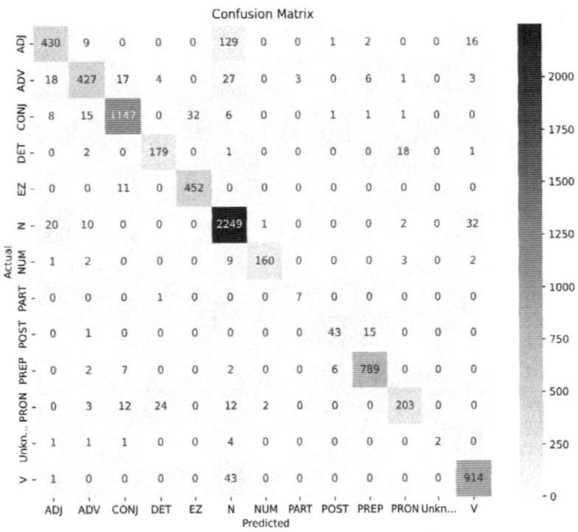


Figure 6: Confusion matrix for Random forest

| | ADJ | ADV | CONJ | DET | EZ | N | NUM | PART | POST | PREP | PRON | Unknown | V |
|---|---|---|---|---|---|---|---|---|---|---|---|---|---|
| **ACC** | 0.97168 | 0.97929 | 0.95391 | 0.98878 | 0.98691 | 0.95003 | 0.99532 | 0.99893 | 0.99693 | 0.99492 | 0.98424 | 0.99947 | 0.98103 |
| **AUC** | 0.8396 | 0.8774 | 0.95 | 0.92651 | 0.95571 | 0.95006 | 0.9092 | 0.5 | 0.81452 | 0.99032 | 0.7865 | 0.6 | 0.94332 |
| **F1** | 0.78842 | 0.81258 | 0.86293 | 0.7931 | 0.90909 | 0.92438 | 0.89489 | 0.0 | 0.77228 | 0.9757 | 0.69271 | 0.33333 | 0.92102 |
| **Precision** | 0.9316 | 0.87047 | 0.79444 | 0.73516 | 0.89908 | 0.9 | 0.98675 | None | 1.0 | 0.96705 | 0.86928 | 1.0 | 0.95063 |
| **Recall** | 0.68339 | 0.7619 | 0.94435 | 0.86096 | 0.91932 | 0.95012 | 0.81868 | 0.0 | 0.62903 | 0.98452 | 0.57576 | 0.2 | 0.8932 |

Table 5: Performance metrics for different POS classes with HMM & Viterbi POS Tagger. Accuracy (ACC) Macro = 0.98319, F1 Macro = 0.74465

| | ADJ | ADV | CONJ | DET | EZ | N | NUM | PART | POST | PREP | PRON | Unknown | V |
|---|---|---|---|---|---|---|---|---|---|---|---|---|---|
| **ACC** | 0.97361 | 0.98568 | 0.98583 | 0.99533 | 0.99367 | 0.96396 | 0.99925 | 0.99864 | 0.99623 | 0.99397 | 0.99291 | 0.9991 | 0.98975 |
| **AUC** | 0.89234 | 0.91405 | 0.97065 | 0.97119 | 0.99119 | 0.96251 | 0.98873 | 0.92255 | 0.80157 | 0.99179 | 0.90472 | 0.5 | 0.97665 |
| **F1** | 0.82893 | 0.87214 | 0.95347 | 0.91014 | 0.95281 | 0.94589 | 0.98141 | 0.70968 | 0.73684 | 0.97294 | 0.85449 | 0.0 | 0.95813 |
| **Precision** | 0.86531 | 0.91525 | 0.95821 | 0.87709 | 0.91974 | 0.93384 | 0.98507 | 0.61111 | 0.94595 | 0.95739 | 0.90196 | None | 0.95695 |
| **Recall** | 0.7955 | 0.8329 | 0.94877 | 0.94578 | 0.98834 | 0.95826 | 0.97778 | 0.84615 | 0.60345 | 0.989 | 0.81176 | 0.0 | 0.95931 |

Table 6: Performance metrics for different POS classes with Logistic regression POS Tagger and Logistic Regression. Accuracy (ACC) Macro = 0.98984, F1 Macro = 0.8213

### B.1 HMM & Viterbi

Table 5 represent class-based metrics for HMM & Viterbi POS tagger and confusion matrix is presented in Figure 4.

### B.2 Logistic Regression

Table 6 represent class-based metrics for Logistic regression POS tagger and confusion matrix is presented in Figure 5.

### B.3 Random Forrest Classifier

Table 4 represent class-based metrics for Random forest POS tagger and confusion matrix is presented in Figure 6.

# Author Index